The International Monetary System

A Conference Sponsored by the
American Enterprise Institute for Public Policy Research

The International Monetary System
A Time of Turbulence

*Edited by Jacob S. Dreyer, Gottfried Haberler, and
Thomas D. Willett*

American Enterprise Institute for Public Policy Research
Washington and London

Library of Congress Cataloging in Publication Data
Main entry under title:

The International monetary system.

    (AEI symposia ; 82E)
    Proceedings of a conference held Feb. 28–29, 1980,
in Washington, D.C.
      1. International finance—Congresses. 2. Foreign
exchange problem—Congresses. I. Dreyer, Jacob S.
II. Haberler, Gottfried, 1900–   . III. Willett,
Thomas D. IV. Series.
HG205 1980   332.4′5   82-13799
ISBN 0-0447-2228-6
ISBN 0-8447-2227-8 (pbk.)

AEI Symposia 82E

Printed in the United States of America

This volume is dedicated to the memory of Wilson E. Schmidt,
a colleague and a friend, whose contributions raised
the level of discourse about numerous issues of public policy.

The Editors

Contents

PART THREE
STUDIES OF SELECTED COUNTRIES

PART FOUR
INTERNATIONAL LIQUIDITY ISSUES UNDER FLOATING

LUNCHEON ADDRESS

PART FIVE

THE OUTLOOK FOR THE DOLLAR AND OTHER INTERNATIONAL ASSETS

PART SIX

NATIONAL ECONOMIC POLICIES IN AN INTERDEPENDENT WORLD

Participants

Sven W. Arndt
University of California at Santa Cruz

Edward M. Bernstein
EMB, Ltd.

John F. O. Bilson
University of Chicago

Stanley W. Black
Vanderbilt University

Karl Brunner
University of Rochester

Ralph C. Bryant
The Brookings Institution

Arthur F. Burns
American Enterprise Institute

Andrew D. Crockett
International Monetary Fund

Rudiger Dornbusch
Massachusetts Institute of Technology

Jacob S. Dreyer
United States Department of the Treasury

Otmar Emminger
Former President, Deutsche Bundesbank

William Fellner
American Enterprise Institute

Michele Fratianni
Indiana University

Jacob A. Frenkel
University of Chicago

Morris Goldstein
International Monetary Fund

Armin Gutowski
HWWA-Institut für Wirtschaftsforschung

Gottfried Haberler
American Enterprise Institute

H. Robert Heller
Bank of America

Dale W. Henderson
Board of Governors, Federal Reserve System

William C. Hood
International Monetary Fund

Helen B. Junz
First National Bank of Chicago

John R. Karlik
United States Department of the Treasury

Michael W. Keran
Federal Reserve Bank of San Francisco

Steven W. Kohlhagen
University of California at Berkeley

Lawrence B. Krause
The Brookings Institution

Richard M. Levich
New York University

Fritz Machlup
New York University

Giovanni Magnifico
Banco d'Italia

Rainer S. Masera
Banca d'Italia

Heinrich Matthes
Duetsche Bundesbank

Ronald I. McKinnon
Stanford University

Allan H. Meltzer
Carnegie-Mellon University

Kurt Schiltknecht
Swiss National Bank

Jeffrey R. Shafer
Board of Governors, Federal Reserve System

Robert Solomon
The Brookings Institution

Richard J. Sweeney
Claremont Graduate School

Roland Vaubel
Erasmus University (Rotterdam)

Douglas G. Waldo
Board of Governors, Federal Reserve System

Henry C. Wallich
Board of Governors, Federal Reserve System

Thomas D. Willett
Claremont Graduate School

John Williamson
Pontificia Universidade Católica do Rio de Janeiro

Preface

Flexible exchange rates have always been controversial. Advocated for a long time by many academic economists, they were often looked upon with suspicion, even hostility, by most practitioners of international finance. In the early 1970s the growing crisis of the pegged exchange rate system forced a reluctant adoption of flexible rates by the major industrial countries. Resort to exchange rate flexibility was a stopgap measure, not a deliberate attempt to reform the international monetary system.

Initially, it was widely assumed that the international monetary system would soon return to some new form of generally pegged rates, albeit perhaps allowing greater scope for exchange rate flexibility.

Experience with floating rates, however, showed them to be a much more viable basis for the evolving international monetary arrangements than critics had anticipated. Not only did greater exchange rate flexibility help cushion the severe international financial shocks of the oil price explosion, but as underlying economic and financial conditions began to stabilize, so did the volatility of exchange rates.

Although criticism of floating rates was never fully muted, appreciation of the contributions that flexible rates could make in reducing a wide range of international monetary problems led to their institutionalization in the Second Amendment of the International Monetary Fund's Articles of Agreement, which recognized flexible rates as an integral element of the new international monetary system.

In 1976 the American Enterprise Institute organized a conference to review the experience of the initial years of floating and to consider some of the major problems involved in the operation of the new flexible rate system, such as international surveillance of exchange rate management to guard against beggar-thy-neighbor policies and the management of international liquidity.

Since the time of that conference, the international monetary climate has shown signs of worsening substantially. The resurgence of strong inflationary pressures in a number of major countries, including the United States, and the reemergence of substantial exchange rate volatility, rapid increases in international liquidity, and diversification of official as well as private currency holdings away from the dollar—all suggest the need for better national and international monetary management. Not surprisingly, criticism of the performance of flexible rates and advocacy of further international monetary reform have increased. With such issues in mind, the American Enterprise Institute decided to hold another conference on February 28 and 29, 1980, in Washington, D.C., to analyze the major causes of the increased stress facing the international monetary system and to discuss strategies for improving the operation of the system. This volume presents the proceedings of that conference.

The conference was divided into six sessions. Gottfried Haberler opened the first session (part 1 of this volume) with an introductory paper in which he discussed the major issues currently facing the international monetary system and placed them in historical perspective. The remaining sessions were devoted to a more detailed exploration of the issues. The second session (part 2) concentrated on a review of the technical literature on the causes and effects of exchange rate volatility, and the third session (part 3) focused on the experiences of several countries with exchange rate flexibility.

The luncheon address, delivered by Otmar Emminger, enriched the participants' understanding of major macroeconomic policy problems by presenting them from the perspective of a central banker operating in an environment of floating exchange rates.

The fourth session (part 4) dealt with the broad issue of international liquidity under floating and, in particular, with the controversy surrounding the proposals to subject the offshore currency markets to some form of supranational control. The fifth session (part 5) was devoted to a discussion of the prospects of various reserve assets—the SDR, the dollar, other major national currencies, and the ECU. The sixth and final session (part 6) was a panel discussion of the various problems inherent in coordinating national economic policies in an interdependent world.

Except for the introductory session, the presentation of papers and commentaries at each session was followed by a floor discussion. The present volume of papers and proceedings follows the format and sequence of the conference with only few exceptions. Emminger's address, published by the American Enterprise Institute as a separate pamphlet under the title *The International Monetary System under Stress: What Can We Learn from the Past?* (May 1980), is reproduced in this volume. A paper by Henry Wallich, appearing in part 4 of this volume, was not presented at the conference. This paper, which is a slightly abridged version of Wallich's congressional testimony on the subject of international regulation of the Eurocurrency markets, constitutes an excellent background for the debate of these issues. The version of the paper by Ronald McKinnon contained in this volume differs substantially from the version presented at the conference. The present version, which has a more sharply focused analytical basis and is more tightly argued than the original version, is included in this volume at the request of the author.

Most sessions conclude with brief summaries of the floor discussions. The summaries are not intended to be a detailed rendition of all remarks, questions, objections, or comments from the floor. They have been provided by the editors to acquaint the reader with the main points focused on in the floor discussions.

THE EDITORS

Part One

An Overview

The International Monetary System Again under Stress

Gottfried Haberler

In 1976 the American Enterprise Institute organized a conference to review the first three years of experience with flexible exchange rates.[1] Advocacy of greater exchange rate flexibility originated in the academic community, but gradually a more receptive attitude toward floating emerged also in banking and business circles. Even those who had been apprehensive initially had to admit that the new system of flexible rates had enabled the world to adjust more easily to a series of shocks—commodity boom, oil crisis, high inflation, and the severe recession of 1974–1975—than would have been possible under the Bretton Woods regime.

Since then the climate has changed again. The reacceleration of inflation in the United States in 1977–1979, the decline, rise, and further decline of the dollar, the emergence of higher inflation rates even in Germany and Switzerland in 1979, and the sharp increase in international liquidity in the past two years have rekindled serious doubts about the present system. Few, if any, recommend a return to a global, Bretton Woods–type system, but many feel strongly that the system of widespread floating does not perform as it was supposed to and needs to be reformed.

In the light of these developments and the resulting changes in perceptions of and sentiments toward the present international monetary system, the American Enterprise Institute decided to convene another conference, once again to take stock, to consider the alleged shortcomings of the system, and to examine some of the reform proposals.

It was proposed that the conference proceed on the assumption that the problem is not to restore a global, Bretton Woods–type system of semifixed exchange rates, but rather to explore how the present system

[1] The proceedings of this conference were later published in a volume entitled *Exchange Rate Flexibility,* Jacob S. Dreyer, Gottfried Haberler, and Thomas D. Willett, eds. (Washington, D.C.: American Enterprise Institute, 1978).

3

of widespread floating has worked and how its working could be improved. Acceptance of widespread floating in an inflationary world is not meant, however, to prejudge the wisdom of the policy of many countries in pegging their currencies to the dollar, the German mark, the French franc, special drawing rights (SDR), and so on, and of others in trying to form a region of exchange stability. That we still live in a world of widespread floating is underscored by the fact that according to International Monetary Fund (IMF) statistics less than one-fifth of world trade is transacted across pegged exchange rates.[2]

Before discussing the operation of the present system and its real and alleged shortcomings, I shall try to put it in broader perspective.

The Present System in Broader Perspective

The renewed doubts concerning the performance of the existing international monetary system of widespread managed floating came in conjunction with a general deterioration of the world economic climate. There is agreement that, contrary to earlier widespread pessimistic expectations (especially in Keynesian circles), the first quarter-century after World War II was a period of almost unprecedented prosperity and growth for the whole Western world, including the less developed countries—in sharp contrast to the dismal record of the twenty years between the two world wars. The euphoria and optimism that had emerged in the 1950s and 1960s changed, however, to pessimism and gloom after the inflationary boom in 1972, the oil shock in 1973, and the worldwide recession in 1974–1975.[3] Some speak of a new crisis of capitalism, others of a new Kondratieff depression; and the fiftieth anniversary of the start of the Great Depression and the crash on the New York Stock Exchange has evoked fears, mainly in journalistic circles, that an economic decline of the same order of magnitude as that of the Great Depression of the 1930s may be in the offing. Few economists take that position, and I myself am convinced that, although not unthinkable, a deep depression is exceedingly unlikely.[4] That is not

[2] International Monetary Fund, *Annual Report 1978*, p. 38.

[3] See Gottfried Haberler, "The Present Economic Malaise," in William Fellner, ed., *Contemporary Economic Problems 1979* (Washington, D.C.: American Enterprise Institute, 1979).

[4] A *deflationary* depression such as the Great Depression of the 1930s is almost unthinkable in our age of inflation. What cannot be ruled out entirely is an *inflationary* depression—that is, a decline in output and employment similar to but much more severe than the inflationary recession of 1973–1975. For reasons that cannot be discussed here, however, I believe that this, too, is unlikely. (See my paper, "The Great Depression of the 1930s: Can It Happen Again?" in Joint Economic Committee, U.S. Congress, *The Business Cycle and Public Policy, 1920-80,* November 28, 1980. Available as Reprint No. 118 (Washington, D.C.: American Enterprise Institute, 1981).

the topic of this conference, however. What I should like to discuss very briefly is why the performance of the world economy during the nearly thirty-five years since World War II—including the recent troubled years—has been so much better than during the interwar period and especially the way in which the various international monetary arrangements during the interwar period and since World War II are related to, or have contributed to, the contrast between the overall economic performance in the two periods.

As to the first point, I believe that there can be no doubt that the most important cause of the exceptional severity of the Great Depression was that, by acts of commission and omission, the monetary authorities in several major countries caused or permitted the money stock to shrink sharply. One need not be an extreme monetarist; Keynesians and monetarists should be able to agree that a reduction of about 30 percent in the money stock, as happened in the United States, would cause a catastrophic slump. Today we are frightened if the target for monetary growth is not reached for a few months; in the 1930s monetary growth was sharply negative for several years.

Note that this formulation leaves open the question of whether it was a monetary factor that started the economic decline in the first place and to what extent mistakes of commission (active measures of deflation) and mistakes of omission (failure to counteract aggressively the deflationary spiral) were responsible for the disaster. These are important questions, but they need not be further discussed on this occasion. What is decisive is that there has been no deflation, no severe contraction of the money supply, since World War II and that no such contraction is likely to be permitted in the future. This is, I believe, the basic reason for the contrast between the interwar and postwar periods.

I now turn to the international aspects and the role of the international monetary arrangements.

It stands to reason—and again Keynesians and monetarists should be able to agree—that a severe depression in major countries was bound to spread to the rest of the world. This is quite clear under a regime of fixed exchanges (gold standard) such as existed at that time. The question remains, To what extent could the spread of the depression have been checked by exchange rate flexibility? This raises another question: To what extent does floating protect a country from deflationary and inflationary shocks from abroad? This question will come up at various points in our discussion, and I shall say a word about it later on. Here I confine myself to pointing to the fact that several countries were able, under the cover of open or disguised devaluation of their currencies, to extricate themselves from the deflationary spiral well before the depression came to an end in the United States.

At any rate, the overall functioning of the "fixed" exchange rate system was disastrous. A series of discontinuous large devaluations of important currencies with longish intervals—the pound sterling in 1931, the dollar in 1933–1934, the gold bloc currencies in 1936, etc.—was bound to maximize the pains of adjustment. Each devaluation improved the situation in the devaluing country for a short while but put heavy deflationary pressure on others, who responded with import restrictions and exchange controls. The result was a protectionist explosion and a contraction of world trade in nominal terms (dollars) to about a third and in real terms to about half the predepression level. During the post–World War II period, in contrast, the volume of world trade has grown rapidly. Only in the recession year 1975 was there a mild decline.[5]

It is misleading to speak of an "international" explanation of the Great Depression in contrast to a "monetary" one, as some writers have done.[6] The monetary deflation in some major countries, primarily in the United States, was the basic factor. The U.S. depression clearly constituted the center of the storm, but there were some epicenters—for example, in Britain (whose economy had been depressed since the ill-advised revaluation of the pound after World War I) and in Germany (where the political consequences of the reparations dispute was a strong depressive force).[7] The depression in the United States, the dominant economic power since World War I, was almost entirely homemade, although at times it was somewhat aggravated by influences from abroad —for example, by the British devaluation in September 1931, which induced the Federal Reserve to take deflationary measures.

There can be no doubt, however, that international complications, the perverse working of the system of "fixed" exchange rates, or rather the uncoordinated exchange rate adjustments or overadjustments (slowly adjustable peg of a beggar-thy-neighbor type), were a powerful intensifying force that for some smaller countries may even have been the principal depressive force.

These horrendous policy mistakes have been avoided in the postwar period. This brings me to the next stage, the Bretton Woods era.

---

[5] See General Agreement on Tariffs and Trade, *International Trade, 1978/79* (Geneva, 1975), table 1, p. 2.

[6] Charles P. Kindleberger "takes exception to the findings of those" who stress monetary policy in the United States and other major countries. He "insists that the origins of the Great Depression were international." Charles P. Kindleberger, "The International Causes and Consequences of the Great Crash," *Journal of Portfolio Management*, Fall 1979, p. 11.

[7] On this point see Gottfried Haberler, *The World Economy, Money, and the Great Depression, 1919–1939* (Washington, D.C.: American Enterprise Institute, 1976), pp. 27-31.

The Bretton Woods System and Its Breakdown

For twenty years the Bretton Woods system worked very well. World trade grew by leaps and bounds as never before and, unlike the situation in the interwar period, a large number of exchange rate changes were accomplished more or less smoothly. Many of these changes were initiated or helped by the good offices of the IMF. The basic factor responsible for the favorable development of the world economy, however, was that the major countries managed their affairs much better than in the interwar period. There was no hyperinflation in a major country, no serious depression in the United States. The German "economic miracle," started in 1948 with the currency reform and the simultaneous abolition of all wartime controls by Ludwig Erhard, had a galvanizing effect on Germany's neighbors in Europe and beyond—both through its direct economic impact and as a dramatic demonstration that liberal policies, what Keynes called "the classical medicine," still work. A Japanese economic miracle of equal proportion, conceived in the same spirit as the German one, had similar beneficial effects. Ten years later, General Charles de Gaulle, following the advice of Jacques Rueff, performed an economic miracle in France.

The rapid worldwide economic recovery from the war was made possible by immediate and generous U.S. aid, later continued under the Marshall Plan. For years the dollar was generally accepted "as better than gold." This statement is underscored by the great popularity in the 1940s and 1950s, even among economists, of the theory of the "permanent dollar shortage," which was especially popular in Britain, where even giants among economists such as J. R. Hicks and D. H. Robertson embraced it,[8] although not in such a crude form as many others.

In practice the Bretton Woods system came to be a gold–dollar exchange standard that lasted as long as the dollar was convertible into gold (for foreign central banks); it became a pure dollar standard after gold convertibility was suspended in August 1971. The dollar standard was never fully accepted, however. The realignment of exchange rates in the Smithsonian Agreement in December 1971 brought the first general devaluation of the dollar vis-à-vis most important currencies, but the patched-up system of "fixed" exchange rates did not last long. In the first quarter of 1973 the Swiss franc and, a little later, the German mark were set afloat, and the Bretton Woods era, the "adjustable peg"

---

[8] J. R. Hicks, "The Long-Run Dollar Problem," Inaugural Lecture, *Oxford Economic Papers* (June 1953); D. H. Robertson, *Britain in the World Economy* (London, 1954). For further references, see P. T. Bauer and A. A. Walters, "The State of Economics," *Journal of Law and Economics* (Chicago), April 1975, p. 4.

system, was followed by a system (or a nonsystem, as some call it) of widespread managed floating of all major currencies.

The immediate cause of the breakdown of the Bretton Woods system, which had in effect become the dollar standard, was that the method of the adjustable or jumping peg could not cope with the strains and stresses caused by the rising tide of world inflation. What might be called the Graham effect[9]—the fact that the adjustable peg system opens the floodgates to disruptive, almost riskless speculation—made the system increasingly unworkable. Because under that system a currency under pressure cannot go up but can only go down, it is easy for speculators to speculate against the central banks, whose hands are tied by the obligation to maintain the par value of the currency. Thus in the last years of the Bretton Woods regime successive changes in exchange rates were preceded and accompanied by increasingly massive flows of speculative capital, entailing an enormous increase in international reserves and thus feeding the flames of worldwide inflation.

Because the Bretton Woods system was inextricably tied up with the U.S. currency, the story of its breakdown is best told in terms of the decline of the dollar.

During the early postwar period, U.S. industries had a quasi-monopoly position and the dollar ruled supreme, but the unexpectedly rapid recovery of Western Europe and Japan confronted U.S. industries with increasing foreign competition; thus the dollar lost some of its bloom and became "more equal." Up to the middle 1960s the U.S. inflation rate was one of the lowest in the world. This began to change after 1965 when the Johnson administration started to finance the escalating war in Vietnam and the equally expensive domestic Great Society programs through inflationary borrowing rather than higher taxes. Gradually the emergence of a significant inflation differential between the United States and some other industrial countries, primarily the three strong-currency countries, Germany, Switzerland, and Japan, became noticeable. This divergence of inflation rates became unmistakable in the later 1970s. After the inflationary explosion in 1972–1974, the U.S. inflation rate had declined from over 12 percent in 1974 to a little below 5 percent in 1976, but it stuck at that level and rose

---

[9] Frank D. Graham was probably the first to point out that, under the adjustable peg, when a serious disequilibrium has developed the direction of a change in the exchange rate is clear and "bear speculators are then presented with that rare and desired phenomenon of a sure thing." Frank D. Graham, "Achilles' Heels in Monetary Standards," *American Economic Review,* March 1940, p. 19. For references to the later literature, see Gottfried Haberler, "The International Monetary System after Jamaica and Manila," in William Fellner, ed., *Contemporary Economic Problems 1977* (Washington, D.C.: American Enterprise Institute, 1977), p. 245.

again sharply when the new administration shifted emphasis from fighting inflation to stimulating the economy by budgetary measures.[10] The three strong-currency countries, on the other hand, continued the anti-inflation policy to bring the rate of inflation down to practically zero in Switzerland, 2 percent in Germany, and 3 percent in Japan.[11] As a consequence of their anti-inflation policy, the three strong-currency countries experienced a slower recovery from the recession than the United States. They accepted a temporary decline in the rate of growth and employment to bring inflation under control—*reculer pour mieux sauter,* as the French say—while the United States impatiently and prematurely reinflated the economy, as Michael Blumenthal now ruefully admits. The divergence of growth and price trends, the joint result of a divergent policy stance, produced red ink in the U.S. balance of payments (heavy trade and current account deficits), which was widely regarded as an alarm signal. No wonder that market participants, both private and official (foreign central banks), became increasingly pessimistic about the future of the dollar and started to diversify their currency holdings. The dollar is especially vulnerable to a loss of confidence because it is still the world's foremost private and official reserve and transactions currency.

The problem of diversification of official and private balances out of the dollar into other currencies (currency portfolio adjustment) has recently received a good deal of attention and will be taken up later in this volume. Now I should like to call attention to the fact that the danger for international monetary equilibrium of a diversification out of dollars into other reserve assets was an early theme of Jacques Rueff and Robert Triffin.[12] In the 1960s Rueff and Triffin were talking of diversification of official reserves into gold under the Bretton Woods regime. The gold conversions at that time (primarily by France under General de Gaulle) were motivated largely by ideological and political rather than financial and economic considerations. The economically motivated reserve diversifications came later when inflation in the United States and the sharp decline of the dollar resulted in large losses (or gains forgone) of dollar holders—losses that were insufficiently compensated by interest differentials. To appreciate the crucial role of U.S. inflation, it is important to keep in mind that what matters is not the

---

[10] This mistake was frankly acknowledged by the administration's chief economic spokesman at the time, former Secretary of the Treasury Michael Blumenthal. See the *Washington Post,* October 30, 1979.

[11] In 1979 these countries experienced a reacceleration of inflation, but their rate of inflation is still far below the U.S. level.

[12] See Robert Triffin, *Gold and the Dollar Crisis: The Future of Convertibility* (New Haven, Conn.: Yale University Press, 1969).

rate of U.S. inflation compared with some broad world or even Organization of Economic Cooperation and Development (OECD) average, a comparison that is not unfavorable for the United States; what matters is a comparison with the inflation rate in a few potential reserve-currency countries—Germany, Japan, and Switzerland—a comparison that is still very unfavorable for the United States.

Whether diversification of official dollar balance (the "Triffin effect") would have become a serious problem if the United States had contained inflation and the dollar had not declined as sharply as it did is doubtful. After the experience of the last five years, however—accelerating U.S. inflation and decline of the dollar—the problem of reserve diversification will probably not soon go away, even if inflation in the United States is reduced to, say, the German rate and the dollar/mark exchange rate settles down to a stable level. It is needless to add that the diversification problem is by no means specific to the system of managed floating, let alone that of free, unmanaged floating; it surely would be much more serious under an adjustable peg than under floating.

The Performance of the Present System of Managed Floating and Proposals for Its Reform

As mentioned in the introduction to this paper, there has lately been much disenchantment with the working of the present system of managed floating. Let me first discuss a criticism that is often made although it is of dubious validity, namely, the complaint that floating has not prevented, or has even caused, world inflation and large inflation differentials between countries. It is true that floating has made large inflation differentials between countries possible because it has enabled some countries to extricate themselves from the spiral of world inflation and has caused higher inflation rates in other countries by making it impossible, or much harder, to "export" inflation to other countries by running large current account deficits.

It will perhaps be objected that some countries have managed to run large current account deficits under floating, the United States being the most conspicuous example. This is true, but the point is that under fixed exchanges the deficits would have been much larger. It should perhaps be pointed out that there are two ways of looking at the U.S. deficits: I have called it a case of a country "exporting" its inflation and thereby alleviating its own inflation. Others regard it as beneficial for the rest of the world, with the United States functioning as a locomotive, albeit an insufficiently powerful one, and pulling the world out of the recession. These two views are not necessarily incompatible, but I cannot go into that problem at this point.[13]

Be that as it may, to say that flexible exchange rates are responsible for the high rate of world inflation in the past six years surely puts the cart before the horse. The phenomenon of high inflation in all countries of the world is deeply rooted in the social, economic, and political climate of our times. High inflation rates entail large inflation differentials because it is inconceivable that many sovereign countries can reach agreement on a common inflation rate of, say, 8 percent or more, which would be necessary to operate a regime of fixed exchange rates in a highly inflationary world. This development has caused the adoption of widespread floating, not the other way around.

It has been said that floating has done very little, if anything, to "insulate a country's level of economic activity from foreign expansion and contraction."[14] It has been argued that "a monetary policy markedly more expansionary than that in the rest of the world is quickly translated into depreciation" of the currency, setting off a vicious circle that forces the country to abandon its expansionary policy.[15]

I find these categoric statements unconvincing. They cannot be reconciled with the facts. Today the main question is whether floating can insulate a country from world inflation. There can be no doubt that floating has done just that for Germany, Japan, Switzerland, and some other countries whose currencies are pegged to the German mark, for example, Austria. It is true that these countries had to accept a temporary reduction in their growth rate as the price for winding down inflation and that in 1979 their inflation went up again slightly after they emerged from the recession. This obviously had nothing to do with the exchange rate regime, however.

On the other hand, floating did not prevent the United States from engineering a rapid recovery. True, the recovery was premature; it set off a rapid reacceleration of inflation and, a year later, a decline of the dollar, especially vis-à-vis the three strong-currency countries; but the real overall depreciation of the dollar was small. It would therefore be entirely unrealistic to speak of the United States as being the victim of a vicious circle in which an excessive depreciation of the dollar in the

[13] I have discussed it in my paper "Reflections on the U.S. Trade Deficit and the Declining Dollar," in William Fellner, ed., *Contemporary Economic Problems 1978* (Washington, D.C.: American Enterprise Institute, 1978).

[14] Jacques R. Artus and John H. Young, "Fixed and Flexible Exchange Rates: A Renewal of the Debate," *IMF Staff Papers,* vol. 26, no. 4 (December 1979).

[15] John Williamson, "World Stagflation and International Monetary Arrangement," mimeographed, 1979, p. 33.

foreign exchange market was a major factor.[16] There is, furthermore, the fact that in the 1930s floating or open or disguised devaluations enabled a number of countries to extricate themselves from the world deflation or, in other words, shielded them from imported deflation.

I conclude that some uncontrovertible facts refute the view that floating does virtually nothing to insulate a country from imported inflation or deflation. But this does not mean that floating shields a country from *all* foreign disturbances. First, obviously, floating cannot protect a country from nonmonetary, real shocks from abroad such as the oil shock or, more generally, changes in the terms of trade. Moreover, such real external disturbances, just like internal ones, can be transformed, primarily though not only through inept policy reactions, into a general pause or recession of the economy. Second, it cannot be excluded that individual exchange rates—the mark/dollar ratio is often mentioned—at times overshoot or undershoot the equilibrium level. This is widely assumed to be the case and is regarded as proof of a basic inefficiency, if not irrationality, of the foreign exchange markets. The charge of excessive volatility of exchange rates, along with the superstructure of vicious or virtuous circles and ratchet effects, will be the subject of parts 2 and 3. I shall therefore not discuss it, other than to say that the papers by Thomas Willett and Richard Sweeney are of crucial importance. The problem of managed versus free float, of the need for and scope of IMF surveillance over exchange rate policies, and other problems depend on whether it is true that there has been much "overshooting," much "over- or undervaluation" of currencies, in other words, whether the exchange markets have been "efficient" or not. It is needless to add that these terms are by no means unambiguous and that they need clarification.

As to reform proposals, few recommend a return to a global, Bretton Woods–type system of adjustable pegs, but on a regional basis it is being tried once again in the European Monetary System (EMS), whose prospects will be discussed in part 5.

A reform proposal under active consideration would lighten the "burden" (if it is one) on the United States stemming from the fact that the dollar is still the foremost international reserve currency. This

16 Just like the deflation of the 1930s, the U.S. inflation of the 1970s was homemade, except for the impact of the oil price rise, which has been greatly exaggerated and is, at any rate, not the consequence of floating. The decline of the foreign exchange value of the dollar is the effect and not the cause of the inflation. Only if there is a large and persistent overshooting, if the exchange rate is driven below the equilibrium rate, could one speak of a separate, independent inflationary effect of floating. Given the large size of the U.S. economy compared with the small foreign sector, however, it is safe to say that the huge dog wags the tiny tail and not the other way around.

12

is to be accomplished by establishing a "substitution account" in the IMF or by moving in the direction of a multicurrency reserve system. Germany, Japan, and Switzerland have been admonished to shoulder some of the "burden" that now weighs exclusively on the United States— a burden that twenty years ago was often characterized (for example, by General de Gaulle) as an "enormous, unwarranted privilege." This problem will be discussed later in this volume.

Another reform proposal, reportedly under active consideration, would tighten the control of international liquidity by international agreement to regulate the Eurodollar market and other offshore currency markets, which raises the problem of the importance of international liquidity in an environment of floating exchange rates. This bundle of problems will be discussed in part 4.

One other reform proposal should perhaps be mentioned, namely, the proposal to make the par value system viable by more frequent changes in exchange rates than had become customary under the Bretton Woods system. It will be recalled that in the reform discussions it was often asserted, for example, in the report of the Committee on Reform of the International Monetary System (Committee of Twenty), that under the Bretton Woods regime exchange rates had become too rigid; countries often waited too long and allowed serious disequilibriums to develop before changing the par values of their currencies. This opened the floodgate for disruptive speculation and gave deficit countries a strong incentive to depreciate their currencies too much rather than too little in order to avoid the danger of having to repeat the painful operation in the near future.[17]

There is much truth in this. The exchange rate pattern under Bretton Woods had indeed become rigid because the basic defect of the adjustable peg system made changes in exchange rates a painful operation that induced countries to postpone changes in the par value as long as possible. This defect, "the Graham effect," cannot be remedied, however, by changing exchange rates more frequently on the average, say, every six months or every year instead of every three or four years. On the contrary, it would probably make things worse by perpetuating and exacerbating turmoil in the foreign exchange market—unless exchange rates were changed at sufficiently short intervals so that the magnitude

---

[17] Surplus countries, on the other hand, had a strong inducement to appreciate the currencies too little rather than too much in order to avoid the risk of being pushed into a deficit. In an inflationary situation this may change. A country with a large international reserve or ample opportunities to borrow abroad may welcome a deficit as an anti-inflation measure (deliberate overvaluation of the currency).

13

of the changes went below a certain low threshold, that is to say, unless one went all the way to a crawling or trotting peg system.

The basic idea of the crawling peg is, it will be recalled, to deny the speculators the easy one-way option, which they enjoy under the adjustable peg, by increasing the frequency of change of exchange rates and making the changes so small that the inducement to speculate can be checked by an appropriate interest differential. The rate of interest is, of course, largely determined by the rate of the ongoing and expected inflation: The more rapid the inflation, the higher the interest rate, and the higher the speed of the crawl or trot of the exchange rate must be.

This is not the place to go more deeply into the economics of the crawling peg, but in my opinion the crawling peg is best regarded as a species of the managed float; it certainly is much closer to the system of floating exchange rates than to that of par values. It is difficult to see how in a highly inflationary environment with rapidly changing inflation rates and changing inflation differentials between countries a "formula variant" of the crawling peg system can work, unless the formula is frequently changed not only with respect to the speed of the crawl (frequency and magnitude of exchange rate changes) but also with respect to the currency or basket of currencies in terms of which the crawl is defined. This in effect turns the formula variant into a "decision variant" of the crawl,[18] which clearly is nothing but a kind of managed float.

There remains the general problem of a managed versus an unmanaged, free float, often described as a dirty versus a clean float. For all practical purposes the case seems to be closed. Practically all countries have managed their float by more or less heavily intervening in the foreign exchange market. Top policy makers continuously make statements to the effect that this or that currency is "clearly" overvalued or undervalued, and they then act on their convictions by intervening heavily in the foreign exchange market; if, as an exception, a country takes the position that it accepts the verdict of the market or that interventions should be confined to smoothing out day-to-day fluctuations and correcting "disorderly" market behavior, the country is accused of benign or malign neglect of its duties.

I confine myself to three short remarks. First, the problem of managed versus unmanaged float should not be regarded as settled. The experience with heavy interventions has not been a happy one; there have been many cases of mismanagement (excessively large inter-

18 The terms "formula variant" and "decision variant" are attributed to John Williamson. See his brilliant paper, "The Crawling Peg in Perspective" (Paper presented at the ANPEC/Ford Conference on the Crawling Peg, Rio de Janeiro, October 1979).

ventions) with highly inflationary consequences. Second, the case should not be prejudged by using the emotive term "clean versus dirty float." I suggest that the term "dirty float" should be reserved for such practices as split exchange markets and multiple exchange rates. The oldest—and, in the opinion of many observers, a very successful—float, that of the Canadian dollar, has never been entirely unmanaged, but there has never been anything dirty about it. Third, one should not dismiss the whole problem of managed versus unmanaged float as meaningless on the ground that even in the complete absence of interventions in the foreign exchange market every float is managed by monetary policy, that is, by the management of the money supply. Some monetarists have taken that position. What they are saying or implying is that it makes no difference whatsoever whether the quantity of money is changed by interventions in the foreign exchange market or by interventions in the domestic securities markets (open market operations). Obviously, there are connections and substitutions between the two types of interventions. Some countries have managed their money supply primarily by interventions in the foreign exchange market (for example, Switzerland), others by open market operations. Abstracting from the possibility that there may be instances of destabilizing speculation in the foreign exchange market, it can be argued that in the final outcome, that is to say, after full steady equilibrium has been reached (if that ever happens), it makes little difference which method is used. For all practical purposes, however, and before a final, steady equilibrium has been reached, it makes a lot of difference whether the money supply is managed by interventions in foreign exchange markets or in the domestic security markets.

Finally, I should like to say a few words on the problem of international coordination of macroeconomic, especially monetary, policy, which will be the topic of the panel discussion in part 6. This problem is related to the old-fashioned argument that fixed exchanges have a strong disciplinary effect on policy makers, putting a damper on inflationary escapades. Under the gold standard the rules of the game were supposed to enforce discipline symmetrically, deficit countries being compelled to tighten money, surplus countries being induced to expand, thus bringing about automatically an international coordination of policies and maintaining or restoring equilibrium in balances of payments. The gold standard was criticized, however, on the ground that in practice the discipline was not symmetrically enforced. Deficit countries run out of reserves and have to contract, but surplus countries can accumulate reserves indefinitely.

Under Bretton Woods the discipline was much weaker. Deficit

15

countries still had a balance-of-payments constraint, but they had the escape hatch of devaluation (in case of a "fundamental disequilibrium") and of exchange control (legal for capital transactions). The abortive and ill-conceived scarce-currency clause was a weak attempt to impose discipline on surplus countries. It was ill conceived (as at least one contemporary commentator on the Bretton Woods charter, Jacob Viner, pointed out) because it envisaged merely direct controls (on current transactions) as a remedy for persistent surplus and not an exchange rate correction. Actually, the practice of the IMF has been much better than the provisions of the charter. In numerous cases the IMF induced countries—mainly developing countries—to change the par value of their currencies (devaluation rather than revaluation) or, in some cases, even recommended floating. The IMF, together with other international institutions and agencies such as the General Agreement on Tariffs and Trade (GATT) and the Organization for Economic Cooperation and Development, provided an extremely useful forum for consultation on and coordination of macroeconomic policies. This surely has contributed to the favorable development of the world economy during the first quarter-century after World War II. We should not exaggerate, however. The success of the Bretton Woods system was due not to international "Keynesian fine-tuning" and the "coordinating mechanism of Bretton Woods"[19] but to the fact that the major countries, primarily the United States, kept their economies on an even keel. The par value system of Bretton Woods collapsed, and widespread floating was reluctantly adopted when U.S. inflation got out of hand and diverged from the inflation rates of other major countries, which had emerged as potential reserve-currency centers. In other words, high world inflation and large inflation differentials between countries due to divergent policies made floating necessary, not the other way around —that is, floating has not caused inflation by "destroying the coordinating mechanism of Bretton Woods."

One of the oldest arguments against floating is that it removes the balance-of-payments constraint and so fosters loose financial policies and inflation. Though it may be true that some countries have over-estimated and abused the freedom from the payments constraint that floating provides, it soon became apparent that, if abused, floating develops its own disciplinary effect. This is true of the United States in particular because, as a consequence of the large foreign-held dollar balances, the dollar is especially vulnerable to a loss of confidence. Thus the two recent major efforts to stem inflation, "the dollar rescue cooperations" of November 1, 1978, and October 6, 1979, were under-

[19] Williamson, "World Stagflation," pp. 31, 33.

taken because the authorities had been alarmed by the sharp decline of
the dollar in the foreign exchange market.

I cannot resist quoting what I wrote in 1974:

> Several economists have pointed out that a falling exchange
> value of a currency under floating is likely to provide a
> stronger inducement for the central bank to curb inflation than
> a declining reserve. For one thing a slump of the value of the
> currency in the exchange market is a much clearer danger
> signal than a declining reserve which can be more easily
> hidden from the public eye. For another, a country with an
> ample reserve can alleviate its inflation by "exporting" some of
> it to other countries, i.e., by increasing domestic supplies
> through larger imports and smaller exports, financing the
> deficit by reserve losses. Under floating on the other hand,
> each country has to swallow the inflation which it generates.
> This provides a strong inducement to curb inflation. These
> conjectures of theorists have recently been confirmed [by the
> chairman of the Federal Reserve Board]. Arthur Burns, not
> an ardent floater, pointed out that under floating "faster infla-
> tion in the United States than abroad would tend to induce a
> depreciation of the dollar, which in turn would exacerbate our
> inflation problem." He drew the conclusion that "under the
> present regime of floating it is *more necessary than ever* to
> proceed cautiously in executing an expansionary policy."
> Burns also noted that "no such intensification can take place
> under a regime of fixed exchange rates as long as international
> reserves remain sufficient to obviate the need for devalua-
> tion." . . . A further comment seems to be in order. The fact
> that floating provides an inducement for the monetary authori-
> ties to step on the brakes does not guarantee that inflation will
> in fact be curbed. A strong inducement to disinflate can
> always be overwhelmed by an even stronger propensity to
> inflate.[20]

This shows that under floating, even in the absence of conscious
efforts toward policy coordination, coordinating disciplinary forces are
at work, although they are much weaker than the harsh discipline of
the gold standard. Attempts at conscious, internationally agreed coordination of macroeconomic policy are going on around the clock on

[20] Gottfried Haberler, "The Future of the International Monetary System,"
Zeitschrift für Nationalökonomie, vol. 34 (Vienna, 1974), pp. 391-92. Available
as Reprint No. 30 (Washington, D.C.: American Enterprise Institute, 1975). Burns's
quotations are taken from his statement before the Subcommittee on International
Finance of the Committee on Banking and Currency of the House of Representatives, April 4, 1974; italics supplied.

several levels, however, from periodic meetings of the heads of state of the five major industrial countries to the various working groups of OECD.

In practice, coordination of macropolicies is clearly a problem of the leading industrial countries, because coordination on a comprehensive, global level where scores of highly inflationary developing countries are included is obviously out of the question. In a decentralized fashion, though, many smaller countries, both developed and less developed, coordinate their policies with that of some major country or countries by pegging their currencies to the dollar, the mark, some other currency, or a basket of currencies. There are, furthermore, the selective but by no means insignificant disciplinary and coordinating pressures exerted by the IMF on countries that are in trouble and are no longer able to finance their deficit by borrowing from private sources.

Not every kind of coordination of macropolicies is desirable, however. The so-called locomotive or convoy policy advocated by the U.S. government in 1977 and 1978, for example, was in my opinion an attempt to impose an undesirable kind of coordination. It will be recalled that the United States asked the strong-currency, low-inflation countries to expand; this in effect was an invitation to join the inflationary convoy.[21] If the advice had been followed, it would have further accelerated world inflation, hardly a solid basis for sustained world prosperity.

The right kind of policy coordination would be for the more inflationary countries, in particular the United States, to reduce their inflation rate to the German, Japanese, and Swiss levels. That would create a large area of comparative price stability, but it would not warrant, in my opinion, a return to a Bretton Woods–type system, because in the present-day world of mixed (semiplanned) economies the requirements for a fixed exchange rate system to work satisfactorily for any length of time are much more exacting than is commonly realized. To understand this it is useful to compare the problems posed by the international adjustment mechanism and fixity of exchange rates between sovereign states, on the one hand, with the virtual absence of such problems inside

---

[21] Naturally, the advice was not formulated so bluntly. It was argued that in view of the existing slack the strong-currency countries could pump up their economies without running the risk of reaccelerating inflation. We do not live in a Keynesian world of mass unemployment where substantial expansion is possible without significant inflationary consequences. This judgment has been confirmed by the fact that when the strong-currency countries in the end, after they had brought the inflation down to an acceptable low level, did take expansionary measures their inflation rate rose again to a level that, although low compared with the U.S. level, they regard as intolerable.

each country on the other hand. There is no exchange rate or adjustment problem (nor are there bothersome inflation or interest differentials) between the East and West Coasts of the United States. The reason is, I believe, that inside each country monetary, fiscal, and other features of macroeconomic policy are fully centralized; whereas for modern sovereign states it is extremely hard, if not impossible, to agree and to stay agreed on the various facets of macroeconomic policy that are necessary to make a fixed exchange rate system work.

I conclude that, even if the inflation differential between the United States and the other potential reserve-currency countries disappears through a reduction of the U.S. inflation rate to approximately the German and Japanese levels, fluctuations of the exchange rates should be allowed to continue.

Two questions arise that require brief answers: First, is it not true that in the past fixed rate systems have worked quite well; and second, will continued fluctuations of exchange rates not lead to continued diversification of reserves and thus perpetuate the turmoil in the exchange market? The answer to the first question is that the fixed rate system, the gold standard, did indeed work quite well in the era of comparative laissez-faire; but it does not follow that it will work between modern mixed economies with their oversized and growing public sector and the far-reaching involvement of public policy in all spheres of economic life. In other words, modern, middle- or old-aged mixed economies whose flexibility has been greatly reduced by the existence of a huge public sector and extensive government interventions and regulations are in much greater need of the additional freedom provided by exchange rate flexibility than were the youthful, flexible economies of the laissez-faire period.

The answer to the second question is that if the U.S. inflation rate comes down to the German and Japanese levels there will be mild *fluctuations* of exchange rates but no longer the presumption of a long-run *trend* of a declining dollar. That will put a strong damper on the diversification of international reserves. Remaining shifts in the currency composition of international reserves can then be remedied by a move in the direction of a multicurrency reserve system and a substitution account in the IMF.

Part Two
Exchange Rate Volatility: Causes and Effects

Introductory Remarks

Perhaps the most frequent charge leveled against the operation of the flexible exchange rate system is that movements of the rates have been too volatile, with consequent damaging effects on international trade and investment and on the pursuit of macroeconomic stability. Parts 2 and 3 focus on these and related issues. The papers presented in part 2 review the technical literature on the causes and effects of exchange rate volatility.

The papers and the subsequent discussion clearly indicate that although the adoption of floating rates has not brought all of the benefits some had hoped for, it has not brought the disasters others had feared. Flexible exchange rates have not eliminated the international transmission of economic disturbances from one country to another, but countries such as Germany and Switzerland do appear to have acquired a greater degree of monetary control as a result of floating. The breakdown in international economic cooperation and the severe damage to international trade that many feared have not materialized. Regarding perhaps the most controversial current issue in this area—the effects of flexible exchange rates on inflation—it is argued that in general the effects of exchange rate variations cannot be determined without knowing their causes and, moreover, that we do not yet have a good idea of the net effects of the adoption of flexible exchange rates on world inflationary pressures.

The Causes and Effects of
Exchange Rate Volatility

Thomas D. Willett

There is great controversy over how well floating exchange rates have been working. Although widespread floating has not brought the extreme disasters that some critics feared, there have been many episodes of considerable exchange rate volatility. Global economic performance over the period of floating has been quite poor, with high rates of inflation and unemployment and low rates of economic growth compared with the previous position of the postwar period. Some argue that the instability of floating rates has been a significant cause of this poor economic performance, whereas others argue that, on the contrary, the instability of exchange rates is primarily a symptom of the instability of the underlying economic and financial fundamentals. Adherents of both schools of thought favor the establishment of more stable underlying conditions. There is, however, a chicken-and-egg problem. The critics of floating tend to argue that a great deal of official exchange-rate management is necessary to create more stable conditions, whereas those who view floating most favorably tend to argue that the major focus should be placed directly on domestic monetary and fiscal policies and that official intervention in the foreign-exchange markets can play a minor role at best in fostering greater global economic stability.

Which of these views is correct? Does the truth lie somewhere between them? One of the principal objectives of this conference is to assess the current state of technical knowledge about the causes and effects of fluctuations in the exchange rate and to discuss implications for national and international policies and needs and strategies for further research. The purpose of this paper is to open a discussion of

Helpful comments on an earlier draft of this paper by Randall Hinshaw, Leon Hollerman, Richard Sweeney, Edward Tower, Paul Wonnacott, and members of the workshop on international and monetary economics at Claremont Graduate School are gratefully acknowledged. The research underlying this paper is being supported in part by a grant from the General Electric Foundation.

these issues. I cannot pretend to offer a detailed technical survey of all of the relevant literature that has been produced in recent years. Both the magnitude and the variety of this research would make it difficult for a single individual to make an adequate survey, even in a book-length manuscript. Happily, however, a number of excellent surveys have been produced in recent years on major aspects of the causes and effects of exchange-rate fluctuations, and we have been fortunate to be able to put together an outstanding panel of experts who are actively engaged in research on various aspects of these questions.

Drawing heavily upon the available surveys (several of which have been written by members of our panel) and on the papers that will appear in the study of exchange rate flexibility that Richard Sweeney and I are editing for the American Enterprise Institute,[1] I shall attempt to offer a perspective on our current state of knowledge and the resulting implications for current policy and future research. I shall offer impressions of where a number of empirical debates currently stand, but in most areas these should be taken primarily as hypotheses for discussion by our panelists rather than as summary judgments based on extensive study of the relevant literature.

Stated in one sentence, my major thesis is that in recent years we have made very important advances in the quality of analysis of exchange rate issues but that in spite of these advances the number of strong policy conclusions that we can draw with confidence at present is disappointingly small. We have been making great strides in clarifying many conceptual issues involved in exchange-rate analysis and in empirically refuting many of the more naive, though often quite popular, views about the causes and effects of exchange rate behavior.

I believe that this progress represents very important research accomplishments and has important policy implications that need much further dissemination for popular and official (and some academic) discussions. These are largely negative policy conclusions, however—as, for example, that one cannot legitimately take deviations from particular purchasing power parity (PPP) indexes as strong evidence of destabilizing speculation and excessive exchange rate volatility, and that in the face of differential inflation trends across countries attempts to maintain a constant exchange rate could lead to distortions rather than to the promotion of efficient resource allocation. Not surprisingly, we have made much less progress in being able to offer positive conclusions about how to identify disequilibrium exchange rates and how best to manage a float. Although for reasons discussed below I think there will always be rather wide limits on how accurately we can assess such questions

[1] Richard J. Sweeney and Thomas D. Willett, eds., *Studies on Exchange Rate Flexibility* (Washington, D.C.: American Enterprise Institute, forthcoming).

with technical (or judgmental) analysis, I would argue that there is still a great deal of mileage for continued research and improved technical analysis to be used by national and international decision makers and that recent developments in exchange-rate analysis have helped pave the way for much productive technical work in these areas over the coming years.

In the second and third sections, I shall briefly characterize the recent experience with floating and the current state of debate and then review some of the major analytic or conceptual advances in exchange rate analysis over the past several decades. I shall argue that, although they have made important contributions in facilitating the rejection of many popular hypotheses about the causes and effects of exchange rate behavior, these developments have left us with a very wide range of uncertainty about the relative explanatory power of more sophisticated hypotheses or analyses. This helps explain why there is such dispersion of judgments among "reasonable people" in the absence of strong evidence.[2]

In the fourth section I shall offer, as a basis for discussion by the panel, a number of propositions about our state of knowledge concerning exchange rate questions and directions for future research. The following is a brief summary of some of my major conclusions.

What has caused the high degree of observed exchange-rate variability? Trends in exchange rates have been heavily influenced by differences in national inflation rates, but even after these considerations have been taken into account there has still been considerable exchange-rate variability as measured by variations in real exchange rates and the small proportion of subsequent spot exchange rate movements explained by forward premiums and discounts. Two of the most popular explanations for large portions of the remaining amount of exchange rate variability are destabilizing or insufficiently stabilizing private speculation and exchange rate overshooting caused by more sluggish adjustment in domestic economies relative to the foreign-exchange market in the face of unanticipated monetary disturbances. These hypotheses suggest that, although a good deal of instability in underlying economic and financial conditions clearly has contributed to exchange-rate variability, exchange-market behavior has substantially magnified rather than merely mirrored the effects of underlying instability.

The prevalence of such causes of exchange-rate volatility should be reflected in predictable patterns of exchange-rate behavior, however, as, for example, in tendencies for short-run deviations from purchasing

---

[2] This is not to argue that there is not still a distressingly large amount of disagreement, because disputants are operating on the basis of highly oversimplified theories and are unaware of much of the relevant theoretical and empirical work that has been done. I wish I could say that this was only a problem in popular discussion and not in academic and official circles.

power parity to be strongly self-reversing and for filter rule and auto-correlation analysis of nominal exchange-rate behavior to uncover unexploited speculative profit opportunities on a risk-adjusted basis. The studies available so far, however, suggest that such patterns of socially undesirable exchange rate dynamics have not dominated the behavior of exchange rates. This evidence does not show that there may not have been particular episodes of substantial exchange-rate variation due to poorly behaved speculation or exchange-rate overshooting in response to unanticipated monetary disturbances, or that all potential speculative profit opportunities were fully exploited. It does in my view quite strongly suggest, however, that such considerations have not been a dominant explanation of observed exchange-rate variability and that the major portion of observed exchange-rate variability has been due to changing expectations of equilibrium real exchange rates.

Factors such as differential rates of income growth and income elasticities of demand for imports, structural shifts in the demand and supply of traded goods, and perceptions of the riskiness of investing in different countries can have very large impacts on equilibrium real exchange rates—that is, on the exchange rate change necessary to offset the balance-of-payments effects of these factors.[3] As is emphasized in modern exchange rate analysis, in efficient markets exchange rates will be dominated by expectations about the effects of current and future developments, rather than merely passively adjusting to clear the market for transactions stimulated by past economic developments. Consequently, given the combination of considerable instability in underlying macroeconomic policies and in microeconomic structural relationships (for example, oil), quite large movements in real exchange rates would be expected, and it would be expected that they would often later be partially or fully reversed in the face of new information.

As was noted above, what would be inconsistent with exchange-market efficiency is that large exchange-rate movements be predictably reversible, and the evidence suggests that this has probably not been the case on a systematic basis.[4]

---

[3] See, for example, Jacques R. Artus and John H. Young, "Fixed and Flexible Exchange Rates: A Renewal of the Debate," *IMF Staff Papers,* vol. 26, no. 4 (December 1979), pp. 654-98; Dean De Rosa, "The Effects of Nonprice Disturbances on Real Exchange Rates," in Sweeney and Willett, *Exchange Rate Flexibility*; Richard J. Sweeney, "Risk, Inflation, and Exchange Rates," in Federal Reserve Bank of San Francisco, *Academic Conference Volume* (1978), pp. 142-61; and Thomas D. Willett, "It's Too Easy to Blame the Speculators," *Euromoney,* May 1979, pp. 111-20.

[4] For similar judgments, see Jacob Frenkel, "Flexible Exchange Rates in the 1970s," in *Stabilization Policy: Lessons from the 1970s and Implications for the 1980s* (St. Louis: Center for the Study of American Business, Washington University, 1980); and Jacob Frenkel and Michael L. Mussa, "Efficiency of Foreign Exchange Markets and Measures of Turbulence," *American Economic Review,* vol. 70, no. 2 (May 1980), pp. 374-81.

On the other hand, we do not have sufficient knowledge about either the specification and parameter of exchange rate models or the content of appropriate expectations about underlying factors to be able to model equilibrium exchange rates with a great deal of confidence. Thus we cannot show conclusively what exchange rate movements were just right on an ex ante basis and what movements were "excessive" on an ex ante basis. Thus we do not have a strong scientific basis at present either to tell officials that they should never intervene in the foreign exchange markets or to tell them when they should intervene. We can be on somewhat stronger ground, however, in suggesting that certain intervention strategies not be followed.

What can we say about the effects of exchange-rate volatility? A major theme of this paper is that exchange-rate variations cannot be analyzed in isolation and that the effects of exchange-rate movements will often depend crucially on the causes. The failure to recognize this point adequately substantially undercuts the value of most of the studies that have been completed to date on the effects of exchange-rate fluctuations on inflation and on the incentives for international trade. Thus, although we can be relatively confident that the move by many countries from pegged to floating exchange rates has not been one of the most important causes of world inflation and has not been a severe discouragement to world trade and the efficiency of global resource allocation, we cannot yet say with great confidence whether the effects of the switch have, on balance, been marginally favorable or unfavorable in these areas.

With respect to policy insulation and the international transmission of disturbances, it appears that the adoption of floating rates has probably tended to offer somewhat greater national independence for a majority of countries but that, because of high capital mobility and the prevalence of real and unanticipated monetary shocks, these effects have been much less strong than many had anticipated. Indeed, the conclusion that the switch from pegged rates to managed floating has had less effect than many people had anticipated could be applied to all of the main categories of effects of alternative exchange-rate systems. This does not mean, however, that the question of exchange rate arrangements and official intervention policies is unimportant.

The paper ends with a brief discussion of policy recommendations based on my reading of the available evidence. I conclude that official exchange-market intervention should be rather limited, except as part of an internationally sanctioned stabilization program or when exchange-rate objectives have a major influence on domestic macroeconomic policies on optimum currency area grounds.

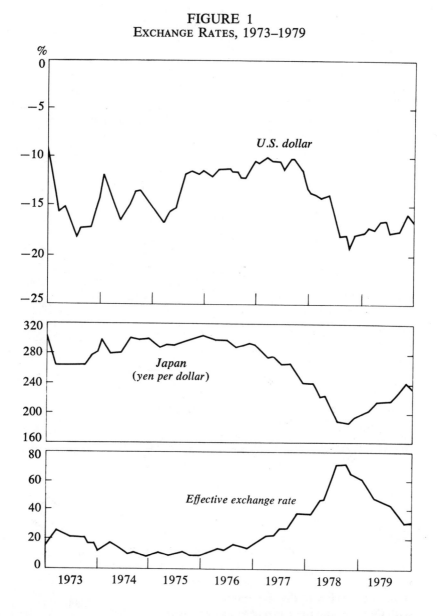

FIGURE 1
EXCHANGE RATES, 1973–1979

NOTE: Exchange rate for each country indicates changes vis-à-vis a group of fifteen major currencies weighted according to the average bilateral manufactures trade of 1978. Changes are in percent from pre-June 1970 parities, based on monthly averages of daily rates.

SOURCE: Conference Board, *Statistical Bulletin* (January 1980).

29

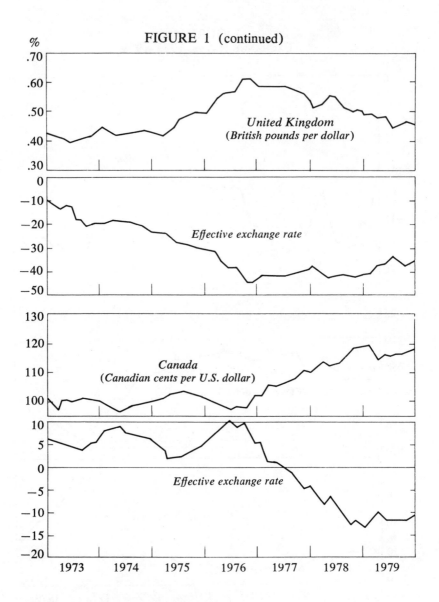

FIGURE 1 (continued)

%

United Kingdom
(British pounds per dollar)

Effective exchange rate

Canada
(Canadian cents per U.S. dollar)

Effective exchange rate

1973   1974   1975   1976   1977   1978   1979

A Brief Overview of the Experience
with Floating and the Current State of Debate

There is still considerable controversy about how well floating rates
work. To be sure, experience has narrowed the range of views about
floating. Floating is neither the extreme disaster reminiscent of the
1930s feared by some of the most extreme critics nor the panacea

FIGURE 1 (continued)

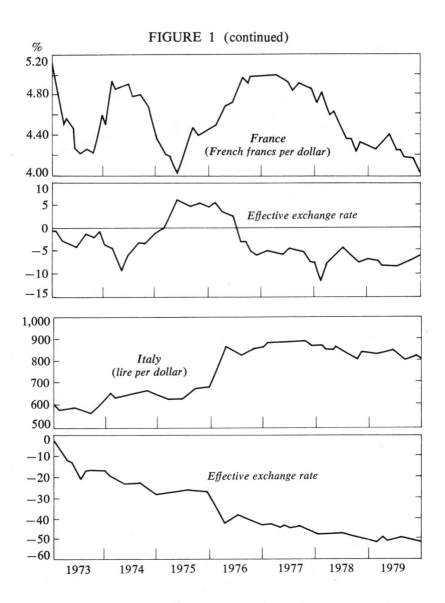

%

France
(French francs per dollar)

Effective exchange rate

Italy
(lire per dollar)

Effective exchange rate

hoped for by some of the more extreme enthusiasts. It has neither brought a breakdown in international economic cooperation and resulting widespread economic warfare and strangling of world trade nor generated complete economic independence, insulating countries from all concerns about economic developments in their trading partners. Though contradicting many popularly expressed views, these results are just what was predicted by the more careful analyses of floating

31

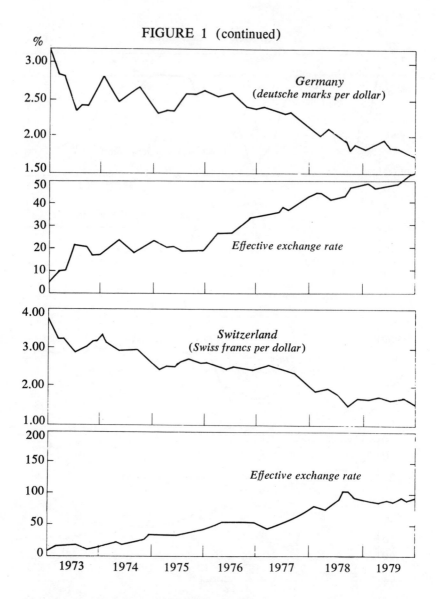

FIGURE 1 (continued)

rates presented during the 1950s and 1960s.[5]

Beyond the refutation of such extreme views, the range of controversy about both the causes and the effects of exchange-rate fluctuations has appeared to narrow rather little. Whereas some critics complain of

[5] For discussion of earlier views of floating rates, see Thomas D. Willett, *Floating Exchange Rates and International Monetary Reform* (Washington, D.C.: American Enterprise Institute, 1977), chaps. 1 and 2, and references cited there.

excessive official management of exchange rates, others complain as much or more about perceived excessive volatility of exchange rates when the private market is left to itself and advocate still stronger official management of exchange rates. Although there is some controversy about the relative roles of stabilizing private speculation versus mild official management, the Canadian experience during the 1950s clearly showed that floating rates need not be inherently unstable in the popular sense of showing great volatility.[6] Our experience with widespread floating during the 1970s has been characterized, however, by a great deal of uncertainty and volatility in the foreign-exchange markets (see figure 1). In a number of instances, bilateral exchange rates have changed by 10 to 20 percent over a period of a few months, and in some instances these changes have been largely reversed in subsequent periods. Although trade-weighted or effective exchange rates for most countries have shown much less percentage variation, they too have tended to show a good deal of variability. Confirming the increase in uncertainty in foreign-exchange markets that this volatility suggests, the predictive performance of forward exchange rates has dropped substantially at least in comparison with the calm days of the adjustable-peg system. Transactions costs, though remaining quite small relative to the value of transactions, have increased substantially in percentage terms.[7]

[6] For recent discussions and analysis of the Canadian experience, see John Pippinger and L. Phillips, "Stabilization of the Canadian Dollar," *Econometrica,* vol. 41 (September 1973), pp. 797-815; Richard J. Sweeney, "Leaning against the Wind: The Case of Canadian Exchange Intervention, 1952-1969," mimeographed (Claremont, Calif.: Claremont Men's College, 1980); and Paul Wonnacott, *The Floating Canadian Dollar* (Washington, D.C.: American Enterprise Institute, 1972).

[7] For recent surveys of the studies on transaction costs and the forecasting performance of forward rates, see Steven W. Kohlhagen, "The Behavior of Foreign Exchange Markets: A Critical Survey of the Empirical Literature," New York University Series in Finance and Economics, 1978; idem, "The Identification of Destabilizing Foreign Exchange Speculation," *Journal of International Economics,* vol. 9 (August 1979), pp. 321-40; Richard Levich, "Tests of Forecasting Models and Market Efficiency in the International Money Market," in Jacob A. Frenkel and Harry G. Johnson, eds., *The Economics of Exchange Rates* (Reading, Mass.: Addison-Wesley, 1978), pp. 129-58; Richard Levich, "Further Results on the Efficiency of Markets for Foreign Exchange," in Federal Reserve Bank of Boston, *Managed Exchange Rate Flexibility: The Recent Experience,* Conference Series, no. 20 (1978); Richard Levich, "The Efficiency of Markets for Foreign Exchange," in Rudiger Dornbusch and Jacob A. Frenkel, eds., *International Economic Policy: Theory and Evidence* (Baltimore: Johns Hopkins University Press, 1979).

For analysis suggesting that most observed exchange volatility has been due to unanticipated "shocks," see Frenkel, "Flexible Exchange Rates"; Frenkel and Mussa, "Efficiency of Foreign Exchange Markets"; Peter Isard, "Expected and Unexpected Changes in Exchange Rates," Federal Reserve Board, International Finance Discussion Papers, no. 145, June 1979; Michael L. Mussa, "Macroeconomic Interdependence and the Exchange Rate Regime," in Dornbusch and Frenkel, *International Economic Policy,* pp. 160-204; and Michael L. Mussa,

Likewise, inflation has remained high on a worldwide scale. Although the growth of international trade does not appear to have slowed noticeably in relation to the growth of gross national product (GNP),[8] domestic investment in a number of countries has been depressed, and it has been charged by some that this was due in good part to exchange rate instability. Furthermore, disagreements about balance-of-payments-adjustment policies and monetary and macroeconomic policy coordination issues have not disappeared by any means. Much concern has been voiced about a perceived tendency toward polarization in economic performance, with floating rates contributing to vicious and virtuous circles in weak and strong countries.

Given the evidence of poor *absolute* performance, it is not surprising that criticism of floating rates remains high. There can be little question that other than avoiding a repeat of the 1930s under rather trying circumstances, the operation of the international economy during the 1970s gave little cause for satisfaction. The key question from the standpoint of evaluating the performance of the international monetary system, however, is to what extent exchange-rate volatility is an independent cause or is merely a symptom of underlying economic and financial uncertainties and instabilities. Defenders of floating can make an extremely strong case that much exchange-market uncertainty and exchange-rate volatility has been inevitable, given the underlying instabilities of national macroeconomic policies and development and the international financial consequences of the huge oil-price increases. There is a good deal of evidence that such indicators of exchange-market uncertainties as transaction costs and predictive accuracy of forward rates vary greatly under both pegged and floating exchange rates, depending on the stability of underlying factors, thus clearly establishing that differences in absolute performance cannot be ascribed fully to the differences in exchange rate systems per se.[9] Likewise, a casual view

---

"Empirical Regularities in the Behavior of Exchange Rates and Theories of the Foreign Exchange Market," in *Policies for Employment Prices and Exchange Rates,* Carnegie-Rochester Conference Series on Public Policy, vol. 11, supplement to *Journal of Monetary Economics* (1979), pp. 9-57.

[8] For surveys and discussions of the studies of the effects of the current experience with floating on international trade and investment, see Artus and Young, "Fixed and Flexible Exchange Rates"; Bela Balassa, "Flexible Exchange Rates and International Trade," in John S. Chipman and Charles P. Kindleberger, eds., *Flexible Exchange Rates and the Balance of Payments: Essays in Memory of Egon Sohmen* (Amsterdam: North-Holland, 1980), pp. 67-80; and Marie Thursby and Thomas D. Willett, "The Effects of Flexible Exchange Rates on International Trade and Investment: A Survey of Historical Views and Recent Evidence," in Sweeney and Willett, *Exchange Rate Flexibility.*

[9] See, for example, Jacob Frenkel and Richard M. Levich, "Transaction Costs and Interest Arbitrage: Tranquil versus Turbulent Periods," *Journal of Political Economy,* vol. 85 (December 1977), pp. 1209-26.

of the experience of the 1970s suggests a noticeable correlation between periods of greater or lesser stability in underlying factors and greater or lesser instability in the foreign-exchange markets. There is now rather widespread recognition that stability of underlying conditions is a necessary condition for exchange-market stability of significant duration and that attempts to maintain rigid exchange rates in the face of divergent economic and monetary conditions can be counterproductive. Official recognition that durable exchange-rate stability must be sought primarily through creating stable underlying conditions rather than exchange-market intervention has been described by Otmar Emminger as a sort of "Copernican revolution" that underlay the Jamaica Agreements on international monetary reforms that officially sanctioned the continuance of generalized floating.[10]

Acceptance of this view, however, still leaves a number of important questions unanswered. Granted that even with ideal private speculation there would have been a great deal of exchange market volatility and uncertainty during the 1970s; but to what extent was actual exchange market volatility exacerbated by poorly behaved speculation due either to destabilizing speculative runs and bandwagons or to an insufficient supply of stabilizing funds to smooth out the effects of temporary phenomena? To what extent did feedback effects cause these instabilities to contribute to further instability in underlying variables? It is easy to argue convincingly that there "should" have been a good deal of exchange market volatility, but it is a quite different matter to argue that virtually all of the observed volatility was due to underlying factors that were themselves largely independent of exchange-market volatility. Likewise, even if it were known ex post that private speculation has worked poorly in a number of instances so that consequent exchange-rate movements were not economically justified, one would like to know to what extent officials could reasonably expect to identify these episodes ex ante. One would also like to know how to weight the relative likelihoods and costs of making the type 1 error of intervening when one should not versus the type 2 error of not intervening when one should.

Many of the evaluations of floating rates have been reminiscent of the earlier days of the monetarist debate in which the failure to distinguish clearly among the trilogy of propositions—"money matters," "money does not matter," and "only money matters"—led to a great deal of miscommunication, with many strong promonetarists and antimonetarists setting up straw men for their opponents and then shooting down the latter two extreme propositions, whereas the real issues were how much money matters and in what ways. I believe that in the last

---

[10] For further discussion on this, see Willett, *Floating Exchange Rates*, pp. 78-81.

few years, however, we have made substantial progress in sweeping away a number of the more naive and extreme versions of exchange-rate hypotheses; for example, it now seems to be widely recognized by officials as well as by academic researchers that it is equally wrong to assert that all exchange-rate depreciations are an independent cause of additional inflation through a vicious circle and to assert that exchange-rate depreciations can never intensify the problem of tradeoffs between short-run inflation and unemployment and thus place pressures on monetary and fiscal authorities for accommodating expansion, which can contribute to a vicious circle or at least to a vicious episode.[11]

The improvement in analytic sophistication of the discussion of policy issues related to exchange rates has not, however, eliminated differences in strongly held views. Many leading experts and officials have argued, for example, that the exchange markets do tend typically to display exaggerated responses to underlying disturbances and that crawling pegs or other forms of heavy official exchange-rate management are needed, whereas many others equally strongly believe that floating rates have generally performed quite well, given the underlying environment, and that at most occasional mild official intervention in the face of temporarily disorderly markets is called for.[12]

---

[11] On this particular issue, see G. Basevi and Paul De Grauwe, "Vicious and Virtuous Circles," *European Economic Review,* vol. 10 (December 1977), pp. 277-301; J. L. O. Bilson, "The 'Vicious Circle' Hypothesis," *IMF Staff Papers,* vol. 26 (March 1979), pp. 1-37; Rudiger Dornbusch and Paul Krugman, "Flexible Exchange Rates in the Short Run," *Brookings Papers on Economic Activity, 3: 1976,* pp. 537-84; Charles Pigott, John Rutledge, and Thomas D. Willett, "Some Difficulties in Estimating the Inflationary Impact of Exchange Rate Changes," mimeographed (Paper presented at the meeting of the Western Economic Association, June 1978)—a revision entitled "The Interrelationships between Price and Exchange-Rate Changes" will appear in Sweeney and Willett, *Exchange-Rate Flexibility*; Henry C. Wallich and JoAnna Gray, "Stabilization Policy and Vicious and Virtuous Circles," in Chipman and Kindleberger, *Flexible Exchange Rates,* pp. 49-66; Willett, *Floating Exchange Rates,* chap. 2; and the discussions in Samuel I. Katz, ed., *U.S.-European Monetary Relations* (Washington, D.C.: American Enterprise Institute, 1979).

[12] There are a number of different hypotheses as to why exchange market responses might be exaggerated. These include destabilizing speculative responses, insufficient stabilizing speculation to smooth out efficiently temporary disturbances and the effects of short-run elasticities that are much lower than long-run ones, and the type of overshooting implied by Dornbusch's model of exchange rate dynamics; see Rudiger Dornbusch, "Expectations and Exchange Rate Dynamics," *Journal of Political Economy* (December 1976). These different causes for exaggerated exchange rate movements may have quite different implications for efficient intervention policies; for example, whereas the first cause (destabilizing speculation) would call for official intervention if sufficient episodes could be clearly identified, the type of overshooting derived from Dornbusch's dynamic model probably would not. For further discussion, see Richard Levich, "An

To what extent are such differences in view inevitable, and to what degree may we hope that a growing body of technical analysis will continue to narrow the bounds of disagreement? How much of the differences in evaluations and policy prescriptions can be ascribed to differences in the particular experiences and economic structures and policy objectives of different countries? After all, we do know from the literature on the theory of optimum currency areas that there are advantages and disadvantages to both fixed and flexible exchange rates and that the relative balance of these costs and benefits can vary substantially from one country to another, depending upon such factors as the openness of the economy, the degree of factor mobility, the sources of disturbances, and the relative weights given to different policy objectives.[13] Thus for example, the effects of a high degree of exchange-rate volatility could be much more severe for a small, open country like Belgium than for a large country with a closed economy such as that of the United States.

Major Developments in Exchange Rate Analysis

At the end of World War II, the weight of academic opinion was strongly against floating exchange rates. The inadvisability of floating rates was widely held to be one of the major lessons of the interwar years. By the 1960s a large majority of international economists (at least in the United States) were in favor of a substantial degree of exchange-rate flexibility. In my recent study, *Floating Exchange Rates and International Monetary Reform,* I attempted to trace the main reasons for this evolution of views and argued that they were attributable in considerable degree to improvements in the sophistication of exchange-rate analysis, improvements in the ways that exchange-rate questions were posed and in the comprehensiveness and conceptual soundness of

Examination of Overshooting Behavior in the Foreign Exchange Market," mimeographed (New York University, 1979); the paper by Richard Sweeney in this volume; and Willett, *Floating Exchange Rates.*

[13] The term "optimum currency areas" was coined by Robert A. Mundell ("A Theory of Optimum Currency Areas," *American Economic Review,* vol. 51, no. 4 [September 1961], pp. 657-65), although many of the basic considerations had been previously advanced in the literature. For further discussion and references to the literature, see Edward Tower and Thomas D. Willett, *The Theory of Optimum Currency Areas and Exchange-Rate Flexibility,* Princeton Special Papers in International Economics, no. 11, May 1976; and Willett, "The Fall and Rise of the Dollar," testimony before the Subcommittee on International Economics of the Joint Economic Committee, U.S. Congress, December 14, 1978; also available as Reprint No. 96, *The Fall and Rise of the Dollar* (Washington, D.C.: American Enterprise Institute, April 1979).

the models used to analyze them. Nor has progress in the quality of analysis slackened since the adoption of floating rates. For example, recent analysis of exchange-rate dynamics and monetary and asset market approaches to exchange rate determination and more widespread focus on real exchange rates have made important contributions in the past few years.

In reviewing major developments in exchange rate analysis, I shall not attempt to delineate a strict historical order. Most of these developments had important precursors (in many cases from such contributors to this volume as Edward Bernstein, Gottfried Haberler, and Fritz Machlup),[14] but I am attempting here to summarize mainstream thinking rather than the history of intellectual contributions. My classification is inevitably somewhat arbitrary. As will be clear from the discussion, many contributions cut across different categories.

The Concept of Optimum Currency Areas. The development of this concept has not allowed us unambiguously to determine the boundaries of optimum currency configurations. Mundell's original emphasis on factor mobility was soon amended to take into account a wide range of often conflicting considerations. These developments did, however, significantly raise the level of debate over exchange-rate issues by emphasizing that such questions could not be profitably debated in the abstract and that the relative costs and benefits of exchange-rate changes and other methods of adjustment would vary depending upon a number of conditions. Although this basic point was certainly known by some of the earlier writers,[15] the breadth of recognition of the point has now increased greatly. This helps to explain, for example, why economists from the United States, which scores very high on the criteria for optimum currency areas, have tended to be much more strongly in favor of floating rates than economists from the smaller European countries. In discussing how floating rates have worked, it is important to remember that they may work differently for different countries.[16]

---

[14] On the recently popular idea of exchange markets adjusting more rapidly to monetary changes than the domestic economy, see, for example, the prewar contributions by Gottfried Haberler (*The Theory of International Trade* [London: William Hodge, 1936]) and Fritz Machlup (*Die Goldkernwahrung* [Halberstadt: H. Meyer's Buchdrunckevei, Abteilung Verlag, 1925]).

[15] See, for example, Milton Friedman's classic article on floating rates, "The Case for Flexible Exchange Rates," *Essays in Positive Economics* (Chicago: University of Chicago Press, 1953), pp. 157-203.

[16] There has been a recent tendency to argue that recognition that no stable long-run tradeoff between inflation and unemployment exists destroys the relevance of the traditional optimum currency area. I do not believe, however, that this destroys the usefulness of optimum-currency-area considerations for a number

38

Incorporation of Capital Account Considerations. A second major development was the incorporation of capital movements into exchange rate analysis. Once this was done, it became clear that, even under floating exchange rates, the Keynesian international transmission mechanism through trade changes would continue to operate, although perhaps in a dampened form. As scholars such as Milton Friedman and Gottfried Haberler emphasized at an early stage, the incorporation of capital flows into the analysis (as long as they were not the result of destabilizing speculation) tended to reduce the differences between fixed and flexible exchange rates on grounds of both resource allocation and macroeconomic stabilization.[17] Indeed, as was emphasized by Modigliani and Askari, with sufficiently high international capital mobility a domestic boom could lead to an appreciation rather than a depreciation of the exchange rate, with the effects of capital inflows more than off-setting the worsening of the trade balance.[18] Emphasis on capital-account considerations also led to important clarifications of stock-flow relationships resulting from the application of the portfolio approach to international capital movements and the monetary and asset-market approaches to exchange rates and the balance of payments.[19]

Movements Away from Viewing the Exchange Rate and Balance of Payments in Isolation. A third major development or set of developments involved a movement away from partial equilibrium analysis of

---

of important policy issues. For further discussion, see Thomas D. Willett, "United States Economic Interests in Crawling Peg Systems" (Paper presented at the ANPEC/Ford Conference on the Crawling Peg, Rio de Janeiro, October 1979), forthcoming in conference volume edited by John Williamson.

[17] For further discussion, see Tower and Willett, *Optimum Currency Areas and Exchange-Rate Flexibility.*

[18] Franco Modigliani and H. Askari, "The International Transfer of Capital and the Propagation of Domestic Disturbances under Alternative Payments Systems," *Banca Nazionale del Lavoro Quarterly Review,* no. 107 (December 1973), pp. 295-310.

[19] Early applications of the portfolio approach to international capital movements were made by Branson, Grubel, Levin, Miller, Willett, and Whitman; see, for example, Fritz Machlup, Walter Salant, and Lorie Tashis, *International Mobility and Movement of Capital* (New York: National Bureau of Economic Research, 1972). One important implication of these papers was that the ability to achieve substantially different effects from monetary and fiscal policy on balance of payments and exchange rate is limited to the short run. For discussion of the later monetary and asset approaches, see J. F. O. Bilson, "Recent Developments in Monetary Models of Exchange Rate Determination," *IMF Staff Papers,* vol. 26 (June 1979), pp. 201-23; Rudiger Dornbusch, "Monetary Policy under Exchange Rate Flexibility," in Federal Reserve Bank of Boston, *Managed Exchange-Rate Flexibility*; Frenkel and Johnson, *Economics of Exchange Rates*; Frenkel, "Flexible Exchange Rates"; and Mussa, "Macroeconomic Interdependence."

the foreign exchange market and the tendency to analyze exchange rates or balance-of-payments developments in isolation. A major corollary of this approach is that the effects of exchange-rate changes will often depend importantly on the cause. Once one drops the traditional Keynesian fixed-price assumption, then a change in the nominal exchange rate need not correspond to a change in real exchange rates. A change in exchange rates that offsets differences in macroeconomic policies may promote rather than distort efficient resource allocation.[20]

Likewise, an exchange rate change that is merely offsetting different domestic trends would be expected, other things being equal, to maintain rather than change the current trade balance. Thus a finding that depreciation did not improve a country's trade balance is not by itself strong evidence that exchange rate adjustments do not work. The depreciation may still have been working in the sense of keeping the trade balance from deteriorating further.[21]

The need to adopt a more general equilibrium framework is likewise crucial for investigating the interrelationships between exchange rate changes and inflation. In the short run it is certainly true that a country's inflation rate will be less if its exchange rate is maintained pegged than if it depreciates. As emphasized by the monetary-approach literature, however, one should focus on long-run equilibrium situations as well as on short-run disequilibrium positions. If the exchange rate is maintained by running down reserves and subsidizing domestic consumption, then, of course, measured inflation would be less over this period. But what about long-run comparisons when resources would have to be recouped? The resultant "pain" later could easily exceed the initial pleasure. It no longer becomes an easy matter to decide whether fixed, or adjustably pegged, or floating rates allow countries to achieve their macroeconomic stabilization objectives with less difficulty over the long run, especially when limits on the export of domestic inflationary or deflationary policies are taken into account.

Furthermore, both the impact and the long-run effects of exchange-rate changes are likely to be affected strongly by the extent to which

[20] For further discussion, see Balassa, "Flexible Exchange Rates"; Charles Pigott, Richard J. Sweeney, and Thomas D. Willett, "Some Aspects of the Behavior and Effects of Floating Exchange Rates" (Paper presented to the Conference on Monetary Theory and Policy, Konstanz, Germany, June 1975); Pigott, Sweeney, and Willett, "The Uncertainty and Distortion Effects of Alternative Exchange Rate Systems," in Sweeney and Willett, *Exchange Rate Flexibility;* and Thursby and Willett, "Effects of Flexible Exchange Rates on Trade and Investment."

[21] For further discussion, see Peter B. Clark, Dennis E. Logue, and Richard J. Sweeney, eds., *The Effects of Exchange Rate Adjustments* (Washington, D.C.: U.S. Treasury, 1977).

they were caused and are accommodated by monetary and fiscal expansion. The extent, for example, to which exchange-rate depreciation is likely to worsen inflationary expectations should depend to a considerable degree on the extent to which it was a result of worsening inflationary expectations in the first place. In a simple rational expectations model with homogeneous expectations, an exchange-rate depreciation caused by domestic monetary expansion would have no independent effect on expectations, contrary to what would be implied by standard Phillips curve–type wage/price blocs based on markup pricing and adaptive expectations. I strongly suspect that for most economies the truth will lie somewhere between these two extreme types of models but that there will be enough of a rational-expectations component to make the effects of exchange rate change often depend on the causes in an empirically important way.[22]

As a consequence, most recent empirical studies on the effects of exchange-rate movements on the volume of international trade and investment and on inflation may offer little useful information.[23] Most of these studies have used nominal exchange rates and treated them as though they were exogenous to domestic macroeconomic developments. They thus implicitly assume that the effects of exchange rate changes can be treated as if they were independent of their causes. On theoretical grounds, we would not expect this to be true for important classes of cases; Charles Pigott, J. Rutledge, and I have found that for the United States at least the use of standard, open-economy, Phillips curve–type models results in quite unstable coefficients, a finding consistent with our view that effects will differ significantly depending on the causes. Using different time periods for estimation, we found price level impact of a one-percentage-point depreciation that varied from less than one to more than twenty basis points and long-run effects that varied from three to fifty-three basis points. Even after deleting the top and bottom 10 percent of the estimates, we found a range of impacts running from four to nineteen basis points and full effects running from eleven to forty-four basis points. Some progress is being made in this area by replacing nominal with real exchange-rate measures, although this does not eliminate all of the important problems, as will be discussed in section 4.

---

[22] For further discussion, see Pigott, Rutledge, and Willett, "Some Difficulties"; and idem, "Some Evidence on the Instability of Estimates of the Inflationary Effects of Exchange Rate Changes," mimeographed (Claremont, Calif.: Claremont Men's College, 1980).

[23] For references to these studies, see Pigott, Rutledge, and Willett, "Some Evidence"; and Thursby and Willett, "Effects of Flexible Exchange Rates on Trade and Investment."

Expectations and Financial Market Efficiency. The final major developments I wish to discuss are increased recognition of the importance of expectations and appreciation of the role of modern finance theory for the analysis of traditional international economic questions. In recent years, there has been a strong resurgence of emphasis on the role of expectations in both domestic and international monetary analysis. Though perhaps best known in the form of the rational-expectations revolution, the crucial importance of the role of expectations is recognized by many who would not be sympathetic to some of the strongest forms of rational expectations modeled in recent years. A major implication for exchange rate analysis is the shift toward viewing the foreign exchange market as a forward-looking financial market that does and should adjust to expectations of future developments rather than serve as just a mechanism for balancing international transactions related to real economic activity and government transfers.

This means that one cannot look at the stability of either nominal or real exchange rates per se as a sound indicator of the efficiency with which the foreign-exchange market is operating. We can conceive of an ideal (though perhaps dull) world in which equilibrium rates would never change, but it is not legitimate to place the blame for the absence of such a world fully on the exchange market. In a changing world, one would want exchange rates to adjust in response to current and expected developments, and a major test for desirable performance would be how well the market did reflect such expectations. Indeed, although at one time speculation was rather widely viewed as something that in destabilizing form could upset the efficient operation of floating exchange rates, it is now recognized that stabilizing private speculation is a necessary condition for floating rates to work well without official intervention. The well-known *J*-curve effects of low trade elasticities in the very short run would mean, for example, that market clearing rates would at a minimum display extreme volatility and would probably be dynamically unstable if it were not for stabilizing speculation.[24]

Another example of the importance of taking expectations into account concerns the relationships between interest rate and exchange rate changes. The conventional wisdom has been that rising interest rates will strengthen a currency, but empirically there does not appear to be any strong simple correlation between interest rate and exchange-

---

[24] For further discussion, see A. J. C. Britton, "The Dynamic Stability of the Foreign Exchange Market," *Economic Journal,* vol. 80 (March 1970), pp. 81-86; Ronald I. McKinnon, *Money in International Exchange* (New York: Oxford University Press, 1979); and Wonnacott, *Floating Canadian Dollar.*

rate changes.[25] Exchange rate depreciation seems to be associated with rising interest rates about as frequently as appreciation. The explanation, of course, is that we would expect a positive association where the increase in nominal interest rates was caused by a tightening of monetary policy and an associated reduction of inflationary expectations and increase in the expected real rate. On the other hand, where the interest-rate increase was caused by anticipations of more rapid inflation, we would expect to see the exchange rate depreciate.[26] Likewise, we would expect that the short-run effects of monetary expansion would depend crucially on whether the expansion was anticipated or unanticipated, just as would the domestic price and employment effects.

The financial-market-cum-expectations approach to the foreign exchange market has made a very important contribution, but it still leaves us at this point with a good deal of scope for disagreement about the experience with floating so far and desirable policy strategies. Though this approach explains why we have had a great deal of exchange rate volatility, given the underlying environment, it does not by itself assure us that the actual amount of volatility has not been greater than would have occurred in an efficient market. Second, the information-processing efficiency of the foreign-exchange market may not be the only important concept of efficiency relevant to the evaluation of exchange rate behavior. I shall briefly discuss these two issues in reverse order.

One important point to make is that financial-market or information-processing efficiency is much more closely related to many traditional international monetary issues than is often realized.[27] At an

---

[25] See Ira J. Kaylin, Charles Pigott, Richard J. Sweeney, and Thomas D. Willett, "The Effect of Interest Rate Changes on Exchange Rates during the Current Float," in Carl H. Stern and others, eds., *Eurocurrencies and the International Monetary System* (Washington, D.C.: American Enterprise Institute, 1976).

[26] For further discussion, see Kathleen H. Brown, "Impact of Changes in the Discount Rate on the Dollar's Foreign Exchange Value," Federal Reserve Board, International Finance Discussion Papers, no. 144 (June 1979); Jeffrey A. Frankel, "On the Mark: A Theory of Floating Exchange Rates Based on Real Interest Rate Differentials," *American Economic Review*, vol. 69 (September 1979), pp. 610-22; Douglas K. Mudd, "Did Discount Rate Changes Affect the Foreign Exchange Value of the Dollar during 1978?" *Federal Reserve Bank of St. Louis Review*, vol. 61 (April 1979), pp. 20-26; idem, "Do Rising U.S. Interest Rates Imply a Strong Dollar?" *Federal Reserve Bank of Saint Louis*, vol. 61 (June 1979), pp. 9-13.

[27] For discussion of financial-market efficiency and of its relationship to the behavior of the foreign exchange market, see Bilson, "Recent Developments"; Eugene Fama, "Efficient Capital Markets: A Review of Theory and Empirical Work," *Journal of Finance*, vol. 25 (May 1970), pp. 383-417; Steven W. Kohlhagen and Thomas D. Willett, "The Costs of Cover and the Question of Forward Rate Bias," in Sweeney and Willett, *Exchange Rate Flexibility*; Levich, "Tests of

earlier conference on exchange-rate flexibility,[28] there was a tendency for a number of participants to consider this question as a relatively minor consideration, perhaps on the order of whether transaction costs were, say, one quarter or three quarters of 1 percent, a small issue compared with the traditional topics of debate about the effects of floating rates. I would argue, though, that it is at the heart of the traditional debate because most of the standard arguments about the adverse economic effects of exchange rate movements on inflation and on resource allocation have been based, at least implicitly, on the assumption that these movements were the result of badly behaved speculation—in other words, that they did not reflect changes in equilibrium exchange rates. There are sufficient ambiguities in the definition of equilibrium and possibilities of externalities resulting from exchange-rate changes, especially in the face of imperfections in domestic adjustment mechanisms, so that there may remain arguments for exchange market intervention even when the foreign exchange market is efficient in the financial market sense, but these additional potential rationales have not been well worked under the assumption of speculative efficiency in the foreign exchange market.[29]

I should perhaps note in passing that a fair portion of the differences in policy recommendations about exchange-rate policies has stemmed from the tendency of authors to take one or two concepts of efficiency as the exclusive focus of analysis. Thus, for example, there are a number of papers on the optimum stabilization criteria and the correlations between domestic and international developments,[30] whereas other analyses of the welfare cost of disequilibrium exchange rates and optimum rates of crawl assume domestic stability and look at the costs

---

Forecasting Models," "Further Results," and "Efficiency of Markets"; idem, "Analyzing the Accuracy of Foreign Exchange Advisory Services: Theory and Evidence," National Bureau of Economic Research, Working Papers Series, no. 336 (April 1979); Dennis Logue, Richard J. Sweeney, and Thomas D. Willett, "The Speculative Behavior of Foreign Exchange Rate during the Current Float," *Journal of Business Research*, vol. 6, no. 2 (1978), pp. 159-74; and the paper by Richard Sweeney in this volume.

[28] Jacob S. Dreyer, Gottfried Haberler, and Thomas D. Willett, eds., *Exchange Rate Flexibility* (Washington, D.C.: American Enterprise Institute, 1978).

[29] See Thomas D. Willett, "Alternative Approaches to International Surveillance of Exchange-Rate Policies," in Federal Reserve Bank of Boston, *Managed Exchange-Rate Flexibility*.

[30] For references and discussion, see Dale W. Henderson, "Financial Policies in an Open Economy," *American Economic Review*, vol. 69 (May 1979), pp. 232-39; Richard J. Sweeney, "Automatic Stabilization Policy and Exchange Rate Regimes: A General Equilibrium Approach," in Sweeney and Willett, *Exchange Rate Flexibility*; Tower and Willett, *Optimum Currency Areas and Exchange-Rate Flexibility*; and papers cited in n. 73, below.

of varying import levels on standard microeconomic welfare criteria[31] or on optimum inflation tax grounds.[32]

I believe that this is an extremely important area for further research, but pending further analysis my judgment would be that the speculative efficiency of the foreign exchange market is the central rather than a relatively minor component of overall exchange market efficiency.

We cannot observe directly whether exchange markets display speculative efficiency or not, but there are ways in which we can bring empirical evidence to bear on the question. There are two basic methods of approach, and though we cannot expect either to be able to discriminate among alternative hypotheses sufficiently sharply and definitively to expect empirical research to resolve all points of disagreement within a few years, they can give us important information on which to base better-informed judgments.

One approach attempts to look directly at what equilibrium rates should be and to compare these with actual exchange rate behavior. This is in effect what commentators are doing when they say that this exchange rate has been pushed down too low or that one has been pushed up too high. The problem of course is that opinions differ. If virtually everyone agreed that a rate is too high or too low, this would be strong evidence of insufficient stabilizing speculation because those with such opinions would be forgoing expected speculative profits. There appear to have been few instances in which this seems likely to have been the case.[33] Generally, the question is how to choose among conflicting opinions. This can never be done with absolute confidence, but statistical analysis of the track records of various forecasters and econometric modeling can provide useful information. Of course, with respect to the former, forecasts can turn out right for the wrong reasons, but it would be highly desirable to know more about forecasting records,

---

[31] John C. Hause, "The Welfare Costs of Disequilibrium Exchange Rates," *Journal of Political Economy*, vol. 74 (August 1966), pp. 333-52; and Harry G. Johnson, "The Welfare Costs of Exchange Rate Stabilization," *Journal of Political Economy*, vol. 74 (October 1966), pp. 512-18.

[32] Donald J. Mathieson, "Is There an Optimal Crawl?" *Journal of International Economics*, vol. 6 (May 1976), pp. 183-202. For discussion of a number of the major concepts of exchange market efficiency that have been used in the literature and suggestions for synthesizing some of them, see Thomas D. Willett and Edward Tower, "The Welfare Economics of International Adjustment," *Journal of Finance*, vol. 26 (May 1971), pp. 287-302; Tower and Willett, *Optimum Currency Areas and Exchange-Rate Flexibility*; Willett, "Crawling Peg Systems"; and idem, *International Liquidity Issues* (Washington, D.C.: American Enterprise Institute, 1980).

[33] See Willett, *Floating Exchange Rates*, pp. 38-40; idem, "Fall and Rise of the Dollar."

especially those of official agencies in terms of both explicit forecasts and inferences based on official intervention policy. Unfortunately, officials seem little inclined to facilitate outside research on these questions (although the U.S. government is more forthcoming than most in making known data on its intervention actions). Furthermore, published reserve changes are generally a very poor proxy for actual official intervention and substitute intervention policies, such as official borrowing and the short-term manipulation of private lending and borrowing incentives.[34] Thus the substantive analysis in the public domain is for private forecasting services.[35]

With respect to econometric modeling, some interesting attempts have been made to tackle this question explicitly,[36] and a great deal of effort has been devoted to econometric modeling of exchange-rate behavior in recent years.[37] Given the combination of the importance of expectations about future developments and uncertainties about the true magnitudes of a number of important structural parameters, however, there can be a very wide range of exchange rates over which it would be hard honestly to say that the rate was clearly overvalued or undervalued, given a plausible range of expectations about future developments.

Thus, for example, the timing of the fall of the dollar during 1977 and 1978 cannot be explained by mechanical linkages with current price and income developments. It can quite plausibly be explained, however, in terms of changing expectations about U.S. inflation, energy policy, and growth differentials between the United States and Europe. The resulting drop in the real exchange rate was well within the range of plausible estimates of what it would take over the medium term to offset the effects of differential income and oil import growth.[38] Given such wide confidence bounds, it is not surprising that officials often argue that exchange rate changes are based on overly pessimistic expectations.

[34] This point has not been sufficiently recognized by empirical researchers.

[35] See, for example, Stephen H. Goodman, "Foreign Exchange Rate Forecasting Techniques," *Journal of Finance,* vol. 34 (May 1979), pp. 415-27; and Levich, "Examination."

[36] See, for example, Kohlhagen, "Identification."

[37] See the recent surveys: Jacques R. Artus, "Methods of Assessing the Long-Run Equilibrium Value of an Exchange Rate," *Journal of International Economics,* vol. 8 (May 1978), pp. 277-99; Bilson, "Recent Developments"; Peter Isard, *Exchange-Rate Determination: A Survey of Popular Views and Recent Models,* Studies in International Finance, no. 42 (Princeton, N.J.: Princeton University, International Finance Section, 1978); Kohlhagen, "Behavior of Foreign Exchange Markets"; and Susan Schadler, "Sources of Exchange Rate Variability," *IMF Staff Papers,* vol. 24 (July 1977), pp. 253-96.

[38] See Willett, "It's Too Easy to Blame the Speculators."

This may certainly be true at times, and I would suspect that the average quality of inside information and technical analysis available to officials in the major countries is considerably higher than for the private sector. On the other hand, there would seem to be more incentives for officials to be overly optimistic and/or to desire that the private sector be overly optimistic than there are incentives for the private sector to be overly pessimistic.

I am very sympathetic to the idea that although we cannot say exactly what the right rate is, it should be possible to identify a wrong rate with a fairly high degree of confidence if it goes sufficiently far astray. The problem is that on scientific grounds the range over which a rate cannot clearly be deemed wrong is quite wide—considerably wider than one might often infer from official pronouncements. As our technical knowledge increases, we should be able to narrow these confidence bounds somewhat. If a more stable environment for expectations were established over time, we might even be able to narrow these bounds considerably. I suspect, however, that there will always be a fairly wide zone over which we cannot identify wrong exchange rates on solid scientific grounds as long as macropolicies are not geared to achieve a specific exchange-rate objective.

If this conclusion is correct, the importance of the second type of approach to analyzing the speculative efficiency of exchange rate behavior is substantially increased. This approach, developed originally to investigate domestic financial and commodity markets, applies time series analysis to look for behavior that would be inconsistent with the efficient-markets hypothesis. The essential point is to attempt to find empirical regularities that suggest unexploited profit opportunities and test the predictions implied by particular hypotheses about badly behaved speculation. Assertions that the foreign exchange markets are dominated by destabilizing bandwagon effects, for example, imply that one should be able to find filter (buy-and-sell) rules that made systematic profits.[39] Runs tests, autocorrelation analysis, and the search for biases in forward-rate predictions are other frequently applied tests.[40]

[39] For further discussion, see J. F. O. Bilson, "The 'Speculative Efficiency' Hypothesis" (University of Chicago, 1979); Bradford Cornell and Kimball Dietrich, "The Efficiency of the Market for Foreign Exchange under Floating Exchange Rates," *Review of Economics and Statistics,* vol. 60 (February 1978), pp. 111-20; Michael P. Dooley and Jeffrey R. Shafer, "Analysis of Short-Run Exchange Rate Behavior, March 1973 to September 1975," mimeographed (Federal Reserve Board, 1976); Levich, "Tests of Forecasting Models," "Further Results," "Efficiency of Markets," and "Accuracy of Foreign Exchange Advisory Services"; Logue, Sweeney, and Willett, "Speculative Behavior"; and the paper by Richard Sweeney in this volume.

[40] I should note that I would expect runs tests to overstate the likelihood of

In evaluating the results of such studies it is very important to distinguish among different possible types of less-than-ideal speculative efficiency. Findings of occasional biased estimates from the forward rate may indicate, for example, only that the speculative schedule is less than perfectly elastic. This might or might not result from risk aversion, which is consistent with the traditional concept of financial market efficiency.[41] Different models suggest different measures for "efficient" risk premiums, which may keep the forward rate from being an unbiased estimator of the future spot rate; and the welfare economics of whether such instances would present a case for ideal government intervention does not yet seem clear. Furthermore, the majority of studies have not found significant biases in the predictions of forward rates, even though their explanatory power has not been high and some studies have found better ex post predictors. Thus on practical grounds I do not think that the research done so far suggests a strong rationale for substantial official intervention on the grounds of possible biases in forward rates.

On the other hand, the existence of large persistent profits from filter rules would suggest that there has been significant destabilizing or insufficiently stabilizing speculation and that official intervention based on such rules would be socially desirable. (From this standpoint, the predictions of the forward rate could be used as the basis for a filter run.) As is discussed in detail in the accompanying paper by Richard Sweeney, the current results from such testing are quite difficult to interpret because we are only beginning to develop tests of statistical significance for filter rules.[42] Another important problem is that we do not yet have good, generally accepted operational measures for distinguishing between diversifiable and nondiversifiable risk and for deciding what are above-normal rates of return on foreign exchange

---

market inefficiency. The standard efficient markets tests are based on the assumption that new bits of information are uncorrelated, whereas I think there are many episodes in which new information is highly serially correlated. This possibility would also affect autocorrelation and filter rate tests and should receive further investigation. Of course, if such runs of information are highly predictable, they would be speculated out in an efficient market. Still, I should not be surprised if in a generally uncertain environment one often found more runs around trend than one would expect under a random walk, but which it would not have been economically profitable on a risk-adjusted basis to speculate out.

[41] See Bilson, "Speculative Efficiency"; Jeffrey A. Frankel, "The Diversifiability of Exchange Risks," *Journal of International Economics* (1979), pp. 379-93; and Kohlhagen and Willett, "Costs of Cover."

[42] See Richard J. Sweeney, "A Statistical Filter Rule Test: The Dollar DM Exchange Rate," mimeographed (Claremont, Calif.: Claremont Men's College, 1980); and P. D. Praetz, "Rates of Return on Filter Tests," *Journal of Finance,* vol. 31 (March 1976), pp. 71-75.

speculation when risk considerations are taken into account. At present we can do little more than reject some of the more extreme hypotheses about the prevalence of large, destabilizing bandwagon effects. The growing length of our data series on floating exchange rates, however, combined with progress in research on the types of technical questions noted above, makes an area with a very high expected payoff for further empirical analysis.

Some Propositions and Conclusions for Discussion

The following propositions summarize my impressions of the current state of empirical evidence on a number of major aspects of the causes and effects of exchange rate behavior during the 1970s and offer some suggestions for further research and for policy strategies. Although I am inclined to believe in the statements presented, a number of them are offered in the spirit of providing a starting point for discussion, to be criticized, amended, and added to rather than as conclusions in which I have 100 percent confidence.

1. The foreign exchange markets have been characterized by an unusually high degree of uncertainty since the widespread adoption of floating rates in the early 1970s, but this has been due more to the underlying environment than to floating rates themselves. Exchange-rate variability has not been greater than that in stock and bond prices.[43] Establishment of greater exchange-rate stability requires establishment of greater stability in the underlying economic and financial environment. The extent to which floating rates themselves have been an independent cause of uncertainty and distortion of economic incentives is not clear from the available evidence.

2. Private speculation appears to have worked fairly well in the sense that the exchange markets have not been generally dominated by the types of destabilizing bandwagons or instabilities due to J-curve effects or other temporary phenomena, or to insufficient stabilizing speculation. The evidence on the stronger forms of speculative-efficiency hypothesis is mixed, however, and it is quite possible that there have been episodes of disorderly markets and less than perfectly elastic speculative schedules that have at times kept spot and forward rates from fully reflecting the mean of speculative expectations. Such biases would not necessarily mean that expectations were not rational or that the markets were not efficient in the financial market sense. Despite a good bit of interesting work in recent years, we do not have a good,

---

[43] See Frenkel, "Flexible Exchange Rates"; and Levich, "Examination."

generally agreed measure of how to calculate "efficient" risk premiums for evaluating the performance of speculation in spot and forward rates.[44]

3. Except when expectations are strongly held by the private market, official exchange market intervention will have a direct effect on foreign exchange rates over and above effects on expectations and monetary aggregates, in contradiction to the assumptions of some of the monetary approach literature.[45] Thus, given the large magnitudes of official intervention, it will be important in analyzing exchange rate behavior to attempt to take into account the effects of official intervention through the construction of exchange market pressure variables (which combine intervention and exchange rate changes), along the lines of Lance Girton and Don Roper and of Michael Connolly and José Dantar da Silveira, or through simultaneous equations estimation of official intervention and exchange rate changes, such as the work of Jacques Artus, William Branson and his colleagues, and Esther Suss.[46]

4. So far there has been little published analysis of the extent to to which official intervention has been stabilizing or destabilizing for different countries and periods. Casual observation suggests there have been examples of both. Systematic evaluation of how well official intervention has worked should be a priority area of research (there will of course be many difficulties both in obtaining data and in evaluating tests of performance).

5. Although there has been much discussion of the possibility of

---

[44] For recent discussions of some of these issues and references to the literature on efficient risk premiums, see Bilson, "Speculative Efficiency"; Cornell and Dietrich, "Efficiency of the Market"; Michael Dooley and Peter Isard, "The Portfolio Balance Model of Exchange Rates," Federal Reserve Board International Finance Discussion Papers, no. 125 (1979); Frankel, "Diversifiability of Exchange Risks"; Kohlhagen and Willett, "Costs of Cover"; and Sweeney, "Statistical Filter Rule Test."

[45] See, for example, Allan H. Meltzer, "The Conduct of Monetary Policy under Current Monetary Arrangement," *Journal of Monetary Economics,* vol. 4, no. 2 (1978), pp. 371-88.

[46] Lance Girton and Don Roper, "A Monetary Model of Exchange Market Pressure Applied to the Postwar Canadian Experience," *American Economic Review,* vol. 67 (September 1977), pp. 537-48; Michael Connolly and José Dantar da Silveira, "Exchange Market Pressure in Postwar Brazil," *American Economic Review,* vol. 69 (June 1979), pp. 448-54; Jacques R. Artus, "Exchange Rate Stability and Managed Floating: The Experience of the Federal Republic of Germany," *IMF Staff Papers,* vol. 23 (July 1976), pp. 312-33; William Branson, Hannan Halttunen, and Paul Mason, "Exchange Rates in the Short-Run: The Dollar Deutschmark Rate," *European Economic Review,* vol. 10 (December 1977), pp. 303-24; and Esther C. Suss, "A Short-Run Model of the Trade-off between Exchange Rate and Reserve Changes," mimeographed (Washington, D.C.: International Monetary Fund, May 1979).

variations in monetary policy having magnification effects that cause exchange-rate changes to overshoot long-run equilibrium values,[47] there are in fact many alternative types of possible exchange-rate dynamics that do not include overshooting.[48] The evidence available so far does not suggest that this type of overshooting has been a major cause of the observed exchange rate variability.[49] We would expect the interest rate and exchange-rate effects of money supply changes to be quite different depending upon whether they were anticipated or not. In future exchange-rate modeling, attempts should be made to divide monetary expansion into expected and unexpected components, as has been begun recently in domestic models looking at inflation and output and employment effects.[50]

6. Conducting analysis in terms of real as well as nominal exchange rates has been an important advance, but the combination of measurement problems and variability of long-run equilibrium real exchange rates keeps PPP indexes by themselves from being a good guide to exchange market intervention.[51]

7. The impact effects of exchange rate changes on domestic prices are larger than was once generally realized, because the tradable-goods sector is much larger for most economies than the percentage of goods actually traded internationally. This does not mean, however, that exchange-rate changes are not effective instruments for balance-of-

[47] See, for example, Dornbusch, "Expectations and Exchange Rate Dynamics."

[48] See, for example, Sven Arndt, "On Exchange Rate Dynamics," *Zeitschrift für Wirtschafts—und Sozialwissenschaften,* vol. 1/2 (1979), pp. 71-93; Robert J. Barro, "A Stochastic Equilibrium Model of an Open Economy under Flexible Exchange Rates," *Quarterly Journal of Economics,* vol. 92 (February 1978), pp. 149-64; Wilfred Eithier, "Expectations and the Asset-Market Approach to the Exchange Rate," *Journal of Monetary Economics,* vol. 5, no. 2 (1979), pp. 259-82; Charles Freedman, "Monetary Policy under Alternative Exchange Rate Regimes: Discussion," in Federal Reserve Bank of Boston, *Managed Exchange-Rate Flexibility*; James C. Ingram, "Expectations and Floating Exchange Rates," *Weltwirtschaftliches Archiv.,* vol. 114, no. 3 (1978); Charles Pigott and Richard J. Sweeney, "International Price Dynamics," mimeographed (Claremont Men's College, 1979); Jürg Niehans, "Exchange Rate Dynamics with Stock-Flow Interaction," *Journal of Political Economy,* vol. 85 (December 1977), pp. 1245-57; and Charles W. Wilson, "Anticipated Shocks and Exchange Rate Dynamics," *Journal of Political Economy,* vol. 87 (June 1979), pp. 639-47.

[49] See Pigott and Sweeney, "International Price Dynamics."

[50] See, for example, Robert J. Barro, "Unanticipated Monetary Growth and Unemployment in the U.S.," *American Economic Review,* vol. 67 (March 1977), pp. 101-15; Charles Pigott, "Rational Expectations and Countercyclical Monetary Policy: The Japanese Experience," Federal Reserve Bank of San Francisco, *Economic Review,* Summer 1978, pp. 6-22; and, explicitly on exchange rate modeling, see Isard, *Exchange-Rate Determination.*

[51] See Willett, "It's Too Easy to Blame the Speculators," and the paper by Sweeney in this volume and references cited there.

payments adjustment for the major industrial countries. Unless offset by changes in macroeconomic policies, exchange-rate changes are capable of causing significant changes in relative prices, at least for most countries that have been independently floating for much of the 1970s. Thus, exchange rate changes do continue to work to promote balance-of-payments adjustments along the lines of traditional analysis (from the perspective of the monetary approach, exchange-rate changes could work through real balance effects even if relative prices were not affected). Much of the often-encountered view that exchange-rate changes are not very effective has probably stemmed from a failure to distinguish between changes that neutralize domestic developments, and thus keep payments positions from worsening further, and changes that go beyond this and cause reductions in imbalances.[52]

8. Most studies of the effects of exchange rate changes on inflation are seriously flawed because they do not attempt to distinguish among their causes. As a consequence, we know relatively little about the extent to which the adoption of floating exchange rates may have tended on balance to worsen or to improve inflation-unemployment relationships. Future research should be directed toward construction of more comprehensive models that attempt to distinguish between the portions of exchange rate movements that are exogenous and those that are endogenous to the domestic inflationary process. This will not be an easy task, but it should be attempted.[53]

9. The effects of the adoption of floating rates on the incentives to inflate are unclear. Though genuinely fixed rates undoubtedly exert strong financial discipline in the absence of rapid increases in international reserves, it seems likely that adjustably pegged or heavily

[52] For recent reviews of empirical studies of the effects of exchange rate changes on trade flows and prices, see A. V. Deardorff and R. M. Stern, "Modeling the Effects of Foreign Prices on Domestic Price Determination: Some Econometric Evidence and Implications for Theoretical Analysis," *Banca Nazionale del Lavoro Quarterly Review*, no. 127 (December 1978), pp. 333-52; Morris Goldstein, "Have Flexible Exchange Rates Handicapped Macroeconomic Policy?" *Special Papers in International Finance*, no. 14, Princeton University (May 1980); P. Hooper and B. Lowrey, "The Impact of the Dollar Depreciation on the U.S. Price Level: An Analytical Survey of Empirical Estimates," Federal Reserve Board International Finance Discussion Papers, no. 128 (January 1979); Robert M. Stern, Jonathan Francis, and Bruce Schumacher, *Price Statistics in International Trade: An Annotated Bibliography* (New York: Macmillan, 1976); and for theoretical analysis of the effectiveness of exchange rate adjustments, see Richard J. Sweeney and Thomas D. Willett, "The Inflationary Impact of Exchange Rate Changes: Some Theoretical Considerations," in Clark, Logue, and Sweeney, *Effects of Exchange Rate Adjustments*, pp. 45-61; and Willett, *Floating Exchange Rates*, chap. 2.

[53] For further discussion, see Pigott, Rutledge, and Willett, "Some Evidence."

managed rates may maximize the incentives to engage in inflationary, political business-cycle activity,[54] and there clearly have been instances in which depreciating exchange rates have disciplined domestic financial authorities. It seems implausible that the adoption of floating rates has been a major cause of the high level of worldwide inflation during the 1970s, but there is little systematic empirical evidence so far on the effects of floating rates per se on discipline and the incentives to inflate.[55] My suspicion is that anyone who now holds strong views on whether pegged or floating rates are likely to cause more inflation has simply not thought about all sides of the question deeply enough.[56]

10. The effects of floating rates on the international transmission of macropolicies and as automatic stabilizers are also unclear. Although traditional balance-of-payments analysis suggested that the exchange rate would depreciate in the face of a domestic boom and thus dampen international transmission through Keynesian trade-balance effects, both the monetary approach and Keynesian analysis with high capital mobility suggest that the exchange rate will appreciate and thus

[54] See Willett, "Crawling Peg Systems"; Thomas D. Willett and John Mullen, "The Effects of Alternative International Monetary Systems on Macroeconomic Discipline and the Political Business Cycle," Claremont Working Papers (Paper presented at the Pennsylvania State Conference on the Political Economy of Domestic and International Monetary Relations, June 1980, forthcoming in the conference volume); and John Mullen and Thomas D. Willett, "The Discipline Debate and Inflationary Biases under Alternative Exchange Rate Systems," in Sweeney and Willett, *Exchange Rate Flexibility.*

[55] See, however, the interesting effort by Stanley Black in *National Policy and Flexible Exchange Rates* (New Haven, Conn.: Yale University Press, 1977); the analysis of the causes of monetary expansion in major industrial countries by Robert Gordon in "World Inflation and Monetary Accommodation in Eight Countries," Brookings Papers on Economic Activity, no. 2 (Washington, D.C.: Brookings Institution, 1977), pp. 2109-468; by Thomas D. Willett and Leroy O. Laney in "Monetarism, Budget Deficits, and Wage Push Inflation," *Banca Nazionale del Lavoro Quarterly Review,* no. 127 (December 1978), pp. 315-31; and by Leroy Laney and Thomas D. Willett, *The Political Economy of Global Inflation: The Causes of Monetary Expansion in the Major Industrial Countries* (Washington, D.C.: American Enterprise Institute, forthcoming).

[56] For recent discussion of the effects of alternative exchange systems on inflation, see Emil-Maria Claassen, "World Inflation under Flexible Exchange Rates," *Scandinavian Journal of Economics,* vol. 78, no. 2 (1976), pp. 346-65; W. M. Corden, "Inflation and the Exchange Rate Regime," *Scandinavian Journal of Economics,* vol. 78, no. 2 (1976), pp. 370-83; idem, *Inflation, Exchange Rates, and the World Economy* (Oxford: Oxford University Press, 1977); A. D. Crockett and Morris Goldstein, "Inflation under Fixed and Flexible Exchange Rates," *IMF Staff Papers,* vol. 23 (November 1976), pp. 509-44; Goldstein, "Have Flexible Rates Handicapped Policy?"; Richard J. Sweeney and Thomas D. Willett, "The International Transmission of Inflation," *Kredit und Kapital,* vol. 9, special supplement, 1976, pp. 441-517; and John Williamson, "World Stagflation and International Monetary Arrangements," mimeographed (1979).

strengthen transmission. So far there does not appear to be a strong, systematic tendency for exchange rates either to appreciate consistently or to depreciate with domestic booms. Although several monetary approach models have found the expected positive signs,[57] other studies have reported many negative signs,[58] and it is in fact likely that the signs will often reverse over different stages of a boom.[59] It is also important to take into account the lags with which changes in trade balances will influence domestic economic activity. Thus, for example, when Joachim Harnack and I extended Edward Tower's and Mark Courtney's empirical measures of the effects of pegged and floating rates as automatic stabilizers to take lagged effects into account, we found that the results were often reversed [60] (see table 1). This should be a profitable area for further research, although I suspect that because of shifts in the pattern of disturbances over time empirical regularities may be hard to find for most countries.

11. Floating rates do appear to have increased the degree of monetary independence for many countries, although the extent of this increase is probably not so great as many people anticipated. This is due to the fact that even under pegged rates many industrial countries displayed a great deal of ability to sterilize payments imbalances in the short run (empirical studies have consistently found a much greater degree of sterilization than would be suggested by the comments of central bankers) and to the fact that monetary policy is not entirely free from external considerations even under floating rates.[61]

[57] See Bilson, "Recent Developments."

[58] See, for example, Henry Goldstein, "Floating Exchange Rates and Modified Purchasing Power Parity," in Federal Reserve Bank of San Francisco, *Academic Conference Volume,* 1978, pp. 166-83.

[59] For recent studies for the United States, see Michael Bazdarich, "Has a Strong U.S. Economy Meant a Weak Dollar?" *Federal Reserve Bank of San Francisco Economic Review,* Spring 1979, pp. 35-46; Robert L. Hetzel and Thomas Lawler, "The Causes of the Dollar Depreciation," *Federal Reserve Bank of Richmond Economic Review,* vol. 65 (May-June 1978), pp. 15-26; and Douglas K. Mudd, "Movements in the Foreign Exchange Value of the Dollar during the Current U.S. Expansion," *Federal Reserve Bank of Saint Louis Review,* vol. 60 (November 1978), pp. 2-7.

[60] Joachim Harnack and Thomas D. Willett, "The Behavior of Flexible Exchange Rates over the Business Cycle during the Current Float," in Sweeney and Willett, *Exchange Rate Flexibility*; and Edward Tower and Mark M. Courtney, "Exchange-Rate Flexibility and Macroeconomic Stability," *Review of Economics and Statistics,* vol. 56 (May 1974), pp. 215-24.

[61] For an interesting recent study of how floating has influenced sterilization policies and references to the literature, see Leroy O. Laney, "National Monetary Independence and Managed Floating Exchange Rates," in Sweeney and Willett, *Exchange Rate Flexibility.*

TABLE 1
The Correlation (C) between Unintended Output and the Balance of Payments

Country[b]	Series	Balance-of-Payments Measures[a]		
		I C	II C	III C
Netherlands	T&C[c]	−.35	−.35	−.02
	0 lag[d]	−.34	−.30	+.36
	1-yr. lag[e]	+.04	+.22	+.33
	3-yr. lag[f]	−.03	−.18	−.16
Belgium	T&C	+.09	+.11	+.21
	0 lag	+.61	+.61	+.40
	1-yr. lag	−.61	−.62	+.01
	3-yr. lag	+.24	+.21	+.21
Ireland	T&C	+.57	+.57	−.56
	0 lag	−.52	−.48	+.26
	1-yr. lag	+.41	+.44	+.31
	3-yr. lag	+.10	+.12	−.25
Denmark	T&C	−.75	−.75	−.75
	0 lag	−.60	−.60	−.53
	1-yr. lag	+.57	+.59	+.43
	3-yr. lag	−.17	−.18	−.16
Switzerland	T&C	−.47	—	−.09
	0 lag	−.62	−.64	+.01
	1-yr. lag	+.15	+.04	−.20
	3-yr. lag	−.09	+.27	−.09
Austria	T&C	−.72	−.72	−.15
	0 lag	−.34	−.35	−.04
	1-yr. lag	+.28	+.23	−.62
	3-yr. lag	+.31	+.20	+.78
Finland	T&C	−.57	−.55	−.39
	0 lag	−.73	−.71	−.60
	1-yr. lag	+.45	+.48	+.15
	3-yr. lag	+.22	+.20	+.02
South Africa	T&C	−.33	−.33	−.63
	0 lag	−.58	−.55	−.57
	1-yr. lag	+.61	+.63	+.39
	3-yr. lag	−.01	−.03	−.37

(table continues)

TABLE 1 (continued)

Country[b]	Series	Balance-of-Payments Measures[a]		
		I C	II C	III C
Germany	T&C	−.65	−.65	+.14
	0 lag	−.79	−.78	−.07
	1-yr. lag	+.17	+.16	−.21
	3-yr. lag	+.18	+.17	−.22
Italy	T&C	−.78	−.78	−.66
	0 lag	−.64	−.59	−.39
	1-yr. lag	+.12	+.17	−.33
	3-yr. lag	+.21	+.17	+.22
Japan	T&C	−.70	−.69	−.49
	0 lag	+.63	−.61	−.64
	1-yr. lag	−.22	−.20	−.39
	3-yr. lag	−.22	−.26	−.55
United Kingdom				
	0 lag	−.68	−.64	−.39
	1-yr. lag	−.40	−.35	−.06
	3-yr. lag	+.35	+.32	+.49
New Zealand				
	0 lag	−.34	−.35	−.40
	1-yr. lag	+.48	+.49	+.01
	3-yr. lag	−.11	−.11	+.21

NOTE: A positive correlation means that a cyclical upturn is accompanied by a balance-of-payments surplus.

[a] As defined in Tower and Courtney, "Exchange-Rate Flexibility," pp. 218-19, only five-year moving average considered.

[b] Listed in same order as in Tower and Courtney's table 1, ibid.

[c] Figures as reported by Tower and Courtney, ibid., table 1, p. 220.

[d] Reestimate of Tower and Courtney series—no lag adjustment; period 1960 to 1970.

[e] Effect of unanticipated balance of payments (BOP) on unintended output lagged by one year; period 1961 to 1970.

[f] Effect of unanticipated BOP on unintended output lagged by three years; period 1961 to 1970.

SOURCE: Joachim Harnack and Thomas D. Willett, "The Behavior of Flexible Exchange Rates over the Business Cycle during the Current Float," in Richard J. Sweeney and Thomas D. Willett, Studies on Exchange Rate Flexibility (Washington, D.C.: American Enterprise Institute, forthcoming).

In analysis of this question, it is important to realize that the issue is whether floating allows a greater degree of monetary independence than pegged rates—not whether floating gives complete independence, which it cannot. Despite the long history of analysis showing that only in the very simplest of models can one expect floating rates to provide complete insulation, it seems that every few years some article discovers a new reason or rediscovers an old reason why floating rates do not give complete insulation and presents this as undercutting the arguments of supporters of floating.[62] In fact, however, though it is a useful analytic development, recognition of currency substitution possibilities has largely the same implications for insulation and monetary policy independence as international capital mobility and adds little to the basic debate about monetary policy under floating rates.[63]

Perhaps the most important clarification of insulation and transmission issues of recent years is greater understanding that it is only with respect to anticipated monetary disturbances and inflation that floating rates may be expected to provide virtually complete insulation, and that the real effects of unanticipated monetary disturbances will have effects on other countries. This suggests that floating is likely to provide much

[62] See, for example, the recent article by Marc Miles, "Currency Substitution, Flexible Exchange Rates, and Monetary Independence," *American Economic Review*, vol. 68, no. 3 (June 1978), pp. 428-36, which makes this argument with respect to currency substitution.

[63] Likewise, I do not think that the recent criticism of flexible rates on currency substitution grounds by John Kareken and Neil Wallace ("International Monetary Reform: The Feasible Alternatives," *Federal Reserve Bank of Minneapolis Quarterly Review*, Summer 1978, pp. 2-7) adds any fundamentally new insight. They convincingly show that, where currency substitution is perfect, floating rates would not be a good idea and argue in effect that in an ideal world currency substitution would be perfect, so that at best floating rates are a second-best solution. Although the authors did not give evidence of familiarity with the theory of optimum currency areas, their argument is essentially that it does not make sense to have floatng rates within an optimum currency area. This is quite true, but I would argue that the evidence is rather overwhelming that the world is not an optimum currency area. It should also be noted that, contrary to the impression given by Kareken and Wallace, advocates of flexible rates like Friedman and Haberler have argued that they could conceive of worlds of high-factor mobility and wage-price flexibility under which genuinely fixed exchange rates would be ideal, so that their arguments for flexible rates were on second-best grounds, although second-best in terms of the world not being ideal, not that there were superior policies given the world as it was (or at least as they saw it). For further discussion of the Kareken and Wallace paper, see Gottfried Haberler, "Flexible Exchange Rate Theories and Controversies Once Again," in Chipman and Kindleberger, *Flexible Exchange Rates*, pp. 29-48, and for extensive discussion of flexible rates as a partial substitute for wage and price flexibility, see Leland Yeager, *International Monetary Relations: Theory, History, and Policy* (New York: Harper & Row, 1976).

more insulation from foreign monetary disturbances in the long run than in the short run.[64]

12. The United States was probably an exception to this tendency toward increased monetary independence. This is because payments imbalances tended to be sterilized automatically, and this along with the large size of the U.S. financial markets gave the United States great scope for short-run monetary independence under pegged rates.[65] The drop of the dollar in 1978 and 1979, however, does appear to have had a significant influence on domestic monetary policy.

13. The effects of the switch to more flexible exchange rates on the effectiveness of monetary and fiscal policy do not appear to be clear. According to the traditional Keynesian fixed-price models of Fleming and Mundell, floating would increase the absolute strength of monetary policy, whereas that of fiscal policy would rise if international capital mobility were low and would fall if capital mobility were high. For the United States, it does not seem clear whether capital mobility is above or below this critical value.[66] More important, however, the basic results of these traditional models have been seriously challenged. Not only may J-curve effects cause the initial effect of exchange-rate depreciation to be contractionary rather than expansionary, thus reducing

[64] For further discussion of these issues, see Peter B. Kenen, "New Views of Exchange Rates and Old Views of Policy," *American Economic Review,* vol. 68 (May 1978), pp. 398-405; Tower and Willett, *Optimum Currency Areas and Exchange-Rate Flexibility;* and Willett, *Floating Exchange Rates,* pp. 53-58.

[65] See, for example, Michael R. Darby, "The Monetary Approach to the Balance of Payments: Two Specious Assumptions," *Economic Inquiry,* vol. 18 (April 1980), pp. 321-26; McKinnon, *Money in International Exchange;* and Thomas D. Willett, "Foreign Activity in United States Treasury Bills: Discussion," *Issues in Federal Debt Management* (Federal Reserve Bank of Boston, 1973), pp. 199-203.

[66] For reviews of the relevant theoretical and empirical work for the United States, see Richard N. Cooper, "Monetary Theory and Policy in an Open Economy," *Scandinavian Journal of Economics,* vol. 78, no. 2 (1976), pp. 146-63; Mussa, "Empirical Regularities"; Thomas D. Willett, "The Eurocurrency Market, Exchange Rate Systems, and National Financial Policies," in Carl H. Stem, John H. Makin, and Dennis E. Logue, eds., *Eurocurrencies and the International Monetary System* (Washington, D.C.: American Enterprise Institute, 1976), pp. 193-221; and the annex by Virginia Farrell, "Capital Mobility and the Efficiency of Fiscal Policy under Alternative Exchange-Rate Systems," also in *Eurocurrencies.* For Canada, see Richard E. Caves and Grant L. Reuber, "International Capital Markets and Economic Policy under Flexible and Fixed Exchange Rates, 1951-70," *Canadian–United States Financial Relationships* (Federal Reserve Bank of Boston, 1971), pp. 9-40. A more recent study by William Dewald and Maurice Marchon, "Monetary and Fiscal Actions: Did Their Relative Importance in the United States Change with Flexible Exchange Rates?" Ohio State University, Working Papers, series 78-42, May 1978, failed to find any substantial effect from the move to floating rates on monetary and budget multipliers in the United States.

rather than increasing the short-run output effects of monetary expansion,[67] but exchange rate depreciation will also speed up, and in some cases can even magnify, the price effects of monetary expansion. Thus in the very short run, monetary expansion seems likely to generate worse inflation-unemployment relationships under floating than under pegged exchange rates, a factor that incidentally could have the beneficial effect of reducing the incentives for political business cycle behavior.[68] By the same token, monetary restraint through the resulting exchange rate appreciation could become more effective in the short run in countering an inflationary spiral.

Over the medium term—that is, after J-curve effects have been reversed—monetary expansion should have stronger output and price effects under floating. Only recently has analysis begun on whether there may be differential impacts on output relative to prices,[69] and much more work needs to be done on this, on the general issue of differential effects of monetary and fiscal policy on domestic economic variables, and on international transmission and policy coordination issues.[70]

14. Although uncertainty has certainly been high in the foreign exchange markets during the 1970s, this has not had a large negative impact on the growth of world trade. Depending upon the nature of disturbances and behavior of speculation, the adoption of floating rates

---

[67] It should be noted, however, that although the nominal trade balance expressed in foreign currency will initially worsen, this is not true of the real trade balance or of the nominal trade balance as expressed in domestic currency. The former is the correct measure for considering the effects of the exchange rate changes on the balance-of-payments and international reserve flows, but it is the latter two measures that are relevant for effects on the domestic economy. The net effect when the real and nominal trade balances move in opposite directions is unclear. For further discussion on this point, see Sweeney and Willett, "Inflationary Impact of Exchange Rate Changes." See also the recent discussion by F. R. Casas, "The Short Run Efficacy of Monetary Policy under Floating Rates Reconsidered," *Journal of International Economics*, vol. 8 (February 1978), pp. 55-63; Jürg Niehans, "Some Doubts about the Efficacy of Monetary Policy under Flexible Exchange Rates," *Journal of International Economics*, vol. 5 (August 1975), pp. 275-81; and Rudiger Dornbusch, "Exchange-Rate Expectations and Monetary Policy," *Journal of International Economics*, vol. 6 (August 1976), pp. 231-44.

[68] See Mullen and Willett, "Inflation–Unemployment Tradeoffs."

[69] See Victor Argy and Joanne Solop, "Price and Output Effects on Monetary and Fiscal Policy under Flexible Exchange Rates," *IMF Staff Papers*, vol. 26, (June 1979), pp. 224-56; and Mullen and Willett, "Inflation–Unemployment Tradeoffs."

[70] Recent discussions include Dornbusch and Krugman, "Flexible Exchange Rates in the Short Run"; Kenen, "New Views and Old Views"; and Willett, "Alternative Approaches."

could either promote or retard international trade and investment as compared with an adjustable peg system. We cannot tell from the research to date whether floating has had marginally favorable or unfavorable effects on the efficiency of resource allocation. This is both because the effects one way or the other appear to be relatively small and because most of the studies undertaken to date have used measures of nominal exchange-rate variability that may not correspond well to the combined price and exchange rate considerations that will influence international trade. Studies are now beginning to use real exchange-rate measures,[71] but there is still a serious need for a more careful formulation of welfare-loss functions in terms of uncertainty and distortion effects and their relation to different measures of real exchange rate variability. It is fairly standard, for example, to assume that costs would be an increasing function of the absolute magnitudes of deviations from equilibrium. To the extent that volatility is excessive because of reversible overshooting, however, the uncertainty effects may be largely diversifiable, and a tendency for a period above equilibrium to be followed by a period below equilibrium could reduce rather than increase some relevant types of economic costs. There are also important questions of how one treats equilibrium changes in real rates. This is another interesting area for future research.[72]

Some Policy Recommendations

In making policy recommendations, it is important to recognize that neither private market nor government activities are likely to be ideal. Though I grant that the private market is often wrong on an ex post basis, my impression is that when there have been strong differences in official and private market views on exchange rates, the private market has usually turned out to be right. I see little support for the view

[71] See, for example, Balassa, "Flexible Exchange Rates"; Donald V. Coes, "The Crawling Peg and Exchange-Rate Uncertainty" (Paper presented at the ANPEC/Ford Foundation Conference on the Crawling Peg, Rio de Janeiro, October 1979, forthcoming in conference volume edited by John Williamson); Peter B. Kenen, "Exchange-Rate Variability: Measurement and Implications," mimeographed (Princeton, N.J.: Princeton University, June 1979); Pigott, Sweeney, and Willett, "Behavior and Effects of Floating Exchange Rates"; idem, "Uncertainty and Distortion Effects of Alternative Exchange Rate Systems."

[72] For further discussion, see Pigott, Sweeney, and Willett, "Uncertainty and Distortion Effects of Alternative Exchange Rate Systems"; and Thursby and Willett, "Effects of Flexible Exchange Rates on International Trade and Investment."

60

that the exchange markets have been subject to frequent periods of massive destabilizing speculation.

The question of whether there has been sufficient stabilizing speculation is more open. My view is that this has not been a persistent problem that has contributed greatly to exchange rate volatility, but that it may very well be a problem from time to time for short periods when the market faces great uncertainty that temporarily reduces the elasticity of speculative funds. When there are imbalances in commercial demand and supply under such circumstances, there could be sizable exchange-rate movements not based on the market's mean expectations about equilibrium exchange rates. This indeed would be my functional definition of disorderly market conditions that would justify official intervention.

How does one use intervention to avoid disorderly markets an operational policy guide when there is no clear-cut set of statistical indicators to define disorderly market conditions? I would suggest the following strategy. When there are sudden exchange rate changes that do not appear related to reasonable changes in expectations, the authorities should intervene to dampen the movement. If the cause of the exchange-rate movement is primarily an imbalance in commercial transactions coupled with a lack of sufficient stabilizing speculation, modest official intervention should have a substantial market impact (and should prove on average to be profitable, adjusted for trend). If modest intervention has little market impact, however, this would suggest that the movement is not primarily the result of insufficient stabilizing speculation, and the authorities should normally back off rather than increase their intervention activities.

When, if ever, should the authorities continue to intervene to counter strongly held private expectations? I would suggest that there are two major types of circumstances. One is when the authorities are undertaking a strong domestic stabilization program, but this is not yet believed by the private market because of past government failures in carrying through such efforts to successful completion. By holding down import price increases, substantial temporary exchange-rate support in such a circumstance could be a significant aid in the speed with which stabilization is achieved in relatively open economies (and by the same token could increase the probability that the policy will in fact be carried through to completion).

The danger with this rationale, of course, is that it is very easy for officials themselves to be overly optimistic and to use exchange-market intervention more as a substitute than as a complement for domestic stabilization policies. To reduce somewhat this danger, I would favor requiring (were it possible) that all such substantial intervention programs be approved by the International Monetary Fund.[73]

[73] For further discussion, see Willett, *International Liquidity Issues.* It is possible that substantial intervention could also be justified in particular instances because of large, prolonged disturbances, which would require larger amounts of stabilizing private speculation than would be available, or because private speculators operated on time horizons that were in some sense "too short." Again, however, the danger of biased views on the part of officials must be weighed against the likelihood of private market failures, and I would favor substantial prolonged intervention by national authorities on these grounds only if they could make a convincing case to the International Monetary Fund. (On the effects of the time horizons of speculators on the extent to which the exchange rate effects of disturbances are smoothed out, see Thomas D. Willett, "Discussion: Oil Prices, Terms of Trade, and Transfers, Static and Dynamic Aspects," in Danny M. Leipziger, ed., *The International Monetary System and the Developing Nations* (Washington, D.C.: U.S. Agency for International Development, 1976), pp. 115–19.

Another complicated area of intervention rationales involves the role of exchange market intervention as a part of optimal policy responses to disturbances on stabilization grounds. One can present a case for exchange market intervention in the face of some types of disturbances (for example, shifts in currency preferences) along the same lines that the relative desirability of stabilizing interest rates versus the money supply depends on the pattern of disturbances. Optimal discretionary national responses may often involve the export of negative externalities to other countries, however. Thus, again on these grounds, I would favor requiring that international approval be secured for large intervention. For recent discussions of the relationships among different types of disturbances and monetary and exchange rate policies of these issues, see David A. Bowers, "Should a Managed Float Use Reserve Levels or Exchange Rate Goals? An Interesting Parallel with Domestic Monetary Policy," *Journal of Political Economy,* vol. 83, no. 5 (1975) pp. 1073-76; Russell S. Boyer, "Optimal Exchange Market Intervention," *Journal of Political Economy,* vol. 86 (December 1978), pp. 1045-55; Ralph C. Bryant, "Financial Interdependence and Variability in Exchange Rates," mimeographed (Washington, D.C.: Brookings Institution, June 1979); Rudiger Dornbusch, "Exchange Rate Rules and Macroeconomic Stability" (Paper presented at the ANPEC/Ford Foundation Conference on the Crawling Peg, Rio de Janeiro, October 1979, forthcoming in conference volume edited by John Williamson); Walter Enders and Harvey Lapman, "Stability, Random Disturbances, and the Exchange Rate Regime," *Southern Economic Journal,* vol. 46 (July 1979), pp. 49-70; Stanley Fischer, "Stability and Exchange Rate Systems in a Monetarist Model of the Balance of Payments," in Robert Z. Aliber, *The Political Economy of Monetary Reform* (New York: Macmillan, 1977); Jacob Frenkel, "International Reserves: Pegged Exchange Rates and Managed Float," in Karl Brunner and Allan H. Meltzer, eds., *Economic Policies in Open Economies,* vol. 9 of the Carnegie-Rochester Conference Series on Public Policy, a supplementary series to the *Journal of Monetary Economics,* vol. 4 (July 1978), pp. 111-40; Henderson, "Financial Policies in an Open Economy"; Ira P. Kaminow, "Economic Stability under Fixed and Flexible Exchange Rates," *Journal of International Economics,* vol. 9, no. 2 (1979), pp. 277-85; Jerome L. Stein, "The Optimum Foreign Exchange Market," *American Economic Review,* vol. 53 (June 1963), pp. 384-402; idem, "Social Welfare under Fixed and Flexible Exchange Rates," in Karl Brunner and Allan H. Meltzer, eds., *Stabilization of the Domestic and International Economy,* supplement to the *Journal of Monetary Economics,* vol. 3 (1977), pp. 267-75; Sweeney, "Automatic Stabilization Policy"; Willett, "Crawling Peg Systems"; and references cited in these papers.

The second type of situation in which, I believe, heavy intervention may be justified is when countries decide on optimum-currency-area grounds to allow exchange-market conditions systematically to play a large role in the determination of national monetary and fiscal policies.[74] Though traditionally discussed in terms of maintaining genuinely fixed rates, such considerations may also justify forms of limited exchange-rate flexibility, such as crawling pegs, under which systematic exchange market intervention is not sterilized but rather is allowed to feed back on domestic monetary and financial conditions. Again the danger, as we have seen in previous efforts to peg exchange rates among the major European countries, is that the political authorities will hope that they can peg rates without serious conflicts between internal and external balance developing but that, when they do, the pegging policy is abandoned.[75]

Such scenarios contribute to destabilizing rather than to stabilizing expectations. It seems quite likely that not all countries fit clearly into categories for which free-floating or full-fledged memberships in a genuine currency area are close approximations to optimality. For such countries a compromise system of limited exchange-rate flexibility may have considerable attractiveness. I believe that postwar experience suggests rather strongly that adjustable pegs or heavy discretionary management that approximates such pegs is unlikely to be an efficient form of compromise. For countries in such halfway-house positions on optimum-currency-area grounds, the relevant question should be the optimal degree of macropolicy coordination and rules for the feedback from exchange-market intervention policies to domestic macropolicies. My reading of the evidence suggests that exchange-market intervention per se (which does not feed back strongly on domestic macropolicies) can contribute only in a quite limited way to improved global economic performance.

Postscript

After this paper was completed, the very useful report by the Exchange Markets Participants' Study Group of the Group of Thirty became available.[76] This report surveys and reports the views of a large number

[74] For recent discussions on this point, see McKinnon, *Money in International Exchange;* and Willett, "Crawling Peg Systems."

[75] On the political incentives for such behavior, see Thomas D. Willett, "Some Aspects of the Public-Choice Approach to International Economic Relations" (Paper presented at the European University Institute Conference on New Economic Approaches to the Study of International Integration, Florence, May 31-June 2, 1979, forthcoming in conference volume edited by Pierre Salmon).

[76] Group of Thirty, *Foreign Exchange Markets under Floating Exchange Rates,* report of the Exchange Market Participants' Study Group (New York: Group of Thirty, 1980).

of participants in the foreign-exchange market, both bankers and businessmen. The conclusions of this survey were generally in agreement with the results of the empirical studies discussed in this paper. The main difference was that the exchange-market participants felt that there was a good deal of short-run exchange-rate overshooting, but they did not appear to believe that the effects of this had been particularly disruptive, and some felt that overshooting had had useful effects in stimulating needed domestic macropolicy changes. Most felt that exchange markets had lost some depth and that long-term forward contracts were less frequent, but most felt that on balance the market had not lost efficiency during floating, although "efficiency" was not precisely defined. Corporate treasurers felt that the market did tend to reflect promptly all available information. Some stressed, however, that this included a good deal of misinformation.

Most participants surveyed felt that floating rates had introduced an additional element of risk but that it was not great. Though a minority reported that the cost of international trade and investment had risen slightly, none reported that the level of international trade or investment had been effected. A great deal of criticism of the record of official exchange-market intervention was reported, but it is interesting that many New York bankers, where official intervention has been the lightest, saw "larger-scale intervention as indispensable to the orderly functioning of the markets." [77] None of the corporate treasurers surveyed felt that he could consistently predict exchange rate movements better than "the market," but a number felt that they could do so "often enough to justify the attempt," and heavy use of PPP comparisons in exchange rate forecasting was reported.

[77] Ibid., p. 5.

Intervention Strategy: Implications of Purchasing Power Parity and Tests of Spot Exchange-Market Efficiency

Richard J. Sweeney

Recent work on purchasing power parity (PPP) and on the efficiency of spot exchange markets and its implications for exchange-market intervention are examined in this paper. As will be shown, the evidence from the PPP literature provides virtually no support for intervention, despite some claims to the contrary. Work on spot exchange-market efficiency does provide at least tentative support for intervention, though further work is necessary, particularly on implementation.

The PPP studies considered here principally involve various kinds of regressions of exchange rates (or their changes) on relative national price levels (or their changes). The cross section and cross section–time series analyses examined can shed no light on the possibility of beneficial intervention. Most of these studies view exchange-rate changes as lagging behind relative national price-level changes, but they cannot distinguish among alternative versions of PPP. It might be plausible, for example, that a country with an inflation trend 5 percent higher than its partner's will experience a 5 percent trend rate of depreciation. If there is a burst of inflation above the given trend, however, will this be (at least partly) reflected in future exchange-rate movements? If the exchange rate will ultimately reflect these price-level developments, perhaps intervention can hasten the movement of the exchange rates. Thus, the important question for intervention is not the relationship in *trends* in inflation and depreciation but the deviations from these trends. Unfortunately, most empirical work does not allow for discrimination between the two cases. One paper that ex-

Thanks are due to Gottfried Haberler, Charles Pigott, and Thomas D. Willett. Work on this paper was supported, in part, by a grant from the General Electric Foundation.

65

plicitly raises these issues of discrimination gives somewhat mixed results but favors the view that trends in relative inflation rates are related to trends in depreciation, rather than the stronger PPP view that deviations from trends are related and might in principle be beneficially affected by intervention.[1]

Many commentators on PPP have seemed to demand "perfection," or (rather) more than is necessary to make PPP useful for intervention. The success of PPP, for example, is often judged according to whether $\hat{b}$, the estimated slope coefficient of the (log of the) exchange rate as a function of relative national price levels, is (statistically) not different from unity.[2] Equations with (positive) highly significant $\hat{b}$'s are often thought to cast substantial doubt on PPP because the $\hat{b}$'s are significantly different from unity. In fact, there are any number of plausible theoretical reasons that the estimated slope coefficient need not (*should* not) equal unity. Only if all equilibrium changes in relative national price levels require equal changes in the equilibrium exchange rate should $\hat{b}$ be (close to) unity. Many price changes do not require this, however, and $\hat{b}$ will then be a sort of weighted average of movements to prices that require and do not require exchange-rate changes. An increase in demand for home money, for example, accompanied by a decrease in the demand for foreign money, requires a fall in home prices and a rise in foreign prices, with an appreciation of the home exchange rate keeping the real exchange rate constant; $\hat{b}$ would tend to unity. If, however, the increase in demand for home money is instead accompanied by a decrease in demand for home output as well as foreign money, home prices rise, foreign prices fall, the real exchange rate depreciates somewhat, and the exchange rate does not fully reflect the change in relative national price levels; $\hat{b}$ tends to be somewhat less than unity in this case. Further, changes in a country's ratio of tradables to nontradables prices will not be fully reflected in exchange-rate changes. In practice, $\hat{b}$ would tend toward a weighted average of the various cases.

Even if the true slope coefficient differs from unity, intervention based on PPP can in principle still make a great deal of sense. What is necessary is that movements in either relative national price levels or the exchange rate give a reliable indication of future movements in the other variables, *and* that the lag be long enough for intervention to help

[1] Charles Pigott and Richard James Sweeney, "Purchasing Power Parity and Exchange Rate Dynamics: Some Empirical Results," mimeographed (Claremont, Calif.: Claremont Men's College, 1979).

[2] See Jacob Frenkel, "Exchange Rates, Prices and Money: Lessons from the 1920's," mimeographed (Chicago: University of Chicago, 1979), and "Flexible Exchange Rates in the 1970's," mimeographed (Chicago: University of Chicago, 1980); and P. Krugman, "Purchasing Power Parity and Exchange Rates," *Journal of International Economics,* vol. 8 (August 1978), pp. 397-407.

shorten the lag and reduce distortions, uncertainty, and the like that are caused by disequilibrium. This is true whether exchange rates are viewed as leading or lagging relative national price levels and, indeed, in cases of complex, mutual leads and lags. (Note that the existence of lead-lag relationships by themselves does not necessarily imply there are any extra costs arising from such relationships. The literature discussed here often assumes that such costs exist. The focus of this paper, however, is on whether the lead-lag relationships exist.)

A closely related demand for perfection is that the PPP equation explain "most," a "great deal," or a "substantial part" of exchange-rate movements. It is often said that exchange rates are determined by many factors beyond PPP, which is surely true. It is further said that real exchange rates vary, as the evidence cited below shows; but the non sequitur is then sometimes advanced that therefore PPP calculations cannot be used for intervention. In particular, there can be substantial, *permanent* deviations from PPP, and yet intervention based on such calculations could in principle be highly useful. The issue turns on whether movements in relative national price levels (or the exchange rate) give *some* useful information about the future evolution of the exchange rate and whether it would be efficient to incorporate this information into the exchange rate faster than the market does.

Time-series analysis of the real exchange rate seems to show no cycles in its changes (though alternative interpretations are possible). This indicates that there is no scope for intervention based on leads and lags between inflation differentials and the exchange rate.[3] Further, it also seems that the contemporaneous relationship between the deviations of inflation differentials around their trend and exchange-rate changes around trend is often minor and may not be significant.

These results are important not only for judging PPP but also for judging spot exchange-market efficiency. The PPP results are seriously different from the implications of the vast majority of "monetary" models as currently formulated. It is frequently charged that usual tests of efficiency are invalid in exchange markets because monetary models can produce results at variance with these tests.[4] One simple

[3] Pigott and Sweeney, "Purchasing Power Parity and Exchange Rate Dynamics"; Frenkel, "Flexible Exchange Rates in the 1970's"; and Richard Roll, "Violations of Purchasing Power Parity and Their Implications for Efficient International Commodity Markets," mimeographed (Los Angeles: UCLA Graduate School of Management, 1978).

[4] R. Levich, "Further Results on the Efficiency of Markets for Foreign Exchange," in *Managed Exchange-Rate Flexibility: The Recent Experience,* Federal Reserve Bank of Boston Conference Series, no. 20, 1978; and R. G. Harris and D. D. Purvis, "Diverse Information and the Market Efficiency in a Monetary Model of the Exchange Rate," mimeographed (Kingston, Ontario: Queen's University, 1978).

test of spot exchange-market efficiency is to test whether there are patterns of correlations in rate changes, the null hypothesis being that there are none. Monetary models very often, however, do imply patterns, so the charge is that such tests are not very useful or significant. There are two responses to this view. First, whether or not properly formulated monetary models *might* make conventional efficiency tests unimportant, the PPP evidence shows that the data do not behave in a way to make these assertions empirically relevant—that is, do not support the basic structure of these monetary models. Empirical considerations suggest that these models are *not* properly formulated. "Overshooting" models typically depend on lags and (quite possibly) on inefficiencies in adjustment of the prices of goods; the implied serial correlation in exchange and inflation rates, however, is not observed. Currency-substitution models can allow wide cycles based on finite elasticities of substitution, but again the data do not show the predicted patterns.[5] Second, these authors misinterpret the point of efficiency tests. These tests do not rule out cycles as long as they can be explained by storage, transactions, and (risk-adjusted) interest costs. With respect to currency-substitution models, the question is whether elasticities are large enough to limit cycles to those explicable by costs. To judge this the efficiency tests must be performed. These models err in making their elasticities parametric rather than having to adjust elasticities to eliminate all cycles not explicable by costs. They are misinterpreted as arguing against efficiency tests rather than supporting these tests to gain insight into whether the elasticities have appropriate values in relation to the patterns and sources of disturbances.

Studies of the efficiency of spot exchange markets have generally shown mixed evidence, with authors' differences in conclusions based to a substantial degree on their *interpretations* of results rather than on differences in results themselves. More "patterns" in serial correlation tests were found than would be expected if there were no genuine underlying relationships. These patterns seemed unstable, however, and might have been the result of the fact that the distributions of disturbances appeared not to be normal but to have "fat" tails (Pareto stable) with larger probability of outliers arising. One approach to resolving this issue was to look directly to see whether there were unexplained profit opportunities.

Unfortunately, these tests also gave conflicting signals. In particular, a number of authors found that for the first three years of the current generalized float, mechanical buy-and-sell rules ("filter" rules)

---

5 Harris and Purvis, ibid.

seemed capable of making substantial profits in most major currencies' markets, even when adjusted for the profits from simply buying and holding the foreign currency.[6] Interpretations of the intervention implications of these profits varied according to whether they seemed disturbingly large, explicable by risk considerations, or consistent in time, all in the judgment of authors. It appears, however, that for the dollar–deutsche mark rate during this period these profits were statistically significant, even when risk is evaluated in terms of the capital asset pricing model.[7] It should be noted, however, that while the significant profits in the dollar–deutsche mark market indicated scope for beneficial intervention, they give little clue by themselves for an appropriate intervention strategy. If, for example, the profits arose from speculative bandwagons, some sort of official leaning-against-the-wind strategy might be appropriate. If the profits arose from the market's failure to incorporate new information and move quickly to a new equilibrium, however, the seemingly paradoxical strategy of "running with the wind," intervening to hasten rises or falls in the exchange rate, might be appropriate. Further empirical work is required to find even approximately optimal guides for intervention.[8] Whether these results hold for other currencies and later periods remains to be seen. At the very least, the results suggest that even intervention as simple-minded as following these mechanical buy-and-sell rules would have helped somewhat in stabilizing the dollar-deutsche mark market.

To summarize the following two sections, on PPP and efficiency, respectively, the following seems true. First, there seems very little support for intervention on the basis of PPP. This view does *not* require that PPP relations have $\hat{b}$ (statistically) close to unity, that PPP explain a large percentage of exchange-rate movements, or that there not be real permanent exchange-rate changes. Rather, time-series evidence shows little in the way of lead-lag relations between changes in relative national price levels and the exchange rate (and relatively little, often nothing, of a contemporaneous relationship). Most cross-section and

---

[6] M. Dooley and J. Shafer, "Analysis of Short-Run Exchange Rate Behavior, March 1973 to September 1975," International Finance Discussion Paper No. 76, mimeographed (Washington, D.C.: Federal Reserve Board, 1976); W. B. Cornell and J. K. Dietrich, "The Efficiency of the Market for Foreign Exchange Rates," *Review of Economics and Statistics,* vol. 60 (February 1978), pp. 111-20; and D. E. Logue, R. J. Sweeney, and T. D. Willett, "Speculative Behavior of Foreign Exchange Rates during the Current Float," *Journal of Business Research,* vol. 6 (1978), pp. 159-74.

[7] R. J. Sweeney, "A Statistical Filter Rule Test: The Dollar-DM Exchange Rate," mimeographed (Claremont, Calif.: Claremont Men's College, 1980).

[8] Ibid.

cross-section–time-series analyses have not been formulated properly to provide evidence. One with a proper formulation finds little support for lead-lag relations.[9] Efficiency tests of the spot exchange market have sometimes been objected to on the basis of empirical implications of monetary approach models. Many of these simple implications, however, seem simply not to hold. Further, efficiency tests are not invalidated by currency-substitution models. Rather, elasticities in these models should take on values consistent with the assumptions underlying efficiency tests.

Spot market-efficiency tests for the first three years of the current float show disturbing signs of inefficiency. Authors disagree, however, as to whether these results are due to inefficiency, to unstable underlying processes or nonnormal error terms, or to the risk to stabilizing speculation. It appears, however, that even taking risk considerations into account, filter rules could have earned statistically significant profits in the first three years of the current float in the dollar–deutsche mark market. It appears, then, that even simple intervention rules would have helped stabilize this market.

Purchasing Power Parity

The old doctrine of PPP has been discussed extensively.[10] This section is not a survey but an overview of PPP with regard to its implications for exchange-market intervention. The section raises two main points. First, what is called the "weak" version of PPP seems preferable to stronger versions that have found some support. In this weak version, trend rates of change in relative national price levels tend to be associated positively with trend rates of depreciation, but deviations around these trends are not. This version of PPP is not favorable to intervention based on PPP calculations. Second, many "monetary" models as they are now formulated imply predictions at odds with the data; in particular, many of the predictions of "overshooting" models are not validated by the data. Some objections to the tests of spot exchange-market efficiency discussed in the final section are based on such models,

---

[9] Pigott and Sweeney, "Purchasing Power Parity and Exchange Rate Dynamics."

[10] Lawrence Officer, "The Purchasing-Power-Parity Theory of Exchange Rates: A Review Article," *IMF Staff Papers*, vol. 23 (March 1976), pp. 1-61; Jacob Frenkel, "A Monetary Approach to the Exchange Rate: Doctrinal Aspects and Empirical Evidence," *Scandinavian Journal of Economics*, vol. 78 (May 1976), pp. 200-24; and Jacob Frenkel, "Purchasing Power Parity: Doctrinal Perspective and Evidence from the 1920s," *Journal of International Economics*, vol. 8 (May 1978), pp. 169-92.

and thus the force of these objections is diminished. In this section some general considerations in PPP testing are first raised; then work in this area, with particular concern for implications for intervention, is discussed and evaluated, and then how well the implication of current monetary models compares with the data is discussed.

General Considerations. Four issues are considered: (1) various strong and weak versions of PPP; (2) index number problems; (3) money-supply disturbances versus changes in relative prices caused by real disturbances; and (4) implications for exchange-market intervention.

Versions of PPP.[11] To illustrate two polar extremes of PPP, consider the simple model

$$\Delta \varepsilon_t = \alpha + \xi_t$$
$$\Delta p_t = \beta + \omega_t$$

where Δp is the change in the (log of the) price level of country i in relation to the price level in the base country, $\Delta \varepsilon$ is the bilateral exchange rate,[12] ξ and ω are random variables, and α and β are intercept terms. In a very strong version of PPP, $\alpha = \beta$, so that if α should shift, β shifts equally, *and* ξ and ω are perfectly correlated; Δp and $\Delta \varepsilon$ are exact images of each other. Note that in this strong version, ω and ξ need not be independent in time—that is, Δp and $\Delta \varepsilon$ could show cyclical patterns with the passage of time. This version offers no scope for intervention based on PPP.

A slightly weaker version allows leads and lags of ω and ξ, with lags in adjustment of α to shifts in β and vice versa. When all such disturbances die away, however, the (log of the) real exchange rate p-ε has not changed—that is, the real exchange rate sometimes shows deviations from PPP, but eventually returns to PPP. This version offers possible scope for intervention to hasten convergence of p-ε to its long-run value. One common version of such intervention views changes in relative national price levels as leading exchange-rate changes;[13] but

[11] Based on Pigott and Sweeney, "Purchasing Power Parity and Exchange Rate Dynamics."

[12] The exchange rate is taken as the number of units of i's currency needed to buy one unit of the base country's currency. Thus, with the U.S. as the base country and Germany as country i, the relative national price level is (say) CPI_G/CPI_{US} (CPI = consumer price index) and the exchange rate is DMs/$.

[13] OPTICA, "Inflation and Exchange Rates: Evidence and Policy Guidelines for the European Community," *OPTICA Report 1976* (Brussels, February 1977). See also Niels Thugesen, "Inflation and Exchange Rates: Evidence and Policy Guidelines for the European Community," *Journal of International Economics*, vol. 8 (May 1978), pp. 301-18.

other views see the exchange market adjusting much more quickly than goods markets. These would lead to different intervention strategies. For convenience only, much of the following discussion assumes $\Delta\varepsilon$ lags Δp.

Yet a weaker version is that in the long run ω and changes in β are (sooner or later) reflected *in part* in α and ξ (or vice versa; there is yet no presumption of causal direction). In the long run, then, there are some permanent changes in the real exchange rate, but a portion of the dynamics in Δp is ultimately reflected in $\Delta\varepsilon$ (and vice versa). To the extent $\Delta\varepsilon$ reflects only with a lag those parts of Δp it will later incorporate, intervention may be helpful.

A weak version asserts that ξ and ω are uncorrelated but that shifts in α and β are at least partly and contemporaneously correlated. Thus, if α and β are given, there will be no detectable relationship between Δp and $\Delta\varepsilon$. A period of above-average inflation in country i will not necessarily be associated with any extra depreciation, either contemporaneously *or* with leads or lags. An increase in the trend rate of (relative) inflation, however—that is, in β—will be associated with a contemporaneous increase in α, the trend rate of depreciation. There is no scope for intervention based on lead-lag PPP relationships.

Which of these versions, or other possible versions, is most consistent with the data? Answers differ in the literature, but the theory and evidence cited below support the weak version.

Index-number issues. Jevons's Law of One Price asserts that identical units of a good will sell for the same price. Identical units of a good sold in different locations, under different conditions, however, are reasonably viewed as different goods and will have different prices. Any aggregation of goods based on criteria different from their having identical dollar prices across countries will show a cross-country dispersion of prices. A shift in relative quantities will thus influence an index dependent on quantities, and a change in the relative price of goods with different qualities will also affect the index. Further, a change in the relative costs of providing differentiating qualities to goods will shift relative prices. This sort of reasoning is well known and allows for changes in relative national price levels, even with a given exchange rate.[14]

With goods appropriately defined so as to be identical across countries, the Law of One Price always trivially ensures PPP. For the purpose of intervention, however, the important PPP question is whether

[14] Frenkel, "A Monetary Approach to the Exchange Rate" and "Purchasing Power Parity."

shifts in relative national prices and in exchange rates have significant relations *beyond* the Law of One Price. As is discussed below, this turns on whether changes in relative national price levels, each measured in its own home currency, are due to money-supply changes or to changes in real demand-and-supply relations (including money-demand shocks).

For PPP purposes, indexes chosen to keep sample goods identical in all respects will not do. Tests with such indexes can measure only opportunities forgone on the basis of commodity arbitrage. Interesting PPP tests can be based only on models in which relative national price levels can potentially change independent of changes in the exchange rate.

Among the most popular candidates for PPP studies are consumer price indexes (CPIs) and wholesale price indexes (WPIs).[15] (Other indexes, such as unit labor costs, gross national product [GNP] deflators, food costs, and export price indexes have been used.) CPIs are sometimes preferred because they give more scope for deviations from PPP, on the grounds they include a smaller percentage of traded goods than do WPIs and hence are less subject to confounding the effects of the Law of One Price with the workings of PPP relationships. In the empirical work discussed below, both CPIs and WPIs were used. There seems to be no notable systematic difference in the overall results, though of course individual results are sometimes affected.[16] In general, the tests are not highly favorable for PPP-based intervention, whatever the index used.

Money supply disturbances versus changes in relative prices. It has long been recognized that the PPP hypothesis is most powerful when money-supply shocks are the main disturbance.[17] It is worthwhile examining this in more detail. Consider a steady state of zero real growth, where the German money supply, M_G, and the U.S. money supply, M_{US}^s, are both constant. Inflation tends, on the average, to be zero in both countries. If all costs of trade are zero in all cases and both countries consume positive amounts of all goods, then the Law of One Price ensures that the real exchange rate would change only

[15] Frenkel, "Purchasing Power Parity."

[16] Frenkel and Krugman used WPIs rather than CPIs. See Frenkel, "Purchasing Power Parity," "Exchange Rates, Prices and Money," and "Flexible Exchange Rates in the 1970's"; and Krugman, "Purchasing Power Parity and Exchange Rates." Roll, "Violations of Purchasing Power Parity and Their Implications," used CPIs. Pigott and Sweeney, "Purchasing Power Parity and Exchange Rate Dynamics," used both.

[17] P. A. Samuelson, "Theoretical Notes on Trade Problems," *Review of Economics and Statistics,* vol. 46 (1964).

because of variations in relative quantities consumed. With significant costs of trade, however, relative prices (measured in the same currency) can then vary, because of traded goods versus nontraded goods, another channel for shifts in relative demands and supplies to affect the real exchange rate.

In a Patinkinesque world, if M_{US}^s doubles, so ultimately does the U.S. price index, however it is chosen. Money-supply changes are neutral in the long run; and the real exchange rate is constant in the long run.[18] PPP theory has genuine predictive power about ε in this case if price-level changes are due in substantial part to money-supply disturbances. In principle, p could vary without any change in M or ε, and ε could vary with no change in p or M; and it is only when such changes are logically possible that PPP becomes more than a triviality (if the Law of One Price holds). If the shocks are predominantly to the money supply, lead-lag relations in Δp and $\Delta \varepsilon$ allow for possibly beneficial intervention on the basis of PPP (neither the very strong nor the weak version of PPP holds).

It is worth exploring a little the effects of disturbances other than to the money supply. If there are shifts in tastes from domestic to foreign goods, the home real exchange rate must depreciate, and because money demand is unaffected in either country, the entire effect is (to a first approximation) on ε and not on p. Suppose, however, that there is an increase in the demand for home goods that is financed (in the sense of Walras's law) by a decline in domestic money demand. A rise in the home price level will eliminate the excess real balances and return the system to equilibrium with a depreciated rate and no change in the real exchange rate. Next, suppose that the home demand for money rises, financed by a fall in demand for home bonds. The excess demand for real balances can be met by a fall in the home price level and appreciation of its exchange rate, leaving the real exchange rate unchanged. Finally, suppose that the home-country aggregate demand rises, financed in part by a fall in demand for home money but also by a fall in demand for home bonds. The home exchange rate appreciates, the home price level rises, and the real exchange rate appreciates. The upshot is that a variety of disturbances, beyond just money-supply shocks, can leave the real exchange rate constant in the long run—but other disturbances

---

[18] Per Meinich, *A Monetary General Equilibrium Theory for an International Economy* (Oslo, Norway: Scandinavian University Books, 1968); and R. J. Sweeney, "Inflation, the Balance of Trade, and the Effects of Exchange Rate Adjustments," in P. B. Clark, D. E. Logue, and R. J. Sweeney (eds.), *The Effects of Exchange Rate Adjustments* (Washington, D.C.: U.S. Treasury, 1976).

will change the real rate. The long-run relation between changes in $\Delta\epsilon$ and Δp will depend on the relative proportions of such shocks.[19]

Implications for intervention. Proposals abound for exchange-market intervention with PPP as an ingredient.[20] As has been pointed out, such intervention makes no sense if the real exchange rate is (essentially) constant in time.[21] Indeed, the best case for such intervention is to have a constant long-run real rate with short-run deviations that are somehow inoptimal and correctable by intervention. To the extent that deviations from PPP represent equilibrium adjustments that are not self-reversing in the long run, the use of PPP calculations for intervention is somewhat damaged, because it is hard to separate permanent changes that ought to be facilitated from temporary ones that ought to be smoothed. Trend changes in the real rate, caused, for example, by productivity differentials, are not difficult to handle,[22] but permanent random changes in the real rate create the risk of counter-productive intervention. This uncertainty, however, serves merely to reduce the optimal amount of intervention, not to eliminate it, as long as some percentage of changes in the real rate are self-reversing.

Possible sources of inoptimal, self-reversing deviations from PPP are (1) differential lags in adjustment of different markets as compared to exchange rates (goods prices are sometimes modeled as adjusting less swiftly *and* in several stages to new information); (2) destabilizing speculation, or insufficient stabilizing speculation, in exchange markets; (3) misguided pricing in goods markets; and (4) combinations of all these. Destabilizing speculation might arise in the absence of disturbances, and business might autonomously make erroneous decisions. More likely causes are suboptimal reactions of decision makers to autonomous disturbances. Successful intervention would require better identification of disturbances (better information or better-processed information) or better-designed reactions than private markets provide. The conventional argument is that better information should simply be

[19] In terms of the section on intervention when $b < 1$, the estimated slope coefficient b when $\Delta\epsilon$ is regressed on Δp depends on the proportion of shocks to Δp that are ultimately reflected in $\Delta\epsilon$; and given this proportion, the correlation of $\Delta\epsilon$ and Δp declines with increases in the total of disturbances to $\Delta\epsilon$.

[20] For example, OPTICA, "Inflation and Exchange Rates."

[21] R. Dornbusch and D. Jaffe, "Purchase Power Parity and Exchange Rate Problems: Introduction," *Journal of International Economics*, vol. 8 (May 1978), pp. 157-62.

[22] Bela Balassa, "The Purchasing Power Parity Doctrine: A Reappraisal," *Journal of Political Economy*, vol. 72 (December 1964), pp. 584-96; and Samuelson, "Theoretical Notes on Trade Problems."

disseminated in the market. The proposition that the government can provide better reactions to information is subject to testing, as will be discussed later.

Statistical Tests of PPP. The design of tests of PPP will differ according to the aspects of PPP in which the author is interested (for example, goods-market arbitrage and the Law of One Price versus the presence of "productivity bias"). One approach to testing PPP is to ask how the data support the case for intervention. As noted before, the best case for intervention turns on a tendency for a constant real exchange rate in the long run (or a real rate where trend movements can easily be discerned) combined with short-run variations in the real rate. As will be discussed later, however, intervention can potentially be useful as long as disturbances to Δp and $\Delta \varepsilon$ around their trends show some relationship *and* there are lead-lag relationships in adjustment of Δp and $\Delta \varepsilon$.

In this subsection three types of investigations of the relationship of p and ε will be examined: (1) simple comparisons of movements in the two variables; (2) cross-section and cross-section–time-series analyses; and (3) time-series analyses. It also shows that beneficial intervention is possible even when the estimated slope coefficient of $\Delta \varepsilon$ regressed on Δp is significantly less than unity and Δp explains only a small percentage of the variance of $\Delta \varepsilon$.

Comparing movements in p and ε. Why not simply regress ε on p (or vice versa) or plot them against each other? [23] In general, this can lead to specious relationships; any detected relationship may not be there at all.

First, suppose

$$\Delta \varepsilon_t = \alpha + \xi_t$$

$$\Delta p_t = \beta + \omega_t,$$

$\alpha = \beta$, and ω and ξ are both white and strictly uncorrelated. This is a weak form of PPP with no suitability for intervention. If $\beta > 0$, p will be rising with the passage of time. But because $\beta = \alpha$, ε will also be rising. If $\beta = 0$ and there are a number of shifts in β, it is quite possible that the estimated OLS slope coefficient of b of ε regressed on p will be statistically significant and not significantly different from unity.

Consider the following experiment, however: In a particular month, p rises twice as fast as average, or $\Delta p_t = 2\beta$. (This means

[23] Hans Genberg, "Purchasing Power Parity as a Rule for a Crawling Peg," mimeographed (Geneva: Graduate Institute for International Studies, 1979).

$\omega_t = \beta$.) Will the currency depreciate faster than average during this month (or any future month)? The regression would say yes, but because ξ and ω are uncorrelated, the expected change in ε is simply α, *not* 2α. Slower depreciation is as likely as faster depreciation.

The change in the real exchange rate is

$$\Delta(p - \varepsilon) = \alpha + \xi_t - \beta - \omega_t = \xi_t - \omega_t,$$

assuming that $\alpha = \beta$. The expected change in the real rate is zero,

$$E\Delta(p - \varepsilon) = E\xi - E\omega = 0,$$

and the changes show no pattern of correlation because ξ and ω do not. Thus, the real rate itself is a random-walk process; the evidence supporting this hypothesis will be discussed later. As is known from the stock-market literature, random-walk processes tend to show apparent cycles that simply are not there. Hence, it is not surprising that the eye can pick out cycles in the real rate, even if such cycles are wholly spurious. The top panel of figure 1 schematically shows a possible cycle from a random-walk process. Suppose the units for measuring the values of p and ε are chosen to set their mean values through the period equal to unity. Then the mean value of $p - \varepsilon = 0$. (Because p and ε are in natural logs, the mean *algebraic* value of the real rate is unity.) The bottom panel of figure 1 shows that the only way the pattern in the top panel can be generated is by apparent cycles in p and ε.[24] Because $p - \varepsilon = 0$ at time t', necessarily $p = \varepsilon$. The fact that $p - \varepsilon$ is falling means ε is rising in relation to p, but because $p - \varepsilon = 0$ at t'', at some time t, $t' < t < t''$, p must be rising in relation to ε. These apparent lead-lag relationships in ε and p are wholly spurious and are implied by the wholly spurious cycles in the real rate.[25]

[24] Where the p and ϵ curves intersect, to give $p - \epsilon = 0$, their values need be equal only to each other, not necessarily to unity, as drawn. Nevertheless, given the hypothetical random walk in the top panel and the decision to scale p and ϵ to set their mean values at unity, p and ϵ tend to intersect on average at unity.

[25] If the model in this section holds, OLS regression of $\Delta\epsilon$ on Δp gives an estimate of $\hat{b}$ where for large samples $E(\hat{b}) = 1/(1 + \frac{\sigma_\omega^2}{\beta})$. Thus, if β and σ_ω σ_ω^2 are the same size, $E(b) = \frac{1}{2}$. Further, if α and β have shifted a number of times, $\hat{b}$ is biased upward from this expression. If there are no shifts in α (and β), then the Durbin-Watson statistic should show high first order serial correlation in the residuals; the expected value of the correlation is unity, which would give first differences of ϵ and p for the transformed data, and give $E(\hat{b}) = 0$. However, shifts in α (and β) will reduce the serial correlation of the residuals leading to less than first differences; indeed, if such shifts are important relative to σ_ω^2, the Cochrane-Orcutt results may well show a significant $\hat{b}$. Distributed lag regressions would show less than instantaneous adjustment, as in, for example, John S. Hodgson and Patricia Phelps, "The Distributed Impact of Price-Level

Cross-section and cross-section–time-series regressions. Numerous cross-section and cross-section–time-series (CS–TS) analyses have purported to show support for strong versions of PPP.[26] Pigott and Sweeney, however, have shown that these results are also consistent with a weak version of PPP—that is, the results provide no evidence on the desirability of intervention.[27] Essentially, the regression is simply picking up the fact that high-inflation countries tend to have high depreciation.

Suppose the above model holds for each country i, with $\alpha_i = \beta_i$ and ξ_i and ω_i independent white noises. Then, if a cross-sectional regression of $\Delta\varepsilon_i$ on Δp_i is run, the estimated slope coefficient is biased upward from zero and can quite plausibly take on values close to unity. Pigott and Sweeney looked at a cross-section of ten countries (the Group of Ten plus Switzerland, minus the United States) with the United States as the base country. Under the weak PPP hypothesis, they found the *expected* estimated slope coefficient $\hat{b}$ to be .92 for CPIs and .81 for WPIs. Intuitively, the inflation performance of a given country during several years will depend on its β as well as ω, and the depreciation of its exchange rate will depend on its α as well as ξ. If high-inflation and low-inflation countries are grouped, it is not surprising to find that they are high-depreciation countries, respectively. This may merely reflect correspondence of α's and β's, and not relations of ω to ξ for a given country.

Some CS–TS studies compare results for various differencing intervals—month-to-month changes in ε versus quarter-to-quarter changes in ε, for example.[28] As the differencing interval is lengthened, $\hat{b}$ tends

---

Variation on Floating Exchange Rates," *Review of Economics and Statistics,* vol. 57 (October 1975), pp. 58-64.

Note that if the above model is modified to $\Delta p_t = \beta + \omega_t + u_t$ $\Delta\varepsilon_t = a + \xi_t + u_t$ where ξ, ω, and u are independent white noises, there is still no potential for beneficial intervention on PPP grounds; Δp and $\Delta\varepsilon$ now show some contemporaneous relationship; $p - \varepsilon$ still shows spurious cycles; and p and ε still show spurious lead-lag relationships. A version of this model with $\Delta\varepsilon$ lagging δp is considered in a later section. M. Friedman and A. Schwartz, *A Monetary History of the United States* (Princeton: Princeton University Press, 1963), suggest cycles in the U.K. real exchange rate relative to the United States. C. Pigott and R. J. Sweeney, "Price and Exchange Rate Dynamics: Theories and Tests," mimeographed (Claremont, Calif.: Claremont Men's College, 1979), argue that Friedman-Schwartz data are consistent with the view that $\Delta(p - \varepsilon)$ is random, so that the observed cycles in $p - \varepsilon$ are spurious.

[26] For example, OPTICA, "Inflation and Exchange Rates"; D. King, "The Performance of Exchange Rates in the Recent Period of Floating: Exchange Rates and Inflation Rates," *Southern Economic Journal* (April 1977), pp. 1582-87; and Arturo Brillembourg, "Purchasing Power Parity Tests of Causalitv and Equilibrium," mimeographed (Washington, D.C.: International Monetary Fund, 1976).

[27] Pigott and Sweeney, "Purchasing Power Parity and Exchange Rate Dynamics."

[28] King, "The Performance of Exchange Rates in the Recent Period of Floating," and Brillembourg, "Purchasing Power Parity Tests of Causality and Equilibrium."

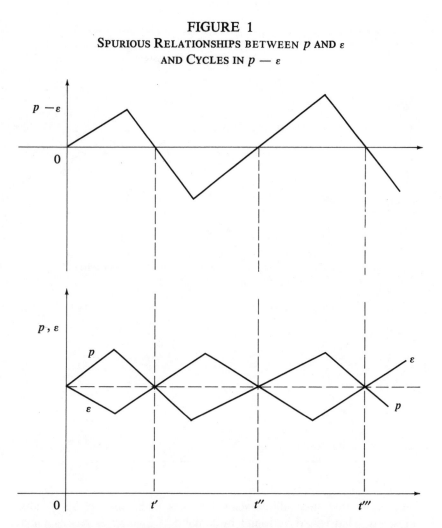

FIGURE 1

SPURIOUS RELATIONSHIPS BETWEEN p AND ε
AND CYCLES IN $p - \varepsilon$

to rise and become significant and not significantly different from unity. On the basis of this pattern it has been argued that PPP holds in a relatively strong form *but* with significant lags—ideal circumstances for intervention to reduce the lags.[29]

As Pigott and Sweeney show, however, such a pattern of regression results are to be expected under weak PPP where $\alpha_i = \beta_i$, and ξ_i and ω_i are independent white noises, and intervention has no rationale.[30]

[29] Hans Genberg, "Purchasing Power Parity under Fixed and Flexible Exchange Rates," *Journal of International Economics,* vol. 8 (May 1978), pp. 247-76, judges these results consistent with those he found using other methods.

[30] Pigott and Sweeney, "Purchasing Power Parity and Exchange Rate Dynamics."

FIGURE 2
Single versus Separate Country Intercepts in Cross-Section Time Series Regressions

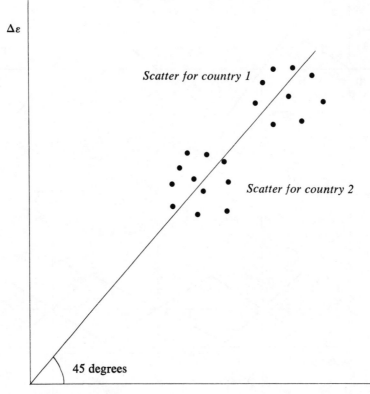

They argue that small differencing intervals make the CS–TS results "close" to what would be found by looking at time-series results for a typical country. If the "weak" version of PPP holds for the typical country, $\hat{b}$ will tend to be insignificant in such time-series work. As the differencing interval is lengthened, the results come closer to cross-sectional results, where $\hat{b}$ is biased upward and can easily be close to unity. Thus the CS–TS results across differencing intervals are to be expected even if the weak version of PPP holds. Hence, because this weak version of PPP is not at all favorable for intervention, these CS–TS studies offer no support or guidance for intervention.

Pigott and Sweeney argue that CS–TS studies have erred in using the same intercept term for each country or estimating $\Delta\varepsilon_i = a + b\Delta p_i$ across countries i. Instead, each country should be allowed its own

80

intercept, with a common $\hat{b}$. If $\alpha_i = \beta_i$ and ξ_i and ω_i are independent white noises, scatter for two countries is shown in figure 2. With a single intercept, the estimated constant is biased downward and the slope upward. With separate intercepts, the slope is expected to be zero. As table 1 shows, using separate country constants gives quite a different picture from a single constant and of the sort predicted by Pigott and Sweeney. They note some anomalies in their empirical results, however; in particular, some $\hat{b}$'s for large differencing intervals are not as small as expected. They conjecture that this may be due to shifts in the α_i and β_i for some countries so that Δp_i and $\Delta \varepsilon_i$ are nonstationary. They turn to time-series analysis of $\Delta \varepsilon$ and Δp in the attempt to resolve the issue.[31]

Analyses of Δp and $\Delta \varepsilon$. These studies show mixed results. Frenkel finds substantial evidence for a strong version of PPP using data from the 1920s, with the estimated slope coefficients of $\Delta \varepsilon$ regressed on Δp not significantly different from unity.[32] Results for the 1970s do not strongly support PPP.[33] In any case, the percentage of variance in exchange-rate changes explained by changes in relative national price levels is quite small.

For approximately the first fifty months of the current float, Pigott and Sweeney, using both WPIs and CPIs, find little cross-correlation relationship between Δp and $\Delta \varepsilon$ for a number of countries among the Group of Ten plus Switzerland, in relation to the United States as base country.[34] This is illustrated by Switzerland in table 2. For other countries in this group, there does seem to be a relation, illustrated by Italy in table 3. It is not clear, however, whether this measured relationship is picking up a correlation between ξ and ω or is due to shifts in α_i and β_i. In the former case, intervention might be appropriate in order to reduce lags and hence deviations of the real exchange rate from its equilibrium value. In the latter case, intervention would likely not be appropriate. Suppose, for example, that Italy embarked on an inflationary program; α and β would both likely rise. Although this would give a measured relationship, intervention would be appropriate only with some genuine relationship of ξ to ω (or some lagged shifts of α relative to β, or vice versa). Pigott and Sweeney argue that the pat-

---

[31] Ibid. The logic can be seen intuitively in figure 2. If the α and β shift for a country and the pre- and post-shift samples are pooled, the $\hat{b}$ is biased upward. What is needed is two intercept terms. Determining when the intercept changes is difficult in practice.

[32] Frenkel, "Purchasing Power Parity" and "Exchange Rates, Prices and Money."

[33] Frenkel, "Flexible Exchange Rates in the 1970's."

[34] Pigott and Sweeney, "Purchasing Power Parity and Exchange Rate Dynamics."

TABLE 1

SLOPE COEFFICIENTS FOR POOLED CROSS-SECTION–TIME-SERIES
REGRESSIONS OF PERCENTAGE RATE OF CHANGE OF EXCHANGE RATES
AS FUNCTIONS OF RELATIVE RATES OF INFLATION,
MARCH 1973–DECEMBER 1976

Difference (months)	CPI	WPI
Country constants constrained to be equal		
1	.18989	.08938
	(.17711)	(.0884)
3	.7377[a][b]	.56165[a]
	(.28896)	(.14298)
6	1.1658[a][b]	.43572[a]
	(.37093)	(.17178)
12	1.51905[a][b]	.6531[a][b]
	(.3818)	(.20328)
18	1.2552[a][b]	.8395[a][b]
	(.1808)	(.13442)
Separate constant for each country		
1	−.06959	.00494
	(.19302)	(.0916)
3	.31094	.4459[a]
	(.36362)	(.1602)
6	.65534	.2351
	(.56956)	(.19905)
12	1.5038	.40769
	(.83811)	(.28118)
18	.71265[a][b]	.3855[a]
	(.2532)	(.17846)

NOTE: Standard errors of estimates are in parentheses.
[a] Significantly different from zero (95 percent).
[b] *Not* significantly different from unity (95 percent).
SOURCE: C. Pigott and R. J. Sweeney, "Purchasing Power Parity and Exchange
Rate Dynamics: Some Empirical Results," mimeographed (Claremont, Calif.:
Claremont Men's College, 1979); the data are from International Monetary Fund,
International Financial Statistics.

terns in table 3 show some evidence of this by displaying traces of nonstationarity attributable to shifts in α and β. *If* this is true, then
differencing both Δp and $\Delta \varepsilon$ would lead to a cross-correlation function
(ccf) that essentially showed no relationship, as in table 4.

Pigott and Sweeney report that for the Group of Ten plus Switzerland, the real exchange rate tends to do a random walk (to a first

TABLE 2

CHANGES IN RELATIVE NATIONAL PRICE LEVELS AND THE
EXCHANGE RATE, SWITZERLAND AND THE UNITED STATES,
APRIL 1973–FEBRUARY 1977

Sample Autocorrelation Functions

Lag	Changes in the Swiss WPI in relation to U.S. WPI	Changes in Swiss–U.S. exchange rate
1	−.10	.19
2	−.05	.07
3	.09	−.06
4	−.13	−.24
5	.08	−.07
6	.24	−.38[a]
7	−.23	.03
8	.04	.05
9	−.13	.03
10	−.23	.14
11	.17	−.13
12	.06	−.08

Sample Cross-Correlation Functions

Lag	Changes in relative WPIs, lagging changes in the exchange rate	Changes in the exchange rate, lagging changes in relative WPIs
0	−.15	−.15
1	.14	.12
2	.11	.12
3	.04	.07
4	.08	−.06
5	−.18	.13
6	.17	.08
7	−.09	.09
8	−.17	−.06
9	.05	−.18
10	−.06	.01
11	.03	−.09
12	−.18	.00

NOTE: N = 47.
[a] Significantly different from zero at the 95 percent confidence level ($2 \sqrt{47} = .29$).
SOURCE: International Monetary Fund, *International Financial Statistics*.

TABLE 3

CHANGES IN RELATIVE NATIONAL PRICE LEVELS AND THE
EXCHANGE RATE, ITALY AND THE UNITED STATES,
APRIL 1973–DECEMBER 1976

Sample Autocorrelation Functions

Lag	Changes in the Italian WPI in relation to U.S. WPI	Changes in the Italian–U.S. exchange rate
1	.29	.46[a]
2	.25	.17
3	.29	−.27
4	.01	−.34[a]
5	−.01	−.15
6	−.05	−.05
7	−.11	.20
8	−.08	.12
9	−.06	.02
10	−.27	−.06
11	.01	−.18
12	.00	−.16

Sample Cross-Correlation Functions

Lag	Changes in relative WPIs, lagging changes in the exchange rate	Change in the exchange rate, lagging changes in relative WPIs
0	.33[a]	.33[a]
1	.21	.53[a]
2	−.00	.30[a]
3	−.15	.17
4	−.01	−.03
5	−.18	−.03
6	.01	−.05
7	.02	.09
8	−.15	.14
9	−.17	.01
10	−.22	.01
11	−.10	−.08
12	−.19	−.05

[a] Greater than $2 \sqrt{45} = .298$, the 95 percent confidence level.

SOURCE: International Monetary Fund, *International Financial Statistics*.

TABLE 4

FIRST DIFFERENCES OF CHANGES IN RELATIVE NATIONAL PRICE LEVELS AND THE EXCHANGE RATE, ITALY AND THE UNITED STATES, APRIL 1973–DECEMBER 1976

Sample Cross-Correlation Functions

Lag	Relative WPIs lagging changes in the exchange rate	Exchange rate lagging changes in relative WPIs
0	−.07	−.07
1	.08	.37 [a]
2	−.05	−.09
3	−.24	.04
4	.26	−.11
5	−.30 [a]	−.03
6	.15	−.13
7	.15	.07
8	−.12	.16
9	.02	−.10
10	−.14	.07
11	.17	.10
12	−.14	.01

[a] Greater than $2\sqrt{44} = .30$, the 95 percent confidence level.
SOURCE: International Monetary Fund, *International Financial Statistics*.

approximation).[35] This is illustrated in tables 5 and 6 by the random rates of change in the real Swiss exchange rate.

Frenkel reports wide variations in $p - \varepsilon$.[36] He notes that for the three countries he considers in relation to the United States (the United Kingdom, France, and Germany) the monthly series on exchange rates appear to do a random walk—that is, $\Delta\varepsilon$ is random. He argues that "national price levels do exhibit a degree of serial correlations."[37] Presumably this argument means that Δp displays measured serial cor-

[35] Pigott and Sweeney, "Price and Exchange Rate Dynamics." Both CPIs and WPIs were examined, with broadly the same results.

[36] Frenkel, "Flexible Exchange Rates in the 1970's." See also Jacob Frenkel and M. Mussa, "Efficiency of Foreign Exchange Markets and Measures of Turbulence," mimeographed (Chicago: University of Chicago, 1979).

[37] Frenkel, ibid. See also M. Mussa, "Empirical Regularities in the Behavior of Exchange Rates and Theories of the Foreign Exchange Market," Carnegie-Rochester Conference Series on Public Policy, vol. 11, supplement to the *Journal of Monetary Economics*, 1979, pp. 9-57.

TABLE 5

LEVEL OF THE REAL EXCHANGE RATE: THE SWISS FRANC
AGAINST THE U.S. DOLLAR, APRIL 1973–FEBRUARY 1977

Lag	Autocorrelation	Partial Autocorrelation
1	.45 [a]	.45 [a]
2	.17	−.05
3	−.17	−.29
4	−.25	−.08
5	−.32 [a]	−.17
6	−.20	−.03
7	−.16	−.12
8	−.00	.01
9	−.02	−.13
10	−.00	−.10
11	.05	.06
12	.11	.12

[a] Standard error: $1/\sqrt{47} = .146$.

SOURCE: International Monetary Fund, *International Financial Statistics*.

TABLE 6

FIRST DIFFERENCE OF THE REAL EXCHANGE RATE:
THE SWISS FRANC AGAINST THE U.S. DOLLAR,
SWITZERLAND, APRIL 1973–FEBRUARY 1977

Lag	Autocorrelation	Partial Autocorrelation
1	.02	.02
2	−.05	−.05
3	−.06	−.06
4	−.20	−.20
5	−.01	−.01
6	−.31 [a]	−.35 [a]
7	−.02	−.06
8	.12	.03
9	.04	−.02
10	.07	−.07
11	−.03	−.05
12	.02	−.07

[a] Significantly different from zero at the 95 percent confidence level.

SOURCE: International Monetary Fund, *International Financial Statistics*.

relation. An interesting question, though, is whether this serial correlation is attributable to shifts in α, that is, whether Δp is nonstationary. The evidence in tables 3 and 4 suggests that this is at least a plausible conjecture. In other work it is argued that a substantial amount of measured serial correlation in CPI (and WPI) inflation rates is due to such nonstationarity.[38]

Frenkel notes either that $p - \varepsilon$ is first-order autoregressive with a large root or that perhaps $\Delta(p - \varepsilon)$ is simply random. Note, however, that his reported autocorrelation functions (acf's) and partial acf's for $p - \varepsilon$ strongly support the latter interpretation (in particular, the acf shows long and large cycles above and below zero). He seems to lean toward the former because this "implies that there are mechanisms which operate to ensure that in the long run purchasing power parities are satisfied."[39] When PPP is considered in its weak and strong versions, however, it is clear that randomness in $\Delta(p - \varepsilon)$ does not mean that PPP does not hold; rather, this is consistent with the weak but not with the strong versions of PPP. Dornbusch's finding of the U.S. dollar–deutsche mark real exchange rate's obeying a first order autoregressive is also consistent with a randomness in $\Delta(p - \varepsilon)$.[40]

Lee states the conventional PPP hypothesis that $\hat{b} = 1$,[41] and then he accountably tries to test this by selecting a period over which changes in the real exchange rate appear to him to be random.[42] This selection, of course, seriously confuses weak and strong forms of PPP and implies nothing about discriminating among various forms.

Roll finds little evidence of lead-lag relationships between $\Delta\varepsilon$ and Δp. Often the $\hat{b}$ at lag zero is small or insignificant or both.[43]

[38] R. J. Sweeney, "Efficient Information Processing in Output Markets: Tests and Implications," *Economic Inquiry,* vol. 53 (July 1978), pp. 313-31, argues that when Δp_{t+1} is regressed on Δp_t, the $\hat{b}$ falls substantially when the sample interval is reduced from 1960-1974 to 1960-1969. This is found for CPIs and WPIs, for the Group of Ten plus Switzerland. The two intervals were selected arbitrarily. More detailed analysis of the U.S. CPI and its components shows similar results. Filter rules run on these indexes (see the final section) found little in the way of profits not explicable on grounds of storage, transactions, and (risk-adjusted) interest costs.

[39] Frenkel, "Flexible Exchange Rates in the 1970's."

[40] R. Dornbusch, "Monetary Policy under Exchange Rate Flexibility," in *Managed Exchange-Rate Flexibility: The Recent Experience,* Federal Reserve Bank of Boston Conference Series, no. 20 (1978), pp. 90-122.

[41] Moon H. Lee, *Purchasing Power Parity* (New York: Marcel Dekker, 1976), p. 2. See his equation 1.1.

[42] Ibid., p. 46.

[43] Roll, "Violations of Purchasing Power Parity and Their Implications."

Studies such as those of Isard and of Richardson find substantial, persistent deviation from PPP using disaggregated price indexes.[44]

To summarize to this point: (1) Evidence of lead-lag PPP relationships seems spurious. (2) There seem to be permanent changes in real exchange rates, and it is at least arguable that "long" cycles in real exchange rates are, in fact, permanent changes. (3) For a number of countries there appears to be no relationship between deviations of Δp and $\Delta \varepsilon$ around their means. (4) For other countries evidence of such a relationship may well be due to correlated shifts in these means (α and β). (5) In any case, it seems likely that $\hat{b}$ is less than unity and that relative price changes explain only a small part of the variance of exchange rates. The two latter points by themselves, however, have no necessary influence on whether intervention might be desirable, as is next discussed.

Intervention when $\hat{b} < 1$ and PPP do not explain a large percentage of exchange rate variance.[45] How do the size of $\hat{b}$ and the measured correlation of $\Delta \varepsilon$ and Δp affect intervention strategy? For concreteness, suppose Δp leads $\Delta \varepsilon$ by one period. It can be shown for quadratic loss functions that decreases in $\hat{b}$ reduce optimal intervention but do not make it zero; and reductions in the $\bar{R}^2$ reduce intervention relative to exchange rate variability but do not make optimum intervention zero.

Suppose relative price and exchange rate movements are modeled as

$$\Delta p_t = \beta + u_t + \omega_t$$

$$\Delta \varepsilon = \alpha + u_{t-1} + \xi_t$$

where $\alpha = \beta$ and u, ω, and ξ are independent and white. This period's

---

[44] P. Isard, "How Far Can We Push the 'Law of One Price'?" *American Economic Review*, vol. 67 (December 1977), pp. 942-48; and J. David Richardson, "Some Empirical Evidence of Commodity Arbitrage and the Law of One Price," *Journal of International Economics*, vol. 8 (May 1978), pp. 341-52. See also Irving B. Kravis and Robert E. Lipsey, "Price Behavior in the Light of Balance of Payments Theories," *Journal of International Economics*, vol. 8 (May 1978), pp. 193-246.

[45] This section simply applies a well-known principle of stochastic control. (Another illustration is Brainard's point about policy's becoming more conservative as uncertainty grows.) The principle is worthwhile making explicitly in order to sort out the objections to PPP-based intervention relating to the question of whether such intervention is at all beneficial from those objections relating to the difficulty of implementing intervention. The general absence of lead-lag relationships between Δp and $\Delta \varepsilon$, found above, renders PPP-based intervention useless at best. The fact that real rates vary, that Δp might explain only a small part of the future $\Delta \varepsilon$'s, or that $\hat{b} < 1$ are not in principle valid objections.

RICHARD J. SWEENEY

u disturbances to Δp show up in next period's $\Delta \varepsilon$ because of lags, and the divergence between the actual and the equilibrium real rate is costly. The equilibrium real rate in t is $(p - \varepsilon)^e_t = w_t - \xi_t + (p - \varepsilon)^e_{t-1}$ and the actual real rate is $[w_t + u_t - \xi_t + (p - \varepsilon)^e_{t-1}]$. One tractable formulation lets the cost of divergence between the actual and the real rate depend positively on the squared deviation between the actual and the equilibrium real rate, or is

$$[w_t + u_t - \xi_t + (p - \varepsilon)^e_{t-1} - w_t + \xi_t - (p - \varepsilon)^e_{t-1}]^2 = (u_t)^2$$

Now, however, let current intervention, I_t, influence $\Delta \varepsilon_t$ (but have no effect on any Δp). Then, $\Delta \varepsilon_t = \alpha + u_{t-1} + \xi_t + I_t,$[46] and the squared deviation between the actual and current real rate is

$$[w_t + u_t - \xi_t - I_t + (p - \varepsilon)^e_{t-1} - w_t + \xi_t$$
$$- (p - \varepsilon)^e_{t-1}]^2 = (u_t - I_t)^2$$

A conventional formulation is to let I_t depend linearly on the observed change in Δp_t, or $I_t = a_o + a_1 \Delta p_t$. Then, the costs of disequilibrium real rates are

$$[u_t - a_o - a_1 \Delta p_t]^2 = [u_t - a_o - a_1 \beta - a_1 u_t - a_1 \omega_t]^2$$
$$= [(1 - a)u_t - (a_o + a_1 \beta) - a_1 \omega_t]^2$$

The expected value of these costs is $(1 - a_1)^2 \sigma^2_u + (a_o + a_1 \beta)^2 + a_1^2 \sigma^2_\omega$. Minimization of expected costs requires $2(a_o + a_1 \beta) = 0$ or $a_o = -a_1 \beta$; and $-2(1 - a_1)\sigma^2_u + 2a_1 \sigma^2_w = 0$, $-\sigma^2_u + a_1 \sigma^2_u + a_1 \sigma^2_w = 0$ or $a_1 = \sigma^2_u / \sigma^2_u + \sigma^2_\omega$ If $\Delta \varepsilon_t$ is regressed on Δp_{t-1} with OLS, $E(\hat{b}) = \sigma^2_u / \sigma^2_u + \sigma^2_\omega$ in large samples. (Note that OLS assumptions are violated here, since the error term in the regression will be correlated with Δp.) Thus if Δp equals its expected value, β, then $I = +a_o + a_1 \beta = -a_1 \beta + a_1 \beta = 0$. If $\hat{b}$ is used to estimate $\sigma^2_u/(\sigma^2_u + \sigma^2_\omega)$, then $\Delta p \neq \beta$ brings intervention $I = \hat{b}(\Delta p - \beta)$.[47] Note that if σ^2 increases, the

[46] The slope coefficient for I is unity simply for convenience. If ε is the (log of the) bilateral U.S. dollar-deutsche mark rate, showing the number of deutsche marks required to buy one dollar, then an increase in I causes the deutsche marks to depreciate. Thus, I is intervention to purchase dollars with the sale of deutsche marks.

[47] Suppose $\omega_t = 0$ and $u_t > 0$. Then, $\Delta p = \alpha + u_t > \alpha$ and $I = \hat{b}u_t > 0$. That is, German inflation is higher than average in relation to U.S. inflation. Thus, either the U.S. or the German authorities enter the exchange market to buy dollars through sales of deutsche marks in order to depreciate the deutsche mark this period, rather than wait for the market to react next period.

Of course, on occasion this will lead to errors. For example, if $\omega_t > 0$ and

variation in I does *not* change on average; as σ^2 rises, the $\overline{R}^2$ of the regression of $\Delta\varepsilon$ on the (lagged) Δp decreases at the same time that $\sigma^2_{\Delta\varepsilon} / \sigma^2_I$ rises. Note also that as σ^2_w rises relative to σ^2_w, or the proportion of disturbances that $\Delta\varepsilon$ and Δp have in common falls, $E(\hat{b})$ declines, or in large samples a decline in $\hat{b}$ is to be expected.

Although $\hat{b}$ affects the amount of desirable intervention and $\overline{R}^2$ affects the amount relative to the variability of exchange rate changes, the desirability of some PPP intervention depends only on the adequacy of the model.[48]

Monetary Models and the Data. It has long been recognized that PPP makes most sense in a world where disturbances arise principally in the money supply. This view of the world is currently best exemplified in "monetary approach" models. Hence, one way of judging PPP is to examine the success of such models. This is done in terms of the results reported above, and the data do not lend much support to such models. Another reason for interest in this topic is its relationship to spot exchange-market efficiency. A number of authors have noted that some monetary models *may* make such tests inappropriate.[49] Efficiency tests of spot exchange markets seem not to be subject to these potential limitations because the data are at variance with many of the implications of these models.

"Monetary approach" models have explicit implications for the acf's and ccf's that should be observed in the data for exogenous and

---

$u_t = 0$, $\Delta p = \alpha + \omega_i > \alpha$ and so $I_t > 0$ and the government mistakenly forces a depreciation of the deutsche mark. This possibility is accounted for in $\hat{b} = \sigma^2 u /\sigma^2_\omega + \sigma^2_\omega$. As σ^2_ω rises, it becomes more likely that any $\Delta p > \alpha$ is due to $\omega_i > 0$, and hence there is less intervention in reaction.

[48] Objections to PPP-based intervention along the lines just discussed may center on two possible views about the model's inadequacy. A small slope coefficient may be taken as indication of model inadequacy, especially if twice the standard error of estimate is "close" to $\hat{b}$. Similarly, a low $\overline{R}^2$ may be taken as indicating inadequacy, especially if the $\overline{R}^2$ is close to what might occur by chance at the chosen confidence level. This is one end of a Bayesian spectrum, with no priors about whether the simple model is adequate. At the other end, some may firmly believe the model is adequate and simply be searching for good estimates of $\sigma^2 u /\sigma^2_u + \sigma^2_\omega$.

A second view of inadequacy is that there is much more going on than the simple PPP equations try to capture. This sort of objection seldom makes clear whether the error terms that capture these other effects meet the conditions of the empirical techniques used or whether the equations are statistically adequate but are simply a starting point for intervention strategy. That is, it is not clear whether such objections are based on technical or policy-making issues or on both.

[49] Harris and Purvis, "Diverse Information and the Market Efficiency in a Monetary Model of the Exchange Rate"; and Levich, "Further Results on the Efficiency of Markets for Foreign Exchange."

endogenous variables. Some of these are examined below for relative national price levels and exchange rates. It is notable that the observed patterns do not correspond to the implied patterns. This lack of fit can be explained in various ways. One view argues that important aspects of reality are neglected in these models and that if they were appropriately augmented, by including fiscal variables and exogenous shocks, for example, they would turn in better, acceptable performances. This is, of course, only conjecture; but even if true, it has two unsettling implications. First, money supply disturbances apparently are not sufficiently important to show up in the data among the welter of other influences. Second, such models cannot be used to interpret observed data: The data do not support such models; and, if the models are interpreted as incomplete, there is no way of telling whether observed behavior is due to money supply changes (and expectations of these) or to the omitted, unstudied variables.

Pigott and Sweeney discuss stochastic versions of two popular monetary models of exchange rate determination.[50] First, prices adjust to clear output markets and exchange rates adjust to clear the exchange market in every period. Second, prices adjust to equilibrium values only with lags, and the exchange rate continuously clears the exchange market. Pigott and Sweeney consider both permanent and transitory, as well as expected and unexpected, changes in the money stock and derive typical acf and ccf patterns as shown in figures 3 and 4. The results of table 2 on acf's and ccf's for Switzerland do not at all conform to these patterns. It might be argued that Italy, in table 3, does more closely conform, but as argued above, this relationship may be spurious (see table 4).

Further results are also inconsistent. Over periods of sixty months, U.S. CPI inflation rates do not show the kind of serial correlation predicted by either model.[51] Changes in exchange rate and interest rates (or interest-rate differentials) seem unrelated. Real exchange rates fail to show the cycles predicted (see table 5).

The data are particularly damaging to "overshooting" models.[52] The serial correlation they predict for various series (inflation, depreciation, real exchange rates, etc.) simply is not there. The cross-correlation evidence similarly is not supportive.

[50] Pigott and Sweeney, "Price and Exchange Rate Dynamics."

[51] See also footnote 14.

[52] See, for example, R. Dornbusch, "Expectations and Exchange Rate Dynamics," *Journal of Political Economy,* 84 (December 1976), pp. 1161-76. For a discussion of various versions of overshooting and their welfare consequences, see R. Levich, "An Examination of Overshooting Behavior in the Foreign Exchange Market," mimeographed (New York: New York University, 1979).

FIGURE 3

AUTOCORRELATION STRUCTURE OF INFLATION RATES

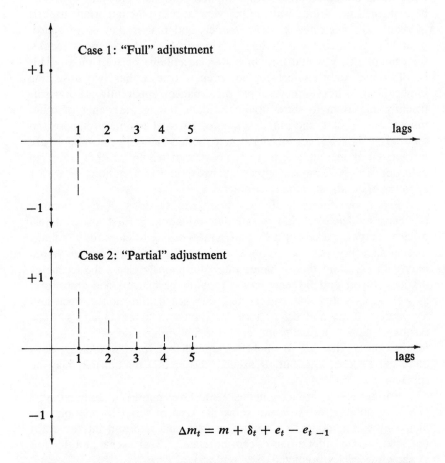

Case 1: "Full" adjustment

Case 2: "Partial" adjustment

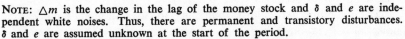

$$\Delta m_t = m + \delta_t + e_t - e_{t-1}$$

NOTE: Δm is the change in the lag of the money stock and δ and e are independent white noises. Thus, there are permanent and transistory disturbances. δ and e are assumed unknown at the start of the period.

The "Efficiency" of Spot Foreign Exchange Markets

The word "efficiency" denotes several different but related concepts in economics.[53] Efficiency here refers to efficiency as used in the finance literature and also to what many writers on exchange markets mean by

[53] T. D. Willett, "Concepts of Efficiency in the Foreign Exchange Market," in preparation.

FIGURE 4
CROSS CORRELATION STRUCTURES OF CHANGES IN PRICES AND EXCHANGE RATES

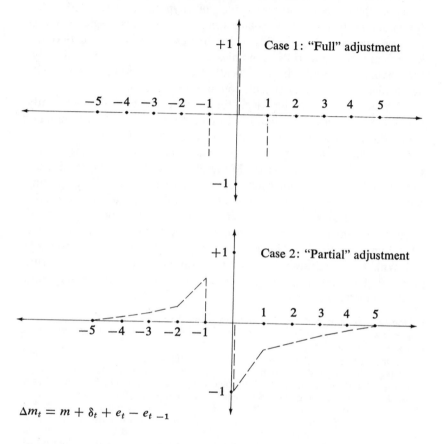

$$\Delta m_t = m + \delta_t + e_t - e_{t-1}$$

stabilizing speculation. The discussion here focuses on spot exchange rates; for surveys of evidence on forward rates, see articles by R. Levich.[54]

General Considerations. Suppose a market efficiently processes information, subject only to storage, (risk-adjusted) interest, and transactions costs. What does this imply about observable behavior of economic

[54] Levich, "Further Results on the Efficiency of Markets for Foreign Exchange" and "Tests of Forecasting Models and Market Efficiency in the International Money Market," in J. Frenkel and H. G. Johnson, eds., *The Economics of Exchange Rates: Selected Studies* (Reading, Mass.: Addison-Wesley Publishing Company, 1978).

variables? Without additional specifications, almost anything is possible. Thus, as is well known, efficiency tests always test a joint hypothesis. This creates the problem of whether to reject the hypothesis of efficiency or one of the other hypotheses if the joint hypothesis is rejected at the chosen significance level. If changes in exchange rates display correlation, for example, perhaps this is due to ups and downs in underlying determinants of the world's economies and not to inefficiency. Similarly, if mechanical buy-and-sell rules "beat" the market, perhaps these profits are justified by the risk of speculation and not by inefficiency.

Efficiency tests are based on the idea that in a market efficiently processing information, individuals cannot make abnormal, or economic, profits on a consistent basis. Further specification is necessary, however, to define what constitutes abnormal profits and to decide if they are made on a consistent basis. Many of the authors of papers dealing with the efficiency of spot exchange markets since generalized floating began in 1973 have reached markedly differing conclusions. Virtually all have found substantial evidence for rejecting the joint hypothesis. Their disagreement centers on whether to reject efficiency or one of the other joint hypotheses. Dooley and Shafer and also Logue, Sweeney, and Willett, for example, present very similar evidence of filter rule profits.[55] The former are more inclined than the latter to ascribe these results to inefficiency.[56]

[55] Dooley and Shafer, "Analysis of Short-Run Exchange Rate Behavior"; and Logue, Sweeney, and Willett, "Speculative Behavior of Foreign Exchange Rates during the Current Float."

[56] For tests of spot exchange-market efficiency during the current float, see the following: Cornell and Dietrich, "The Efficiency of the Market for Foreign Exchange Rates"; J. Westerfield, "Empirical Properties of Foreign Exchange Rates under Fixed and Floating Rate Regimes," mimeographed (Philadelphia: Federal Reserve Bank, 1975); I. Giddy and G. Dufey, "The Random Behavior of Flexible Exchange Rates: Implications for Forecasting," *Journal of International Business,* vol. 6 (Spring 1976), pp. 1-32; John Burt, Fred R. Kaen, and G. Geoffrey Booth, "Foreign Exchange Market Efficiency under Flexible Exchange Rates," *Journal of Finance,* vol. 32 (September 1977), pp. 1325-30; John Burt, "Foreign Exchange Market Efficiency under Flexible Exchange Rates: Reply," *Journal of Finance,* vol. 34 (June 1979), pp. 791-93; Marc A. Miles and D. Sykes Wilford, "Foreign Exchange Market Efficiency under Flexible Exchange Rates: Comment," *Journal of Finance,* vol. 34 (June 1979), pp. 787-89; D. E. Logue and R. J. Sweeney, " 'White Noise' in Imperfect Markets: The Case of the Franc/Dollar Exchange Rate," *Journal of Finance,* vol. 32 (June 1977), pp. 761-68; R. J. Sweeney, "Report on Technical Studies on Speculation and Market Efficiency," in J. S. Dreyer, G. Haberler, and T. D. Willett, eds., *Exchange Rate Flexibility* (Washington, D.C.: American Enterprise Institute, 1978); Logue, Sweeney, and Willett, "Speculative Behavior of Foreign Exchange Rates during the Current Float"; and W. A. Allen and C. A. Enoch, "Some Recent Evidence on Short-run Exchange Rate Behavior," *Manchester School of Economic and Social Studies,* vol. 46, no. 4 (December 1978), pp. 364-91. For the 1920s, see William Poole, "Speculative Price as Random Walks: An Analysis of Ten Time Series of Flexible Exchange Rates," *Southern Economic Journal,* vol. 33 (1967), pp. 468-78.

In this section, first results of serial correlation and filter rule tests are discussed. Then the risk premiums to be used in judging filter tests are discussed. Some authors have argued that serial correlation tests are inappropriate because some models (typically monetary approach models) can be developed that show serial correlation patterns.[57] It is argued that such models do not accord well with the data (as the previous section showed) and hence may be empirically irrelevant. It is also argued that these theoretical models have *not* had imposed on them the restrictions required for efficiency; thus, they throw little light on questions of efficiency.

Serial Correlation Tests. Let ε be, say, the (log of the) dollar–deutsche mark spot exchange rate at times t. One frequently used test of efficiency examines the correlation of $\Delta\varepsilon_t$ and $\Delta\varepsilon_{t-i}$ over the N sample observations, for $i = (0, n)$ where n ($<$N) is variously chosen in different studies. The hypothesis tested is that the population autocorrelation function is zero at all lags. Since before 1970, however, it has been well known that lack of serial correlation is neither necessary nor sufficient for efficiency.[58] As for sufficiency, correlation measures linear relationships, and inefficiency may result from a nonlinear relationship. Regarding necessity, the $\Delta\varepsilon$ may be generated by a nonstationary process consistent with efficiency, and the nonstationarity will show up as correlation that does not reflect inefficiency.

To illustrate the problems caused by nonstationarity in the mean, consider the top panel of figure 5. For $t < t'$ the exchange-rate process is given by $\Delta\varepsilon_t = \alpha + \xi_t$, where α is a constant. Because day-to-day storage, transactions, and interest costs are low in the spot foreign-exchange market, the population acf for $\Delta\varepsilon$ should show only very small relationships; the scatter of observed points should be random about α up to t', giving an insignificant sample acf approximately 95 percent of the time (at the 5 percent significance level) if usual t and Q tests are tried on a large number of samples *and* the process ξ_t is normal. At t', α shifts up to α'. With ξ still essentially uncorrelated, the sample acf for $t > t'$ will still tend to shown no significant serial correlation. The acf for the entire sample, however, *will* tend to show measured serial correlation; this indicates the shift in α, not any serial correlation in ξ. This is shown in the bottom panel of figure 5. For the period $0 \le t < t'$, the scatter centers around α and shows no relationship of $\Delta\varepsilon_t$ to $\Delta\varepsilon_{t+1}$. The scatter

---

[57] Harris and Purvis, "Diverse Information and the Market Efficiency in a Monetary Model of the Exchange Rate"; and Levich, "Further Results on the Efficiency of Markets for Foreign Exchange."

[58] E. F. Fama, "Efficient Capital Markets: A Review of Theory and Empirical Work," *Journal of Finance*, vol. 25, no. 2 (May 1970), pp. 383-417.

FIGURE 5
SERIAL CORRELATION TESTS AND NONSTATIONARITY

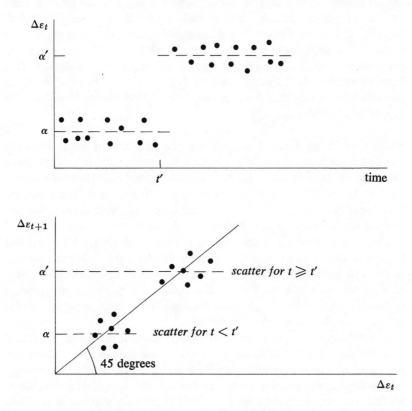

for $t' \leq t$ similarly centers around α' and shows no relationship. When the samples are pooled, however, the regression of $\Delta\varepsilon_{t+1}$ on $\Delta\varepsilon_t$ tends to show significant positive correlation.

All of the authors surveyed found measured serial correlation at various lags. Some took this as evidence of inefficiency. Others argued that the mean of $\Delta\varepsilon$ was not stationary. Many noted that the distribution of $\Delta\varepsilon$ was not normal and may not have a finite variance.[59] In the latter case the statistical tests based on normality would be biased against the null hypothesis, and rejection of efficiency might be unwarranted.[60]

[59] Dooley and Shafer, "Analysis of Short-Run Exchange Rate Behavior"; and Logue, Sweeney, and Willett, "Speculative Behavior of Foreign Exchange Rates during the Current Float."

[60] Fama, "Efficient Capital Markets" and B. Mandelbrot, "The Variations of Certain Speculative Prices," *Journal of Business,* vol. 26 (October 1963), pp. 394-419.

Further, some studies found significant serial correlation coefficients at lags that seemed to make no economic sense. Perhaps these ought to be viewed as due to sampling variability.

Because some of the joint hypotheses must be rejected, the search turns to which are the most likely candidates. Shifts in the mean rate of depreciation can be explained on (weak) PPP grounds. If the United States begins to inflate faster in relation to Germany, β falls and α would be expected to fall, resulting in some measured but spurious serial correlation. Alternatively, suppose the riskiness of U.S. assets rises in relation to Germany's. To offset this risk, the yield on U.S. assets should rise while that on German assets falls. In terms of holding deutsche marks, the yield in relation to dollars is simply α, so α would be expected to fall.[61] One approach to the problem of a shift in mean is to look at the real exchange rate, where shifts in α and β should be (at least partially, if not necessarily fully) offsetting. As reported above, changes in the real rate appear random, as would be expected with efficiency.

Under the null hypothesis the nonnormality of $\Delta\varepsilon$ would mean that ω is nonnormal. Alternatively, ω may be normal, but the variance of ω, σ_ω, may shift from time to time. This will show "peakedness" around the mean and "fatter" tails than a normal distribution. Further, this peaked, fat-tailed sample distribution looks as though it could come from a distribution that has an infinite variance.

σ_ξ^2 might shift for a number of reasons. σ_ξ^2 is based in part on expectations, and these may become more variable in times where either the private economy or policy becomes more uncertain and increases in the actual variability of the private economy or policy cause similiar increases in σ_ξ^2.

A number of studies have noted instability in sample variances. Logue, Sweeney, and Willett, for example, noted that the dollar–deutsche mark rate showed sample variances of 0.7616, 0.4473, 0.1872 over the thirds of the (approximately) first three years of the float, and

---

[61] It might be objected that an increase in the trend rate of dollar depreciation is implausible in the absence of increased U.S. monetary expansion. R. J. Sweeney, "Risk, Inflation and Exchange Rates," in *Proceedings of the 1978 West Coast Academic/Federal Reserve Economic Research Seminar* (San Francisco: Federal Reserve Bank, 1979), however, showed that the short-run effect of an increase in risk is to raise the required real rate of return on assets in the United States in relation to that abroad (in this example, α falls). In Sweeney, "Risk, Capital Formation and Exchange Rates," mimeographed (Claremont, Calif.: Claremont Men's College, 1979), the long-run result is a fall in the country's capital stock and real output. Thus, both Δp and $\Delta \varepsilon$ can take on higher trend values as real output falls in relation to a given time path of the money stock.

of 0.4684 for this overall period;[62] simply observing these changes in sample variance cannot reveal whether the population variance is infinite or has simply shifted periodically. They argue, however, that the statistically significant autocorrelation coefficients shift around a good bit. This is evidence of the instability of the process: Either the "significant" coefficients are really spurious and are due to the non-normal distribution, or there is some significant serial correlation; but the pattern jumps around in such an uncertain, confusing way that the patterns cannot be exploited for abnormal, consistent profits. The problem is that these conjectures cannot be proved any more than rival conjectures—or, rather, none has been empirically formulated and tested.

Why bother with such tests? This is a good question, with perfectly adequate answers. Past experience with other markets, preeminently the U.S. stock markets, showed the power of such tests. In other words, the possible problems discussed above with the joint hypotheses seemed not to be important. For spot exchange markets, it is now clear that either there are inefficiencies *or* other hypotheses must be rejected. Surely this is good to know.

Further, the unresolved questions of just which of the hypotheses to reject are *not* questions that cannot be answered, either in principle or in practice. Little progress has been made, however, in directly tackling the other parts of the joint hypotheses. Instead, an alternative approach has been to use filter rules to see whether the possible inefficiencies detected in serial correlation tests are economically meaningful in the sense of generating abnormal profits.

Filter-Rule Tests. It has long been argued that the appropriate test of seeming inefficiencies is whether there are any unexploited systematic (consistent) profit opportunities remaining after taking full account of transactions costs;[63] and an obvious extension is to include storage costs, opportunity costs in terms of other assets, and risk premiums to reflect differential risks of alternative assets. Filter rules are a way to implement this approach.

A longstanding complaint has been that filter rules have no confidence bounds. This is true but somewhat misleading. If the rate of return on an asset is random with $\alpha > 0$, then the filter rule loses α percent every period the investor is out of the asset. With a large number of observations and an $\alpha > 0$, any filter-rule profits make a market suspect. Thus, these tests had an implicit confidence bound that filter

[62] Logue, Sweeney, and Willett, "Speculative Behavior of Foreign Exchange Rates during the Current Float."

[63] E. F. Fama and M. Blume, "Filter Rules and Stock Market Trading," *Journal of Business,* vol. 39 (January 1966), pp. 226-41.

rules should not make any net profits. It remained true, though, that there was no way to judge whether detected profits were statistically significant. Indeed, Praetz in 1976 pointed out that a filter might provide abnormally high percentage rates of return even if the absolute profits were less than the buy-and-sell strategy's.[64] Intuitively, suppose buy-and-hold earned 0.0011 percent per day, on average, for 1000 days, the alternative asset paid 0.0 percent, the investor was out of the asset 95 percent of the time, and the rate of return on the filter rule was 0.001 percent—only slightly less than buy-and-hold. Startling returns must have been made on the 50 days the investor was in the asset. At that time Praetz, however, did *not* provide a statistical test of filter-rule profits and was somewhat pessimistic about filter tests' usefulness.[65]

Praetz later did provide a statistical test, but he was still pessimistic because his test required knowledge of the population mean rate of return α.[66] Sweeney argued that Praetz's test also required that the sample buy-and-hold mean equal α and provided a generalized test not dependent on knowledge of α.[67] Results of the two sorts of tests—those without confidence bounds and those with—are discussed later.

Judgmental filter tests. Virtually all studies of the first several years of the present float found filter profits disturbingly high from the point of view of efficiency. Table 7 shows sample results from Logue, Sweeney, and Willett.[68] Some authors judged these results inconsistent with efficiency. Others argued that the results across periods were not stable.[69] In table 7, for example, the profitable rules from the first period were unprofitable in the second period (though they were again profitable in the third period). Also, the most profitable rules changed from period to period.

Cornell and Dietrich argued that perhaps these filter profits were due to risk premiums; that is, the filter profits did not represent genuine

---

[64] P. Praetz, "Rates of Return on Filter Tests," *Journal of Finance,* vol. 31 (March 1976), pp. 71-75.

[65] Ibid.

[66] P. Praetz, "A General Test of a Filter Effect," *Journal of Financial and Quantitative Analysis,* vol. 14 (June 1979), pp. 385-94.

[67] Sweeney, "A Statistical Filter Rule Test."

[68] Logue, Sweeney, and Willett, "Speculative Behavior of Foreign Exchange Rates during the Current Float." Dooley and Shafer, "Analysis of Short-Run Exchange Rate Behavior," found similar results as did Cornell and Dietrich, "The Efficiency of the Market for Foreign Exchange Rates."

[69] Logue, Sweeney, and Willett, ibid; and Sweeney, "Report on Technical Studies on Speculation and Market Efficiency," in *Exchange Rate Flexibility,* Dreyer, Haberler, and Willett, eds.

TABLE 7

NET FILTER RULE PROFITS: GERMANY

(based on daily data, April 1, 1973–January 7, 1976)

Buy/Sell Rule (percent)	Whole Period	First Subperiod	Second Subperiod	Third Subperiod
0.5	13.70	8.04	−3.55	−6.81
1.0	24.32	18.38	−2.32	4.83
1.15	14.03	6.94	−4.88	10.20
2.0	22.80	7.71	2.63	9.47
3.0	14.73	11.48	−2.85	4.62
4.0	14.39	9.41	0	3.61
5.0	6.01	12.90	0	2.48
6.0	−1.08	1.51	0	0
7.0	−10.93	−8.34	0	0
10.0	0	0	0	0
15.0	0	0	0	0
Average filter-rule profit	18.78	12.33	11.93	−5.49
Buy-and-hold	9.87	7.28	12.93	−9.31

NOTE: Profits are net of the gains from buy-and-hold. For example, in the whole period, the 0.5 percent filter rule began with $100 and immediately bought deutsche marks; it ended with $123.57, for a profit of $23.57. Buy-and-hold profits are seen to be $9.87 (= $109.87 − $100), so net profits are $13.70. Note that the rule puts one in the foreign currency at the start of the period; so, for example, a 10 percent rule yields zero net profits since one holds deutsche marks to the very end of the period. This procedure prevents us showing negative net profits when buy-and-hold profits are positive and the filter is so large that no transactions are made; that is, one never buys into the foreign currency.

SOURCE: Logue, Sweeney, and Willett, "Speculative Behavior of Foreign Exchange Rates under the Current Float."

economic profits.[70]   When Cornell and Dietrich estimated such premiums in the context of the capital asset pricing model (CAPM), however, the profits still appeared quite large, though they still viewed the results as consistent with efficiency.

Thus, these filter tests basically left authors relying on personal judgment regarding which profits appeared unduly large.

Statistical filter tests. Praetz viewed his filter test as valid only when it was known that $\alpha = 0$ (in present notation);[71] however, he held out some hope of obtaining sufficiently good estimates of α to use the tests when $\alpha \neq 0$. Sweeney suggested a test that does not require either

[70] Cornell and Dietrich, "The Efficiency of the Market for Foreign Exchange Rates."

[71] Praetz, "A General Test of a Filter Effect."

that α be known or that $\alpha = 0$;[72] further, he argued that the Praetz test is really valid only when α equals the sample mean *and* this equality is known. One way he suggested for altering Praetz's test is to allow α not to equal the sample mean, which makes the test equivalent to Sweeney's test.

Sweeney examined only the dollar–deutsche mark rate for April 1, 1973, to January 6, 1976;[73] the test results are thus severely limited as to the coverage of period and country. The results, however, emphatically contradict the hypothesis of efficiency in this case (see table 8).[74] Furthermore, unpublished results available from the author show that subdividing periods into the first third and the final two-thirds, as in table 7, still leaves significant profits.[75] Perhaps further tests will find cases of insignificant profits, particularly for later periods; but it seems harder to maintain the hypothesis of efficiency as a general characterization of spot exchange markets. Nevertheless, these detected profits might be dismissed as a normal return on speculation.

Risk premiums and filter-rule profits. Filter-rule profits can always be conjectured to represent risk premiums. These premiums can be judged only in terms of some theory of how risk is incorporated in assets' returns. The most popular model currently is probably the CAPM (in one of its versions, in this case an international version).[76]

[72] Sweeney, "A Statistical Filter Rule Test."

[73] Ibid.

[74] Returns were not adjusted for differential interest earnings on short-term assets in the two countries. Previous work suggests that such adjustment makes little difference; most of the "action" is in the exchange rate, and any bias thus introduced is negligible. See Dooley and Shafer, "Analysis of the Short-Run Exchange Rate Behavior," and Logue and Sweeney, " 'White Noise' in Imperfect Markets."

The sample statistic is $x = a_F - a + fa$, where a_F is the per period rate of return on the filter rule, a is the per period rate of return on buy-and-hold, and F is the fraction of days the buyer is out of the market. Under the (joint) null hypothesis that the market is efficient *and* the rates of return are randomly distributed, $E(x) = 0$.

The sampling distribution of x for a given value f has the standard deviation $\sigma_x = [f(1-f)]^{1/2} \dfrac{\sigma}{N^{1/2}}$, where σ is the standard deviation of the per period rates of return to buy-and-hold and N is the sample size. σ_x is approximated by $\hat{\sigma}_x$ with the sample $\hat{\sigma}$ substituted for σ; with a sample of $N = 692$, this is a very good approximation.

[75] That is, the profits from the first third of the sample were significant, as were those from the final two-thirds.

[76] On the international CAPM, see B. Solnik, *European Capital Markets: Toward a General Theory of International Investment* (Lexington, Mass., 1973), and R. Roll and B. Solnik, "A Pure Foreign Exchange Asset Pricing Model," *Journal of International Economics* (1977), pp. 161-69.

TABLE 8

THE U.S. DOLLAR–DEUTSCHE MARK EXCHANGE RATE
(APRIL 1, 1973–JANUARY 7, 1976)

Filter Buy-and-Sell (percent) (1)	Profit per $100 (U.S. dollars) (2)	Average Rate of Return per day (a_F) (3)	$f = (N$ out $\div N)$ (4)	$X = a_F - a + fa$ (5)	$2\hat{\sigma}_x$ (6)	Number of transactions (round trips) (7)
10	9.87	.0143	0.0	0	0	1
5	15.88	.0230	0.6575	.0181	.02472	3
4.5	8.10	.0117	0.6228	.0063	.02525	4
4	24.26	.0351	0.3179	.0254[a]	.02426	4
3.5	18.41	.0266	0.7240	.0227	.0235	5
3	24.60	.0356	0.4595	.0279[a]	.02597	6
2.5	38.16	.0557	0.4884	.0479[a]	.02604	8
2	32.67	.0472	0.5405	.0406[a]	.02597	11
1.5	23.90	.0345	0.5246	.0277[a]	.02602	22
1	34.19	.0494	0.5202	.0425[a]	.02602	33
0.5	23.57	.0341	0.4711	.0265[a]	.02601	88

NOTE: $N = 692$ days; $\hat{\sigma}_x = [f(1-f)]^{1/2} \frac{\hat{\sigma}}{N^{1/2}}$; $\hat{\sigma} = .6844$; $a_F =$ filter-rule average rate of return; $a =$ buy-and-hold average rate of return.

[a] Significant at the 95 percent confidence level with $\hat{\sigma} = .6844$.

SOURCE: R. J. Sweeney, "A Statistical Filter Rule Test: The Dollar–DM Exchange Rate," mimeographed (Claremont, Calif.: Claremont Men's College, 1980).

Statements are often made that leave the impression that use of the filter rule might be expected to earn a return above buy-and-hold because the filter rules' returns are risky. In terms of the CAPM, this conjecture is incorrect. Any extra risk due to using the rule is non-systematic risk, and the expected return from bearing this risk is zero.

In this framework, the observed per period rate of return (in terms of dollars) of holding deutsche marks provides an estimate of the equilibrium rate of return, and the zero returns on holding dollars are, of course, fixed. Switching back and forth between the two assets is expected to give simply a weighted average of the two expected rates of return. The real question is: Given the variability of the rate of return on deutsche marks, does this weighted average perform better than expected? This is essentially Sweeney's approach.[77] The separate question of a risk premium does not arise.[78]

Efficiency Tests: Real and Monetary Shocks, Permanent and Transitory Disturbances. Harris and Purvis built a currency substitution model in which the only assets are various national moneys.[79] They show that disturbances (real or monetary) have different effects depending on whether they are transitory or permanent, expected or unexpected. A transitory increase in the U.S. money supply will cause the dollar to depreciate, for example. People will realize, however, that the dollar

[77] Sweeney, "A Statistical Filter Rule Test."

[78] The joint hypothesis is that the exchange market is efficient and that the distribution from which exchange rates are drawn is stationary. With negligible transactions and storage and interest costs, the changes should be random. The additional hypothesis that the CAPM holds implies that the mean' rate of change of the exchange rate depends on the risk-free rate of return, the expected return on the (international) "market," and on the exchange markets' beta. The observed per period rate of return is a good measure of this expected rate of return under the (triple) null hypothesis.

The CAPM implies there is no sense in holding a risky portfolio other than the "market" portfolio. Trying to fit currency speculators into the CAPM framework violates its logic by implying they are rewarded for not holding the market portfolio.

The confusion seems to arise because of the CAPMs separate positive and normative roles. As a positive theory, it asserts that the return to currency speculation is the weighted (by f) average of holding dollars and deutsche marks, as in table 8. In its normative role, it allows a speculator in a single, small, inefficient market in a web of efficient markets to judge whether speculation in this one market pays an adequate return in terms of the speculation's (systematic) risk. However, if exchange markets are inefficient, this inefficiency clearly violates the assumption of a small, inefficient market in a web of efficient markets, and the usefulness of the CAPM as a guide vanishes.

[79] Harris and Purvis, "Diverse Information and the Market Efficiency." For another currency substitution model, see G. A. Calvo and C. A. Rodriguez, "A Model of Exchange Rate Determination with Currency Substitution and Rational Expectations," *Journal of Political Economy,* vol. 85 (June 1977), pp. 617-26.

will eventually appreciate to its previous level, and they will begin to substitute dollars for deutsche marks. Thus the dollar initially falls (but not as much as it would if the change were permanent) and then eventually returns to its previous level.

Harris and Purvis argue that we might then observe cycles in exchange-rate changes *and* that these cycles would be consistent with efficiency.[80] Hence serial correlation tests could incorrectly reject efficiency.

The importance of this point turns on two issues: First, is the model empirically relevant? Second, is it theoretically adequate to discuss the issue of efficiency? The answer seems to be no for both questions. As discussed in a previous section, the data do not seem to conform to many of the direct implications of such monetary approach models.

Perhaps more important, the Harris and Purvis work does not discuss or explicitly use the implications that efficiency has for the structure of their model. In particular, they treat the elasticity of substitution coefficients as parametric. In fact, they should be endogenous. In the experiment of a transitory increase in the money supply, one influence restraining the degree of substitution is fear that the increase is permanent. If all increases were known to be temporary, there would be greater substitution and smaller falls in the rate. Indeed, in a currency substitution model where moneys are held only as assets and there are no alternative assets, this absence of risk should lead to infinite elasticities and no variation in the rate.

The important question in such models is whether the elasticities have the appropriate magnitudes. One way of judging this is through observed cycles in exchange-rate changes. If $\Delta\varepsilon$ is stationary, can the observed patterns be explained by storage, transaction, and interest costs (where these latter are taken as risk-adjusted opportunity costs)? A similar point is true for filter tests. Rather than using the Harris and Purvis argument which invalidates such tests, it is proper to use such tests to judge if the world is efficient in terms of Harris and Purvis's own model.

Conclusions

This paper examines two bodies of evidence relevant to intervention in the spot exchange market: the empirical literature on purchasing power parity (PPP) and work on the efficiency of spot exchange mar-

[80] Harris and Purvis, "Diverse Information and the Market Efficiency in a Monetary Model of the Exchange Rate."

kets. The evidence is somewhat mixed, of course, but the PPP literature seems to provide little basis for intervention strategy. Tests of spot exchange-market efficiency for the early years of the float do show signs that intervention might have improved some markets' performances.

Much of the PPP literature reviewed concerns lead-lag relations between relative national price levels and exchange rates. Often the investigation bears either on the estimated slope coefficient of the exchange rate (ε) regressed on relative national price levels (p) or on the relationship between changes in these two variables.

For PPP-based intervention to be potentially beneficial, there must be some believable, detectable lead-lag pattern. It is not at all necessary that $\hat{b}$ be close to unity or that p explain a substantial part of ε (or vice versa). Further, there can be permanent changes in real exchange rates with PPP-based intervention still potentially useful.

Simply comparing levels of p and ε can be misleading, in much the same way that the eye can pick out plausible but spurious cycles in levels of U.S. stock prices. Cross-section and cross-section–time-series regressions have often given distorted impressions of the power of PPP relationships because of the studies' implicit assumptions that all countries have the same trend rates of depreciation and relative inflation. When econometric allowance is made for the fact that these rates differ across countries, the seeming PPP relationship is greatly weakened. Careful time-series analysis of $\Delta\varepsilon$, Δp, and the real exchange rate shows little in the way of the lead-lag relationships that would allow useful PPP-based intervention. Indeed, often any contemporaneous relationship is small or insignificant or both.

Studies of spot exchange-market efficiency have cast doubts on the hypothesis. Because all such tests necessarily test a joint hypothesis of efficiency and other hypotheses, however, authors have differed on whether to reject efficiency or to accept it and reject another hypothesis. Serial correlation tests of changes in spot exchange rates found more structure than expected. The structure appeared unstable, however, and the error terms did not seem normally distributed. Various filter-rule tests cast further doubts, since many rules seemed to show substantial profits (beyond buy-and-hold) earned in many exchange markets during the first three years of the float. Profitable rules showed instability across periods, as did profit levels, however, and it was suggested that perhaps the profits were not abnormal but were due to the risk borne by speculators. It was noted, in addition, that conventional filter tests lacked confidence bounds. The one test with confidence bounds (for the dollar–deutsche mark rate for the first three years of the float) found statistically significant, persistent profits. Further, these profits could not be explained by risk, at least in the context of the capital asset pricing model. Of course, more such testing is needed on other currencies and for later periods. Tentatively, however, spot exchange markets showed as least some signs of inefficiency that could indicate scope for beneficial intervention. The form and extent of appropriate intervention is by no means clear.

Bibliography

Balassa, Bela. "The Purchasing Power Parity Doctrine: A Reappraisal." *Journal of Political Economy* 72 (December 1964), pp. 584–96.

Brainard, W. "Uncertainty and the Effectiveness of Policy." *American Economic Review,* May 1967, pp. 411–25.

Brillembourg, Arturo. "Purchasing Power Parity Tests of Causality and Equilibrium." Mimeographed. International Monetary Fund, 1976.

Burt, John. "Foreign Exchange Market Efficiency under Flexible Exchange Rates: Reply." *Journal of Finance* 34 (June 1979), pp. 791–93.

———; Kaen, Fred R.; and Booth, G. Geoffrey. "Foreign Exchange Market Efficiency under Flexible Exchange Rates." *Journal of Finance* 32 (September 1977), pp. 1325–30.

Calvo, G. A. and Rodriguez, Carlos A. "A Model of Exchange Rate Determination with Currency Substitution and Rational Expectations." *Journal of Political Economy* 85 (June 1977), pp. 617–26.

Cornell, W. B., and Dietrich, J. K. "The Efficiency of the Market for Foreign Exchange Rates." *Review of Economics and Statistics* 60 (February 1978), pp. 111–20.

Dooley, M., and Shafer, J. "Analysis of Short-Run Exchange Rate Behavior, March, 1973, to September, 1975." International Finance Discussion Paper No. 76. Mimeographed. Federal Reserve Board, 1976.

Dornbusch, R. "Monetary Policy Under Exchange Rate Flexibility." In *Managed Exchange-Rate Flexibility: The Recent Experience,* Federal Reserve Bank of Boston Conference Series, no. 20 (1978), pp. 90–122.

———. "Expectations and Exchange Rate Dynamics." *Journal of Political Economy* 84 (December 1976), pp. 1161–76.

———, and Jaffe, D. "Purchase Power Parity and Exchange Rate Problems: Introduction." *Journal of International Economics* 8 (May 1978), pp. 157–62.

Fama, E. F., and Blume, M. "Filter Rules and Stock Market Trading." *Journal of Business* 39 (January 1966), pp. 226–41.

Frenkel, Jacob. "Exchange Rates, Prices and Money: Lessons from the 1920s." Mimeographed. Chicago: University of Chicago, 1979.

———. "Flexible Exchange Rates in the 1970s." Mimeographed. Chicago: University of Chicago, 1980.

―――. "A Monetary Approach to the Exchange Rate: Doctrinal Aspects and Empirical Evidence." *Scandinavian Journal of Economics* 78 (May 1976), pp. 200–24.

―――. "Purchasing Power Parity: Doctrinal Perspective and Evidence from the 1920s." *Journal of International Economics* 8 (May 1978), pp. 169–92.

―――, and Johnson, H. G., eds. *The Economics of Exchange Rates: Selected Studies*. Reading, Mass.: Addison-Wesley Publishing Co., 1978.

―――, and Mussa, M. "Efficiency of Foreign Exchange Markets and Measures of Turbulence." Mimeographed. Chicago: University of Chicago, 1979.

Friedman, M., and Schwartz, A. *A Monetary History of the United States*. Princeton: Princeton University Press, 1963.

Genberg, Hans. "Purchasing Power Parity under Fixed and Flexible Exchange Rates." *Journal of International Economics* 8 (May 1978), pp. 247–76.

―――. "Purchasing Power Parity as a Rule for a Crawling Peg." Mimeographed. Geneva: Graduate Institute for International Studies, 1979.

Giddy, I., and Dufey, G. "The Random Behavior of Flexible Exchange Rates: Implications for Forecasting." *Journal of International Business* 6 (Spring 1976), pp. 1–32.

Harris, R. G., and Purvis, D. D. "Diverse Information and the Market Efficiency in a Monetary Model of the Exchange Rate." Mimeographed. Queen's University, 1978.

Hodgson, John S., and Phelps, Patricia. "The Distributed Impact of Price-Level Variation on Floating Exchange Rates." *Review of Economics and Statistics* 57 (October 1975), pp. 58–64.

Isard, P. "How Far Can We Push the 'Law of One Price'?" *American Economic Review* 67 (December 1977), pp. 942–48.

King, D. "The Performance of Exchange Rates in the Recent Period of Floating: Exchange Rates and Inflation Rates." *Southern Economic Journal,* April 1977, pp. 1582–87.

Kravis, Irving B., and Lipsey, Robert E. "Price Behavior in the Light of Balance of Payments Theories." *Journal of International Economics* 8 (May 1978), pp. 193–246.

Krugman, P. "Purchasing Power Parity and Exchange Rates." *Journal of International Economics* 8 (August 1978), pp. 397–407.

Lee, Moon H. *Purchasing Power Parity*. New York: Marcel Dekker, 1976.

―――. "Further Results on the Efficiency of Markets for Foreign Exchange." In *Managed Exchange-Rate Flexibility: The Recent Experience,* Federal Reserve Bank of Boston Conference Series, no. 20, 1978.

107

————. "Tests of Forecasting Models and Market Efficiency in the International Money Market." In *The Economics of Exchange Rates: Selected Studies.* Edited by J. Frenkel and H. G. Johnson. Reading, Mass.: Addison-Wesley Publishing Co., 1978.

Levich, R. "The Efficiency of Markets for Foreign Exchange." In *International Economic Policy: Theory and Evidence.* Edited by R. Dornbusch and J. Frenkel. Baltimore: Johns Hopkins University Press, 1979.

————. "An Examination of Overshooting Behavior in the Foreign Exchange Market." Mimeographed. New York: New York University, 1979.

Logue, D. E., and Sweeney, R. J. " 'White Noise' in Imperfect Markets: The Case of the Franc/Dollar Exchange Rate." *Journal of Finance* 32 (June 1977), pp. 761–68.

————, eds. *The Effects of Exchange Rate Adjustments.* Washington, D.C.: U.S. Treasury, 1976.

————, and Willett, T. D. "Speculative Behavior of Foreign Exchange Rates during the Current Float." *Journal of Business Research* 6 (1978), pp. 159–74.

Mandelbrot, B. "The Variations of Certain Speculative Prices." *Journal of Business* 26 (October 1963), pp. 394–419.

Meinich, Per. *A Monetary General Equilibrium Theory for an International Economy.* Oslo, Norway: Scandinavian University Books, 1968.

Miles, Marc A., and Wilford, D. Sykes. "Foreign Exchange Market Efficiency under Flexible Exchange Rates: Comment." *Journal of Finance* 34 (June 1979), pp. 787–89.

Mussa, M. "Empirical Regularities in the Behavior of Exchange Rates and Theories of the Foreign Exchange Market." Carnegie-Rochester Conference Series on Public Policy, vol. 11, Supplement to the *Journal of Monetary Economics,* 1979, pp. 9–57.

Officer, Lawrence. "The Purchasing-Power-Parity Theory of Exchange Rates: A Review Article." *IMF Staff Papers* 23 (March 1976), pp. 1–61.

OPTICA. "Inflation and Exchange Rates: Evidence and Policy Guidelines for the European Community." *OPTICA Report 1976,* Brussels, February 1977.

Pigott, C., and Sweeney, R. J. "Price and Exchange Rate Dynamics: Theories and Tests." Mimeographed. Claremont, Calif.: Claremont Men's College, 1979.

————. "Purchasing Power Parity and Exchange Rate Dynamics: Some Empirical Results." Mimeographed. Claremont, Calif.: Claremont Men's College, 1979.

Poole, William. "Speculative Price as Random Walks: An Analysis of Ten Time Series of Flexible Exchange Rates." *Southern Economic Journal* 33 (1967), pp. 468–78.

———. "The Stability of the Canadian Flexible Exchange Rate." *Canadian Journal of Economics* 33 (1967), pp. 205–17.

Praetz, P. "A General Test of a Filter Effect." *Journal of Financial and Quantitative Analysis,* June 1979, pp. 385–94.

———. "Rates of Return on Filter Tests." *Journal of Finance* 31 (March 1976), pp. 71–75.

Richardson, J. David. "Some Empirical Evidence of Commodity Arbitrage and the Law of One Price." *Journal of International Economics* 8 (May 1978), pp. 341–52.

Roll, Richard. "Violations of Purchasing Power Parity and Their Implications for Efficient International Commodity Markets." Mimeographed. UCLA Graduate School of Management, 1978.

———, and Solnik, B. "A Pure Foreign Exchange Asset Pricing Model." *Journal of International Economics,* 1977, pp. 161–69.

Samuelson, P. A. "Theoretical Notes on Trade Problems." *Review of Economics and Statistics* 46 (1964).

Solnik, B. H. *European Capital Markets: Towards a General Theory of International Investment.* Lexington, Mass.: Lexington Books, 1973.

Sweeney, R. J. "Efficient Information Processing in Output Markets: Tests and Implications." *Economic Inquiry* 53 (July 1978), pp. 313–31.

———. "Inflation, the Balance of Trade, and the Effects of Exchange Rate Adjustments." In *The Effects of Exchange Rate Adjustments.* Edited by P. B. Clark, D. E. Logue, and R. J. Sweeney. Washington, D.C.: U.S. Treasury, 1976.

———. "Report on Technical Studies on Speculation and Market Efficiency." In *Exchange Rate Flexibility.* Edited by J. S. Dreyer, G. Haberler, and T. D. Willett. Washington, D.C.: American Enterprise Institute, 1978.

———. "Risk, Capital Formation and Exchange Rates." Mimeographed. Claremont, Calif.: Claremont Men's College, 1979.

———. "Risk, Inflation and Exchange Rates." In *Proceedings of the 1978 West Coast Academic/Federal Reserve Economic Research Seminar.* San Francisco: Federal Reserve Bank, 1979.

———. "A Statistical Filter Rule Test: The Dollar-DM Exchange Rate." Mimeographed. Claremont, Calif.: Claremont Men's College, 1980.

Thygesen, Niels. "Inflation and Exchange Rates: Evidence and Policy Guidelines for the European Community." *Journal of International Economics* 8 (May 1978), pp. 301–18.

Westerfield, J. "Empirical Properties of Foreign Exchange Rates under Fixed and Floating Rate Regimes." Mimeographed. Philadelphia: Federal Reserve Bank, 1975.

Willett, T. D. "Concepts of Efficiency in the Foreign Exchange Market." In preparation.

Commentary

Jacob A. Frenkel

The papers by Thomas D. Willett and by Richard J. Sweeney deal with some of the fundamental issues concerning our recent experience with flexible exchange rates. They deal with the causes and the effects of exchange rate volatility, with the efficiency of the foreign exchange market, and with the purchasing power parity theory. In my remarks I will interpret the evidence concerning exchange rate volatility and purchasing power parities in terms of the theory of exchange rate determination, and I will conclude with a brief discussion concerning the policy implications.[1]

The central insight of the modern approach to the analysis of exchange rates is the notion that the exchange rate, being the relative price of two durable assets (moneys), can be best analyzed within a framework that is appropriate for the analysis of asset prices. A key characteristic of the price of an asset is its strong dependence on expectations concerning the future. In an efficient market for assets, new information concerning the future is reflected immediately in current prices, thus precluding unexploited profit opportunities from arbitrage. The strong dependence of current prices on expectations about the future is unique to the determination of durable asset prices that are traded in organized exchange; it is not a characteristic of price determi-

I am indebted to the National Science Foundation, grant SOC 78-14480, for financial support. The views expressed are those of the author and not necessarily those of the National Bureau of Economic Research.
[1] For a further elaboration, see Michael L. Mussa, "Empirical Regularities in the Behavior of Exchange Rates and Theories of the Foreign Exchange Market," Carnegie-Rochester Conference Series on Public Policy, vol. 11, supplement to *Journal of Monetary Economics* (1979), pp. 9-57; Jacob A. Frenkel and Michael L. Mussa, "Efficiency of Foreign Exchange Markets and Measures of Turbulence," *American Economic Review*, vol. 70, no. 2 (May 1980); and Frenkel, "Flexible Exchange Rates in the 1970s," *Stabilization Policy: Lessons from the 1970s and Implications for the 1980s* (St. Louis: Center for the Study of American Business, Washington University, 1980).

nation of nondurable commodities (like fresh fish). The strong dependence of asset prices on expectations also implies that, during periods that are dominated by "news" that induces frequent changes in expectations, asset prices exhibit large fluctuations. Because exchange rates are viewed as asset prices, they will also exhibit a relatively large degree of volatility during periods that are dominated by news that alters expectations. With this perspective the recent volatility of exchange rates is not a mystery; rather, it reflects the volatile character of the 1970s, which witnessed great turbulence in the world economy and great uncertainty about the future course of economic and political events.

The evidence reported by Willett, Sweeney, and others lends support to the hypotheses that the foreign exchange market behaves as an efficient-asset market and that much of the volatility of exchange rates reflects frequent and large changes in expectations concerning the future. Forward exchange rates seem to be unbiased forecasts of future spot rates, and the forecast errors do not seem to contain systematic patterns that can be used to improve predictions. As such, forward exchange rates may be viewed as a reasonable measure of expectations concerning the future value of the currency. The magnitude of the forecast errors is substantial, however. Only a small fraction of the actual change in exchange rates is accounted for by the previous period's forward premium or discount on foreign exchange given the hypothesis that the lagged forward premium or discount reflects all the relevant information available in the previous period, it follows that the forecast error reflects news that, by definition, could not have been predicted. This is indeed what seems to have happened in the market for foreign exchange as well as in other futures markets.

What can we predict about the future evolution of exchange rates? There is only one reasonable answer: We can predict that exchange rates (or their rate of change) will change. As is typical of other efficient markets, this is all that one can say because market participants forecast a specific future change in the price of an asset, and competition ensures that these expectations are reflected immediately in current prices; further changes remain unpredictable. This notion that current exchange rates and the information that they convey tend to become obsolete at a rapid pace is illustrated by the following quotation from George J. Goschen taken from the preface to the third edition of his classic book, *The Theory of Foreign Exchanges:* "The few weeks which have elapsed since the second edition have again proved the rapidity with which the situation of the 'Foreign Exchanges' may be reversed, and the difficulty of selecting durable illustrations."[2]

[2] George J. Goschen, *The Theory of Foreign Exchanges,* 3d ed. (London, 1864).

For the sake of the history of economic thought, it should be noted that the unique role of expectations in determining current exchange rates has been well understood by previous generations. Thus in explaining the large changes that took place upon Napoleon's landing from Elba, John Stuart Mill wrote:

> On the news of Bonaparte's landing from Elba, the price of bills advanced in one day as much as ten percent. . . . This great price was an equivalent . . . for the anticipated difficulty of producing [gold] to send; the expectations being that there would be such immense remittances to the Continent in subsidies and for the support of armies, as would press hard on the stock of bullion in country.[3]

Similarly, the error of explaining current exchange rates by the balance of trade rather than by the more fundamental determinants (demand and supplies of the various assets and particularly expectations) underlay the bullionist controversy of the early nineteenth century and led Knut Wicksell to describe the evolution of the theory as a retrogression:

> Indeed, the theory may have even be said to have retrogressed. . . . there was an inclination to ascribe even the gigantic deviations of the exchange rates above or below Parity which were witnessed in the World War almost exclusively to considerations of trade and credit, without bearing in mind—as Goschen had expressed pointed out that the really large fluctuations in rates of exchange . . . always presuppose a positive deterioration—be it actual or merely anticipated, in the value of the country's currency.[4]

Unfortunately, the tendency to "explain" the evolution of exchange rates in terms of developments of the balance of trade is still popular. In contrast, the analytical framework that incorporates the renewed emphasis on the role of expectations implies that in analyzing the relationship between the balance of trade and the exchange rate a key distinction should be made between anticipated and unanticipated components of the balance of trade. Only the latter component is expected to induce a strong change in the exchange rate because only the unanticipated component reflects news that may be relevant for the formation of expectations and, thereby, for the determination of the value of the currency.

[3] John Stuart Mill, *Principles of Political Economy*, 5th ed. (London: Parker and Co., 1862), bk. 3, chap. 20.
[4] Knut Wicksell, "The Riddle of Foreign Exchanges," in his *Selected Papers on Economic Theory* (London: Routledge & Kegan Paul, 1958; reprint ed., New York: Augustus M. Kelley, 1969).

Have exchange-rate fluctuations been excessive? It should be obvious that in order to answer this question we need a standard for comparison. If a relevant yardstick is the extent of variation of national price levels, then indeed exchange rates have fluctuated excessively. From June 1973 through the end of 1979, for example, the average absolute monthly percentage change of the dollar/pound, the dollar/French franc, and the dollar/DM exchange rates exceeded 2 percent per month. In comparison the average absolute monthly percentage changes for wholesale and consumer price indexes and for the ratios of national price levels were only about half that of the corresponding exchange rates. As a result, adherence to a narrow interpretation of the purchasing power parity theory results in the conclusion that exchange rate variations were excessive. The asset-market approach suggests, however, that a relevant yardstick should be the variations of other asset prices rather than commodity prices. During the same period the average absolute percentage changes in the various stock market indexes have been about twice the corresponding changes in exchange rates. By this standard, exchange rates have not fluctuated excessively.

The distinction between commodity prices and asset prices is fundamental for interpreting the deviations from purchasing power parities that were reported by Richard Sweeney. As is well known, changes in commodity prices are serially correlated whereas changes in exchange rates are not. The "stickiness" exhibited by commodity prices need not reflect any market imperfection; rather, it may reflect the cost of price adjustment that leads to finite nominal contracts. Likewise, it may reflect the results of a confusion between nominal and real shocks or between permanent and transitory shocks. In addition, commodity price indexes are less sensitive to changes in expectations because they include commodities with a low degree of durability. It follows, therefore, that when there are frequent and significant changes in expectations exchange rates adjust immediately and commodity prices do not. Exchange rates reflect expectations about future circumstances, whereas prices reflect present circumstances. This different response implies that large fluctuations of exchange rates are likely to be associated with large deviations from purchasing power parities. These large deviations reflect the intrinsic difference between commodity and asset prices. It is noteworthy that Gustav Cassel, the most vocal proponent of the purchasing power parity theory, recognized the unique role that expectations play in inducing deviations from parities:

A depreciation of currency is often merely an expression for discounting an expected fall in the currency's internal purchasing power. . . . The international valuation of the currency will,

then, generally show a tendency to anticipate events, so to
speak, and becomes more an expression of the internal value
the currency is expected to possess in a few months, or perhaps
in a year's time.[5]

With this interpretation it seems that intervention in the foreign exchange
market that ensures that exchange rates conform with purchasing power
parities would be a mistaken course of policy. If commodity prices do
not adjust fully in response to exogenous shocks, it seems that a large
adjustment of exchange rates serves a useful role because it provides
the outlet for the pressure that otherwise would have been reflected in
commodity prices.

Given the expected large deviations, what is left of the purchasing
power parity theory, and what role should it play in guiding policy? It
is clear that it should not be viewed as a theory of exchange rate determination because it specifies a relationship between two endogenous
variables without providing the details about the processes that bring
it about. It is also clear that it does not provide a guide for day-to-day
or month-to-month fluctuations of exchange rates. Further, when the
economy experiences real structural changes that require adjustments
of relative prices, purchasing power parities may not be satisfied even
in the long run. Its usefulness is in providing a guide as to the general
trend of exchange rates in particular in circumstances where the main
shocks underlying the trend are of a monetary origin. As for the conduct
of macroeconomic policy, it serves as an important reminder that the
exchange rate and the price level cannot be divorced from each other
and that policies that affect the trend of domestic prices in relation to
foreign prices are likely to affect the exchange rate in the same manner.
Recent experience suggests that this reminder is still necessary and is
not trivial.

Emphasis on the fact that exchange rates and prices are both
endogenous variables is important in view of the recent allegations that
flexible exchange rates have been inflationary. Both exchange rates and
prices respond to the same set of shocks, and both can be influenced by
a similar set of policies. The fact that exchange rates adjust faster than
commodity prices reflects the known phenomenon that asset markets
clear relatively quickly. This fact does not imply that as an economic
matter the chain of causality runs from exchange rates to prices. It is
again noteworthy that the basic fact that exchange rates and prices are
determined simultaneously has been recognized long ago and was ex-

---

[5] Gustav Cassel, *Money and Foreign Exchange after 1919* (London: Macmillan,
1930), pp. 149-50.

pressed forcefully by Gottfried Haberler: "One should not say as supporters of the theory of PPP are fond of doing that the rise in prices is the primary phenomenon, and that the depreciation of exchange is merely an effect of this. The two changes bear a functional relation to one another and are both effects of the same cause." [6]

The recognition that exchange rate fluctuations reflect the underlying circumstances rather than creating them is fundamental. It implies that, for a given conduct of macroeconomic policy, the basic choice is not between costly turbulence and free tranquillity but between alternative outlets to the underlying turbulence. If the source of evil were the variability of exchange rates, then pegging the rate would have been the simple and the feasible solution. The experience with the Bretton Woods system indicates that this is not the case. One could argue, however, that the obligation to peg the rate would alter the conduct of policy by introducing discipline. Experience suggests, however, that national governments are unlikely to be disciplined by the exchange rate regime; rather, the exchange rate regime is more likely to adjust to whatever discipline national governments choose to have.

Government policy can make a positive contribution to reducing costly and unnecessary variations of exchange rates by adopting more stable and predictable patterns of policies. This is particularly relevant in the case of exchange rates because, as was argued earlier, current exchange rates reflect expectations concerning future events and future policies. Current policy instability may induce expectations for future policy instability and, thereby, have a magnified effect on current exchange rates. When policies are erratic and unpredictable, monetary policy exerts real side effects. Put differently, money is felt when it is out of order; when it is in order, it only serves as a veil over the real equilibrium of the economy. This unique property of money is best summarized by the following quotation from John Stuart Mill:

> There cannot, in short, be intrinsically a more insignificant thing, in the economy of society, than money; except in the character of a contrivance for sparing time and labour. It is a machine for doing quickly and commodiously, what would be done, though less quickly and commodiously, without it: and like many other kinds of machinery, it only exerts a distinct and independent influence of its own when it gets out of order. [7]

The role of policy is to ensure that money is in order, and this can be achieved by following a predictable, stable course of policy. Following

[6] Gottfried Haberler, *The Theory of International Trade* (London: William Hodge, 1936), p. 60.

[7] Mill, *Principles of Political Economy,* bk. 3, chap. 7.

such a course will not eliminate variations of exchange rates, nor will it ensure that exchange rates conform with the predictions of the purchasing power parity theory. It will, however, reduce some of the unnecessary and costly fluctuations that are induced by unstable and erratic policies.

John F. O. Bilson

Thomas Willett emphasizes that the floating exchange rate experience has induced a large quantity of new research on the economic determinants of the exchange rate. He also states—correctly, I believe—that this literature has had relatively little influence on policy analysis because of its apparent lack of consensus. In these comments, I should like to expand on these points by answering two questions: (1) What do we know about the determination of the exchange rate? (2) Why do we not know what we do not know?

In answer to the first question, which is certainly the easier of the two, it is important to distinguish between the strong academic consensus on the equilibrium determinants of the exchange rate and the sharp controversy surrounding the dynamics of adjustment toward the equilibrium value. Almost all of the modern theories of the exchange rate have the same steady-state properties; where they differ is in the short-run dynamics. The equilibrium value of the exchange rate that arises out of the asset-market theories is generally of the following simple form:

$$S(*/\$) = [M(*)/M(\$)][Y(\$)/Y(*)][V(*)/V(\$)]$$

where $S(*/\$)$ is the number of units of foreign currency required to purchase one dollar, M is the quantity of money, Y is the level of real income, and V is the velocity of circulation. This formula has a distinct monetarist tinge in its terminology, but similar expressions in different accents can be found in the nonmonetarist writings on exchange rates. This equation is the fundamental valuation formula for foreign exchange—the quantity theory of the exchange rate—and, like the quantity theory, it is a tautology until the determinants of velocity are specified. To paraphrase Jacob Frenkel, the equation states that the exchange rate, as the relative price of two moneys, is determined by the relative supplies and relative demands of the two moneys.

This valuation formula has gained wide acceptance because its predictive power is high in "laboratory" experiments in which the

The views expressed are solely the responsibility of the author and are not necessarily those of the National Bureau of Economic Research.

TABLE 1
PREDICTED AND ACTUAL EXCHANGE RATES FOR 1978

Country	$S(*/\$)$	$M(*)/$ $M(\$)$	$Y(\$)/$ $Y(*)$	$V(*)/$ $V(\$)$	Predicted	Error (%)
France	4.51	4.39	1.10	0.90	4.35	3.70
West Germany	2.01	3.52	0.93	0.60	1.96	2.31
Japan	210.47	258.45	1.15	0.63	187.25	11.69
Switzerland	1.79	9.74	0.70	0.25	1.70	4.89
United Kingdom	0.52	0.31	1.57	1.11	0.54	3.82

NOTE: In these calculations, S is the exchange rate, H is the quantity of high-powered money per capita, Y is the dollar value of GNP per capita, and V is derived from a velocity equation of the form $V = a \exp(b/i)$. The parameters a and b were estimated from an ordinary least squares equation for seventeen advanced industrial countries. The fitted value is the product of the preceding three columns, and the final column gives the percentage error of the model in predicting the actual exchange rate. Further details of this model are available from the author.
SOURCE: Author.

sample variance of the right-hand-side variables is large enough to dominate any short-run adjustment dynamics. As an example of this type of analysis, consider the cross-sectional variation between the exchange rates of the major currencies in 1978. The relevant statistics are given in table 1. This relatively simple model does a creditable job of accounting for cross-sectional differences in exchange rates between the major currencies. The major factor is clearly the relative quantity of money, which is defined in the calculations as the relative quantity of high-powered money per capita. In addition, the model demonstrates that countries with high levels of real per capita income tend, other things being equal, to have a strong exchange rate. Hence, despite the utterances of some Federal Reserve officials, there is no conflict between the standard of living and the value of the currency. Finally, countries with low velocities, induced by low interest rates, tend, *ceteris paribus,* to have strong currencies. In the long run, the lesson is that high interest rates reflect inflationary expectations and that an inflationary currency is a weak currency.

To my mind, these calculations summarize the state of academic knowledge about exchange rates. At best, the academic is able to provide a plausible range for the value of a currency with confidence limits of around 10 percent. Within this range, it appears to be very difficult to predict the value of the exchange rate. Because the empirical evi-

117

dence is uninformative in this range, a large number of contrasting theoretical models can offer equally plausible theories of exchange rate dynamics. We simply do not have enough empirical knowledge to distinguish between them.

This brings me to my second question: Why do we not know what we do not know? What we do not know is how exchange rates adjust in the short run. Here, then, is why we do not know. The best approach to take in answering the question is to make use of an analogy with the equity market. In equity markets, the equivalent valuation formula to the quantity-theory equation is the price/earnings ratio, which relates the price of an equity share to the number of shares issued and the earnings of the corporation. Price/earnings ratios do a creditable job of predicting the equity share prices of various companies on the New York Stock Exchange, and they are equally useful for certain comparative statics exercises including, for example, the effect on price of a stock split. Equity market participants have long learned, however, that price/earnings ratios are of little value in predicting the path of equity prices because equity prices predominantly change in response to new information about the future path of earnings.

This is also the case in the foreign exchange market. Basically, the spot exchange rate will reach a short-run equilibrium when its expected change is small. Hence, expectations are the primary influence on exchange rates in the short run. Because we know almost nothing about the way in which expectations are formed, we also know almost nothing about the short-run dynamics of the exchange rate.

The final important question is: Should we care? The answer to this question depends upon one's purposes. For short-run speculation, or for short-run official intervention, the lack of information is disturbing. For a more farsighted, stable control of the value of the exchange rate, however, all that is required is a knowledge of the long-run fundamentals. There is, after all, very little difference between the policy that stabilizes the price of foreign exchange and the policy that stabilizes other prices in the economy. Although intervention in the foreign-exchange market, credit controls, or even wage/price controls may have some effect in the short run, long-term control requires a reduction in the rate of growth and the variability of the money supply. In the long run, this tried-and-true policy prescription has a unit probability of success.

I have dwelt at length on the consensus view of the determinants of the equilibrium value of the exchange rate for a number of reasons. First, it sheds light on the intervention issue discussed in Willett's paper. The equilibrium approach suggests that intervention will be successful only if it influences the underlying fundamental determinants of the exchange rate. In the absence of offsetting domestic credit policies, foreign exchange market intervention should alter the exchange rate in the desired direction, but—and this is an important point—the same effect could also be reached by domestic monetary policy alone. There is consequently no difference between successful intervention and control of underlying conditions. Second, I detect a tendency in both the Willett and Sweeney papers to be overly concerned with short-run dynamics arising in the form of destabilizing speculation, forecasting errors, and deviations from purchasing power parity. The approach that I would prefer is long-run because I believe that the transmission of the academic consensus on the long-run determinants of the exchange rate to both public and private participants in the market would stabilize exchange rates by reducing the heterogeneity of expectations.

Morris Goldstein

One of the main points of Thomas Willett's paper is that the effects of exchange-rate volatility cannot be discussed in isolation from the causes. In a sense, however, I have been asked to do just that. Specifically, my assignment is to discuss the effects of exchange-rate volatility on international trade flows and on domestic inflation rates. Following that, I will make a few general remarks about what can be done about exchange-rate volatility.

Effects of Exchange Rate Volatility on International Trade Flows

As Willett correctly points out, prior to the introduction of floating rates in early 1973, there was great apprehension that floating rates would be highly volatile rates and that high exchange-rate volatility in turn would inhibit the volume of international trade.

In retrospect, the critics of floating rates appear to have been half right. Floating rates have indeed proved to be highly volatile rates, at least in the short run. On the other hand, exchange-rate volatility does not appear to have had any inhibiting effect on international trade flows, at least as regards industrial countries.

Three types of evidence support this conclusion. The first of these are the empirical studies that have tested directly for the *independent* effect of exchange-rate uncertainty on the volume of imports and exports of the industrial countries, after holding the other known determinants of trade flows constant (that is, levels of real economic activity at home

The views expressed in this paper are solely those of the author and do not necessarily represent the views of the International Monetary Fund.

and abroad, and relative traded goods prices).[1] The measures of exchange rate uncertainty used are either indicators of short-run exchange-rate variability (simple standard deviations or variances of nominal bilateral or effective exchange rates) or convenient proxies for exchange-rate uncertainty itself, such as the forward exchange rate minus the spot exchange rate at the maturity of the forward contract—namely, the forecasting error of the forward rate. For neither measure have these studies produced any significant effect of exchange-rate uncertainty on the volume of trade.[2]

A second piece of evidence is obtained by comparing price elasticities in trade equations estimated for the period of fixed rates with those for the period of floating rates. Some observers have argued that because much exchange-rate volatility under floating rates is short-term and reversible, producers and consumers of traded goods will respond only to those exchange rate changes they deem to be "permanent."[3] Two implications of this hypothesis are that the size of price elasticities should be smaller under the floating rates than under fixed rates and that the response of trade flows to (observed) changes in exchange rates should be slower under floating rates. Suffice it to say that at this point there seems to be no evidence of such differences in price elasticities or time lags as between the fixed and floating rate periods.[4]

[1] Peter B. Clark and Charles J. Haulk, "Flexible Exchange Rates and the Level of Trade: A Preliminary Analysis of the Canadian Experience," mimeographed (U.S. Treasury, March 1972); John H. Makin, "Eurocurrencies and the Evolution of the International Monetary System," in Carl H. Stem, John H. Makin, and Dennis E. Logue, eds., *Eurocurrencies and the International Monetary System* (Washington, D.C.: American Enterprise Institute, 1976); Peter Hooper and Steven W. Kohlhagen, "The Effect of Exchange Rate Uncertainty on the Prices and Volume of International Trade," *Journal of International Economics,* vol. 8 (November 1978), pp. 483-511.

[2] One important qualification to this conclusion should be mentioned. When the change in exchange rate uncertainty is large and when exchange rate uncertainty is measured with respect to the real rather than the nominal exchange rate, a significant depressing effect of exchange rate uncertainty on the allocation of production as between exports and the domestic market has been identified; see the recent study on Brazil by Donald V. Coes, "The Crawling Peg and Exchange-Rate Uncertainty" (Paper presented at the ANPEC/Ford Foundation Conference on the Crawling Peg, Rio de Janeiro, October 1979). Coes found that the large decrease in real exchange-rate uncertainty after the adoption of a crawling peg in 1968 had a strong positive effect on the export propensity of Brazilian manufacturing producers. I am indebted to John Williamson for drawing my attention to this study.

[3] For example, Jürg Niehans, "Some Doubts about the Efficacy of Monetary Policy under Flexible Exchange Rates," *Journal of International Economics,* vol. 5 (August 1975), pp. 245-81.

[4] See Morris Goldstein, "Have Flexible Exchange Rates Handicapped Macroeconomic Policy?" *Special Papers in International Finance,* no. 14 (Princeton, N.J.: Princeton University, May 1980).

The third and most informal type of evidence comes from economists who specialize in forecasting trade flows. One may ask these trade forecasters what they do differently now that they have to forecast trade in an environment of floating rates. Similarly, one may inquire whether their forecasting equations have perceptibly gone "off track" since the introduction of floating rates. As far as I can determine, the answer to both questions is again no.

All of this does not deny that there have been periods under floating rates when economists did become somewhat disenchanted with the ability of exchange rate changes to equilibrate current account imbalances. I refer here particularly to the 1976–1978 period, which saw both large nominal exchange rate changes and sticky current account imbalances for the three largest industrial countries (the United States, Germany, and Japan). By now, however, I think there is general agreement that the poor performance during that period can be explained in terms of: (1) the fact that real changes in exchange rates during 1976–1978 were much smaller than nominal changes (real changes in exchange rates are of course what matters for trade flows); (2) the distinction between short-run and long-run price elasticities (elasticities for one year being only about half as large as those for two to three years); (3) the fact that cyclical real income movements in the United States and its main trading partners (other G-10 countries) overwhelmed and frustrated relative price movements during that period; [5] and (4) the effects that large current account imbalances themselves had on the size of changes in exchange rates through the effect of the former on exchange-rate expectations.

In sum, I share Willett's conclusion that the effects of exchange rate volatility on international trade appear to have been minimal, and far less damaging than was expected. [6]

---

[5] During 1967-1973, the average annual percentage change in U.S. real gross national product was 3.8 percent whereas that for the other G-10 countries plus Switzerland (weighted by 1972-1976 trade shares) was 6.3 percent. In contrast, during 1975-1978, the corresponding figures for the United States and foreign industrial countries were 5.1 and 3.6 percent, respectively. See Edwin M. Truman, "Balance-of-Payments Adjustment from a U.S. Perspective," Paper presented at the Conference on Europe and the Dollar in World-wide Disequilibrium, Basel, May 1979.

[6] Having said that, I should also introduce the caveat that the volume of international trade need not be synonymous with global welfare. If, for example, short-run exchange rate movements induce traders to respond to relative price signals that bear little relation to longer-run comparative advantage ("false-trading," as Ronald McKinnon calls it), the volume of trade can increase while global welfare decreases. See Ronald McKinnon, *Money in International Exchange* (New York: Oxford University Press, 1979).

Effects of Exchange Rate Volatility on Inflation Rates

There is a whole range of issues and important questions under this general heading, and I will touch on just a few of them.[7] On balance, Willett is critical of the view that exchange-rate volatility has exacerbated the domestic inflation problem. Let me just spell out what I think makes sense about the effect of exchange-rate changes on inflation rates and what does not.

To begin with, I do not think it can be denied that exchange-rate movements can have rapid and sizable effects on countries' import prices, domestic prices, money wages, and export prices. A consensus estimate would be that a 10 percent change in import prices (expressed in domestic currency) will within a year lead to a 1.5–4 percent change in consumer prices, with the United States at the low end of the range and the smaller, more open industrial economies (Italy, the United Kingdom, Belgium, the Netherlands) at the upper end of the range. These effects of exchange rate changes on domestic prices also appear to be getting larger and faster.[8] Part of this reflects the secular increase in openness in most industrial countries. From 1960 to 1977, for example, there was an increase of about 40 percent in ratios of trade to gross national product for industrial countries.[9]

A second argument that makes sense is that flexible rates increase the slope (steepness) of the short-run Phillips curve. That is, they shorten the time lag between money supply changes and domestic price changes. This happens because increases in the money supply under floating rates are transmitted rapidly into exchange rate depreciation, driving up import prices and domestic prices. This restricts the scope of antirecessionary action, particularly in the post-1975 situation where most industrial countries have faced high inflation and high unemployment simultaneously. I think this short-run adverse effect is more important than Willett's long-run "silver lining," which says that the steeper slope of the short-run Phillips curve also limits the ability of the authorities to manipulate the economy for short-run political advantage; for example, if the money supply is pumped up prior to elec-

[7] A more comprehensive discussion of the effects of the exchange rate regime on inflation can be found in A. D. Crockett and Morris Goldstein, "Inflation under Fixed and Flexible Exchange Rates," *IMF Staff Papers*, vol. 23 (November 1976), pp. 509-44.

[8] P. Robinson, T. Webb, and M. Towsend, "The Influence of Exchange Rate Changes on Prices," *Economica*, vol. 46 (February 1979), pp. 27-50.

[9] N. Fieleke, "The International Transmission of Inflation," in *Managed Exchange-Rate Flexibility: The Recent Experience*, Federal Reserve Bank of Boston Conference Series No. 20 (October 1978).

tion time, the increase in prices may come before the increase in employment that was the original intention of such expansion.

Let me now identify two arguments about the effects of exchange rate volatility on inflation that make less sense.

The first of these claims that changes in exchange rates *cause* changes in inflation. The problem here is that once one realizes that exchange rates are endogenous, one has to ask what made the exchange rate depreciate in the first place. We have learned that it is easy to get an "optical illusion" that exchange rates are driving inflation rates when in fact *both* developments are joint reflections of excess monetary expansion. In this sense I heartily agree with Willett that we need a more general equilibrium view of the problem.

The other argument I wish to criticize is the so-called ratchet hypothesis. This hypothesis argues that short-run fluctuations in exchange rates impart an inflationary bias to the world economy because exchange-rate depreciations lead to increases in import and domestic prices whereas exchange-rate appreciations do not induce any fall in domestic prices in the appreciating countries.

This argument sounds good but is not really supported by the empirical evidence. Import prices do appear to fall after exchange rate appreciations, and domestic prices do not seem to react differently to positive versus negative changes in import prices.[10]

I think there is some confusion in the ratchet hypothesis between the statement that downward price inflexibility is a problem and the statement that flexible rates exacerbate this problem. I support the first statement but not the second. The real problem is, rather, that workers and producers today believe that modern governments can sustain contractionary demand policies for only short periods. Hence, long-term expectations about inflation are not much affected by these policies, and neither are present rates of inflation.

Proposals for Dealing with Exchange Rate Volatility

In a nutshell, I think there are two things, one active and one passive, that we can do about exchange-rate volatility. On the active side, countries can adopt more stable underlying economic and financial policies, and they can take a long-term view of macroeconomic policies. The rationale for this is straightforward. Because present exchange rates are heavily dependent on future expected exchange rates and

[10] See Morris Goldstein, "Downward Price Inflexibility, Ratchet Effects, and the Inflationary Impact of Import Price Changes," *IMF Staff Papers,* vol. 24 (November 1977), pp. 569-612.

because future expected rates are heavily dependent on future expected macroeconomic policies, present policies operate on exchange rates in part by affecting expectations about future policies. Therefore, if the conduct of macroeconomic policy is unstable, great uncertainty about future policies is generated and hence instability in exchange rates is also induced because there is no firm anchor for long-term expectations.

The passive part involves becoming resigned to the idea that the exchange-rate market is an asset market and that it may exhibit fluctuations that are similar to those in other asset markets even when macroeconomic policies are coordinated across countries. That is, we must realize that stable monetary policies are a necessary but not a sufficient condition for exchange-rate stability. As long as we have unexpected developments ("news") that affect expected future exchange rates, present exchange rates will also fluctuate. To draw an analogy with changing perceptions about unemployment, we have come to recognize that the full-employment unemployment rate is not zero. Similarly, short-run exchange rate variability should not be expected to be absent even in "orderly exchange markets," and these exchange rate fluctuations may well be the least costly response to certain types of disturbances.

Jeffrey R. Shafer

I would like to focus on the implications of research on exchange market efficiency, and exchange rate behavior more broadly, for official intervention policy.

We have two papers as background. Thomas Willett has given us a militantly centrist ("anyone who currently holds strong views . . . has simply not thought about all sides of the question deeply enough") and eclectic view of our understanding of exchange markets. I find nothing important to quarrel with in it. Richard Sweeney's paper gave me problems at a number of points, but rather than dwell on them I should like to consider an alternative to what I take to be its central premise: that the case for official exchange market intervention rests on the existence of cycles in real exchange rates or of speculative inefficiency in spot-exchange markets. The study of the time series properties of exchange rates provides an indication of the types of models within which questions such as the role of intervention could be addressed. The evidence in Sweeney's paper, in my earlier paper with Michael

This paper represents the views of the author, not those of the Federal Reserve Board or its staff.

Dooley,[1] and in a number of other papers, for example, suggests that exchange markets may not satisfy the conditions that would prevail in a market where expectations were rational, adjustment was instantaneous, and assets denominated in different currencies were viewed as perfect substitutes. But it cannot substitute for the construction and testing of alternative structural models within which the costs and benefits of intervention can be evaluated.

Before this thought is developed further, it is important to be concrete about what is meant by intervention. The question of the role of exchange market intervention can be distinguished from monetary policy only if we consider sterilized intervention. Ronald McKinnon has recently reviewed the case for unsterilized intervention—gold-standard rules of the game, if you will—as a normative prescription.[2] The issue he raises is whether exchange market pressures largely reflect shocks to which *domestic* monetary policy should respond. The response could be made not only through intervention but also through domestic open market operations, discount window policy, and so on. Willett, Sweeney, and most others who have addressed the question in recent years have asked, "Given a domestic monetary policy (Is there anyone left who would not define such a policy in terms of some aggregate?), can authorities, should authorities, sell or buy home currency securities for foreign currency securities?"

Willett says he believes that such intervention can affect exchange rates. He does not say by how much and for how long. Indeed, the evidence is slim. One way to look for an answer would be to ask what conditions would have to hold for intervention to affect spot exchange rates. The answer in the context of asset models of exchange rate determination is that there must be distinct demands for outside securities—that is, claims on governments—denominated in different currencies. If such distinct demands exist, changes in relative supplies should cause changes in relative expected returns. The search for such alterations in expected returns is the search for the "risk factor" because the existence of risk aversion and undiversifiable currency risk is what provides a satisfying theoretical basis for belief in distinct demands for currencies.

My impression is that this search has not been very successful. Jeffrey Frankel in a recent paper fails to reject the hypothesis that there

[1] Michael P. Dooley and Jeffrey R. Shafer, "Analysis of Short-Run Exchange Rate Behavior, March 1973 to September 1975," International Finance Discussion Paper No. 76 (Washington, D.C.: Federal Reserve Board, February 1976).

[2] Ronald I. McKinnon, "Dollar Stabilization and American Monetary Policy," Paper presented to the American Economics Association meetings, December 1979, Atlanta, Ga.

is not risk premium.[3] I do not think, and Frankel has not claimed, that this should be taken as the last word on the subject. Nonetheless, the lack of empirical support is not comforting for those of us who have assumed that currencies are imperfect substitutes.

Empirical work in this area has been hampered by several factors:

• a still brief period of floating exchange rates, which is clearly marked by structural instability

• central bank reactions, also variable over the period, such that, unless simultaneous equations techniques are used, regressions tend to show that purchases of a currency are associated with a declining exchange value rather than a rising exchange value

• the expectational nature of exchange rate relationship, which introduces difficult statistical problems

• central bank reluctance to provide more complete data, which would permit researchers to conduct good series for outside supplies of assets

Two of my Federal Reserve colleagues, Peter Hooper and John Morton, are now making use of inside information to make a direct estimate of the effects of intervention. They find support for a short-run effect that persists for several months, but it is not a large one. The evidence of a permanent effect is shaky. Perhaps there are sufficient short-run rigidities in financial markets to give intervention some leverage, but over periods of several quarters investors respond on a larger scale to bring exchange rates into line with price and trade developments. If this is so, it would account for the evidence in the data, admittedly inconclusive, for speculative inefficiency in exchange markets. I would argue that if intervention has only a short-run effect the need for intervention is also only short-run. Official foreign-currency operations can be reversed in time without adverse consequences. Thus the questions of the possibility of effective intervention and the desirability of intervention are closely related, if not identical.

I would link the case for intervention to further development of this sort of evidence rather than to evidence of the existence of a stable time series model for real exchange rates, as Sweeney does in the first part of his paper.

To consider this suggestion in another light, the kinds of forces that could conceivably affect exchange rates might be listed:

[3] Jeffrey A. Frankel, "A Test of the Non-existence of the Risk Premium in the Foreign Exchange Market," mimeographed (Berkeley: University of California, February 1980).

- general uncertainty causing a loss of focus to expectations and, perhaps as a consequence, greater volatility
- portfolio shifts in demand
- responses to changes in rates of return
- changes in real factors—oil shocks, productivity, taste changes, etc.
- diverging price levels

I would personally consider the case for intervention to be strongest for the first of these disturbances and nonexistent for the last. Right now authorities have very little evidence on which to rely to distinguish these various kinds of shocks. Nonetheless, it is a fair inference that, the larger is a movement that cannot be clearly accounted for by recognizable price or trade developments, the stronger is the case that at least part of the movement is of the sort that can and perhaps should be met with intervention. Thus a strategy of stiffening resistance to cumulative movements, taking account of price developments and trend developments in trade, seems appropriate. Lack of effectiveness should also be taken as a sign to back off. This is essentially Willett's suggestion.

What are the costs of authorities' being wrong and resisting a fundamental rate movement? If the market is really efficient, there are none on an expected-value basis. Intervention will fail, and from the level of any given day the exchange rate will be as likely to rise as to fall. It is only when intervention might sometimes be appropriate— that is, when there are significant differences that build up in expected rates of return for different currencies—that there is a risk that central banks may often both be wrong and consistently lose money. A central bank strategy that consistently loses money is likely to add to exchange rate instability as well.

These observations emphasize to me the need for better empirical models of exchange rate behavior to distinguish financial from real disturbances if intervention is to make a better contribution to exchange market, and hence to macroeconomic, stability. In the meantime authorities will continue to function in an environment of great uncertainty. Caution would be warranted.

I would emphasize, again, that the issue of intervention must be distinguished from the issue of the extent to which authorities should seek to retain the domestic-policy freedom that exchange rate flexibility permits, given the much-discussed price consequences. The answer to this distinct question certainly depends on the sensitivity of a country's prices to exchange rate movements and on the costs of adjustment through exchange rate change rather than by other means. Countries of different size, with different degrees of openness, and with different domestic price and wage processes clearly differ in this regard.

127

Richard M. Levich

I have been asked to focus my comments on overshooting and foreign exchange market efficiency. Most of my remarks will be general in nature; however, I shall address several specific comments to the papers presented by Thomas Willett and Richard Sweeney.

The term "overshooting" has become popular in both academic and business discussions of the behavior of floating exchange rates. As is often the case with economic terminology, there is no unique or standardized definition of overshooting. In this paper I shall sketch out four alternative concepts of overshooting in order to illustrate that how we judge overshooting—specifically, whether it is a symptom of a troubled and inefficient foreign exchange market that imposes extra costs on the system and requires an active intervention policy to be corrected—depends on the definition that we adopt. The four definitions of overshooting may be stated briefly as follows:

1. The current spot-exchange rate (S_t) does not equal its official policy target (S'_t).

2. The current spot-exchange rate (S_t) does not equal some long-run equilibrium rate $(\overline{S})$ that may be based on purchasing power parity or another long-run model.

3. The equilibrium exchange-rate change that occurs in the short run (ΔS_{sr}) exceeds the equilibrium exchange-rate change in the long run (ΔS_{lr}).

4. The actual exchange-rate change that occurs in the marketplace (ΔS_t) exceeds the equilibrium exchange-rate change $(\Delta S'_t)$ required if the market had full information about economic structure and disturbances.

Although the first definition recalls a necessary aspect of gauging the performance of economic policy, it begs many questions concerning the derivation of S'_t. If, for example, S'_t reflects unfeasible or unattained targets for external and internal balance, then there are clear reasons why S_t and S'_t are unequal. For these reasons, this definition of overshooting cannot be used to identify market inefficiencies.

The second definition follows from the observation that $\overline{S}$ is a relatively quiet series whereas S_t is relatively volatile, making frequent and extended departures from $\overline{S}$. Although we may define this as overshooting, there is substantial ambiguity concerning the underlying causes of this exchange rate behavior, its costs on the economy, and the benefits from eliminating it. If we maintain that $\overline{S}$ is the true, equilibrium exchange rate, then economic costs exist when the market fails to

128

establish $S_t = \overline{S}$. Interestingly, overshooting of this type could be explained by two very different stories: a shortage of speculative capital, so that transactions to stabilize S_t around $\overline{S}$ are not sufficient, or an excess of speculative capital, so that speculative bandwagons that push S_t far from $\overline{S}$ are frequent. In either case unexploited profit opportunities exist for speculators who recognize the divergence between S_t and $\overline{S}$.[1]

There may, however, be numerous economic reasons why a particular $\overline{S}$ (and purchasing power parity [PPP] is a popular candidate here) is not an appropriate standard for short-run exchange rate changes.[2] Suppose, for example, that exchange rates are always set so that the Law of One Price holds for tradable commodities.[3] If the number of tradable commodities is small relative to the number of goods in the consumer price index (CPI), then an index based on tradable goods (namely, the exchange rate, S_t) will naturally be more volatile than an index based on many goods (namely, the purchasing power parity rate computed using the CPI, $\overline{S}$). In this model, disparities between S_t and $\overline{S}$ reflect (1) that the CPI is calculated based on many goods prices whereas, in the short run, the exchange rate may be determined by a small number of traded-goods prices, and (2) that the change in the relative price of tradable versus nontradable goods represents a market equilibrium. In this case, "overshooting" loses its pejorative connotation.

Our third definition of overshooting focuses on changes in price rather than their level. It recalls a simple story from introductory microeconomics: Assuming that the supply of good X is fixed in the short run, if demand increases the initial price change exceeds the

[1] Demonstrating empirically that the market does not establish a fair price ($S_t \neq \overline{S}$) is extremely difficult. Most empirical tests have been unable to reject market efficiency in favor of an alternative hypothesis. See, for example, Richard M. Levich, "Further Results on the Efficiency of Markets for Foreign Exchange," in Federal Reserve Bank of Boston, *Managed Exchange Rate Flexibility: The Recent Experience,* Conference Series, no. 20 (1978). These tests of market efficiency are really tests of a joint hypothesis, however. That is to say, when we observed that $S_t \neq \overline{S}$, we cannot be sure whether this is because S_t is set too high (or low) and/or our estimate of $\overline{S}$ is too high (or low). Therefore, this definition of overshooting is not likely to be an operational success. It is too easy to be led to the efficient-market tautology: A price set by a freely competitive market must be a fair price, and so overshooting or undershooting is impossible.

[2] *Measured* deviations from PPP (as opposed to ex ante, unexploited profit opportunities) can be rationalized in many ways: differences in national consumption bundles, changes in quality, dissimilarity between domestic and export products, differences between quoted and transaction prices, differences in foreign trade credits, and changes in taxes, tariffs, or tastes, to name only a few. See Ronald I. McKinnon, *Money in International Exchange* (New York: Oxford University Press, 1979), chap. 6.

[3] This example follows from Bradford Cornell, "Relative Price Changes and Deviations from Purchasing Power Parity," *Journal of Banking and Finance,* September 1979, pp. 263-80.

change required for long-run equilibrium. The important lesson of this story is that, at every moment, price is adjusting to equate supply and demand. No unexploited profit opportunities exist. The increase in price provides the incentive for production to expand to its higher long-run level. In this case, "overshooting" is beneficial, and it would be undesirable to try to smooth prices. In a market economy, the price change is simply the channel through which costs associated with the increase in demand are made visible. Given that the demand for good X has increased, there is no presumption that *extra* adjustment costs are imposed on the system because of the large initial price change. Rather, we presume that the price change eliminates the need for queuing, rationing, or other allocation schemes that are less efficient.

The recent models of exchange rate dynamics by Rudiger Dornbusch and the portfolio-balance approach by Pentti J. K. Kouri and William H. Branson illustrate this notion of exchange rate overshooting.[4] A common feature of these economic models is that one or more channels of adjustment is impaired. In the Dornbusch model, goods prices are assumed to change very slowly relative to asset prices, whereas in portfolio-balance models desired increases in foreign assets must be accumulated over time through the current account. The policy implications to draw from these models are similar in spirit to our earlier simple story—that is, these models of exchange rate determination are equilibrium models; short-run exchange rate changes are determined endogenously, given the exogenous disturbance and the ability of other channels to share the burden of adjustment over time. In the context of these models, it appears that exchange rate overshooting consistent with our third definition does not impose *additional* adjustment costs on the system.[5]

[4] See Rudiger Dornbusch, "Expectations and Exchange Rate Dynamics," *Journal of Political Economy,* December 1976, pp. 1161-76; Pentti J. K. Kouri, "The Exchange Rate and the Balance of Payments in the Short Run and the Long Run," *Scandinavian Journal of Economics,* vol. 78, no. 2 (May 1976), pp. 280-304; William H. Branson, "Exchange Rate Dynamics and Monetary Policy," in Assar Lindbeck, ed., *Inflation and Employment in Open Economies* (Amsterdam: North-Holland Publishing Company, 1979).

[5] As a technical matter, when an economic time series follows a mean-reverting process and futures prices are set equal to expected spot prices, the prices of short-term futures contracts will be more volatile than the prices of long-term futures contracts—which is overshooting by definition 3. Current weather conditions, for example, may greatly affect the volatility of spot and near-term futures prices for wheat while the price of five-year futures will show little change. See Paul A. Samuelson, "Is Real-World Price a Tale Told by the Idiot of Chance?" *Review of Economics and Statistics,* January 1976, pp. 120-23, for a formal proof; and D. J. S. Rutledge, "A Note on the Variability of Futures Prices," *Review of Economics and Statistics,* January 1976, pp. 118-20; and Katherine Miller, "The Relation between Volatility and Maturity in Futures Contracts," in Raymond M. Leuthold, ed., *Commodity Markets and Futures Prices* (Chicago: Chicago Mercantile Exchange, 1979), for empirical evidence.

In the real world, exchange rates are based on incomplete information. Our fourth and last definition equates overshooting with actual exchange rate changes that are too large relative to the change required, given complete information. Recall that the classic definition of an efficient market is one in which prices "fully reflect" available information. Our last definition of overshooting therefore requires that actual prices do not reflect *all* information—that is, the market is not "strong-form" efficient. When a market price is not set to reflect *all* information, costs resulting from resource misallocations are entailed. If, however, information itself is costly to collect and process, it is rational for investors to be less than fully informed. Therefore, the existence of overshooting (definition 4) need not lead to additional adjustment costs.

Two strands of theoretical literature are relevant for definition 4. First is the type of macroeconomic model that experiences either temporary or permanent monetary and real disturbances and that allows for different information sets across economic agents and sectors.[6] In this setting, it can be demonstrated that the realized time path of the exchange rate may vary considerably from the "full-information" path. Overshooting of type 4, however, will exist only if agents misinterpret economic disturbances so as to require large exchange rate changes. It is also possible that in assessing the temporary/permanent, monetary/real characteristics of a disturbance, economic agents will select the combination that minimizes the required exchange rate change. If agents do not consistently misjudge the nature of disturbances, it seems that overshooting and undershooting should be equally likely.

The second type of models related to definition 4 are those that analyze capital market behavior under heterogeneous expectations. In the model developed by Stephen Figlewski, traders are assumed to have heterogeneous information as well as diverse price expectations, risk aversion, predictive ability, and wealth.[7] The price of an asset is determined by the combined "dollar votes" of all traders who possess varying pieces of information, rather than by an omniscient trader who sees and accurately processes *all* information. It is this process of combining pieces of information that results in the actual market price diverging from the full-information price. The model suggests that, when there is a wide range of forecasting ability or a wide diversity of expectations among agents, then actual market prices may deviate relatively far from full-information prices.

[6] Richard G. Harris and Douglas I. Purvis, "Diverse Information and Market Efficiency in a Monetary Model of the Exchange Rate," Queen's University Discussion Paper, no. 309, July 1978.

[7] Stephen Figlewski, "Market 'Efficiency' in a Market with Heterogeneous Expectations," *Journal of Political Economy*, August 1978, pp. 581-97.

Empirical testing for this type of overshooting will be difficult to execute and interpret for policy purposes. It may be possible with the aid of hindsight to find episodes during the 1970s in which exchange rates were too volatile and investors overlooked opportunities to earn unusual profits. As Willett correctly stresses in his paper, however, exchange rate determination must be viewed ex ante. We must investigate whether exchange rates were too volatile, given the incomplete information available when prices were set. This might raise a related question: Did investors collect the optimal amount of information, or would additional expenditures on information have led to unusual profits (and a reduction in overshooting)?

The above discussion suggests a proper role for government: to increase the timely distribution of accurate information and to follow monetary and fiscal policies that are predictable over the relevant horizon. These policies should increase the homogeneity of expectations and reduce the likelihood of overshooting. Governments also might choose to intervene in the foreign exchange market based on their inside information (similarly to a firm that repurchases its own stock). This raises larger philosophical questions that can be left for later discussion.

To summarize, according to definitions 3 and 4, "overshooting" behavior is consistent with an equilibrium model. In practice, definitions 1 and 2 will often gauge exchange rate behavior relative to a standard that is improperly or incompletely specified, such as a naive PPP standard. It seems reasonable to assume that if we used an exchange rate standard that was specified more properly the *measured* degree of "overshooting" according to definitions 1 and 2 would be reduced substantially. Large deviations of market exchange rates from naive standards or large short-run fluctuations in exchange rates per se do not imply that *extra* adjustment costs are imposed on the system. When associated with an equilibrium model, overshooting is more a symptom of underlying forces than an independent cause of costly economic adjustment. This is not to argue that large, albeit equilibrium, exchange rate changes represent an ideal state of the world. Clearly, society would gain if fundamental economic variables could be predicted more accurately, if structural economic linkages were known with greater certainty, and if the prices and quantities of other variables were more free to adjust. Taking the preceding factors as given, however, our objective is for optimal exchange rate fluctuations rather than minimal fluctuations. Thus our concern with overshooting is tantamount to our concern with "disequilibrium" prices in any situation. Viewed in this way, tests of overshooting are equivalent to tests of exchange market efficiency.

With this as background, let me offer a few specific comments about the Willett and Sweeney papers. My introductory comments very much support Willett's statement that exchange rate changes cannot be analyzed in isolation. A discussion of deviations from PPP, overshooting, and intervention requires us to specify the underlying economic structure. Sweeney's analysis of deviations from PPP and the lag structure of price changes and exchange rate changes, though interesting in its own right, is difficult to interpret without more knowledge of the economic structure. Are large deviations from PPP and long adjustment lags the sign of an inefficient market or simply a rational response to underlying forces? Unless we know the answer to this question, the empirical results will not help us judge the merits of government intervention or the merits of a faster convergence to PPP. Moreover, the empirical analysis should attempt to control for government intervention that occurred over the sample period. It is possible that actual or anticipated intervention led to an increase in exchange rate volatility and that a reduction in intervention will have the desired effect of calming exchange markets.

One further empirical point concerns the time series of exchange rate changes predicted by certain overshooting models. According to definition 3, in response to a once-and-for-all change in the money supply, the initial positive (negative) exchange rate change should be followed by a long sequence of negative (positive) changes. The empirical observation that day-to-day changes are often random for many exchange rates does not rule out the possibility of overshooting. This is simply because the market receives news every day of permanent and temporary changes for all exogenous variables. This setting does not match the laboratory of a once-and-for-all change in a single variable.

Let me shift my focus toward tests of foreign exchange market efficiency. Sweeney suggests that significant risk-adjusted profits exist by following simple filter rule trading strategies. If this is the case, Sweeney argues that intervention may be warranted. I have always felt that filter rule tests are very tricky to interpret. This is because very often the researcher reports only the final profits without indicating the risk involved. Several points should be stressed. First, in the foreign exchange market, transaction costs and overnight interest rates should be accounted for, because both of these variables can become large.

Second, the risk associated with filter rule trading is difficult to measure. The trader is, in effect, trying to capitalize on his knowledge of market timing by switching back and forth between, for example, U.S. dollars and deutsche marks (DM). Following this strategy, the trader may judge market timing correctly in all n periods or incorrectly in all n periods. It is clear that this active strategy exposes the trader to a wider (more risky) range of favorable and unfavorable outcomes than had he passively held a balanced portfolio of U.S. dollar and DM assets.[8] Therefore, traders who follow a filter rule strategy must *expect* to earn returns that exceed the returns from a passively held portfolio of similar composition.[9] The market is inefficient if the *extra* returns earned by following an active trading strategy rather than holding a passive portfolio are unusually large relative to the *extra* risks that are incurred.[10]

Finally, it must be demonstrated that unusual filter rule trading profits exist in an ex ante sense. My interpretation of the empirical evidence is that expected returns and risks for a randomly selected currency and time period are highly dependent on the magnitude of the filter. It is not clear that *unusual* filter rule profits discovered over an in-sample period provide any assurances that these unusual profits can be replicated in the postsample period.

The major factor detracting from our studies of foreign exchange market efficiency is our lack of an adequate measure of foreign exchange risk and an adequate model for pricing it. Some simple examples will

[8] Consider a two-period model in which an investor desires a $\beta = 0.5$ portfolio. One strategy is for the investor to divide his wealth evenly between the risk-free asset $\beta = 0$ and the market portfolio $\beta = 1$ in both periods. Second, the investor could hold only the risk-free asset in period 1 and only the market portfolio in period 2. Third, the investor could choose the market portfolio in period 1 and the risk-free asset in period 2. Although all three strategies have the same expected return, strategy 1 has the lowest risk. The investor with strategy 1 achieves "time-diversification" gains; by holding a steady-target risk portfolio, he avoids the risk of a low market return in period 1 (with strategy 3) or in period 2 (with strategy 2).

[9] Over 100 trading days, for example, the filter rule may advise us to be long DM on 75 days and long U.S. dollars on 25 days. The filter rule trader must expect that his returns will exceed the returns on a passive portfolio with composition 75 percent DM and 25 percent U.S. dollars. The example is not exact because the filter rule trader need not predict his currency positions 100 days in advance.

[10] One way to test for the presence of timing expertise is simply to count the number of periods in which timing advice is successful (r) in a sample of n periods. If $p = r/n$ is significantly greater than 0.5, then timing expertise exists. This technique has the advantage of not attributing large price swings and high returns to the forecaster, because he is predicting only the direction and not the magnitude of price changes. For an application of this approach to professional foreign exchange advisory services, see Richard M. Levich, "Analyzing the Accuracy of Foreign Exchange Advisory Services: Theory and Evidence," in R. Levich and C. Wihlborg, eds., *Exchange Risk and Exposure* (Lexington, Mass.: D. C. Heath and Company, 1980). A more technical discussion of the value of market timing is presented in Robert C. Merton, "On Market Timing and Investment Performance, Part I: An Equilibrium Theory of Value for Market Forecasts," M.I.T. Sloan School of Management Working Papers, nos. 1076-79, August 1979.

illustrate the difficulty in measuring the aggregate risk of foreign exchange. In a world with 100 bushels of corn, for example, investors may trade thousands or millions of futures contracts. In the aggregate, however, only 100 bushels of corn are at risk and earn the realized rate of return for those who maintain a long forward position; the risk and return of all other forward contracts cancel in the aggregate. Alternatively, suppose there are two commodities, corn and wheat, produced by two groups of farmers. The corn and wheat farmers could trade future supplies of their final outputs, thus assuring desired consumption of both commodities and reducing aggregate risk.

What is a proper analogy for foreign exchange? I think most of the key points can be seen in the following example.

Assume there is a U.S. investor in London who plans to repatriate a £1 million dividend in ninety days when the exchange rate is expected to be \$2.00/£. Unless there is a U.K. investor who wishes to repatriate \$2 million from New York to London in ninety days, the U.S. investor must locate someone who currently is in portfolio balance, yet who may be induced to exchange British sterling for U.S. dollars in ninety days. The supplier of the forward dollars may demand compensation for altering his currency portfolio (assuming that he holds dollar balances to purchase dollar-denominated goods, and sterling balances are in imperfect substitute for this purpose), and the U.S. investor, assuming risk aversion, will be willing to pay it. In this case, the U.S. investor may sell his sterling at, say, \$1.98 even though he expects the price to be \$2.00 in ninety days. The two cents per pound sterling is the compensation paid to the supplier of forward dollars for altering his initial currency portfolio and taking on additional risk. This suggests that investors select a currency portfolio simultaneously with their desired international consumption pattern. Risk is associated with the quality of a currency's purchasing power to achieve desired consumption.

It is to be hoped that the current research on the measurement and pricing of foreign exchange risk will continue. These issues represent a crucial barrier to our understanding of foreign exchange market efficiency.

Summary of the Discussion

In the general discussion following the commentaries there was considerable agreement that we know much more about the factors affecting long-run trends in exchange rates than about the short-run behavior. To improve our knowledge of the latter, it was constantly emphasized that we need to distinguish clearly between anticipated and unanticipated changes in policies and economic conditions.

Considerable attention also was given to the question of the degree of diversifiability of exchange risk and nature of risk premiums in the foreign-exchange market. It was pointed out that these questions have important implications for investigating exchange rate behavior and evaluating the efficiency of the foreign exchange market. Although a good bit of interesting analysis has been done in this area in recent years, many of these questions remain unanswered. The floor discussion revealed that the accumulated empirical evidence was interpreted by most discussants as having been quite strong against the adequacy of the purchasing power parity as a guide to equilibrium exchange rates and against claims that the foreign-exchange markets have been persistently dominated by destabilizing speculation. Nevertheless, a number of discussants pointed out that, so far, we have neither conclusive evidence of a high degree of efficiency of the foreign-exchange markets nor objective criteria for identifying conditions under which official intervention might be desirable. In the absence of such evidence and criteria, not surprisingly, a wide range of views was expressed.

In spite of noticeable differences in views expressed by the discussants, a rather widespread agreement emerged that the predominant cause of exchange-rate fluctuations has been the instability in underlying economic and financial conditions, rather than irrational and exaggerated speculative behavior. Indeed, to the extent that there may have been serious deficiencies in the behavior of speculation under flexible rates, this is probably as much the result of too little stabilizing speculation as it is the result of actively destabilizing speculation. Opinions were expressed that the current state of research does seem to indicate strongly that most of the exchange rate variations we observed under floating have been the result of real and monetary disturbances, which can cause considerable changes in equilibrium real—that is, inflation-adjusted—exchange rates, thus implying, as mentioned earlier, that purchasing power parity calculations do not provide a good measure of equilibrium exchange rates.

The floor discussion also indicated that we still have not clearly identified the various costs of exchange rate fluctuations. In response to concern that the adoption of flexible rates has worsened the problem of inflation by leading to a steepening of the short-run inflation/unemployment trade-off, for example, it was pointed out that this could conceivably have the beneficial effect of reducing the incentives for the adoption of politically motivated inflationary policies. Opinions were also expressed to the effect that in evaluating the consequences of flexible exchange rates, it is important to distinguish between the instability generated by the exchange-rate system per se and the instabilities in underlying economic conditions and policies. Whichever the cause, one notable development in recent years has been a substantial increase in resources and attention devoted by the private sector to foreign-exchange trading, forecasting, and management. Finally, the floor discussion revealed that although questions of the appropriate scope and strategies for official exchange market intervention remained controversial, there was general agreement that the most important requirement for creating greater exchange-rate stability is the restoration of greater macroeconomic stability in the major industrial countries.

Part Three
Studies of Selected Countries

Introductory Remarks

The issues of causes and consequences of exchange rate flexibility discussed in part 2 pose different policy dilemmas for different countries and, accordingly, evoke different responses from national policy makers. Certainly, whether or not exchange-rate volatility is judged excessive would depend, among other things, on the commodity composition and geographical distribution of a country's foreign trade or the degree of openness of its financial markets. Similarly, the strength of inflationary consequences of changes in exchange rates would be perceived differently by different countries, depending on a multitude of structural and institutional factors.

The purpose of part 3 is to provide concrete policy perspectives on the issues of causes and effects of exchange-rate volatility and to analyze those issues from the vantage points of particular countries. Even though responses to exchange-rate fluctuations since 1973 by various countries have displayed a dazzling diversity, because of time constraints the policies of only a few countries could be analyzed in the requisite detail. The United States, West Germany cum Switzerland, and Japan were selected, not only because their currencies are the most important ones in international finance but also because the experiences of these countries typify policy quandaries faced by weak-currency and strong-currency issuers. Although each of the papers presented in part 3 reviews the experience with floating since its inception, emphasis is focused on the cause of exchange-rate changes and policy debates and measures that have taken place in the past three years.

The Experience with Floating: The 1973-1979 Dollar

Steven W. Kohlhagen

The decade of the 1970s began and ended with international financial turbulence. The period of floating exchange rates began in March 1973 after a four-year period of exchange-rate crises in response to disequilibrium exchange rates that had built up as a result of increasingly divergent macroeconomic performances across countries. The decade ended in an atmosphere of financial concern about rising worldwide inflation, falling real growth rates, escalating oil prices, and disrupted oil markets. In addition, the international political crises in Iran and Afghanistan at the end of 1979, together with expectations about inflationary pressures, sent the price of gold careening upward in disorderly and disturbed markets as some worried international investors sought refuge from currencies.

A careful examination of the events in the intervening years clearly reveals that floating exchange rates did not solve the underlying international financial problems that led to their adoption. Nor did they completely free countries from the effects of those problems. On the other hand, there is no clear alternative to managed floating for the early 1980s. In fact, many argue that much of the criticism that has been leveled at the current system is due more to a misunderstanding of how the foreign-exchange markets function and what their appropriate role should be than to any systematic failure in market behavior. Nevertheless, there have been frequent claims of disorderly and poorly functioning markets. In this paper the behavior of the U.S. dollar

I have benefited greatly in the writing of this paper from discussions with Morris Goldstein, Peter Hooper, Val Koromzay, Bill Nordhaus, and Ralph Smith. I would also like to thank the Institute of Business and Economic Research, University of California at Berkeley, for its support; Robin Layton for her invaluable research assistance; and several members of the staff of the Federal Reserve Board, especially Pat Decker and Peter Hooper, for their assistance in obtaining the data.

markets during the period of the 1973–1979 float is examined in the light of these issues and claims.

The U.S. economy and the U.S. dollar are special cases. There are few, if any, generalizations available for application to other currencies from the dollar experience. The size of the U.S. economy, its relatively small proportion of international trade, and the reserve role of the dollar make the situation in the United States unique.

The initial problem raised by the uniqueness of the U.S. situation is that of determining against what the dollar's performance is to be measured. A German, Japanese, or United Kingdom case study would presumably analyze the bilateral exchange rate of that country against the dollar. Such an approach for the dollar is clearly impossible. Because any dollar bilateral exchange-rate time series is essentially a case study of the other—that is, the nondollar—currency, we must use some weighted average of all currency values for measuring dollar performance. The only alternative to this multilateral approach would be to present a series of dollar cases: the dollar/yen case, the dollar/mark case, the dollar/pound case, the dollar/franc case, and so on. Unfortunately, there are many multilateral indexes available, none of which is universally accepted as the most appropriate, and there are no clear-cut criteria for selecting among the available versions.[1] In this study, we use the Federal Reserve Board's multilateral trade-weighted index. There are several reasons for this choice.

First, the development of the weighting scheme has been the product of years of careful economic analysis, and its rationale has been well documented.[2] Second, the inclusion of the ten major trading partners of the United States captures the major disruptions to the U.S. external accounts during the period, without including so many countries that it would have been impossible to make the comparisons of domestic and foreign underlying fundamentals that are presented in this paper. And, third, consistent daily and periodic averages are routinely provided by the Federal Reserve Board on request and were thus easily available for analysis.

---

[1] For a discussion of the issues involved in selecting the currencies to include, the most appropriate weighting procedures, and the best techniques for estimating the weights, see Peter Hooper and John Morton, "Summary Measures of the Dollar's Average Exchange Value," *Federal Reserve Bulletin*, vol. 64, no. 10 (October 1978).

[2] Ibid. This index is a geometric average of the dollar exchange rates for Belgium, Canada, France, Germany, Italy, Japan, the Netherlands, Sweden, Switzerland, and the United Kingdom. The weights are derived from the proportion of the 1972-1976 total trade for each of the countries as a proportion of total trade for all of the countries.

FIGURE 1

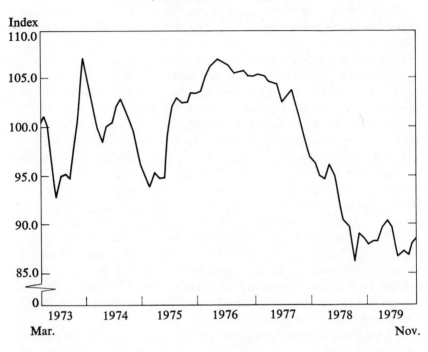

The next section of this paper discusses the actual dollar movements during the 1973–1979 period and the reasons frequently given by private and official market analysts for those movements. The following section analyzes whether actual movements have been excessive (1) compared with any possible alternatives to floating during the period, (2) in relation to underlying fundamental determinants, (3) in any sense of financial market efficiency, or (4) in the sense that they adversely affected U.S. macroeconomic performance or constrained U.S. policy making. The last section presents some concluding comments.

The Dollar: 1973–1979

Figure 1 shows the path of the trade-weighted dollar from 1973 to 1979. Data are monthly averages of trade-weighted averages of daily quotations throughout the period. The period of August 15, 1971 (the date of the Nixon speech ending dollar convertibility into gold and imposing

144

wage/price controls), to March 1973 (the beginning of general floating among the major currencies) was a period of occasional floating and generalized attempts to repeg currencies—the Smithsonian agreement of December 1971, for example.

By February and March of 1973 it became increasingly clear to country after country that pegging currencies was not possible in an atmosphere of financial crisis brought on by years of policies inconsistent with fixed exchange rates, then-existing disequilibrium rates, and large movements of financial capital in response to expectations of imminent parity changes. In retrospect, it is also possible that the 1971 devaluation and subsequent macroeconomic policy changes were inadequate to bring about external equilibrium for the United States.[3] The foreign-exchange markets were closed several times, parities were readjusted in last attempts to salvage fixity, and, finally, by March 1973 all central bankers allowed the international financial system to slip (or fall) into a period of generalized free floating against the dollar.

In the face of a large U.S. current-account deficit, and with little official intervention, the dollar fell dramatically during the first three months of the float. By summer many officials were reluctant to allow their currencies to appreciate much further against the dollar, and central bankers (including the U.S. Federal Reserve System) announced that they would intervene to resist any further movements in that direction. The dollar had fallen 11 percent between April 3 and July 6, 1973 (17.9 percent since January 19).

These announcements, coupled with improvements in the U.S. external accounts, including a sizable U.S. trade surplus, were associated with a recovery in the dollar's value during the third quarter of 1973. In October, the Organization of Petroleum Exporting Countries (OPEC) announced its dramatic oil embargo, which resulted in the enormous oil price increases by the beginning of the following year. The market's expectation that the U.S. economy could better cope with this shock than many of its trading partners, plus the improvement in the U.S. external balance, drove the dollar back up above its prefloat levels by the end of 1973 (the dollar rose 16.5 percent between October 23, 1973, and January 21, 1974).

In 1974, the dollar depreciated 11.4 percent from January 21 to May 13, largely as an adjustment to the rapid appreciation of the previous three months and partly as a result of the lifting of U.S. capital

[3] See Edwin M. Truman, "Balance-of-Payments Adjustments from a U.S. Perspective: The Lessons of the 1970s," International Finance Discussion Paper, no. 152 (Washington, D.C.: Board of Governors of the Federal Reserve System, June 1979).

controls and evidence of relatively higher inflation in the United States than in Germany and some of the other, smaller countries. Coordinated (and announced) intervention by the U.S., German, and Swiss central banks, evidence of some German banks in trouble because of foreign exchange losses, and record-level U.S. interest rates were variously accorded responsibility for the substantial (6.8 percent) subsequent recovery in the dollar from May 13 to September 5.

From September 5, 1974, to March 3, 1975, despite substantial intervention, the dollar depreciated 10.3 percent. Sharply declining relative U.S. interest rates were generally assigned responsibility by "the market" for this six-month movement, during which the U.S. external accounts were moving into surplus. In retrospect, this does not seem to be a very satisfactory explanation. It might therefore be more meaningful to view the May–September 1974 dollar appreciation of 6.8 percent as a market adjustment to tightening U.S. credit conditions and the January 1974–March 1975 net dollar depreciation of 15.1 percent as the relevant long-term movement associated with the increasing U.S. inflation rate and continued current-account deficit.

The dollar then rose 15.9 percent from March 3, 1975, to June 4, 1976, on the strength of increasingly large U.S. current-account surpluses, a dramatic improvement in the relative U.S. inflation performance, and relatively better overall performance by the U.S. economy than by its major trading partners. At one point within this period, from June 30 through September 29, 1975, the dollar actually rose at an annual rate of 43 percent!

The period from September 29, 1975, through September 14, 1977, was one of remarkable stability. The trade-weighted dollar during this two-year period was never on any day more than 2.9 percent higher or lower than 104.6 (March 1973 = 100). This dollar stability occurred despite a period of much higher exchange rate instability in Europe, due mainly to political factors, and despite very large U.S. current account deficits. The markets apparently recognized the special stabilizing role played by these U.S. deficits in equilibrating world trade imbalances brought on by the OPEC surpluses. In addition, economic activity in the United States was relatively stronger than in its major trading partners, and U.S. inflation was lower for much of the period (consumer price index [CPI] inflation for the two years beginning September 1975 was at an annual rate of 6.1 percent for the United States and was 8.9 percent on a trade-weighted basis for its major trading partners). Finally, official purchases of dollars by foreign central banks were extremely large during the latter part of the period.

In the face of the increasingly large U.S. payments deficits and signs of increasing U.S. inflationary pressures, the dollar fell slowly but in a clearly orderly manner from June 4, 1976, to September 1977— a total depreciation of 3.4 percent. This slow, steady depreciation turned into an avalanche late in 1977. The specific triggering action in the summer of 1977 that arguably changed the nature of the dollar markets was the conflicting statements by U.S. officials about the desirability of dollar depreciation. Secretary Michael Blumenthal, in particular, was perceived to be saying that dollar depreciations would not be unjustified.

Although these policy statements may have been responsible for changing market expectations about the short-run position of the dollar, they were not responsible for the protracted one-year dollar collapse. From September 14, 1977, until October 30, 1978, the dollar dropped by 21.1 percent (15.5 percent in the last five and a half months alone), despite huge amounts of intervention. This was more than the precipitous 17.9 percent drop in the first six months of 1973. The basic reason for the long-term slide was the deterioration in the economic fundamentals of dollar determination.

The trade balance, which had gone from a $9 billion surplus in 1975 to a $9 billion deficit in 1976, seemed to be headed for close to a $30 billion 1977 deficit by late in the year (it actually turned out to be an unprecedented $31.1 billion). The current account, positive since 1972, when it had been in deficit by $6 billion (in no other year had a current-account deficit ever been greater than $1.8 billion), seemed headed for a greater than $10 billion deficit (it turned out to be an astonishing $15.3 billion). Such external deficits are the "traditional" explanation for the dollar's decline, driving the dollar lower through both an increase in the supply of dollar holdings abroad and their contributions to reduced confidence in the dollar.[4]

Whereas the 1976 U.S. deficits were viewed as temporary and with gratitude by a world still trying to finance the OPEC shock, the 1977 deficits were viewed as unsustainable and not reversible without exchange rate adjustment. Despite the fact that the bulk of the deficit could be explained by the faster U.S. recovery from the 1974–1975 recession, by late 1977 and early 1978 this cyclical effect did not seem likely to be eliminated soon.[5]

[4] See Mordechai E. Kreinen, "United States Foreign Economic Policy: An Overview," Seminar Paper no. 124 (Stockholm: Institute for International Economic Studies, August 1979).

[5] Michael Bazdarich ("Has a Strong U.S. Economy Meant a Weak Dollar?"

Also by late 1977, inflationary pressures were increasing once again in the United States, and, whereas inflation rates were rising in all major countries, U.S. inflation rose significantly above that of its principal trading partners. The markets came to feel that the Carter administration was unlikely to use macroeconomic policies effectively to deal with the inflation problem. The October 24 unveiling of the administration's anti-inflation program was viewed as anything but re-assuring, and the dollar fell another 3.9 percent in the week immediately following the president's speech.

On November 1, 1978, the administration announced that it had put together a $30 billion rescue package, composed of deutsche marks, Swiss francs, and Japanese yen. While tightening domestic monetary policies, the administration pledged, in conjunction with foreign central banks, to intervene massively if necessary to resist further unwarranted dollar depreciations. U.S. officials felt that further depreciations were unwarranted at that time because both private and official forecasts implied that economic fundamentals were already turning around. The exchange rate seemed to be moving on the basis of rumors and growing uncertainty about administration policies rather than on expectations of economic fundamentals. In addition, the administration was more certain than market participants of its resolve to eliminate the inflation problem. In the face of such a disorderly market, the administration felt obligated to prevent further unwarranted depreciations both because it believed that such depreciations were themselves inflationary and be-cause of its responsibilities as the manager of the world's reserve currency.

The dollar markets, seemingly relieved that the administration's policy of benign neglect toward the dollar had ended and interpreting the November 1 package as a choice of recession over further inflation and dollar weakness, rallied dramatically. The dollar rose 7.7 percent in the first week and over 9 percent by November 30.

Despite increasing inflation and higher OPEC oil prices, the dollar had appreciated to 10.9 percent above its October 30, 1978, low by May 29, 1979. This was attributable mainly to the improving U.S. trade and current accounts, the increasing signs of slower U.S. growth, and the sense that the U.S. economy was in a relatively good position to deal with the intermittent supply shortages resulting from the instabilities in Iran. In March the European Monetary System (EMS) began operation with little apparent effect on the dollar's value, despite the feeling of

---

Federal Reserve Bank of San Francisco Economic Review, Spring 1979, pp. 35-46) provides an alternative view to this normally maintained notion that the strong U.S. economy was responsible for the weak dollar.

many that it had been created in response to concerns about the 1977–1978 dollar slide and fluctuations.

The dollar resumed its 1977–1978 slide in the early summer of 1979 in response to the 60 percent increase in OPEC prices, the increasingly bad news on U.S. inflation, and the political uncertainties generated by the Iran–U.S. confrontation late in 1979, returning to its end-of-1978 levels by late September.

On October 6 the Federal Reserve System unveiled a dramatic new monetary policy aimed at targeting monetary aggregates rather than interest rates, in an attempt to try to control inflation more effectively than had the administration's antiinflation program up to that time. Whereas the November 1 initiative had been aimed primarily at the symptoms of the dollar fall in an attempt to calm a disorderly market, it was claimed that the October 6 policy was aimed at the fundamental problem of resolving inflation. The true test of the efficacy of the new policy will come only over time, as the resolve of the administration and the Federal Reserve is revealed in the marketplace. The dollar rallied briefly in response to the new policy (up to 3.4 percent, peaking on October 30) before it began declining again, primarily as a result of political instability arising from the Iranian and Afghan crises, concern about further OPEC price rises, and fear of possible OPEC diversification out of dollars. These political uncertainties were reflected in the near-panic conditions in the gold (and other commodity) markets in late 1979 and early 1980. The price of gold skyrocketed against not only the dollar but all currencies.

In summary, faced with the adjustment requirements of the international financial disequilibriums of the late 1960s and the early 1970s, the OPEC shock, and rising worldwide inflation, the dollar followed a sine wave–type pattern from March 1973 to September 1975, fluctuating at roughly ±9½ percent of its March 1973 value. In retrospect, it is difficult to imagine a workable alternative to the amount of exchange rate fluctuations experienced in that period—successful attempts at greater fixity would most likely have required restrictive exchange and capital controls. The two-year period of stability that followed was noteworthy for its lack of problems for the dollar. Under the surface, of course, the U.S. external disequilibrium and inflationary pressures were growing. These would later manifest themselves in a prolonged dollar slide, beginning in September 1977. To the extent that there is interest in those aspects of floating that have led to unhappy experiences for the U.S. dollar, the major focus would apparently have to be on the period leading up to September 1977 and carrying on to the end of this sample, or the beginning of 1980.

149

Has Exchange-Rate Volatility Been Excessive?

To assess whether or not the 1973–1979 U.S. dollar has been characterized by excessive volatility, one must answer the question: Compared with what? Are we interested in comparing the actual path of the dollar with that which would have occurred under a historical analysis of other possible counterfactual exchange rate regimes? Or are we interested in the volatility of the dollar in comparison with the volatility of its underlying determinants? Or are we interested in the functioning of international capital markets, relative to an ideal notion of financial market efficiency? Or are we interested in the effects of exchange-rate volatility on macroeconomic activity and policy options? In this section each of these questions is analyzed in turn.

Alternatives to the Float for the 1973–1979 Dollar. With respect to comparing the actual observed dollar exchange rate over the past seven years with some other possible alternative, it seems unlikely for the early part of the period (1973–1975) that an alternative that involved less—or more restricted—floating was realistically available. Intervention by both the Federal Reserve System and other central banks was quite significant. Underlying shocks and divergent macroeconomic policies and performances were enormous relative to the previous twenty-five-year postwar experience. Exchange-rate movements, rather than exchange, capital, and goods controls, were a necessary and, in fact, probably a desirable buffer against these factors.

During the stable two-year period from late 1975 to late 1977, it is likely that central banks *preferred* managed floating to any alternative. Central banks accumulated $18 billion and $37 billion worth of dollar assets in 1976 and 1977, respectively, as a means of ensuring that U.S. deficits rather than dollar depreciation coupled with larger deficits in other countries would finance the OPEC surpluses. Had private market participants been faced with a choice of whether or not to accumulate these dollar assets at then-existing exchange rates and interest rates, the dollar would most certainly have fallen lower than it had by the fall of 1977. The corresponding 1977 and 1978 U.S. external deficits would have been considerably lower. Whether or not the subsequent 1978–1979 dollar problems would have been eased if central bankers had allowed some of the dollar depreciation to occur earlier in response to growing U.S. deficits is a subject worth pursuing. In other words, more rather than less floating may quite possibly have been desirable in the 1975–1977 period.

Since 1977 the attractiveness of actual experience is less clear. Considerable dollar depreciation over the past two years was clearly necessary to correct the rapidly growing trade disequilibriums in the major countries. In conjunction with this exchange-rate adjustment, real output growth in the United States needed to fall relative to that abroad, and the United States needed to arrest the increase in domestic inflationary pressures and to reduce its oil import bill. By mid-1978 the first two factors had moved in the right direction, but the markets had serious doubts about the ability of the Carter administration to manage the inflation and oil import problems successfully. These doubts pushed the dollar lower than officials felt was necessary to equilibrate the external imbalance.

The bulk of international financial assets is denominated in dollars. Thus, the value of the dollar has a central function in determining the value of assets held by both private and official market participants. Therefore, concern about a weak dollar has at times generated fear about diversification out of dollars and price increases in traded goods whose prices are denominated in dollars. Depreciation of the dollar as an adjustment to a temporary U.S. external equilibrium may, as a result of the dollar's special place in the system, lead to even further downward pressure on the dollar than would normally be necessary. In the view of some, then, the ability of the United States to be in temporary disequilibrium without eventually generating excessive exchange rate movements may be seriously limited.

To conclude, however, from the 1977–1979 falling-dollar episode that there could, or even should, be greater management of exchange rates is to overlook several factors. First, as mentioned above, some dollar depreciation may have been necessary to adjust to the disequilibriums generated by the 1975–1977 intervention. Second, even though the Federal Reserve did not actively manage the dollar, foreign central banks did. Dollar assets held by foreign central banks grew by over $30 billion in the two quarters after September 1977 alone, while the dollar was falling roughly 5 percent. In the previous seven quarters, while the dollar was more or less stable, foreign official dollar assets in the United States grew by about $40 billion.[6] From April to September 1978, however, while the dollar was falling by roughly 15 percent,

[6] Peter Hooper and John Morton ("Fluctuations in the Dollar: A Model of Nominal and Real Exchange Rate Determination," mimeographed [Washington, D.C.: Federal Reserve Board, October 5, 1979]) note that "exchange market intervention by foreign central banks during 1977-78 resulted in a net increase of foreign official holdings of dollar-denominated assets amounting to more than twice the flow of funds associated with the U.S. current account deficit during the period."

151

foreign officials were suddenly net sellers of dollar assets in the United States.

Third, it is quite likely that by late 1977, and certainly by the second quarter of 1978, a basic source of dollar weakness was not only the trade deficits but also concern over the ability of the administration to develop and manage effective energy and antiinflation policies. If the cyclical portion of the trade imbalance had been clearly expected to be fully reversed and if the U.S. domestic house had been in order— with inflation rates falling rather than rising in the first half of 1978, with an energy program moving on line that was perceived to be comprehensive—the dollar depreciation through the first half of 1978 in conjunction with declining relative rates of growth in the United States might well have been sufficient to bring about external equilibrium eventually.[7] U.S. domestic economic policies, however, or at least the market's perceptions of these policies, contributed significantly to the continued dollar slide through the first ten months of 1978.

In fact, the November 1, 1978, dollar rescue package was essentially an administration statement of exactly this point. The administration felt that market participants either were not utilizing available information or were discounting it too heavily. The relative U.S. growth rate was slowing; the trade and current account deficits, though at unacceptably high 1978 levels, were substantially improving into 1979; the volume of oil imports in 1978 was falling from 1976 and 1977 levels; the National Energy Act was in place; and, most important, the administration was dedicated to solving inflation and to making the new antiinflation program work. It thus announced that it would massively resist any further unwarranted dollar depreciations that, it felt, would exacerbate U.S. inflationary pressures and undermine the stabilizing role that the dollar holds in the international monetary system.

Significantly, no fundamental new policies were really announced on November 1, 1978. To be sure, the $30 billion support package was new (until that time, the U.S. Treasury and Federal Reserve simply did not have large enough foreign exchange assets to sell against dollars to have a significant market impact), but it was not aimed at fundamental economic factors. In fact, U.S. policy had for years been to intervene in disorderly markets, and a strong case can certainly be made, and in fact *was* made by the administration, that the markets in October 1978

---

[7] See Thomas D. Willett, *The Fall and Rise of the Dollar*, Reprint No. 96 (Washington, D.C.: American Enterprise Institute, 1979), for a more complete exposition of this notion that fully justified expectations about the future course of the U.S. economy could justify the depths of the 1978 dollar depreciation and the need for a U.S. policy response.

were disorderly. The accompanying tightening of monetary policy was essentially cosmetic, merely reinforcing previous restrictive policies, and was quickly dominated by further tightening through 1979 as inflationary pressures escalated. In sum, the November 1 initiative, rather than being a fundamental change in the U.S. posture toward floating rates, was an attempt to shake a disorderly market into its senses by pointing out the depth of official commitment to policies already existing and improvements already in motion in fundamental underlying factors.

Even with the escalating inflation of 1979, the dollar's two-year skid did end on November 1, 1978. Almost a year later, even with double-digit inflation, the political turmoil in Iran, and a 60 percent increase in oil prices, the dollar was somewhat above its October 1978 lows. "Further unwarranted dollar depreciations" had been successfully resisted. The underlying fundamental problem of inflation was worse, however, and, in contrast to the November 1 initiative, the October 6, 1979, initiative was billed as a fundamental change in U.S. antiinflation policy, which, if successful, would be likely to ensure longer-term strength and stability of the dollar.

In summary, during the period since 1977, the alternative to a rapidly falling dollar, which at times may have been disorderly, was likely to be not greater intervention but a greater policy emphasis on improving the underlying fundamentals. If the market's perception of these policies was incorrect, as the Carter administration felt it was in October 1978, then it made sense so to inform the market. Until, however, there was clear evidence of a turnaround in the current account and trade balances and until there was an anti-inflation program toward which market participants could at least take a wait-and-see attitude, such an attempt would have met with little success. Without these preconditions, it is unlikely that a more active interventionist strategy by the United States would have been successful between the fall of 1977 and November 1, 1978. Before that, it was unnecessary, as, for better or for worse, it was being done for the United States by foreign central banks.

The Volatility of Underlying Determinants. One disturbing aspect of trying to analyze how the dollar has behaved in relation to some ideal is that economists do not currently have a generally accepted model of exchange rate determination. And even those models that have been empirically tested are usually studies of bilateral rather than multilateral exchange rates.[8]

[8] See Steven W. Kohlhagen, "The Behavior of Foreign Exchange Markets: A Critical Survey of the Empirical Literature," New York University Series in

One notion about exchange-rate determination that has retained its appeal through generations of economists is the purchasing power parity theory (PPP).[9] Without belaboring the point unnecessarily, the basic notion is the intuitive one that, in the absence of transport costs, differential risks, and barriers to trade, a product should sell for the same price in all countries at current exchange rates (or its price should change by the same proportion across countries at current exchange rates). Observed prices may differ from PPP for a host of reasons, including those mentioned previously, plus measurement errors, differences in quality of products across countries, indexing problems, and delivery lags.[10] If an exchange rate adjusted for relative prices (namely, the so-called real exchange rate) were to change dramatically, it might indicate that there are measurement problems with the particular indexes chosen, that there are serious impediments to trade, or that the exchange rate is at times at inappropriate levels.

Figure 2 shows the "real" trade-weighted dollar (adjusted by trade-weighted relative CPIs) for the current float. The real exchange rate looks very much like the nominal exchange rate path in figure 1. The drop in the value of the real dollar highlights the fact that the weakness of the nominal dollar has occurred despite a faster rise in foreign consumer prices in relation to U.S. consumer prices. From March 1973 through July 1978, the real dollar fluctuated at 95 plus or minus 11.5 percent (March 1973 = 100). In the second half of 1978, it fell outside this range for the first time during the current float, to 20 percent below its summer 1976 high, and has never again risen into the earlier range.

This sharp drop is open to a wide variety of interpretations. Tradable goods, rather than consumer goods, should be the relevant products for such an analysis; trade is undertaken on a bilateral, not a multilateral, basis, and there may be resulting errors in this figure because of averaging; also, there is no way to disprove the alternative hypothesis that in fact the real dollar was overvalued from 1973 to 1977 and only

---

Finance and Economics, no. 3 1978, and Jacob A. Frenkel and Harry G. Johnson, eds., *The Economics of Exchange Rates* (Reading, Mass.: Addison-Wesley, 1978), for discussions of existing empirical models.

[9] See the surveys by Peter Isard, *Exchange-Rate Determination: A Survey of Popular Views and Recent Models,* Studies in International Finance, no. 42 (Princeton, N.J.: Princeton University, International Finance Section, 1978); Kohlhagen, "Behavior of Foreign Exchange Markets"; and Lawrence H. Officer, "The Purchasing Power Parity Theory of Exchange Rates: A Review Article," *IMF Staff Papers,* vol. 23, no. 1 (March 1976), pp. 1-60, and the references cited therein.

[10] See, especially, Peter Isard, "How Far Can We Push the 'Law of One Price'?" *American Economic Review,* vol. 67, no. 5 (December 1977), pp. 942-48.

FIGURE 2
MONTHLY AVERAGE REAL (ADJUSTED FOR CPIS)
TRADE-WEIGHTED DOLLAR EXCHANGE RATE
(MARCH 1973 = 100)

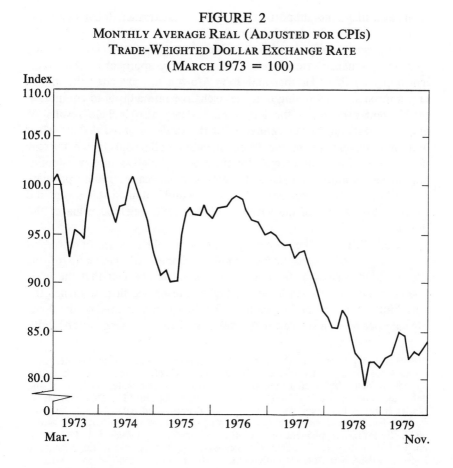

late in 1978 reached its "equilibrium" value of 82.5. On the other hand, some depreciation in the real dollar was clearly necessary to equilibrate the external accounts. Dornbusch has concluded from somewhat similar results for all industrialized countries that there *are* significant short-run changes in competitiveness due to a lack of integration between the wage/price process and exchange rate determination and long-run changes in relative price levels due to differential productivity growth or terms-of-trade changes.[11] Nevertheless, the figure implies that sometime in 1978 the real dollar reached unprecedentedly low

[11] Rudiger Dornbusch, "Issues in International Finance: Who and What Controls the Dollar?" (Cambridge: Massachusetts Institute of Technology, April 1979); idem, "Monetary Policy under Exchange Rate Flexibility," Working Paper no. 311 (Washington, D.C.: National Bureau of Economic Research, 1979).

levels and may lend support to the notion that further dollar depreciations were unwarranted at that time.

One particularly fruitful and increasingly popular direction for
empirical exchange rate models is the monetary approach.[12] An excellent paper by Peter Hooper and John Morton has extended the monetary approach by assuming that the exchange rate adjusts to equilibrate
the current account in the long run.[13] They also include results of
empirical tests on the determination of the *trade-weighted* dollar. They
find that movements of the trade-weighted dollar during the current
float are explained quite well by their tests: relative money supplies
and demands among the United States and its major trading partners
and adjustments to current account disequilibriums explain on the
order of 90 percent of the variance of the trade-weighted value of the
dollar.

Both PPP and the monetary approach yield a series of variables
that can be considered underlying determinants of the value of the
dollar. Many critics of floating have pointed to the fact that the variability of exchange rates has been higher during the float than has the
variability of the underlying factors. Table 1 confirms this for the floating rate period as a whole for the dollar and the following set of funda-

[12] See, among others, J. F. O. Bilson, "The Monetary Approach to the Exchange
Rate: Some Empirical Evidence," *IMF Staff Papers*, vol. 25, no. 1 (March 1978),
pp. 48-75; idem, "Rational Expectations and the Exchange Rate," in Frenkel and
Johnson, *Economics of Exchange Rates;* John F. O. Bilson, "The Deutsche Mark/
Dollar Rate: A Monetary Analysis," in Karl Brunner and Allan H. Meltzer, eds.,
Policies for Employment, Prices, and Exchange Rates, Carnegie-Rochester Series
on Public Policy, supplement to *Journal of Monetary Economics*, vol. 11 (1979),
pp. 59-101; Jeffrey A. Frankel, "On the Mark: A Theory of Floating Exchange
Rates Based on Real Interest Differentials," *American Economic Review*, vol. 69,
no. 4 (September 1979), pp. 610-22; Jacob A. Frenkel, "A Monetary Approach
to the Exchange Rate: Doctrinal Aspects and Empirical Evidence," *Scandinavian
Journal of Economics*, vol. 78, no. 2 (1976), pp. 200-224; idem, "The Forward
Exchange Rate, Expectations, and the Demand for Money: The German Hyper-
inflation," *American Economic Review*, vol. 67, no. 4 (September 1977), pp. 653-
70; Michael Keran, "Money and Exchange Rates, 1974-79," *Federal Reserve
Bank of San Francisco Economic Review* (Spring 1979), pp. 19-34; Steven W.
Kohlhagen, "The Identification of Destabilizing Foreign Exchange Speculation,"
Journal of International Economics, vol. 9, no. 3 (August 1979), pp. 321-40;
Michael Mussa, "Macroeconomic Interdependence and the Exchange Rate Re-
gime," in Rudiger Dornbusch and Jacob A. Frenkel, eds., *International Economic
Policy: Theory and Evidence* (Baltimore: Johns Hopkins University Press, 1979),
pp. 160-204; Alan C. Stockman, "Risk, Information, and Forward Exchange
Rates," in Dornbusch and Frenkel, *International Economic Policy;* and Robert J.
Hodrick, "An Empirical Analysis of the Monetary Approach to the Determina-
tion of the Exchange Rate," in Frenkel and Johnson, *Economics of Exchange
Rates.*

[13] Hooper and Morton, "Fluctuations in the Dollar."

TABLE 1
AVERAGE ABSOLUTE MONTHLY PERCENTAGE CHANGES IN ECONOMIC VARIABLES, 1973–1979

Variable	Period						
	1973:3–1978:12	1973:3–1975:9	1975:10–1977:8	1977:9–1978:12	1973:3–1977:8	1973:3–1979:11	1977:9–1979:11
Trade-weighted dollar	1.367	1.8887	.4684	1.6475	1.2838	1.3051	1.3478
Trade-weighted dollar adjusted for relative CPIs	1.428	1.992	.5962	1.5300	1.3976		
U.S. money supply (M-1)	0.920	.8970	.9494	.9239	.9193		
Trade-weighted foreign money supply (M-1s)	0.934	.8736	.9644	1.0067	.9123		
U.S. CPI	0.640	.7500	.4958	.6372	.6417		
Trade-weighted foreign CPIs	0.7622	.9235	.7170	.5146	.8356		
U.S. industrial production index	0.8053	.8309	.8571	.6814	.8420		
Trade-weighted foreign industrial production indexes	0.9345	.9529	.9655	.8542	.9582		
Relative money supplies (item 3 ÷ item 4)	1.2249	1.2236	1.3933	.9818	1.2959		
Relative CPIs (item 5 ÷ item 6)	0.3272	.3556	.3239	.2769	.3420		
Relative industrial production indexes (item 7 ÷ item 8)	0.9446	.9955	1.0131	.7472	1.0030		

NOTE: CPI = consumer price index.
SOURCE: Data are monthly averages, as provided by the Federal Reserve Board.

mental underlying factors: domestic money supply, foreign money supply, relative money supplies, domestic prices, foreign prices, relative prices, domestic economic activity (monthly industrial production), foreign economic activity, and relative economic activity. The figures are average absolute monthly percentage changes for each variable for each sample period.

Precisely what these data imply about the functioning of the foreign exchange market is by no means clear, however. There is currently no generally accepted notion of (1) what variables should be included in the complete list of underlying determinants, and (2) what the appropriate ratio should be between the variability of these underlying determinants and the variability of the exchange rate. Rudi Dornbusch, John Bilson, Pentti Kouri, Michael Mussa, and Susan Schadler, among others, have discussed models that generate overshooting behavior by exchange rates that implies a potentially greater variability of exchange rates than that of underlying variables.[14] This result derives principally from a relatively faster adjustment in the asset market than in the goods market. To this point, however, no author has claimed that the elimination of the resultant exchange-rate variability is either possible or desirable. The data presented in table 1, then, are a potentially interesting characterization of the dollar's behavior, rather than a test of the appropriateness of dollar variability.

For the floating period as a whole, the average absolute monthly exchange rate change was 50 percent greater than the average monthly money supply change, either in the United States or abroad; about twice the domestic or foreign monthly price change; and about 50 percent to 60 percent more than the foreign or domestic monthly change in industrial production. Whereas it was about the same as the average monthly change in relative money supplies, it was about 50 percent more than the monthly change in relative industrial production and more than four times the average monthly change in relative prices. For the floating period before the recent dollar slide (March 1973/August 1978), these figures are all slightly lower but with roughly the same magnitude.

If we divide the floating period into its logical three segments—

---

[14] Rudiger Dornbusch, "Expectations and Exchange Rate Dynamics," *Journal of Political Economy*, vol. 84, no. 6 (December 1976), pp. 1161-76; J. F. O. Bilson, "A Monetary Approach to the Exchange Rate" (Ph.D. diss., University of Chicago, 1976); Pentti J. K. Kouri, "The Exchange Rate and the Balance of Payments in the Short Run and the Long Run," *Scandinavian Journal of Economics*, vol. 78, no. 2 (1976), pp. 280-304; Michael Mussa, "The Exchange Rate, the Balance of Payments, and Monetary and Fiscal Policy under a Regime of Controlled Floating," *Scandinavian Journal of Economics*, vol. 78, no. 2 (1976), pp. 229-48; and Susan Schadler, "Sources of Exchange Rate Variability: Theory and Empirical Evidence," *IMF Staff Papers*, July 1977, pp. 253-96.

the 1973–1975 early adjustment period, the 1975–1977 stable period, and the 1977–1978 dollar slide [15]—we have a somewhat different picture. In the early period, whereas the relative money supplies, prices, and economic activity variables were about as volatile as for the period as a whole (although average domestic and foreign price change were each about 20 percent higher), the monthly average exchange-rate change was about 40 percent higher than for the period as a whole. During the 1977–1978 dollar slide, the average changes in relative money supplies, prices, and industrial production were considerably lower than at any other time in the sample. The average monthly exchange-rate changes were 70 percent, six times, and twice as large, respectively, during this most recent period. This is somewhat misleading, because the exchange-rate figures for 1979 are not included. If these are included, they show that average exchange-rate changes for the 1977–1979 period were 18 percent lower than for only the 1977–1978 period (and, in fact, if the 1979 period is included, then the average monthly exchange-rate change for the period as a whole is reduced by 4½ percent).

The 1975–1977 period is shown to be remarkable for its exchange rate stability—the dollar changed by less than ½ percent per month on the average during the two-year period. This average monthly exchange-rate change was less than the variability of any fundamental variable during the same period, with the exception of the change in relative prices, and it was only 45 percent larger in that case.

These data, in general, highlight the volatility of the exchange rate during the float, especially during the 1973–1975 and 1977–1979 periods. The major generalization that suggests itself is that perhaps the exchange markets are quite volatile in relation to underlying variables, particularly in periods immediately following sustained intervention by authorities that prevents necessary exchange rate adjustment (that is, the periods immediately after 1970–1973 and 1976–1977).

There is one aspect of this general question of excessive volatility that has been essentially unexplained in the literature—namely, what is the amount of day-to-day or week-to-week exchange-rate variability that may be necessary to ensure that the desired amount of medium-term to long-term exchange rate flexibility is possible? [16] The reason

[15] Current data for all ten variables for each of the eleven countries were available only through 1978. The exchange rate data were available through November 1979.

[16] I am indebted to Bill Nordhaus for generating the development of this line of questioning and analysis. Preliminary experimental work on this particular question was completed in 1978 at the Council of Economic Advisers by Val Koromzay, Wanda Tseng, and me, under his direction.

for abandoning the fixed but adjustable system in favor of a floating regime, for example, was to ensure that the necessary long-run exchange rate flexibility was possible without the extreme short-run instability that had characterized the markets of the late 1960s and early 1970s.

Given alternative macroeconomic goals across countries and the underlying variability of economic fundamentals, if it were desirable that exchange rates should have enough flexibility to move on the order of, say, 10 percent a year, how much do they *need* to be free to move on a monthly basis? week to week? day to day? Clearly, if 10 percent a year is desirable or necessary, restricting month-to-month movements to ½ percent may inevitably lead to cumulative disequilibriums and eventually necessitate sharp exchange-rate adjustments that may be undesirable.

Experimental empirical work on this question at the Council of Economic Advisers for the Swiss franc, yen, pound sterling, and deutsche mark against the dollar (March 1973–December 1978) analyzed the one-day, two-day, three-day, five-day, ten-day (and so on, up to two-year) variance of each exchange rate divided by the length of the period for each case.[17] Presumably, in a well-behaved market the variation of one-day changes in the exchange rate would not be dramatically different from the ten-day or four-hundred-day variation adjusted for the length of the lag. The simple, nonrigorous hypothesis was that a currency that was highly volatile in the long run should be relatively volatile in the short run, whereas a currency that was stable in the long run should not be so volatile in the short run.

Their results are presented in figure 3. The Swiss franc has been roughly invariant to the length of the time lag, the largest variance being for the two-and-a-half- to nine-month range. Short-term Swiss franc variability has clearly not been excessive in relation to long-term movements. For the yen and the pound sterling, on the other hand, short-term variability has been relatively low as compared with longer-term movements, and for the deutsche mark, a case could be made that the two-and-a-half- to five-month variability has been excessive in relation to short-term and long-term movements. For all currencies throughout the entire period of the float, however, short-term variability does not seem to have been excessive in relation to long-term changes.

One particularly important qualification to these results is that, for much of the period, the central banks of each of the four countries were intervening to limit day-to-day changes in the exchange markets.

---

[17] That is, they compared the one-day variance to the two-day variance divided by two, the three-day variance divided by three, the one-hundred-day variance divided by one hundred . . . the n-day variance divided by n.

FIGURE 3
Variance of Bilateral Exchange Rates for Various Lags

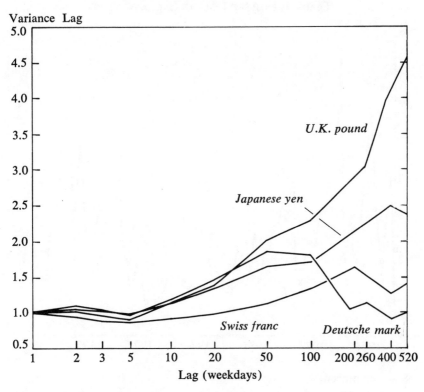

NOTE: Normalized so that the one-day variance equals 1.0.

The low day-to-day variance, especially for the yen, may be explained by this intervention activity. To the extent that they were successful, the variances for the shorter exchange rate movements represented in figure 3 understate the movements that would have existed in a free float. The effect on the variability of longer-term movements of "sitting on" short-term movements is not clear. To the extent, however, that preventing short-term exchange rate movements may at times limit the kind of long-term flexibility that may be desirable, it may eventually lead to larger short- to medium-term exchange rate changes in response to accumulated disequilibriums than would otherwise have been necessary.

From a slightly different point of view, the largest twelve-month change in the monthly average dollar up to now was the 14 percent

FIGURE 4

MONTHLY AVERAGES OF ABSOLUTE CHANGES IN DAILY TRADE-WEIGHTED DOLLAR EXCHANGE RATES

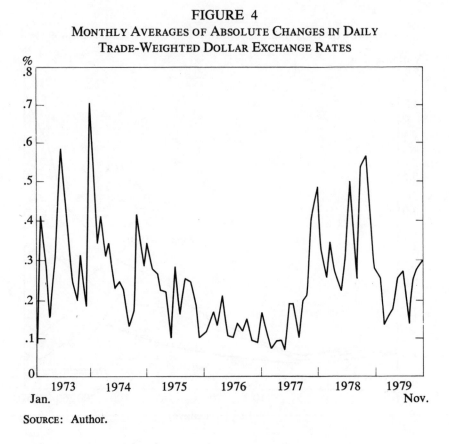

SOURCE: Author.

depreciation after October 1977. If such *maximum* annual changes are not undesirable, does the roughly 1.3 percent average absolute change in the monthly average dollar shown in table 1 seem excessive? I think not. Even if each monthly change were in the same direction, the average monthly change would have to be on the order of 1.1 percent to permit the rate to move 14 percent in one year. Even the 1.9 percent and the 1.6 percent average monthly changes in March 1973–September 1975 and September 1977–December 1978 may not be seen to be so excessive in this light—especially as both experiences followed periods when exchange rates were being managed by central bankers in order to reduce some fluctuations that, in retrospect, may have been necessary for adjustment.

Many critics of floating have claimed that short-run fluctuations in general, and the day-to-day fluctuations in particular, have been

162

excessive. The evidence in figure 4 clearly shows that, whereas daily movements have been quite large at times during the float, they have been quite stable at other times. Figure 4 shows the average absolute daily percentage exchange-rate changes for the trade-weighted dollar for each month during the float. This figure graphically illustrates once again the stability of the 1975–1977 period in relation to the 1973–1975 period of adjustment to past disequilibriums, OPEC, and the float and to the recent 1977–1979 period of dollar weakness. Day-to-day changes were much less during the stable period, partly as a result of an increasing ability of market participants to live with floating, especially as much of the exchange rate adjustment that was necessary in light of the changes and shocks of 1970–1975 had been completed by 1975, and partly as a result of increasing management of the dollar by foreign central banks during the period.

As stated previously, by late 1977 the increasingly large U.S. external disequilibrium was a clear reality, administration officials were perceived to be giving conflicting signals about the appropriateness of dollar adjustment, and the market was feeling increasingly less confident about the ability of the administration to deal effectively with the growing problems of inflation and the U.S. external imbalance. As can be seen in figure 4, despite very large amounts of official intervention through the first quarter of 1978, daily exchange-rate changes returned, in late 1977, almost to the levels of the 1973–1975 period.

Some critics have also charged that there has been significant destabilizing speculation during the current float. This has not been rigorously substantiated as a general problem during the float. In an earlier study, I have shown that tests of this hypothesis that have appeared in the literature have not been correctly specified.[18] Specifically, no test has correctly designed a technique for identifying the characteristics of the exchange rate in the absence of speculation. I demonstrated that evidence of behavior such as overshooting, bandwagons, excessive volatility in general, and excessive volatility relative to economic fundamentals in particular is not evidence of the existence of destabilizing speculation.

The opposite claim, that there has been an insufficient amount of stabilizing speculation during the float, has also been made.[19] This

---

[18] Kohlhagen, "The Identification of Destabilizing Foreign Exchange Speculation," *Journal of International Economics* (August 1979).

[19] For a thorough discussion of the legitimacy of these claims, see Thomas D. Willett, *Floating Exchange Rates and the International Monetary Reform* (Washington, D.C.: American Enterprise Institute, 1977), pp. 32-40; James Burtle, "Some Problems in Living with a System of Floating Exchange Rates," mimeo-

would seem to be a difficult claim to substantiate rigorously. Nevertheless, during times when markets are dominated by uncertainty, episodes where stabilizing speculation is reduced to inadequate levels, causing resultant fluctuations to be excessive, are not impossible.[20] In fact, the Carter administration all but explicitly pointed to insufficient stabilizing speculation as a rationale for the November 1 initiative.[21] The administration characterized the dollar markets in the summer and fall of 1978 as being dominated by a posture of one-way movements and an air of uncertainty that dominated economic fundamentals. The announced intent of the November 1 policies was in fact to allow the dollar's value to be determined once again by the course of economic fundamentals rather than by rumor, uncertainty, and resulting dominant one-way positions.

Market Efficiency. The evidence is still mixed and quite inconclusive as to whether or not the foreign exchange markets have been efficient in the financial sense during the current float.[22] Some authors have reported results rejecting the hypothesis of efficiency, and some have not been able to reject it. Some of the methodology has been poorly, and sometimes even inappropriately, applied from other financial market literature. Profits have been found in some spot markets and not in others. In many studies, tests to account for risk have been poorly devised, and indeed most authors ignore this factor completely. Most research into forward market efficiency has found the forward rate to

---

graphed (W. R. Grace and Co., May 1974); Fred Hirsh and David Hinshaw, "Floating Rates: Expectations and Experience," *Three Banks Review* (June 1974); Ronald M. McKinnon, "Floating Exchange Rates, 1973-74: The Emperor's New Clothes," in Karl Brunner and Alan Meltzer, eds., *Institutional Arrangements in the Inflation Problem,* supplement to *Journal of Monetary Economics* (1976); and especially McKinnon, *Money in International Exchange* (New York: Oxford University Press, 1979).

[20] See especially McKinnon, *Money in International Exchange.*

[21] See also Willett, "Fall and Rise of the Dollar"; idem, "It's Too Easy to Blame the Speculators," *Euromoney,* May 1979, pp. 111-20.

[22] See Kohlhagen, "Behavior of Foreign Exchange Markets"; and especially Richard Levich, "On the Efficiency of Markets for Foreign Exchange," in Dornbusch and Frenkel, *International Economic Policy,* pp. 246-67; and Levich, "The Efficiency of Markets for Foreign Exchange: A Review and Extension," in Donald R. Lessard, ed., *International Financial Management* (Boston: Warren, Gorham, and Lamont, 1979), for comprehensive reviews of this literature. Efficiency is a concept associated with actual market activities, which of course are conducted in a bilateral rather than a multilateral market context. The presumption here, not supported rigorously, is that if bilateral markets are efficient (not efficient) for bilateral tests, they are efficient (not efficient) in a multilateral sense.

be a poor but unbiased predictor of the future spot rate.[23] On the other hand, some authors have found evidence of a forward-rate bias, which, if not correctly adjusted for risk, implies little if anything about market efficiency.[24]

To quote from Levich:

[These] empirical results . . . provide evidence that the market is volatile and that large profit opportunities are possible. However, they do not provide convincing evidence that the market is inefficient. In part, this may reflect a problem in statistical methodology. The statistical tests may not be powerful enough to reject market efficiency, even if they should. This may be because it has been difficult to specify precisely the alternative hypothesis. . . . In the short run, we know that the foreign exchange market does not fully reflect *all* information. Traders invest in information, they take positions, time passes, wealth shifts, and the exchange market generally moves closer to a full reflection of all information. The test that checks to see if this process is evolving rationally has yet to be devised.[25]

In sum, whereas most empirical tests have been unable to reject market efficiency in favor of an alternative hypothesis, this literature is not yet at a stage where it can definitively contribute to an analysis of the behavior of the dollar during the current float.

Effects of Exchange Rate Volatility on the U.S. Economy. In analyzing the effects of floating exchange rates on the U.S. economy—or on any economy—one must clearly distinguish between the effects of floating exchange rates per se and the effects of the underlying international financial instability and the higher divergence of macroeconomic performances that made floating necessary and desirable in the first place. The necessity and the difficulty of this task are presented as *the* major caveat to analysis of this sort by Morris Goldstein in his excellent survey of these issues:

---

[23] Dornbusch ("Issues in International Finance") attributes this to the fact that unanticipated developments are "news" to the market and thus the forward rate is, in general, closer to the contemporaneous spot rate than to the subsequent spot rate at the maturity of the forward contract.

[24] See Steven W. Kohlhagen and Thomas D. Willett, "The Determination of the Forward Exchange Rate and the Cost of Using the Foreign Exchange Markets," in Richard J. Sweeney and Thomas D. Willett, eds., *Studies in Exchange-Rate Flexibility* (Washington, D.C.: American Enterprise Institute, forthcoming).

[25] Levich, "Efficiency of Markets," p. 272.

But care needs to be taken to avoid confusing the *period* of flexible rates with the effects of flexible rates themselves. Specifically, one wants to be able to distinguish between the proposition that macroeconomic policy in general has become less effective in industrial countries during the floating rate period and the proposition that flexible rates per se have made macroeconomic policy less effective.[26]

This section analyzes the effects of the floating dollar on U.S. unemployment, foreign trade, insulation from external shocks, independence of policies, ratchets, policy discipline, and the existence of vicious and virtuous circles.

Except where noted, it is my contention that the effects of fluctuating exchange rates are less on the economy of the United States than on the economies of its major trading partners.[27] This is the case because it has a much larger, much less open economy. A given exchange-rate change (either against an individual currency or against all currencies) simply does not affect the same proportion of total economic activity as it does in other countries where foreign activity is more important and the frequency of foreign exchange–denominated transactions is larger.[28] Evidence on the effects of floating on other countries, then, may not apply so strongly to the U.S. case.

With respect to the effects of floating exchange rates on U.S. unemployment, there would seem to be little reason to expect that there has been much if any effect. Goldstein summarizes this general contention in the following way:

> There is little in the way of theoretical argument, even less in empirical work, to suggest that flexible rates have had a major influence on unemployment rates in industrial countries. . . . This is not to say that the level of the exchange rate does not have strong effects on sectoral employment in individual coun-

[26] Morris Goldstein, "Have Flexible Exchange Rates Handicapped Macroeconomic Policy?" *Special Papers in International Economics,* no. 14 (Princeton, N.J.: Princeton University, June 1980). This paper is a comprehensive review of the macroeconomic effects of floating exchange rates in the major industrialized countries. See also Willett, "The Fall and Rise of the Dollar," for a comprehensive discussion of these issues.

[27] This contention would seem to be supported by the fact that intervention activity has been less for the United States than for its major trading partners.

[28] Peter Hooper and Steven W. Kohlhagen ("The Effect of Exchange Rate Uncertainty on the Prices and Volume of International Trade," *Journal of International Economics,* vol. 8 [1978], pp. 483-511) report econometric evidence on the effects of exchange-rate uncertainty on tradable goods prices, which they interpret to imply that high proportions of both U.S. exports and U.S. *imports* are denominated in dollars.

tries. Surely, the large amount of official intervention that has taken place over the floating rate period . . . has something to do with countries' attempts to obtain and to hold a competitive relative price advantage for their workers in export and import-competing industries. But this latter event has more to do with how individual countries manage their floating rates than with the properties of flexible rates themselves.[29]

Similarly, there is little if any evidence that greater exchange rate uncertainty as a result of floating exchange rates has had a negative effect on U.S. trade. Whereas, theoretically, we expect to see reduced trade associated with greater price uncertainty, studies by Peter Clark and Charles Haulk, John Makin, and Peter Hooper and the present author have found no evidence of such an effect.[30] Of course, simple exchange rate fluctuations are not an accurate measure of trade risk, even in the short run. Deviations from purchasing power parity or forward-rate forecasting errors (as used in some of the work cited above) would be better measures of risk, and it is by no means clear that the former measure has been greater under the floating-rate period than during the pegged period. An obvious caveat to the work in this area so far is that the experience with floating up to now has been too short to test whether or not any negative effects on trade are longer run in nature. In addition, with fixed rates that are held at disequilibrium levels, the existence or expectation of necessary exchange and capital controls may have a greater chilling effect on trade than do exchange rate fluctuations.

It is clear that flexible rates have provided much less insulation against some external disturbances than had at first been assumed, especially for smaller, open economies. This is especially true, the greater is capital mobility and the more the disturbances are a result of foreign fiscal rather than monetary policies. The most dramatic example of this is the stagflationary effects of the successive oil shocks on each of the industrialized economies. In response, policy makers

[29] Goldstein, "Have Flexible Rates Handicapped Policy?"

[30] Peter B. Clark and Charles J. Haulk, "Flexible Exchange Rates and the Level of Trade: A Preliminary Analysis of the Canadian Experience," mimeographed (Washington, D.C.: U.S. Treasury, 1972); John H. Makin, "Eurocurrencies and the Evolution of the International Monetary System," in Carl H. Stem, John H. Makin, and Dennis E. Logue, eds., *Eurocurrencies and the International Monetary System* (Washington, D.C.: American Enterprise Institute, 1976); and Hooper and Kohlhagen, "Effect of Exchange Rate Uncertainty." Akbar Akhtar and Bluford Putnam ("Money Demand and Foreign Exchange Risk: The German Case, 1972-1976," mimeographed [Federal Reserve Bank of New York, September 1979]) do report results for a reduction in money demand (in Germany) as a result of increased exchange risk.

have been faced with a choice of two unpalatable paths. They have, in general, not had the opportunity to choose between accepting the adjustment costs and insulating their economies from the shocks through exchange rate adjustment.

With respect to insulation for the United States in particular, Peter Kenen shows that the effects of some external disturbances on the U.S. economy are on the order of half as large under floating as they were with fixed rates.[31] In summary:

> We still have a lot to learn about the insulating properties of flexible rates against external shocks and disturbances, especially in quantitative terms. It is abundantly clear however from the experience of the last six years that the old textbook view of flexible rates as insulators par excellence against a wide variety of foreign disturbances should be abandoned. . . . The fact that flexible rates can provide less insulation than was previously supposed means that on balance the case for active policy against foreign disturbances (including use of exchange market intervention) has been strengthened. This is especially true for the smaller, more-open economies where foreign disturbances transmitted via the exchange rate are apt to have the relatively largest impact on domestic variables.[32]

It is less true for the United States.

Advocates of floating rates promised more independent monetary policies. Certainly the larger divergences of macroeconomic performances between the more and less restrictive monetary policy countries for the past seven years would support this contention. On the other hand, the ability of the United States in the more recent past to pursue a relatively expansionary monetary policy has been limited by both domestic political pressures and concerns about international responsibilities for the value of the dollar.

The inappropriateness of short-term interest rate targets with floating was also pointed out by the 1979 U.S. experience. Rising U.S. interest rates reflected market expectations of continued, if not rising, U.S. inflation rates and accompanying dollar weakness. Official concern over the length and depth of the oncoming recession created pressures to resist the upward pressure on interest rates while officials still publicly claimed to be pursuing a tight anti-inflationary policy. The attempt to fight inflation and maintain a strong dollar while resisting upward interest-rate pressures was clearly inconsistent. It was subsequently

[31] Peter B. Kenen, "New Views of Exchange Rates and Old Views of Policy," *American Economic Review*, vol. 68 (May 1978), pp. 398-406.
[32] Goldstein, "Have Flexible Rates Handicapped Macroeconomic Policy?"

announced on October 6, 1979, that the traditional U.S. interest rate target approach had been abandoned in favor of a monetary-aggregates target. It simply was not possible to interpret correctly—and, in fact, target—short-term interest rates without considering expectations on domestic inflation and future exchange rate movements.[33] Here, however, inconsistent policies, not floating rates, caused the problem. In fact, it can be argued somewhat convincingly that the floating rate provided support to domestic political pressures to put into place those tight policies that were being claimed.

Although domestic monetary policies have, in general, been more independent with floating than before, it is clear that they have not been completely independent of neighboring policies. The U.S. current account deficits of 1977–1979 were at least partly (and some would maintain totally) a result of nonsynchronized monetary policies. The subsequent dollar fall has certainly had an effect on later policies.

The general results are summarized very well by Goldstein:

> In sum, it seems clear in retrospect that the case for the efficacy of monetary policy under flexible rates was subject to a certain amount of false advertising. Early models did not take sufficient account of the slow response of trade flows to exchange rate changes, of the wage-price feedbacks of exchange rate changes, of the limits imposed by high substitution between domestic and foreign assets (including currencies), and of expectations about exchange rates and money supply changes themselves. At the same time, if one normalizes for the probability that monetary and fiscal policy are in general less effective than they used to be in controlling real variables, it is still probably so that monetary policy is more effective under flexible rates than under fixed rates. The few empirical studies that are able to make such a comparison . . . generally find that monetary policy has more powerful effects on both real output and prices under flexible rates, and there is a strong suspicion that the differences between the two regimes would be more pronounced for those countries with abnormal inflation rates.[34]

Critics of floating rates have claimed that the downward inflexibility of wages and prices has produced inflationary ratchet effects in the impact

---

[33] Ronald M. McKinnon ("Exchange Rate Instability, Trade Imbalances, and Monetary Policies in Japan and the United States," September 1978) points to this problem in the 1976-1978 yen/dollar markets, when authorities incorrectly concluded from high U.S. interest rates in relation to Japanese rates that there were excess Japanese liquidity and tight U.S. monetary conditions rather than vice versa.

[34] Goldstein, "Have Flexible Rates Handicapped Policy?"

of exchange-rate fluctuations. That is, when the exchange rate depreciates, it raises tradable goods prices and eventually wages and other domestic prices as well. Alternatively, when there is an appreciation (for example, simultaneously for its trading partners) and tradable goods prices fall, wages and other domestic prices do not fall, and thus there is no concomitant deflationary pressure.

The existence of such a phenomenon seems dubious at best. First, this logic cuts into a simultaneously determined set of variables at an arbitrary point in the process. Exchange rates, wages, and domestic prices are all simultaneously determined. It is not correct to assign lines of causation arbitrarily across these variables. Price inflation and exchange-rate depreciation are associated with each other and, in general, are both caused by changes in underlying exogenous variables. Second, even if the level of wages and prices *were* rigid downward, in an inflationary world it is unlikely that wage rate *increases* and price *increases* are unable to fall. Exchange-rate appreciation would not be expected to, and does not have to, lead to falling prices and wages, but it should be associated with downward pressure on rising rates of domestic price and wage increases. Specifically for the United States, econometric work has yet to uncover any evidence of ratchet effects.[35] In summary:

> There is not much evidence that flexible exchange rates are an important contributory factor to this problem at least directly. . . . if there is a ratchet effect associated with flexible rates, it would have more to do with their "discipline" effects on government's behavior than with any price-cost asymmetries induced by short-run rate fluctuations.[36]

This discipline hypothesis, that floating rates are inflationary because they do not provide the discipline of reserve losses that exist under fixed rates, is one of the oldest concerns about floating.[37] Before we turn to

[35] James Tobin, "The Wage-Price Mechanism: Overview of the Conference," in Otto Eckstein, ed., *The Econometrics of Price Determination* (Washington, D.C.: Board of Governors of the Federal Reserve System, 1972); F. Ripley and L. Segal, "Price Determination in 395 Manufacturing Industries," *Review of Economics and Statistics,* August 1978, pp. 263-71; Morris Goldstein, "Downward Price Inflexibility, Ratchet Effects, and the Inflationary Impact of Import Price Changes," *IMF Staff Papers,* November 1977, pp. 569-612; and Dean De Rosa and Michael Finger, "Commodity Price Stabilization and the Ratchet Effect," *World Economy,* January 1978, pp. 195-204.

[36] Goldstein, "Have Flexible Rates Handicapped Macroeconomic Policy?"

[37] Egon Sohmen, "International Monetary Problems and the Foreign Exchanges," Special Papers in International Economics, no. 4 (Princeton University, International Finance Section, April 1963); Gottfried Haberler, "Integration and Growth of the World Economy in Historical Perspective," *American Economic*

the recent U.S. experience, it is worth repeating Goldstein's insightful conclusions on this issue for the floating countries in general:

> In summary, there are good arguments on both sides of the reserve discipline issue and the evidence does not point strongly in one direction. Much of the argument hinges on distinctions between purely flexible and truly fixed exchange rates and these distinctions are blurred in a comparison of managed floating and adjustable par values. . . . It seems more than coincidental that since the disappearance of fixed rates, there has been an active search in high-inflation countries for some type of *institutional* mechanism that would provide some discipline against inflation—be it tax-based incomes policies, pre-announced money supply targets, IMF letters of intent, the European Monetary System, or even a constitutional amendment for a balanced budget.[38]

Now add to this list, in the U.S. case, the switch in monetary targets from short-term interest rates to monetary aggregates as of October 6, 1979.

The discipline provided to the United States by external disequilibriums is inextricably linked to the reserve role of the dollar. The United States is simply not a typical deficit country. The United States during the late 1960s is the "classic counterexample" to the general notion that balance-of-payments deficits with fixed exchange rates tend to induce restrictive domestic policies.[39] In fact, the U.S. response in 1971 to continued external disequilibrium was not more restrictive policies but the unsuccessful use of wage and price controls and temporary exchange rate flexibility leading shortly to changed exchange rate parities.

Because the U.S. economy is relatively closed, because there was no alternative to the float and resulting path of the dollar from 1973 to 1975 that was both desirable and feasible, and because the dollar was so stable during the 1975–1977 period, the external sector provided few if any constraints to U.S. policy before 1978.

The period of the 1978–1979 dollar slide has been a different story, however. With the dollar falling steadily, and at times rapidly, its value began to be of concern to U.S. policy makers. There were two

---

Review, March 1964; and Leland Yeager, "Discipline, Inflation, and the Balance of Payments," in Nicholas A. Beadles and L. Aubrey Drewry, eds., *Money, the Market, and the State: Essays in Honor of James Muir Waller* (Athens: University of Georgia Press, 1968), pp. 1-34.

[38] Goldstein, "Have Flexible Rates Handicapped Policy?"

[39] Ibid.

major reasons why the dollar's weakness became a policy problem. First, dollar depreciation not justified by underlying fundamentals was viewed as inflationary. In general, it is estimated that a 10 percent exogenous dollar depreciation (for example, as a result of incorrect expectations or overshooting) will result in a one- to one-and-a-half-percentage-point increase in the U.S. price level within one to two years.[40] Because by early 1978 the Carter administration was starting to target the control of inflation as its foremost economic priority, the prevention of excessive dollar depreciation increasingly became an important element in that policy.[41]

This became a particularly important concern in late October 1978 when the dollar plummeted in response to the announcement of the antiinflation policy. It was the administration's contention that the economic fundamentals were already falling in line: the external deficit, though still large, was already beginning to fall, and forecasts indicated that it would decrease even further in 1979; and the new antiinflation program was then in place. Further, administration officials felt that: (1) private market participants were in agreement on the turnaround of the balance-of-payments deficit; (2) private participants were also in agreement that the slide of the dollar would soon end, but their market activities were self-limited by the considerable uncertainty about U.S. commitments to end inflation; and (3) the administration had more information about that commitment and the likelihood of its ultimate success. They therefore felt that their responsibility to limit inflationary pressures, especially at that time, required that they intervene in the disorderly markets so as to convey the extent of their resolve.

Second, the administration was concerned about its responsibility to (1) the value of the dollar, the main international financial reserve asset, and (2) an orderly evolution toward any changes in the international monetary system if they became necessary or desirable. Here the problem centered on the role of the U.S. dollar as the main reserve asset and store of value in the international financial system. As the slide of the dollar accelerated through late 1977 and the first half of 1978, discussion of such phenomena as official diversification out of dollar reserves, oil pricing in a basket of currencies rather than in dollars,

[40] See Peter Hooper and Barbara Lowry, "The Impact of Dollar Depreciation on the U.S. Price Level: An Analytical Survey of Empirical Estimates," International Finance Discussion Papers, no. 128 (January 1979), and references cited therein.
[41] In fact, if factors such as policy pronouncements could successfully cause the exchange rate to rise above (or prevent it from falling to) the level justified by economic fundamentals, then this could *reduce* inflationary pressures somewhat.

and even the silly proposal that oil *receipts* be in a basket of currencies rather than in dollars began to receive attention in financial circles.[42]

To the extent that U.S. external deficits and associated dollar weakness generate such excessive nervousness about the dollar's value as a public and private unit of account and store of value, resulting diversification out of dollars may create excessive depreciations. That is, the central role of the dollar may give the United States fewer degrees of freedom than other countries in running external deficits during a floating-rate period. In that sense, more rather than less discipline may be imposed on U.S. policies than would otherwise be the case. Viewed in this context, the 1977–1979 experience may have been quite undesirable for the United States merely as a result of its central role in the floating-exchange-rate regime. For any other country, the 1977–1978 deficit, due in large part to faster U.S. real growth rates, could possibly have been equilibrated by a more gradual decline in both the exchange rate and the real growth rate, whereas the current account deficit could have been tolerated for a somewhat longer period.[43]

The sharp reduction in U.S. growth rates in 1979 and 1980 was at least partly a result of the tighter monetary and fiscal policies, which were even tighter than they might otherwise have been as a result of the dollar weakness. This is not to say that such externally induced

---

[42] Announcing that oil receipts will not be accepted in dollars makes sense only if OPEC is trying to hurt the value of the dollar or the international monetary system as a specific economic or political weapon (as Iran was trying to do in November 1979). Otherwise, the major effect on OPEC's wealth (assuming the dollar were to fall as a result of such an announcement) is to drop the value of all of OPEC's dollar-denominated net assets. Given existing institutional arrangements, the receipts could be converted to any currency desired by the seller at the time of receipt at existing exchange rates anyway. Thus, as long as the price in real terms on the date payable is fixed, the real value of the receipts is invariant to the currency of denomination. The major financial effect on OPEC of such a decision is likely to be negative. Even announcing a shift in oil pricing from dollars to a basket has limited financial appeal, because it is likely to drive down the value of OPEC's investments unnecessarily in the short term. The same effect on receipts could be achieved by changing the dollar price of oil at more frequent intervals to reflect worldwide inflation, exchange rate changes, and changing conditions in the oil market, without making the composition of the pricing formula a public or political matter. Shifting to a basket publicly may make political sense, but it is not likely to be financially beneficial to OPEC.

[43] It remains largely a mystery to me why an economic entity as fundamentally strong as the U.S. economy cannot run an annual excess of payments over receipts of less than 0.8 percent (the 1977 current-account deficit as a proportion of 1977 GNP) in as rich a financial market as currently exists in the international financial system without generating the sort of excitement that occurred in 1978-1979. The question of the size of deficit that is sustainable in the current environment is a potentially fruitful area for future research.

discipline was not a welcome force for those concerned about the serious inflation problem in the United States. It is quite possible, though, that a soft, or at least a softer, landing might have been possible without it.

With respect to U.S. responsibilities toward the evolution of the international monetary system, U.S. officials in the Carter administration consistently claimed that they were not committed to maintaining the dollar at the center of the system. They were, however, committed to seeing that any necessary transitions were not disorderly. This therefore precluded merely allowing the value of the dollar to tumble until officials were forced to take action to change the system in an environment not conducive to constructive evolution. Therefore, the necessity to maintain an orderly dollar market without excessive depreciation had induced some discipline on actions, especially toward domestic inflation, that might otherwise not have existed.

The final major policy issue in the discussion of the effects of floating exchange rates has been the existence of vicious and virtuous circles.[44] To my mind, there are two major problems with the contention that these phenomena have represented significant problems during the current float.[45] First, in order for even an exogenous exchange rate depreciation to be inflationary in any causal sense, the monetary authority must act to accommodate the initial effect.[46]

Second, observers of vicious circles usually fail to give sufficient consideration to the fact that exchange rate changes and the inflation rate are both endogenous variables in the economic system. A reduced-

[44] A vicious circle is the existence of the following sequence of events: exchange depreciation, which causes inflation, which causes further exchange depreciation, followed by further inflation, etc. (not necessarily starting at that point). A virtuous circle is the opposite, with exchange appreciation and deflationary pressures.

[45] For a more complete discussion of both the virtues and the faults inherent in this literature, see Goldstein, "Have Flexible Rates Handicapped Policy?"; Willett, *Floating Exchange Rates*; and references cited therein.

[46] On this point about monetary accommodation, see Robert J. Gordon ("World Inflation and Monetary Accommodation in Eight Countries," Brookings Papers on Economic Activity, no. 2 [Washington, D.C.: Brookings Institution, 1977], pp. 409-78), who notes that Germany and Japan tend to follow countercyclical monetary policies, whereas Italy and the United Kingdom follow accommodating policies (p. 448). See also the Bank for International Settlements, *Forty-seventh Annual Report* (Basel, 1977), pp. 38, 40. Henry C. Wallich and JoAnna Gray ("Stabilization Policy and Vicious and Virtuous Circles," International Finance Discussion Papers, no. 152 [Washington, D.C.: Board of Governors of the Federal Reserve System, September 1979]) similarly conclude that "the most extensive form of vicious circle can be expected to occur in countries that have suffered significant negative shocks to aggregate demand and that, in addition, put a relatively heavy weight on maintaining output and employment at or above their full employment levels despite a high degree of wage indexation." Vicious circles then occur in similarly minded countries that receive positive real shocks and in countries seriously determined to control increasing inflationary pressures.

174

form general equilibrium model would thus show both to be functions of the same set of exogenous variables (namely, the underlying fundamental determinants). To the extent that there was an exogenous component of the exchange rate change, it would be inflationary (although *how* inflationary would be determined by the extent of monetary accommodation), but the amount of inflation *associated with* a given amount of exchange depreciation would be different for a given one-unit change in each exogenous variable in the system.[47] Exchange depreciation does not *cause* inflation, which, in turn, does not *cause* further exchange depreciation, etc. A one-percentage-point increase in the growth rate of the domestic money supply will, however, cause a certain amount of inflation and exchange depreciation; a one-percentage-point increase in oil prices will cause a different amount of inflation and exchange rate change; an exogenous productivity shift will cause yet another change in inflation rates and exchange rates; and so on. Along this line, Bilson develops a model and presents evidence supporting the contention that the U.K. and Italian 1973–1976 "vicious-circle" experience was a result of expansionary domestic money supplies.[48]

Even if vicious circles were a problem in general—and Goldstein contends that "much of the controversy . . . is traceable to misconceptions about the importance of exchange rates"[49]—they have clearly not been a problem for the U.S. economy. Assuming all of the vicious-circle conditions and using the Hooper and Lowry result cited earlier,[50] a 10 percent exogenous dollar depreciation could cause a 1 to 1½ percent increase in the U.S. price level. If the 1½ percent increase in U.S. prices would then cause as much as a 1½ percent dollar depreciation, this could then, in turn, cause up to a 0.15 percent rise in the price level. That is, after the first full round, the effects would at most be negligible in the United States.

In summary, dollar movements have, at least at the end of the decade, provided some discipline to domestic policies that appear to have reinforced domestic pressures. The sharp 1977–1978 depreciation certainly worsened the inflation performance of the period slightly, at least against the alternative of no or less exchange depreciation. On balance, though, for the period as a whole, it would not seem to be

---

[47] That is, the partial derivative of the inflation rate with respect to exchange rate depreciation.

[48] J. F. O. Bilson, "The 'Vicious Circle' Hypothesis," *IMF Staff Papers*, March 1979, pp. 1-37.

[49] Goldstein, "Have Flexible Exchange Rates Handicapped Macroeconomic Policy?"

[50] Hooper and Lowry, "Impact of Dollar Depreciation on U.S. Price Level."

correct to conclude that dollar fluctuations had significantly affected either the U.S. macroeconomic performance or policy choices in an adverse manner.

Concluding Comments

In analyzing the experience with the 1970s period of managed floating exchange rates, it can reasonably be concluded that, at least for the U.S. dollar, when the foreign-exchange markets have been allowed some reasonable scope for functioning without inappropriate official guidance, they have performed more or less satisfactorily. The experience has not been as unhappy as that claimed for many other currencies. The 1973–1975 period was characterized by wide fluctuations, but these were not inappropriate in light of the contemporary and immediately preceding instabilities, shocks, and disequilibriums. The 1975–1977 period was largely one of stability for the dollar, with foreign central banks essentially managing the dollar within a "narrow band." Only during the 1977–1978 period did the dollar experience the types of behavior that had led some to criticize seriously the floating rate experience in other countries. Whereas this experience appears to have been at least partly a result of a high degree of uncertainty on the part of private participants, it was also a function of the fact that foreign officials actively prevented the rate from falling earlier in 1976 and 1977. In addition, the volatility of the dollar and uncertain market expectations were both functions of the uncertainty surrounding U.S. policies on energy, macroeconomic stabilization, and inflation.

The key question, of course, is this: Have managed floating exchange rates equilibrated external disequilibriums without generating excessive exchange-rate movements? The answer for the United States is apparently yes for 1973–1977 and probably no for 1977–1978. The reasons for the adverse experience in 1977–1978 fall into roughly three categories: (1) domestic policy, (2) international economic factors, and (3) the central role of the dollar in the international financial system.

With respect to domestic macroeconomic policy, there is no question that uncertainties about the future course of critical U.S. policies toward macroeconomic stabilization in general, and inflation and energy specifically, had adverse effects on the dollar market in the late 1970s. The policy implications are obvious in theory; political realities may make them difficult to accomplish in practice. If private market participants are to be able to form strongly held expectations on the future path of exchange rates, they must be able to form strongly

176

held expectations on the future course of underlying economic variables and policies. To the extent that leadership in economic policy is perceived to be highly uncertain, economic policies to be unpredictable, and official forecasts to be unbelievable, exchange-rate expectations will be weakly held, and exchange rate movements are likely to be larger than otherwise.

The principal lesson from the experience of the late 1970s with respect to international economic factors is that increased divergences in macroeconomic performances are possible but probably not without significant exchange-rate fluctuations.[51] It follows quite simply that if policy makers feel that the costs of these resultant exchange-rate fluctuations are excessive, they must find ways to manage exchange rates (more successfully) so as to reduce them, or they must better coordinate their macroeconomic policies and the macroeconomic performances of their economies. Given past experience with exchange-rate management, including, if not especially, the 1975–1977 management of the dollar by foreign central banks and the subsequent dollar slide, macroeconomic coordination may be the only realistic alternative if exchange rate volatility is undesirable. That is, unhappily, the degree of macroeconomic independence and exchange rate volatility may be positively correlated.

The special function of the dollar as a reserve currency, international means of payment, and store of value almost certainly reduces the scope for exchange rate adjustment of significant external disequilibriums without some international financial concern about dollar variability. Rumors of official diversification out of dollars, not to mention the fact of diversification itself, put downward pressure on the dollar during the 1978–1979 depreciation. Merely being the center currency country may restrict the size of an external deficit that can realistically be expected to be equilibrated by exchange depreciation without creating undue concern about further depreciation.

The Carter administration made clear its willingness to allow the international monetary system to evolve, even if that meant that the dollar must move from center stage. The only qualification was that the evolutionary process could not be disorderly. U.S. policy was thus to contribute constructively to the evolutionary process while working to prevent or resist episodes of excessive or unnecessary dollar decline that might result. Work on the International Monetary Fund Substitution Account was intended to be one such step in enabling the system to have the needed flexibility in this evolutionary process. The

[51] See also Council of Economic Advisers, *Economic Report of the President* (Washington, D.C., January 1979); and Truman, "Balance-of-Payments Adjustment."

177

European Monetary System is both a symptom of the need for this evolutionary process and a vehicle for its development. In the meantime, managed floating is the only short-term option.

The 1970s experience offers a number of lessons about the appropriate amount and types of official exchange rate management. Two of these apply directly to the U.S. case. First, there is no "right rate" for equilibrating a specific external account.[52] One exchange-rate depreciation may yield current-account equilibrium in a certain period. A somewhat larger depreciation will bring about an equilibrium in less time while generating higher growth in the interim. On the other hand, a smaller depreciation may take longer to bring about equilibrium but yield lower inflationary pressures during the adjustment period. The "correct" choice will depend on policy makers' assessment of domestic policy goals and the costs of adjustment.

The second lesson is related to this first point. If other countries manage one's exchange rate, they may manage it at a rate that is not desirable from the viewpoint of long-run domestic policy. This is the lesson of the 1975–1977 period of dollar stability. Though foreign central banks intervened to prevent their currencies from appreciating against the dollar, an enormous U.S. external deficit developed. By 1977 some U.S. officials, committed to a policy of intervening only in disorderly markets, began suggesting that a lower dollar might be desirable or necessary in order to equilibrate what was beginning to appear to be a sizable deficit. These statements, coupled with an increasing awareness of the size of the disequilibrium and increasing uncertainty about U.S. policies, induced the beginning of what became the dollar slide in the fall of 1977. This deep depreciation did not even slow down until it was abruptly halted on November 1, 1978, when President Carter declared that the United States was going to take an active interest in the management of the dollar.

The clear lesson is that if it is desirable for a currency to be managed, the management should be coordinated among central banks. More important, if a currency is to be managed, one of the participants should certainly be the central bank that issues and has ultimate responsibility for the currency that is being managed.

This is not to say that the dollar needs more active management. On the contrary, arguably, the problem with the 1977–1979 dollar was that it had received too much management in the immediately preceding period. The United States either could not or would not exercise its prerogative in 1976–1977 to prevent overmanagement of its currency

[52] I am indebted to my former colleague Val Koromzay for pointing out the significance of this notion.

or to participate with other central banks to ensure that the amount and type of management were appropriate.

As we enter the decade of the 1980s, U.S. policy makers have two responsibilities in this area. First, if they want to put an end to dollar weakness, they must bring domestic inflation under control. This is consistent with both current domestic macroeconomic requirements and political pressures. Second, they must ensure that, *if and only if* it is clearly desirable for the dollar to be managed officially, the Federal Reserve System must participate to ensure that such management is in the best interests of the United States. This is consistent with insisting that long-run exchange market intervention by the European Monetary System entail neither net purchases nor net sale of dollars without prior coordination with the U.S. Federal Reserve System. This also requires that, insofar as is possible, international financial policy makers should work to enable any evolution of the international monetary system to proceed in an environment that ensures as much flexibility as is possible and that minimizes the probability of disorderly market developments. This is likely to require patience on the part of officials, the patience to see that institutional changes are gradual, the patience to see that market participants (including officials) continuously have several desirable alternatives with respect to the determination of the denomination of their assets and liabilities, and the patience not to intervene in markets when inappropriate or in order to defend indefensible or inappropriate exchange rates.

West Germany's and Switzerland's Experience with Exchange Rate Flexibility

Roland Vaubel

For any student of exchange-rate flexibility in the 1970s, West Germany and Switzerland must be of particular interest. Switzerland was the first European country to let its currency float indefinitely (in January 1973) as well as to return to an exchange-rate target (in October 1978). Germany was the first European country to experiment with flexible exchange rates (in fall 1969 and again from May to December 1971). It followed Switzerland into "permanent" exchange-rate flexibility toward the dollar and most other currencies with a lag of two months; and with the same lag it reestablished exchange-rate targets for major European Community (EC) currencies in December 1978 (in the context of the European Monetary System).

Both the Swiss franc (SF) and the deutsche mark (DM) experienced a considerable appreciation in the exchange markets: The annual compound average rate of effective appreciation (MERM) from 1973I to 1979III amounted to 9.8 percent for the franc and 6.2 percent for the mark. The nominal appreciation primarily reflected the fact that, at 3.7 percent and 4.6 percent, respectively, annual consumer price inflation in Switzerland and Germany was much lower than in all other major industrial countries. But there was also a real effective appreciation on a consumer price basis: 3.7 percent per year for the franc and 0.8 percent per year for the mark; the real appreciation was 0.9 percent and 1.2 percent, respectively, in the period 1966II–1972IV.[1]

I thank Jacqueline Rijsdijk, Cees Bangma, and especially Fred Bär for highly competent research assistance; Eduard Bomhoff for helping to organize the computational work; and Hans Genberg, Georg Junge, Heinz Müller, and the Bank for International Settlements for kindly supplying urgently needed data.
[1] For sources, see the statistical appendix to this paper.

Finally, any list of such common experiences should mention that the German Bundesbank and the Swiss Nationalbank were the first central banks to adopt and announce target rates of growth for monetary aggregates (in December 1974 and January 1975, respectively).

These are obvious similarities, but there is one important and obvious difference: the Swiss economy is much smaller than that of West Germany. In 1978, the gross domestic product (GDP) of Switzerland amounted to only about 13 percent of that of Germany. This has important consequences for the costs and benefits of exchange-rate flexibility.

In the first place, because of its smaller GDP, Switzerland's money supply (M-1) is equal to about a third of Germany's money supply, so that any given international shift in the demand for their currencies affects the Swiss price level and exchange rate much more strongly than the German price level and exchange rate, other things being equal.[2] Second, because the Swiss ratio of exports to GDP (35.3 percent) is even larger than the German equivalent (27.2 percent), a given rate of change in exports demanded by the world as a result of a temporary (real) exchange rate change vis-à-vis the rest of the world implies a larger rate of change for Swiss real income than for German real income. Moreover, being more open with respect to trade, the Swiss economy is more susceptible to exchange rate risk than the German economy.[3] It is notably for these reasons that most economists would predict that the net benefits of exchange rate flexibility—as compared with genuinely(!) fixed exchange rates—tend to be larger for a major economy like Germany than for the small Swiss economy.[4] The following sections will bring evidence to bear on this point.

The next section presents the record of Swiss and German exchange rate developments, monetary policies, and international trade in 1973II–1979III. It shows that, although Switzerland's and Germany's exchange-

---

[2] Note also, however, that under fixed exchange rates a small country is less capable of affecting world monetary growth and inflation. Herbert Giersch, "On the Desirable Degree of Flexibility of Exchange Rates," *Weltwirtschaftliches Archiv*, no. 2, 1973.

[3] For the general point, see Gottfried Haberler, *Der Sinn der Indexzahlen* (Tübingen, 1927), p. 104; idem, *Der internationale Handel* (Berlin, 1933), p. 41.

[4] Robert A. Mundell, "The Theory of Optimum Currency Areas," *American Economic Review*, vol. 51, no. 4 (1961), and Ronald I. McKinnon, "Optimum Currency Areas," *American Economic Review*, vol. 53, no. 4 (1963), have also argued that, in a small economy, there is less chance to exploit money illusion for employment purposes. However, this aspect seems to have been far less important in the 1970s than in the 1960s, and there is little evidence that the German or the Swiss monetary authorities aimed at the exploitation of money illusion during the period of exchange rate flexibility.

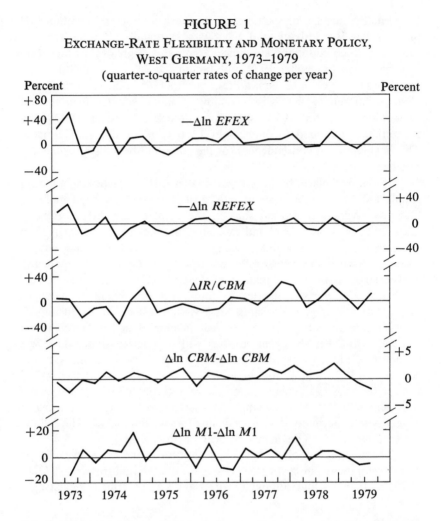

FIGURE 1

EXCHANGE-RATE FLEXIBILITY AND MONETARY POLICY,
WEST GERMANY, 1973–1979

(quarter-to-quarter rates of change per year)

rate experiences were quite similar, their reactions to this experience
differed in important respects.

The last section presents a stylized theoretical and econometric
analysis of the causes of Swiss and German exchange rate experience.[5] It
notably tries to quantify the effects that international shifts in the demand
for Swiss francs and German marks have had on their inflation rates and
on their exchange-rate changes in relation to the dollar. The analysis

[5] The last section draws on a larger study by the present author: "International
Shifts in the Demand for Money, Their Effects on Exchange Rates and Price
Levels, and Their Implications for the Preannouncement of Monetary Expansion,"
Weltwirtschaftliches Archiv, no. 1, 1980.

FIGURE 2

EXCHANGE-RATE FLEXIBILITY AND MONETARY POLICY, SWITZERLAND, 1973–1979

(quarter-to-quarter rates of change per year)

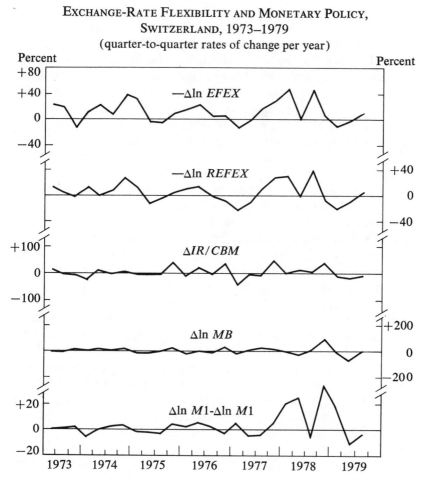

also focuses on the question of whether and, if so, how economic policy makers should try to identify, and to react to, such international shifts in the demand for money and whether the Bundesbank's and the Nationalbank's present views on this problems can be defended.

German and Swiss Exchange Rate
Experience and Its Effects: Some Basic Evidence

Exchange Rate Experience. The upper panels of figures 1 and 2 show the quarter-to-quarter changes in the DM and SF effective exchange rates ($-\Delta\ln EFEX$) as annual rates of change (a minus sign indicates appreciation). As can be seen, exchange-rate fluctuations were larger for the franc than for the mark; the mean absolute rate of change is 15.4 percent for the franc but only 11.8 percent for the mark.

The larger exchange-rate changes for the Swiss franc could be the result of the fact that the Swiss inflation rate was lower than the German inflation rate and therefore deviated more from the average inflation rate of its trading partners. For this reason, the corresponding real effective exchange rate changes on a CPI basis ($- \Delta \ln REFEX$) have been drawn in the second panels of these graphs, and various measures of real exchange-rate stability are reported in table 1. As can be seen, the mean absolute rate of quarterly change is now smaller for both countries, but it is still larger for the smaller economy.

Those who are aware of the existence of long-run equilibrium real exchange-rate trends will be interested to see that the variance of real exchange-rate change is also much larger for Switzerland than for Germany, both on a quarterly and on an annual basis. Thus the higher mean absolute rate of real exchange-rate change for Switzerland reflects not merely the higher Swiss trend rate of real exchange-rate appreciation but also larger deviations from this trend. Finally, as the figures for the mean absolute change in the rate of real exchange-rate changes indicate, Switzerland also suffered most from real exchange rate fluctuations in terms of quarter-to-quarter and year-to-year jumps in the rate of real exchange-rate change.

Even more interesting than the comparison between Germany and Switzerland is an intertemporal comparison. It shows that, on all six measures, real exchange-rate stability has been much smaller from 1973 onward than during the preceding period of equal length; with one exception, all F-ratios are highly significant, most of all, again, for Switzerland.

Real exchange-rate instability should not be confused with exchange-rate risk. Changes in exchange rates, whether real or nominal, may be expected. The available evidence, however, shows very clearly that if, for example, the forward rate is assumed to be an unbiased predictor of the future spot rate, forecast errors concerning the exchange rate vis-à-vis the dollar have on the average been much larger under floating rates than under the adjustable peg.[6] For the mark, for example,

[6] Robert Z. Aliber, "The Firm under Pegged and Floating Exchange Rates," *Scandinavian Journal of Economics* (1976), no. 2; idem, "Floating Exchange Rates: The Twenties and the Seventies," in John S. Chipman and Charles P. Kindleberger, eds., *Flexible Exchange Rates and the Balance of Payments* (North Holland, 1980); and Richard M. Levich, "Tests of Forecasting Models and Market Efficiency in the International Money Market," in Jacob A. Frenkel and Harry G. Johnson, eds., *The Economics of Exchange Rates* (Reading, Mass.: Addison-Wesley, 1978).

TABLE 1
MEASURES OF REAL EXCHANGE RATE STABILITY, 1966–1979

	West Germany			Switzerland		
	1973II–1979III	1966III–1972IV	F-ratio	1973II–1979III	1966III–1972IV	F-ratio
Quarterly changes						
Mean absolute rate of real exchange rate change	1.96	0.85	—	2.81	0.76	—
Variance of rate of real exchange rate change	6.97	1.70	4.10**	12.07	0.84	14.37**
Mean absolute change in rate of real exchange rate change	2.69	1.12	—	3.44	0.87	—
Annual changes	1973–1979	1966–1972	F-ratio	1973–1979	1966–1972	F-ratio
Mean absolute rate of real exchange rate change	2.57	1.84	—	7.13	1.74	—
Variance of rate of real exchange rate change	14.16	7.10	1.99	50.45	3.37	14.97**
Mean absolute change in rate of real exchange rate change	3.75	2.23	—	9.37	2.38	—

** Significant at 1 percent level.
SOURCES: See statistical appendix.

the mean absolute value of the percentage difference between the actual dollar spot rate and the dollar spot rate predicted ninety days ago was 4.6 percent during the period 1973–1978 and only 2.1 percent during the period 1967–1972. For the Swiss franc, the average forecast error in 1973–1978 amounted to 5.2 percent and was thus still higher than the DM forecast error, although it had been lower in 1965–1972. As Aliber shows, it was also higher than the forecast errors in 1922III–1926IV (1.4 percent), when the Swiss franc was on a flexible rate.[7]

[7] Aliber, "Floating Exchange Rates."

185

While it probably cannot be denied that exchange-rate risk has been larger under the flexible-exchange-rate regime in force since 1973 than under the adjustable-peg system preceding it, it does not, of course, follow that high exchange-rate risk is an intrinsic feature of flexible exchange rates. The postwar experience of such countries as Canada and Austria (or of Switzerland, the Netherlands, and the United Kingdom in the 1920s) demonstrates this point. The reason that flexible exchange rates are nevertheless most often associated with larger exchange-rate risk is not that they necessarily increase uncertainty or instability but that they are typically adopted *because* the economic situation has become unusually turbulent or unstable and *because* all other exchange-rate regimes perform worse in such circumstances. Among the special factors that put the international monetary system under unusual stress in the 1970s were the Vietnam war, inflation in the United States, the real exchange-rate changes induced by the rapid rise in the price of oil and other raw materials, and the very different policy reactions to these shocks in the various industrial countries.

Exchange Rate Flexibility and Monetary Policy. How did the monetary authorities in Germany and Switzerland react to the exchange-rate changes of their currencies? Both the Bundesbank and the Nationalbank intervened heavily in the foreign-exchange markets in order to reduce exchange rate changes. Although nominal ($\Delta\ln EFEX$) and real ($\Delta\ln REFEX$) effective exchange-rate changes showed an extremely significant positive correlation with each other (see table 2), the interventions of both central banks ($\Delta IR/CBM$ and $\Delta IR/MB$) were triggered by nominal rather than real exchange rate changes, thus revealing some remnants of exchange-rate illusion. Although the Bundesbank's reaction was immediate and significant at the 1 percent level, the Swiss response was statistically insignificant and often occurred with a lag of one quarter (see table 2).[8] Nevertheless, as a proportion of central bank money or the monetary base, respectively, the mean absolute change in Swiss international reserves (29.8 percent per year) has been much larger than the German mean gross intervention outside the snake (11.8 percent per year).[9] In short, the Nationalbank has been much more reluctant to intervene in response to exchange-rate changes, but its gross interventions carried much more weight than those of the Bundesbank if account is taken of the smaller Swiss monetary base.

[8] For further evidence with respect to Germany, see Jacques R. Artus, "Exchange Rate Stability and Managed Floating: The Experience of the Federal Republic of Germany," *IMF Staff Papers*, no. 2, 1976; and Harmen Lehment, *Devisenmarktinterventionen bei flexiblen Wechselkursen* (Tübingen: Kieler Studien, 1980).

[9] For the calculation of these variables, see the appendix.

TABLE 2

EXCHANGE RATE FLEXIBILITY AND MONETARY POLICY, 1973II–1979III

West Germany: Simple Correlation Coefficients

	$\Delta\ln EFEX^a$	$\Delta\ln REFEX^a$	$\Delta IR/CBM$	$\Delta\ln CBM -$ $\Delta\ln CBM$
$\Delta\ln EFEX^a$	+ .951**			
$\Delta IR/CBM$	− .533**	− .515**		
$\Delta\ln CBM$				
$-\ \overline{\Delta\ln CBM}$	+ .266	+ .134	+ .329	
$\Delta\ln$ M-1				
$-\ \overline{\Delta\ln \text{M-1}}$	+ .377	+ .406	− .040	+ .579**

Switzerland: Simple or Partial[b] Correlation Coefficients

	$\Delta\ln EFEX^{a,c}$	$\Delta\ln REFEX^{a,c}$	$\Delta IR/MB^c$	$\Delta\ln MB^c$
$\Delta\ln REFEX^a$	+ .926**			
$\Delta IR/CBM$	− .264	− .251		
	(L: − .254)	(L: − .330)		
$\Delta\ln$ MB^a	− .111	+ .047	+ .452*	
	(L: − .364)	(L: − .437*)		
$\Delta\ln$ M-1				
$-\ \overline{\Delta\ln \text{M-1}}$	+ .025	+ .091	+ .311	+ .562**
	(L: − .716**)	(L: − .696**)	(L: + .388)	(L: + .359)

* Significant at 5 percent level only.
** Significant at 1 percent level.
[a] A positive sign indicates a depreciation.
[b] The partial correlation coefficient is given because the dependent variable ($\Delta\ln MB$) is not deseasonalized; three seasonal dummies are included as explanatory variables.
[c] L: the left-hand variable is lagged one quarter.

It seems that this reluctance reflects notably Swiss intervention abstinence from mid-1974 to mid-1975 when—in contrast to 1977IV–1978IV—the Nationalbank resisted all demands for large-scale interventions to mitigate the remarkable (nominal and real) appreciation of the franc. As will be shown in figure 4, the reason for this refusal can be found not in a weaker response of export orders and export volumes— the response was marked in both periods—but in the fact that in 1974–1975 Switzerland was still suffering from rapid inflation (about 8.4 percent), whereas in 1977–1978, with price-level stability regained, the Swiss authorities seem to have thought that they could better afford the inflation risk of a more expansionary monetary policy.

Did the German and Swiss monetary authorities try to sterilize at least part of the effect that their interventions would otherwise have on central bank money or the monetary base, respectively? Once more, table 2 reveals a characteristic difference between the German and the Swiss stances on monetary policy. Whereas, in the Swiss case, the positive correlation between foreign-exchange interventions (as a proportion of the monetary base) and the rate of growth of the monetary base ($\Delta \ln MB$) is significant, it is insignificant for Germany (where the deviation from target or, in 1973–1974, from the annual average of central bank money growth ($\Delta \ln CBM - \overline{\Delta \ln CBM}$) is used). Accordingly, the correlation with exchange-rate changes becomes positive for German central bank money growth (minus target), whereas it stays negative in the Swiss case.[10] Indeed, if a lag of one quarter is allowed for, the negative correlation between Swiss nominal and especially real exchange rate changes and the growth of the monetary base is close to the 5 percent significance level. In short, the Swiss authorities, on the "small-country assumption," essentially accepted the domestic monetary effects of their foreign exchange intervention; they used interventions as an instrument of domestic monetary policy. The German authorities, in contrast, sterilized the domestic monetary effects of their interventions to a considerable extent; by implication, they must have viewed their interventions as an instrument to affect foreign monetary policies.[11]

The very significant positive correlation between the central bank money or monetary-base variables on the one hand and the deviation of M-1 monetary expansion from the explicit or implicit target ($\Delta \ln M\text{-}1 - \overline{\Delta \ln M\text{-}1}$) that is reported in table 2 reveals a considerable and approximately equal stability for the money multiplier in both countries. Owing to the small weight of interventions and its stronger propensity to

10 It may be objected that this difference is probably due to the different definitions of the monetary variables. This objection carries no force, however, because $\overline{\Delta \ln CBM}$ has been virtually constant at about 8 percent; 1974 is the only exception.

11 For a more detailed analysis of the Bundesbank's sterilization policies, see Lehment, "Devisenmarktinterventionen." With respect to the Bretton Woods period, this issue has been investigated by Manfred Willms, "Controlling Money in an Open Economy: The German Case," *Federal Reserve Bank of Saint Louis Review*, 1971, no. 2. My paper, "The Return to the New European Monetary System: Objectives, Incentives, Perspectives," in Karl Brunner and Allan H. Meltzer, eds., *Monetary Institutions and the Policy Process* (Amsterdam, 1980) has shown that in the European snake, the Bundesbank's monetary policies were hardly deflected from target through foreign exchange interventions.

TABLE 3

STABILITY AND TRENDS OF MONETARY EXPANSION, 1966–1979

(M-1 seasonally adjusted)

	West Germany			Switzerland		
	1973II–1979III	1966III–1972IV	F-ratio	1973II–1979III	1966III–1972IV	F-ratio
Quarterly changes						
Variance of rate of monetary expansion	44.27	44.04	1.01	178.40	65.71	2.71**
Mean absolute change of rate of monetary expansion	5.66	5.91	—	11.20	7.02	—
Annual changes						
Variance of rate of monetary expansion	11.36	14.02	.81	24.46	25.06	.98
Mean absolute change of rate of monetary expansion	4.67	2.76	—	6.53	3.59	—
Compound rates						
Compound average rate of monetary expansion (per year)	10.3	9.4	—	4.4	10.6	—
Compound average rate of CPI inflation (per year)	4.7	3.5	—	4.2	4.5	—

** Significant at 1 percent level.

SOURCES: Federal Reserve Bank of St. Louis; IMF *International Financial Statistics.*

sterilize, however, the Bundesbank's $\Delta \ln$ M-1 $- \overline{\Delta \ln \text{M-1}}$ is now highly positively correlated with exchange-rate changes, whereas the correlation in the Swiss case is close to zero contemporaneously and significantly negative with a lag of one quarter. In other words, German monetary policy (deviations) determined exchange-rate changes rather than the reverse, and Swiss monetary policy (deviations) reacted more to exchange-rate developments. Because Swiss exchange-rate changes were less due to money-supply changes, they must have been due to money-demand changes to a larger extent than German exchange-rate changes.

189

Exchange-rate flexibility gives the national monetary authorities the freedom to stabilize monetary expansion and thereby the price level (provided the demand for money grows at a stable rate).[12] Have the German and Swiss authorities grasped this opportunity? As table 3 demonstrates, the answer depends on whether annual or quarterly changes are analyzed and on whether stability is measured by the variance around the trend or by the period-to-period changes of monetary expansion. The variances of the annual rates indicate a small (insignificant) reduction of instability, whereas the year-to-year changes signal a considerable increase. As for the quarterly changes, both measures show that the variability of German monetary expansion has hardly changed but that monetary expansion in Switzerland has become significantly more variable. Apparently the Swiss authorities have aimed at stability of monetary expansion only, if at all, on an annual basis, using quarterly deviations from the annual target trend to mitigate exchange rate changes.[13] As Genberg and Roth have demonstrated, such a policy can be successful only if and to the extent that the expectations of private agents are not rational.[14]

All measures of stability demonstrate that Switzerland has always experienced less stability of monetary expansion than Germany and that the change in variability from 1966III–1972IV to 1973II–1979III has been less favorable for Switzerland than for Germany. As can be seen in table 4, Switzerland has also been far less successful in implementing its monetary targets.[15] Although Switzerland experienced a more variable monetary expansion than Germany, it succeeded—unlike Germany—in attaining both a markedly lower average rate of monetary expansion [16] and a lower rate of inflation than in 1966III–1972IV. The Swiss authorities used the opportunity of exchange rate flexibility to achieve low rates of monetary expansion and inflation more effectively

---

[12] This assumption will be tested in the last section.

[13] It might be objected to this interpretation that, for example, according to Michele Fratianni and M. Nabli, "Money Stock Control in the EEC Countries," *Weltwirtschaftliches Archiv*, no. 3, 1979, money stock control has also been much more difficult on a quarterly basis than on an annual basis. This does not explain, however, why the difference between annual and quarterly variability is so much larger in the Swiss case than in the German case.

[14] Hans Genberg and J. P. Roth, "Exchange-Rate Stabilization Policy and Monetary Target with Endogenous Expectations," *Schweizerische Zeitschrift für Volkswirtschaft und Statistik*, no. 3, 1979.

[15] The reverse is true if the special case of 1978 is excluded, however.

[16] To some extent the higher variability of monetary expansion must have been the price of the faster monetary deceleration, but the faster deceleration does not explain why variability has been higher during the deceleration than during the acceleration and why the Swiss deviations from target were larger.

TABLE 4

TARGET AND ACTUAL RATES OF MONETARY EXPANSION, 1974–1980
(percent)

Period	Target Rate	Actual Rate	Deviation
West Germany: Central Bank Money			
1974IV–1975IV	8.0	9.5	1.5
1975 average–1976 average	8.0	9.2	1.2
1976 average–1977 average	8.0	9.0	1.0
1977 average–1978 average	8.0	11.4	3.4
1978IV–1979IV	6–9	6.5	1.0[a]
1979IV–1980IV	5–8	4.9	1.6[a]
Average deviation			1.62
Switzerland: Monetary Base			
December 1974–December 1975	6.0	6.2	0.2
1975 average–1976 average	6.0	3.8	2.2
1979 average–1980 average	4.0	−2.4	6.4
M-1			
December 1974–December 1975	6.0	5.9	0.1
1975 average–1976 average	6.0	8.0	2.0
1976 average–1977 average	5.0	5.4	0.4
1977 average–1978 average	5.0	16.2	11.2
Average deviation[b]			3.95

[a] Deviation from midpoint of target band.

[b] In 1975 and 1976, the deviations for the monetary base and M-1 are each given a weight of one-half.

than the German authorities. With only 4.7 and 4.2 percent inflation, respectively, however, both countries reaped a considerable part of the potential benefits of exchange-rate flexibility in relation to the dollar, which during the same period inflated at an annual rate of 8.4 percent. In 1966III–1972IV, by way of contrast, German and Swiss inflation had been very close to U.S. inflation (4.1 percent).

To summarize this part of the analysis, it can be stated that for Germany and Switzerland the only benefits of exchange-rate flexibility— although extremely important ones—have been much lower inflation rates than they would otherwise have had, as well as relaxation of restrictions on capital movements in 1974. These benefits have to be set against the cost of larger real exchange-rate variability and exchange-rate risk as well as—in the case of Switzerland—the potential cost of a

FIGURE 3

Exchange-Rate Flexibility and International Trade, West Germany, 1973–1979

(quarter-to-quarter rates of change per year)

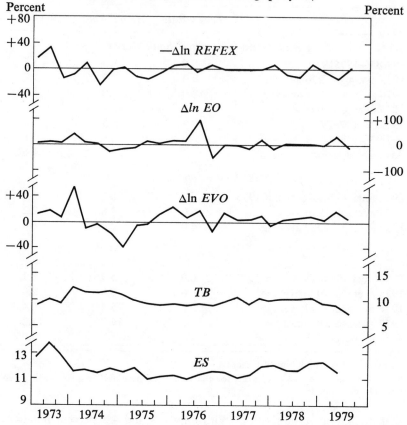

more variable rate of monetary expansion. For countries whose residents have far more assets and liabilities denominated in the domestic currency than in foreign currencies, the benefit of less purchasing-power risk is likely to exceed the cost of more exchange-rate risk.

Exchange Rate Flexibility and International Trade. Have the larger real exchange-rate fluctuations destabilized German and Swiss foreign trade? As figures 3 and 4 and table 5 demonstrate, it is impossible in the case of Germany to discover a sizable positive effect of (unusual) real exchange-rate changes (depreciation) on the rate of growth of (new)

192

FIGURE 4

EXCHANGE-RATE FLEXIBILITY AND INTERNATIONAL TRADE,
SWITZERLAND, 1973–1979

(quarter-to-quarter rates of change per year)

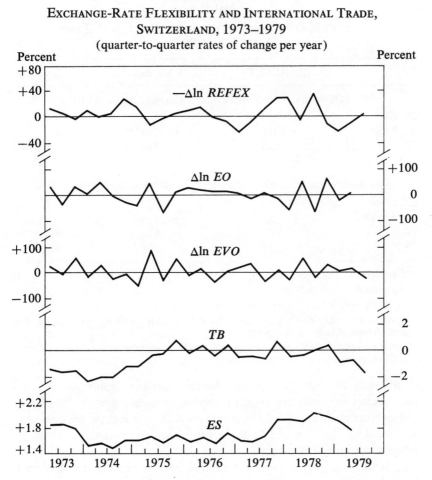

export orders in manufacturing (*EO*) or of export volumes (*EVO*) and on the trade balance (*TB*) or Germany's share in world exports (*ES*) within the same quarter. For Switzerland, in contrast, such an effect can be traced with respect to both export orders (in the engineering industry) and export volumes; in the latter case this immediate effect is even significant.

Table 6 allows for reaction lags of up to three years. In the case of Germany, real exchange-rate variations (beyond long-run trend) seem to exert a positive influence on the growth of export orders and of export volumes after about six to eight quarters, in the latter case even

193

TABLE 5

EXCHANGE RATE FLEXIBILITY AND INTERNATIONAL TRADE, 1973II–1979II

	Δln REFEX[a]	Δln EO	Δln EVO
West Germany: Simple or Partial[b,c] Correlation Coefficients			
Δln EO[b]	+ .124		
Δln EVO[b]	− .018	+ .598**	
TB	+ .095	− .038	− .066
ES[c]	− .491*	− .074	+ .087
Switzerland: Simple or Partial[b,c] Correlation Coefficients			
Δln EO[b,c]	+ .384		
Δln EVO[b,c]	+ .559*	+ .318	
TB[c]	− .006	− .134	+ .052
ES[c]	− .237	− .158	+ .112

* Significant at 5 percent level only.
** Significant at 1 percent level.

[a] A positive sign indicates a depreciation.

[b] Partial correlation coefficient: the left-hand variable is also regressed on the rate of change of real world exports.

[c] Partial correlation coefficient: because the left-hand variable is not deseasonalized, it is also regressed on three seasonal dummies.

significantly so. Neither the trade balance nor the export share, however, shows a significant positive impact over this period. If export *values* react positively at all,[17] the lag seems to be ten to twelve quarters. The positive effect on the trade balance after one quarter is likely to reflect the response of imports.

With respect to Switzerland, the evidence is more uniform. Apart from the immediate positive effect on export orders and export volumes (which does not carry through into the trade balance or the export share), there is another positive effect after about six quarters that affects export volumes, the trade balance, and the export share.

To summarize, it can be stated that the response of international trade to real exchange rate changes is stronger and more immediate for Switzerland than for the larger and less open German

[17] Whatever may be the price elasticities in the long run, there is no cogent theoretical reason why export values and the real exchange rate should be positively correlated; for if the real exchange rate appreciates as a result of a shift of world demand in favor of the country's products, real appreciation does not indicate a deterioration of competitiveness but an improvement of competitiveness.

TABLE 6
LAGGED RESPONSES OF INTERNATIONAL TRADE TO
REAL EXCHANGE RATE CHANGES
($+$ = depreciation)

Lag in Quarters	Dependent Variable			
	$\Delta\ln EO$[a]	$\Delta\ln EVO$[a]	TB[a]	ES[a]
West Germany: Simple or Partial[a] Correlation Coefficients				
0	+ .124	− .018	+ .095	− .491*
1	− .133	− .043	+ .304[b]	− .560**
2	− .375	− .548**	− .235	− .132
3	+ .057	− .022	− .395	+ .037
4	+ .128	− .079	− .415	− .355
5	+ .094	+ .074	− .430	− .226
6	+ .040	+ .578*[b]	− .479*	− .110
7	+ .234	+ .310	− .455	− .489
8	+ .317[b]	+ .481	− .125	− .198
9	− .403	− .222	+ .094	+ .090
10	+ .091	− .249	+ .180	+ .196
11	+ .038	− .290	+ .300	+ .285[b]
12	− .708**	− .407	+ .259	+ .118
Switzerland: Simple or Partial[a] Correlation Coefficients				
0	+ .384[b]	+ .559*[b]	− .006	− .237
1	− .248	+ .028	− .005	− .331
2	+ .089	− .313	+ .009	− .396
3	+ .105	− .154	+ .060	− .129
4	− .261	− .410	+ .100	+ .112
5	− .196	+ .003	+ .182	+ .258
6	+ .106	+ .508	+ .217[b]	+ .440[b]
7	+ .046	+ .452	+ .059	+ .364
8	− .086	− .114	− .322	+ .244
9	+ .264	− .370	− .477	+ .160
10	− .522	− .618*	+ .092	+ .315
11	− .317	− .075	+ .071	+ .260
12	+ .212	+ .663	− .166	+ .164

* Significant at 5 percent level only.
** Significant at 1 percent level.
[a] See table 4.
[b] Most significant coefficient of hypothesized sign.

economy. Although it must be admitted that the empirical analysis of this section leaves room for more sophistication[18] and that the estimation of a "full" model would probably yield somewhat different coefficients of correlation, the qualitative findings reported here are unlikely to be substantially modified. Rather, a more detailed analysis will be devoted to the causes of German and Swiss exchange rate variations and the implications for the variability of monetary expansion rates.

Exchange Rate and Monetary Policy in the Presence of International Shifts in the Demand for Money

The Policy Problem for "Strong-Currency Countries." Since 1978 at the latest, policy makers in Germany and Switzerland have been aware of the problem that international shifts in the demand for money pose for a policy of exchange-rate flexibility with preannounced monetary expansion. In that year, the central banks of both countries missed their monetary targets by record margins (see table 4) "in the interest of exchange-rate developments."[19] Both central banks attributed their difficulties, at least partially, to "substantial shifts in foreign demand" for their currencies.[20] Whereas the Bundesbank was converted to explicit target bands rather than point targets,[21] the Nationalbank adopted a minimum exchange rate target in relation to the mark and

[18] The terms of trade or a real exchange rate measured with respect to wage cost could appropriately be used in place of the real exchange rate measured with respect to the CPI, for example. For two recent studies along these lines, see Alfred C. Steinherr and C. Morel, "The Reaction of Prices and of the Balance of Payments to Revaluation of the Deutsche Mark," *Weltwirtschaftliches Archiv*, no. 3, 1979; and Henner Kleinewefers and E. Locher, "Untersuchungen zur Frage der Konkurrenzfähigkeit der schweizer Exporte bei flexiblen Wechselkursen," *Schweizerische Zeitschrift für Volkswirtschaft und Statistik*, no. 3, 1979. In public discussions, however, it is usually the deviations from (dynamic) purchasing power parity on a CPI basis that are considered the main defect of flexible exchange rates.

[19] Schweizerische Nationalbank, *Bericht des Direktoriums über die Wirtschafts und Währungslage*, August 24, 1978, p. 6; similarly, Deutsche Bundesbank, *Monatsbericht* [monthly report], September 1978, p. 9; November 1978, p. 6; December 1978, pp. 8, 11f.

[20] Schweizerische Nationalbank, Referat von Dr. F. Leutwiler an der Generalversammlung der Schweizerischen Nationalbank, April 26, 1979, p. 3; Fritz Leutwiler, Interview, *The Banker*, February 1979; Deutsche Bundesbank, *Monatsbericht*, June 1978, p. 17; Geschäftsbericht für das Jahr 1978, p. 52; and notably *Monatsbericht*, November 1979, pp. 26-34. The German Sachverständigenrat claimed at a very early stage that such shifts had been taking place and that they should be accommodated by money supply policy (Jahresgutachten 1978/79, paras. 404, 406, etc.).

[21] Of course, the point target had always been meant as the midpoint of a band, also by the Nationalbank; see Kurt Schiltknecht, "Monetary Policy under Flexible Exchange Rates: The Swiss Case" (Paper presented at the Seventh Konstanz

refused to announce a money-supply target for 1979. It made clear, however, that it viewed the exchange rate target not as an alternative to price-level stability but as another means of achieving medium-term price-level stability,[22] while at the same time protecting the (short-run) competitiveness of the Swiss export industry.[23]

The policy problems posed by international shifts in the demand for money have been foreseen by several authors[24] and can be described as follows. A shift in the demand for money from currency A to currency B must, other things unchanged, raise the price of currency B and lower the price of currency A. With regard to the exchange rate—that is, the relative price between two moneys—this means that currency B must appreciate with respect to third currencies and even more so with respect to currency A. With regard to the relative price of money in terms of goods, let us assume that the two price levels would have remained constant in the absence of the international shift in the demand for money. It then follows that the rise in the relative price of currency B implies a fall in the price level of country B; analogously,

---

Seminar on Monetary Theory and Monetary Policy, June 1979), published in German translation as "Die Geldpolitik der Schweiz unter dem System flexibler Wechselkurse," *Schweizerische Zeitschrift für Volkswirtschaft und Statistik,* no. 1, 1977, p. 7. Schiltknecht also suggested that the width of the implicit band should be larger, the more open the economy (ibid.) and that foreign demand for the currency is an important factor in this respect (p. 24). See also Schiltknecht, "Von der Kreditpolitik zur Geldmengenpolitik: Die Geldpolitik der Schweizerischen Nationalbank in den letzten zehn Jahren," *Kredit und Kapital,* no. 3, 1978, p. 299.

[22] Schweizerische Nationalbank, *Monatsbericht,* January 1979, p. 3.

[23] Schweizerische Nationalbank, *Bericht des Direktoriums über die Wirtschafts und Währungslage,* September 21, 1979, p. 10.

[24] See, notably, Arthur Laffer, "Optimal Exchange Rate Systems" (Paper presented at the American Economic Association Meeting, Atlantic City, September 1976); Herbert Giersch, "Exchange-Rate Surveillance," in R. A. Mundell and J. J. Polak, eds., *The New International Monetary System* (New York: Columbia University Press, 1977); David T. King, B. H. Putnam, and D. S. Wilford, "A Currency Portfolio Approach to Exchange Rate Determination: Exchange Rate Stability and the Independence of Monetary Policy," Federal Reserve Bank of New York, Research Paper no. 7733, July 1977, reprinted in Bluford H. Putnam and D. Sykes Wilford, eds., *The Monetary Approach to International Adjustment* (New York: Praeger Publishers, 1978); John F. O. Bilson, "The Current Experience with Floating Exchange Rates: An Appraisal of the Monetary Approach," *American Economic Review,* vol. 68, no. 2, 1978; Lance Girton and Don Roper, "Theory and Implications of Currency Substitution," Federal Reserve Board International Finance Discussion Paper, no. 86, 1976, rev. May 1978; idem, "Substitutable Monies and the Monetary Standard," in M. P. Dooley, H. M. Kaufmann, and R. E. Lombra, eds., *The Political Economy of Policy Making: Essays in Honor of Will E. Mason* (Beverley Hills, London, 1979); and Marc Miles, "Currency Substitution, Flexible Exchange Rates, and Monetary Independence," *American Economic Review,* vol. 68, no. 3, 1978.

the fall in the price of currency A implies a rise in the price level of country A. Because the exchange rate tends to react faster than the two commodity price levels, moreover, international shifts in the demand for money tend to produce transient real exchange-rate changes, which temporarily affect the international competitiveness of the countries' export- and import-competing industries; and even in the absence of such differences in adjustment speeds, shifts in the foreign demand for a currency that lead to net monetary movements in the balance of payments will tend to affect the real exchange rate and international competitive positions so that the current account balance can change by the same amount as the capital account. To fix monetary expansion in advance is to validate the assumption of *ceteris paribus* with regard to the rate of growth of the money supply.

International shifts in the demand for money are thus another cause of international economic interdependence under flexible exchange rates besides the real factors making for changes in the terms of trade and capital movements.[25] It is of course not true, however, that international shifts in the demand for money destroy the "independence of monetary policy" or "monetary autonomy" under flexible exchange rates (as has been claimed).[26] Although the demand for money may be internationally interdependent, money supply is *not* under flexible exchange rates. Each national monetary authority is thus in principle free, as it is not under fixed rates, to attain its preferred price-level target by adjusting money supply to money demand. This is not to deny that such a policy creates identification problems; these will be analyzed in turn.

DM and SF Exchange Rate Changes and International Shifts in the Demand for Money. The determinants of private demand for foreign moneys have been estimated in a number of studies, but none of them is capable of indicating the size of the effect that international shifts in the demand for money have on exchange rates.[27] Another group of studies tries to locate these shifts by estimating domestic money-demand

[25] That such interdependencies had not been denied by the advocates of exchange rate flexibility is shown by a rereading of Milton Friedman, "The Case for Flexible Exchange Rates," *Essays in Positive Economics* (Chicago: University of Chicago Press, 1953), p. 199.

[26] See, for example, Laffer, "Optimal Exchange Rate Systems," p. 9; and King, Putnam, and Wilford, "Currency Portfolio Approach to Exchange Rate Determination," p. 4.

[27] Mordechai E. Kreinin and R. F. Gilbert, "The Demand for Foreign Currency Holdings by European Banks," *Southern Economic Journal*, no. 1, 1971; Pentti J. K. Kouri and M. G. Porter, "International Capital Flows and Portfolio Equilibrium," *Journal of Political Economy*, no. 2, 1974; K. Alec Chrystal, "Demand for International Media of Exchange," *American Economic Review*, no. 5, 1977;

ROLAND VAUBEL

functions, or transformations thereof, and by analyzing the resulting forecast errors.[28] This approach is inadequate because such forecast errors may also reflect domestic shifts in the demand for money. International shifts cannot be identified as a mere residual but must be allowed for explicitly in a total demand-for-money function.[29]

The model. Money supply in currency i (M_i) is defined to be held by domestic residents (M_i^D) as well as by foreigners (M_i^F):

$$\frac{M_i}{P_i} = \frac{M_i^D}{P_i} + \frac{M_i^F}{P_i} \tag{1}$$

Miles, "Currency Substitution"; Marc Miles and Marion B. Stewart, "The Effects of Risk and Return on the Currency Composition of Money Demand," *Weltwirtschaftliches Archiv,* no. 4, 1980; idem, "Currency Substitution: Some Further Results and Conclusions," *Southern Economic Journal,* no. 1, 1981; Roland Vaubel, *Strategies for Currency Unification: The Economics of Currency Competition and the Case for a European Parallel Currency* (Tübingen: Kieler Studien, vol. 156, 1978); Arturo Brillembourg and S. M. Schadler, "A Model of Currency Substitution in Exchange Rate Determination, 1973-1978," *IMF Staff Papers,* no. 3, 1979; and Guillermo Ortiz and L. Solís, "Inflation and Growth: Exchange-Rate Alternatives for Mexico," in John Williamson, ed., *Exchange Rate Rules: The Theory, Performance, and Prospects of the Crawling Peg* (New York: St. Martin's Press, 1981).

[28] Peter Trapp et al., Überwindung der Konjunkturschwäche in der Bundesrepublik Deutschland," *Die Weltwirtschaft,* no. 2 (1978); Harmen Lehment, "Devisenmarktinterventionen"; and Bruce Brittain, "International Currency Substitution and the Apparent Instability of Velocity in Some Western European Economies and in the United States," *BIS Working Papers,* no. 2, (Basel: Bank for International Settlements, 1980).

[29] *Theoretical* analyses that allow for money demand from residents of other currency areas are Russell S. Boyer, "Substitutability between Currencies and between Bonds: A Theoretical Analysis of Gresham's Law," mimeographed, February 1973, reprinted as "Currency Mobility and Balance of Payments Adjustment," in Putnam and Wilford, *Monetary Approach,* pp. 4ff.; Guillermo A. Calvo and C. A. Rodriguez, "A Model of Exchange-Rate Determination under Currency Substitution and Rational Expectations," *Journal of Political Economy,* no. 3, 1977; Jürg Niehans, "Purchasing-Power Parity under Flexible Rates," in Peter Oppenheimer, ed., *Issues in International Economics* (Boston: Oriel Press, 1980); and Jacob A. Frenkel and K. Clements, "Exchange Rates in the 1920s: A Monetary Approach," in M. June Flanders and Assaf Razin, eds., *Development in an Inflationary World* (New York, 1980). Frenkel has also repeatedly used the forward discount to explain money demand during the Weimar hyperinflation: "The Forward Exchange Rate, Expectations and the Demand for Money: The German Hyperinflation," *American Economic Review,* vol. 67, no. 4 (1977); "Further Evidence on Expectations and the Demand for Money: The German Hyperinflation," *Journal of Monetary Economics,* no. 1, 1979; "The Forward Premium on Foreign Exchange and Currency Depreciation during the German Hyperinflation," *American Economic Review,* vol. 70, no. 2 (1980). For an extension of Frenkel (1977), see also Andrew Abel, Rudiger Dornbusch, John Huizinga, and Alan Marcus, "Money Demand during Hyperinflation," *Journal of Monetary Economics,* no. 1, 1979, and Robert E. Cumby and John Huizinga, "Currency Substitution during Hyperinflation: Empirical Evidence," 1981, mimeographed.

199

The demand for real balances from domestic residents is assumed to depend not only on the domestic volume of transactions and wealth (both proxied by real income, y_i) and on the opportunity cost of holding the domestic money rather than financial and real assets (proxied by the domestic nominal interest rate, i_i) but also on the opportunity cost of holding the domestic money rather than foreign money (proxied by the difference between the domestic (i) and the world (w) nominal interest rates, which is assumed to approximate the expected inflation differential):

$$M_i^D / P_i = c\, y_i^{\eta_i} \exp[-\,\varepsilon_i i_i - \lambda_i (i_i - i_w)] \qquad (2)$$

If we assume covered interest parity, money demand from foreigners can be written analogously as follows:

$$M_i^F / P_i = k\, y_{j+k}^{\theta_i} \exp[-\,\delta_i i_i - \mu_i (i_i - i_w)] \qquad (3)$$

It should be noted that the interest-rate differential is a valid proxy of relative opportunity costs not only for non-interest-bearing money balances but also for those interest-bearing money balances that are subject to reserves on which no interest or a less-than-market rate of interest is paid and that the interest-rate differential may reflect opportunity cost not only in terms of expected yield but also in terms of risk because currencies tend to involve less purchasing-power risk, the smaller their mean expected rate of inflation and depreciation.[30] Taking rates of change of equations 1 to 3, we obtain equations 4 to 6:

$$\hat{M}_i - \hat{P}_i = \frac{M_i^D}{M_i}(\hat{M}_i^D - \hat{P}_i) + \frac{M_i^F}{M_i}(\hat{M}_i^F - \hat{P}_i) \qquad (4)$$

$$\hat{M}_i^D - \hat{P}_i = \eta_i \hat{y}_i - (\varepsilon_i + \lambda_i)\Delta i_i + \lambda \Delta i_w \qquad (5)$$

$$\hat{M}_i^F - \hat{P}_i = \theta_i \hat{y}_{j+k} - (\delta_i + \mu_i)\Delta i_i + \mu_i \Delta i_w \qquad (6)$$

Substituting equations 5 and 6 into equation 4, we have the complete money-demand equation:

$$\hat{M}_i - \hat{P}_i = \eta_i \frac{M_i^D}{M_i}\hat{y}_i + \theta_i \frac{M_i^F}{M_i}\hat{y}_{j+k} - \left[(\varepsilon_i + \lambda_i)\frac{M_i^D}{M_i}\right.$$

$$\left. + (\delta_i + \mu_i)\frac{M_i^F}{M_i}\right]\Delta i_i + \left[\lambda_i \frac{M_i^D}{M_i} + \mu_i \frac{M_i^F}{M_i}\right]\Delta i_w \qquad (7)$$

[30] The reason is that a falling price level is considered improbable (at least in the long run). Thus a fall in the mean expected inflation rate is equivalent to a reduction of the dispersion of expected inflation rates below the mean and around the mean. For a list of empirical studies and supporting evidence, see Vaubel, "Strategies for Currency Unification," p. 183, n. 2.

In equation 7 demand for money from foreigners is reflected by θ, λ, μ, and δ, where θ relates to flow demand induced by portfolio growth, where λ and μ capture demand for currency substitution, and where δ allows for demand for substitution between currency i and financial or real assets in other countries. Whereas the coefficient of Δi_w reflects only cross-currency shifts in the demand for money, the coefficient of Δi_i also captures demand for substitution between domestic money on the one hand and domestic and foreign nonmonetary assets on the the other hand. For simplicity, we shall adopt the symmetry assumption $\lambda_i = \mu_i = \sigma_i$.

As a next step, let us postulate that, in long-run steady-state equilibrium, the demand for money equals the supply of money and that monetary expansion can be considered exogenous. Solving for the steady-state equilibrium inflation rate ($\hat{P}^*_i$), we can now write:

$$\hat{P}^*_i = \hat{M}_i - \eta_i \frac{M_i^D}{M_i} \hat{y}_i - \theta_i \frac{M_i^F}{M_i} \hat{y}_{j+k}$$
$$+ (\varepsilon_i \frac{M_i^D}{M_i} + \delta_i \frac{M_i^F}{M_i} + \sigma_i) \Delta i_i - \sigma_i \Delta i_w \qquad (8)$$

In the absence of a steady state, the inflation rate is known to adjust with a lag to (unexpected)[31] variations in the rates of change of the explanatory variables.

Instead of estimating the fraction of inflation adjustment that takes place within the same quarter, as would be the case in a partial adjustment model, we shall estimate the typical lag (z) with which the dynamic disequilibrium is overcome:

$$\hat{P}^*_{i,t+z} = \hat{M}_{i,t} - \eta_i \frac{M_{i,t}^D}{M_{i,t}} \hat{y}_{i,t} - \theta_i \frac{M_{i,t}^F}{M_{i,t}} \hat{y}_{j+k,t}$$
$$+ (\varepsilon_i \frac{M_{i,t}^D}{M_{i,t}} + \delta_i \frac{M_{i,t}^F}{M_{i,t}} + \sigma_i) \Delta i_{i,t} - \sigma_i \Delta i_{w,t} \qquad (9)$$

Like all single-equation estimates of money demand, this one, too, can yield unbiased estimates only to the extent that not only monetary

[31] In the empirical implementation, an attempt was made to attribute the lag only to *unexpected* monetary expansion and real income growth, the former being estimated on a quarterly basis from a Box-Jenkins model. Quite implausibly, however, "expected" monetary expansion did not prove to be correlated with the inflation rate without a lag either. Because "expected" monetary expansion was mostly estimated to equal last quarter's actual monetary expansion, the main effect of using autoregressively estimated expected monetary expansion seems to be a shortening of the lag but not a pricing behavior according to autoregressive expectations. In view of the impossibility of arriving at a plausible estimate of unexpected monetary expansion, actual monetary expansion is used in its place.

expansion but also growth in real income and the change in the nominal interest rate are exogenous to the model. Fortunately, we know from many simultaneous-equation estimates that the single-equation bias is small.

The equation for the (spot) exchange rate (s) will be directly stated in terms of rates of change:

$$\hat{s}_{i,j,t} = E(\hat{P}^*_i) - E(\hat{P}^*_j) + \alpha_i \Delta i_{i,t} - \alpha_j \Delta i_{j,t} - K_{i,j} \qquad (10)$$

It allows for three sources of (statistical) deviations from dynamic purchasing power parity:

• *Temporary real exchange rate changes due to lagged price-level adjustment:* Since the price level adjusts with a lag whereas the exchange rate adjusts almost instantaneously to monetary changes, unexpected and, to a lesser extent, expected changes in the determinants of the inflation rate and of the nominal rate of exchange-rate change push the real exchange rate (as measured by one of the conventional price indexes) away from its equilibrium path until the inflation rate has attained its new equilibrium. Thus, dynamic purchasing power parity can at most be assumed to hold on an expected basis.

• *Once-and-for-all real exchange-rate changes due to imperfect substitutability between money and nondurables:* Whereas money is a durable asset, most of the items that enter conventional price indexes are nondurables. Thus, for example, a change in long-term inflation expectations should affect the spot exchange rate more than the price level.[32] In equation 10 this difference of impact is reflected by $\alpha_i \Delta i_{i,t} - \alpha_j \Delta i_{j,t}$.

• *Permanent-trend real exchange rate changes due to international shifts in the supply of, and the demand for, goods:* Even in the absence of transportation costs, trade restrictions, and other barriers to trade, the law of one price holds only for identical goods. Because the consumer price indexes used to deflate nominal money supplies are based on baskets of goods and services whose composition differs from country to country even at a very disaggregated level, it cannot be surprising that, between many industrialized countries, real exchange rates change (on a CPI basis) at a long-term trend rate of several percent a year.[33] Those trend changes are captured by the constant term $K_{i,j}$.

[32] I owe this hypothesis to Eduard Bomhoff.

[33] See, for example, Roland Vaubel, "Real Exchange-Rate Changes in the European Community: The Empirical Evidence and Its Implications for European Currency Unification," *Weltwirtschaftliches Archiv,* no. 3, 1976, reprinted in

Because $E(\hat{P}_i{}^*)$ and $E(\hat{P}_j{}^*)$ in equation 10 are the future equilibrium inflation rates rationally expected to prevail once current money
demand and supply have worked themselves out, the current values of
the deterministic component of equation 9 can be put in their place:[34]

$$\hat{s}_{i,j;t} = (\hat{M}_{i,t} - \hat{M}_{j,t}) - (\eta_i \frac{M_{i,t}^D}{M_{i,t}} - \theta_{ji} \frac{M_{j,t}^{FI}}{M_{j,t}}) \, \hat{y}_{i,t}$$

$$+ (\eta_j \frac{M_{j,t}^D}{M_{j,t}} - \theta_{ij} \frac{M_{i,t}^{FJ}}{M_{i,t}}) \, \hat{y}_{j,t} - (\theta_{ik} \frac{M_{i,t}^{FK}}{M_{i,t}} - \theta_{jk} \frac{M_{j,t}^{FK}}{M_{j,t}}) \, \hat{y}_{k,t}$$

$$+ (\varepsilon_i \frac{M_{i,t}^D}{M_{i,t}} + \delta_i \frac{M_{i,t}^F}{M_{i,t}} + \sigma_i + \alpha_i) \Delta i_{i,t}$$

$$- (\varepsilon_j \frac{M_{j,t}^D}{M_{j,t}} + \delta_j \frac{M_{j,t}^F}{M_{j,t}} + \sigma_j + \alpha_j) \Delta i_{j,t}$$

$$- (\sigma_i - \sigma_j) \Delta i_{w,t} - K_{i,j} \tag{11}$$

If we further simplify and assume $\sigma_i = \sigma_j$, we obtain the final *reduced-
form equation for the rate of change of the spot exchange rate*:

$$\hat{s}_{i,j;t} = - K_{i,j} + (\hat{M}_{i,t} - \hat{M}_{j,t}) - (\eta_i \frac{M_{i,t}^D}{M_{i,t}} - \theta_{ji} \frac{M_{j,t}^{FI}}{M_{j,t}}) \, \hat{y}_{i,t}$$

$$+ (\eta_j \frac{M_{j,t}^D}{M_{j,t}} - \theta_{ij} \frac{M_{i,t}^{FJ}}{M_{i,t}}) \, \hat{y}_{j,t} - (\theta_{ik} \frac{M_{i,t}^{FK}}{M_{i,t}} - \theta_{jk} \frac{M_{j,t}^{FK}}{M_{j,t}}) \, \hat{y}_{k,t}$$

$$+ (\varepsilon_i \frac{M_{i,t}^D}{M_{i,t}} + \delta_i \frac{M_{i,t}^F}{M_{i,t}} + \sigma_i + \alpha_i) \Delta i_{i,t}$$

$$- (\varepsilon_j \frac{M_{j,t}^D}{M_{j,t}} + \delta_j \frac{M_{j,t}^F}{M_{j,t}} + \sigma_j + \alpha_j) \Delta i_{j,t} \tag{12}$$

Since the monetary approach to exchange rates assumes perfect substitutability between foreign and domestic bonds and thus covered interest
parity in international capital markets so that $(1 + i_i)/(1 + i_j) =$
$f_{i,j}/s_{i,j}$ or, as an approximation, $\Delta i_i - \Delta i_j = \hat{f}_{i,j} - \hat{s}_{i,j}$, and if we

revised form in *Journal of International Economics*, no. 2, 1978; idem, *Strategies
for Currency Unification*; Hans Genberg, "Purchasing-Power Parity under Fixed
and Flexible Exchange Rates," *Journal of International Economics*, no. 2, 1978;
idem, "Purchasing-Power Parity as a Rule for a Crawling Peg"; Paul R. Krugman,
"Purchasing Power Parity and Exchange Rates," *Journal of International Economics*, no. 4, 1978; and Alexander K. Swoboda, "Exchange-Rate Flexibility in
Practice: A Selective Survey of Experience since 1973," in Herbert Giersch, ed.,
Macroeconomic Policies for Growth and Stability: A European Perspective
(Tübingen: Mohr, 1981). See also the introduction to this paper.

[34] In equation 11, $M_j{}^{FI}$ denotes money j held by foreign residents of country I;
$M_j{}^{FK}$ money j held by foreigners resident in all countries other than I; etc. Thus:
$M_j{}^{FI} + M_j{}^{FK} = M_j{}^F$.

assume the components of the coefficients of $\Delta i_{i,t}$ and $\Delta i_{j,t}$ in equation 12 to be equal, we may alternatively estimate the following equation:

$$\hat{s}_{i,j;t} = \cfrac{1}{1 + \varepsilon_{i,j}\, M_{i,j;t}^{D}\,/M_{i,j;t} + \delta_{i,j}\, M_{i,j;t}^{F}\,/M_{i,j;t} + \sigma_{i,j} + \alpha_{i,j}}$$
$$\left[-K_{i,i} + (\hat{M}_{i,t} - \hat{M}_{j,t}) - (\eta_i \frac{M_{i,j;t}^{D}}{M_{i,j;t}} - \theta_{ji}\frac{M_{j,t}^{FI}}{M_{j,t}})\,\hat{y}_{i,t} \right.$$
$$+ (\eta_j \frac{M_{i,j;t}^{D}}{M_{i,j;t}} - \theta_{ij}\frac{M_{i,t}^{FJ}}{M_{i,t}})\,\hat{y}_{j,t} + (\varepsilon_{i,j}\frac{M_{i,j;t}^{D}}{M_{i,j;t}}$$
$$\left. + \delta_{i,j}\frac{M_{i,j;t}^{F}}{M_{i,j;t}} + \sigma_{i,j} + \alpha_{i,j})\,\hat{f}_{i,j} \right] \qquad (13)$$

The exchange rate equations 11–13 show that international shifts in the demand for money reduce the exchange-rate effect of differences in real income growth (through θ) but that they increase the exchange-rate effect of changes in exchange rate expectations (through σ). The size of θ and σ can be estimated only in the price-level equation, however, and δ cannot be estimated at all.

The estimation. The estimates relate to the dollar exchange rate of the mark and the Swiss franc in 1973II–1978II.

Each M_i^F comprises not only claims of foreign nonbanks in currency i on banks in the country issuing currency i but also Eurocurrency claims of nonbanks in currency i, provided currency i is not the claimant's own national currency.[35] Because data for own-currency claims on banks in the Eurocurrency market are available only for the dollar, the own-currency component had to be estimated for the other currencies. The method of estimation and all data sources are described in the statistical appendix.

M_i^D relates to M2 (excluding balances held by foreigners). All money-supply series and real-income series are deseasonalized. The money-supply figures are measured in national currency. The world nominal interest rate is approximated by the weighted average of nominal interest rates in seven countries, the weights being given by real income (as a proxy).

Table 7 reports the best exchange-rate estimates obtained after exclusion of all variables whose coefficients were insignificant and did

[35] The German money supply data include foreign currency deposits of German nonbanks with German banks. Data on their volume and currency composition are not published, but they are known to be very small.

TABLE 7
EXCHANGE RATE EQUATIONS, 1973II–1978II

Dependent Variable	Explanatory Variables	$\dfrac{R^2}{\bar{R}^2}$	D.W.

Explanatory Variables with Short-Term Interest Variables

$$\hat{s}_{DM/\$} \quad -2.489 + .061 (\Delta i_{DM}^S - \Delta i_\$^S) + 1.320\,\hat{y}_{US}$$
$$(1.89) \quad (.08) \qquad\qquad (1.42)$$
$R^2 = .101$, $\bar{R}^2 = .001$, D.W. $= 1.82$

$$\hat{s}_{SF/\$} \quad -3.580 + 1.598 (\Delta i_{SF}^S - \Delta i_\$^S) + 2.049\,\hat{y}_{US}$$
$$(4.24^{**}) \quad (3.96^{**}) \qquad\qquad (3.46^{**})$$
$R^2 = .615^{*}$, $\bar{R}^2 = .551$, D.W. $= 1.95$

Explanatory Variables with Forward Exchange Rate Variable

$$\hat{s}_{DM/\$} \quad -.022 + .966\,\hat{f}_{DM/\$} - .067\,\hat{y}_D + .077\,\hat{y}_{US}$$
$$(.20) \quad (56.94^{**}) \quad (.55) \qquad (.82)$$
$R^2 = .996^{*}$, $\bar{R}^2 = .995$, D.W. $= 1.54$

$$\hat{s}_{SF/\$} \quad -.096 + .033\,(\hat{M}_{SF} - \hat{M}_\$) + .946\,\hat{f}_{SF/\$} - .002\,(\hat{y}_{CH} - \hat{y}_{US})$$
$$(.99) \quad (.51) \qquad\qquad (56.67^{**}) \qquad (.10)$$
$R^2 = .996^{*}$, $\bar{R}^2 = .995$, D.W. $= 2.07$

Implicit "Structural" Coefficients

$$\varepsilon_{i,j}\frac{M_{i,j}^D}{M_{i,j}} + \delta_{i,j}\frac{M_{i,j}^F}{M_{i,j}} + \sigma_{i,j} + \alpha_{i,j}$$

	Intercept	$M_i - M_\$$	$\eta_i\dfrac{M_i^D}{M_i} - \theta_{ji}\dfrac{M_j^{FI}}{M_j}$	$\eta_{1j}\dfrac{M_j^{FI}}{M_j} - \theta_{ij}\dfrac{M_j^D}{M_j}$	$\dfrac{M_i^{FJ}}{M_i}$	$\dfrac{M_i^{FK}}{M_i}$	$\theta_{ik}\dfrac{M_i^{FK}}{M_i} - \theta_{jk}\dfrac{M_j^{FK}}{M_j}$
$DM/\$$	-5.50	0	-16.75	$+19.25$	0		$+249.00$
$SF/\$$	-1.78	$+.61$	$.03$	0	0		$+17.52$

NOTE: t-values in parentheses.
* Significant at 5 percent level only.
** Significant at 1 percent level.

205

not take the hypothesized sign. If the change in the short-term[36] interest-rate differential is used (equation 12), the DM equation is totally unsatisfactory, whereas the SF estimate yields significant coefficients for three variables explaining more than 60 percent of the variations of $\hat{s}_{SF}$. In both equations, the constant term—correctly—indicates a considerable real appreciation trend. None of the equations, however, takes a money-supply variable; the probable explanation seems to be the reaction of foreign-exchange interventions to exchange-rate changes noted previously.

If the rate of change of the forward rate $(\hat{f})$ is substituted for the change in the interest-rate differential (see equation 13), the explanatory power of the estimates improves dramatically (to 99.6 percent), but all variables other than $\hat{f}$ now take insignificant coefficients. This result indicates that interest rates and thus interest-rate differentials and forward discounts/premiums vary much less than the spot and forward rates themselves and that the exchange rate is dominated by expectations ("speculation").

Using the fact that

$$\frac{1}{1 + \varepsilon M^D/M + \delta M^F/M + \sigma + \alpha}$$

$$= 1 - \frac{\varepsilon M^D/M + \delta M^F/M + \sigma + \alpha}{1 + \varepsilon M^D/M + \delta M^F/M + \sigma + \alpha} = 1 - \hat{b}_f$$

(where $\hat{b}_f$ is the estimated coefficient of $\hat{f}_{ij}$ in table 7), we can compute the implicit "structural" coefficients as presented in the lower panel of table 7. Unfortunately, the income and expectation variables all take less plausible values than in the equations using interest-rate differentials, and the same is true for the DM intercept. The only improvement is the money-supply coefficient in the SF equation, which is consistent with the unity postulate.

In the price-level equations we have to allow for a lag. Although the time lag cannot plausibly be supposed to differ among the various money demand and supply variables within each equation, there is no need to assume that the common lag of those variables will be the same for both currencies. It was found that the best fit was obtained when using a seven-quarter moving average for the German explanatory variables and a twelve-quarter moving average for the Swiss explanatory variables. Each moving average includes the current quarter and gives the same weight to each quarter included. Explanatory variables that took insignificant coefficients with a "wrong" sign were again

---

[36] Long-term interest rates were also tried but yielded less satisfactory results.

excluded. The following results were obtained (t-values are given in parentheses):

$$\hat{P}_D = \underset{(1.27)}{.512} + \underset{(2.51^*)}{.587 \, \hat{M}_{DM}} - \underset{(2.22^*)}{7.867 \, \hat{y}_{j+k} M^F_{DM} / M_{DM}}$$

$$+ \underset{(2.36^*)}{1.348 \, \Delta i_{DM}} - \underset{(2.62^*)}{2.066 \, \Delta i_w}$$

$$R^2 = .454^* \qquad D.W. = 1.66$$

$$\hat{P}_{CH} = \underset{(.94)}{- 1.089} + \underset{(2.13^*)}{1.170 \, \hat{M}_{SF}} - \underset{(.22)}{.088 \, \hat{y}_{CH} M^{\bar{D}}_{SF} / M_{SF}}$$

$$+ \underset{(3.00^{**})}{3.572 \, \Delta i_{SF}} - \underset{(1.76)}{2.455 \, \Delta i_w}$$

$$R^2 = .610^{**} \qquad D.W. = 2.08$$

As can be seen, the world-interest-rate variable (Δi_w) figures importantly in both equations;[37] moreover, the foreign-income variable takes a significant coefficient in the DM equation. To measure the contribution that these world or foreign variables make toward the equations' explanatory power, the inflation rates were regressed only on these variables. The resulting coefficients of determination amount to 13.2 percent (DM) and 57.2 percent (SF) of the total equations' explanatory power. Because in the DM equation the coefficient of the world-interest-rate variable (that is σ) is larger in absolute terms than the coefficient of the domestic-interest-rate variable (that is, $\varepsilon M^D / M + \delta M^F / M + \sigma$), the explanatory power of demand for DM currency substitution cannot be isolated. For the Swiss franc, however, the estimates are consistent: using the β-weights as approximations to the relative contributions to explanatory power,[38] the results would indicate that cross-currency shifts in the demand for money contributed about 54 percent of the equation's explanatory power and account for about a third of the variations of the Swiss inflation rate.

A similar procedure can be applied to determine the weight of cross-currency shifts in the demand for money in the exchange-rate equations (using the forward rate variable). It yields the result that international shifts in the demand for the Swiss franc account for at least a seventh of the variations of the SF/$ exchange rate changes.

---

[37] An analogous analysis was undertaken for the dollar, pound sterling, French franc, lira, and guilder, but in no case did the coefficient of Δi_w come close to being significant.

[38] This procedure is chosen because, owing to collinearity between Δi_{SF} and Δi_w, the R^2s for $\hat{P}_{SF}$ and Δi_{SF} and for $\hat{P}_{SF}$ and Δi_w add to more than the R^2 (.610) for the complete equation.

The results of this section indicate that the mark and the Swiss franc —unlike all other currencies considered—have been subject to significant international shifts in the demand for money. Several of the estimated coefficients take implausible values, however, or are even inconsistent within or between the equations. Although the estimates may be the best available, they cannot be considered reliable. The deficiencies may be due to (1) inadequate sample size, (2) omission of important variables, (3) the choice of too broad a monetary aggregate, (4) simultaneity bias, and (5) the significant collinearity among several explanatory variables. Little can be done about 1, 3, and 5, but a fuller model and simultaneous-equation estimation may yield some improvements.

Policy Options in the Presence of International Shifts in the Demand for Money. How, if at all, should the Bundesbank and the Nationalbank have reacted to the international shifts in the demand for their currencies? A number of optional policy responses should be considered.

Option 1: Announcements net of international shifts in the demand for money. Given that price-level stability is the only ultimate aim of monetary policy, the "ideal" solution would probably be to preannounce target rates of monetary expansion only net of international shifts in the demand for the national money and to offset all such shifts through compensatory money-supply adjustment. The central banks could still follow a clear and predictable rule for domestic money-supply growth according to the expected growth of the domestic demand for real balances, thus stabilizing monetary-policy expectations and even dampening those short-run fluctuations in output that are not due to monetary-policy instability; but at the same time they would prevent temporary and permanent international shifts in the demand for money (and expectations thereof) from destabilizing national price levels or exchange rates (and expectations thereof).

The problem about this approach is that international shifts in the demand for money cannot be directly observed. In particular, it is not possible to infer from changes in money balances held by foreigners[39] whether foreign demand for the money has changed and in which direction. If, for example, more marks are held by foreigners, this is consistent with both an increase and a decrease of foreign demand for marks; for if at the same time residents' demand for marks decreases and

[39] As has been mentioned, even these cannot be accurately identified. This is because the Eurocurrency statistics do not indicate the precise size of short-term deposits in a currency held by foreign nonbanks. Moreover, what external currency-market data there are become available only on a quarterly basis and with a lag of five months.

does so by more than foreigners' demand for marks, foreigners' nominal holdings of marks will increase (with the DM depreciating), although foreign demand for real mark balances is falling.[40] Of course, this difficulty is merely one implication of the more fundamental point that balance-of-payments statistics (that is, actual quantity movements between countries) do not permit any conclusions about total demand for, and supply of, a money or, for this reason, about its exchange rate.

Option 2: Announcements allowing for expected international shifts in the demand for money. Because international shifts in the demand for money can be verified not from monetary statistics but only, if at all, by tracing such shifts back to their determinants, central banks may base the formulation of their money-supply targets on estimates of the coefficients and the likely values of these determinants (foreign income, foreign interest rates), just as they now tend to allow for expected domestic demand for substitution between money and nonmonetary assets due to changes in the domestic interest rate. According to Schiltknecht, the Nationalbank has actually followed such an anticipatory feedback rule.[41] This may explain why the Nationalbank adopts its monetary target always a few weeks after the Bundesbank.

The problem about this course of action is that, as has been shown earlier, it does not seem possible to generate reliable estimates of the relevant parameters, the more so as a change in the policy is likely to change the parameters. In order to allow for errors about the size of the parameters and, probably even more important, about the future values of the variables concerned, central banks may declare their money supply targets conditional upon whether their parameter estimates prove to be correct. As Finn Kydland and E. C. Prescott have shown, however, iterative adjustment of the parameters may fail to produce convergence.[42] Moreover, if the possibility is to be excluded that central banks (*ab-*) use forecast errors about the values of the determinants to justify deviations from the money supply target that, in fact, are of a discretionary nature, they would have to be asked to announce also the parameter estimates so that the public can verify the feedback rule that is used for the revision of targets.

[40] The empirical evidence for seven major countries in 1973II-1978II shows that, except in the case of sterling, nominal exchange rate changes were not significantly correlated with changes in money balances held by nonresidents of the two countries concerned. See Vaubel, "International Shifts in the Demand for Money."

[41] Schiltknecht, "Monetary Policy under Flexible Exchange Rates," p. 8.

[42] Finn E. Kydland and E. C. Prescott, "Rules Rather Than Discretion: The Inconsistency of Optimal Plans," *Journal of Political Economy*, no. 3, 1977.

209

Option 3: Shorter announcement periods and/or wider target bands. In the presence of intense uncertainty, economic agents tend to shorten the time horizon of their commitments or to insist on escape clauses. The same may hold for the commitments that monetary-policy makers undertake. Whereas Giersch has considered the possibility of shorter announcement periods (or, rather, of not lengthening announcement periods, which he would otherwise have preferred),[43] the Bundesbank has chosen a target band. Just as economic agents are well advised, however, to prefer indexed contracts to shorter maturities and vaguer commitments whenever the source of the increased uncertainty can be measured by ex post indexes, so the monetary authorities would better explain in advance which indicators (indexes) they intend to use to adjust their targets and what their parameters in the feedback rule are (option 2).

Option 4: Announcements of monetary expansion subject to price-level constraints. If, as is assumed here, price-level stability is the aim of monetary policy, there can be no doubt that monetary targets have to be revised if they prove to be (more than temporarily) inconsistent with that aim. The price level, however, is not only the ultimate and, therefore, the only incontrovertible indicator of the appropriateness of monetary policy; it is also a (too) late indicator. If inflation or deflation is already developing (for some time) or if disinflation is already proceeding at an excessive and disruptive speed, revision of monetary targets and policy will come too late to stop the process from continuing for at least another year. What one would like to have is an "early warning indicator" of errors about international shifts in the demand for money.

Option 5: Nominal exchange rate targets. These considerations explain why some authors have wondered whether the problems raised by unpredictable international shifts in the demand for money could be solved by returning from preannounced monetary expansion to pegged exchange rates and why the Swiss Nationalbank has acted in this spirit by setting a ceiling for the DM/Swiss franc exchange rate it would tolerate.[44] Exchange-market pressure would then register international shifts in the demand for money immediately, and the monetary authorities would merely have to adjust their money supplies so as to keep the exchange rate constant. Whereas demand for substitution between

---

[43] Giersch, "Exchange-Rate Surveillance," para. 14.
[44] See Laffer, "Optimal Exchange Rate Systems," p. 35; and Giersch, "Exchange-Rate Surveillance," para. 11.

domestic money and financial assets would be satisfied through open-market operations, demand for currency substitution would be met through foreign-exchange interventions or through open-market operations of opposite sign in both countries concerned.[45]

Although these arguments make sense as far as they go, they can hardly serve to justify the Nationalbank's policy in 1978–1979. After all, the exchange rate target was declared vis-à-vis another currency (the DM), which was subject to similar international shifts of money demand away from the dollar. By linking to the monetary policy of the Bundesbank, which was just as helpless in this situation as the Nationalbank itself, the Swiss authorities obviously could not solve their problem. They could only hope to share it. Thus the Bundesbank and the Nationalbank shared the error of increasing monetary expansion in 1978 to such an extent that inflation in 1979 accelerated by more than the oil price increases of that year could justify.[46]

Because money demand shifted from the dollar to the Swiss franc and the deutsche mark, an obvious possibility would have been to adopt an exchange-rate target with respect to the dollar, and to some extent the dollar purchases by the two central banks must of course be interpreted in this sense. To fix an exchange rate in relation to the dollar would have meant, however, to import U.S. monetary policy and inflation, that is, to go from bad to worse.

---

[45] Note the analogy with Poole's recommendation of nominal interest rate targets in the face of unstable domestic portfolio behavior; see William Poole, "Optimal Choice of Monetary Policy Instruments in a Simple Stochastic Macro Model," *Quarterly Journal of Economics*, no. 2, 1970. The analogy is recognized by Russell S. Boyer ("Optimal Foreign-Exchange Intervention," *Journal of Political Economy*, no. 6, 1978), who concludes from a model not allowing for currency substitutability that foreign-exchange intervention is appropriate only to the extent that disturbances (are expected to) occur in the money market and, more generally, that interventions ought to concentrate on the market in which disturbances are (expected to be) largest. This view is also taken by Stanley W. Black ("The Analysis of Floating Exchange Rates and the Choice between Crawl and Float," in Williamson, *Exchange Rate Rules*) and Hans Genberg ("Purchasing-Power Parity as a Rule for a Crawling Peg," ibid.).

[46] Various members of the Bundesbank and the Nationalbank have indicated that the domestic price level will be allowed to rise to the extent that the deterioration of the terms of trade reduces real income and the demand for money. See, for example, Schiltknecht, "Von der Kreditpolitik zur Geldmengenpolitik," p. 7; and Otmar Emminger, interview with Finanz und Wirtschaft, Zürich, September 29, 1979, reprinted in Deutsche Bundesbank, *Auszüge aus Presseartikeln,* no. 74, 1979. This intention has explicitly been endorsed by the German Sachverständigenrat (1979-1980, para. 182). It is based on the view that the loss of real income or wealth, which the deterioration of the terms of trade implies, should be borne by the owners of domestic monetary and real assets. If that is accepted, symmetry requires that the price level be permitted to *fall* when the terms of trade improve.

Alternatively, the Bundesbank and the Nationalbank might have considered a preannounced crawling peg vis-à-vis the dollar,[47] where the speed of the crawl would have reflected the desired inflation-rate differential plus the considerable[48] real exchange-rate trend in relation to the dollar. But such a preannouncement would have been promising only if monetary policy in the United States and real exchange-rate variations in relation to the dollar had seemed rather predictable in that year. They were not, however, and this is precisely why foreign demand for the dollar was especially volatile at that time. In short, a preannounced crawling peg would have been a satisfactory solution to the problem only if the problem had not existed in the first place.

Option 6: Announcement of monetary expansion subject to real exchange rate constraints. In view of the difficulties that uncertainty about foreign monetary policies implies for a preannounced crawling peg with respect to nominal exchange rates, some economists—notably the Optica Group appointed by the EC Commission and the German Sachverständigenrat (Council of Economic Advisers)—have suggested that unpredictable international shifts in the demand for money should be dealt with by announcing monetary targets subject to the condition that the *real* exchange rate does not change very much.[49] Indeed, both the Bundesbank and the Nationalbank have indicated that their intervention policy vis-à-vis the dollar aims at real exchange-rate stability.[50]

To use real exchange-rate criteria to deal with international shifts in the demand for money is directly analogous to using real interest rate criteria to deal with shifts in portfolio preferences between the domestic currency and other domestic assets. In both cases, relative price changes are assumed to signal changes in money demand. Such changes, however, may also be of a nonmonetary nature, and although there is a trend component in postwar real exchange rate changes, not all "large and abrupt"[51] deviations from it signal monetary shocks and ought to be

[47] This possibility has also been considered by Giersch, "Exchange-Rate Surveillance," para. 58.

[48] In 1973-1978, the real appreciation of the SF and the DM vis-à-vis the dollar amounted to 8.6 percent and 4.5 percent per annum, respectively.

[49] Optica Report 1976, Study Group on Optimum Currency Areas, *Inflation and Exchange Rates,* Commission of the European Communities, D.G. II (Brussels, 1977), pp. 83ff., esp. p. 88. Sachverständigenrat zur Begutachtung der gesamtwirtschaftlichen Entwicklung, 1978-1979, Stuttgart, Mainz, paras. 405-6, 411.

[50] Deutsche Bundesbank, *Monatsbericht,* June 1979, p. 39; Fritz Leutwiler, interview with *Schweizerische Handelszeitung,* September 27, 1979.

[51] This is the Sachverständigenrat's indicator for international shifts in the demand for money (1978-1979, para. 406).

avoided.[52] A large and abrupt real exchange-rate change is likely to be due to: (1) a sudden international shift in the demand for goods and services ("fashion"); (2) a sudden supply shock (for example, an oil-price change caused by the collapse of the OPEC cartel, a discovery of new oil reservoirs, or a political upheaval); and/or (3) an international difference in unexpected changes of the supply of, and demand for, money.

If one of the first two causes applies, the case against a counteractive monetary policy is the same as in the case of trend-oriented real exchange rate changes. If the third cause applies, three cases have to be distinguished. If, first of all, the real exchange-rate change is due to an unexpected and divergent acceleration (or deceleration) of *monetary expansion abroad,* domestic monetary policy should not try to prevent the temporary real appreciation of the domestic currency because to do so would mean to join the foreign countries in their monetary acceleration or deceleration and thus to abandon the domestic price-level target. If, second, the real exchange-rate change is due to unexpected changes in the real determinants of *demand for the foreign money,* a monetary policy designed to avoid real exchange rate changes is likely to imply full transmission of any foreign real shock[53] and, quite possibly, a larger shock to the home country's output than a do-nothing policy.[54] If these two types of monetarily induced real exchange-rate changes are to be prevented from having an unmitigated, though temporary, effect on the domestic price level, domestic money-supply adjustment would have to be partial, its extent depending on the effective weight that import prices occupy in the national price index to be stabilized.[55]

Thus full money-supply adjustment can only be justified if and to the extent that the abrupt and larger-than-normal real exchange rate change must be attributed to an unexpected change in the demand for the domestic money, for example, to an *international shift in the demand for money* between the domestic currency and foreign assets. Because,

---

[52] For critiques of the Optica proposal, see Jürg Niehans, "Dynamic Purchasing Power as a Monetary Rule," in John S. Chipman and Charles P. Kindleberger, eds., *Flexible Exchange Rates and the Balance of Payments* (North Holland, 1980); Harmen Lehment, "Devisenmarktinterventionen"; Roland Vaubel, "A Europe-wide Parallel Currency," in Samuel I. Katz, ed., *U.S.-European Monetary Relations* (Washington, D.C.: American Enterprise Institute, 1979), pp. 181-83; and Genberg, "Purchasing-Power Parity as a Rule for a Crawling Peg," pp. 30-31.

[53] See Enno Langfeldt and Peter Trapp, "Überlegungen zum Kurs der Geldpolitik bei Veränderungen des Währungsraums," mimeographed (Kiel: Institute of World Economics, April 1979), p. 5.

[54] See the numerical example used by Niehans in "Dynamic Purchasing Power," pp. 15-17.

[55] I owe this point to discussions with Reinhard Fürstenberg.

however, "large and abrupt" changes in the real exchange rate are by no means necessarily due to such shifts and disturbances, they cannot be, as such, an automatic indicator of the need for a deviation from the target rate of monetary expansion.[56]

Option 7: Measures to reduce currency substitutability. In view of these difficulties, it must be tempting to deal with the policy problem posed by unpredictable international shifts in the demand for money through measures to reduce currency substitutability. This is the "solution" that Kareken and Wallace have advocated[57] and that the Nationalbank and, to a lesser extent, the Bundesbank have tried with little success.[58]

In 1979 the Bundesbank temporarily launched a campaign to convince the German public and foreign monetary authorities that everything must be done to prevent the mark from taking over a larger part of the dollar's position as an international currency, and especially as an official reserve currency. It gave three major reasons for its policy stance:

> • Owing to the limited capacity of our money and capital markets there would from the outset be a danger of the investment or withdrawal . . . of DM reserves consistently putting an undue strain on the viability of these markets. This would entail fluctuations in liquidity and interest rates which would not be desirable for the domestic economy and which the

[56] With respect to Germany, this conclusion appears to be supported by Lehment's finding that unexplained reductions in the domestic income velocity of M1 were not usually accompanied by real exchange rate appreciation in 1973-1978. As Lehment admits, however, his residuals cannot be interpreted as an indicator of international shifts in the demand for money because they may also reflect demand shifts between money and domestic nonmonetary assets and because, owing to the use of a monetary aggregate (M1) that does not include foreigners' holdings of the money, they must temporarily signal an unexplained *increase* of the demand for real balances (i.e., an unexplained reduction of velocity) when the increase in residents' holdings of the money is in fact due merely to a *reduction* of foreigners' demand for the money.

[57] John Kareken and Neil Wallace, "International Monetary Reform: The Feasible Alternatives," *Federal Reserve Bank of Minneapolis Quarterly Review,* Summer 1978, p. 7. For a critique, see Gottfried Haberler, "Flexible Exchange Rate Theories and Controversies Once Again," in John S. Chipman and Charles P. Kindleberger, eds., *Flexible Exchange Rates and the Balance of Payments* (North Holland, 1980).

[58] From the end of 1974 to the end of 1979, the Nationalbank imposed a negative interest rate on foreigners' SF deposits in excess of historical ceilings. In Germany, the acquisition by nonresidents of domestic money-market paper and domestic bonds maturing within four years was subject to authorization, and in principle the Bundesbank did not grant such authorization.

Bundesbank would not always be able to offset. . . . Germany's economic policy makers would eventually be faced with the choice either of allowing the exchange rate of the DM to rise consistently faster than was justified by the inflation differential and tolerating the resultant shifts in the structure of the domestic economy (which would have disastrous economic policy consequences . . .) or of restraining the movement of the exchange rate . . . which would entail the risk of an inflationary expansion of the domestic money stock.

• Compared with the risks of assuming the reserve function, the possible advantages for a country [such as] Germany . . . are rather questionable. . . . In the case of Germany, . . . the view that the country of issue . . . derives seigniorage from its reserve role . . . would be a highly theoretical notion. On the one hand, the assets held in DM would normally bear a considerable real rate of interest and therefore not be without cost. On the other, the reserve role of a currency is incompatible in the long run with deficits on current account. . . . Sustained large-scale current account deficits would very soon lead to a loss of confidence and thus preclude the build-up of a reserve currency from the start. So far Germany has derived no significant real economic benefit from the investment of monetary reserves in DM, if only because the German current account has almost always been in substantial surplus. . . . The accumulation of DM reserves by foreign central banks has therefore mainly been reflected in the dollar holdings of the Budesbank. At the moment interest rates on these are higher than those on DM liabilities to foreign monetary authorities, but hitherto this interest rate advantage has not nearly offset the decline in the dollar against the DM. . . . Germany has thus relieved the diversifiers of the exchange risk on their dollar assets without receiving any quid pro quo.

• A "system" of several reserve currencies, such as would be the outcome of an unrestrained diversification process, would be a highly unstable structure, exposed to the risks of constant exchange rate unrest and uncontrolled development of international liquidity. . . . The limitation of the reserve role of the DM is therefore not only in the German interest; it seems to be desirable from an international point of view as well.[59]

[59] These are quotations from Deutsche Bundesbank, "The Deutsche Mark as an International Investment Currency," Monthly Report, November 1979, p. 33. The arguments have recurred in various speeches by members of the Bundesbank Direktorium and the federal chancellor.

The first and the last argument have been echoed by the president of the Swiss Nationalbank with respect to the Swiss franc.[60]

The *first* argument rather aptly states the policy problems mentioned above that are raised by unpredictable and not directly identifiable shifts in the demand for money across currencies. It conceals, however, the strictly temporary nature of all real exchange-rate changes that may be caused by such shifts; their duration is no longer than the lag of price-level adjustment. For this reason, even serious policy errors with regard to international money-demand shifts will hardly have "disastrous consequences."

More generally, the Bundesbank's appraisal of the costs that a larger international role for the mark might have for Germany reveals a high degree of risk aversion. The Bundesbank's attitude resembles that of a (non-?) banker who refuses to accept deposits because banking involves intermediation risk. More generally, it resembles that of a (non-?) entrepreneur who refuses to produce (for example, money) because errors about optimal output may lead to losses. More specifically, monopolists and particularly civil servants may refuse to enter competitive markets because they prefer a quiet life.

Second, as for the benefits for Germany, is it true that Germany would not earn more external seigniorage? Seigniorage gains are by no means confined to the issuers of assets that do not bear interest. Seigniorage is the "monopoly" profit from the production of money. Any money producer who faces a less than perfectly elastic demand for his product—that is, for whose product there are no perfect substitutes—can gain seigniorage. An increase in foreign demand for its currency or assets denominated in its currency enables the issuing country to borrow at a lower cost—that is, at a lower real interest rate—from foreign savers than it otherwise could.[61] The extent to which the increase in net short-term capital imports leads to an increase of private long-term capital exports or to an increase in net imports of goods is irrelevant to the seigniorage issue. An increase in income is an increase in income regardless of whether it is consumed or saved.

If the savings are badly invested, the original income gain may of course be wasted or even turned into a loss. In the past such losses have recurred because the Bundesbank has issued its marks in exchange

---

for U.S. treasury bills rather than German government debt.[62] Is the Bundesbank essentially complaining about its own mistaken investment policies? If the past is a guide to the future, it would be in Germany's interest to leave the export of capital to the private sector.

Alternatively, if the gain is consumed and a current account deficit develops, this need not undermine international confidence in the mark. The mark will weaken in the exchange market only if the Bundesbank permits the supply of marks to increase more than foreign and domestic demand for them.

Third, is international currency competition undesirable from an international point of view? Competition disciplines those who try to supply their product at too high a price. It is a check on those money producers who raise the opportunity cost of holding money through inflation and who reduce their output—that is, real balances.[63] If international shifts in the demand for money have been responsible for the dollar's and sterling's weakness in the exchange markets, they have played an important role in inducing the Federal Reserve System and the Bank of England to correct their monetary policies. International shifts in the demand for money are not the cause of monetary instability but its consequence and symptom and serve as an important element of the corrective feedback mechanism. Where "voice" does not help, "exit" usually does.[64] By permitting "entry" and "exit," the Bundesbank and the Nationalbank can do the world a service.

Why then do both central banks object to an extended international role for their currencies? A public-economics approach yields two complementary explanations. The first is that all competition is a public good and that currency competition is an international public good: the

[62] International reserves currently account for about 70 percent of the Bundesbank's assets. Lehment ("Devisenmarktinterventionen") has calculated that in 1970-1978 the Bundesbank's foreign exchange reserves were subject to larger depreciation losses (DM44 billion) than they earned interest (DM33 billion) and that interest earnings would have been DM10 billion higher if the Bundesbank had held German government debt instead of dollars. The total loss (DM54 billion) is equivalent to 30 percent of German federal government debt outstanding at the end of 1978.

[63] These ideas are developed in much more detail in Friedrich A. von Hayek, *Choice in Currency: A Way to Stop Inflation,* Occasional Papers, no. 48 (London: Institute of Economic Affairs, 1976); idem, *Denationalization of Money,* Hobard Paper Special, no. 70 (London: Institute of Economic Affairs, 1976, rev. and enlarged 1978); Girton and Roper, "Theory and Implications of Currency Substitution"; idem, "Substitutable Monies and the Monetary Standard," 1978; Roland Vaubel, "Free Currency Competition," *Weltwirtschaftliches Archiv,* no. 3, 1977; idem, *Strategies for Currency Unification.*

[64] Compare Albert O. Hirschman, *Exit, Voice, and Loyalty: Responses to Decline in Firms, Organizations, and States* (Cambridge: Harvard University Press, 1970).

benefits accrue to all money holders and are largely external to the entering country. Second, within the country, the benefits are reaped primarily by private money holders (a reduced inflation tax), private borrowers (improved "terms of finance") and possibly by taxpayers (increased external seigniorage), whereas the cost in terms of increased monetary policy risks falls squarely on the central bankers, the more so because bureaucrats tend to be held responsible for the errors they commit rather than the opportunities they miss.

Conclusion. The analysis of the various policy options shows that there is no neat short-term solution to the policy problems caused by international shifts in the demand for money. The only neat solution is of a medium-term or long-term nature: the return to price-level stability in all major industrial countries. Europe in addition might reduce its problems by replacing the existing inflating national currencies by a common currency. In contrast, an adjustable-peg system (like the European Monetary System) is certainly no answer to the problem.[65]

If U.S. monetary policy became more predictable (and, by implication, less inflationary)[66] and if the hope were well founded that real shocks in the world economy (and thus equilibrium deviations from international real exchange rate trends) will be much smaller in the 1980s than in the 1970s, individual European countries might, for the time being, adopt a preannounced crawling peg vis-à-vis the dollar. The latter hope at least seems to be a pious one, however.

How then might national monetary authorities deal with international shifts in the demand for money as long as the neat solutions are not attainable? Because such shifts seem to be neither sufficiently predictable nor even clearly verifiable, should monetary policy authorities behave as if these shifts did not exist and firmly stick to their traditional targets, even where there is evidence that the shifts are substantial? Or should money-supply targets be made "conditional" on real exchange-rate performance? Should they be given up altogether?

The author agrees with those who consider monetary preannouncement an indispensable precondition for a satisfactory functioning of a flexible exchange rate system. Without credible *long-term* preannouncement of the rules governing future monetary expansion, expectations are unstable and exchange rates erratic.[67] To the extent that international

[65] This point has been argued in more detail in Vaubel, "Return to the New European Monetary System," sec. 1.

[66] See above, n. 30.

[67] This was predicted by Meade twenty-five years ago: "The system of fluctuating

shifts in the demand for money can be shown to be a function of some more or less predictable variables, such as real income growth at home and abroad and international interest-rate relatives, such shifts should be taken into account when formulating the money-supply targets (option 2). The targets should then be revised automatically according to the estimated parameters (which should be published) if those variables take other values than expected. The results of this section, however, provide no basis for the hope that international shifts in the demand for money may be traced back to a sufficiently simple and reliable relationship. As long as such a relationship cannot be found, international shifts in the demand for money of small economies require that preannounced targets be subject to an implicit or explicit emergency clause. An emergency would arise if there were persistent deviations from the intended price level or—preferably within the limits of a monetary target band—if an exceptionally large and intolerably disruptive temporary real exchange-rate change could plausibly be attributed *only* to large international shifts in the demand for money. Such a retreat from unconditional monetary preannouncement is not without risks.[68] As Friedman noted in 1967,

> monetary policy can contribute to offsetting major disturbances in the economic system arising from other sources . . . though experience is not very encouraging that it can do so without going too far. . . . Experience suggests that the path of wisdom is to use monetary policy explicitly to offset other disturbances only when they offer a "clear and present danger."[69]

---

exchange rates will operate with fully smooth effectiveness only if it is built on the fairly solid foundation of reasonable domestic stability in the main countries. . . . If [money holders] cannot rely upon reasonable stability in the general level of domestic prices and costs, then they will have to speculate not only on the future of domestic underlying real factors, but also upon the future of domestic financial policies. . . . It is possible that this speculation against the currency may itself give rise to the very evils whose expectation has motivated the speculation in the first place." (James E. Meade, "The Case for Variable Exchange Rates," *Three Banks Review*, no. 27, 1955, pp. 19-20).

[68] This is witnessed by the fact that the Bundesbank uses the limited discretion afforded by the target band to respond also to developments other than international shifts in the demand for money.

[69] Milton Friedman, "The Role of Monetary Policy," *American Economic Review*, vol. 58, no. 1, 1968, p. 14. In a sense, of course, international shifts in the demand for money are always due to monetary policy, but it may be changes in *foreign* monetary policy that induce them.

Statistical Appendix: Concepts and Sources

CBM   Central bank money, *Germany,* seasonally adjusted. Source: Deutsche Bundesbank, *Monatsberichte.*

EFEX   Effective exchange rate (units of domestic currency per unit of trade-weighted foreign currencies), MERM. Source: International Monetary Fund, *International Financial Statistics.*

EO   Incoming export orders (values). *Germany:* manufacturing industry, seasonally adjusted. Source: Deutsche Bundesbank, *Saisonbereinigte Wirtschaftszahlen. Switzerland:* engineering industry. Source: *Verein Schweizerischer Maschinenindustrieller.*

ES   Export share in world exports (values at market exchange rates vis-à-vis U.S. dollar). Calculated from IMF *International Financial Statistics.* The same is true for the rate of change of world export volumes.

EVO   Export volumes. *Germany:* seasonally adjusted. Source: Deutsche Bundesbank, *Saisonbereinigte Wirtschaftszahlen. Switzerland,* source: Schweizerische Nationalbank, *Monatsberichte.*

MB   Monetary base, *Switzerland.* Source: Schweizerische Nationalbank, *Monatsberichte.*

M1   Demand deposits and currency in circulation. *Germany:* seasonally adjusted. Source: Deutsche Bundesbank, *Saisonbereinigte Wirtschaftszahlen. Switzerland,* source: Schweizerische Nationalbank, *Monatsberichte* (except table 3; see sources indicated there).

REFEX   Real effective exchange rate on CPI basis. Sources: 1966–1978, Genberg; for definition, see Genberg, "Purchasing-Power Parity under Fixed and Flexible Rates"; 1979, Schweizerische Nationalbank, *Monatsberichte;* and own estimates.

TB   Trade balance (values in national currency). *Germany:* seasonally adjusted. Source: Deutsche Bundesbank, *Saisonbereinigte Wirtschaftszahlen. Switzerland,* source: Schweizerische Nationalbank, *Monatsberichte.*

ΔIR Changes in international reserves. *Germany:* Change in foreign-exchange reserves minus change in net liabilities with respect to foreign monetary authorities minus DM interventions in the snake and European Monetary System, respectively. Sources: Deutsche Bundesbank, *Monatsberichte,*

Geschäftsberichte; Otmar Emminger, "The D-Mark in the Conflict between Internal and External Equilibrium, 1948–1975," Essays in International Finance, no. 122 (Princeton, N.J.: Princeton University, June 1977), table 5; *Switzerland:* Changes in international reserves. Source: Schweizerische Nationalbank, *Monatsberichte.*

Δln   All rates of change relate to the preceding quarter and are expressed as rates of change per annum.

Money supply held by residents domestically (monthly data). Germany, M2 seasonally adjusted. Source: Deutsche Bundesbank, *Saisonbereinigte Wirtschaftszahlen.* Switzerland, M1 plus savings deposits. Source: Schweizerischen Nationalbank, *Monatsberichte,* own seasonal adjustment.

Claims on foreign banks (by currency, by nationality of creditor, type of claimant, in Eurocurrency system versus in country of origin, etc.). Source: Bank for International Settlements; end of quarter data, own seasonal adjustment.

Real income. Germany: real GNP, seasonally adjusted. Source: Deutsche Bundesbank, *Monatsberichte.* Switzerland: real industrial production, seasonally adjusted. Source: OECD/MEI.

Consumer price indexes. Source: IMF/*International Financial Statistics* (*IFS*).

Forward exchange rates vis-à-vis U.S. dollar (90 days). Source: IMF/*IFS.*

Interest rates. Eurodollar, London (90 days). Source: IMF/*IFS.* All other currencies: In order to avoid discrepancies between the results from equations 12 and 13 that might result from imperfect covered interest arbitrage, the interest rates for all other currencies were calculated from the Eurodollar interest rate and the forward exchange rate under the assumption of standardized covered interest parity.

Total money supply (M_i). This is the sum of money supply in currency i held domestically by (nonbank) residents ($= M_i^D$), claims of foreign nonbanks in currency i on banks in country i ($= M_i^{LXI}$), claims of nonbanks in currency i on banks in the Eurocurrency system ($= M_i^{LXE}$). For the Swiss franc, only data on claims of all foreigners on banks in Switzerland are available; the nonbank claims (M_{SF}^{LXI}) were calculated by assuming that the nonbank share for the Swiss franc is the same as for the current average of the other currencies.

221

For M_i^{LXE}, the nonbank share is reported only for the dollar and the total of the other six currencies. It was therefore assumed that the share of nonbank creditors in total creditors was the same for those six currencies.

Foreign currency claims of nonbanks on foreign banks (M_i^F). These were calculated in three steps. In the first step, total foreign currency liabilities of European banks were purged for each currency (except the dollar, for which the relevant statistics are available) of those foreign currency liabilities that are denominated in the home currency of the creditor. This was done by regressing the total Eurocurrency claims of the nationals of each country on total Eurocurrency claims in their home currency and on total Eurocurrency claims in the other currencies over the period 1967I–1978II (the intercept was suppressed). Total Eurocurrency claims in that home currency were then purged of that constant part (given by the variable's regression coefficient) that can be attributed to currency nationals. Thus the following own-currency proportions were estimated for the foreign-currency liabilities of European banks by currency: 0.033 percent for the DM and 0.301 percent for the SF. For the dollar a regression of Eurodollar claims of U.S. residents on total Eurodollar claims yielded an average own-currency proportion of 0.083. It should be noted that the purging of Eurocurrency deposits in the DM and the SF does not affect their rates of change over time.

In a second step, the purged series—namely, foreign-currency claims on the Eurocurrency system—were multiplied by the proportion of Eurocurrency claims held by nonbanks, which had already been used to calculate M_i^{LXE} for each currency.

Finally, the resulting foreign-currency claims of nonbanks on the Eurocurrency system were added to the foreign currency claims of nonbanks on banks in the country issuing the currency (M_i^{LXI}) to yield M_i^F.

The Value of the Yen

Michael W. Keran

The purpose of this paper is to examine the exchange value of the yen since the movement to flexible exchange rates. The paper is divided into two sections. The first, which is concerned with exchange-rate policy, explores the views of the Japanese government on intervention in the exchange market. The second section deals with exchange-rate determination and, in particular, with the dominant market forces operating on the exchange rate.

The conclusions to be drawn from the first section are that the Japanese have gradually withdrawn from the position of determining a target exchange rate and that, as a result, market forces have played an increasingly important role in the determination of the exchange rate. In the second section it will be shown that the most important market forces determining the exchange rate are the underlying monetary disturbances determined by monetary policy in the United States and Japan and real shocks affecting the terms of trade associated, in particular, in recent years with the price of oil.

Japan's Exchange-Rate Policy

Has Japan attempted to manage its exchange rate since 1973 as a deliberate instrument of policy, or was the exchange rate determined primarily in the marketplace by the normal forces of supply and demand? If market forces dominated, this does not, of course, rule out the fact that macroeconomic policies (but not exchange-rate policies per se) were an important element in influencing the exchange rate.

Exchange-Rate Strategies. There are at least three potential strategies for foreign exchange-market intervention: (1) to prevent disorderly

The views expressed in this paper are those of the author and not necessarily those of the Federal Reserve Bank of San Francisco or the Federal Reserve System.

markets; (2) to slow the market adjustment by "leaning against the wind"; (3) to establish either a moving or a fixed exchange-rate target. I will argue that although strategies 1 and 2 are still being followed, strategy 3 has been abandoned. There are three elements in this argument. First, the economic case for exchange-rate management has largely been dissipated by changing economic circumstances. Second, the political pressure toward setting exchange-rate targets has been largely neutralized by the rise in new special-interest groups. Third, given Japan's major moves toward liberalization of trade and capital, the technical ability to hit an exchange-rate target is limited.

Economic considerations. In a period of relatively low inflation and underuse of labor, government actions to expand output and exports provide an obvious neomercantilist case for targeting an undervalued exchange rate. In the 1950s and 1960s Japan had a "dual labor market": a high-wage, high-productivity advanced sector associated with exports and a low-wage, low-productivity sector associated with (potential) import-competing and service industries. An undervalued yen was considered an appropriate tool for expanding employment in the high-wage sector.

In the present environment, in which the dual labor market has virtually been eliminated and wages are roughly the same throughout the export and service industries, the rationale for artificially induced export growth is greatly weakened. Furthermore, the economic costs of an undervalued yen are more apparent when inflation is high. One potential antiinflation policy would be to target an increasingly overvalued yen.

Japan does not appear to have suffered a loss of international market shares as a result of an almost 60 percent appreciation of the yen between 1971 and 1978. Japan's exports as a share of the exports of industrial countries have increased from 10.3 percent to 12.1 percent during that seven-year period. This macroindicator confirms the casual impression that Japanese exports have continued to sell well on the basis of quality, if not price. The Japanese have done well in the flexible rate environment.

Political considerations. The dominant political forces in Japan are the interests of producers rather than the interests of consumers. In the past it was believed that the interests of producers were dominated by export considerations and that they therefore encouraged an undervalued yen. In recent years, however, there has been a strong surge of interest on the part of producers on the import side. This change has reflected in a particularly striking way the changed role of the Japanese

224

trading companies. In the present market environment, the most success-ful Japanese exporters, such as those in automobiles and machinery, tend to handle export sales through their own foreign sales networks. As a result, trading companies have tended to lose out on the most rapidly growing export markets. The traditional trading company–related export industries—sundry goods, textiles, and steel—are relatively weak export industries now. In response to these market factors, trading companies have increased their concentration on imports. They now are important in the marketing of oil, for example. This has come about because as the Organization of Petroleum Exporting Countries (OPEC) has taken greater control of the sale of oil, there has been a shift from long-term contract markets to spot markets for Japanese oil imports, and the trading companies handle most of the spot-market purchases of oil. In general, the shift in emphasis by the trading companies from heavy involvement in exports to heavy involvement in imports has created a strong and important group interested in avoiding an under-valued exchange rate.

In another example, even the traditional export industries, such as steel, are also importers of raw materials. They have benefited from appreciation of the yen in the form of reduced costs of their inputs. Furthermore, the U.S. trigger pricing system, imposed to reduce Japanese competition with U.S. steel producers, has led to higher export prices and improved the profits of the Japanese steel industry. (The Japanese steel industry now enjoys monopoly rents, thanks to the U.S. Treasury.)

Since the emergence of producer interest groups on the import side, balancing the longstanding producer interest group on the export side, there now appears to be an equal balancing of special interests in support of appreciation or depreciation of the yen.

Technical considerations. Japanese officials who are used to hav-ing a strong influence on domestic economic conditions have found their ability to influence the exchange rate substantially limited. There is a feeling among officials of the Bank of Japan that the massive amount of intervention they have been willing to engage in has had only a temporary effect on the exchange value of the yen. The average month-to-month variation of the yen has been at least as great as that of the Swiss franc, a currency in which intervention by the central bank has been modest until recently. The one time the Bank of Japan intervened sufficiently to hold the exchange rate unchanged was August 15–29, 1971. In that brief period, international currency holdings of the Bank of Japan literally went off the chart, rising 69 percent in ten trading days. When the Bank of Japan withdrew after that massive interven-tion, the value of the yen appreciated immediately.

225

In the period since the move to flexible exchange rates in 1973, there has been a substantial net increase in the international reserve holdings of the Bank of Japan. It is difficult, however, to attribute this to attempts to hold down the rate of appreciation of the yen. It may, in fact, represent no more than normal growth in demand for international reserves associated with growth in the value of international transactions. Most countries have exhibited a rise in international reserve holdings during the same period, whether or not their currencies have appreciated. This suggests a demand motive for increasing reserves rather than an intervention motive. Recent research suggests that the demand for international reserves continues to be a function of the level and variance of the international transactions even in an era of flexible exchange rates.[1]

Implications for the Exchange Rate. The logical consequence of the decision not to target the exchange rate is to have it determined in the marketplace. Japanese officials assert that if market determination of exchange rates is to be efficient and to represent a competitive equilibrium, there should be as little government interference as possible. These same officials assure foreign visitors that they are taking every precaution to avoid influencing the foreign exchange markets—either directly in reducing exchange controls or indirectly to avoid "moral suasion."

Government officials describe Japan's position on exchange controls as follows: With respect to the current account, import liberalization has been largely completed with the exception of the limited number of agricultural products. Nontariff barriers are also coming down. Japan has become at least as open as the average of the Western European countries. With respect to the capital account, liberalization can be divided into two classes: first, the easing of restrictions on Japanese residents' purchase of foreign securities; second, the easing of restrictions on the purchase of Japanese securities by foreigners.

The Japanese have followed a general trend toward capital liberalization of the first class (purchase of foreign securities by Japanese residents); they have no intention of reversing this action unless they are faced with an unexpectedly severe threat to the yen, which might add greatly to the rate of inflation or cause a loss in international confidence in the yen.

[1] Jacob A. Frenkel, "The Monetary Approach to the Exchange Rate: Doctrinal Aspects and Empirical Evidence," in Jacob Frenkel and Harry G. Johnson, eds., *The Economics of Exchange Rates* (Reading, Mass.: Addison-Wesley, 1978).

With respect to the second class of actions—the easing of restrictions on the purchase of Japanese securities by foreigners—some backtracking has occurred from time to time. It is emphasized, however, that this class of restrictions is perfectly consistent with the actions that the Europeans, especially the Germans and the Swiss, have taken to discourage capital inflows into their currencies when there was an appreciation.

Intervention behavior. Do the statements of official government intent match actual behavior? Has intervention, supported by capital controls, been systematically directed toward hitting a target exchange rate? Or has liberalization of trade and capital progressed so far that intervention, beyond a strategy of leaning against the wind, is no longer a viable choice? In an IMF staff paper this proposition is tested and the conclusion is reached that Japanese intervention was of the leaning-against-the-wind variety through 1976.[2] A simple extension of those tests through 1979 supports the assumption that the strategy still applies.

An intervention strategy of leaning against the wind would mean that the exchange rate on the average through longer periods—such as six months—would most likely be independent of the level of intervention. This does not preclude the possibility, however, that exchange rates during shorter periods—say one month—would be affected by intervention. This possibility was tested by estimating exchange-rate and reserve relations for intervals of one month and six months. The results, using data from July 1973 to July 1979, indicate no statistical difference between the one-month and six-month coefficient values.

This test would not distinguish whether the behavior of the Bank of Japan was different in those periods when the yen appreciated than in those periods when the yen depreciated. A target exchange-rate policy can be implemented only by resisting exchange-rate appreciation and taking no action when the exchange rate depreciates. Thus, an additional test was to split the sample period into months of appreciation and months of depreciation and reestimate the same equation. The results indicate that there was no statistically significant difference in either the constant term or the slope coefficient between months of appreciation and months of depreciation.

The conclusions to be derived from these results are (1) that there is strong empirical evidence in support of a strategy of leaning against the wind by the Bank of Japan; (2) that there is some evidence—admitted to be indirect—that the monthly average value of the yen was

[2] P. J. Quirk, "Exchange Rate Policy in Japan: Leaning against the Wind," *IMF Staff Papers,* November 1977.

227

not significantly affected by intervention; (3) that to the extent that the exchange rate has been influenced by intervention, the results reported in the next section will be biased. The extent of the bias is apt to be small, however, because the effect of intervention (if not zero) was certainly not large.

Determination of the Exchange Rate

In its most general form, the exchange rate can be thought of as the price that clears the market for the international supply of and demand for goods and services and financial assets. An excess supply would depreciate the exchange rate; excess demand would appreciate the exchange rate. This international market can be modeled with the use of the balance of payments identity. A balance of payments surplus would represent excess demand for goods, services, and financial assets of a country. Conversely, a balance of payments deficit would imply an excess supply. We shall consider three alternative approaches to exchange rate determination:

1. the portfolio approach
2. the income/expenditure approach
3. the monetary approach

Each theory of exchange-rate determination can use the balance-of-payments identity as a starting point. Table 1 summarizes the differences among these three approaches and shows how each is related to the balance-of-payments identity. The column headings show the markets that are analyzed (money, goods, and bonds and other assets). The stub lists alternative approaches to modeling the exchange rate. The X's indicate which markets are analyzed by which model.[3] Analysis of the supply-and-demand behavior in each market will specify those factors that determine the exchange rate according to the model. As a general proposition, behavior in the goods market determines the trade (or current-account) balance, behavior in the bond (or asset) market determines the capital account, and behavior in the money market determines change in international reserves. To close the system, we also know that in a fixed-rate regime the change in international reserves must by definition equal the current account plus the capital account of the balance of payments. In a flexible-rate regime the change

---

[3] This refers to explicit analysis. It is recognized that certain implicit assumptions are also made about the markets that are not explicitly modeled. Specifically, Walras's law assumes that equilibrium in $N - 1$ markets implies equilibrium in the Nth market.

TABLE 1
ALTERNATIVE APPROACHES TO DETERMINATION OF THE EXCHANGE RATE

	Market		
Approach	Money	Goods	Bonds and other assets
1. Income/ expenditure		X	
2. Portfolio		X	X
3. Monetary	X		
Foreign-exchange market	International reserves/ exchange rate	Current account (trade balance)	Capital account

in the exchange rate is a function of the current and capital accounts of the balance of payments.

The simple income/expenditure approach focuses primarily on the goods market and through this the effect of the current account on the exchange rate. The portfolio approach is the most comprehensive in the sense that it integrates both the goods and the bond markets to analyze capital- as well as current-account effects on the exchange rate. Finally, the monetary approach considers, not the components of the balance of payments directly, but rather the need to clear any domestic excess supply of money in the foreign-exchange market, through either a change in international reserves or a change in the exchange rate.

Although each approach views the economy in a different way, any of these approaches can be made logically consistent with the others. The key question is which approach provides the most useful way of organizing the empirical evidence better to understand the operation of the economy in general and the determination of exchange rates in particular.[4]

[4] This discussion analyzes the yen/dollar exchange rate rather than the trade-weighted exchange rate for the following reasons: (1) much of the recent theoretical literature is presented in terms of the bilateral exchange rate; (2) from a policy point of view, the key exchange rate for Japan is that with the dollar; (3) a multilateral trade-weighted index of the yen's foreign exchange value moves closely with the yen/dollar rate.

The Portfolio Approach. A major change in professional economic opinion in recent years is reflected in the shift in focus from the goods market and the current account to the bond market and the capital account as the major determinants of the exchange rate. This shift is explicit in the portfolio approach and implicit in the monetary approach.

The portfolio approach considers both the goods and the bond markets. The goods-market analysis determines the exchange rate that equalizes the supply and demand for goods—that is, equilibrium in the trade (or current account) balance. Asset-market analysis determines the exchange rate that equalizes the desired and actual stock of bonds— that is, equilibrium in the capital account of the balance of payments.

The exchange rate that is consistent with equilibrium in both the goods and the bond markets may not always be the same. Because asset markets adjust more quickly than goods markets, the exchange rate in the short run is determined in the asset market. In the long run, both markets must be in equilibrium at the same exchange rate by means of a dynamic adjustment process that works along the following lines: Assuming an initial condition of long-run equilibrium in both goods and bond markets, a change in the relative supply of assets in one country will induce a rise in real interest rates, an inflow of capital, and appreciation of the exchange rate. This appreciation would throw the goods market out of equilibrium by creating a trade deficit (or a smaller surplus). Gradually, however, the cumulative trade deficit (which creates an excess supply of domestic bonds available to foreigners) will depreciate the exchange rate back toward its old level. Eventually foreign demand for domestic bonds would be cleared through an increase in the quantity of bonds held rather than through the exchange rate. In the long run, the goods and bond markets would be back in equilibrium at the old exchange rate.

Testing of the portfolio approach is still in an early stage. I do not feel qualified to explore the empirical relations until there is a greater sense of professional agreement on the appropriate empirical measures.

The monetary approach, with its focus on the supply and demand for money, does not have the "structural richness" to distinguish explicitly between adjustments in the bond and in the goods markets. It is consistent, however, with the portfolio approach. Before considering the monetary approach, we should first see whether the income/ expenditure approach provides an adequate explanation of the exchange value of the yen.

The Income/Expenditure Approach. The income/expenditure approach is based on early Keynesian models of the goods market and focuses on the current account, more specifically on the trade-balance component of the balance of payments. There are historical and theoretical reasons for this approach. Historically, in the case of fixed exchange rates, most of the variation in the balance of payments in Japan and in other non-reserve-currency countries has been associated with variations in the balance of trade.[5] It was not unnatural to assume that this same relation would hold in a period of flexible exchange rates.

Theoretically, there are two links between the balance of trade and the exchange rate. One is the "income effect," in which the dominant influence runs from the balance of trade to the exchange rate; the other is the substitution, or relative-price, effect, which goes from the exchange rate to the balance of trade. With the income effect, a decline in income and imports will improve the balance of trade and lead to an appreciation of the exchange rate; with the substitution effect, an exchange-rate appreciation will lead to substitution of exports for imports and a decline in the balance of trade. In the short run, however—that is, through the business cycle—the income effect generally dominates the substitution effect, because it usually takes longer for prices than for income to affect trade flows.[6] Figure 1 shows that the income effect appears to dominate in the Japanese case, because normal trade surpluses have been associated with yen appreciation and deficits with yen depreciation. It has been asserted in Japanese policy circles that the

[5] Under a fixed- (or adjusted-peg-) exchange-rate regime, there was a relatively close link between the trade balance and the overall balance of payments because of business-cycle considerations. A business cycle expansion in income would eventually induce a rise in imports in excess of exports and a decline in the balance of trade. Except in the relatively rare instances where there was an expectation of exchange-rate change, there would be only a moderate offsetting capital inflow due to higher than average interest rates. Thus a decline in the trade balance generally was associated with a decline in the balance of payments, which induced the monetary authorities to follow a tighter monetary policy. The resulting decline in income and imports would restore the trade balance to its trend value. This quasi–gold standard behavior would ensure that a country's price level would stay in line with prices of major trading partners. This ensured approximate purchasing power parity with a fixed exchange rate.

The major exception to this adjustment mechanism was the United States, since the dollar was the major reserve currency in the system. U.S. trade deficits did not induce changes in U.S. monetary policy. Thus in the late 1960s U.S. prices got out of line with those of its major trading partners and led to strong expectations of exchange-rate change to reestablish purchasing power parity. This destroyed the post–World War II fixed-exchange-rate regime.

[6] Substitution-effect equations were estimated with the trade balance as the dependent variable. These results indicate that it takes from eighteen to twenty-four months for a change in the exchange rate to affect the trade balance. The elasticity is approximately 2.0 for the trade balance in real terms and 1.0 for the trade balance in nominal terms. Thus the Marshall-Lener conditions are satisfied. As indicated in the text, the income effect from the trade balance to the exchange rate is complete in just six months.

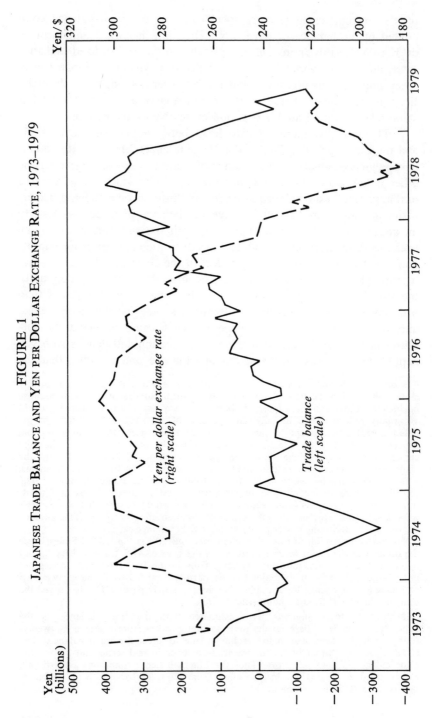

FIGURE 1

JAPANESE TRADE BALANCE AND YEN PER DOLLAR EXCHANGE RATE, 1973–1979

close association between the exchange rates and the trade balance validates the income/expenditure approach in the Japanese case. A close association is confirmed by the regression analysis of the balance of trade and the exchange rate for the period July 1974 to August 1979.

$$\Delta \ln (¥/\$)_t = -.005 - \sum_{j=0}^{6} .79 \, \Delta \ln (EX/IM)_{t-j}$$

$$(-2.0) \qquad (-4.2)$$

$$\bar{R}^2 = .221$$
$$SE = .0203$$
$$DW = 1.56$$

The exchange rate is defined as yen per dollar, and the balance of trade is defined as the ratio of exports to imports (EX/IM). The equation was estimated in the equivalent of monthly percent change form. It shows a close association between the change in the exchange rate and the change in the balance of trade, with a relatively short six-month time lag.

This apparently strong income-effect relation between the balance of trade and the exchange rate is suspect, however, because of the well-known J-curve effect. When the yen appreciates, there will be an immediate rise in the price of Japanese exports denominated in dollars and a fall in the price of Japanese imports denominated in yen. Thus, whether the balance of trade is measured in dollars or in yen, an appreciation will be associated with an "improved" trade balance and a depreciation with a "deteriorating" trade balance. The more pronounced the movements in the exchange rate (such as in Japan's case), the greater will be the short-run J-curve effect on the balance of trade, tending to bias the estimated coefficient value toward 1. In the regressions described above, the fact that the best statistical results were obtained with a six-month time lag and a coefficient close to 1 in absolute value is consistent with a strong short-run J-curve effect.

To eliminate this bias, the simplest solution is to estimate the relationship with a balance of trade adjusted to remove the contemporaneous effect of the exchange rate. This can be done by using the real balance of trade.[7] Figure 2 shows the relation between the real balance of trade and the exchange rate from 1973 to 1979. A summary of the regression results is reported below:

$$\Delta \ln (¥/\$)_t = -.006 - \sum_{j=0}^{6} .22 \, \Delta \ln (EX^*/IM^*)_{t-j} \quad \bar{R}^2 = -.050$$

$$(-.7) \qquad\qquad SE = .0232$$

$$DW = 1.34$$

[7] Real exports and imports are equal to their nominal values divided by the price index for exports and imports respectively. Since these are calculated in yen, the import price index implicitly includes an adjustment for exchange-rate change.

FIGURE 2
JAPANESE/U.S. REAL TRADE BALANCE AND EXCHANGE RATE, JANUARY, 1973–JUNE, 1979

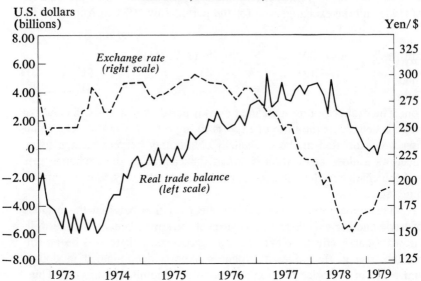

Both figure 2 and the regression results testify to the fact that there is no statistically significant relation between the real balance of trade and the exchange rate. While this result is clearly not conclusive, it does suggest that at least some of the apparently close association between the movements in the balance of trade and in the exchange rate is a statistical artifact associated with the *J*-curve effect.

The procedure for removing the *J*-curve effect also removed all other terms-of-trade influences from the trade balance. Only the pure income effects of the trade balance are allowed to affect the exchange rate. The real balance of trade is clearly incomplete as a measure of all the potentially real factors that could operate on the exchange rate. This oversight will be corrected as the monetary approach is examined.

The Monetary Approach. The monetary approach is based on two propositions. The first is that long-run inflation is a monetary phenomenon. The second is that relative national price levels are a dominant factor in determining the exchange rate between two currencies—that is, purchasing power parity will hold. These two propositions can be illustrated with a simple three-equation model (in log form) for the yen–dollar exchange rate.

234

$$\bar{P}_J = ME_J = (Ms - md^*)_J \qquad (1)$$

$$\bar{P}_{US} = ME_{US} = (Ms - md^*)_{US} \qquad (2)$$

$$(\yen/\$) = (\bar{P}_J - \bar{P}_{US}) + T \qquad (3)$$

Equations 1 and 2 say that the long-run equilibrium price level $(\bar{P})$ is determined by the excess supply of money (ME), which is defined as the difference between the *nominal* money supply (Ms) and the *real* money demand (md^*) in both the United States and Japan. Equation 3 says that the yen–dollar exchange rate is equal to the relative long-run price levels in the United States and Japan. This is long-run purchasing power parity. In addition, the exchange rate is also influenced by the real terms of trade (T). The last term summarizes all the potential real shocks that could affect the exchange rate.

One real shock that has been important since 1973 and that could have a large potential effect on the yen–dollar exchange rate is the real price of oil. Japan is completely dependent upon imported oil. While the dependency of the United States has been rising, it is still no more than 50 percent dependent on imports. At the same time, Japan relies more heavily on oil as a source of energy than does the United States. On both accounts, a rise in the real price of oil would be expected, other things being equal, to have a more severe adverse effect on the Japanese trade surplus than on the U.S. balance of trade and thus tend to depreciate the yen in relation to the dollar. This same oil shock could easily have the opposite effect on the dollar in relation to the British pound because the United Kingdom is nearly oil independent. In the empirical section, we will use the real price of oil as one obvious real-terms-of-trade shock on the yen–dollar exchange rate.

The monetary effects on exchange rates operate through two separate avenues. In the long run, monetary policy operates through the goods market, the current account, and purchasing power parity. In the short run, monetary factors operate through the bond market, the capital account, and real interest rates. These two influences will be considered in turn.

The long-run link between monetary developments and purchasing power parity is well understood and accepted. Equilibrium in the current account and in the goods market requires that the exchange rate adjust to reflect divergences in national price trends between countries. The neutrality of money requires that, if the money supply is doubled, all prices will also double or, alternatively, the purchasing power of money will decline by half. For this proposition to hold for all goods, both domestic and foreign, the exchange value of a currency must fall by half in relation to the value of the foreign currency (assuming, for simplicity, that there are no changes in the excess supply of money abroad). Thus, there is a close link in the long run between the domestic purchasing power of a currency, reflected in the domestic price level, and the international purchasing power of a currency, reflected in its exchange value with other currencies.

It is in the short-run relation between monetary developments and exchange rates that a good deal of controversy exists. The short-run variation in exchange rates is much greater than that of underlying relative national price levels, which suggests that no goods-market phenomenon is in operation. Rather, the evidence suggests that the exchange rate is behaving more like the price in an asset market and can respond quickly to new information. But what is the new information to which the exchange market is responding? Some would argue that new information regarding inflation expectations will affect the exchange rate. A sudden surge of excess monetary growth can lead to a rise in inflation expectations that will depress the value of the currency in the foreign-exchange markets. This explanation, however, is implicitly based on a segmented-markets theory, in which the exchange markets and domestic financial markets respond differently. To the extent that inflation expectations are sufficiently well founded and financial market participants respond to them, there will be a parallel rise in inflation expectations and in market interest rates. An investor with a diversified international portfolio of assets will therefore be compensated for the higher expected rate of inflation in the United States with higher nominal interest rates. The exchange market participants will respond to inflation expectations only to the extent that they are not imbedded in domestic market interest rates—that is, to the extent that the two markets are segmented.

Another explanation for short-run exchange-rate movements is shifts in portfolio preferences between assets denominated in different currencies. The portfolio preference approach, however, only begs the question to the extent that it does not deal with the factors that may cause the shift in preferences. If a shift in preferences is due to a change in inflation expectations, we are back to the issues discussed in the previous paragraph. If the shift in preferences is due to a change in real interest rates, then it is important to consider what factors may have caused a shift in real rates.

It is the proposition in this paper that short-run monetary developments, by way of their effect on real interest rates, are the principal factors that drive a short-run wedge between purchasing power parity and the observed value of the exchange rate.

236

Conceptually, monetary effects can be broken down into two components: expected and unexpected changes in money.[8] Expected monetary changes determine long-run purchasing power parity and current long-term interest rates by way of long-run inflation expectations. There will be no bond-market or asset-market response to exchange rates unless there are segmented markets, as discussed above.

Unexpected monetary growth will affect the exchange rate by way of the bond or asset market and not immediately in the goods market. The delayed response in the goods market is due to the well-recognized adjustment lags with respect to changing production, consumption, and inventory decisions in response to unexpected developments. The bond market, in contrast, is not impeded by a high adjustment cost and can respond quickly to new information. An unexpected increase in money will have the unambiguous effect of increasing domestic liquidity, depressing domestic real interest rates, and, other things being equal, reducing the exchange rate.[9]

In summary, the expected component of money will affect exchange rates through purchasing power parity and the goods market, while the unexpected component will affect the exchange rate by way of the liquidity effect in the bond market. Given that the magnitude and direction of impact of both components of money are approximately the same, a challenging empirical problem can be sidestepped. It is unnecessary to attempt to measure these two separate influences.

Another measurement problem, however, cannot be so easily disposed of—namely, the definition of excess money. Conceptually the definition is clear—excess money is the difference between the nominal money supply and the real money demand. The latter is determined by real income and a representative market interest rate. For the purposes of this paper, I will rely on earlier work of my own that suggests that only the long-run trend in the real demand for money is relevant in determining exchange rates.[10] Business-cycle or transitory changes in money demand will not affect the long-run equilibrium price

[8] For detailed discussion of the author's views on the impact of monetary disturbances on exchange rates, see Michael W. Keran and Stephen Zeldes, "The Effects of Monetary Distrubances on Exchange Rates, Inflation, and Interest Rates," in *Federal Reserve Bank of San Francisco Economic Review,* Spring 1980.

[9] The move in real interest rates will not necessarily be paralleled by a move in nominal interest rates. The unexpected increase in money will also have increased short-run inflation expectations since the price level is now expected to be higher in the future than it was before. The net effect of the unexpected change in money on the nominal interest rate will depend on the relative magnitudes of the liquidity and inflation expectation effects.

[10] See Michael W. Keran, "Money and Exchange Rates, 1974–79," *Federal Reserve Bank of San Francisco Economic Review,* Spring 1979.

FIGURE 3
Excess Money, Prices, and the Exchange Rate

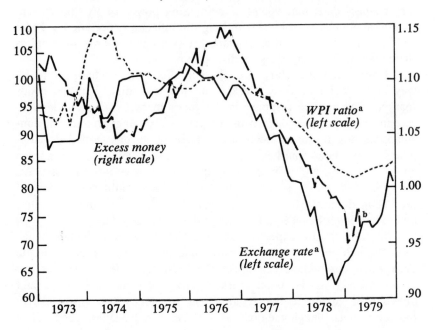

NOTE: The scale for excess money is derived from the coefficient value relating money to exchange rates.
[a] 1975=100.
[b] Break in the series.

level and, therefore, will not affect either actual or expected purchasing power parity. Furthermore, in the long run, when prices adjust to a monetary disturbance, the real supply of and demand for money will be equal. Putting these two points together, we can measure the real demand for money as a moving average of the growth rate of the real money stock. A three-year moving average is used in the work reported here.

If 1975 is used as a base year, an excess money measure for both the United States and Japan can be constructed as the difference between the actual nominal money stock and the trend growth in the real money stock. (Money-stock data are from *International Financial Statistics,* money plus quasi money.) The ratio of these measures of excess money for the United States and Japan is our monetary disturbance. In figure 3 this monetary disturbance is plotted against the yen–dollar exchange rate. The monetary measure appears to be in good

238

conformity with the exchange rate most of the time. Regression analysis confirms this proposition for the data from July 1974 to March 1979. The summary results, in both level and change forms, are as follows:

$$\bar{R}^2 = .982$$
$$SE = .0219$$

$$\ln (¥/\$)_t = 5.34 + \sum_{j=0}^{6} 2.09 \ln(ME_J/ME_{US})_{t-j} \qquad DW = 1.45$$
$$\quad\quad\quad\quad (74.9) \qquad\quad (3.5) \qquad\qquad\qquad\qquad Rho = .96$$

$$\Delta\ln (¥/\$)_t = -.006 + \sum_{j=0}^{6} 1.45 \Delta\ln(ME_J/ME_{US})_{t-j} \quad \bar{R}^2 = .037$$
$$\quad\quad\quad\quad (-1.6) \qquad\quad (2.0) \qquad\qquad\qquad\qquad SE = .0222$$
$$\qquad\qquad\qquad\qquad\qquad\qquad\qquad\qquad\qquad\qquad\qquad DW = 1.47$$

Lags were chosen on the basis of earlier work by the author in which it was shown that a six-month lag produced the minimum standard error. The coefficient of the monetary disturbance (excess money in Japan in relation to excess money in the United States) is statistically significant in both the level and the change forms of the equation. The value of the coefficient expected on the basis of pure purchasing-power-parity considerations is 1.0. The actual value of 2.1 in the level form is consistent with overshooting. The 1.4 coefficient in the change form, however, is not sufficiently different from 1.0 to give strong support to the overshooting hypothesis. More on this subject below.

In this equation, the real terms-of-trade effect operates only through the constant term or the error term. In the level equation, the terms of trade are assumed to be unchanged throughout the estimation period, except for random and temporary variations. In the change form, the terms of trade are assumed to change at a constant average rate in time. Neither of these assumptions is realistic, especially since December 1978, when the price of oil began its dramatic rise. Drawing from earlier discussions, a direct measure of one important terms-of-trade influence can be added to the equation above in the form of the real price of oil. The effect on the exchange rate would occur as soon as the change in prices was anticipated to be lasting enough to have an appreciable effect on the balance of trade. This means that even a real shock can be transmitted immediately to the exchange rate through the financial markets for the same reasons as monetary disturbances.

The best measure would be the spot price of oil rather than the long-term contract price of oil, because it would more accurately reflect the rapidly changing nature of the volatile oil market. Spot oil-price data are not available for years earlier than 1979. As a substitute, however, the spot price of gasoline, which has been available on a monthly basis since 1974, is used. This price is quoted on the Rotterdam market in U.S. dollars. To convert to real series, it is deflated by the U.S. wholesale price index (WPI). Adding the real price of oil to the earlier equations (in level and change form) gives the following results:

$$\ln(¥/\$)_t = 5.7 + \sum_{j=0}^{6} 2.37 \ln(ME_J/ME_{US})_{t-j} \qquad \bar{R}^2 = .98$$
$$(4.1) \qquad\qquad\qquad SE = .0219$$
$$+ \sum_{i=0}^{3} .20 \ln Poil^*_{t-i} \qquad\qquad DW = 1.43$$
$$(2.4) \qquad\qquad\qquad Rho = .95$$

$$\Delta\log(¥/\$)_t = -.009 + \sum_{j=0}^{6} 1.48 \,\Delta\log(ME_J/ME_{US})_{t-j}$$
$$(-2.5) \qquad (2.0) \qquad\qquad \bar{R}^2 = .117$$
$$+ \sum_{i=0}^{4} .32 \,\Delta\log Poil^*_{t-i} \qquad SE = .0216$$
$$(3.0) \qquad\qquad DW = 1.48$$

These results show that the real price of oil (*Poil**) has had an important, if temporary, effect on the yen–dollar exchange rate. For every increase of 1 percent in the real price of oil, the yen will depreciate in relation to the dollar during the next three to four months by between 0.2 and 0.3 percent. As shown in figure 4, the change form of the equation tracks the yen–dollar exchange rate rather well during the estimation period, which ends in March 1979. (A break in the *International Financial Statistics* money-supply series for the United States made estimation beyond this date impossible.) A dynamic simulation was performed from March 1979 to December 1980, which is also shown in figure 4. Actual values of real oil prices and Japanese excess money and a proxy of U.S. excess money were used through December 1979. The simulation results in 1980 are based on assumptions about the values of exogenous variables. The real price of oil is assumed to be unchanged from its January 1980 value. The Japanese nominal money supply is assumed to grow at the same rate as in 1979 (12 percent), and the U.S. money supply is assumed to grow at the midpoint of the 1980 target range (7½ percent).

Taking the simulation at face value would suggest a rate of ¥200 to the dollar by the end of 1980. If the simulation is adjusted for forecast errors as of January 1979, the simulated value at the end of 1980 would be ¥220 to the dollar. The simulations should not be interpreted as forecasts of the yen–dollar exchange rate unless one is prepared to accept the assumptions with respect to the oil price and money supplies that are used in these simulations.[11]

[11] Text as of February 1980. The actual exchange rate as of December 1980 was ¥210 to the dollar.

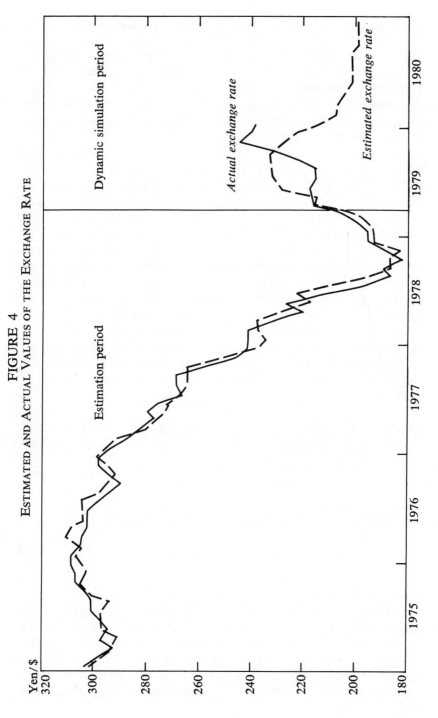

FIGURE 4
ESTIMATED AND ACTUAL VALUES OF THE EXCHANGE RATE

Yen/$

Dynamic simulation period

Estimation period

Actual exchange rate

Estimated exchange rate

320
300
280
260
240
220
200
180

1975   1976   1977   1978   1979   1980

The evidence on overshooting with respect to the yen–dollar exchange rate is indirect. The coefficient linking money to exchange rates is greater than 1.0 in the level form and not significantly greater than one in the change form. The expectations of a 1.0 coefficient are based on assumptions that monetary neutrality with respect to prices also applies to exchange rates. Although this is a correct theoretical proposition, it may not hold in empirical estimation because of errors in measuring the excess money supply. One way to test for possible errors in monetary measures is to estimate relative price equations between the United States and Japan using the same monetary variable as in the exchange-rate equation. The lags in the price equation are expected to be longer than those in the exchange-rate equation because the goods market takes longer to adjust to a monetary disturbance than the bond market does. If the coefficient in the price equation is not significantly different from 1, this suggests that we have an accurate measure of excess money and that there is overshooting in the exchange markets. If the coefficient in the price equation is greater than one, however, and not significantly different from the coefficient in the exchange-rate equation, this suggests that the explanation is not so much overshooting as a bias in the measure of the excess money supply.

To test for these possible alternatives, let us set up an equation that estimates the relative national wholesale price indexes in Japan and the United States with respect to the monetary disturbances and the real price of oil.

$$\ln (P_J/P_{US} = -.053 + 1.38 \sum_{}^{18}\ln(ME_J/ME_{US}) \qquad \bar{R}^2 = .996$$
$$(-1.5) \quad (7.1) \qquad\qquad\qquad SE = .0046$$
$$+ .08 \sum_{}^{6} \ln(Poil^*) \qquad\qquad DW = 1.27$$
$$(3.3) \qquad\qquad\qquad\qquad\qquad Rho = .97$$

$$\Delta\ln(P_J/P_{US} = -.004 + 1.12 \sum_{}^{18}\Delta\ln(ME_J/ME_{US})$$
$$(-1.6) \quad (3.9) \qquad\qquad\qquad \bar{R}^2 = .54$$
$$+ .14 \sum_{}^{6} \Delta\ln(Poil^*) \qquad SE = .0040$$
$$(3.6) \qquad\qquad\qquad\qquad DW = 2.24$$
$$Rho = .41$$

There are a number of things to comment on: (1) The lag between excess money and relative national price levels is eighteen months. While this is, as expected, substantially longer than the lag between excess money and exchange rates, it is much shorter than the lags of three to four years usually observed in such analysis. This relatively short lag may well be due to the fact that this equation was estimated with data from a period of flexible exchange rates. The prices of internationally traded goods (which make up a significant share of both indexes) are determined in a world market and thus are more directly influenced by exchange rates than are consumer prices. In a flexible-rate regime, the exchange rate responds to a change in excess money relatively quickly. Thus, wholesale prices that include a significant share of internationally traded goods will respond more quickly on the average to a monetary disturbance under flexible rates than under fixed rates. (2) The coefficient on the excess money variable in the level form of the equation is significantly lower in the price equation than in the exchange-rate equation (1.38 versus 2.37). This result supports the existence of overshooting. The coefficient value in the change form, however, is about the same in both the price and the exchange-rate equations (1.12 versus 1.48) and not significantly different from 1. This result does not support overshooting. (3) The real price of oil has a statistically significant and positive effect on the relative national price levels.

Why should the price of oil have a greater effect on Japanese than on U.S. wholesale prices? Three factors explain this result.[12] (1) Oil has a bigger weight in the Japanese wholesale price index than in that of the United States. (2) Controls on prices of domestic oil in the United States mean that oil prices, on the average, would increase faster in Japan. (3) Because Japan is more dependent on imported oil than is the United States, its real terms of trade and, therefore, real permanent income will be affected more adversely. As a result, the real demand for money will decline more in Japan than in the United States, and excess money will be greater for any given nominal money supply.

Returning to the exchange-rate overshooting question, the equations in change form do not support such an explanation. Given an increase in excess money, overshooting will occur only if the liquidity effect is greater than the inflation expectations effect on short term interest rates. The results suggest that the two influences have been roughly offsetting, and thus overshooting is not systematically observed with respect to the yen–dollar exchange rate.

Is this result not inconsistent with the observed greater variability of exchange rates in relation to actual price levels? No. Greater variability of exchange rates in relation to price levels is not a priori evi-

---

[12] A possible source of statistical bias is that the real price of oil is deflated by the U.S. wholesale price index, which is also part of the dependent variable. This does not appear to be significant because the lag on the real oil prices is six months and the contemporaneous effect is not statistically significant.

dence of exchange-rate overshooting. It may simply reflect the fact that the asset market, which dominates the exchange rate in the short run, reacts to incoming information more promptly than the goods market, which dominates the relative national price levels. This can be seen very roughly as the difference between observing movements in a time series that has been smooth with a six-month average versus an eighteen-month average; the longer the moving average, the smoother the series will appear to be.

Monetary Policy and the Exchange Rate

What was the monetary policy behavior that underlay the observed variations in the excess money supply in Japan in relation to money supply in the United States? In the summer of 1975, both countries faced a common set of economic problems—two or more years of double-digit inflation and the recent emergence of a business-cycle recession, which was the worst in the post–World War II period. Initially the two governments responded to these twin problems in the same way: with an easing of monetary policy.

As a result, excess money supply—that is, the nominal money supply adjusted for changes in real demand for money—grew at virtually the same rate in the two countries through the end of 1976. After that, monetary policy became more expansionary in the United States, perhaps as a result of the new administration's economic priorities. As shown in figure 3, excess money increased much more rapidly in the United States than in Japan during 1977–1978. The response of the foreign-exchange market to this divergence in monetary policies was a quick and dramatic appreciation of the yen. This was not an isolated occurrence, for the dollar also depreciated against the deutsche mark and the Swiss franc for substantially the same monetary reason.[13]

In at least partial response to these exchange-rate developments, a major change in U.S. policy, first announced in November 1978 and later reinforced and strengthened in October 1979, stabilized the excess money supply in the United States in relation to the money supply of Japan. On the basis of purely monetary factors, however, this would have stabilized only the yen–dollar exchange rate. The principal weakness in the yen during 1979 was due to real-terms-of-trade shocks associated with the rise in the price of oil. As these real factors were largely neutral for the European countries, this may explain why the dollar continued to be relatively weak against the deutsche mark and the Swiss franc and strong against the yen during 1979.

[13] See Keran, "Money and Exchange Rates."

Conclusion

The exchange value of the yen will be determined by two types of influences: first, direct government actions through central bank intervention; second, private market behavior. The evidence reviewed here suggests that, although intervention by the Bank of Japan has been substantial, it has been of the leaning-against-the-wind variety. The Japanese government has not systematically attempted to aim for a particular exchange rate. Furthermore, there is circumstantial evidence that this leaning-against-the-wind strategy has not had any significant effect on the monthly average value of the yen–dollar exchange rate.

These propositions suggest that a major portion of the movement in the yen is attributable to private market forces. Given the very sharp fluctuations that have been observed in the yen–dollar rate, the question arises whether this represents private speculation of a steamroller, self-fulfilling variety unrelated to underlying fundamentals. The evidence suggests that such is not the case. Much of the movement in the exchange value of the yen in relation to the dollar can be explained by economic fundamentals. Specifically, divergent monetary policies in the United States and Japan explain much of the appreciation of the yen during 1977 and 1978, and real supply-side shocks associated with oil prices explain much of its depreciation during 1979.

The policy implications of this study are clear. As most of the variation in the yen–dollar exchange rate is the result of divergence in monetary policy followed in the United States and Japan, stabilizing the exchange rate is primarily a function of establishing consistent monetary policies between the two countries.

Bibliography

Bilson, John F. "The Monetary Approach to the Exchange Rate: Some Empirical Evidence." *IMF Staff Papers,* March 1978, pp. 48–75.
———. "Recent Developments in Monetary Models of Exchange Rate Determination." *IMF Staff Papers,* June 1979, pp. 201–23.
Dornbusch, Rudiger. "Expectations and Exchange Rate Dynamics." *Journal of Political Economy,* December 1976, pp. 1161–76.
———. "Monetary Policy under Exchange Rate Flexibility." In Federal Reserve Bank of Boston, *Conference on Managed Exchange-Rate Flexibility,* October 1978.
Frankel, Jeffrey. "On the Mark: A Theory of Floating Exchange Rates Based on Real Interest Rate Differentials." *American Economic Review,* September 1979.

Frenkel, Jacob A. "The Monetary Approach to the Exchange Rate: Doctrinal Aspects and Empirical Evidence." In *The Economics of Exchange Rates,* edited by Jacob Frenkel and Harry G. Johnson. Reading, Mass.: Addison-Wesley, 1978.

Johnson, Harry G. "The Monetary Approach to Balance of Payments Theory." In *The Monetary Approach to the Balance of Payments,* edited by Jacob Frenkel and Harry G. Johnson. Toronto: University of Toronto Press, 1976.

Keran, Michael W. "Money and Exchange Rates, 1974–79." *Federal Reserve Bank of San Francisco Economic Review,* Spring 1979.

Keran, Michael W., and Zeldes, Stephen. "Effects of Monetary Disturbances on Exchange Rates, Inflation, and Interest Rates." *Federal Reserve Bank of San Francisco Economic Review,* Spring 1980.

Quirk, P. J. "Exchange Rate Policy in Japan: Leaning against the Wind." *IMF Staff Papers,* November 1977.

Sweeney, Richard J. "Risk, Inflation, and Exchange Rates." In *Proceedings of the West Coast Academic/Federal Reserve Economic Research Seminar,* held at the Federal Reserve Bank of San Francisco, November 2–3, 1978.

Commentary

Lawrence B. Krause

I shall discuss two papers, that of Steven Kohlhagen, "The Experience with Floating: The 1973–1979 Dollar," and that of Michael Keran, "The Value of the Yen."

In the first part of the Kohlhagen paper, an explanation of movements of the dollar in exchange markets during the floating period with which I fully agree is presented. The complications involved in managing the dollar that grow out of its role as a reserve and vehicle currency are a legacy of the past that must and, in my view, will change. The evolution to a multiple key currency system has not been helped by the Bundesbank, which has resisted an enhanced role for the deutsche mark. Germany and other countries should facilitate the use of their currencies by other countries and foreign residents and, through cooperation with the monetary authorities of other key currency countries, make a multiple currency system work for the benefit of all countries.

One major deficiency of the floating period can be traced, as suggested by Kohlhagen, to massive foreign-exchange-market interventions in 1976 by the United Kingdom, Italy, and Japan and during most of 1977 by Japan. Excessive amounts of dollars were bought, which led to the rigidification of the dollar exchange rate when it should have fallen. If the dollar had been permitted to fall, the U.S. policy actions of November 1, 1978, might have occurred twelve or eighteen months earlier, and U.S. inflation would have been much reduced. A second deficiency was the failure of the United States to respond immediately to the decline of the dollar that began at the end of 1977. American policy makers failed to recognize the information implied by the decline of the dollar, namely, that excessive amounts of dollars were being created. They sustained their macroeconomic policies as though the dollar had not fallen, when they should have enforced greater restraint. Of course, the two deficiencies were related. If foreign central banks had thought that the United States itself would react to a decline of the dollar, they would have been less inclined to intervene themselves. On the other hand, American authorities came to expect other countries to intervene and thus felt little pressure to change basic policies Presumably that experience will not be forgotten, and the dollar will be managed better in the future.

One minor point concerns short-term volatility of the dollar during the period. If each day when the dollar changed by 1 percent or more (a rough indication of excess volatility) is counted, then a number of such episodes were reactions to government actions that the private market was unable to anticipate correctly. Thus volatility may be not only a failure of markets but also a failure of government policy.

Kohlhagen, in his section on policy, current-account deficits, and exchange-rate movements, suggests that the market was too intolerant of U.S. deficits in 1977–1978 and in his note 43 suggests that the United States ought to be able to run a deficit equal to 0.7 percent to 1 percent of gross national product (GNP) without undermining markets. To the contrary, I believe that the market was too tolerant of U.S. deficits. U.S. policy makers continued to misjudge the economy, repeatedly making the mistake of underestimating the strength of the economy. Is this not enough to question the wisdom of future policy actions as well? Furthermore, an equilibrium position for the U.S. current account would be a significant surplus, given much higher real rates of return to capital in other countries than in the United States. Thus the deviation from equilibrium as represented by a current account deficit equal to 1 percent of GNP is very great indeed.

Kohlhagen concludes that by and large the system has worked in a satisfactory manner; but excessive volatility and overshooting of exchange-rate movements can be destabilizing. If this is to be avoided, then some minimum degree of macroeconomic coordination (of course, not currency intervention) is necessary among countries. If the world is very contractionary, for instance, then the United States must also be somewhat contractionary because economic interdependence does not permit the United States or any other country to deviate greatly from the major thrust of the world economy.

The paper on the yen by Michael Keran begins with a general statement that currency values are determined by supply and demand for a currency; one cannot quarrel with that. He concludes that major movements in the yen/dollar rate were caused by relative monetary policies of Japan and the United States and by changes in the price of oil. That conclusion also is eminently reasonable. One can take issue, however, with some of the analysis that falls between the introduction and the conclusion. Keran recognizes that the usefulness of particular theories of exchange-rate determination depends on how well they simplify reality because, with elaboration, all theories can be made equivalent. He sets up a horse race between two of the three theories he mentions: the income/expenditure approach and the monetary approach. The portfolio balance theory was not modeled. Keran found that the income/expenditure approach (when corrected for *J*-curve effects) was less successful than the monetary approach in explaining movements of the yen. The conclusion may be correct, but the race was unfair. The income/expenditure model used by Keran was simplicity itself, with only trade balances used as an explanatory variable. On the other hand, the monetary approach used a concept of excess money supply that involves a complex demand for money function. Though reality is no doubt even more complex than either model, if they are to be compared, at least as much sophistication should be built into the income/expenditure model as was involved in the monetary model.

Keran observes that the Japanese authorities intervened heavily in the exchange market without being able to stop the exchange rate from changing and thus were unsuccessful in reaching a target rate— even if they had a target. The Japanese authorities merely leaned against the wind without changing direction. Why did the Japanese behave in this fashion? This intervention strategy is almost certain to cause trading losses for the central bank, and this may be the purpose: the cost of exchange rate flexibility is thus socialized. As long as it is primarily Japanese citizens rather than foreigners who gain at the expense of the Bank of Japan, a welfare argument can be made for absorbing the cost in this fashion.

Finally, a point must be made as to some of the cost of excessive exchange rate volatility and overshooting in the yen/dollar rate that falls on neither the United States nor Japan. For a country such as the Philippines, the real cost of an overshooting yen/dollar rate can be substantial. The Philippines trade about equally with Japan and the United States and thus do not belong to a single optimal currency area. Although some substitution does occur at the margin, certain products are bought from and sold to Japan and different ones from and to the United States. Thus, when the yen/dollar rate changes, substantial internal terms-of-trade changes occur that impose tremendous adjustment costs. Many countries in the Pacific are in this position. Thus it is incumbent on the United States and Japan not to permit a continuation of the overshooting of the exchange rate, and they should moderate it by closer macroeconomic coordination.

Stanley W. Black

Trying to understand exchange markets and international monetary relations is a complicated exercise that requires study of both market behavior and macroeconomic policy. A broad approach that combines both aspects is essential. The papers by Steven Kohlhagen and Michael Keran set about this task for the United States and Japan, each using a somewhat different methodology.

Kohlhagen describes what happened to the dollar from 1973 to 1979, relating his discussion to macroeconomic events of the decade—what I would call a blow-by-blow description. In addition he gives us some measures of the relative volatility of exchange rates and the underlying macroeconomic phenomena. Keran, in contrast, sets his analysis of the yen/dollar rate in a simple monetarist framework, after bowing first in the direction of alternative theories of exchange rate determination. Kohlhagen's paper, which I enjoyed very much, takes an eclectic approach, bringing in many different factors and points of view, so that it is sometimes hard to tell whether he is right or wrong on a specific point. Although this is an inherent problem with eclecticism, Keran's clarity suffers from the opposite problem.

On the whole, Kohlhagen's descriptive analysis of the dollar from 1973 to 1979 is plausible, but I would differ with him on several points of detail. His description of the sharp fall in the dollar from March to June 1973 omits the significant tightening of German monetary policy that occurred with the beginning of the float, a tightening that was not equally matched in the United States. The total absence of U.S. intervention should also be given some "credit."

The description of the dollar depreciation from January 1974 to March 1975 as a consequence of faster U.S. inflation and the current account deficit seems wrong, certainly on the first point. U.S. inflation was lower than average in this period. To some extent, the January 1974 dollar peak was due to overreaction to the oil price rise.

Nor can I accept the assignment of blame for the 1977–1979 fall in the dollar to central bank intervention in 1975–1977. Though I believe that Japan intervened too much in 1976 and Britain and Italy too much in 1977, aside from these cases this was the period of *least* intervention during the entire decade. The main cause is to be found rather in divergent macroeconomic policies, in my opinion.

Finally, I believe that Kohlhagen has underestimated the importance of the November 1, 1978, change in U.S. policy. The author argues that the policy merely attacked the symptoms of the problem. I disagree. One week earlier the administration had announced, with

250

much fanfare, an anti-inflation program consisting of wage/price guide-lines and a call for budgetary discipline. The president's only comment on monetary policy at the time was that "interest rates are too high." The ensuing debacle forced the president to announce personally an unprecedented 1 percent rise in the discount rate for *external* reasons, which had always taken a back seat to domestic goals.

Furthermore, the commitment to substantial foreign currency borrowing was a major step, as was agreement to begin intervening in yens. The issuance of Carter bonds was a reluctant admission that private capital was unwilling to finance the U.S. deficit without an exchange rate guarantee. Our own willingness to bet on the dollar was an important signal to private markets, as was our willingness to step up the scale of intervention. In my view, significant U.S. participation in central bank intervention is a necessary condition for a viable floating-rate regime, though it is far from a sufficient condition.

Kohlhagen asks the fundamental question: "Have managed floating exchange rates equilibrated external disequilibriums without generating excessive exchange-rate movements?" His answers for the United States are: "apparently yes for 1973–1977 and probably no for 1977–1978." I must disagree with both these judgments. Though the dollar rose and fell during the period 1973–1977 after adjustment for relative price changes, as shown by his figure 2, it did not really change significantly until 1977–1978. The main contribution to U.S. external disequilib-riums in the early 1970s came from the devaluations of 1971 and early 1973, not from floating. The recent drop in the dollar, though "exces-sive" by some standards, has helped external disequilibriums.

To conclude my remarks on the Kohlhagen paper, let me note that it points usefully to the major factors that must be dealt with in judging the performance of the floating dollar: expectations, domestic macro-economic policy, oil prices, and the reserve role of the dollar. I do believe, however, that it fails to address the issue of whether floating itself contributed to divergent macroeconomic behavior.

Turning to Keran's paper, I felt somewhat as though it were a Bible story written by one of my fundamentalist neighbors in Nash-ville. The conclusions seem to be built in before the analysis is done. The argument against a target-rate policy, for example, is simply that— an argument. It does not prove that the Japanese authorities did not engage in targeting. Nor does the equation in the section headed "Intervention behavior," which tests no alternative hypothesis to "lean-ing against the wind." My own work shows a significant role for a target rate during this period.

Keran's discussion of alternative theories of the exchange rate seems fair enough, though one is hardly surprised that the monetary approach comes out as his first choice. I personally find a pure quantity-theory approach to the price level and a purchasing-power-parity theory of the exchange rate to be rather oversimplified. I am not surprised, therefore, when the coefficient of relative excess money is inconsistent with the theory. Perhaps if the data were averaged into two- or three-year moving averages, the coefficients would approach the theoretical expectation applying to such a long-run theory.

Although I can agree with the long-run implications of the analysis of the yen/dollar rate, I believe that we are still left at sea with respect to the short-run determinants of the rate.

Robert Solomon

Steven Kohlhagen undertakes to appraise the working of floating exchange rates since March 1973 by examining fluctuations in the U.S. dollar. In general, I am in agreement with his appraisal, but I am not sure that a nonbeliever—an opponent of floating—would be persuaded by his arguments. Let me select a few important propositions and comment on them.

After reviewing the ups and downs of the dollar from March 1973 to the present, Kohlhagen decides, quite appropriately, to focus on the episode of steep depreciation from September 1977 through October 1978, when the trade-weighted dollar exchange rate fell about 20 percent.

One point that Kohlhagen makes over and over again is that other central banks intervened too heavily in the two years before September 1977 to prevent their currencies from appreciating. If, instead, they had let the dollar decline earlier, he asserts, the U.S. deficit would have been smaller and the dollar would have dropped less sharply in 1977–1978.

Here I am puzzled, as is Stanley Black, by a factual question: Did foreign central banks intervene to support the dollar in 1976–1977? According to the *Federal Reserve Bulletin,* foreign official dollar holdings in the United States (and that is a satisfactory measure for present purposes as the other industrial countries presumably do not place dollars in the Euromarkets) increased $11.2 billion in 1976 and $19.2 billion in the first nine months of 1977. In Western Europe, there was no increase at all in 1976, and there was an increase of about $15 billion in 1977. Most of the latter can be accounted for by the reserve accumulation of the United Kingdom, which was hardly a dollar-supporting operation. Japan's foreign exchange reserves increased only $3.3 billion in 1976 and $1.3 billion in the first nine months of 1977.

Thus I believe that Kohlhagen exaggerates the extent to which foreign monetary authorities were managing the float in 1976–1977.

I find Kohlhagen's position on purchasing power parity (PPP) to be a bit unclear. Although he presents a figure showing that the real exchange rate moved very closely with the nominal exchange rate, he then informs us that "PPP and the monetary approach yield a series of variables that can be considered underlying determinants of the value of the dollar." This seems to contradict what the figure reveals. Furthermore, I have just completed a book on exchange rates and inflation in which PPP is carefully examined and is shown to have rather little explanatory power in both the short run and the long run.

Let me say a word about what the Federal Reserve did on October 6, 1979. Kohlhagen tells us several times that the Federal Reserve abandoned an interest-rate target in favor of a monetary-aggregates target. In fact, it has used monetary-aggregates targets for years. The change last October was from manipulating the federal funds rate as a way of meeting the targets to acting directly on bank reserves for this purpose.

Kohlhagen concludes that the "excessive depreciation" of the dollar induced the U.S. authorities to adopt stronger anti-inflation policies than they might otherwise have adopted. The same point, in relation to overshooting, has been made in a recent report of the Group of Thirty on foreign exchange markets. I have characterized this policy effect of alleged overshooting in the words of Oscar Wilde: "Nothing succeeds like excess."

I was struck by the fact that, in his discussion of vicious and virtuous circles, Kohlhagen does not once mention wages. I had the impression that "real wage resistance"—to use Hicks's term—played an essential role in vicious circles and in the theoretical models of vicious circles.

Let me add that vicious and virtuous circles are not independent of each other. Virtue requires an appreciating exchange rate, but an appreciating exchange rate in turn requires that at least one other country have a depreciating exchange rate. Thus virtue sets up the conditions for vice, and vice versa.

Finally, let me add a brief word on "policy coordination." This is a term that seems to mean all things to all persons. In the present context, it is often prescribed as a way of bringing about more stable exchange rates. This approach puts the cart before the horse, in my view. If policy coordination is properly defined and implemented, its purpose is presumably to improve the performance of the world economy in terms of output and inflation. The exchange-rate effects would, I should think, be incidental.

Heinrich Matthes

In discussing the interesting papers presented at this session, I consider it my function to speak from the specific standpoint of the Bundesbank. I shall necessarily give greater attention to Roland Vaubel's paper than to the other two, if only because I have nothing really controversial to say about Kohlhagen's and Keran's papers.

I share Kohlhagen's views and findings to a very great extent, especially his contention that "the central role of the dollar may give the United States fewer degrees of freedom than other countries in running external deficits during a floating-rate period." I would in fact go so far as to say that the external constraint for the United States is at present greater than it ever was during the period of fixed exchange rates. This being so, it should not really be "largely a mystery" to Kohlhagen that the U.S. deficit on current account generated "the sort of excitement that occurred in 1978–1979." In this case, I think, one is bound to agree with the German Council of Economic Experts, which stated in its annual report for 1978/1979 that the U.S. current-account deficits would not have presented any problems at all if the dollar had not been endangered in its position as the key currency. "The crux of the problem is U.S. inflation. Both to devalue the world's huge dollar holdings by inflation and to remain the key currency country—that cannot be done at the same time."[1]

Kohlhagen's positive assessment of the first few years of floating must also be endorsed from the German point of view. Major upheavals in the world economy were handled without any dangerous chain reactions in international financial relationships. On the contrary, current and capital transactions between Western countries even increased considerably. Thus floating exchange rates proved to be the mechanism that enabled the world economy to go on working satisfactorily in spite of serious problems. From the German viewpoint it was also noticeable that, during a period of about three years after the transition to floating, the deutsche mark did not appreciate more than was consistent with the change in the price differential between Germany and its principal trading partners. The system of floating exchange rates therefore worked quite satisfactorily in its initial phase.

During this period, however, it became increasingly obvious to the weak-currency countries, in particular, that the transition to floating had not brought them the additional degrees of freedom in their domestic employment and growth policies that they had originally

---

[1] German Council of Economic Experts, Annual Report, 1978/1979, para. 340.

expected it to yield. Instead, the familiar vicious-circle problems soon meant that exchange-rate policy had to be dropped as a means of safeguarding an expansionary economic policy. As a logical consequence, many of these countries tried from early 1976 onward to stabilize their exchange rates more and more. In view of the persistent inflation differentials, there emerged from this—in sharp contrast to the situation in the 1930s—a tendency to keep the exchange rate overvalued for as long as possible. For the United States this caused a specific "redundancy problem," that is, the management of the dollar by foreign central banks "at a rate that is not desirable from the viewpoint of long-run domestic policy," as deplored by Kohlhagen, for the period from 1975 to 1977. One cannot but agree with this finding; as we know, the Bundesbank was not involved in this "management." The necessary learning process in the United States was certainly greatly delayed by this development.

What effect did the transition to floating exchange rates have on German monetary policy? Figure 1 shows that in the first phase (from the beginning of 1973 to the end of 1975) the cumulative monetary reserves of the Bundesbank did not rise at all—despite huge current-account surpluses and two monetary crises during that period. Only the second of these crises led to significant nonbank, short-term, capital inflows.

This brings me to an extremely important point that is often overlooked, even in many theoretical models: Not every purchase of foreign exchange by the Bundesbank brings about monetary expansion as we understand it. Only if the corresponding funds flow to domestic nonbanks do they immediately become money, for only in this case do the banks' liabilities to residents increase, and only this is counted as money according to the German definition of the money stock. The situation is quite different when the funds flow primarily to banks, as they have almost always done since 1977 (figures 2 and 3). In this case nonbanks are not initially affected at all by the speculative inflows, and the central bank is obviously in a much stronger position because, in principle, it can control the liquidity of the banking system. This is particularly true for a monetary constitution like Germany's, where the government component of central bank money is negligible. This, in turn, implies that the central bank may decide at its discretion whether to consider any inflow of liquidity to the banking system caused by external factors in formulating its general strategy toward liquidity. If the Bundesbank refrains from any intervention in the foreign exchange markets, it must meet the banks' central bank money requirements generated by the stability-oriented growth of the money stock—at

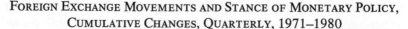

FIGURE 1

FOREIGN EXCHANGE MOVEMENTS AND STANCE OF MONETARY POLICY,
CUMULATIVE CHANGES, QUARTERLY, 1971–1980

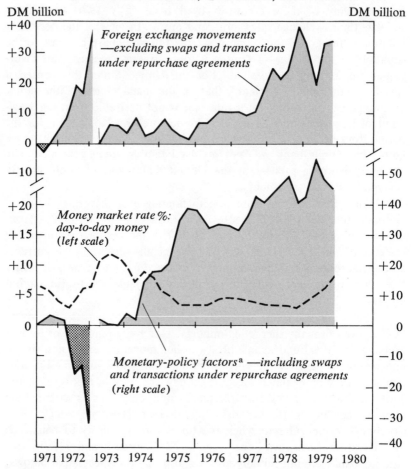

present these requirements amount to about DM8 billion a year—by buying other assets.

Apart from the banks' trend-induced central bank money needs, however, there are also considerable seasonal fluctuations in bank liquidity in the course of the year, such as those associated with the tax payment dates (the government's accounts are kept at the central bank) or with the sharply oscillating currency circulation. Needless to say, such seasonal fluctuations in the banks' central bank money requirements must also be smoothed out by the Bundesbank, and they normally

FIGURE 1 (continued)

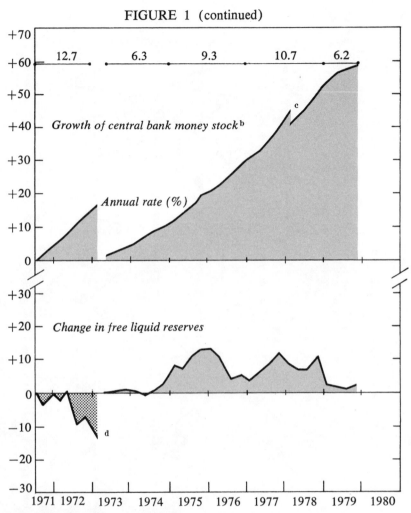

a Includes lombard loans.
b Currency in circulation and minimum reserves on domestic liabilities at constant reserve ratios; seasonally adjusted.
c Statistically adjusted; as of March 1978 banks' cash balances of domestic notes and coins are deductible from the minimum reserves.
d Adoption of floating exchange rates in March 1973.
SOURCE: Monthly report of the Deutsche Bundesbank, various issues.

lead to corresponding movements in the central bank's balance sheet. Hence in the framework of such seasonal variations the central bank evidently has an additional degree of freedom for offsetting foreign exchange inflows and outflows by means of otherwise necessary corre-

FIGURE 2

CAPITAL TRANSACTIONS AND BALANCE-OF-PAYMENTS EQUILIBRIUM, QUARTERLY, 1974–1979

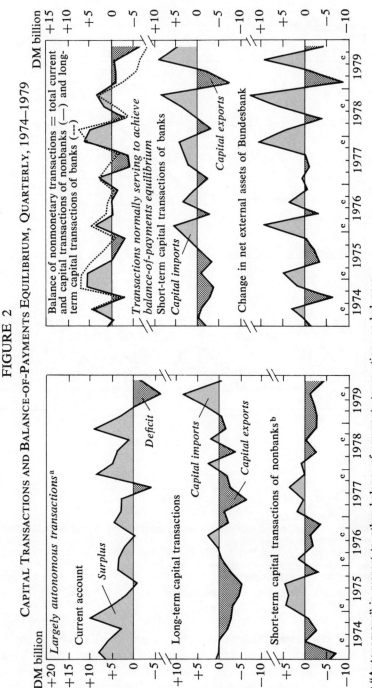

[a] "Autonomous" in respect to other balance-of-payments transactions or balances.
[b] Including the balancing item of the balance of payments.
[c] Phases of heavier, partly speculative, inflows of foreign exchange from abroad.
NOTE: Minus sign (−) indicates a deficit.

FIGURE 3

MAJOR PAYMENTS BALANCES, 1974–1979

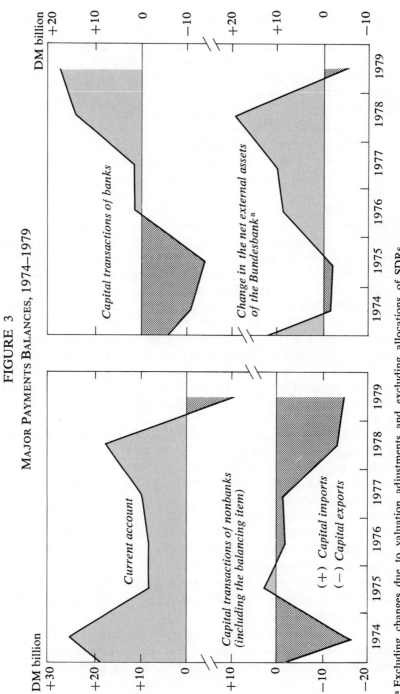

^a Excluding changes due to valuation adjustments and excluding allocations of SDRs.

sponding financing operations, without immediately causing any disturbances for monetary policy. In fact, serious problems do not arise for monetary policy until the trend of the Bundesbank's interventions exceeds the magnitude of some DM8 billion a year. Figure 1 shows that this did not happen between the beginning of 1973 and autumn 1977. The cumulative inflow of foreign exchange to the Bundesbank in this period came to some DM10 billion.

During the second phase of the period of interest here, namely, from the beginning of 1977 to the late autumn of 1978—the time of the "locomotive" debate—the central bank apparently tolerated a fairly massive increase in liquidity, to judge from figure 1. This took place against the background of an insufficiently firm base for the economic upswing. The fact that a sustained upswing did not get under way, despite the efforts of economic policy (in which expansionary fiscal policy also had some part), was not least due to the dampening effect on economic activity of the appreciation of the deutsche mark in real terms. The monetary pump priming in this period was certainly not inconsiderable. Not only did the monetary reserves go up by about DM28 billion, but the Bundesbank also provided the banks with some DM7 billion of "base money" in the course of other transactions; this accommodated a growth of the central bank money stock that quite substantially overshot the monetary growth target (from the beginning of 1977 to the end of 1978 the central bank money stock expanded at a seasonally adjusted annual rate of almost 11 percent, which was several percentage points more than the monetary growth target at that time).

In connection with this policy, the money market rates controlled by the Bundesbank reached a low for the 1970s (figure 1). The monetary crises of that period (in autumn 1977 and autumn 1978) greatly increased the Bundesbank's foreign-exchange reserves, but they hardly affected nonbanks' short-term capital transactions (figures 2 and 3). The heavy national demand for money at that time—and only this is measured according to the German money-stock concept—was thus caused entirely by domestic factors. The speculative funds mainly flowed in through short-term capital transactions of banks—a channel that does not directly affect the monetary growth target and that the Bundesbank in principle has under control, if it is prepared to accept the exchange rate consequences.

Then, as now, the strategic monetary-policy target variable of the Bundesbank was the central bank money stock—that is, currency in circulation and required minimum reserves on the *domestic* liabilities

260

of banks (at constant reserve ratios).[2] The central bank money stock is not, however, a "monetarist" monetary base concept—that is, a variable on which the banks may still build up something—but rather a money stock concept sui generis that reflects, besides the cash component, the money creation that has already taken place in the banking system.[3] This makes it clear that the Bundesbank cannot control the central bank money stock *directly* through the mysterious working of multipliers and that the growth of this variable obeys the same laws as those that apply to the other monetary aggregates.

In the last analysis the only thing that matters is that setting appropriate basic interest-rate conditions influences the portfolio decisions of banks and nonbanks in such a way that the money creation process takes place on the desired quantitative scale. This demonstrates that the control process is highly complex and that it is often difficult to be as accurate as one might wish, particularly in the shorter run. The Bundesbank consequently uses a long-term objective as a guide for its monetary policy, namely, an annual target.

Judging from the experience of 1977–1978, however, there may well be fairly long periods in which the Bundesbank must strike a balance between what appears necessary in the light of the monetary growth target and what in the end cannot be justified after all in view of the sluggish economy and unsatisfactory level of employment. The fact that, in reconciling such short- and medium-term aspects of its policy in 1977–1978, the Bundesbank had to tolerate quite considerable divergences from the monetary growth target announced at the beginning of the year has already been mentioned. As early as its annual report for 1977 the Bundesbank expressed its concern about this and pointed out that it was not impossible that the sharp increase in liquidity at that time involved the danger of creating scope for inflation in the longer run.

Even so, it was not until December 1978 that the Bundesbank was able to change its course definitively. This shows that even a quantitative control strategy does not relieve a central bank of the necessity of constantly deciding whether the policy it is pursuing is acceptable in the light of the underlying objectives of economic and social policy. This economic policy "balancing act" between what has undoubtedly proved to be right in the medium run and what appears inescapable in the

[2] Reserves on nonresidents' deposits are thus made available outside the monetary growth target, as suggested by Vaubel, so that currency substitution by nonresidents does not have a *direct* impact on the growth of the domestic money stock.

[3] The required minimum reserves at constant reserve ratios can apparently be viewed as an index of the development of deposits, the demand, time, and savings deposits being weighted with the reserve ratios (namely, in the ratio 4:3:2).

short run is of course particularly difficult at times of serious disequilibriums, such as we have experienced since the first oil crisis.

One of the reasons the Bundesbank was able to tolerate a fairly brief overshooting of the target at that time was of course that the Bundesbank's preeminent objective, price stability, was not directly threatened because of the strong tendency of the deutsche mark to appreciate in real terms during that period. In the autumn of 1978, when it seemed more apparent that the upswing was at last reasonably firmly based, the Bundesbank—as mentioned—soon changed its course.

Experience since the end of 1978 seems to imply that, given sufficient domestic room for maneuver, the Bundesbank remains in principle in a strong position with respect to the banks. Problems in the external field have caused us comparatively little trouble since the late autumn of 1978, in spite of a crisis in the European Monetary System and another dollar crisis. As figure 3 indicates, our policy was not undermined from abroad in the field of nonbank transactions at any time during 1979, although the turnaround in the German current account admittedly played a significant part in this. In the overall capital transactions of nonbanks (including the balancing item), there were even outflows amounting to some DM13 billion in 1979. Together with the deficit on current account, this meant that roughly DM22 billion was withdrawn from the entire nonbank sector through external current and capital transactions. In fact, monetary expansion declined by half in that period. The "monetary cloak," which widened excessively in 1977–1978, has thus become much more tight fitting.

This may have made it clear that the *direct* potential disruptive impact of external developments on German monetary policy is often overrated under conditions of largely flexible exchange rates, and Vaubel too does not seem to me to have entirely avoided this danger. Our inadequate knowledge of the *national* money demand function or the coefficients of the domestic variables still causes us far more concern in conducting day-to-day monetary policy. Even the money demand function estimated by the Kiel Economic Research Institute, for instance, leaves almost half of the variance unexplained.[4] Without doubt, though, the external economic dislocations of the past few years have greatly hampered monetary policy *indirectly*. In view of the obvious deflationary effects of a persistent real appreciation of the deutsche mark, the Bundesbank lost a number of political degrees of freedom in its

---

[4] I may refer in this context to the 1978 annual report of the Bundesbank, where certain conjectures were made about some possible influences in the domestic sphere, such as "spreading effects" and sectoral demands for money.

shorter-term control of the central bank money stock. Given the strong external ties of the German economy and the competitive pressure exerted by imports owing to the real appreciation of the deutsche mark, the short-lived overshooting was quite safe (incidentally, the structural problems caused by that pressure are not mentioned by Vaubel at all). The Bundesbank's immediate stability policy objective was therefore not in danger. In spite of a largely accommodating Bundesbank policy during this period, however, the money stock target had at least the useful result that the Bundesbank did what it had to do only with a very guilty "medium-term conscience."

In conclusion, let me make a few brief remarks on the problem of the reserve role of the deutsche mark, which is discussed by Vaubel toward the end of his paper. In Vaubel's opinion the attitude of the Bundesbank resembles that of a "(non-?) banker who refuses to accept deposits because banking involves intermediation risk." Vaubel comes to this view because, as he thinks, "real exchange-rate changes that may be caused by such shifts" are "strictly temporary." In the context of a long-term equilibrium-theory concept, though, even a pronounced real appreciation of a currency lasting two to three years may be "strictly temporary." If this point of view is adopted, then almost all efforts of official economic policy are a delusion. It is tempting to cite Keynes's famous view about the long run, in which, as is well known, we are all dead. After all, the problem of practical economic policy consists in the fact that such a long run does not exist. Economic policy makers almost always respond only to disturbances that are "strictly temporary" in relation to a long-term equilibrium approach but that in the short run may well yield wrong signals for the use of resources and thus lead to losses.

In my opinion, therefore, a country of the size of Germany—especially since its current account is now in lasting deficit—cannot assume the role of a reserve-currency country without sooner or later destroying the basis of confidence necessary for assuming such a role. (It should be borne in mind that even the United States, during the period when the dollar was developing into the key currency, consistently recorded current-account surpluses.) Therefore, because a permanent "seigniorage gain," which would always have to be accompanied by corresponding imports of real resources, is unattainable for Germany, our situation presumably corresponds more to that of a banker who has no use for additional deposits or to that of an enterprise that cannot usefully invest additional funds. In these circumstances we do not find Vaubel's "plea for international currency competition" very convincing, quite apart from the fact that competition between David and

Goliath is doomed to failure from the start, unless David's historical tactics of despair are regarded as a practicable approach.

In my view Germany would, rather, be faced with severe economic policy problems in the long run were voluntarily to assume more key currency functions under present circumstances. For a while Germany could of course live beyond its means and import real resources from abroad; in the somewhat longer term, however, it would have to pay a heavy price for doing so, namely, a lasting distortion of the structure of the German economy for exchange rate reasons. While the deutsche mark was developing into a key currency, German competitiveness would increasingly be impaired by unrealistically high exchange rates, which would push up the deficit on current account even further. If action finally had to be taken against the external disequilibriums, there would be no basis from which to do so, because the corresponding industrial capacity would have been destroyed beforehand. In the end, therefore, the voluntary assumption of reserve-currency functions by a country of the locational structure of Germany is self-defeating. That these considerations are not purely theoretical is shown by the example of the United Kingdom, which has hardly derived much long-run benefit from the *voluntary* assumption of a key currency role. Although we in principle reject the idea of the deutsche mark as a reserve currency, we are not unrealistic. At the moment, in particular, we have little reason to be especially alarmed in the slightly shorter term about the reserve currency issue.

May I quote, in closing, the governor of the Deutsche Bundesbank on this question: "We are not particularly pleased about [the growing role of the deutsche mark as a reserve currency]. However, we must learn to live with it, and to a certain extent we can. The alternative, after all, would be restrictions on the freedom of capital movements—a notion we reject."[5]

Kurt Schiltknecht

Roland Vaubel has presented an interesting paper. As far as I know, this is the first paper that analyzes the German and Swiss monetary policies systematically. On the whole, I share most of Vaubel's conclusions. There are, however, a few points that might be worth discussing in some detail. First of all, I should like to comment upon the

---

[5] Karl Otto Pöhl, at the Annual Banquet of the Overseas Bankers Club, London, February 4, 1980, reprinted in *Deutsche Bundesbank Press Review,* no. 12 (February 6, 1980).

analysis of the so-called basic facts. These comments will be followed by some remarks related to the section on international shifts in the demand for money and their implication for monetary policy. Finally, I should like to explain very briefly why we at the Swiss Nationalbank have chosen a monetary base target for this year instead of an M1 target as in the years 1975 to 1978.

In the section entitled "Exchange Rate Flexibility and Monetary Policy," a few coefficients of correlation are presented to shed some light on the different responses of German and Swiss authorities to exchange-rate changes. In my opinion it would have been worthwhile to formulate an explicit money-supply model for the two countries before carrying out correlations between money stock variables and exchange rates. If such money supply models had been formulated, Vaubel would have realized that some of the statistical differences he found are more the outcome of different institutional frameworks in the two countries and less the outcome of different responses to exchange-rate changes by the national monetary authorities.

I should like to elaborate a bit on this point by comparing two of the variables used in the analysis, the central bank money stock and the monetary base. At first sight, there is no great difference between the definition of the central bank money stock in Germany and the definition of the monetary base in Switzerland. In practice, however, the differences are substantial. Whereas in Switzerland banks have only limited access to the rediscount and Lombard facilities offered by the central bank—in other words, the Swiss Nationalbank controls the monetary base—this is, at least in the short run, not the case in Germany. The required reserves in Germany tend to be higher, moreover, than the amount needed by the banks for transactions and precautionary purposes, whereas the opposite is true for Switzerland. If the required reserves are higher than the amount needed for transactions, banks normally will not hold any reserves in excess of required reserves. If, for example, the German Bundesbank intervenes in the foreign-exchange market, the banks acquire excess reserves. Because it is costly to hold excess reserves, banks will lower their reserves almost immediately to the required level by repaying central bank credit. Therefore, the central bank money stock does not respond in the short run to intervention purchases in the foreign-exchange market.

If, on the other hand, the Swiss Nationalbank intervenes in the foreign-exchange market, there is an immediate response in the monetary base, owing to the fact that the amount of outstanding central bank credit is so small that there is no possibility of banks' using the excess reserves for repaying central bank credits. Therefore, in Switzerland changes in the monetary base immediately indicate central bank actions. This is not the case in Germany. There, the central bank money stock changes only if the demand for currency or the demand for required reserves varies. Thus, under the German system the central bank money stock tends to lag the actions of the Bundesbank. If one measures, as Vaubel did, the policy response to exchange-rate changes, using the monetary base for Switzerland and the central bank money stock for Germany, one must get different results. How conclusive such differences are remains at least an open question.

Let me now turn to the model that Vaubel has formulated to estimate the changes in the demand for money. The crucial part of the model is his formulation of inflationary expectations. From a few casual observations during the past few years, I draw the conclusion that this formulation is not appropriate. Let me elaborate a bit. When forming inflationary expectations, market participants face a difficult forecasting problem. In a world characterized by different monetary-policy strategies, different definitions of monetary aggregates, and high variability of growth rates in the money stock, it is very difficult to know whether a change in the observed growth rate of a monetary aggregate is permanent or transitory or whether any particular inflation rate will be the outcome of the specific growth rates. Considering these uncertainties, market participants are likely to make use of other information as well. Specifically, the performance of a central bank over the past years will be of some relevance for forming expectations about future inflation rates. If—as was the case for Switzerland and Germany—the growth in the money stock during three consecutive years is more or less on target, if the inflation rate is down to a few percentage points, and if every deviation from the money stock target tends to be corrected within a few months, then a deviation from the money stock target will at first be judged as temporary. In contrast, if a central bank has a bad record, then a change in the growth rate of the money stock is likely to be judged as permanent, especially if there is an increase in the growth rate. This asymmetry in respect to the evaluation of an observed growth rate of the money stock should be introduced into the model.

If, for example, an increase in the monetary base is judged as transitory, market participants will not in the short run adjust their portfolios. This means that the increase in the money supply affects the interest rates only at the very short end of the yield curve. If the same increase in the monetary base were judged as permanent, then the whole interest-rate structure would be affected. From this example it might be obvious that it is inappropriate to use only one short-term interest rate in the money-demand or the exchange rate equation as Vaubel did.

Finally, I should like to explain very briefly why the Swiss National-bank has chosen a monetary-base target for this year instead of an M1 target.[1] An analysis of the prediction error of our money multiplier model[2] has shown that the prediction errors are correlated with the dollar exchange rate. Because the money multiplier model does not include a variable for exchange-rate expectations, this correlation might indicate that the money stock is affected by exchange-rate expectations. As a working hypothesis, we have assumed that this conclusion is correct. Under such conditions, a realistic short-run money-stock target can be formulated only if the influence of exchange-rate expectations on the money stock can be accurately predicted. Because this is not possible, it is difficult to know whether a deviation from the money-stock target is due to a change in exchange-rate expectations or to an inappropriate monetary policy. In view of such uncertainties, it is clear that a deviation in the money stock from its target should not be rectified immediately by changing the monetary base. From such findings we draw the conclusion that in the presence of (especially) short-run shifts in the demand for Swiss francs, a monetary-base target is an optimal target.

[1] See, for this point, George Rich and Kurt Schiltknecht, "Targeting the Monetary Base: The Swiss Experience," mimeographed (Zurich, 1980).

[2] See, for a description of the money multiplier model, H. J. Bütler, J. F. Gorgerat, H. Schiltknecht, and K. Schiltknecht, "A Multiplier Model for Controlling the Money Stock," *Journal of Monetary Economics*, vol. 5, no. 3 (July 1979), pp. 327-41.

Summary of the Discussion

In the general discussion that followed the commentaries, the commentators addressed three main points: the reasons for scant empirical support for the theory of purchasing power parity (PPP), the evaluation of effects of exchange-rate volatility on international trade, and the importance of currency substitution for exchange-rate determination.

Empirical Validation of PPP Relationships

Several statements were made, both by the authors of papers presented in part 3 and by the commentators, to the effect that in most cases studied the evidence of relationships postulated by the PPP theory was weak. This led a number of participants in the conference to express doubts about the usefulness and applicability of the theory itself. Jacob Frenkel made a distinction, however, between the fact that purchasing power parity appears not to hold and the inference that the theory is not valid. He stated that this fact is not so much a test of the validity of a specific theory of exchange rate determination as it is a reflection of the nature of the shocks that disturbed the world economy in the 1970s. Given the frequency and intensity of real shocks during the past decade, it is not surprising, Frenkel maintained, that PPP relationships failed to hold in either the short run or the long run.

John Bilson expanded Frenkel's argument by pointing out that real shocks generally entail changes in relative prices, and hence deviations from purchasing power parity. Because such relative price changes in the 1970s were large, so also were the deviations from parity relationships. These deviations, for example, accounted for about 30 percent of the inflation differential between West Germany and both the United States and the United Kingdom. Parenthetically, Bilson argued that the observed failure of the PPP theory to hold does not undermine the soundness of monetary models of exchange rate determination because the fundamental idea underlying these models is not the PPP relationship but the idea that the economic system is homogeneous in its monetary magnitudes.

John Makin pointed out that the function of the PPP theory in determining an exchange rate is to filter out the obvious monetary factors. What is left, and what Frenkel, Bilson, and others call real factors, is often treated as a residual about which we do not know very much. He suggested that it is important to divide these real factors into a systematic component—currency substitution, oil price changes, and so on—and a nonsystematic component and then to proceed with measuring the systematic real factors and their relative weights in explaining deviations of exchange rates from their PPP relationships.

Michael Keran, defending the model employed in his paper against the commentators' criticism, indicated that he did exactly what Bilson and Makin suggested. He modeled the "monetary" component of expectations by using changes in relative growth rates of money in the United States and Japan. Relying on the homogeneity property of money mentioned by Bilson, Keran took these changes as a proxy for future changes in the price relationship between the two countries and, consequently, the yen/dollar exchange rate. He augmented his essentially monetary model, however, by taking into account at least one expected "real" shock: the future differential effect of announced oil price increases on the economies of the two countries.

The Effects of Exchange Rate Volatility on International Trade

A discussion of this topic was prompted by a remark by John Williamson, who took exception to the proposition that floating exchange rates have had no substantial adverse impact on international trade. He mentioned that a recent study by Carlos Diaz-Alejandro produces results that are at odds with this proposition.

Williamson's line of criticism was taken up by Ronald McKinnon within a broader context of selecting proper criteria for evaluating the performance of flexible exchange rates. McKinnon found it erroneous to look at a rising volume of trade in recent years and to conclude from this trend that flexible exchange rates have had no harmful effect on the efficiency of international trade. He pointed out that unanticipated fluctuations in exchange rates are just one aspect of monetary instability, which in his view contributed decisively to the slowdown in productivity growth afflicting all industrial nations. In drawing an analogy between international and purely domestic monetary instability, he invoked a proposition, well established in the economic literature, that unexpected or unpredictable inflation leads to serious resource misallocation within a country because producers and consumers cannot distinguish absolute from relative price changes. As a result—and this is the primary cost of

269

inflation—economic agents are likely to make bad choices in deciding on purchasing and selling goods and services. In the international arena, if producers and traders are unable to distinguish between permanent and transitory changes in the exchange rates, they are likely to make bad decisions regarding purchases of inputs and the shipment of goods produced. McKinnon observed that the volume of domestic commerce intensifies in a highly inflationary situation, but that does not mean that the gain from increased commerce is a net social gain. Similarly, the rising volume of international trade is by no means an indication of increased gains from trade. On the contrary, in his view, there has been a decline in the efficiency of trade, which he attributes to exchange-rate volatility.

Bilson expressed support for McKinnon's view. He pointed out that a substantial part of the increase in the volume of trade between 1973 and 1979 was due to a very large increase in oil prices. Realistic evaluation of effects of exchange-rate volatility on international trade should take as the point of departure not the volume of trade, but rather some price measures. He invoked the results obtained by Peter Isard and Jacques Artus which indicate large and persistent changes in relative prices even for homogeneous products. These changes in relative prices have apparently not been eliminated by offsetting movement in exchange rates.

Thomas Willett agreed that the volume of trade is not an appropriate criterion for assessing the effect of exchange-rate flexibility on trade. He argued that we would expect exchange-rate volatility to have some adverse effect on trade efficiency but pointed out that the relevant question is: To what extent is exchange-rate volatility an *independent* cause of distortions in allocation of resources? In his view, these distortions arise mainly from external shocks and instability in official policies rather than from the operation of the exchange-rate system. He stressed that McKinnon's argument is a case against exchange-rate uncertainty, not against exchange-rate flexibility. In fact, a flexible exchange-rate regime may well lead to less uncertainty than any of the feasible alternative arrangements, given the course of underlying policies.

The Importance of Currency Substitution

Referring to the empirical results contained in Roland Vaubel's paper, Dale Henderson expressed his longstanding skepticism about the reasoning underlying the currency-substitution argument. According to Henderson, it seems more logical for someone who wants to take a long position in some currency to acquire an interest-bearing asset rather than cash or demand deposits. It also seems quite implausible to him that residents of a country would actually acquire significantly greater amounts of foreign currencies for transaction purposes. His skepticism was reinforced by Roland Vaubel, whose results showed upward shifts in demand functions for German marks (DM) and Swiss francs but failed to find matching downward shifts in demand functions for other currencies. Henderson did not contest Vaubel's findings, but he was doubtful that they constitute a confirmation of explicit shifts between the transaction media of various countries. Vaubel's findings are due, rather, Henderson suggested, to institutional peculiarities in Germany and Switzerland. He noted that, especially in the case of Switzerland, it was exceedingly difficult for foreigners to establish interest-bearing accounts denominated in Swiss francs. The Swiss interest rate has been very low anyway, moreover, and has not provided much more of an incentive than a non-interest-bearing account. In this connection Henderson remarked that in both Germany and Switzerland not only deposits held by foreigners but also those held by residents went up substantially (thus reinforcing the upward shift, discovered by Vaubel, in the demand-for-money function). He appeared to be puzzled by this finding, and the one possible explanation of this phenomenon offered by Henderson was that somehow it must be easier to get oneself defined as resident for the purpose of holding a simple demand deposit than for the purpose of opening an interest-bearing account.

Vaubel took as a point of departure a statement by Otmar Emminger concerning the Bundesbank's definition of the money supply concept (which excludes deutsche mark–denominated deposits held by foreigners). Vaubel remarked that this definition of the money supply does not make it invariant with respect to shifts in demand for various currencies. In his view such shifts have to do not only with the behavior of foreigners but also with the behavior of residents. In fact, Vaubel pointed out, if exchange-rate expectations are on the whole homogeneous among residents of different countries, a shift in foreign demand for German marks would be accompanied by a shift in demand by Germans out of, say, dollars. Moreover, he said, an increase in the demand for German marks (or Swiss francs) by foreigners would result in an appreciation of the deutsche mark, which, in turn, might affect exchange-rate expectations of residents of Germany or lead to rebalancing of their portfolios, that is, to a shift in their demand for German marks. Vaubel concluded that such shifts among currencies (whether held in interest-bearing or non-interest-bearing form) are relevant to both inflation and the exchange rate and should not be ignored by the Bundesbank in the conduct of monetary policy.

Part Four

International Liquidity Issues under Floating

Introductory Remarks

In addition to a number of issues associated with exchange rate volatility discussed in parts 2 and 3, a major set of international monetary issues concerns a perceived lack of control over the volume of international liquidity, both official and private, and the prospects for increased monetary instability resulting from an accelerated trend toward a multiple currency reserve system.

It has been argued that the Second Amendment to the International Monetary Fund (IMF) Articles of Agreement, which officially sanctioned the new international monetary system based on flexible exchange rates, was dangerously deficient in not paying sufficient attention to these issues. Some proposals for further reforms of the international monetary system include the restoration of some form of convertibility of currencies into international reserve assets and other methods of greater international control over official international reserve holdings, international regulation of the Eurocurrency markets, and the creation of a substitution facility in the IMF to convert current holdings of dollars into special drawing rights (SDR) with the hope of thus enhancing the role of the SDR and at the same time reducing the incentives for switching from dollars into other currencies, such as the deutsche mark or the yen.

These issues are discussed in parts 4 and 5. Part 4 concentrates on international regulation of official international liquidity and of the Eurocurrency markets. The problem of control of official liquidity is considered by John Williamson. The remaining three papers deal with the issue of international regulation of Eurocurrency markets. The first of them, "The Need for Control over the Eurocurrency Market" by Henry C. Wallich, is an abridged version of his testimony of July 12, 1979, before the Subcommittees on Domestic Monetary Policy and International Trade, Investment, and Monetary Policy of the House Committee on Banking, Finance, and Urban Affairs. This paper was not presented at the conference itself, but Governor Wallich kindly agreed to have it included in the present volume. In the editors' judgment his testimony constitutes an excellent (and compact) statement of the problem.

The two papers following Henry Wallich's testimony should be seen against this background. The first, by Dale W. Henderson and Douglas G. Waldo, contemplates the consequences of Eurocurrency reserve requirements for monetary control. The second paper, by Ronald I. McKinnon, takes a critical look at various proposals for Eurocurrency control. The version of McKinnon's paper included in this volume differs substantially from the version actually presented at the conference. The new version was prepared originally for the Monetary Authority of Singapore, but because it has a sharper analytical focus and, especially, stronger implications for U.S. monetary policy than the original version, the editors thought it appropriate to satisfy McKinnon's request for substitution.

Part 4 concludes with extensive remarks by five commentators and a lively floor discussion.

The Growth of Official Reserves and the Issue of World Monetary Control

John Williamson

It is a historical fact, documented in section 1 of this paper, that by virtually any concept official international reserves have expanded enormously in the past decade and are continuing to rise rapidly. It is also a historical fact, so familiar as to need no documentation, that the past decade has witnessed global inflation without precedent except during major wars. The central question addressed in section 2 is whether responsibility for the inflation can be attributed to the reserve explosion, as is contended by the school of thought recently described as "international reserve monetarism." Although I would certainly not deny that the defense of the dollar at an overvalued level prior to 1973 was an important cause of the generalization of world inflation, I argue that there is neither theoretical nor empirical evidence linking global reserves to world inflation, especially under present arrangements. The conclusion one can draw is that a coherent world monetary policy, in the sense of an assurance that the world money supply will expand at an appropriate rate, cannot be achieved by establishing and exercising collective control of the volume of world reserves. An alternative possible strategy for achieving the same goal, involving internationally agreed-upon and collectively consistent targets for the creation of credit in participating countries, is sketched in section 3.

Past Reserve Growth

Table 1 presents statistics regarding official reserves of the International Monetary Fund (IMF) "world" from 1959, the year when the Bretton Woods system effectively began to operate after the restoration of European convertibility, until the latest date for which statistics are

277

TABLE 1

The Growth of Official Reserves, 1959–1979
(SDR billions)

Row	Description	1959	1964	1969	1970	1971	1972	1973	1974	1975	1976	1977	1978	Nov. 1979
1	Gold (at SDR35 per ounce)	37.6	40.5	38.9	37.0	35.9	35.6	35.6	35.6	35.5	35.3	35.4	35.6	32.5
2	Foreign exchange	16.1	24.2	33.0	45.4	75.0	95.9	101.5	126.3	136.9	159.8	200.0	220.7	204.9
3	Reserve positions in IMF	3.3	4.2	6.7	7.7	6.3	6.3	6.2	8.8	12.6	17.7	18.1	14.8	12.4
4	SDRs	—	—	—	3.1	5.9	8.7	8.8	8.9	8.8	8.7	8.1	8.1	11.6
5	ECUs	—	—	—	—	—	—	—	—	—	—	—	—	32.1
6	Total	57.0	68.9	78.7	93.2	123.1	146.6	152.1	179.5	193.8	221.6	261.7	279.4	293.5
	Memorandum items													
7	Total excluding OPEC	54.5	66.3	74.6	88.2	115.3	136.6	140.1	141.1	145.5	165.5	199.5	233.2	241.3
8	Total excluding gold	19.4	28.4	39.8	56.3	87.2	111.0	116.5	144.0	158.3	186.2	226.3	243.8	261.0
9	Total with gold at market value	57.0	68.9	78.9	95.8	132.0	177.0	230.7	333.5	300.7	322.2	394.2	474.1	554.8

NOTE: Figures relate to end of year, except for 1979.
SOURCE: *International Financial Statistics*, 1979 Yearbook, and International Monetary Fund.

available, November 1979. Row 1 shows gold holdings, valued at the old official price of SDR35 an ounce. Row 2 shows foreign exchange, aggregated over currencies and between that held in the issuing country and offshore. Rows 3 and 4 show reserve assets created by the IMF, and row 5 shows the European Currency Units (ECU) first created in 1979 within the context of the European Monetary System. The sum of these five items, shown in row 6, constitutes the total of world reserves as that concept has been measured traditionally.

The memorandum items display three alternative concepts of world reserves. The first of these excludes reserves of the oil-exporting countries, on the argument that the reserves of these countries serve more as long-term investments than as working balances or as a basis for expansion of the domestic money supply. The second concept excludes gold, on the argument that certainly since August 1971, and arguably since March 1968, gold has not satisfied the widely accepted definition of a "reserve asset" as one that "can be used, directly or through assured convertibility into other assets, to support [a country's] rate of exchange when [its] external payments are in deficit." [1] The third concept includes gold at its current market value. Personally, I regard this measure as indefensible, given that as far as major central banks (at least) are concerned gold has conspicuously lost the attribute of liquidity that is the prime characteristic of a reserve asset, but I suppose some economists may not accept this reasoning. It is, in any event, interesting to see the expansion in the value of reserves that, on this concept, has been provoked by the speculative bubble in the gold market.

The story documented in table 1 will be familiar to participants in this conference. During the 1960s, gold reserves first stagnated, then started to decline, but the buildup of dollar holdings (and to some extent of claims on the IMF) led to a moderate expansion, averaging some 3.3 percent a year, in total reserves. This situation, however, was commonly regarded as unsustainable for reasons popularized by Triffin, and hence in due course the SDR was created in order to permit an orderly expansion of international liquidity.[2] The first SDRs were allocated in 1970 as part of a three-year program. As it happened, however, the attempt to peg the dollar at an overvalued exchange rate, coupled with active U.S. use of monetary policy to expand domestic demand, led to a simultaneous explosion of foreign-exchange holdings, almost doubling total reserves in the three-year period prior to the adoption of generalized

[1] Group of Ten, *Report of the Study Group on the Creation of Reserve Assets,* 1965, p. 21.

[2] Robert Triffin, *Gold and the Dollar Crisis* (New Haven, Conn.: Yale University Press, 1960).

floating in March 1973. The move to floating was followed by a pause in reserve growth. At the aggregate world level, this pause was very brief, but, excluding the oil exporters (row 7), it lasted some three years. In 1976, however, the general expansion of foreign exchange reserves resumed. In 1979 it was reinforced by a new allocation of SDRs and, more important, by the creation of ECUs within the European Monetary System. Of course, if the concept of reserves in row 9 is taken seriously, the increase in the value of gold has dwarfed all other factors.[3] Even those, however, who would reject row 9 cannot avoid the conclusion that reserves have continued to grow very rapidly.

International Reserve Monetarism

The standard argument in favor of creation of a new reserve asset during the debate of the 1960s was the desirability of being able to deliberately expand international liquidity in order to influence world macroeconomic conditions.[4] At the turn of the decade, Johnson and Mundell were taking it as axiomatic that an expansion of reserves would increase the world price level at least proportionately [5]—a proposition I once termed the "international quantity theory." Willett has recently used the term "international reserve monetarism" for the more general proposition that the level of international reserves has a sufficiently systematic and powerful influence on global economic aggregates to make control of the world reserve stock a potential policy instrument.[6] The validity of this thesis is the topic of this section.

It is of course easy to specify circumstances in which international reserve monetarism would be justified. The obvious case is that of a pure gold standard, in which reserves consist exclusively of gold and all

[3] At the beginning of the week in which this was written, total reserves on this concept must have reached some SDR875 billion. (But within three days reserves fell, on the row 9 concept, by more than SDR100 billion!)

[4] See, for example, Triffin, *Gold and the Dollar Crisis;* J. Marcus Fleming, "Towards Assessing the Need for International Reserves," Essays in International Finance, no. 58 (Princeton, N.J.: Princeton University, 1967); *International Reserves: Needs and Availability,* (Washington, D.C.: International Monetary Fund, 1970).

[5] Harry G. Johnson, *Inflation and the Monetarist Controversy* (Amsterdam, 1972), chap. 3; IMF, *International Reserves: Needs and Availability;* Robert A. Mundell, *Monetary Theory: Inflation, Interest, and Growth in the World Economy* (Pacific Palisades, Calif.: Goodyear Publishing Co., 1971). They in fact argued that faster reserve expansion would promote inflation, hence increase the opportunity cost of reserve holding, hence reduce desired levels of real reserves, and hence increase prices more than proportionately to the reserve expansion.

[6] Thomas D. Willett, *International Liquidity Issues* (Washington, D.C.: American Enterprise Institute, 1980).

countries maintain a fixed exchange rate in relation to gold by a systematic policy of holding a constant ratio of gold to money, thus inflating or deflating the money supply when they are gaining or losing reserves, respectively.[7] Granted the presumption (which will not be queried in this paper—we are all monetarists now!) that nominal income is roughly proportionate to the money supply in each country, it follows that in equilibrium world income will be proportionate to world reserves and hence that any possibility of varying world reserves will provide also a way of influencing global aggregate income. If in addition one makes the monetarist assumption that output is determined exclusively by real forces, one would endorse not just international reserve monetarism but also the international quantity theory.

It is obvious enough that the present international monetary non-system bears no resemblance whatsoever to a pure gold standard. There has since 1973 been a running debate as to whether these differences are not such as to destroy international reserve monetarism.[8] My own views have evolved gradually, to the point that I can no longer believe, for the following reasons, that the lack of control of reserves is of any consequence.

There are a series of traditional arguments for querying whether the relation between aggregate reserve supplies and global income should be as close as that between domestic money and domestic income.[9] These traditional arguments are: that ratios of reserves to money may vary between countries, so that the distribution as well as the level of reserves will matter; that central bank desires for reserves are in large measure conventional, implying that the desired level of reserves may be ratcheted up when a country experiences higher reserves;[10] that the number of important central banks is small, so that one cannot rely on the law of large numbers to generate a systematic reaction of the system to portfolio disequilibrium; and that monetary authorities, unlike private agents, have a stabilization objective high in their priorities, which may lead them to ignore or mute their reactions to a portfolio disequilibrium. These arguments are convincing enough in showing

[7] Constant gold/money ratios in each country would imply a constant gold/money ratio at the global level only when the distribution of reserves was in equilibrium, except in the case where the ratios were equal across countries.

[8] See especially Robert A. Mundell and J. J. Polak, *The New International Monetary System* (New York: Columbia University Press, 1977); Willett, "International Liquidity Issues."

[9] See, for example, J. Marcus Fleming in IMF, *International Reserves,* or Willett, "International Liquidity Issues."

[10] Fritz Machlup, "The Need for Monetary Reserves," *Banca Nazionale del Lavoro Quarterly Review,* September 1966.

why one should expect a relatively loose relationship between world reserves and world money, but whether they suffice to destroy international reserve monetarism is as much an empirical question as whether variations in velocity suffice to destroy the usefulness of the quantity theory.

An important point that has not to my knowledge been recognized in the existing literature concerns the payment of interest on reserves. The fact that gold pays no interest implies that under a pure gold standard liquidity can be secured only by sacrificing earnings. This means that each central bank has both a pecuniary incentive to avoid holding excess reserves and a prudential incentive to ensure adequate reserves, which in conjunction lend plausibility to the assumption of a constant ratio of reserves to money. This logic becomes progressively less compelling, however, as the interest rate paid on reserves rises toward an economic rate, because the pecuniary incentive to avoid excess reserves is eroded. It is surely true (despite the remaining shortfall in the SDR interest rate below the average on the major currencies in the basket) that yields on reserves are today close to competitive levels.

The point that has received most discussion is of course that of the move from pegged to floating exchange rates. It had traditionally been argued that floating rates would remove the need to use, and hence presumably the desire to hold, official reserves. Experience of managed floating quickly demonstrated that this was erroneous and that intervention continued under floating on a scale broadly similar to that previously prevailing. Three studies have now attempted to assess econometrically the effect of the move to floating on the demand for reserves. All three have concluded that there remains enough regularity in the demand for reserves to continue thinking in terms of a reserve demand function. Heller and Kahn found that the advent of floating had brought some reduction in the demand for reserves,[11] whereas Frenkel's study and that of Bilson and Frenkel found no evidence of a change in the reserve demand function.[12]

[11] H. Robert Heller and Moshin S. Khan, "The Demand for International Reserves under Fixed and Floating Exchange Rates," *IMF Staff Papers,* December 1978.

[12] Jacob A. Frenkel, "The Demand for International Reserves under Pegged and Flexible Exchange Rate Regimes and Aspects of the Economics of Managed Float," in D. Bigman and T. Taya, eds., *The Functioning of Floating Exchange Rates: Theory, Evidence, and Policy Implications* (Cambridge, Mass.: Ballinger Publishing Co., 1980); John F. O. Bilson and Jacob A. Frenkel, "Dynamic Adjustment and the Demand for International Reserves," NBER Working Paper no. 407 (Cambridge, Mass.: National Bureau of Economic Research, 1979).

Existence of a reserve demand function, and even of evidence that departure of actual reserves from the target level prompts a systematic adjustment process,[13] is *not,* however, sufficient to justify international reserve monetarism. That requires in addition that the induced adjustment take the particular form that it did under the gold standard: namely, that a reserve shortage (surfeit) induces domestic monetary contraction (expansion). With a flexible exchange rate, however, there is no need to adopt this strategy, because an alternative method of remedying the reserve shortage is for the monetary authority to enter the exchange market and buy some more reserves, accepting the necessary depreciation of its currency. Naturally there may be times when the authorities are reluctant to do this because of an implicit target level for the exchange rate. Nevertheless, a decision to choose floating reflects a conviction that the rate of exchange is a target variable of less importance than the supply of money and hence implies that the latter is less likely to be influenced by the reserves available at a given exchange rate than under a fixed exchange rate regime.

What seems to me to be the fundamental point may be expressed as follows. In a world of fixed exchange rates, the growth of each country's money stock is ultimately governed by the growth of its international reserves:[14] this is a corollary of the well-known theorem that permanent sterilization is not consistent with the maintenance of a fixed exchange rate. Reserves and domestic credit are *complements.* In contrast, under floating, domestic credit expansion (DCE) tends to be a *substitute* for reserve acquisition, if the central bank has either a money supply target or an interest-rate target. An expansion of global reserves reflects a decision by central banks that on balance they prefer a larger part of an exogenously determined volume of monetary expansion to take a form that will depreciate their currencies on the exchange markets; but it does not increase the world money supply.

There is yet another reason, of a comparable order of importance to the advent of floating, for rejecting international reserve monetarism: the growth of capital mobility. Where capital mobility is high enough, the variables that have traditionally been deemed relevant to the determination of reserve demand, such as the variability of exports or the level of imports, lose all importance. Liquidity needs can be satisfied from the liability as well as the asset side of the balance sheet, because an assured ability to borrow provides a near-perfect substitute for holdings of an asset that can assuredly be realized. The external

[13] Bilson and Frenkel, "Dynamic Adjustment."
[14] This formulation was stimulated by Gottfried Haberler in Mundell and Polak, *New International Monetary System.*

283

constraint on economic policy no longer stems from the level of reserves but stems from the net borrowing that the country can undertake without undermining its creditworthiness. In this environment there is no reason to suppose that reserve policy, such as allocation or cancellation of SDRs, would exert any significant influence on countries' macroeconomic policies; it would simply induce them to manipulate their capital flows in order to reestablish the reserve levels preferred on portfolio grounds. In short, control of reserves without complementary control of international borrowing would produce effects that were no more than cosmetic.

The implication of the foregoing discussion seems to me to be clear. Despite the emphatic rejection of the views of the Radcliffe committee in the domestic context in which they were advanced,[15] it is exactly such a vision that is appropriate at the international level. There is no world "monetary base" that determines the world money supply and that can or should be controlled by collective international decision, as international reserve monetarism contends; rather, world economic conditions will be influenced by the general state of liquidity—the cost and availability of loans—as much as by the stock of liquid assets. Obviously, this is not to argue (any more than the Radcliffe committee would have done) that a reserve expansion that produced a positive net wealth effect would not have expansionary effects on world demand. In particular, a Radcliffean view is consistent with a conviction that Prime Minister Barre's reported proposal to remonetize gold at a price close to the current market level must be expected to have inflationary results and should accordingly be resisted.

I am aware of three attempts to test "international reserve monetarism" empirically. The first was undertaken by Parkin and concluded that the link between reserves and money supplies was far too weak to sustain the thesis.[16] The second and third are by Heller, who concluded that his results substantiated the theory.[17] The result in Heller's 1976 paper, the controversial link of the theory between international reserves and the world money supply, is as follows:

[15] Committee on the Working of the Monetary System, *Report,* London, 1959. 1959.

[16] J. Michael Parkin, "International Liquidity and World Inflation in the 1960's," paper presented to SSRC (UK)/Royal Economic Society Conference on International Liquidity, 1975.

[17] H. Robert Heller, "International Reserves and Worldwide Inflation," *IMF Staff Papers,* March 1976; idem, "Further Evidence on the Relationship between International Reserves and World Inflation," in Michael Boskin, ed., *Economics and Human Welfare: Essays in Honor of Tibor Scitovsky* (New York: Academic Press, 1979).

$$M_t = 7.34 + 0.08R_t + 0.14R_{t-1}$$
$$(0.62)\ (0.05)\quad (0.05)$$

$$\bar{R}^2 = 0.57;\quad D - W = 2.01;\quad SEE = 1.72;\quad \rho = 0.30$$

where M is the annual percentage change in the world money supply, R is the annual percentage change in world reserves measured in dollars, and standard errors are shown in parentheses. This equation implies that, over the period 1951–1974 to which it was fitted, each 1 percent increase in reserves stimulated an increase of only 0.22 percent in money, rather than the 1 percent increase predicted by international reserve monetarism; it also implies that over 90 percent of all monetary expansion was "explained" by the constant term rather than by reserve growth! Thus, the equation can hardly be interpreted as providing support for any but the weakest form of international reserve monetarism, despite the fact that the period over which it was estimated largely antedated the adoption of floating exchange rates and was marked by high capital mobility only in its later years. In his 1979 paper, Heller finds a slightly higher coefficient on reserve changes (0.36), but the results are broadly similar. Hence, I conclude that such empirical evidence as exists is consistent with the conclusion drawn from the theoretical discussion.

An Alternative Approach to World Monetary Control

The conclusion that the only acceptable view of international liquidity is Radcliffean rather than monetarist does not necessarily imply a Radcliffean unconcern with monetary aggregates. The latter attitude has been rather generally deemed unacceptable at the national level, which perhaps suggests that it should also be rejected at the world level. The two views can be reconciled by recognizing that the important world monetary aggregate is the *world money supply,*[18] whereas what the Radcliffean view of international liquidity implies is that there is no possibility of influencing the world money supply via manipulation of the level of reserves.

One possibility that may be dismissed rather briefly is that of seeking to supplement reserve control by control of international borrowing in order to seek to reestablish a link between reserves and the world money supply. Such a policy could be criticized as prone to discriminate between countries: Obviously, those countries most vul-

---

[18] W. H. L. Day and H. Robert Heller, "The World Money Supply: Concept and Measurement," *Weltwirtschaftliches Archiv,* no. 4 (1977).

nerable to restrictive limits on foreign borrowing would be the capital importers, even when they have strong allocational reasons for running current account deficits in the interest of accelerating development. More fundamentally, however, one must doubt whether action directed at only one of the four reasons for rejecting international reserve monetarism discussed in the preceding section would be sufficient to change the conclusion. If world control of the world money supply is regarded as a desirable objective, one will surely have to contemplate more far-reaching reforms than placing limits on international borrowing.

Before we discuss how this objective might be achieved, it is natural to pause briefly to consider whether the objective can be considered rational. Why might one argue that an individual country has an interest in appropriate growth of the world money stock and not merely of the money issued by its central bank?

The answer lies in interdependence. Demand in each country depends on the money supplies of its trading partners, not merely its domestic money supply. Monetary assets issued by other central banks may be held by its residents and thereby contribute even to domestic demand. Recent British discussion on the interpretation of the money supply figures since the abolition of exchange control illustrates the ambiguity of national monetary targets in an age of high capital mobility. Furthermore, changes in foreign monetary conditions can sharply influence a country's real exchange rate.

The advantages can be illustrated most graphically by considering the phenomenon of currency substitution, which appears to be a factor of considerable and growing empirical importance. The optimum response to a desired portfolio switch between currencies is to finance it through reserve changes that are not sterilized; this causes national monetary aggregates to alter, but there is no presumption that it will have the slightest impact on aggregate demand in either country. This would not be true if such a switch were financed but sterilization policies were adopted, and especially not if those sterilization policies differed between the two countries. And it would certainly not be true if the switch were not financed but left to provoke changes in the exchange rate; Swiss experience in 1978 illustrates just how violent the resulting real exchange rate changes can be. In the end Switzerland abandoned its monetary target—and no doubt, given the absence of any sort of coherent international monetary policy, inflated the world money supply in the process.

It is hoped that the above sketch of the case for seeking a world monetary target is sufficient to suggest that the objective is one that might be worth pursuing if it were feasible. The question that will now be considered is how it might be pursued.

An elementary accounting identity states that $M_i = R_i + C_i$, where M = money supply, R = reserves, C = domestic credit, and the subscript i refers to the ith country. The traditional strategy relies on controlling $\sum_i R_i$ and trusting that C_i is systematically related to R_i. It has already been argued that this supposition is untenable and that therefore the traditional strategy is impractical. An alternative strategy, suggested by some of the writings of McKinnon, would be to place internationally agreed-upon limits on the C_i.[19] If reserves were defined net, so that total world reserves were unable to change (except by SDR allocations, which do not produce a direct monetary expansion), control of each individual C_i would ensure control of $\sum M_i$, the world money supply. Money could be redistributed, but not created or destroyed, through payments surpluses and deficits, because DCE targets imply a proscription on sterilization.

Two basic questions require consideration.[20] The first concerns the principles that should be used to calculate target rates of DCE. It would seem to me essential to base these targets on a formula, rather than on ad hoc negotiation, given the number of countries that might be involved (though no doubt there could be provisions for special cases to be agreed upon with the fund). I suggest four elements that might enter a formula for the permitted level of DCE as a proportion of the money supply:

Following McKinnon, one would certainly want to include an allowance for each country to satisfy the increase in its own demand for money due to real growth. The first element in the formula should therefore be the product of the country's estimated trend rate of real growth and its estimated income elasticity of demand for money.

McKinnon's second element is an allowance for inflation. Because he was envisaging the proposal as a support for a fixed exchange rate

---

[19] Ronald I. McKinnon, "On Securing a Common Monetary Policy in Europe," *Banca Nazionale del Lavoro Quarterly Review,* March 1973; idem, "Dollar Stabilization and American Monetary Policy," *American Economic Association Papers and Proceedings,* May 1980.

[20] Another important set of questions that I do not go into here concerns the accounting conventions needed to secure a net definition of reserves. This would be bound to raise the problem of the Euromarkets. Let me just state that in my view short-term bank deposits held in the Euromarkets by nonbanks should certainly be deemed to be a part of the world money supply and hence would need to be controlled in an appropriate way consistent with the treatment of onshore bank deposits.

system, the inflation element in his case consisted of a common target rate of inflation.[21] Naturally, this would need to be modified for application to a system in which countries were not committed to the maintenance of fixed exchange rates but wished to allow exchange rate variations at least to the extent necessary to compensate for differential rates of inflation. Individual countries would thus have their own individual target inflation rates, with a presumption that differences between these would be neutralized by exchange rate changes. Although target rates of inflation might differ between countries, they would need to be chosen by a uniform principle. The principle that seems most appropriate is that of building in a gradualist anti-inflationary policy by requiring that past inflation be partially, but only partially, financed. This element of the target would therefore be equal to some agreed-upon fraction α of an appropriate measure (gross domestic product deflator?) of the immediately preceding rate of inflation.

A third element that might be urged, at least by economists of a Keynesian orientation, would represent a contribution to anticyclical policy. This might be introduced by adding (subtracting) a number equal to an agreed parameter β multiplied by the estimated deflationary (inflationary) gap. The deflationary/inflationary gap to be used here might be that for the individual country concerned or that for the world as a whole, or some weighted average of the two. Use of the figure for the world as a whole might seem rational to those who believe that interdependence is now too great to make national anticyclical policies viable.

Finally, it might be desired to use monetary policy to reinforce the adjustment process, even over and above the natural reinforcement provided by the nonsterilization inherent in following a DCE target rather than a money supply target. My own view is that, because the external constraint on policy now stems from creditworthiness rather than liquidity, it is natural to define the target for adjustment in terms of the current account rather than the level of reserves. This implies the need to define current-account targets. Most of the criticisms leveled at this proposal in the past have been unbelievably simplistic, sometimes amounting to no more than the trite observation that current account balance is not in general a sensible target in an age of capital mobility. I do not believe that it is more difficult to establish sensible order-of-magnitude estimates of "underlying" capital flows—the average

---

[21] It is understood that allowance would need to be made for slightly differing target rates of overall inflation consistent with an equal rate of price increase for traded goods, because of different rates of productivity increase between sectors and countries.

inflow or outflow that seems called for on grounds of resource allocation, modified where necessary by creditworthiness considerations—than
of the other magnitudes necessary for any intelligent macroeconomic
management.[22] An appropriate current balance target might also include, besides the estimated underlying capital outflow, an allowance
for partial reversal of the past cumulative deviation of the current
balance from its target, so as to limit cumulative deviations without
imposing unrealistic demands for rapid adjustment. An allowance
might also be added for the effect of temporary factors beyond the
country's own control—crop failure or the effect of the world con-
juncture on exports or import prices. This would reintroduce the important principle (which was embodied in the phrase "fundamental
disequilibrium" but has been rather lost sight of since Jamaica) that
short-run disequilibriums should be financed rather than adjusted.
Furthermore, because export variations caused by *other countries'*
deviations from full employment are outside a country's control whereas
variations in imports or exports caused by a country's *own* deviation
from full employment are clearly not, the formula would tend to increase aggregate current balance targets during a world boom and
to decrease them during a world recession, which should contribute
to stabilization.

If a formula for DCE similar to the one I have outlined were to be
adopted and adhered to by all countries, the world money supply would
increase by enough to finance real growth, plus a fraction of the in-
herited rate of inflation, plus or minus an anticyclical component stemming either directly from the third element or indirectly, via modifica-
tion of current balance targets, from the fourth. All other elements
would cancel out. The world money supply would be immune to payments imbalances, currency substitution, and intervention policies.
There would be a common international commitment to a gradualist
anti-inflationary strategy, which would not be compromised by some
countries' intervention.

The second basic question that requires attention concerns the
acceptability of such a system to the United States. Prohibition of
sterilization would strike at the heart of the special position of the dollar
that made a passive policy acceptable to the United States. If other
countries were dissatisfied with their rate of monetary growth, they
would be able to intervene and acquire reserves and thus accelerate

[22] These other magnitudes can virtually be read off from the discussion of the
determinants of target DCE: the growth rate of capacity, the income elasticity
of demand for money, and the natural rate of unemployment (necessary for
estimating the deflationary gap).

their monetary expansion. The rules would then require the United States to accept a corresponding reduction in its money stock. One could hardly expect the United States to accept such a set of rules.

There are two possible ways around this difficulty. The first would involve modifying the exchange-rate regime so as to limit intervention to occasions when it was implicitly judged to be acceptable to the United States. One way of achieving this would be through adoption of the reference-rate proposal. Another would be to return to a regime of pegged exchange rates. I take it for granted that the only such system worthy of consideration is the crawling peg,[23] because the sudden elimination and perhaps also the subsequent complete suppression of inflation differentials is far too painful to make fixed rates an option, and the speculative pressures that killed the adjustable peg are hardly likely to abate in the future. In the event of a return to a pegged-rate system, however, a system of DCE targets would have the great attraction of making it possible to extend unlimited credit to a country whose currency was under speculative attack without eroding its monetary discipline, thus greatly enhancing the credibility of exchange-rate commitments. Indeed, I find it difficult to conceive of the stability-minded countries even considering a return to pegged rates without a discipline such as this being in place.

The other possible way around the difficulty would be to use a set of DCE targets as a base for the exercise of IMF surveillance rather than as a set of binding commitments. Most economists have long regarded monetary policy (including exchange-rate policy) as the natural area on which to concentrate surveillance, because it is the area with the largest and quickest international spillover effect. As far as one can judge, however, multilateral surveillance has up to now been so ad hoc as to be of dubious value. If the process is ever to play a serious role in coordinating the policies of different countries, it is surely necessary that it be based on some systematic conceptual framework capable of showing the interrelatedness of the crucial policy decisions of the separate nations. Even if the idea of a formula to determine binding national DCE targets is rejected as utopian, I hope that the more

[23] I have to disagree sharply with Gottfried Haberler's classification of the crawling peg as a species of managed float. The difference is quite fundamental. Under a crawling peg, the central bank assumes a responsibility to intervene to whatever extent is necessary in order to prevent the rate from moving outside of a defined range, which for any moment of time is well specified and public; under a managed float, the central bank has no responsibility to intervene but can decide at each moment whether, in what quantity, and at what rate to intervene (Gottfried Haberler, "The International Monetary System Again under Stress," in this volume).

modest idea that it might provide a currently lacking coherence to the surveillance process will receive attention.

Concluding Remarks

In the first half of this paper I argued rather strongly that international reserves cannot be regarded as a world "monetary base" governing the evolution of the world money supply: a Radcliffean view of international liquidity is more appropriate than "international reserve monetarism." The second half should be regarded as altogether more tentative—as raising and exploring issues rather than as offering definitive solutions. Essentially, four issues are at stake: (1) Should one want to control the "world money supply," interpreted as an appropriately weighted sum of national money supplies, at the world level? (2) If so, how can this be achieved? I suggest an international agreement to base domestic credit expansion on a set of commonly agreed principles. (3) Under what circumstances would such a mechanism make sense? Because the reserve position of the dollar would make such an agreement intolerable to the United States without a more structured exchange-rate regime than currently prevails, it may be that introduction of such a mechanism would be feasible only as part of a return to a system based on (crawlingly) pegged exchange rates. (4) Even without a return to a structural international monetary system, could the type of calculation suggested in response to question 2 provide the basis for a coherent surveillance process?

The Need for Control over the Eurocurrency Market

Henry C. Wallich

U.S. monetary authorities have monitored the development of the Euro-dollar market since its birth in the 1950s and its expansion into a market for several Eurocurrencies.

I would like first to address some general questions about the Eurocurrency market that are often asked. I will then turn to the possible need for better control of the market from a monetary policy standpoint. In addition, since concern is also expressed from time to time regarding the adequacy of supervision to assure the safety and soundness of banks participating in Eurocurrency banking, I shall briefly touch on this aspect.

Principal Features of the Eurocurrency Market

The Eurocurrency market is an international banking market in bank deposits and loans that are denominated in currencies other than the currency of the country where the bank is located—for example, dollar deposits and loans of banking offices in London. The phrase "Euro-currency" developed because the market originated in Europe, chiefly as a market for Eurodollars. Eurodollars still account for about three-quarters of the Eurocurrency market, with about half of the remainder being Euromarks. Also, some deposits in the market are denominated in pounds sterling, Swiss francs, and other major currencies. I will focus my comments on the Eurocurrency market as a whole with the reminder that at present it is largely, but not exclusively, a market in dollars.

What is now considered the Eurocurrency market extends beyond Europe to include banking activities in major industrial countries world-wide and in offshore banking centers such as the Bahamas, the Cayman Islands, Hong Kong, and Singapore. Still, the Eurocurrency market does not embrace all of international banking activity. Traditionally, international banking has been conducted through the taking of deposits from foreigners and lending to foreigners in the currency of the country where the bank is located. This form of banking continues. On the other hand, some Eurocurrency activity is not international at all and occurs within a country's domestic market; deposits are taken from residents and loans made to residents denominated in dollars or other foreign currencies.

The Eurocurrency liabilities of banks usually take the form of time deposits of large size. Eurocurrency deposits are not generally used to make payments directly, and only a relatively small part are in immediately available funds that can be used directly to economize on conventional checking account balances. Thus, for the most part they cannot be considered money in the narrow sense of M-1. The closest analogy, in U.S. monetary statistics, is perhaps with large negotiable certificates of deposit, which are included in M-4. However, negotiable CDs can be issued by U.S. banks only with a maturity of one month or more while one-third of all Eurocurrency deposits have a remaining maturity of less than one month. Thus, Eurocurrency deposits may be said to have more of a money-like quality than large CDs.

How Large is the Eurocurrency Market?

The scale of the Eurocurrency market is often misunderstood. For instance, one measure of size often cited—its so-called gross size—represents the total of foreign currency liabilities of banks in industrial countries reporting to the BIS plus those of certain offshore branches of U.S. banks. This figure exceeded $800 billion at the end of 1978. However, it is inflated by a large volume of interbank activity that neither contributes to the liquidity of the nonbank public nor is associated with any extension of credit to nonbanks. On these grounds, we exclude interbank liabilities such as correspondent balances and federal funds from U.S. domestic money and credit aggregates. One should similarly adjust downward the stock of Eurocurrency liabilities. Commonly cited measures produced by the BIS and others put the net size of the Eurocurrency market in the neighborhood of $400 billion. However, these measures still overstate the monetary significance of the market because they net out only banks' liabilities to other banks within the reporting area. Eliminating, insofar as possible, liabilities to banks and central banks outside the reporting area yields a measure of net monetary liabilities in the Eurocurrency market of roughly $150 billion to $175 billion as of the end of 1978. Of this amount, about one-third is counted in the monetary statistics of some country. Thus, today the so-called stateless money in the Eurocurrency market, that which is not counted in national monetary statistics, is on the order of $100 billion to $120 billion.

The net credit provided to nonbanks through the Eurocurrency market, estimated at about $225 billion to $250 billion as of the end of 1978, is larger than its net monetary liabilities. The difference arises largely because of sizable deposits of central banks in the market. While these deposits do not constitute part of the net monetary asset holdings of nonbanks, they do provide a source of funds that can be used to make loans and, to the extent that they are largely deposits of central banks of smaller countries, they are more likely to be shifted among currencies.

The numbers I have cited tend to shrink one's perception of the Eurocurrency market compared with the impression that is often conveyed, but the importance of the market should not be underestimated. The absolute numbers involved are large. Moreover, Eurocurrency holdings and credits have been growing more rapidly than the domestic monetary and credit aggregates of the United States and of most other countries. For example, from the end of 1974 to the end of 1978, Eurocurrency liabilities to nonbanks are estimated to have grown at an average annual rate of about 18½ percent, compared with growth in M-1 and M-4 in the United States at average annual rates of 6.3 percent and 8.5 percent respectively over the same four-year period. This trend can be expected to continue unless checked. Thus, the existence of the Eurocurrency market increasingly will have to be taken into account in formulating and executing domestic monetary policies; issues of surveillance, supervision, and control of the Eurocurrency market will continue to be in the foreground of domestic and international financial policy.

Is the Eurocurrency Market Out of Control?

Because Eurocurrency banking is not subject to reserve requirements or various other restrictions, such as liquidity ratios or credit ceilings, which various monetary authorities employ to facilitate the execution of domestic monetary policies, it is often alleged that the Eurocurrency market is a source of uncontrolled liquidity. However, because of its close links with domestic markets for bank funds, the Eurocurrency market is, in fact, directly subject to the influence of domestic monetary policies in countries of financial importance.

Observation of interest rates confirms the prediction of economic theory that Eurocurrency interest rates should be closely tied to interest rates in the domestic market for comparable assets denominated in the corresponding currency. Relatively stable differentials are normally observed, and these differentials reflect costs in the domestic market arising from reserve requirements and other regulations that do not exist in the Eurocurrency market.

These close links between domestic and "Euro" interest rates are maintained by flows of funds between domestic markets and the Eurocurrency market. For example, when domestic U.S. interest rates rise, depositors have an incentive to switch funds from Eurodollar deposits to domestic U.S. bank deposits and commercial paper. Some borrowers shift their borrowing to the Eurodollar market, and banks themselves move funds raised in that market to the U.S. credit market. These responses put upward pressure on Eurodollar interest rates until the normal relationship with domestic U.S. rates is restored. In practice, the adjustment is virtually instantaneous. Thus, the dampening effect of higher U.S. interest rates on credit demand and spending is felt in the Eurodollar market as well as in the U.S. market.

While the transmission of domestic monetary influences to the Eurocurrency market is very real and effective, there is a somewhat paradoxical tendency for the growth of the market to accelerate relative to the domestic banking market when monetary policy becomes more restrictive and interest rates rise. In the case of Eurodollars this phenomenon is a consequence of two features of the U.S. monetary system: first, requirements that member banks hold non-interest-bearing reserves and, second, restrictions on deposit interest rates (particularly the prohibition of interest payments on deposits of less than 30 days' maturity).

As a result of reserve requirements, member banks incur additional costs in bidding for large deposits domestically compared with the costs of raising funds in the Eurodollar market since a portion of funds raised at home must be held in nonearning form. Monetary restraint in the United States, either in the form of a higher federal funds rate or in the form of higher reserve requirements, pushes up these additional costs of domestic banking and induces banks to shift their funding efforts to the Eurodollar market even though deposit interest rates for dollars in that market may rise by at least as much as in the domestic market. With higher market interest rates generally, demand deposits tend to be attracted from the U.S. banking system to the Eurodollar market since such deposits cannot, by law, earn interest in the United States. Similar reactions occur in the response to monetary tightening in other countries although the specific factors differ from country to country. These effects constitute one reason, although by no means the only reason, why the Eurocurrency market has grown so rapidly over the past decade when inflation has risen and brought with it historically high nominal interest rates.

As interest rates rise, the Eurocurrency market is not the only financial channel that gains a competitive advantage. Domestic U.S. financial flows through channels not subjected to member bank reserve requirements or interest rate restrictions—such as the commercial paper market, finance companies, and money market mutual funds—are also favored.

Despite the tendency of the Eurocurrency market to grow relatively more rapidly when domestic interest rates rise, it is still true that monetary restraint is effective. When the Federal Reserve tightens monetary policy, it forces interest rates to rise and growth of domestic member bank deposits to slow. The expansion of the Eurodollar market will slow less than that of the domestic market in response to higher interest rates, and the Eurodollar market may grow faster than it otherwise would if enough banking activity shifts to it from the U.S. market. Nevertheless, it will normally be the case that the application of domestic restraint will reduce the growth of the two markets taken together.

Does the Eurocurrency Market Create Problems for Domestic Monetary Policy?

While the Eurocurrency market is linked to domestic markets and subject to control through the impact of domestic monetary policy on interest rates, it does pose problems for monetary policy. My judgment is that these problems have been of only moderate significance to date, but they are increasing. Moreover, the Eurocurrency market adds to inflationary pressures because liabilities to nonbanks in this market are rising faster than domestic money supplies. In the present inflationary environment we must look closely at every source of inflationary tendency.

Let me identify some of the ways in which the Eurocurrency market complicates the execution of monetary policy. The presence of a Eurocurrency market confronts domestic monetary authorities with a dilemma. They could, in principle, act in such a way as to provide for the desired growth of liquidity, taking account of both the domestic market and the Eurocurrency market. One problem that the Federal Reserve would encounter in following such an approach would arise because we cannot gauge well the extent to which growth in the Eurocurrency market affects spending in the United States. Dollars held or borrowed in the Eurocurrency market could be spent anywhere in the world, not just in the United States. On the other hand, it is likely that growth in the nondollar portion of the market would stimulate spending in the United States at least marginally. Other monetary authorities face the same uncertainties.

Perhaps an even more serious problem in carrying out a monetary policy that takes explicit account of the Eurocurrency market would arise because of the uneven effects of restrictive policy on the domestic and Eurocurrency markets. Those smaller domestic banks and their customers that have less access to the Eurocurrency market than the large international banks and their U.S. and foreign customers would absorb a disproportionate share of the burden of a restrictive policy. This inequity, in turn, would undermine support for an appropriate counterinflationary monetary policy.

Moreover, if monetary authorities focus exclusively on the growth of domestic aggregates, ignoring the effects of the more rapid growth of liabilities to nonbanks that is occurring in the Eurocurrency market, they may facilitate more expansionary and more inflationary conditions than they intend, or may be aware of. Indeed, there is a risk that, over time, as the Eurocurrency market expands relative to domestic markets, control over the aggregate volume of money may increasingly slip from the hands of central banks. Thus, it would be prudent to have available instruments for controlling the Eurocurrency market as we have for controlling domestic monetary aggregates. This is one of the principal reasons for seriously considering the need for reserve requirements against Eurocurrency deposits on an international basis.

What Role Does the Eurocurrency Market Play in Exchange-Rate Developments?

The existence of the Eurocurrency market as a liquid and efficient mechanism for international financial dealings has certainly had an important influence on exchange-rate developments in recent years. It would be wrong, however, to view the market itself as having given rise to new stabilizing or destabilizing forces. Rather it has acted as a conduit and amplifier through which both stabilizing and destabilizing financial flows have been felt in exchange markets with greater speed and intensity.

The size of current-account deficits in recent years has been unprecedented. Without an efficient international financial market to channel funds from countries in surplus to those in deficit, exchange-rate pressures at times would have been even greater than they were.

297

The Eurocurrency markets have played an important role in moving excess savings to private and official borrowers in countries with current-account deficits.

At other times international capital flows have exacerbated pressures in exchange markets that have arisen to some extent from the need to finance current-account deficits. In some of these episodes the capital movements undoubtedly have reflected a reasonable market view that authorities were attempting to maintain untenable exchange-rate relationships. In other episodes, however, market psychology has appeared to drive exchange rates to unwarranted levels—movements that have subsequently been reversed. The international character and the liquidity of the Eurocurrency market have tended to swell the volume of funds moving through exchange markets at such times.

What Measures Could Be Taken to Deal Better with the Eurocurrency Market?

The thrust of my discussion of the Eurocurrency market has been to reject as unfounded the extreme view that the market is an unrestrained source of monetary and exchange-market instability but to recognize that its existence makes the execution of monetary policy more difficult. There is a danger that, if measures are not taken to moderate the growth of the Eurocurrency market, the problem will grow over time and the prospects for controlling inflation will worsen correspondingly. Thus, careful monitoring of the Eurocurrency market is in order, and careful consideration should be given to making monetary restraints on the Eurocurrency market move more in parallel with restraints on domestic markets. In considering various approaches we should be mindful of several factors.

First, any approach adopted should take account of and seek to preserve the benefits that flow from the existence of the market. I have only alluded to these benefits, but they are considerable. The market is extremely competitive and efficient. It facilitates movements of large volumes of funds from savers to investors across national borders at low cost. In doing so it helps to finance temporary current-account imbalances and improve the efficiency of investment worldwide. It also exerts competitive pressure on domestic banking systems to be more responsive to their customers and to become more efficient.

Second, any approach adopted should have a good prospect of contributing significantly to broad control over the volume of international liquid assets and credit. Little would be achieved, and a great burden would be placed on some institutions, if part of the market were restricted and another part were left unrestrained to take up the slack, or if Eurocurrency banking activity could easily be shifted into new unrestricted forms. Similarly, any burden imposed should be as low as possible and should apply equally and equitably to all banks operating in the Eurocurrency market. Thus, for example, it has not seemed desirable to restrict the scale of U.S. banks' participation in the Eurocurrency market so long as banks of other major countries were unfettered.

The Federal Reserve has, of course, the responsibility to consider the safety and soundness of U.S. banks abroad when reviewing proposals of banks to expand their international operations. Together with the Comptroller of the Currency, the Federal Reserve also examines the lending, funding, and management of U.S. banks abroad and considers the consolidated worldwide positions of U.S. banks in assessing their overall condition. Foreign central banks often believe that they do not have the authority to oversee the foreign operations of their banks as closely as we do in the United States, but they are moving, in some cases with the support of new grants of authority, to adopt approaches similar to ours.

Third, measures that were applied only to Eurodollars and not to all Eurocurrencies would have limited effectiveness and might well introduce new instabilities into international financial markets. Although depositors and bankers see Eurodollars, Euromarks, and Eurosterling as being quite different and are not indifferent among these Eurocurrencies, forward markets in foreign exchange offer a ready means of achieving any desired foreign exchange position regardless of the actual currency of a deposit. Hence, restrictions on the availability of one Eurocurrency would induce some who wished to hold that currency to move into deposits denominated in other currencies and then to acquire the desired currency through a forward contract.

Taking account of these considerations, the Federal Reserve has been examining the advantages and disadvantages of various ways that the Eurocurrency market might be brought under greater control. One technique we have explored would entail placing reserve requirements on the Eurocurrency liabilities of banks' head offices, branches, and affiliates no matter where located. Those countries whose banks and banking affiliates have a significant, or potentially significant, presence in international markets would be expected to act in concert with respect to their banks. Deposits accepted from banks that were subjected to the requirement could be exempted. The objective would be to slow down the growth of deposits from outside the covered banks and the corresponding growth of credit by putting the Eurocurrency market more nearly in a position of competitive equality with domestic banking markets. If this approach were accepted by the important countries, it would minimize the likelihood that large, parallel, but reserve-free markets would emerge through banks with head offices in nonparticipating countries.

The reserve requirement approach seems to be the most effective of several that might have merit. An alternative, unilateral approach would be to reduce the competitive advantage of the Eurocurrency market by removing reserve requirements and interest rate restrictions on those domestic deposits for which Eurocurrency deposits are close substitutes. However, this would have the disadvantage of giving up an important monetary policy instrument. Other possible international approaches might be to impose special restraints on Eurocurrency loans or deposits in relation to capital, or to specify some kinds of liquidity ratios that would have to be observed in Eurocurrency banking.

Reserve Requirements on Eurocurrency Deposits: Implications for Eurodeposit Multipliers, Control of a Monetary Aggregate, and Avoidance of Redenomination Incentives

Dale W. Henderson and Douglas G. Waldo

In this paper a two-country model of international financial markets is employed to analyze some implications of placing reserve requirements on Eurocurrency deposits. The features of this model are described in section 1. Many earlier analyses of the Eurocurrency markets focused on the Eurodeposit multiplier, the response of equilibrium holdings of Eurodeposits to an autonomous shift from domestic deposits into Eurodeposits.[1] The analysis in the second section is a continuation of

The model employed in this paper is a substantially modified version of one developed by Henderson and Lance Girton, which is discussed briefly in Dale W. Henderson, "Eurodollars, Petrodollars, and World Liquidity and Inflation: A Comment," in Karl Brunner and Allan H. Meltzer, eds., *Stabilization of the Domestic and International Economy*, Carnegie-Rochester Conference Series on Public Policy, vol. 5 (Amsterdam: North-Holland Publishing Company, 1977), pp. 311-318. The authors have benefited greatly from discussions of many of the issues considered in this paper with Stephen Axilrod, Michael Dooley, Richard Froyen, Lance Girton, Don Roper, Jeffrey Shafer, and Roger Waud. Helpful suggestions were received from Peter Clark, Walter Enders, Pentti Kouri, Harvey Lapan, Thomas Pugel, and Clas Wihlborg. This paper represents the views of the authors and should not be interpreted as reflecting the views of the Board of Governors of the Federal Reserve System or other members of its staff.

[1] Among the studies that consider the Eurodeposit multiplier, as well as many other important topics suggested by the existence and rapid growth of the Eurocurrency markets, are Charles Freedman, "A Model of the Eurodollar Market," *Journal of Monetary Economics,* vol. 3, no. 2 (April 1977), pp 139-161; John Hewson and Eisuke Sakakibara, *The Eurocurrency Markets and Their Implica-*

this tradition; there the model is used to trace the implications of a shift from domestic demand deposits to Eurodollar deposits for the equilibrium holdings of Eurodollar deposits and total Eurocurrency deposits. The approach of recent contributions to the analysis of monetary policy making has been to evaluate alternative operating procedures and suggested changes in financial regulations under various assumptions about the relative magnitudes of different kinds of shocks to the economy.[2] This is the approach adopted in the third section, where the effects of changes in Eurocurrency reserve requirements on the deviations of a monetary aggregate from a chosen target value are investigated.[3] There is it assumed that the authorities set the supply of

---

tions (Lexington, Mass.: Lexington Books, 1975); Rainer S. Masera, "Deposit Creation, Multiplication and the Euro-dollar Market," *A Debate on the Euro-dollar Market,* Quaderni di Ricerche, no. 11 (Rome: Ente per gli Studi Monetari, Bancari e Finanziari Luigi Einardi, 1973), pp. 123-189; Jürg Niehans and John Hewson, "The Eurodollar Market and Monetary Theory," *Journal of Money, Credit and Banking,* vol. 8, no. 1 (February 1976), pp. 1-27.

[2] This approach to the evaluation of alternative monetary policy regimes originated in William Poole, "Optimal Choice of Monetary Policy Instruments in a Simple Stochastic Macro Model," *Quarterly Journal of Economics,* vol. 84, no. 2 (May 1970), pp. 197-216, and has subsequently been developed and applied by many analysts. It has been used to analyze the implications of alternative reserve requirement systems for money stock stabilization in Richard Froyen and Kenneth J. Kopecky, "Reserve Requirements and Money Stock Control with a Flexible Deposit Rate," mimeographed (Department of Economics, University of North Carolina, 1979); Ira Kaminow, "Required Reserve Ratios, Policy Instruments, and Money Stock Control," *Journal of Monetary Economics,* vol. 3, no. 4 (October 1977), pp. 389-408; Kenneth Kopecky, "The Relationship between Reserve Ratios and the Monetary Aggregates under Reserves and Federal Funds Operating Targets," Staff Economic Studies, no. 100 (Washington, D.C.: Board of Governors of the Federal Reserve System, 1978); Daniel E. Laufenberg, "Optimal Reserve Requirement Ratios Against Bank Deposits for Short-Run Monetary Control," *Journal of Money, Credit and Banking,* vol. 11, no. 1 (February 1979), pp. 99-105; and Lawrence F. Sherman, Case M. Sprenkle, and Bryan E. Stanhouse, "Reserve Requirements and Control of the Money Supply," *Journal of Money, Credit and Banking,* vol. 11, no. 4 (November 1979), pp. 486-493, and for real output stabilization in Ernst Baltensperger, "Macroeconomic Effects of Reserve Requirements" (University of Heidelberg, June 1980); Arthur J. Rolnick, "Evaluating the Effectiveness of Monetary Reforms," *Journal of Monetary Economics,* vol. 2, no. 3 (July 1976), pp. 271-296; Anthony M. Santomero and Jeremy J. Siegel, "Bank Regulation and Macroeconomic Stability," *American Economic Review,* vol. 71, no. 1 (March 1981), pp. 39-53; and Case M. Sprenkle and Bryan E. Stanhouse, "A Theoretical Framework for Evaluating the Impact of Universal Reserve Requirements," *Journal of Finance,* vol. 36, no. 4 (September 1981), and in a related study of the implications of alternative definitions of a monetary aggregate for real output stabilization, Don E. Roper and Stephen J. Turnovsky, "The Optimum Monetary Aggregate for Stabilization Policy," *Quarterly Journal of Economics,* vol. 95, no. 2 (September 1980), 333-354.

[3] It is not an objective of this paper to consider the advisability of this kind of operating strategy under which a monetary aggregate is viewed as an intermediate target. Cogent criticisms of this strategy are provided in Ralph Bryant, *Money*

high-powered money in an attempt to achieve a desired value for a monetary aggregate, which is their intermediate target. Deviations between the actual and desired values arise because the authorities have incomplete current information about the shocks that buffet the financial system. In the first three sections one possible system of Eurocurrency reserve requirements is analyzed. In the fourth section it is demonstrated that under some alternative systems the imposition of Eurocurrency reserve requirements may give rise to an incentive for Eurocurrency deposits denominated in one or the other currency to be redenominated so that all Eurocurrency deposits are denominated in a single currency. This section also includes a discussion of how to structure Eurocurrency reserve requirements so as to avoid giving rise to redenomination incentives. The last section contains some conclusions.

The Model

The model is a description of financial dealings among agents in two countries, the United States and Germany, denominated in two currencies, the dollar and the deutsche mark (DM). The exchange rate (E) is defined as the dollar price of the DM. The seven groups of agents whose behavior is portrayed are U.S. nonbanks, German nonbanks, U.S. banks' home-country offices (U.S. banks), German banks' home country offices (German banks), U.S. and German banks' foreign affiliates (Eurobanks), the U.S. central bank (Federal Reserve), and the German central bank (Bundesbank). In addition it is assumed that the U.S. (German) Treasury issues a stock of dollar-denominated (DM-denominated) securities designated by $\bar{B}$ ($\bar{F}$). Eighteen financial instruments will be mentioned, but simplifying assumptions and the balance sheet constraints of the agents imply that attention can be focused on the markets for only two instruments, U.S. high-powered money and German high-powered money.

---

and Monetary Policy in Interdependent Nations (Washington, D.C.: Brookings Institution, 1980); Matthew B. Canzoneri, "The Intermediate Control Problem," *Journal of Money, Credit and Banking,* vol. 9, no. 2 (May 1977), pp. 368-371; Benjamin M. Friedman, "Targets, Instruments, and Indicators of Monetary Policy," *Journal of Monetary Economics,* vol. 1, no. 4 (October 1975), pp. 443-473; and John Kareken, Thomas Muench, and Neil Wallace, "Optimal Open Market Strategy: The Use of Information Variables," *American Economic Review,* vol. 63, no. 1 (March 1973), pp. 156-172. The implications of Eurocurrency reserve requirements for the stabilization of real outputs are investigated in Dale W. Henderson and Douglas G. Waldo, "Reserve Requirements on Eurocurrency Deposits: Implications for the Stabilization of Real Outputs," in Jagdeep S. Bhandari and Bluford H. Putnam, eds., *Economic Interdependence and Flexible Exchange Rates* (Cambridge, Mass.: MIT Press, forthcoming).

TABLE 1

BALANCE SHEETS OF THE AGENTS AND
MARKET-CLEARING CONDITIONS FOR THE FINANCIAL INSTRUMENTS

					Instruments				
Agents	H	EA	B	EF	D	T	EG	EU	L
U.S. banks	H^B		B^B	EF^B	$-D^B$	$-T^B$			L^B
German banks		$\overset{*}{EA}{}^{B}$	$\overset{*}{B}{}^{B}$	$\overset{*}{EF}{}^{B}$			$-\overset{*}{EG}{}^{B}$	$-\overset{*}{EU}{}^{B}$	
Eurobanks	H^A								
U.S. nonbanks	H^N		B^N	EF^N	D^N	T^N		$EU^N - L^N$	
German nonbanks		$\overset{*}{EA}{}^{N}$	$\overset{*}{B}{}^{N}$	$\overset{*}{EF}{}^{N}$		$\overset{*}{T}{}^{N}$	$\overset{*}{EG}{}^{N}$	$\overset{*}{EU}{}^{N} - \overset{*}{L}{}^{N}$	
Federal Reserve	$-H^C$		B^C						
Bundesbank		$-\overset{*}{EA}{}^{C}$	$\overset{*}{B}{}^{C}$	$\overset{*}{EF}{}^{C}$					
U.S. Treasury			$-\overline{B}$						
German Treasury				$-\overline{EF}$					

NOTE: E = exchange rate
  H = U.S. high-powered money
  A = German high-powered money
  B = U.S. treasury securities
  F = German treasury securities
  D = U.S. banks' dollar demand deposits
  T = U.S. banks' dollar time deposits
  G = German banks' DM demand deposits
  U = German banks' DM time deposits
  L = U.S. banks' dollar loans

The balance sheets of the agents and the market-clearing conditions for the financial instruments are described here and are summarized in table 1, which also contains a list of all the financial instruments included in the model. Because balance sheets must be expressed in a single currency, all DM-denominated magnitudes are converted to dollars. Summing the entries in the row for a given group of agents in

TABLE 1 (continued)

Instruments									
EP	V	EX	Y	EZ	Q	ES	I	EJ	W
							I^B		$-W^B$
$\overset{*}{EP}{}^B$								$\overset{*}{EJ}{}^B$	$-\overset{*}{W}{}^B$
	$-V^A$	$-EX^A$	$-Y^A$	$-EZ^A$	Q^A	ES^A	$-I^A$	$-EJ^A$	$-W^A$
$-EP^N$	V^N	EX^N	Y^N	EZ^N	$-Q^N$	$-ES^N$			$-W^N$
$-\overset{*}{EP}{}^N$	$\overset{*}{V}{}^N$	$\overset{*}{EX}{}^N$	$\overset{*}{Y}{}^N$	$\overset{*}{EZ}{}^N$	$-\overset{*}{Q}{}^N$	$-\overset{*}{ES}{}^N$			$-\overset{*}{W}{}^N$
									$\overset{*}{W}{}^C$
									W^T
									$\overset{*}{W}{}^T$

$P =$ German banks' DM loans
$V =$ short-term Eurodollar deposits
$X =$ short-term Euro-DM deposits
$Y =$ long-term Eurodollar deposits
$Z =$ long-term Euro-DM deposits
$Q =$ Eurodollar loans
$S =$ Euro-DM loans
$I =$ U.S. banks' dollar loans to Eurobanks
$J =$ German banks' DM loans to Eurobanks
$W =$ net worth in dollars

table 1 yields the balance sheet constraint for that group of agents; therefore, the sum of the entries in each row must be identically equal to zero. The sum of the entries in the last column of table 1 must also be identically equal to zero because the sum of the net worths of banks and nonbanks must always be equal to the sum of the net worths of the German central bank and the two treasuries. For the model to be in equilibrium, each remaining column must sum to zero. How the variables in the model change to ensure that these conditions are fulfilled will be explained.

U.S. banks (row 1), whose holdings are designated with the superscript B, have as liabilities dollar demand deposits, dollar time deposits, and a net worth item measured in dollars and as assets dollar high-powered money, dollar loans, U.S. treasury securities, German treasury securities, and dollar claims on the Eurobanks.

German banks (row 2), whose holdings are designated with asterisks, as are all German holdings, and with the superscript B, have as liabilities DM demand deposits, DM time deposits, and a net worth item measured in dollars and as assets DM high-powered money, DM loans, German treasury securities, U.S. treasury securities, and DM claims on the Eurobanks.

The Eurobanks (row 3), whose holdings are designated with the superscript A, have as liabilities short-term Eurodollar deposits, short-term Euro-DM deposits, long-term Eurodollar deposits, long-term Euro-DM deposits, dollar borrowings from U.S. banks, DM borrowings from German banks, and a net worth item measured in dollars and as assets U.S. high-powered money, Eurodollar loans, and Euro-DM loans.

Throughout, it is assumed that all banking institutions are risk-neutral price takers with zero intermediation costs and that the interest rates on demand deposits at banks in both countries are fixed at zero. Initially, it is assumed that each central bank pays interest on required bank reserves at a rate equal to the rate on treasury securities denominated in its country's currency and that even when the exchange rate is flexible all private agents *expect* the exchange rate to remain unchanged.[4] Under these assumptions, the interest rates associated with all the variable-rate financial instruments must be equal to a single representative interest rate (r). Only when this condition is met will individual U.S. banks, German banks, and Eurobanks expect neither profits nor losses from accepting all kinds of interest-bearing deposits, engaging in all types of interbank borrowing, and holding all forms of assets assumed to be specific to their category of banking institution.[5]

---

[4] The assumption that all private agents expect the exchange rate to remain unchanged could be replaced by the assumption that the expected rate of change in the exchange rate is nonzero but exogenous without altering any of the conclusions in sections 1, 2, and 3. The analysis in section 4 is consistent with a non-zero expected rate of change in the exchange rate. See also note 8, below.

[5] The profits and losses of banks do not affect the wealth of nonbanks participating in the market for traded financial assets because it is assumed that the risk-neutral owners of banks do not sell shares to risk-averse holders of traded financial assets and do not hold traded financial assets.

306

U.S. nonbanks (row 4), whose holdings are designated by the superscript N, allocate their net worth among all the financial instruments except DM currency, DM demand deposits at German banks, and interbank loans denominated in dollars and DM.[6] German nonbanks (row 5), whose holdings are designated with an asterisk and the superscript N, allocate their net worth measured in dollars among all the financial instruments except dollar currency, dollar demand deposits at U.S. banks, and interbank loans denominated in dollars and DM. The symbol θ $(\overset{*}{\theta})$ is employed to represent the ratio of U.S. (German) residents' *net* dollar assets to their net worth measured in dollars. It is assumed that θ $(\overset{*}{\theta})$ lies between zero and one so that U.S. (German) residents' net holdings of both dollar and DM assets are positive.

The Federal Reserve (row 6), whose holdings are designated by the superscript C, has U.S. treasury securities as an asset and high-powered money as a liability. The Bundesbank (row 7), whose holdings are designated with an asterisk and the superscript C, has German treasury securities and U.S. treasury securities as assets and DM high-powered money as a liability. The net worth item measured in dollars $(\overset{*}{W}{}^{C})$ moves to offset the effects of changes in the exchange rate on the value of the Bundesbank's assets so that the DM value of German high-powered money remains unchanged.

Now consider the demands by U.S. and German nonbanks for the various financial instruments. Because our assumptions regarding banking institutions imply that all interest rates move together in lockstep, these demands can be taken to depend on the single representative interest rate. The demands for the various financial instruments by nonbanks in each country also depend on the net worth of nonbanks in that country and that country's exogenous real output. As examples, consider the desired holding of dollar currency by U.S. nonbanks,

$$H^N = H^N(r, W^N, y) \qquad (1a)$$

and the desired holding of DM currency by German nonbanks expressed in dollars,

$$EA^{*N} = EA^{*N}\left(r, \frac{\overset{*}{W}{}^N}{E}, \overset{*}{y}\right) \qquad (1b)$$

where y $(\overset{*}{y})$ represents U.S. (German) real output. All desired holdings

[6] It could be assumed that U.S. (and German) nonbanks hold all financial instruments, but, unless additional assumptions about the relative magnitudes of parameters were made, some of the results we derive could not be obtained. It could not be proved, for example, that the interest rate responsiveness of the demands for the two kinds of high-powered money are definitely negative.

of financial instruments by nonbanks are given by analogous expressions.

U.S. nonbanks and German nonbanks regard all the instruments in their portfolios as *strict gross substitutes*.[7] Whenever the interest rate on a given asset (liability) rises, the desired holding of that asset (liability) rises (falls) and the desired holdings of all other assets (liabilities) fall (rise) while the desired holdings of all liabilities (assets) rise (fall). It is also assumed that for each financial instrument *the own-rate effect exceeds the sum of cross-rate effects*. This assumption implies that if all variable interest rates rise by the same amount, as they must because of the foregoing assumptions, then the desired holdings of each interest-bearing asset must rise, the desired holding of each interest-bearing liability must fall, and the desired holdings of currency and demand deposits must fall.

The functions describing U.S. and German nonbanks' desired holdings of financial instruments are assumed to be linearly homogeneous in net worth so that the fraction of their net worth allocated by nonbanks in either country to each of the financial instruments they hold is independent of the level of their net worth. It has been assumed that both U.S. and German nonbanks have positive net asset positions in both dollars and DMs. This assumption implies that when the dollar depreciates, that is, when E rises, W^N rises ($\overset{*}{W}{}^N/E$ falls), so U.S. residents' (German residents') desired holdings of each financial instrument rise (fall) when measured in dollars (DMs).[8]

---

[7] The assumption that, for example, dollar deposits at U.S. banks and Eurodollar deposits are imperfect substitutes is crucial for our analysis. This assumption is plausible and empirically supportable. The two types of deposits have somewhat different payment provisions and are subject to different political risk factors. Furthermore, legal restrictions have some effect on depositors' decisions about where to place their funds. Factors such as these may explain why nonbanks actually hold dollar certificates of deposit issued by U.S. banks and Eurodollar deposits despite a rate of return differential that usually exactly reflects U.S. reserve requirements. Furthermore, there is substitution in favor of Eurodollar deposits when the return differential rises as nominal interest rates rise. The assumption that, for example, dollar loans from U.S. banks and Eurodollar loans are imperfect substitutes is less important. It does make the location of booking of dollar loans determinate. The conclusion regarding the quantity of Eurocurrency loans in section 2 depends on this assumption. The other conclusions of the paper are independent of this assumption, however. It is not immediately apparent why a borrower would care where his loan was booked. Further investigation that focuses on tax laws and other determinants of bank and borrower behavior may be required in order to arrive at a more adequate explanation of why loans are booked where they are.

[8] Short-run financial models of the type explored here yield appealing predictions about the effects of various shocks on the exchange rate when assumptions are made that ensure that when the dollar depreciates the demand for U.S. (German) high-powered money measured in dollars (DMs) rises (falls). One very simple set of assumptions that guarantees that a dollar depreciation has these effects is the pair of assumptions just discussed in the text. Alternatively, it could be

U.S. nonbanks' demands for dollar currency, dollar demand deposits, and short-term Eurodollar deposits are assumed to be positively related to exogenous U.S. output. Exogenous U.S. output is assumed to be equal to a constant $(\bar{y})$, plus a stochastic disturbance term (λ), which will be referred to in the following analysis:

$$y = \bar{y} + \lambda \tag{2}$$

Exogenous German output is assumed to be equal to a constant $(\overset{*}{\bar{y}})$.

Three conditions must be fulfilled in equilibrium. First, the demand for U.S. high-powered money must equal the supply:

$$H^o = H^N + H^B + H^A \tag{3a}$$

Second, the demand for German high-powered money measured in dollars must equal the supply measured in dollars:

$$E\overset{*}{A}{}^o = E(\overset{*}{A}{}^N + \overset{*}{A}{}^B) \tag{3b}$$

Third, the sum of private demands for U.S. and German treasury securities measured in dollars must equal the amount of these assets measured in dollars available to private agents:

$$\bar{B} - B^o - \overset{*}{B}{}^o + E(\bar{F} - \overset{*}{F}{}^o) = B^N + \overset{*}{B}{}^N + B^B + \overset{*}{B}{}^B$$
$$+ E(F^N + \overset{*}{F}{}^N + F^B + \overset{*}{F}{}^B) \tag{4}$$

These three conditions are sufficient for equilibrium in all financial markets, and only two of them are independent. First, equilibrium is guaranteed in all markets except those for government securities and high-powered money because as long as interest rates are locked together banking institutions will accept all the deposits and make all the loans that nonbanks want, and U.S. and German banks will accommodate the desired borrowings of the Eurobanks. Thus, when all interest rates are the same, the sum of each of the columns in table 1 except the first four is identically equal to zero. Second, if equation 4 holds, both security markets are in equilibrium because banks regard

---

assumed that the demand for U.S. (German) high-powered money depends negatively (positively) on the expected rate of depreciation of the dollar. Then it could be assumed that exchange rate expectations are regressive so that the expected rate of depreciation of the dollar depends positively on the gap between a constant "normal" value of the exchange rate and its current value. Under these assumptions, actual dollar depreciation would increase (decrease) U.S. (German) high-powered money demand if this demand were independent of net worth or if expectations effects dominate any perverse valuation effects arising from negative net foreign asset positions or any negative response of U.S. (German) high-powered money demand to increases in net worth.

German and U.S. treasury securities as being the same asset.[9] Third, when account is taken of the balance sheet constraints, the sum of the excess demands for high-powered money and both securities is identically equal to the sum of the sums of all columns in table 1 except the first four, which is identically equal to zero. Hence, only two of the equilibrium conditions are independent.

The two independent equilibrium conditions that are used in what follows are the equilibrium conditions for the U.S. and German high-powered money markets. To complete the description of the model it is necessary to specify the demands for U.S. and German high-powered money by banking institutions. It is assumed that the demands for U.S. and German high-powered money by U.S. banks, German banks, and Eurobanks are equal to required reserves.[10] U.S. banks hold the U.S. high-powered money implied by required reserve ratios on their demand deposits (k_D) and on the time deposits they accept from U.S. residents (k_T).[11] German banks hold the German high-powered money implied by required reserve ratios on their demand deposits ($\overset{*}{k_G}$) and on the time deposits they accept from German residents ($\overset{*}{k_U}$). Eurobanks hold the U.S. high-powered money implied by required reserve ratios on their short-term Eurodollar deposits accepted from U.S. residents (k_V) and on their long-term Eurodollar deposits accepted from U.S. residents (k_Y). It is assumed that the reserve ratio for dollar (DM) demand deposits is greater than or equal to the reserve ratio for dollar (DM) time deposits of U.S. (German) residents and the reserve ratios for short-term and long-term Eurodollar deposits of U.S. residents ($k_D \geqslant k_T, k_V, k_Y; \overset{*}{k_G} \geqslant \overset{*}{k_U}$).

The final version of the two high-powered money market equilibrium conditions is obtained by substituting the bank demands for U.S.

[9] The last condition is based on the assumption that total government security holdings are treated as the residual item on the balance sheets of U.S. and German banks. If another item, say, lending to the Eurobanks, were chosen as the residual item, the third equilibrium condition would be different, but it would still be linearly dependent with equations 3a and 3b.

[10] Excess reserves for both U.S. and German banks are ruled out for simplicity. They could be included with relatively little difficulty. If it were assumed that no interest was paid on excess reserves, the qualitative effects of interest rate changes on desired holdings of excess reserves would be the same as those on desired holdings of currency. Under this assumption, none of the results of the paper would be affected by the inclusion of excess reserves.

[11] It could be assumed that all time deposits at U.S. banks were reservable, but, unless additional assumptions were made about the relative magnitudes of parameter values, some of the results we derive could not be obtained. It could not be proved, for example, that the interest rate responsiveness of the demand for U.S. high-powered money is definitely negative.

310

and German high-powered money just described, the nonbank behavioral relations, and expressions for H^C and $\overset{*}{EA}{}^C$ from the central bank balance sheets into equations $3a$ and $3b$ to obtain equations $5a$ and $5b$:[12]

$$B^C = H^N + k_D D^N + k_T T^N + k_V V^N + k_Y Y^N$$
$$- (k_D - k_V)\alpha - k_D\gamma - k_V\beta - \eta \tag{5a}$$

$$\overset{*}{F}{}^C + \frac{1}{E}\,(\overset{*}{B}{}^C + \overset{*}{W}{}^C) = \overset{*}{A}{}^N + \overset{*}{k}_G \overset{*}{G}{}^N + \overset{*}{k}_U \overset{*}{U}{}^N \tag{5b}$$

where α, γ, β, and η are stochastic disturbance terms that will be referred to in the analysis below.

An initial equilibrium in world financial markets is represented by the intersection of the H_0H_0 and A_0A_0 schedules at a_0 in panel 1 of figure 1. The HH schedule shows the pairs of the interest rate and the exchange rate for which the demand for U.S. high-powered money is equal to a fixed supply. The HH schedule must have a positive slope under the assumptions of this paper. A depreciation of the dollar (rise in E) increases the demand for U.S. high-powered money. The depreciation raises U.S. residents' demands for all types of reservable dollar deposits measured in dollars because it increases their net worth measured in dollars. In order to reduce the demand for U.S. high-powered money to its previous level, the interest rate must rise.

It must be established that an increase in the interest rate reduces the demand for U.S. high-powered money. The interest rate responsiveness of the demand for U.S. high-powered money (H_r) is given by

$$H_r = H_1^N + k_D D_1^N + k_T T_1^N + k_V V_1^N + k_Y Y_1^N \tag{6}$$

which can be rewritten as

$$H_r = k_D \left(\frac{1}{k_D} H_1^N + D_1^N + \frac{k_T}{k_D}\, T_1^N + \frac{k_V}{k_D}\, V_1^N + \frac{k_Y}{k_D}\, Y_1^N \right) \tag{7}$$

Given the assumptions about U.S. residents' demands for financial instruments, it is an implication of the balance sheet constraint for U.S. residents that

$$\overset{(-)}{H_1^N} + \overset{(-)}{D_1^N} + \overset{(+)}{T_1^N} + \overset{(+)}{V_1^N} + \overset{(+)}{Y_1^N}$$

$$\equiv -\overset{(+)}{B_1^N} + \overset{(-)}{L_1^N} + \overset{(-)}{Q_1^N}$$

$$- E(\overset{(+)}{F_1^N} + \overset{(+)}{U_1^N} - \overset{(-)}{P_1^N} + \overset{(+)}{X_1^N} + \overset{(+)}{Z_1^N} - \overset{(-)}{S_1^N}) < 0 \tag{8}$$

---

[12] For a version of equation 4 in a form comparable to equations $5a$ and $5b$, see appendix A.

312

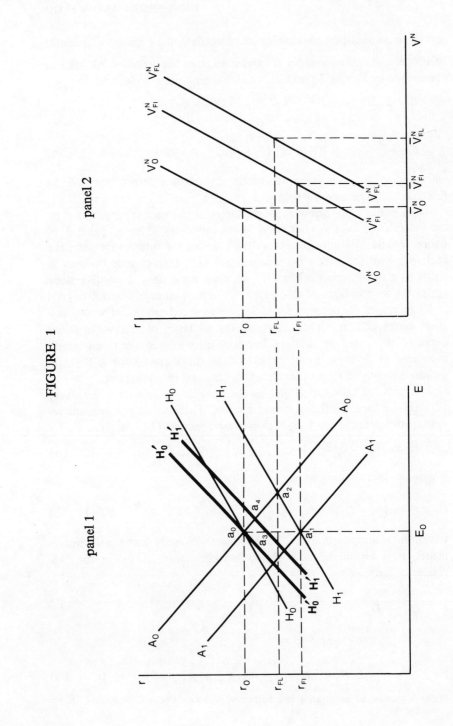

FIGURE 1

H_r must be negative because the weighted sum of interest rate responsiveness in parentheses on the right-hand side of equation 7 is more negative than the unweighted sum of the same interest rate responsiveness on the left-hand side of equation 8 because the weight on the negative $H_1{}^N$ is greater than one, whereas the weights on the positive $T_1{}^N$, $V_1{}^N$, and $Y_1{}^N$ are less than or equal to one.

The AA schedule shows the pairs of the interest rate and the exchange rate for which the demand for German high-powered money is equal to a fixed supply. The AA schedule must have a negative slope. A depreciation of the dollar reduces the demand for German high-powered money. The depreciation lowers German residents' demands for all types of reservable DM deposits measured in DMs because it reduces their net worth measured in DMs. In order to increase the demand for German high-powered money to its previous level, the interest rate must fall. That a decline in the interest rate increases the demand for German high-powered money can be established by an argument analogous to the one used to establish the sign of the interest rate responsiveness of the demand for U.S. high-powered money.

As preparation for the analysis below it is useful to consider the effects of a reduction in the U.S. demand for high-powered money. The HH schedule shifts down from H_0H_0 to H_1H_1 because at each exchange rate the interest rate must be lower in order to reestablish equilibrium in the market for U.S. high-powered money. Under fixed exchange rates, the new equilibrium is at point a_1. The shift down in the demand for U.S. high-powered money causes the interest rate to decline. The drop in the interest rate gives rise to excess demand for German high-powered money. As a result of this excess demand, there is pressure on the dollar to depreciate. In order to prevent a depreciation of the dollar, the Bundesbank undertakes an intervention operation that satisfies the excess demand for German high-powered money. This operation involves a purchase of U.S. treasury securities from nonbanks in return for German high-powered money.[13] The AA schedule corresponding to

---

[13] That is, it is assumed that a change in the Bundesbank's holdings of U.S. treasury securities results in an equal absolute change in German high-powered money and no change in U.S. high-powered money. This assumption that the Bundesbank does not sterilize at all and that its actions amount to complete sterilization of U.S. high-powered money is probably the most appealing simple assumption that can be made. Alternatively, it could be assumed that the supplies of both kinds of high-powered money are sterilized partially but not completely, and this assumption would lead to some changes in our results. Models in which the supplies of both kinds of high-powered money can be sterilized completely are somewhat more complex than the one considered here; see those employed by Freedman, "Model of Eurodollar Market," and Hewson and Sakakibara, *Eurocurrency Markets*.

the new higher supply of German high-powered money is A_1A_1. In the case of fixed exchange rates the interest rate falls by the full amount necessary to restore equilibrium in the market for U.S. high-powered money.

Under flexible exchange rates the new equilibrium following a shift down in the demand for U.S. high-powered money is at point a_2. The Bundesbank undertakes no intervention operation, so the dollar depreciates. This depreciation of the dollar increases the demand for U.S. high-powered money, so the interest rate does not fall by the full amount necessary to restore equilibrium in the U.S. high-powered money market at the initial exchange rate (E_0). The depreciation of the dollar reduces the demand for German high-powered money, so the demand for German high-powered money does not exceed the fixed supply even though the interest rate is lower.

Eurodeposit Multipliers under Fixed and Flexible Exchange Rates

The effects of a shift in U.S. nonbanks' portfolio preferences away from dollar demand deposits at U.S. banks and toward short-term Eurodollar deposits are traced in the two panels of figure 1. The effects of the shift on the interest rate and the exchange rate are shown in panel 1. The shift in portfolio preferences reduces the demand for U.S. high-powered money because the reserve ratio for short-term Eurodollar deposits is less than the reserve ratio for dollar demand deposits. It is assumed that the size of the shift is such that it causes the HH schedule to move down from H_0H_0 to H_1H_1. The interest rate falls under both fixed and flexible exchange rates, and the dollar depreciates under flexible exchange rates.

The effects on U.S. residents' equilibrium holdings of short-term Eurodollar deposits are shown in panel 2. The case of fixed exchange rates is examined first. This case is particularly interesting because the assumption of fixed exchange rates facilitates a comparison with the closed-economy case of a shift out of demand deposits into time deposits.

Under fixed exchange rates U.S. residents' demand for short-term Eurodollar deposits shifts from V_0^N to V_{FI}^N in panel 2. Their holdings at the new equilibrium must be higher $(\overline{V}_{FI}^N > \overline{V}_0^N)$, but the increase is less than the original shift in demand because the interest rate decline discourages the holding of short-term Eurodollar deposits. A shift out of dollar demand deposits can be represented by an increase in α in equation 5a. The increase in U.S. residents' holdings of short-term Eurodollar deposits under fixed exchange rates (FI) is given by

$$\frac{dV^N}{d\alpha}\bigg|_{FI} = V_1^N \frac{dr}{d\alpha}\bigg|_{FI} + 1 \tag{9}$$

where

$$\frac{dr}{d\alpha}\bigg|_{FI} = \frac{k_D - k_V}{H_r} < 0 \tag{10}$$

If we make use of equations 10 and 6, equation 9 can be rewritten as

$$0 < \frac{dV^N}{d\alpha}\bigg|_{FI} = \frac{1}{H_r}(H_1^N + k_D D_1^N + k_T T_1^N + k_D V_1^N + k_Y Y_1^N) < 1 \tag{11}$$

An argument analogous to the one used to establish that H_r is negative can be used to establish that the weighted sum in parentheses in equation 11 is negative. This weighted sum is less than H_r in absolute value because the positive V_1^N is weighted by k_D which is greater than k_V. This result for the multiplier for U.S. nonbanks' holdings of short-term Eurodollars illustrates the familiar contention that the largest possible multiplier for U.S. nonbanks' holdings of Eurodollars given a shift in U.S. nonbanks' preferences from dollar demand deposits to Eurodollar deposits under fixed exchange rates is positive but less than one. Under the additional plausible assumption that $k_Y \leqslant k_V$, there are increases in U.S. nonbanks' holdings of both all Eurodollar deposits and all Euro-currency deposits measured in dollars, but, because of the interest-rate decline, these increases are less than the increase in their holdings of short-term Eurodollar deposits. This result can be proved by making use once again of the balance sheet constraint for U.S. residents. Thus, if $k_Y \leqslant k_V$, the qualitative effects of a shift out of dollar demand deposits and into short-term Eurodollar deposits on the equilibrium holdings of Eurodollar and Eurocurrency deposits by *U.S. residents* are the same as the effects of a shift out of demand deposits and into time deposits on the equilibrium holdings of time deposits in a closed economy.

When the behavior of German nonbanks is taken into account, however, it becomes clear that there is a difference between the qualitative results for a shift into short-run Eurodollar deposits in an open economy and those for a shift into time deposits in a closed economy. The decline in the interest rate causes German nonbanks to reduce their holdings of short-term Eurodollar deposits, so the total of all nonbanks' holdings of short-term Eurodollar deposits may actually fall as a result of the interest-rate decline caused by the shift in U.S. residents' portfolio preferences:

$$0 \lesseqgtr \frac{d(V^N + \overset{*}{V}{}^N)}{d\alpha}\bigg|_{FI} = \frac{dV^N}{d\alpha}\bigg|_{FI} + \frac{\overset{*}{V}{}_1^N (k_D - k_V)}{H_r} < 1 \tag{12}$$

315

A fortiori, the total of all nonbanks' holding of Eurodollar deposits and Eurocurrency deposits measured in dollars may fall. This possibility illustrates another familiar contention that for some measures of the Eurodollar or Eurocurrency market the multiplier may actually be negative.[14] The possibility that holdings of time deposits may fall does not arise in the case of a shift out of demand deposits into time deposits in a closed economy.

It is interesting to note that, whatever happens to the total of Eurocurrency deposits, the total of Eurocurrency loans must rise because of the decline in the interest rate. Thus, by at least one measure of size, the size of the Eurocurrency markets must increase no matter what happens to the total of Eurocurrency deposits. Of course, if the total of Eurocurrency deposits falls or if Euroloans rise more than Eurodeposits, Eurobanks increase their borrowings from U.S. and German banks to the extent necessary to fund their increased loans to nonbanks.

Under flexible exchange rates the depreciation of the dollar shifts the demand for Eurodollar deposits out from V_0^N farther than V_{FI}^N to a position like V_{FL}^N. The short-term Eurodollar deposit multiplier may now be greater than one, as shown in panel 2. All multipliers for Eurodollar deposits and for Eurocurrency deposits measured in dollars are raised, and the likelihood of a negative multiplier for total nonbank Eurodollar deposits or total Eurocurrency deposits measured in dollars is reduced. Eurocurrency loans measured in dollars rise, but the increase may be less or more than with a fixed exchange rate because the interest rate declines by less but the depreciation of the dollar raises nonbanks' Eurocurrency loan demand measured in dollars. An unavoidable ambiguity that has plagued analysts of the Eurocurrency markets is also evident; for example, even when the total of Eurocurrency deposits measured in dollars rises it may fall when measured in DM. We would be in a better position to know what to make of this possibility if we understood more fully the implications of changes in nominal deposit or loan totals measured in any given currency.

Eurocurrency Reserve Requirements and the Control of a Monetary Aggregate

In order to determine the circumstances under which monetary authorities might find it desirable to place a reserve requirement on Eurocurrency deposits it is necessary to describe the environment in which

[14] This possibility would still exist if German residents' holdings of short-term Eurodollar deposits were reserved.

monetary policy is formulated. Assumptions are made about the operating strategy for monetary policy, about the types of disturbances faced by policy makers, and about the implementation of the operating strategy.

As an operating strategy the monetary authorities in several countries set the instruments under their direct control in order to achieve desired values for one or another monetary aggregate over well-defined periods of as short as a month or as long as a year. Therefore, it seems useful to consider how the expected degree of success of such an intermediate-target strategy is affected by the introduction of Euro-currency reserve requirements. Specifically, it is assumed that the U.S. authorities attempt to achieve a desired value for M1', defined as U.S. residents' holdings of currency, demand deposits, and short-term Eurodollar deposits.[15] The effects of changes in the reserve requirement on short-term Eurodollar deposits on the deviations of M1' from its target value are investigated.

As has often been observed, in models such as the one investigated in this paper the U.S. authorities could always hit an intermediate target value for M1' exactly in the absence of uncertainty. So that meaningful and tractable questions can be addressed it is assumed that the U.S. high-powered money demand function is affected by stochastic shifts in U.S. nonbanks' desired holdings of financial instruments. Five kinds of shifts are considered, each of which is represented by a separate disturbance term: (1) shifts between dollar demand deposits and short-term Eurodollar deposits, represented by α; (2) shifts between short-term Eurodollar deposits and nonreservable instruments, represented by β; (3) shifts between dollar demand deposits and nonreservable instruments, represented by γ; (4) shifts between dollar currency and nonreservable instruments, represented by η; and (5) shifts in the demands for all reservable assets resulting from shifts in exogenous U.S. output, represented by λ. It is useful to observe that shifts between dollar currency and nonreservable instruments have the same effects as would shifts in the supply of U.S. high-powered money through open market operations. The stochastic variables representing the five kinds of shifts are assumed to have zero expected values and to be mutually and serially uncorrelated.

A single method for the implementation of the operating strategy of

[15] Attention is focused on a single monetary aggregate for simplicity. It could be assumed that another monetary aggregate, for example, M1 defined as the U.S. residents' holdings of currency plus demand deposits, was the intermediate target, but the results of the analysis would not be as unambiguous or intuitively appealing. See note 18, below.

the U.S. monetary authorities is considered. It is assumed that they cannot observe M1' in the current period. They use the supply of U.S. high-powered money as their policy instrument.[16] The supply of high-powered money is set before the values of the disturbances emerge in any period so that the expected value of M1' is equal to a desired value $\tilde{M1}'$. If the desired value of M1' is changed, a different amount of U.S. high-powered money must be supplied. When the values of the disturbance terms emerge in any period, the implied value for M1' is, in general, different from $\tilde{M1}'$. The sizes of deviations of M1' from its desired (and expected) value resulting from the various stochastic shifts depend on the parameters of the high-powered money demand functions, on the parameters of the demand function for M1', on the exchange rate regime, and on the levels of the reserve requirements.

The purpose of this section is to determine how deviations of M1' from its desired value are affected when the U.S. authorities raise the reserve ratio for short-term Eurodollar deposits held by U.S. residents (k_V). It is assumed that k_V can be varied within a range that has a lower limit of zero and an upper limit of the exogenous reserve requirement on demand deposits.[17] Given the assumption that the disturbance terms representing the stochastic shifts are mutually uncorrelated, it is possible to consider the effect of an increase in k_V when each of the stochastic shifts is the only source of uncertainty. These effects can then be combined to obtain the overall effect of an increase in k_V. For simplicity, it is assumed that the reserve ratios for dollar time deposits at U.S. banks and for long-term Eurodollar deposits held by U.S. residents are zero throughout this section.

The same general approach is used in the analysis of each source of deviations of M1' from its desired value. First, for each type of disturbance an example is chosen that leads to the same size reduction in the demand for U.S. high-powered money at the initial value of k_V.

[16] It could be assumed instead that the U.S. authorities use the interest rate as their policy instrument. If this assumption were made, then the deviations of M1' from its desired value would be independent of the levels of all reserve ratios, including k_V. Because the purpose of this section is to investigate the effects of changes in k_V on such deviations, the case in which the interest rate is the policy instrument is not considered here. It would be interesting to extend the analysis of this paper to compare the variance of M1' when U.S. high-powered money is the policy instrument and k_V is set at its *optimal* value with the variance of M1' when the interest rate is the policy instrument in order to determine circumstances under which one policy instrument would be preferred to the other. Also, reserve requirements are used as the policy instrument by some countries, notably Germany. A different approach would be required to analyze the effects of varying the reserve requirement on Eurodollars in response to changes in the desired value of a monetary aggregate.

[17] This limitation is consistent with proposals that have been considered recently.

Thus, for all disturbances the shift in the HH schedule given the initial k_V can be represented by the shift from H_0H_0 to H_1H_1 in panel 1 of figure 1. Second, the implications of the shift for M1' are described. Although the impact effects on M1' vary among disturbances, the induced change in M1' at the initial k_V is the same for all disturbances because the interest rate decline and, under flexible exchange rates, the depreciation of the dollar are the same. Third, the effects of an increase in k_V on the size of the interest rate decline and, under flexible exchange rates, on the amount of dollar depreciation required to restore equilibrium are determined. These effects arise because an increase in k_V alters the impact effect of disturbances on the demand for U.S. high-powered money and the responsivenesses of this demand to changes in the interest rate and the exchange rate. The change in the impact effect and, therefore, in the size of the shift in the HH schedule is different, depending on the source of the disturbance. The changes in both the interest rate responsiveness and the exchange rate responsiveness and, therefore, in the slope of the HH schedule are, however, the same for all disturbances. The final step in the analysis of each disturbance is to spell out the implications of the new equilibrating adjustments of the interest rate and the exchange rate for the size of the induced change in M1'.

Because the effects of an increase in k_V on the interest rate responsiveness and the exchange rate responsiveness of the demand for U.S. high-powered money are the same no matter what type of disturbance is under consideration, it is useful to describe these effects and their implications for the slope of the HH schedule at the outset. When k_V is increased, the interest rate responsiveness of the demand for U.S. high-powered money is lowered in absolute value. This interest rate responsiveness is a weighted sum of the interest rate responsivenesses of the demands by U.S. residents for currency, dollar demand deposits, and short-term Eurodollar deposits, where each of the deposit demand responsivenesses is weighted by the relevant reserve requirement. It has been shown that the weighted sum is negative even though the interest responsiveness of U.S. residents' demand for short-term Eurodollar deposits is positive. When k_V is increased, the weighted sum remains negative but becomes less negative because the weight on the positive component is increased. When k_V is increased, the exchange rate responsiveness of the demand for U.S. high-powered money becomes more positive. This exchange rate responsiveness is a weighted sum of the exchange rate responsivenesses of the demands by U.S. residents for currency, dollar demand deposits, and short-term Eurodollar deposits, where each of the deposit demand responsivenesses is weighted

319

by the relevant reserve requirement. The weighted sum is positive because all of the exchange rate responsivenesses are positive. When k_V is increased, the weight on a positive component is increased. Because the interest rate responsiveness of the demand for U.S. high-powered money is lowered in absolute value and the exchange rate responsiveness is increased when k_V rises, the slope of the HH schedule becomes more positive, as illustrated by the $H'_0H'_0$ schedule in panel 1 of figure 1.

The first disturbance to be considered is a shift by U.S. residents out of dollar demand deposits into short-term Eurodollar deposits. This disturbance causes the HH schedule to shift down from H_0H_0 to H_1H_1 in panel 1 of figure 1. The interest rate declines under both fixed and flexible exchange rates, and the dollar depreciates under flexible exchange rates. Although the disturbance under consideration has no impact effect on M1', the changes in the interest rate and the exchange rate induce M1' to rise under both fixed and flexible exchange rates.[18]

Now consider how the size of the increase in M1' is affected by a rise in k_V. As explained above, a rise in k_V increases the slope of the HH schedule by the same amount, no matter what the source of the disturbance. This increase is represented by the rotation of HH from H_0H_0 to $H'_0H'_0$. In the case of a shift out of dollar demand deposits into short-term Eurodollar deposits, a rise in k_V also reduces the downward shift in the HH schedule at a given exchange rate, as shown by the shift in HH from $H'_0H'_0$ to $H'_1H'_1$ ($a_0a_3 < a_0a_1$). The downward shift tends to be smaller because the reduction in the difference between k_D and k_V decreases the impact effect of the disturbance on the demand for U.S. high-powered money. The downward shift tends to be larger because the interest responsiveness of the demand for high-powered money is reduced in absolute value. The reduction in the impact effect outweighs the reduction of the absolute value of the interest rate responsiveness, so the downward shift in the HH schedule is definitely smaller:

$$\frac{d(dr/d\alpha|E = E_0)}{dk_V} = \frac{d[(k_D - k_V)/H_r]}{dk_V}$$

$$= -\frac{1}{(H_r)^2}[H_r + (k_D - k_V)V_1^N] > 0 \quad (13)$$

[18] Under flexible exchange rates M1' tends to rise less because of the smaller decline in the interest rate, but tends to rise more because of the depreciation of the dollar. It can be proved that when the exchange rate is fixed and $k_T = k_Y = 0$, M1 defined as U.S. residents' holdings of currency plus demand deposits falls, but by less than the shift down in demand. When the exchange rate is flexible and $k_T = k_Y = 0$, M1 tends to fall less because of the depreciation of the dollar but tends to fall more because the interest rate decline is smaller.

FIGURE 2

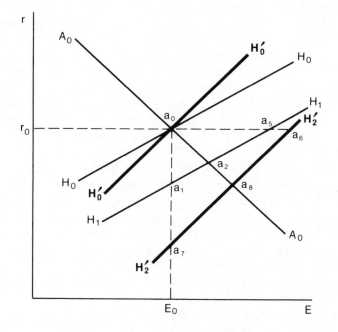

Consequently, the new equilibrium under fixed exchange rates (point a_3) involves a smaller interest rate decline, and the new equilibrium under flexible exchange rates (point a_4) involves a smaller interest rate decline and less dollar depreciation.

Thus, in the case of a shift by U.S. residents from dollar demand deposits to Eurodollar deposits, the rise in M1′ above its desired value is less when k_V is higher. Because such shifts have no impact effect on M1′, the smaller interest rate decline and, under flexible exchange rates, the smaller dollar depreciation imply a smaller total effect on M1′.

The second disturbance to be considered is a shift by U.S. residents from short-term Eurodollar deposits to nonreservable instruments. Figure 2 is employed in the analysis of this disturbance. As before, it is assumed that this disturbance leads to a shift down in the *HH* schedule from H_0H_0 to H_1H_1 at the initial value of k_V. M1′ declines under both fixed and flexible exchange rates because the fall in the interest rate and, under flexible exchange rates, the depreciation of the dollar only partially offset the negative impact effect on the demand for

321

M1' of the shift in portfolio preferences.[19] The impact effect of the disturbance on the demand for U.S. high-powered money is k_V times the impact effect on the demand for M1'. The absolute value of the interest rate responsiveness of the demand for U.S. high-powered money is greater than k_V times the absolute value of the interest rate responsiveness of the demand for M1' because the reserve requirements for currency (one) and demand deposits exceed k_V. Thus, under fixed exchange rates, the interest rate decline that clears the market for U.S. high-powered money is less than the one that would be required to keep M1' constant. Under flexible exchange rates the dollar must depreciate when the interest rate declines in order to keep the market for German high-powered money in equilibrium. This depreciation increases the demand for U.S. high-powered money and the demand for M1'. The induced exchange rate effect on the demand for U.S. high-powered money is greater than k_V times the induced exchange rate effect on M1' because the reserve requirements for currency and demand deposits exceed k_V. Thus, under flexible exchange rates, the interest rate decline and dollar depreciation that clear the market for U.S. high-powered money and maintain equilibrium in the market for German high-powered money are less than those that would be required to keep M1' constant.

An increase in k_V raises the slope of the HH schedule by an amount represented by the rotation of HH from $H_0 H_0$ to $H'_0 H'_0$, as before. In the case of a shift out of Eurodollar deposits and into non-reservable instruments, an increase in k_V increases the amount by which the HH schedule shifts to the right at a given interest rate, as shown by the shift of HH from $H'_0 H'_0$ to $H'_2 H'_2$ ($a_0 a_6 > a_0 a_5$). The shift tends to be larger because the impact effect of the disturbance on the demand for U.S. high-powered money is increased with a larger k_V. The shift tends to be smaller because the exchange rate responsiveness of the demand for high-powered money is increased. The increase in the impact effect outweighs the increase in the exchange rate responsiveness, so the HH schedule definitely shifts farther to the right:

$$\frac{d(dE/d\beta | r = r_0)}{dk_V} = \frac{1}{(H_E)^2} [H_E - k_V V_2^N W^N (1 - \theta)] > 0 \quad (14)$$

The new equilibrium under fixed rates (point a_7) involves a larger interest rate decline that clears the market for U.S. high-powered money (point a_8) involves a larger interest rate decline and more dollar depreciation.

[19] See appendix B for an algebraic derivation of this result.

FIGURE 3

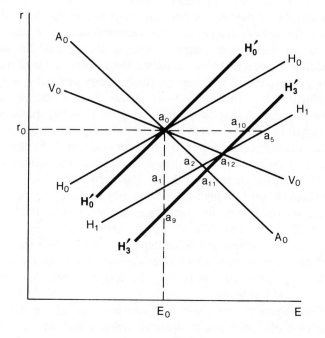

Thus, in the case of a shift by U.S. residents from Eurodollar deposits to nonreservable instruments, the decline in M1′ below its desired value is less when k_V is higher. The negative impact effect of the disturbance on M1′ is unchanged. The overall decline in M1′ is less, however, because the larger induced interest rate decline and, under flexible exchange rates, the larger induced dollar depreciation offset a greater fraction of the negative impact effect.

The third disturbance to be considered is a shift by U.S. residents out of dollar demand deposits into nonreservable instruments. Figure 3 is employed in the analysis of this disturbance. Once again it is assumed that the disturbance leads to a shift down in the HH schedule from H_0H_0 to H_1H_1 at the initial value of k_V. Under fixed exchange rates M1′ definitely declines because the fall in the interest rate only partially offsets the negative impact on the demand for M1′ of the shift in financial instrument preferences, but under flexible exchange rates M1′ may fall or rise.[20] The impact effect of this disturbance on the demand for U.S. high-powered money is k_D times the impact effect on the demand for

[20] See appendix B for an algebraic derivation of this result.

M1'. The absolute value of the interest rate responsiveness of the demand for U.S. high-powered money is greater than k_D times the absolute value of the interest rate responsiveness of the demand for M1' because the reserve requirement for currency exceeds k_D and because the positive interest rate responsiveness of the demand for short-term Eurodollar deposits that tends to reduce the absolute value of the interest rate responsiveness of U.S. high-powered money demand is weighted by k_V, which is less than k_D. Thus, under fixed exchange rates, the interest rate decline that clears the market for U.S. high-powered money is too small to keep M1' from falling. Under flexible exchange rates the induced exchange rate effect on the demand for U.S. high-powered money may be greater than or less than k_D times the induced exchange rate effect on the demand for M1'. The induced exchange rate effect on the demand for U.S. high-powered money tends to be greater because the reserve requirement for currency is greater than k_D but tends to be less because k_V is less than k_D. Thus, under flexible exchange rates, the interest rate decline and dollar depreciation that clear the market for U.S. high-powered money and maintain equilibrium in the market for German high-powered money may be less or more than those that would keep M1' constant.

Once again an increase in k_V raises the slope of the HH schedule. In the case of a shift out of demand deposits and into nonreservable instruments, an increase in k_V increases the amount by which the HH schedule shifts down at a given exchange rate and reduces the amount by which the HH schedule shifts to the right at a given interest rate, as shown by the shift of HH from $H_0'H_0'$ to $H_3'H_3'$ ($a_0a_9 > a_0a_1$ and $a_0a_{10} < a_0a_5$). An increase in k_V has no effect on the impact effect of the disturbance, but it reduces the absolute value of the interest rate responsiveness of the demand for high-powered money and increases the exchange rate responsiveness. The new equilibrium under fixed exchange rates (point a_9) involves a larger interest rate decline.

Under flexible exchange rates an increase in k_V may increase the interest rate decline and dollar depreciation, as at point a_{11}, or reduce these adjustments. In order to isolate the factors that determine whether the adjustment of the interest rate and the exchange rate is larger or smaller, it is useful to consider an additional schedule. The V_0V_0 schedule shows the pairs of the interest rate and the exchange rate that are consistent with unchanged holdings of short-term Eurodollar deposits by U.S. residents; a depreciation of the dollar raises the demand for Eurodollar deposits, so the interest rate must decline in order to reduce demand to its previous level. This schedule is useful in analyzing the disturbance under consideration because the H_1H_1 schedule and the

$H_3'H_3'$ schedule shift by the same distance $(a_0 a_{12})$ along the $V_0 V_0$ schedule. Setting the total differential of the demand for U.S. high-powered money equal to zero yields

$$(H_1^N + k_D D_1^N + k_V V_1^N) \, dr \tag{15}$$
$$+ (H_2^N + k_D D_2^N + k_V V_2^N) W^N (1 - \theta) dE - k_D d\gamma = 0$$

If U.S. residents' holdings of Eurodollar deposits are to remain constant, then whenever E changes, r must change so that the resulting pair of E and r lies on the $V_0 V_0$ schedule.

$$V_1^N dr + V_2^N W^N (1 - \theta) dE = 0 \tag{16}$$

Solving equation 16 for dr and substituting the result into equation 15 yields

$$[(H_1^N + k_D D_1^N) \, (- V_2^N W^N (1 - \theta)/V_1^N)$$
$$+ (H_2^N + k_D D_2^N) W^N (1 - \theta)] dE = k_D d\gamma = 0 \tag{17}$$

Thus, any changes in r and E that keep the demand for short-term Eurodollars constant and reestablish equilibrium in the market for U.S. high-powered money at some arbitrary value of k_V also reestablish equilibrium at all values of k_V.

The slope of the VV schedule may be less negative than the slope of the $A_0 A_0$ schedule, as shown in figure 3, or more negative. If the slope of the VV schedule is less (more) negative than the slope of the AA schedule, then the intersection of $H_1 H_1$ and $H'_3 H'_3$ lies above (below) and $A_0 A_0$ schedule; and because the slope of the $H'_3 H'_3$ schedule is more positive than the slope of the $H_1 H_1$ schedule, the intersection of $H'_3 H'_3$ and $A_0 A_0$ lies below (above) point a_2. Consequently, when the slope of the VV schedule is less (more) negative than the slope of the $A_0 A_0$ schedule, a higher k_V leads to an increase (decrease) in the interest rate decline and dollar depreciation under flexible exchange rates.

Thus, in the case of a shift by U.S. residents from demand deposits to nonreservable instruments, an increase in k_V may reduce or increase the resulting deviation of M1' from its desired value. If the exchange rate is fixed, then an increase in k_V reduces the decline in M1' below its desired value. If the exchange rate is flexible, the slope of $V_0 V_0$ is less (more) negative than the slope of $A_0 A_0$ and M1' declines, then an increase in k_V reduces (increases) the decline in M1'. If the exchange rate is flexible, the slope of $V_0 V_0$ is less (more) negative than the slope of $A_0 A_0$ and M1' rises, then an increase in k_V increases (reduces) the rise in M1'.

The fourth disturbance to be considered is a shift by U.S. residents out of currency into nonreservable instruments. Recall that this disturbance has the same effect as would an open market operation that increased the supply of U.S. high-powered money. Once again this disturbance leads to a shift down in the HH schedule from H_0H_0 to H_1H_1 at the initial k_V in figure 3. M1' may fall or rise under both fixed and flexible exchange rates because the fall in the interest rate and, under flexible exchange rates, the depreciation of the dollar may only partially offset or may more than offset the negative impact effect on M1' of the shift in portfolio preferences.[21] The impact effect of this disturbance on the demand for U.S. high-powered money is equal to the impact effect on the demand for M1'. The absolute value of the interest rate responsiveness of the demand for U.S. high-powered money may be greater or less than the absolute value of the interest rate responsiveness of the demand for M1'. It tends to be less because the negative interest rate responsiveness of demand deposits receives a weight of k_D rather than one, but it tends to be greater because the positive interest rate responsiveness of the demand for short-term Eurodollar deposits receives a weight of k_V rather than one. Thus, under fixed exchange rates the interest rate decline that clears the market for U.S. high-powered money may be less or greater than the one that would be required to keep M1' constant. Under flexible exchange rates the induced exchange rate effect on the demand for U.S. high-powered money is less than the induced exchange rate effect on the demand for M1' because k_D and k_V are less than one. Nonetheless, under flexible exchange rates, the interest rate decline and dollar depreciation that clear the market for U.S. high-powered money and maintain equilibrium in the market for German high-powered money may be less or more than those that would keep M1' constant.

The analysis of the effect of an increase in k_V on the interest rate decline and, under flexible exchange rates, the depreciation of the dollar caused by a shift out of currency and into nonreservable instruments is exactly equivalent to the analysis when the shift under consideration is a shift out of demand deposits into nonreservable instruments. In the cases of both shifts an increase in k_V does not change the impact effect of the shift on the demand for U.S. high-powered money. Furthermore, the increase in k_V alters the interest rate responsiveness and the exchange rate responsiveness in the same way. Therefore, the change in the slope of the HH schedule and the shifts of the HH schedule at a constant exchange rate and at a constant interest rate are exactly the same.

---

[21] See appendix B for an algebraic derivation of this result.

Thus, in the case of a shift by U.S. residents from currency to nonreservable instruments, an increase in k_V may reduce or increase the resulting deviation of M1' from its desired value. If the exchange rate is fixed and M1' declines below (rises above) its desired value, then an increase in k_V reduces (increases) the decline (rise) in M1'. If the exchange rate is flexible, the slope of V_0V_0 is less (more) negative than the slope of A_0A_0, and M1' declines, then an increase in k_V reduces (increases) the decline in M1'. If the exchange rate is flexible, the slope of V_0V_0 is less (more) negative than the slope of A_0A_0, and M1' rises, then an increase in k_V increases (reduces) the rise in M1'.

The fifth and final disturbance to be considered is a shift down in exogenous U.S. output. This shift is a weighted sum of shifts out of dollar currency, dollar demand deposits, and short-term Eurodollar deposits into nonreservable instruments, where the weights are the income responsivenesses of currency, demand deposits, and short-term Eurodollar deposits, respectively.[22] Recall that in the first section it is assumed that the demand for each of these assets is positively related to output. The effects of each of the three component shifts on M1' have been analyzed. Under fixed exchange rates, if a shift out of currency into nonreservable instruments lowers M1', then the total effect of a shift down in US. output is to lower M1'. Otherwise, whether M1' is lowered or raised depends on the relative sizes of the effects of the three component shifts and their weights. Under flexible exchange rates, if shifts out of currency and demand deposits into a nonreservable instrument lower M1', then the total effect of a shift down in U.S. output is to lower M1'. If shifts out of either currency or demand deposits or both raise M1', then whether M1' is lowered or raised depends on the relative sizes of the effects of the three component shifts and their weights.

If a shift down in U.S. output causes M1' to decrease (increase) under fixed exchange rates, an increase in k_V lowers (raises) the amount of the decrease (increase) because it increases the interest rate decline induced by each of the three component shifts. If a shift down in U.S. output under flexible exchange rates causes M1' to decrease (increase), an increase in k_V lowers (raises) the amount of the decrease (increase) if it increases (decreases) the interest rate decline and dollar depreciation resulting from the three component shifts. A rise in k_V always increases the interest rate decline and dollar depreciation resulting from a shift out of short-term Eurocurrency deposits under flexible exchange rates. A rise in k_V increases the interest rate decline and dollar depreciation resulting from the other two component shifts if the slope of the V_0V_0 schedule is less negative than the slope of the A_0A_0 schedule. If

[22] See appendix B for an algebraic derivation of this result.

327

the slope of the V_0V_0 schedule is more negative than the slope of the A_0A_0 schedule, the interest rate decline and dollar depreciation resulting from a shift down in U.S. output may increase or decrease depending on the relative sizes of the component effects and their weights.

Eurocurrency Reserve Requirements and Avoidance of Redenomination Incentives

In this section it is shown that under some Eurocurrency reserve requirement systems there may be an incentive to redenominate Eurocurrency deposits so that all Eurocurrency deposits are denominated in a single currency. Such an incentive is to be avoided because redenomination could defeat the purpose of imposing the reserve requirement or could lessen the information content of movements in a monetary aggregate. Redenomination incentives can be avoided by setting up a reserve requirement system so that, no matter what the currency denomination of a deposit, the burden of holding reserves against that deposit is the same.

Suppose a Eurobank accepts dollars from a customer and assumes a future dollar liability to that customer. The bank can book this liability in at least two ways: as a dollar deposit or as a covered DM deposit, that is, as a DM deposit combined with a forward contract that commits the bank to sell the customer dollars for DMs. In order to decide how to book its dollar liability, the bank will compare the payments and the returns associated with the two alternatives.

If the liability is booked as a dollar deposit, the payment to the customer is the Eurodollar deposit rate (r_V). If the liability is booked as a covered DM deposit, the payment is the Euro-DM deposit rate (r_X), plus the forward discount on the dollar (δ), which is the payment associated with the forward contract.[23] If depositors are indifferent between dollar and covered DM deposits, then the deposit rates and the forward discount must satisfy the condition for covered interest parity,

$$r_V = r_X + \delta \qquad (18)$$

[23] The forward discount on the dollar is the forward dollar price of a DM, less the spot dollar price of a DM, divided by the spot dollar price of a DM. Assumptions made earlier imply that risk-neutral banks would bid the forward discount equal to the expected rate of depreciation of the dollar, so for there to be a forward discount on the dollar private agents must expect the dollar to depreciate. This last statement would have to be modified slightly if difficulties raised by Jensen's inequality were taken into account. If banks were not risk neutral, the forward discount would not have to equal the expected rate of depreciation. The results of this section depend on covered interest arbitrage, however, and therefore are valid whether or not the forward discount equals the expected rate of depreciation.

and the payments under both booking alternatives are the same. Because the reserve requirement system does not directly affect the payments under the two alternatives, an incentive to choose one alternative over the other must arise from a comparison of the returns the bank receives from investing the deposited funds.

The returns on the investment of deposited funds under various reserve requirement systems are presented in table 2. First, consider the system used in the earlier analysis, which is labeled Case a. Under the dollar deposit alternative, the bank puts a fraction of the deposit (k_V) into reserves and earns a return equal to the return on a representative dollar asset $(r_\$)$. This return might be, for example, the rate of interest on a treasury bill of the same maturity as the deposit. The remaining fraction of the deposit $(1 - k_V)$ is invested in the representative asset and earns the same return as the return on reserves. Under the DM alternative, the bank invests all of the deposit in the representative asset. Under both alternatives the returns are the same. Hence, under this system there is no incentive to redenominate dollar deposits as DM deposits that are matched by forward contracts. If no interest were paid on reserves, however, banks and U.S. citizens would have an incentive to redenominate all dollar deposits of Eurobanks as unreserved DM deposits that are matched by forward contracts. In this case redenomination would defeat the purpose of the reserve requirement scheme, which is to alter the parameters of the demand for high-powered money so as to reduce fluctuations in a monetary aggregate that includes the dollar liabilities of Eurobanks to U.S. residents.

Next, consider a system where the Eurodeposits of residents of both countries denominated in both currencies are reserved, reserves are held in the currency of the deposit, and the required reserve ratios are equal. This is Case b in table 2. If the bank books the dollar liability as a dollar deposit, then it earns a fraction $(1 - k)$ of the return on the representative asset. If the bank books the dollar liability as a covered DM deposit, then it earns the same return on the fraction of the deposit not held in reserves. The bank, however, has accepted dollars, holds reserves in DMs, and has a future dollar liability. Thus, the bank must convert dollars to DMs spot and DMs to dollars forward, thereby earning a return on its required reserves equal to the forward discount on the dollar. Under this system a positive (negative) forward discount on the dollar creates an incentive to redenominate dollar deposits (DM deposits) as DM deposits (dollar deposits) that are matched by forward contracts. If the currency denomination of Eurocurrency deposits switches back and forth with changes in the forward discount, then monetary authorities who take account of Eurocurrency deposits

329

TABLE 2
RETURN ON THE INVESTMENT OF DEPOSITED FUNDS UNDER VARIOUS EUROCURRENCY RESERVE REQUIREMENT SYSTEMS

Case	Interest Payments on Reserves	Currency of Reserves	Reservable Assets	Reserve Requirements	Return on Investment of Deposited Funds	
					Eurodollar deposit	Covered Euro-DM deposit
a	$r_\$$	Dollars	U.S. residents' short-term Euro-dollar deposits	$k_V \neq 0$, $k_X = 0$	$r_\$(1 - k_V) + k_V r_\$$	$r_\$$
b	None	Currency of deposit	All short-term Eurocurrency deposits	$k_V = k_X = k$	$r_\$(1 - k) + k(0)$	$r_\$(1 - k) + k\delta$
c	None	Currency of deposit	All short-term Eurocurrency deposits	$k_V = k_X r_{DM}/r_\$$	$r_\$(1 - k_V) + k_V(0)$	$r_\$(1 - k_X) + k_X\delta$
d	None	Dollars	All short-term Eurocurrency deposits	$k_V = k_X = k$	$r_\$(1 - k) + k(0)$	$r_\$(1 - k) + k(0)$
e	$r_\$$ on dollars r_{DM} on DMs	Currency of deposit	All short-term Eurocurrency deposits	$k_V = k_X = k$	$r_\$(1 - k) + k r_\$$	$r_\$(1 - k) + k(r_{DM} + \delta)$

denominated in their country's currency when formulating policy might receive confusing signals.[24]

The kind of redenomination incentive that arises in Case b can be avoided in several ways. One way is to vary one of the reserve requirements so as to offset the return arising from the forward discount, Case c. Specifically, the reserve requirement on, for example, dollar deposits (k_V) should be varied so that the product of the dollar reserve requirement and interest rate on the representative dollar asset is equal to the product of the DM reserve requirement and the interest rate on the representative DM asset (r_{DM}):

$$k_V r_\$ = k_X r_{DM} \qquad (19)$$

Varying k_V in this way equalizes the net burdens of holding reserves against the two types of deposits. The burden of holding reserves against a dollar deposit is equal to the interest forgone because reserves must be held, $k_V r_\$$. The net burden of holding reserves against a DM deposit is equal to the interest forgone because reserves must be held, $k_X r_\$$, minus the return to holding reserves arising from the forward discount, $k_X \delta$. Net burdens are equalized if

$$k_V r_\$ = k_X (r_\$ - \delta) \qquad (20)$$

Covered interest arbitrage between representative assets ensures that the difference between the interest rates on representative assets exactly reflects the forward discount:

$$r_\$ = r_{DM} + \delta \qquad (21)$$

Solving equation 21 for δ and substituting the result into equation 20 yields equation 19. A larger discount on the dollar, for instance, implies a higher representative rate on dollar assets and a lower reserve requirement on dollar deposits. Although variable reserve requirements are a way of avoiding the redenomination incentive, they might be difficult to implement.

A second way to avoid the redenomination incentive that arises in Case b is to hold all reserves in the same currency, Case d, or a market basket of currencies. If, for instance, reserves are held in dollars there will be no conversion from dollars to DMs associated with holding

---

[24] It might be argued that if the nonbank public regards home currency deposits and covered foreign currency deposits as perfect substitutes, then both should be included in the definition of a monetary aggregate. Forward contracts and foreign currency deposits can be held for reasons other than the evasion of reserve requirements, however, and the reason these instruments are being held cannot be inferred simply from an inspection of a bank's balance sheet.

reserves against covered DM deposits, no differential return resulting from currency conversion, and, therefore, no redenomination incentive. Note that the single currency or market basket approach would make it difficult if not impossible for monetary authorities in individual countries to use the monetary base as an instrument to influence monetary aggregates that include Eurodeposits denominated in the home currency and held by residents.

A third way to avoid the redenomination incentive that arises in Case *b* is to pay interest on reserves at a rate equal to the representative rate for assets denominated in the same currency as the reserves, Case *e*. Under the DM deposit alternative, the bank would still have to convert dollars to DMs on the spot market and DMs to dollars on the forward market because reserves must be held in DMs. Thus, the bank's reserves would earn the forward discount on the dollar, plus the rate on the representative DM asset (r_{DM}) under the DM deposit alternative. Under the dollar deposit alternative, the bank's reserves would earn the return on the representative dollar asset. Because covered interest arbitrage in the market for representative assets ensures that the difference between the interest rates on representative assets exactly reflects the forward discount, the rates of return on reserves are the same, and there is no redenomination incentive.

Some Conclusions

The development of closer links between domestic and Eurocurrency markets has provided an incentive for further investigation of the implications of placing reserve requirements on Eurocurrency deposits. In this paper a two-country model of international financial markets has been employed to make a contribution to that investigation. Most of the paper was devoted to the analysis of a particular system of Euro-currency reserve requirements. Under that system the only Eurocurrency reserve requirement was one on the short-term Eurodollar deposits of U.S. residents, and interest was paid on all required reserves. First, several Eurodeposit multipliers were derived. Then the implications of raising the reserve requirement on short-term Eurodollar deposits for control of a particular monetary aggregate were traced. This aggregate, designated M1', was the sum of U.S. residents' holding of currency, demand deposits, and short-term Eurodollar deposits. The remainder of the paper was devoted to a discussion of the redenomination incentives that may arise under some alternative Eurocurrency reserve requirement systems and of ways to avoid these incentives.

Some conclusions can be drawn about the effects of an increase in the reserve requirement on U.S. residents' short-term Eurodollar deposits (k_V) on the Eurodeposit multipliers associated with a shift from dollar demand deposits to short-term Eurodollar deposits by U.S. residents. These conclusions are obtained by combining some of the results obtained in the earlier sections. In section 2 it was shown that under fixed exchange rates Eurodeposit multipliers are smaller the larger the interest rate decline resulting from this shift and that under flexible exchange rates the multipliers for various Eurodeposit totals measured in dollars are smaller, the larger the interest rate decline and are larger the greater the amount of dollar depreciation. In section 3 it was shown that an increase in k_V reduces the interest rate decline under both fixed and flexible exchange rates and reduces the amount of dollar depreciation under flexible exchange rates. Thus, under fixed exchange rates, an increase in k_V raises all the Eurodeposit multipliers, whereas under flexible exchange rates it may raise or lower these multipliers.

For some values of the parameters of the model, an increase in k_V definitely improves control of M1′; that is, this increase unambiguously reduces the deviations of M1′ from its desired value, no matter what the source of the disturbance. First, consider the case of fixed exchange rates. When U.S. residents shift out of demand deposits into Eurodollar deposits, M1′ rises. An increase in k_V reduces the interest rate decline resulting from this shift and therefore damps the rise in M1′. Four other types of disturbances remain. Shifts out of Eurodollar deposits or demand deposits into nonreservable instruments lower M1′; shifts out of currency into nonreservable instruments and, therefore, shifts down in output *may* lower M1′. A rise in k_V increases the interest rate decline resulting from all four shifts. Thus, if M1′ declines as a result of all four types of shifts, then an increase in k_V damps the decline in M1′.

Now consider the case of flexible exchange rates. When U.S. residents shift out of demand deposits into Eurodollar deposits, M1′ rises. An increase in k_V reduces the interest rate decline and dollar depreciation resulting from this shift and, therefore, damps the rise in M1′. Four other types of disturbances remain. A shift out of Eurodollar deposits into nonreservable instruments lowers M1′; shifts out of demand deposits or currency into nonreservable instruments and, therefore, shifts down in output *may* lower M1′. A rise in k_V increases the interest rate decline and dollar depreciation resulting from a shift out of Eurodollar deposits. A rise in k_V *may* increase both the interest rate decline and dollar depreciation resulting from shifts out of demand deposits and currency and, therefore, from shifts down in output. Thus, if M1′ declines as a result of all four types of shifts and if an increase in

k_V increases the interest rate decline and dollar depreciation resulting from all four kinds of shifts, then an increase in k_V damps the decline in M1′.

If the conditions just described are met, an increase in k_V damps the deviations of M1′ from its desired value for all values of the parameters of the model that satisfy the conditions, no matter what the relative magnitudes of the variances of the disturbance terms representing the five kinds of shifts. If these conditions are not met, an increase in k_V may still reduce the variance of M1′. Whether or not the variance of M1′ is reduced depends, however, on both the parameters of the model and the relative magnitudes of the variances of the disturbance terms representing the five kinds of shifts. Although an analysis of the circumstances under which the variance of M1′ would be reduced if the conditions stated above are not met has not been presented, the ingredients for such an analysis have been provided.

For some alternative Eurocurrency reserve requirements systems under which no interest is paid on required reserves, banks and non-banks may have an incentive to redenominate Eurocurrency deposits denominated in one currency so that all Eurocurrency deposits are denominated in a single currency. Such redenomination incentives occur when the burdens of holding reserves against deposits denominated in different currencies are not the same. Reserve-holding burdens can be equalized and redenomination incentives avoided by adopting a system of variable reserve requirements, by specifying that reserves must be held in a single currency or basket of currencies, or by paying interest on required reserves at a rate equal to the rate on the representative asset denominated in the currency in which reserves must be held.

It would be useful to extend the analysis of this paper in several ways. It has been assumed that the authorities employ the intermediate target strategy of controlling M1′ in attempting to achieve their ultimate objective, which might be the stabilization of output. Well-known objections have been raised to the use of such an intermediate target strategy. Perhaps the most useful extension of the analysis of this paper would be to explore the implications of Eurocurrency reserve requirements for the direct stabilization of an ultimate target variable such as output. For direct stabilization the supply of high-powered money is set so that the expected value of output is equal to its desired value, and no attempt is made to achieve a particular value for an intermediate target variable such as a monetary aggregate. Other useful extensions would include more detailed investigations of some of the alternative

Eurocurrency reserve requirement systems presented earlier and considerations of all the Eurocurrency reserve requirement systems in more general models of international financial markets.

Appendix A

In this appendix a version of the equilibrium condition that states that the sum of private demands for U.S. and German treasury securities measured in dollars must equal the sum of supplies of these assets measured in dollars comparable to equations 5a and 5b is derived. The first step is to specify the demands for U.S. and German treasury securities by U.S. and German banks. U.S. banks' demand for the sum of the two types of treasury securities, which they regard as perfect substitutes, is equal to their net worth, plus the deposits they accept, minus their required reserves and the loans they make to both nonbanks and Eurobanks:

$$B^B + EF^B = W^B + (1 - k_D)D^N + (1 - k_T)T^N$$
$$+ \overset{*}{T}{}^N - L^N - \overset{*}{L}{}^N - I^A \qquad \text{(A1)}$$

German banks' demand for the sum of the two types of treasury securities, which they regard as perfect substitutes, is equal to their net worth, plus the deposits they accept, minus their required reserves and the loans they make to both nonbanks and Eurobanks:

$$\overset{*}{B}{}^B + E\overset{*}{F}{}^B = \overset{*}{W}{}^B + E[(1 - \overset{*}{k}_G)\overset{*}{G}{}^N + (1 - \overset{*}{k}_U)\overset{*}{U}{}^N$$
$$+ U^N - \overset{*}{P}{}^N - P^N - J^A] \qquad \text{(A2)}$$

It is also useful to note that Eurobanks' demand for the sum of loans denominated in dollars from U.S. banks and the dollar equivalent of loans denominated in DMs from German banks, which they regard as perfect substitutes, is equal to the loans they make to nonbanks, plus their required reserves, minus their net worth and the deposits they accept from nonbanks:

$$I^A + EJ^A = Q^N + \overset{*}{Q}{}^N - W^A - (1 - k_V)V^N - \overset{*}{V}{}^N - (1 - k_Y)Y^N$$
$$- \overset{*}{Y}{}^N + E(S^N + \overset{*}{S}{}^N - X^N - \overset{*}{X}{}^N - Z^N - \overset{*}{Z}{}^N) \qquad \text{(A3)}$$

The desired version of the treasury securities market equilibrium condition is obtained by substituting three items into equation 4: banks' demand for combinations of U.S. and German treasury securities, given by equations A1 and A2; the Eurobanks' desired holdings of combina-

335

tions of dollar and DM interbank loans, given by equation A3; and nonbank behavioral relations. These substitutions yield equation A4:

$$\bar{B} - (B^C + \overset{*}{B}{}^C) + E(\bar{F} - \overset{*}{F}{}^C) = W^B + \overset{*}{W}{}^B + W^A$$
$$+ B^N + \overset{*}{B}{}^N - L^N - \overset{*}{L}{}^N - Q^N - \overset{*}{Q}{}^N + \overset{*}{T}{}^N + \overset{*}{V}{}^N$$
$$+ \overset{*}{Y}{}^N + E(F^N + \overset{*}{F}{}^N - P^N - \overset{*}{P}{}^N + U^N - S^N - \overset{*}{S}{}^N$$
$$+ X^N + \overset{*}{X}{}^N + Z^N + \overset{*}{Z}{}^N) + (1 - k_D)D^N + (1 - k_T)T^N$$
$$+ (1 - k_V)V^N + (1 - k_Y)Y^N + (1 - k_G)E\overset{*}{G}{}^N$$
$$+ (1 - k_U)E\overset{*}{U}{}^N \tag{A4}$$

Appendix B

In this appendix algebraic expressions for the effects of four of the five disturbances on M1' under fixed and flexible exchange rates are derived.

A shift out of short-term Eurodollar deposits into nonreservable instruments: Under fixed exchange rates (*FI*) the effect of this disturbance is given by

$$\frac{dM1'}{d\beta}\bigg|_{FI} = M1'_r \frac{dr}{d\beta}\bigg|_{FI} - 1 \tag{B1}$$

where

$$M1'_r = H^N_1 + D^N_1 + V^N_1 < 0 \tag{B2}$$

Equation B1 can be rewritten as

$$\frac{dM1'}{d\beta}\bigg|_{FI} = \frac{1}{k_V}\left(H_r \frac{dr}{d\beta}\bigg|_{FI} - k_V \right) + \frac{1}{k_V}\big[(k_V - 1)H^N_1$$
$$+ (k_V - k_D)D^N_1 \big]\frac{dr}{d\beta}\bigg|_{FI} < 0 \tag{B3}$$

where

$$H_r = H^N_1 + k_D D^N_1 + k_V V^N_1 \tag{B4}$$

In order for equilibrium to be reestablished in the market for U.S. high-powered money, the first term on the right-hand side of equation B3 must be zero and $dr/d\beta|FI$ must be negative, so the second term on the right-hand side of equation B3 is negative.

Under flexible exchange rates (*FL*) the effect of this disturbance is given by

$$\frac{dM1'}{d\beta}\bigg|_{FL} = M1'_r \frac{dr}{d\beta}\bigg|_{FL} + M1'_E \frac{dE}{d\beta}\bigg|_{FL} - 1 \tag{B5}$$

where

$$M1'_E = (H_2^N + D_2^N + V_2^N)W^N(1-\theta) > 0 \qquad (B6)$$

If the market for German high-powered money is to remain in equilibrium, $(dr/d\beta|FL)$ and $(dE/d\beta|FL)$ must satisfy

$$\left.\frac{dE}{d\beta}\right|_{FL} = -\frac{\overset{*}{A_r}}{\overset{*}{A_E}}\left.\frac{dr}{d\beta}\right|_{FL} \qquad (B7)$$

where $\overset{*}{A_r}$ and $\overset{*}{A_E}$ are, respectively, the interest rate responsiveness and the exchange rate responsiveness of the demand for German high-powered money. Given equation B7, equation B5 can be rewritten as

$$\left.\frac{dM1'}{d\beta}\right|_{FL} = (M1'_r - M1'_E\frac{\overset{*}{A_r}}{\overset{*}{A_E}})\left.\frac{dr}{d\beta}\right|_{FL} - 1 \qquad (B8)$$

or as

$$\left.\frac{dM1'}{d\beta}\right|_{FL} = \frac{1}{k_V}[(H_r - H_E\frac{\overset{*}{A_r}}{\overset{*}{A_E}})\left.\frac{dr}{d\beta}\right|_{FL} - k_V] + \frac{1}{k_V}\{[(k_V-1)H_1^N$$

$$+ (k_V - k_D)D_1^N] - [(k_V-1)H_2^N + (k_V-k_D)D_2^N]$$

$$\times \frac{\overset{*}{A_r}}{\overset{*}{A_E}}W^N(1-\theta)\}\left.\frac{dr}{d\beta}\right|_{FL} < 0 \qquad (B9)$$

where

$$H_E = (H_2^N + k_D D_2^N + k_V V_2^N)W^N(1-\theta) > 0 \qquad (B10)$$

In order for equilibrium to be reestablished in the market for U.S. high-powered money, given that the market for German high-powered money remains in equilibrium, the first term on the right-hand side of equation B9 must be equal to zero and $dr/d\beta|FL$ must be negative, so the second term on the right-hand side of equation B9 is also negative.

A shift out of dollar demand deposits into nonreservable instruments: Under fixed exchange rates the effect of this disturbance is given by

$$\left.\frac{dM1'}{d\gamma}\right|_{FI} = M1'_r\left.\frac{dr}{d\gamma}\right|_{FI} - 1 \qquad (B11)$$

337

which can be rewritten as

$$\frac{d\mathrm{M1}'}{d\gamma}\Bigg|_{FI} = \frac{1}{k_D}(H_r\frac{dr}{d\gamma}\Bigg|_{FI} - k_D) + \frac{1}{k_D}[(k_D - 1)H_1^N$$

$$+ (k_D - k_V)V_1^N]\frac{dr}{d\gamma}\Bigg|_{FI} < 0 \qquad (B12)$$

The first term on the right-hand side of equation B12 must be equal to zero, and $dr/d\gamma|FI$ must be negative, so the second term on the right-hand side of equation B12 must be negative.

Under flexible exchange rates, the effect of this disturbance is given by

$$\frac{d\mathrm{M1}'}{d\gamma}\Bigg|_{FL} = \mathrm{M1}'_r\frac{dr}{d\gamma}\Bigg|_{FL} + \mathrm{M1}'_E\frac{dE}{d\gamma}\Bigg|_{FL} - 1 \qquad (B13)$$

which can be rewritten as

$$\frac{d\mathrm{M1}'}{d\gamma}\Bigg|_{FL} = \frac{1}{k_D}[(H_r - H_E\frac{\overset{*}{A}_r}{\overset{*}{A}_E})\frac{dr}{d\gamma}\Bigg|_{FL} - k_D]$$

$$+ \frac{1}{k_D}\{[(k_D - 1)H_1^N + (k_D - k_V)V_1^N]$$

$$- [(k_D - 1)H_2^N + (k_D - k_V)V_2^N]$$

$$\times \frac{\overset{*}{A}_r}{\overset{*}{A}_E}W^N(1 - \theta)\}\frac{dr}{d\gamma}\Bigg|_{FL} \lesseqgtr 0 \qquad (B14)$$

The first term on the right-hand side of equation B14 must equal zero, and $dr/d\gamma|FL$ must be negative, but with $dr/d\gamma|FL < 0$ the second term on the right-hand side of equation B14 may be positive if the negative term

$$-\frac{1}{k_D}[(k_D - k_V)V_2^N]\frac{\overset{*}{A}_r}{\overset{*}{A}_E}W^N(1 - \theta) \qquad (B15)$$

is large enough relative to the other three positive terms that are multiplied times $dr/d\gamma|FL$. Note that if $k_V = k_D$, $d\mathrm{M1}'/d\gamma|FL$ is negative.

A shift out of dollar currency into nonreservable instruments: Under fixed exchange rates the effect of this disturbance is given by

$$\frac{d\mathrm{M1}'}{d\eta}\Bigg|_{FI} = \mathrm{M1}'_r\frac{dr}{d\eta}\Bigg|_{FI} - 1 \qquad (B16)$$

which can be rewritten as

$$\left.\frac{d\mathrm{M1'}}{d\eta}\right|_{FI} = (H_r \left.\frac{dr}{d\eta}\right|_{FI} - 1) + [(1 - k_D)D_1^N$$

$$+ (1 - k_V)V_1^N] \left.\frac{dr}{d\eta}\right|_{FI} \lessgtr 0 \quad \text{(B17)}$$

The first term on the right-hand side of equation B17 must be equal to zero, and $dr/d\eta|FI$ must be negative, but with $dr/d\eta|FI < 0$ the second term on the right-hand side of equation B17 is positive unless $(1 - k_V)V_1^N > |(1 - k_D)D_1^N|$.

The effect of a rise in η on M1' under flexible rates is given by

$$\left.\frac{d\mathrm{M1'}}{d\eta}\right|_{FL} = \mathrm{M1'}_r \left.\frac{dr}{d\eta}\right|_{FL} + \mathrm{M1'}_E \left.\frac{dE}{d\eta}\right|_{FL} - 1 \quad \text{(B18)}$$

which can be rewritten as

$$\left.\frac{d\mathrm{M1'}}{d\eta}\right|_{FL} = [(H_r - H_E \frac{\overset{*}{A}_r}{\overset{*}{A}_E}) \left.\frac{dr}{d\eta}\right|_{FL} - 1]$$

$$+ \{[(1 - k_D)D_1^N + (1 - k_V)V_1^N]$$

$$- [(1 - k_D)D_2^N + (1 - k_V)V_2^N]$$

$$\times \frac{\overset{*}{A}_r}{\overset{*}{A}_E} W^N (1 - \theta)\} \left.\frac{dr}{d\eta}\right|_{FL} \lessgtr 0 \quad \text{(B19)}$$

The first term on the right-hand side of equation B19 must be equal to zero, and $dr/d\eta|FL$ must be negative, but with $dr/d\eta|FL < 0$ the second term on the right-hand side of equation B19 will be positive unless $(1 - k_V)V_1^N$, which is positive, outweighs the other three terms, which are multiplied times $dr/d\eta|FL$, which are all negative.

A shift down in exogenous U.S. output: Under fixed exchange rates the effect of this disturbance is given by

$$\left.\frac{d\mathrm{M1'}}{d\lambda}\right|_{FI} = \mathrm{M1'}_r \left.\frac{dr}{d\lambda}\right|_{FI} - \mathrm{M1'}_y \quad \text{(B20)}$$

where

$$\mathrm{M1'}_y = H_3^N + D_3 + V_3^N \quad \text{(B21)}$$

It can be shown that it is possible to rewrite $dr/d\lambda|FI$ as

$$\frac{dr}{d\lambda}\bigg|_{FI} = H_3^N \frac{dr}{d\eta}\bigg|_{FI} + D_3^N \frac{dr}{d\gamma}\bigg|_{FI} + V_3^N \frac{dr}{d\beta}\bigg|_{FI} \qquad \text{(B22)}$$

so that equation B20 can be rewritten as

$$\frac{dM1'}{d\lambda}\bigg|_{FI} = H_3^N (M1'_r \frac{dr}{d\eta}\bigg|_{FI} - 1) + D_3^N (M1'_r \frac{dr}{d\gamma}\bigg|_{FI} - 1)$$

$$+ V_3^N (M1'_r \frac{dr}{d\beta}\bigg|_{FI} - 1) \gtreqless 0 \qquad \text{(B23)}$$

Thus, the effect of a shift down in exogenous U.S. output on M1' can be expressed as a weighted sum of the effects of shifts out of currency, demand deposits, and short-term Eurodollar deposits into nonreservable instruments, where the weights are the positive income responsivenesses of currency, demand deposits, and short-term Eurodollar deposits, respectively. The effect of each of the three component shifts on M1' under fixed exchange rates has been analyzed here, and by referring to that analysis it can be determined that the sign of the weighted average of those effects is ambiguous and under what conditions this weighted average is negative.

Under flexible exchange rates, the effect on M1' of this shift is once again a weighted sum of the effects of the same three kinds of shifts where the weights are income responsivenesses:

$$\frac{dM1'}{d\lambda}\bigg|_{FL} = H_3^N [(M1'_r - M1'_E \frac{\overset{*}{A_r}}{\overset{*}{A_E}}) \frac{dr}{d\eta}\bigg|_{FL} - 1]$$

$$+ D_3^N [M1'_r - M1'_E \frac{\overset{*}{A_r}}{\overset{*}{A_E}}) \frac{dr}{d\gamma}\bigg|_{FL} - 1]$$

$$+ V_3^N [(M1'_r - M1'_E \frac{\overset{*}{A_r}}{\overset{*}{A_E}}) \frac{dr}{d\beta}\bigg|_{FL} - 1] \lesseqgtr 0$$

$$\text{(B24)}$$

From the analysis above, it can be determined that the sign of this weighted average is ambiguous and under what conditions it is negative.

Offshore Markets in Foreign Currencies and National Monetary Control: Britain, Singapore, and the United States

Ronald I. McKinnon

During the 1960s and most of the 1970s, many writers concluded that unregulated or lightly regulated markets in foreign currencies—loosely referred to collectively as Eurocurrencies—provided invaluable international financial services without significantly undermining control over national money.[1] This conclusion applied to countries providing the market site: Britain and Singapore are the prototypes analyzed herein. It also applied to those countries issuing internationally convertible currencies—notably the U.S. dollar—that are traded in European, Asian, and other offshore markets. Recent and proposed changes in banking regulations, however, and financial problems in the United States and Britain warrant a reassessment of the way Euromarkets impinge on national monetary policies.

To avoid including too many diverse countries, I shall consider the regulatory problems faced by the U.S. Federal Reserve Bank on

I should like to thank officials of the Monetary Authority of Singapore, Wong Pakshong and Ng Kok Song, for useful information. Helmut Mayer of the Bank for International Settlements and C. A. E. Goodhart of the Bank of England also provided helpful criticism. None, however, is responsible for the main arguments advanced in this paper.

[1] See, for example, Alexander K. Swoboda, "The Euro-Dollar Market: An Interpretation," Essays in International Finance, no. 64 (Princeton, N.J.: Princeton University, February 1968); Jürg Niehans and John Hewson, "The Eurodollar Market and Monetary Theory," *Journal of Money, Credit and Banking*, vol. 8, no. 1 (February 1976), pp. 1-27; Ronald I. McKinnon, "The Eurocurrency Market," Essays in International Finance, no. 125 (Princeton, N.J.: Princeton University, December 1977), reprinted as chap. 9 in McKinnon, *Money in International Exchange: The Convertible Currency System* (New York: Oxford University Press, 1979).

the one hand, and by the Bank of England and Monetary Authority of Singapore on the other. The appropriate strategy for monetary control is now quite different in each of the two cases, but they are related to one another.

My principal conclusion is that central banks in both sets of countries must learn to control "money" rather than "credit." First, the proliferation of unregulated Eurodeposits—which are basically credit instruments and not money—tends to undermine any controls on purely domestic flows of credit. Second, free Euromarkets are essential to the international financial system, and extending credit controls to them would be counterproductive. Third, the extension of even modest reserve requirements to Eurocurrency deposits, which are similar to interest-bearing certificates of deposit rather than checking accounts, would destabilize the demand for any one central bank's monetary base. The ebb and flow of international credit—for example, the changing surplus of the Organization of Petroleum Exporting Countries (OPEC) —through the Euromarkets is too unpredictable. If endogenously determined, this variable flow of credit—reflecting international borrowing and lending—is itself neither inflationary nor deflationary.

Focusing then on money, the national means of payment that is controllable, I shall discuss how ultraliberal financial entrepôts—such as Britain and Singapore—may best secure monetary stability. Because of the ease with which residents may substitute domestic currency deposits for foreign in conveniently located neighborhood banks, the demand for domestic money (and the exchange rate) is potentially quite unstable. Hence, I argue that the centerpiece of domestic monetary policy should be a stabilized exchange rate with some "hard" foreign money. By standing ready to buy or sell foreign exchange on demand, and by allowing the domestic monetary base to adjust to such interventions, the monetary authority can automatically match the supply of domestic money to the shifting demand for it. One then gives up on any purely national monetary rule such as a target rate of interest or a fixed rate of growth in a particular domestic monetary aggregate.

This exchange-rate strategy, appropriate for a financial entrepôt, is insufficient, however, for the "center" country whose currency is being actively traded in the Euromarkets. The last section of this paper discusses how the United States should evolve a more independent system for controlling the supply of dollars, narrowly but inclusively defined to be the domestic means of payment. This monetary independence is necessary because, first, the United States is still a relatively closed economy and, second, the world dollar standard needs an independent anchor. Because the United States has this intrinsically more difficult problem of securing monetary control, the Federal Reserve Bank should make a sharper distinction between money and credit than would be necessary for a smaller economy with a fixed exchange rate. The administrative difficulty in making this distinction leads to the conclusion that the legalization of Eurocurrency trading within the United States itself would be most unwise.

The Changing Regulatory Environment

In the 1980s, the international worth of unregulated Eurocurrency transacting remains unchallenged as long as purely national banking systems continue to be tightly regulated. Indeed, the Asian and Eurocurrency markets are the centerpiece of the international capital market. Under floating exchange rates, the foreign exchange departments of commercial banks throughout the world use interbank Eurocurrency deposits and loans from a few offshore centers to cover forward any net foreign exchange exposure incurred in servicing their retail clients.[2] Without such an efficient hedging facility, exchange fluctuations and the associated currency risk would have been much more damaging to foreign trade. In times of individual stress, developing countries and small eastern European countries receive large net Eurocredits—increasingly in the form of syndicated loans. Most important of all, in times of collective international stress set in motion by the successive oil crises, the unhindered recycling of financial surpluses of oil-exporting countries to the rest of the world remains a remarkable achievement of the Asian and Eurocurrency markets.

That said, what occurred in the late 1970s and early 1980s to warrant a reassessment of the uneasy coexistence of free Euromarkets and more tightly regulated national banking systems? Throughout most of the 1970s, both Britain and Singapore had used exchange controls to separate the domains of their domestic currencies from offshore transactions. The United Kingdom severely restricted British nationals from acquiring foreign currency securities, notably dollars: These could be purchased only in limited circumstances at a substantial premium over the regular commercial exchange rate between sterling and dollars. Concomitantly, U.K. exporters were required to repatriate all current earnings back into sterling within a short time, depending on the nature of export financing. Tourists and immigrants were similarly restricted. Between July and October 1979, however, all these exchange controls were abolished. British residents were free to arbitrage between unregulated foreign currency deposits and tightly regulated sterling de-

[2] McKinnon, "Eurocurrency Market."

posits! The premium on investment dollars vanished. Because this foreign exchange liberalization further undermines any policy based on purely domestic monetary targets, I shall devote an entire section to an analysis of how sterling should be managed.

Less precipitously, but no less comprehensively, the Monetary Authority of Singapore has progressively liberalized the exchange controls on capital account that, in the early 1970s, restricted Singapore residents from borrowing or depositing in foreign currencies, particularly in those Singapore banks known as Asian currency units (ACUs). These ACUs are specifically authorized to deal only in foreign currencies; they remain free of reserve requirements or lending restrictions and are the institutional basis for the rapidly burgeoning Asian currency market that is mainly denominated in U.S. dollars to serve nonresidents. As of June 1978, however, Singapore residents can freely make deposits with or accept loans from the ACUs. Because Singapore's financial and fiscal strategy is such a neat microcosm of the systematic separation of offshore and onshore transactions *without* loss of domestic monetary control, we shall analyze the Singapore strategy before going on to the unresolved British conundrum.

Finally, what recent financial events may have upset monetary management in the United States? In October 1979, the Federal Reserve System placed a supplemental 8 percent marginal reserve on the managed liabilities of all member banks resident in the United States. These managed liabilities were defined to include U.S. certificates of deposit, repurchase agreements, and direct Eurocurrency borrowing. In March 1980, these new reserve requirements were extended to virtually all American financial institutions—including nonmember banks and money-market funds. In addition, direct credit controls were imposed. After sharply reducing U.S. bank lending and money growth, these extraordinary measures were rescinded as of July 1980. In the interim, however, U.S. banks were at a grave competitive disadvantage compared with unregulated European and Asian dollar banks, which remained free to make loans to, or accept deposits from, American residents. The disadvantage of carrying non-interest-bearing reserves is aggravated in a time of high nominal rates of interest reflecting inflationary expectations.

Recognizing this competitive imbalance, the U.S. Federal Reserve Bank proposed to extend a "modest" reserve requirement to European and Asian dollar deposits owned by nonbanks.[3] To be effective, the

[3] Henry C. Wallich, "Statement on the Eurocurrency Market," U.S. Congress, House of Representatives, Subcommittees on Domestic Monetary Policy and on International Trade, Investment, and Monetary Policy of the Committee on Banking, Finance, and Urban Affairs, July 1979.

cooperation of authorities in offshore centers around the world—particularly those in London and Singapore—would be needed. Not surprisingly, the American proposal was not favorably received and remains in abeyance—perhaps wisely so. The competitive imbalance is nonetheless real, however, and it could again be aggravated by credit controls in times of economic stress. More important, the problem of avoiding international price inflation is not resolved.

Another recent (1980) American proposal for offsetting the "unfair" regulatory advantages enjoyed by Eurobanks in attracting dollar deposits, is to allow unregulated international banking facilities (IBFs) in the United States to accept dollar (and possibly foreign currency) deposits owned by nonresidents. These nonresident dollar deposits would be free of local usury laws, taxes, and the reserve requirement that the Federal Reserve (and state governments) normally imposes on deposits owned by resident American firms and households. The idea is to attract foreign-owned dollar deposits "back from" their overseas havens. This proposed IBF (as put forward by a group of New York banks) is much stronger than having pure Eurodeposits confined to foreign money. Neither Britain nor Singapore has offshore facilities in sterling and Singapore dollars, respectively. Thus, having unregulated U.S. dollar deposits conveniently located in the United States may well further undermine the Federal Reserve's control over the (regulated) American banking system as explained below.

Before discussing American financial policy, however, let us consider the impact of more conventional Euromarkets in foreign currencies on the monetary policies of Singapore and Great Britain.

The Asian Currency Market and Monetary Control in Singapore

With the final abolition of exchange controls on nonbank residents of Singapore on June 1, 1978, what remains to separate the domain of foreign currency transactions from that of Singapore dollars? In effect, separation now depends on confining ACUs to acceptance of deposits in foreign currencies only and making certain important fiscal distinctions between residents and nonresidents.

Financial institutions operating in the Asian dollar market out of Singapore are required to keep a separate set of accounts (in U.S. dollars) called Asian currency units. Banks that are pure ACUs may accept deposits and make loans only in foreign currencies; such limited-license banks are not subject to reserve requirements or any other significant restriction on their assets or liabilities. They can, however, deal with Singapore residents as well as nonresidents. A slightly broader

345

license allows "offshore banks" to operate as ACUs and, although they are not allowed to accept deposits in Singapore dollars, they can freely make loans in Singapore dollars to domestic residents or nonresidents. The terms of reference, however, of the offshore banks (as with pure ACUs) confine them to wholesale banking.

Finally, domestic full-service banks, which can open branches at will, solicit retail custom from Singapore residents in Singapore dollars; they often own an ACU with a separate set of books. In their dealings in Singapore dollars, domestic banks (and finance companies) are subject to reserve requirements on their eligible liabilities, which are defined as the total amount of nonbank deposits (including certificates of deposit), less the net interbank deposits including interbank borrowings. These requirements are: (1) a 6 percent non-interest-bearing cash reserve to be held with the Monetary Authority of Singapore (MAS); (2) a 10 percent primary liquid asset requirement (notes and coin, excess cash reserves held with the MAS, call loans, and short-term treasury securities); and (3) a 10 percent second tier of liquid assets including excess items under *b,* commercial bills, and longer-term government securities.

Although these requirements seem substantial—particularly those under 2 and 3—they are mainly *interest-bearing* reserves. Because there are no usury laws in Singapore, interest rates are close to their equilibrium levels, and having to hold government or other short-term liquid securities is not a great disadvantage for the banks. The MAS does allow a cartel of commercial banks to agree not to pay interest on demand deposits, however—a prohibition that could become more destabilizing if expected price inflation and nominal rates of interest in Singapore become greater than those of the outside world. Then such an interest prohibition, coupled with expected exchange depreciation, would encourage residents to switch out of Singapore dollars into foreign currencies.

Fortunately, however, price inflation in Singapore has been less than that in the United States. The Singapore dollar has appreciated relative to the U.S. dollar in the last ten years. In 1951, 3.1 Singapore dollars exchanged for one American dollar, and this rate stayed constant until 1970. Then, without a very definite trend, this exchange rate changed to 2.1 by June of 1980. Hence, domestic residents have had little incentive to switch into foreign currencies because of the relatively tight money policy pursued by Singapore's monetary authority—a virtual necessity for the survival of the domestic currency in small offshore centers without exchange controls but with normal reserve requirements against deposits in domestic currency.

Although the Singapore dollar has appreciated against the "benchmark" U.S. dollar because of excessively high American price inflation, the MAS still intervenes in the short run on a week-to-week basis to smooth fluctuations between these two currencies and with the Japanese yen. Hence, the monetary base in Singapore dollars is largely endogenized by this desire to maintain an orderly foreign exchange market. That is, instead of setting firm *internal* rules for rates of monetary growth—such as 5 percent a year—the MAS allows the monetary base to adjust to reflect foreign exchange interventions. If the MAS buys American and sells Singapore dollars, the domestic monetary base expands commensurately; and such a "dependent" monetary policy is appropriate for a highly open entrepôt economy whose domestic prices are completely dominated by the flow of imports and exports.

Various fiscal and tax incentives have evolved through time to ensure that ACUs (and offshore banks) gain more from dealing with nonresidents in comparison with residents. On the ACU part of their income, banks are subject to a corporate profits tax of 10 percent derived from loans to nonbank nonresident customers, whether or not such profits are remitted abroad. The normal corporate profits tax is 40 percent on all other corporate businesses in Singapore, including domestic banking as well as loans by ACUs to nonbank domestic residents. This reduced 10 percent tax greatly strengthens the ability of ACUs to compete for international business from nonresidents, whose deposits are also exempt from Singapore estate taxes and stamp duties.

Although they are significant in encouraging foreign currency banks serving nonresidents to locate in Singapore, special low rates of profits taxation need not be crucial. Margins are very small on interbank borrowing and lending—say, less than one-quarter of 1 percent. As long as the profit base for tax purposes is defined after expenses are subtracted, however, a moderate tax rate need not be an impossible burden. Far more important is the levying of withholding taxes on interest paid on deposits in ACUs held by nonresidents: "Taxes on gross interest are a far more serious deterrent to offshore business. A withholding tax, even at a modest rate of 5%, would kill any offshore business more surely than a 50% tax on net profits." [4]

However modest, any withholding tax that is imposed on interest received by nonresidents will be very large in relation to the profit margins of the ACUs and to the deposit yields in Singapore in relation to those of competing offshore centers. Thus, the absence of withholding on interest income accruing to nonresidents is a key legal provision

[4] John F. Chown and Thomas Kellen, *Offshore Investment Centers*, 3d ed. (London: Banker Research Unit, 1979), p. 2.

for any successful "offshore" or "Euro" banking facility. Indeed, the Asian dollar market was started back in 1968 when Singapore removed its 40 percent withholding tax on nonresident interest income from the newly licensed ACUs.

Without exchange controls, of course, it becomes imperative for Singapore to maintain the 40 percent withholding tax on *domestic* nonbank residents who own foreign currency deposits in ACUs. Then any artificial incentives for residents to evade domestic taxes by switching to foreign currency deposits in conveniently close ACUs is eliminated. (They may still evade domestic taxes, however, by switching to foreign currency deposits in competing offshore centers that are less easily monitored by the Singapore authorities.) Nonbank foreigners, on the other hand, are discouraged from holding interest-bearing deposits in Singapore dollars because they would be liable for the 40 percent withholding levy. Thus is fiscal separation maintained: Foreigners are given strong incentives to transact only with ACUs in foreign moneys, whereas domestic residents are not given artificial incentives to move out of Singapore dollars—subject to the caveat that the economic burden of domestic reserve requirements remains modest (and that taxpayers find it somewhat inconvenient to hold foreign currency deposits illicitly abroad).

Even with this separation, however, the nature of entrepôt trade encourages nonbank Singapore enterprises to take substantial foreign currency positions in ACUs. In table 1, we note that their deposits in ACUs are equivalent to US$1.1 billion and that their loans from ACUs are US$0.8 billion at the end of 1979; whereas M_3 in Singapore dollars, broadly defined to include term deposits in Singapore banks, amounted to the equivalent of US$8 billion in 1979 (see table 2). By this standard, the foreign currency deposits owned by Singapore residents are significant and will continue to grow relatively rapidly in the future. Such ACU deposits, however, are best considered as *credit instruments:* very large term deposits owned by business firms with negotiated rates of interest.

The actual *means of payment* within Singapore itself—checking accounts plus coin and currency in Singapore dollars—at the end of 1979 amounted to the equivalent of US$2.6 billion in claims on domestic Singapore banks. In contrast, checking accounts in the ACUs are negligible. Hence, ACUs do not displace the Singapore dollar in providing the actual means of payment and standard of domestic value. In effect, having an unregulated offshore market undermines whatever control the Singapore authorities may have had over flows of credit based on term deposits in the domestic economy—whether in Singapore dollars or in foreign currencies. Yet, by maintaining the real purchasing power

TABLE 1
ASIAN DOLLAR MARKET DEPOSITS, LOANS, AND ADVANCES
TO NONBANK CUSTOMERS, 1968–1979
(millions of U.S. dollars)

End of Period	Loans and Advances			Deposits		
	Total	Residents of Singapore	Non-residents	Total	Residents of Singapore	Non-residents
1968	1.4	n.a.	n.a.	17.8	14.6	3.2
1969	0.9	n.a.	n.a.	97.9	45.3	52.6
1970	13.9	n.a.	13.9	243.7	87.0	156.7
1971	188.8	58.7	130.1	237.8	62.3	175.5
1972	600.9	157.6	443.3	398.7	118.0	280.7
1973	1,226.1	184.9	1,041.2	912.8	296.4	616.4
1974	2,697.7	349.9	2,347.8	1,614.2	488.7	1,125.5
1975	3,472.5	375.8	3,096.7	2,067.7	583.9	1,483.8
1976	4,386.6	508.1	3,878.5	1,960.3	364.8	1,595.5
1977	5,281.2	517.5	4,763.7	2,254.6	334.1	1,920.5
1978	6,376.8	793.7	5,583.1	3,600.0	777.8	2,822.2
1979	8,484.0	792.5	7,691.5	5,771.4	1,080.4	4,691.0

NOTES: Interbank lending at the end of 1979 was US$28 billion in the Asian dollar market; interbank deposits, US$29.4 billion; n.a. = not available.
SOURCE: Monetary Authority of Singapore.

of the Singapore dollar better than that of the U.S. dollar, the Monetary Authority of Singapore preserves the effective domain of domestic money as a means of payment among residents.

The absence of control over foreign credits granted to, or received from, Singapore residents is no cause for concern in a small entrepôt economy. Any burst of net credits to Singapore residents leading to higher spending will simply result in a widening of the current account deficit and a matching inflow of goods to relieve any domestic inflationary pressure. The domestic money supply then endogenously adjusts, through foreign exchange transactions by the Monetary Authority of Singapore, to the higher spending levels. The system is fully consistent for preserving financial stability if the exchange rate is stable. The same monetary control mechanism would not apply, however, to an economy where trade restrictions abounded so that external credits did not quickly result in a net inflow of goods or to one (like the United States) where foreign trade is a small proportion of gross national product (GNP). Moreover, chronic price inflation and exchange depreciation, as has sometimes occurred in Britain, would quickly cause domestic transactors to switch into foreign moneys.

TABLE 2

MONEY SUPPLY, 1968–1979

(millions of Singapore dollars)

End of Period	M_1	M_2	M_3
1968	1,172.3	2,734.1	n.a.
1969	1,341.7	3,252.9	n.a.
1970	1,574.3	3,782.6	4,072.1
1971	1,759.9	4,204.6	4,615.1
1972	2,384.8	5,281.7	5,795.8
1973	2,632.7	6,103.2	6,765.5
1974	2,585.8	6,924.8	7,753.8
1975	3,472.2	8,164.2	9,186.5
1976	4,000.0	9,202.5	10,837.3
1977	4,412.1	9,806.3	12,030.5
1978	4,925.9	10,862.3	13,830.2
1979	5,706.1	12,899.5	16,646.2

NOTE: n.a. = not available.
SOURCE: Monetary Authority of Singapore.

The Eurocurrency Market and Monetary Instability in Great Britain

The British financial system—inclusive of Eurocurrency transactions centered in London—is much bigger and more complex than that associated with Singapore. Hence, nothing but the broadest overview of British policy is attempted here. Suffice it to say that the British impose no withholding tax on interest earned by nonresidents on their foreign currency deposits in London, nor are there any official reserve requirements against these deposits. Because in the later 1950s the British were the first to evolve this system of free offshore transactions in foreign money, the Eurocurrency market centered in London is by far the world's largest.

On the other hand, there exist reserve requirements against sterling deposits: cash (claims against the Bank of England) or certain short-term securities such as treasury bills. Because the Bank of England does not control the stock of treasury bills in the system and had no separate set of pure cash requirements after 1971, the manipulation of short-term rates of interest has been the Bank's primary instrument of monetary control. Rather than a direct concern with stabilizing the sterling exchange rate, in recent years the Bank's target variable is limiting the rate of growth in M_3—a rather broadly defined sterling aggregate that includes currency at one extreme and interest-bearing term deposits of
350

large denomination (which compete directly with Eurocurrency deposits) at the other. The Bank has not been successful, however, in meeting its M_3 growth targets—typically overshooting rather than undershooting.

Hence, in the 1970s various ad hoc measures—called the "corset"— were introduced to influence incremental flows of bank lending in sterling. Though complex, these measures amounted to a changing set of official cash reserve requirements on new bank loans based on the acquisition of new "managed liabilities"—interest-bearing deposits. Increasingly ineffective, this restraint on intermediation by domestic banks was completely undermined by the abolition of exchange controls in October 1979. British borrowers could then go directly to London banks in the Euromarket to satisfy their needs for sterling or foreign money; British savers could buy foreign currency deposits that were not subject to the corset. Seeing its futility, the Bank of England abolished the corset in June 1980. Although this abolition of credit restrictions was much needed to restore the basic competitiveness of domestic British banks vis-à-vis their European offspring, the Bank of England is still without a coherent analytical framework for domestic monetary control.

Under these newly liberalized financial circumstances, how can the domain of sterling be preserved as a means of payment and stable standard of value in Britain? I shall consider, first, the necessity of free commodity trade and, second, the desirability of a monetary policy based on a stable exchange rate.

Because the British have, perhaps correctly, given up on any form of exchange or credit control, a necessary condition for financial stability is that they maintain a completely open stance toward foreign commodity trade. Somewhat quixotically, the intimate link between extreme financial liberalization on the one hand and the maintenance of free commodity trade on the other is not mentioned in the voluminous and highly charged current debate on how the Bank of England should conduct monetary policy. But with no restraint on Eurobank lending to Britons in any currency, and with a potentially high degree of currency substitution in the portfolios of Britons between sterling and foreign currency assets in London banks, the U.K. government is now hard pressed to apply any *direct* financial constraints for matching aggregate demand and supply in the domestic British economy.

Fortunately, a potentially powerful indirect mechanism exists: the current account of the balance of payments. If British firms or the British government receive new bank credits—whatever the currency of denomination—the pressure of excess demand on British resources will be relieved by imports rising relative to exports—a current account deficit. This in turn will reduce the net private financial wealth and

351

spending of Britons as their international net indebtedness increases.[5] A key ingredient in this adjustment process, however, is that trade remain free and that the economy remain highly open to the international flow of goods and services. Although the British economy is not as naturally open to foreign trade as Singapore's entrepôt economy, Britain's increasing integration with Europe makes it a good deal more open than the United States. Indeed, in 1979 Britain's ratio of imports to GNP was 29 percent, that of the United States only 9 percent. Hence, in the absence of protectionism, reliance on a changing balance of trade to offset inflationary or deflationary pressure in Britain would seem feasible.

Although a necessary condition for financial stability in Britain, liberal trading policies are not by themselves sufficient. How is the value of sterling in relation to that of foreign money that are also easily traded in Britain to be established? After becoming financially open, Britain must eliminate erratic changes in spot exchange rates and in relative interest differentials, which reflect anticipated future exchange rate changes. Otherwise, there will be an ebb and flow of "hot" money in and out of sterling—and the domain of sterling transactions may well contract on net balance.

Early in 1979, for example, when it became apparent that a "hard-money" Tory government was going to be elected and that sterling was becoming a "petrocurrency" due to the sharp run-up in the price of oil, the international demand for sterling assets increased sharply. Even quasi-legal holdings of foreign currency assets owned by Britons themselves were repatriated. In the face of this increased demand, sterling began to rise sharply in the foreign exchange markets: The demand for the Bank of England's monetary base rose. Rather than respond by increasing the supply of base money, however, the Bank of England found itself committed to a fixed Friedman growth rule.[6] The Bank resisted, somewhat unsuccessfully as it turned out,

[5] Ronald I. McKinnon, "Portfolio Balance and International Payments Adjustment," in Robert A. Mundell and Alexander K. Swoboda, eds., *Monetary Problems of the International Economy* (Chicago: University of Chicago Press, 1969), pp. 199-234.

[6] Unfortunately, the heated debate in Britain between the Bank of England (Cmnd. 7858) and its critics (Brian Griffiths, "The Monetary Base and U.K. Money Supply Control," *Banker,* December 1979, pp. 23-32, and Brian Griffiths and others, "Reforming Monetary Control in the United Kingdom," *Banker,* April and May 1980, pp. 75-90) has focused on ways of bringing the growth in M_3 under control. The Bank designed its reserve requirements so that interest rates are the only feasible instrumental variable, whereas the critics believe that banking regulations should be redesigned so that the monetary base can be used to control M_3. That the exchange rate itself should be the primary target of monetary policy seems outside the scope of the debate.

the terrific pressure coming through the sterling part of the British banking system to create more interest-bearing term deposits that dominate M_3. Hence, the sterling exchange rate rose sharply by about 20 percent against the dollar to reach $2.40 as of September 1980, the same level as 1967—despite much greater price inflation in Britain in the interim. This rise in the external value of sterling occurred at a time when Britain was suffering a wage explosion with great concern that its industry was becoming internationally uncompetitive. Yet, the government did not want to be seen abandoning its tight money policy by letting the monetary base increase faster than its proscribed "closed-economy" growth rule based on M_3

Clearly, with completely open financial policies, the Bank of England should smooth the foreign exchange rate as the focal point of its monetary policy. The ebb and flow of movements out of, or into, sterling should be accommodated in much the same way as the Monetary Authority of Singapore buys and sells foreign exchange to stabilize the value of the Singapore dollar. These purchases and sales of foreign exchange would then govern short-term movements in the British monetary base. As long as these foreign exchange interventions were not sterilized in their domestic monetary effect, they would be fully credible. The Bank of England would then no longer need to define money precisely, whether M_1 or M_3, because no single aggregate would be the target of domestic policy.

"Tight" money should be redefined as a sustained tie to a hard convertible currency like the deutsche mark, or perhaps as slow exchange appreciation against a weaker one like the U.S. dollar. In either case, the British monetary base—but not the exchange rate—would fluctuate according to the ebb and flow in the demand for sterling through the foreign exchanges. At the present time, a completely autonomous monetary growth rule based on purely domestic criteria fails to account for Britain's special position as the center of the Eurocurrency market without exchange controls to insulate the money market in sterling.

Having accepted the principle of foreign-exchange smoothing, the exact target for the Bank of England's foreign-exchange policy can then be discussed at a somewhat lesser level of importance.

Because the American dollar is the principal currency traded in the Euromarkets out of London, a case can be made for stabilizing the pound vis-à-vis the dollar in order to minimize currency substitution. Indeed, preventing sharp changes in the *forward* discount of the pound against the dollar and hence preventing continual changes in interest differentials would be at the heart of such a monetary stabilization program.[7] If need be, this informal dollar parity (defined within a wide band) could be adjusted if the dollar appreciates or depreciates sharply against other convertible currencies. Alternatively, if secular price inflation in the United States seems too high vis-à-vis Britain, the Bank of England could allow market pressure to induce slow secular appreciation of sterling against the dollar—a policy much like that followed by the Swiss authorities in their similar position as a financial entrepôt. Though they adhere formally to a target rate of growth in in their domestic money supply, from time to time the Swiss avoid rapid appreciation by allowing their domestic money supply to expand sharply in response to heavy foreign demand for Swiss francs. In 1978, for example, the narrowly defined Swiss money supply increased over 19 percent as the franc tended to appreciate in the foreign exchange market; Swiss domestic price inflation remained negligible because such a monetary increase is not inflationary if the international demand for one's money has increased commensurately.

A somewhat more imaginative technique to resolve the foreign exchange indicator problem would be for Her Majesty's Government to announce its intention to join the new European Monetary System (EMS) at some specified future time—say, two years hence. This would of course establish a future fixed exchange rate against the deutsche mark (DM). Britain, however, as of September 1980, starts off with nominal short-term rates of interest on sterling assets that are as much as eight or ten percentage points higher than those on DM assets. The market currently expects sterling to fall in relation to the deutsche mark, and Britain should enter the EMS only after its exchange rate and interest rates are properly aligned.

To accomplish this, suppose the Bank of England announces a once-and-for-all downward crawl in the sterling/DM exchange rate over, say, the next two years. The beginning rate of crawl would reflect the present differential in short-term rates of interest, which would diminish through time. The two-year calendar for the ever-decreasing rate of downward crawl would be unalterably fixed, however, and would come to an end the day Britain formally joined the EMS. By the date of entry, the interest differential should have been squeezed to the vanishing point and the sterling/DM exchange rate would be set at a more competitive level for Britain. Because the crawl is tailored to the interest differential, no significant capital inflows or outflows would be

[7] In Ronald I. McKinnon, "Currency Substitution and Instability in the World Dollar Standard," *American Economic Review,* forthcoming, I show how changes in expected future movements in exchange rates lead to strong currency substitution.

induced—but the sterling monetary base would be endogenously determined by these foreign exchange transactions.[8]

In summary, there are two necessary conditions for monetary stability in the open financial circumstances in which Britain (and Singapore) finds itself. First, with the complete freedom to move capital in or out of Britain, free commodity trade must be maintained to allow the current account of the balance of payments to adjust the aggregate demand and supply of commodities—whatever currency is used as numeraire. Second, in the presence of virtually unlimited possibilities for currency substitution, the relative value of sterling in terms of some hard currency should be maintained directly by the Bank of England—with the monetary base adjusting passively to these foreign exchange transactions. "Tight" money should be redefined in terms of the exchange rate rather than in terms of a constant rate of growth in some purely domestic monetary aggregate.

The Case against Eurocurrency Markets in the United States

What is appropriate for Singapore and Britain as centers for the Asian and Eurocurrency markets, however, most certainly does not generalize to the United States, that country whose money is most commonly traded in these same Euromarkets. More than other countries issuing convertible currencies, the United States must exercise a high degree of domestic independence in determining the real purchasing power of the American dollar, and the presence of separate Eurofacilities within the United States itself may well undermine this independence. Why should the American situation be so different?

First, if many other countries—but particularly small ones—run dependent monetary policies, at least one major country must independently determine the purchasing power of its own money if the world's price level is to be determinate. From a global point of view, the system needs an anchor. True, the United States may find it difficult to manage the world dollar standard without the explicit cooperation of one or two major trading partners,[9] but at least this subset

[8] For a more complete discussion of the mechanics of the crawling peg, see Ronald I. McKinnon, "Monetary Control and the Crawling Peg," in John Williamson, ed., *Exchange Rate Rules: The Theory, Performance and Prospects of the Crawling Peg* (New York: Macmillan, 1981), pp. 38-49.

[9] Ronald I. McKinnon, "A New Tripartite Monetary Agreement or a Limping Dollar Standard?" Essays in International Finance, no. 106 (Princeton, N.J.: Princeton University, 1974); and McKinnon, "Currency Substitution and Instability in the World Dollar Stand," *American Economic Review* (forthcoming).

of countries must run an independent policy to which others—particularly financial entrepôts—can adjust.

Second, the United States is not small and open enough to rely mainly on international arbitrage in goods and services to peg the internal American price level. Rather, the balancing of aggregate demand and supply in U.S. commodity markets must be internally managed by appropriate countercyclical fiscal policy on the one hand, and by careful matching of the supply of and the demand for dollars held by American residents on the other. How best to maintain monetary control within the center country itself is my main concern in the remainder of this paper.

More or less by historical accident, "Euro" or offshore trading of foreign currencies has not so far been of any significance in the United States. To be sure, foreign banks licensed to operate in the United States maintain the occasional non-interest-bearing checking account in foreign currencies for their foreign customers, but there is no significant borrowing and lending in foreign currencies at flexible equilibrium rates of interest among American banks that is the heart of a Eurocurrency market. Quite simply, American monetary and fiscal authorities decided against chartering special corporate entities, such as Singapore's Asian currency units, that are given tax concessions and special exemptions from federal and state reserve requirements, usury laws, loan limitations, and other detailed regulations governing domestic banks. Although certain Edge Act subsidiaries of American banks are exempt from prevailing restraints on multistate banking in order to serve the international interests of their corporate clients, the Federal Reserve Bank has typically frowned on the uninhibited solicitation of foreign currency deposits by American banks.

Besides these restraints on the supply of Euroservices within the United States, the effective demand for them is limited. The U.S. dollar itself is the principal currency traded in the Asian and Eurocurrency markets, accounting for between 70 and 80 percent of all such transactions. This reflects the dollar's unique role as an international currency of invoice and a vehicle currency in spot and forward foreign-exchange transactions, as well as its dominance in official reserves. Hence, the incipient demand for regulation-free transactions in currencies other than the dollar within the United States is not nearly so intense as the demand for free dollar transactions in the Asian and Eurocurrency markets outside the United States. Therefore, the social need for Eurotransactions in the United States is less—although regulated American banks often chafe against their competitive disadvantages in comparison with their unregulated overseas brethren.

This competitive disadvantage is made unnecessarily acute because the Federal Reserve Bank does not make a sharp enough distinction between money and credit in its purely domestic banking regulations. Term deposits, for example, must be of a large minimum size to escape usury laws (regulation Q) and even then are subject to fluctuating—albeit modest—reserve requirements. Hence, Americans and foreigners are induced to hold dollar term deposits in the Cayman Islands and the Bahamas, undercutting business that might otherwise flow to New York. Similarly, dollar holdings in other major offshore centers such as Singapore and London are unnaturally augmented, but here the problem is less acute because much of the business is interbank and would be less inhibited by the U.S. regulations. The first-best solution is for the Federal Reserve to eliminate all interest rate restrictions and reserve requirements on credit-market instruments, that is, on term deposits of more than a few days maturity, available to American residents and nonresidents alike.

Rather than correct the basic regulatory distortion, however, the Federal Reserve proposes (November 1980) a strictly second-best solution:

> Under the Fed's plan, banks would be permitted to take deposits from and make loans to nonresidents, including overseas subsidiaries of U.S. companies, through specially designated offices in the U.S., to be known as international banking facilities (IBFs). The Fed would waive reserve requirements and interest rate ceilings, while state legislatures would give banks a tax break on this kind of business. To date, only New York State has passed such legislation. When fully operational, IBFs could attract nearly $70 billion in deposits, the amount now held at Caribbean branches of U.S. banks.[10]

Instead of outlining all the kinks in the IBF legislation, let us consider one unusual feature: the legislation proposes unregulated international banking facilities (primarily) in the domestic currency of the host country! An unregulated market in U.S. dollar deposits among "nonresidents" will compete with a regulated market in U.S. dollars among residents. So-called nonresidents, however, will include the foreign subsidiaries of U.S. corporations! More than an orthodox Eurofacility that is confined to foreign currencies, as described for Britain and Singapore, the dollar-based IBF system will be an open invitation to undercut the domain of the regulated part of the American banking system as firms and individuals use various subterfuges to

[10] *Business Week,* December 8, 1980, p. 34.

establish nonresident intermediaries. Worse yet, insofar as there is growth of unregulated demand deposits or checking accounts in the IBFs, unlike the Eurocurrency markets outside the United States, IBFs could be a more direct threat to the Federal Reserve's control over the actual means of payment within the U.S. economy.

Nor is a more orthodox Eurofacility in foreign currencies within the United States a good idea. The Federal Reserve Bank would undermine its own efforts to secure *independent* control over the real purchasing power of the American dollar. There are no exchange controls on American nonbank residents. Hence, American nonbank firms and households, as borrowers or depositors, could easily move between a highly regulated dollar-based banking system and an unregulated banking system based on foreign money to which they had convenient access in the United States itself. The degree of potential currency substitution would be high but of unknown magnitude in practice. The domain of dollar transactions in the United States would erode because of the detailed reserve requirements, usury laws, and other restrictions on American banks. This could easily destabilize the demand for U.S. dollars by American residents and destabilize the derived demand for the Federal Reserve's base money. Furthermore, the introduction of the proposed IBF could be significantly more destabilizing in this last respect.

Securing the real purchasing power of the U.S. dollar depends, however, on the ability of the Federal Reserve Bank to directly control the supply of base money—say, by discretionary open market operations—to match the correctly projected demand for dollars by American residents at a stable price level. The obverse is that the aggregate supply and demand for goods by nonbanks within the United States itself is balanced, which in turn dominates the American rate of price inflation because of the more or less "closed" nature of the American economy, despite the international importance of the dollar. Thus does the dollar price level become an independent datum in the international financial system.[11]

Whether by accident or by design, the American monetary authorities had been correct in forestalling the development of a Eurocurrency market in the United States. Such a market would complicate their task of monetary management without offsetting social benefits—par-

---

[11] Again, I should note that, although the world system requires the United States to be an independent balance wheel, monetary cooperation with one or two American trading partners might enhance the ability of the Federal Reserve to achieve this end. McKinnon, "A New Tripartite Monetary Agreement"; and McKinnon, "Currency Substitution."

ticularly as most of these benefits already obtain from the London and Singapore markets. Yet, even "distant" Euromarkets in dollars pose potential problems for the Federal Reserve; and to the resolution of those problems I now turn.

The Case against the Use of "Credit" Controls
by American Monetary Authorities

An undeniable aspect of having free European and Asian dollar markets is that they may substitute to some extent for purely domestic financial intermediation in the United States. To what extent has the Eurodollar market provided a means of payment for domestic transactions within the United States, and to what extent has it been a source of liquidity to nonbanks that might compete with money or quasi money in the United States—or indeed in other industrial countries? As I discussed more carefully in an earlier paper, Eurodollar deposits have almost never been used for drawing checks.[12] On the contrary, the transfer of funds within the Eurodollar system uses checks drawn on American banks as its means of payment. Drafts drawn on Eurobanks do not circulate in the United States, and thus fears that Eurodollars provide a competing form of money narrowly defined like a demand deposit or a NOW account are ill founded. Of course, this situation might change if, say, the taxation of demand deposits in the United States, against which non-interest-bearing reserves must be held, were to sharply escalate because of dollar price inflation. Hence, the situation should be carefully monitored by the Federal Reserve: Data should be collected on whether American nonbank firms and individuals own "Euro" checking accounts in, say, London or Singapore. Before 1979, however, there was no evidence that they do on any significant scale.

Because Eurodeposits are very large—typically more than $1 million—and bear interest throughout a given term to maturity, they are more akin to time deposits in U.S. banks, such as certificates of deposit. In this non-monetary or quasi-monetary aspect of banking, there obviously has been some shift in purely domestic American business from New York to the Asian and European dollar markets. It remains quite convenient, however, for American borrowers and depositors to deal primarily with domestic banks. Table 3 makes clear that Eurocurrency holdings by nonbanks were, by the end of 1978, just a tiny fraction of national monetary aggregates of the major industrial countries. To quote Helmut Mayer on table 3: "Identified deposits by private non-

[12] McKinnon, "Eurocurrency Market."

TABLE 3

World Monetary Aggregates and Nonbank Deposits in the Eurocurrency Markets

(billions of U.S. dollars, end of 1978)

	Money (1)	Money plus Quasi Money (2)	Foreign Currency Deposits with Domestic Banks (3)	Other Euro- deposits (4)	(3) + (4) (5)	(4) as Percentage of (2) (6)	(5) as Percentage of (2) (7)
Belgium–Luxembourg	29.2	53.8	3.0	2.1	5.1	3.9	0.5
Canada	25.2	93.8	8.7	0.8	9.5	0.9	10.1
France	134.6	261.0	1.3	1.6	2.9	0.6	1.1
Germany	123.8	470.3	1.6	2.8	4.4	0.6	0.9
Italy	138.1	243.4	0.8	1.3	2.1	0.5	0.9
Japan[a]	354.2	918.4	3.0e	0.2	3.2e	0.0	0.3
Netherlands	30.6	84.7	2.0	1.2	3.2	1.4	3.8
Sweden	9.7	34.7	0.4	0.3	0.7	0.9	2.0
Switzerland	46.7	122.0	3.1	6.9	10.0	5.7	8.2
United Kingdom	56.0	114.6	9.3	1.8	11.1	1.6	9.7
United States	364.6	963.3	0.0	26.5[b]	26.5	2.8	2.8
Subtotal for eleven countries listed	1,312.7	3,360.0	33.2	45.5	78.7	1.4	2.3
World total[a]	1,700e	4,200e	—	—	115	—	2.7

Note: Eurocurrency deposits with banks in the Group of Ten countries (other than the United States) and with banks in Austria, Denmark, Ireland, and Switzerland.

[a] e = estimates.

[b] Including deposits by U.S. nonbanks with the branches of U.S. banks in the Caribbean.

Source: IMF, International Financial Statistics, in Helmut Mayer, "Credit and Liquidity Creation in the International Banking Sector," Economic Papers, no. 1 (Basel: Bank for International Settlements, November 1979), p. 23.

bank residents of the Group of Ten totalled $79 billion, or, on average, 2.3 percent of money plus quasi money." [13]

[13] Helmut W. Mayer, "Credit and Liquidity Creation in the International Banking Sector," Economic Papers, no. 1 (Basel: Bank for International Settlements, November 1979), p. 22.

Only in extreme situations where the regulation of time deposits in the United States becomes unduly onerous or distinctly irrational is there danger of a large-scale shift in time deposits from New York to London. One such example occurred in 1969 when regulation Q was still being applied to U.S. certificates of deposit and there was a sharp rise in money-market rates of interest above their "Q" ceilings. This induced a large outflow of nonbank deposits from New York to London, which were then lent back to American firms. Fortunately, this flow unwound the next year, when the interest ceiling on certificates of deposit was discontinued. For a brief period in 1980, a similar problem existed because of the temporary 8 percent marginal reserve requirement on interest-bearing managed liabilities of U.S. banks, including certificates of deposit. Before 1979, however, this kind of switching had not been a serious problem in "normal" circumstances.

What these experiences indicate is that American authorities should sharply distinguish between money and instruments of credit.[14] Money can be used as a means of payment to third parties and needs to be carefully controlled, whereas term deposits with flexible market-clearing rates of interest are less liquid credit instruments and should remain unregulated to remain competitive-at-a-distance with the European and Asian dollar markets. It is sufficient for the American authorities to control narrowly defined M_1 in dollars carefully—which is possible (in ways to be discussed later)—while letting domestic and international flows of credit be completely free. Then the IBF would be redundant.

An alternative way of reducing this tension in the financial markets would be to impose reserve requirements on all classes of Eurodeposits, including time deposits and certificates of deposit, held by nonbanks— as was recently unofficially suggested by Governor Henry Wallich.[15] The weakness in this American proposal for Eurocurrency control revolves around the conceptual failure of the American authorities (and British as well as others) to make a distinction between the monetary and nonmonetary liabilities of the banking system. Credit expansion based on the creation of nonmonetary liabilities is neither expansionary nor contractionary for the economy as a whole. As long as there is an act of saving by the holder of the term deposit that releases funds for spending by other units, the endogenous expansion or contraction of such credits does not undermine the monetary and price level control of the central bank. Of course, forced-draft expansion of bank credits by the central bank's injecting base money into the system, which ex-

---

[14] H. Robert Heller, "Money and Credit in the Euromarkets: A Demand Approach," Group of Thirty, Background Paper (August 1979).

[15] Wallich, "Statement on Eurocurrency Market."

pands M_1 and credits based on it, then causes a complementary portfolio increase in time deposits and bank credits based on them, is indeed inflationary. If, however, under a floating exchange rate the central bank carefully controls M_1 for which the demand is stable, an ebb and flow of domestic credit based on endogenous changes in nonmonetary bank liabilities is perfectly consistent with domestic money stability. Hence, a reserve requirement tax on such credit intermediation is quite inappropriate.

To be even more critical, a reserve requirement on pure credit transactions would tend to undermine the monetary control of each participating central bank. Precisely because the ebb and flow of credit—particularly international credit of the kind that OPEC extends indirectly to third countries—is highly variable, it is not desirable that the demand for each country's base money reflect this instability—hence the case for abolishing such requirements on "domestic" credit transactions without extending them to Euromarkets and without establishing special regulation-free domestic IBFs.

On Securing Control over the Money Supply in the United States

With the passage in May 1980 by the U.S. Congress of a new monetary control act (H.R. 7), the Federal Reserve Bank would finally seem to have the legal authority it needs to control all American institutions that might issue "money"—deposits that can be used to make payments to third parties. Having made a careful distinction between credit instruments and money, the Federal Reserve should then control "money" very inclusively, whether owned by foreigners or by domestic nationals.

The money stock is coin and currency, plus any bank account—interest-bearing or non-interest-bearing—owned by households or nonbank firms on which checks can be drawn and payments made to third parties. This would include penalty-free overdraft facilities and any provision for automatically switching funds from passbook savings accounts into checking accounts. It would also include loans using term deposits as collateral as well as certain kinds of repurchase agreements on government securities that allow owners of demand deposits to write checks in excess of the nominal amount of funds on hand in the account. Very short-dated term deposits—of, say, less than three days' maturity—owned by nonbanks might also be included in this monetary category. All items thus classified as money, whether in banks, credit unions, or mutual funds, would then bear a modest uniform reserve requirement—say, 6 to 8 percent. (To some extent, the newly broadened definition of M_1 introduced by the Federal Reserve is a step toward this more inclusive definition of money.) This, then, should serve to stabilize the demand for the Federal Reserve Bank's own base money.

A 6 to 8 percent reserve requirement on checking accounts is unlikely to put an undue burden on American banks in comparison with their unregulated "Euro" offspring overseas. Unlike what might happen in the IBF proposed for New York, we have seen that very little pressure now exists for competing checking accounts to develop in Euromarkets. Communications technology could change, however, or American price inflation could escalate to increase the burden of non-interest-bearing reserves on domestic American banks and induce Americans to write dollar checks on accounts overseas as a means of payment within the United States.

To guard against this uncomfortable possibility and to increase the efficiency of the American financial system, the Federal Reserve Bank could pay interest (at "market" rates) on all *required* reserves held with it. In addition, American commercial banks could be encouraged to pay competitive rates of interest to their checking account customers. Then, as market rates of interest escalated with price inflation, American depositors would have minimal incentive to shift their checking accounts to unregulated markets abroad, such as those existing in Singapore and London.[16] The independent power of the Federal Reserve to stabilize the purchasing power of the American dollar would be enhanced as the ebb and flow of international currency substitution were reduced.

[16] I am indebted to Helmut Mayer for stressing this positive approach to the problem of keeping American M_1 under the control of the Federal Reserve. In an earlier draft of this paper, I had considered a distant second-best solution: to impose similar non-interest-bearing reserve requirements on foreign currency checking accounts held in major financial centers abroad. This would require complex international agreements, however, unlike the best solution of simply paying interest on required reserves.

Commentary

Allan H. Meltzer

Two interesting papers in part 4 treat different aspects of the Eurodollar market.[1] Ronald McKinnon describes some of the services performed by the market and distinguishes between money and credit. The distinction is elementary but important because it is often neglected. Neglect has given rise to incorrect inferences about the effect of the Eurodollar market on inflation, as McKinnon notes. Dale Henderson and Douglas Waldo analyze the effect of putting reserve requirements on Eurodollars. They show that, in a model with a single rate of interest and fixed exchange rates, reserve requirements on Eurodollars reduce the variance of the money stock—demand deposits and currency—around its target value. With fluctuating exchange rates, the result is ambiguous. One point should be emphasized but is not: The effect of reserve requirements on Eurodollars depends on monetary and other institutional arrangements and on assumptions about the new substitutes that will develop in response to the change. McKinnon points out that taxation of interest payments, liberalization of trade, and other arrangements cannot be neglected.

Intermediation. Intermediation produces differences between money, defined as currency and demand deposits, and bank credit, defined as the earnings assets of all banks. To show how Eurodollars affect bank credit and money, I start from the consolidated balance sheet.[2] Let R be bank reserves, E be bank earning assets (credit), and D and T be demand and time deposits, respectively. Then,

$$E = D + T - R \tag{1}$$

[1] I have written a postscript to discuss the paper that Ronald McKinnon preferred to substitute for the paper given at the conference. I have modified my comments to reflect the change, but extensive revision was not required. In the postscript, I comment on the additional material offered by McKinnon.

[2] This section is based on the traditional Brunner and Meltzer analysis of intermediation that is available in several papers.

is the consolidated balance sheet for the banks, including as banks all issuers of deposits subject to check. If we add and subtract currency, C, we have

$$E = (C + D) + T - (R + C) \tag{2}$$

The sum $C + D$ is money; the sum $R + C$ is the monetary base. The growth of any type of time deposits—intermediation—increases credit (E) in relation to money at a given value of the base. T includes all time deposits, Euromarket and domestic, on the banks' balance sheets.

A shift from demand deposits to time deposits reduces money but leaves credit unchanged, if there are no further effects of the shift. Lower reserve requirements for time deposits than for demand deposits imply that the shift increases time deposits in relation to demand deposits; credit rises in relation to money. The reason for the change is the difference in reserve requirements. With no reserve requirements on Eurodollar deposits and with reserve requirements on domestic deposits, the shift from one to the other releases excess reserves and permits money to expand or forces contraction. A central bank can, if it chooses to do so, control the base and prevent the entire change in money or credit, but it cannot do both.

The example shows that conclusions about the effects of intermediation depend on regulations and on policies. If the analysis is extended to show explicitly the many types of time deposit—passbook accounts, certificates of deposit, and Eurodollars—equation 2 becomes larger, but the same principle applies. Regulation of interest rates, differences in reserve requirements, and other regulated costs are a principal reason that changes in the public's desired mix of financial assets change money and credit by different amounts.[3]

With fluctuating exchange rates, countries can control the base if they choose to do so. There need be no effect of intermediation on the base. With fixed exchange rates, shifts between Eurodollars and domestic certificates of deposit can change the distribution of international reserves and the monetary base.

I see no problem of defining credit and the domestic money stock in the presence or absence of Eurodollars. Banks may choose not to consolidate all of the liabilities and assets of overseas branches on their balance sheet. If this is a general practice, the total assets and liabilities of banks are understated, but money, defined as currency and demand

[3] The real service yield on money is larger than the service yield on time deposits; that is to say, money is a medium of exchange. Changes in the rate of inflation may affect the desired composition of financial assets in an unregulated (but insured) banking system.

deposits of domestic residents, is affected only if offshore banks or Eurobanks issue deposits, subject to check, denominated in domestic currency units. McKinnon and others assure us that this is not commonly done.

In the absence of regulation and controls of interest payments on deposits and required reserves, banks would offer rates related to the real services rendered by particular deposits and the cost of providing those services. Term-to-maturity, or expected holding periods, would surely be one of the features that affect nominal yields on deposits. In the absence of restrictions on interest payments and other regulations, banks have an incentive to alter rates paid in response to market rates; changes in interest rates would become more frequent and portfolio changes less frequent. Those who want deposits available on demand— a real service—would sacrifice interest payments. Currency and demand deposits of domestic residents would be clear enough to identify and to control if *proper methods of control were used*.

Regulation and Control of Money. The Eurodollar market appears to grow fastest when it is most advantageous to avoid the prohibitions and restrictions imposed by central banks and governments, particularly the U.S. government. The growth of the market is, in part, a result of innovation that reduced the excess burden of regulation. Nevertheless, some of the burden remains. It is less costly to change relative rates of interest than to shift balances between institutions, and it is wasteful to use resources to develop institutions and practices that circumvent regulations and restrictions.

The discussion of intermediation alerts us to the fact that any study of the effects of regulation of Eurodollars or of the effect of reserve requirements on Eurodollars depends on the set of regulations and restrictions that accompanies the reserve requirements on Euro-dollars. Henderson and Waldo, for example, show that the effect of reserve requirements on Eurodollars is different when exchange rates fluctuate and interest is not paid on required reserves than when required reserves bear interest. The third and fourth sections of the Henderson and Waldo paper rely on the assumption that domestic time deposits (and long-term Eurodollar deposits) are not subject to reserve requirements. It is not surprising that Henderson and Waldo find that shifts between bank liabilities subject to reserve requirements induce less variance in interest rates than shifts between deposits subject to reserve requirements and other deposits. Under flexible rates, variability of exchange rates substitutes for some of the variability of interest rates.

If asset shifts are induced by reserve requirements, imposing additional reserve requirements will not, generally, reduce the deadweight loss. The reason is that the cost of differences in reserve requirements and prohibition of interest payments changes with the rate of inflation and the development of unregulated assets. Henderson and Waldo do not consider this problem.

I believe the effect of new substitutes is important. The extension of reserve requirements to Eurodollars will increase the risk borne, or the cost paid, by asset owners who circumvent the regulation by shifting to covered foreign currencies instead of lower-yielding Eurodollars.[4] To avoid the shift, all financial assets must be subject to equivalent reserve requirements. This is not only unlikely; it is impossible in a world of maximizers.

Recent experience supports this view. When regulation Q was extended to savings and loan associations and mutual savings banks, the extension was justified as a means of preventing competition for deposits. A main result was the development and expansion of less-regulated substitutes, including Eurodollars, money market funds, and overnight repurchase agreements. The profitability of the thrift institutions has not been protected. The cost of regulation is a tax on the owners or on the remaining depositors.

A more general consideration comes from the theory of taxation. Reserve requirements are a tax on the owners of capital in financial institutions. Such taxes distort the allocation of resources. Imposing comparable taxes on competing institutions does not, under most circumstances, remove the distortion. The distortion is likely to increase, together with the amount of resources used to circumvent the tax.

The best way to reduce the relative size of the Eurodollar market is to remove interest rate controls on deposits, pay competitive market interest rates on the required reserves of domestic banks, or eliminate reserve requirements. Henderson and Waldo, at some points in their analysis, recognize the benefits that these changes would bring, but they do not draw the proper conclusion. One reason is that they do not consider allocative efficiency or the burden imposed by regulations and controls.

Elimination of domestic reserve requirements and other reforms that reduce deadweight losses would not eliminate the Eurodollar mar-

---

[4] Controls or reserve requirements on Eurodollars by a single country, or small group, illustrate the point. The reserve requirements reduce the yield of the deposits subject to reserve requirements much more than they reduce the stock of Eurocurrency.

ket. As McKinnon notes, the Eurodollar market is more than just a means of escaping regulation. The market provides real services efficiently and is therefore likely to remain and grow if unregulated or to be replaced by an alternative if taxed or regulated out of existence by concerted action of all central banks and governments.

Postscript. Many of the issues in the present version of Ronald McKinnon's paper overlap the issues in the paper he delivered at the conference. In this section I comment on some of the additional issues raised in the version herein, particularly the conclusions he draws for monetary policy in Britain and the United States. Although I do not agree with several of McKinnon's conclusions, I fully agree with the emphasis he gives to liberal trade arrangements. McKinnon pays too little attention to efficiency and growth and emphasizes the average, rather than the marginal, share of trade in an economy, but he makes the right recommendation when he urges countries to permit substitution of foreign for domestic goods to facilitate adjustment to financial and monetary change.

The core of McKinnon's argument is that liberal trade policies are not sufficient for financial stability. Financial stability is not defined precisely, but the context suggests that fluctuations in exchange rates are less desirable than fluctuations in monetary aggregates. I cannot find where McKinnon is very definite about his reasons for preferring one to the other, but there is no doubt about his conclusion. He praises the Singapore Monetary Authority for choosing fixed, but adjustable, exchange rates, and he urges the Bank of England to do the same: "In the presence of virtually unlimited possibilities for currency substitution, the relative value of sterling in terms of some hard currency should be maintained directly by the Bank of England—with the monetary base adjusting passively to these foreign exchange transactions." McKinnon does not add a fiscal policy to his monetary policy, and he does not point out that the Bank of England cannot continue to act as lender of *first* resort to the government and the banking system. These omissions remove his analysis a long way from practice because, in practice, the Bank of England fixes a short-term interest rate and buys all the government debt offered by the market at that rate of interest. As a consequence, neither the base nor the exchange rate is controlled.[5]

I am not sure what McKinnon means by the statement: "Unlimited possibilities for currency substitution" arise because Britain is a

[5] At the time of writing (December 1980), Mrs. Thatcher's government has asked the Bank to reconsider its policy procedures.

"Eurocurrency" center.[6] Nor do I accept that the location of a Eurocurrency center in Britain makes monetary control or floating more costly to Britons. A fixed exchange rate increases the possibilities for substitution between domestic and foreign assets by offering convertibility at a fixed rate. With fixed rates, the central bank must permit "unlimited substitution" at a fixed price; domestic prices and base money are subject to more, and exchange rates to less, day-to-day variability. With floating rates, the base is controlled, the price level is less variable, and the banks issue or contract intermediary (time) deposits when there is a net capital flow to or from London. As equation 2 shows, bank earning assets rise relative to money when time deposits expand and contract relative to money when time deposits fall. Strict control of the base does not keep money or credit constant; both depend on the behavior of banks (intermediaries) and the public. Fluctuating exchange rates shift exchange-rate risk to the private sector but do not eliminate substitution between foreign and domestic assets or short-term capital movements. It is true that when exchange rates are permitted to change currency substitution can never be as close to perfect as under fixed exchange rates if there is, at least, some cost to hedging exchange rate risk.

In a small, less developed, open economy such as that of Singapore, individuals may be indifferent about whether they allow the home price level to fluctuate because the growth of base money fluctuates or, alternatively, permit relative prices to fluctuate because the exchange rate fluctuates. Britain is richer than Singapore and has a larger share of nontraded services in gross national product, so it may be more desirable for Britain to reduce fluctuations in money wages and in the prices of final goods and accept the social cost caused by fluctuations in exchange rates. Hedgers and specialists are available to reduce the costs and, if the hedgers and speculators are efficient, the costs are minimized.

Switzerland is a small open economy that sells financial services to the world. Stability of purchasing power in relation to that of the dollar enhances the value of the financial services Switzerland sells; the value of the services would decline if the Swiss chose to stabilize the dollar exchange rate. Switzerland also sells durable manufactured goods to Germany and other countries of the Common Market, however. Exchange-rate stability reduces the variability of the relative prices and costs of Swiss and non-Swiss producers. Hence, Switzerland chooses to let the dollar exchange rate fluctuate and to stabilize the mark/franc exchange rate, for months or years at a time.

The example of Switzerland brings us to a conclusion quite different

[6] I use the term "Eurocurrency" to refer to time deposits denominated in foreign units of account.

from the conclusion reached by McKinnon. The sale of financial services and the amount of intermediation by Swiss banks are increased by *floating* the Swiss franc in relation to the dollar. A stable British price level would, I believe, also increase the attractiveness of London as a center for Eurocurrency and other financial services.

In his discussion of the United States, McKinnon comes very close to the argument that I just made for Britain and Switzerland. He is, of course, correct if he claims that, with a stable dollar price level, the United States would have a comparative advantage in the financial-services industry. The dollar is a principal medium of international exchange and unit of account. A dollar with stable purchasing power for goods would lower the cost of using the medium of exchange as a store of value.

McKinnon's final sections discuss the control of money in the United States. He favors a policy of controlling the monetary base to achieve a stable price level, and he notes, correctly, that large capital flows to and from the United States often resulted from the combination of high inflation and controls that prohibit payment of interest on demand deposits and on required reserves, limit the payment of interest on time deposits, and raise the cost of intermediation in the United States relative to the cost abroad. In the absence of controls, interest rates and exchange rates would adjust and capital flows would be smaller.

McKinnon argues, however, that a "Eurocurrency" market in the United States would reduce Federal Reserve control of (narrowly defined) money. His argument is that substitution between domestic money and Eurocurrency would reduce stability of the demand function for money on which the Federal Reserve must rely to control money. He recognizes that "Eurocurrency deposits" are usually a million dollars or more each and are time deposits, not demand deposits or currency. He recognizes, also, that intermediation changes bank credit in relation to money and does not affect the demand for narrowly defined money if the exchange rate is allowed to adjust and banks are permitted to pay interest on demand deposits. The problem he fears is that in the future inflation "could escalate to increase the burden of non-interest-bearing reserves . . . and induce Americans to write dollar checks on accounts overseas as a means of payment within the United States."

Inflation will escalate only if the Federal Reserve fails to control money. If the Federal Reserve combines this failure with a prohibition of interest on required reserves, people will seek opportunities to avoid holding or using dollars. The availability of a substitute means of payment would, under the circumstances McKinnon posits, increase welfare.

370

The source of the problem is inflation and regulation, and the proper solution is to reduce both. Rate changes are a low-cost substitute for portfolio reallocation and innovation to avoid controls. I believe that the moral McKinnon should draw differs from the one he does draw. Remove the restrictions in the United States and reduce inflation, so that the public willingly holds and uses the familiar forms of money as a medium of exchange.

H. Robert Heller

John Williamson addresses the important question whether the increase in official reserves during the last decade caused the sharp increase in world inflation during the same period. He argues that there is neither theoretical nor empirical evidence for linking global reserves to inflation and concludes that he "can no longer believe . . . that the lack of control of reserves is of any consequence."

He then cites my previous findings on the relation between international reserves and worldwide inflation as supporting his view that there is no association between reserve growth and world monetary expansion and consequent global inflation.[1] In that paper I argued, and believe it still to be true and supported by the available evidence, that "international reserve increases played a significant role in the recent world-wide inflation, [but] it should be recognized that other factors played important roles as well."[2]

More detailed subsequent work showed that a 10 percent increase in reserves results in a 3–4 percent increase in the world monetary base.[3] Within a period of four years, the same 10 percent increase in reserves causes an increase in global inflation of 3–4 percent as well. This clearly does not mean that increases in reserves are the exclusive cause of world inflation, but it implies that they are an important cause. Controlling the growth of reserves to a greater extent than heretofore would therefore not eliminate world inflation but would make a contribution toward reducing it.

These conclusions are confirmed by the existence of a relatively

---

[1] H. Robert Heller, "International Reserves and World-Wide Inflation," *IMF Staff Papers*, March 1976; published earlier as International Monetary Fund Document DM/75/63, July 1975.

[2] Ibid., p. 85.

[3] H. Robert Heller, "Further Evidence on the Relationship between International Reserves and World Inflation," in Michael J. Boskin, ed., *Economics and Human Welfare: Essays in Honor of Tibor Scitovsky* (New York: Academic Press, 1979).

stable and well-behaved demand-for-reserves function on behalf of monetary authorities for a wide variety of country groups.[4]

In his paper John Williamson goes on to argue that "the external constraint on economic policy no longer stems from the level of reserves but stems from the net borrowing that the country can undertake without undermining its creditworthiness." Of course, it should be observed that a country's ability to borrow and its level of reserves are not two unrelated factors. One need not even think of cases in which countries have directly pledged part of their international reserves as collateral for official international loans (compare, for example, Italy and Portugal), but most assuredly every commercial banker will take a careful look at the country's international reserves before making a sovereign loan commitment. Again, there is no one-for-one correspondence between the level of reserves and the amount of credit that a country might be able to obtain, but there certainly is a relation between the two variables.

This brings me to the last point I wish to make with respect to the Williamson paper. His assertion that "there is no reason to suppose that reserve policy, such as allocation or cancellation of SDRs, would exert any significant influence on countries' macroeconomic policies" is certainly not well founded.

If his view were correct, then why should there be any opposition to closing down the SDR department? For that matter, why would countries object to a hundredfold increase in its size. I cannot believe that either suggestion would find any significant support among nations —for the simple reason that the level of reserves does matter for both an individual country and the world community.

In regard to the papers by Dale Henderson and Douglas Waldo and by Ronald McKinnon on Eurodollars and the desirability of controlling the growth of these and similar currency markets, I believe that an important distinction must be drawn between money and credit in the off-shore markets. I expressed this view first in June 1979 in my testimony on the Eurocurrency Market Control Act of 1979,[5] and I am happy to see that Professor McKinnon supports this view.

Much damage has been done by researchers of so-called alternative concepts of the money supply ranging all the way from M1 to M16. It should be recognized, however, that Federal Reserve regulation Q is

---

[4] H. Robert Heller and Moshin S. Khan, "The Demand for International Reserves under Fixed and Floating Exchange Rates," *IMF Staff Papers,* December 1978.

[5] H. Robert Heller, "Statement on the Eurocurrency Market Control Act of 1979," U.S., Congress, House of Representatives, Subcommittees on Domestic Monetary Policy and on International Trade, Investment, and Monetary Policy of the Committee on Banking, Finance, and Urban Affairs, June 1979.

not without responsibility in that it artificially enhanced the stability of the broader monetary aggregates at the expense of the narrowly defined money supply. Regulation Q has made life more difficult not only for bankers but also for economists, and it should be repealed.

Recent research by the staffs of the Federal Reserve Banks of San Francisco and New York has shown that control over money is all that is needed to influence the rate of inflation.[6] In contrast, controlling credit adds little effectiveness to Federal Reserve policy. It follows that there is little reason to control the quantity of credit but that the Federal Reserve should concentrate on controlling the money supply. Credit, after all, is the result of abstaining from spending—and can therefore hardly be the ultimate cause of inflation. Instead, credit is the precondition of investment, which in turn is a necessary precondition for an expansion of aggregate supply and productive capacity—and therefore represents a powerful force for the reduction of inflationary pressures.

In the international sphere there is the additional argument that international capital flows—which are the result of decisions by foreign nations concerning saving and investment—should not be taxed in the form of reserve requirements (or otherwise) by the U.S. government. In the current world environment, this would imply the taxation of the lending oil-exporting countries or the borrowing developing countries.

In that context the effort by the U.S. House of Representatives to eliminate taxation of saving in the form of reserve requirements should certainly be applauded. Just as domestic reserve requirements on time deposits are superfluous, so are reserve requirements on time deposits in the Euromarkets.

In contrast, reserve requirements on transaction balances may serve some useful purpose as they may be needed to enhance the degree of monetary control that the central bank can exercise. Of course, the same degree of monetary control may be exercised under a regime of interest-paying reserve requirements as under a system of non-interest-paying reserve requirements. Paying interest on reserves would remove many of the inequities and discontinuities of the present regulatory framework while ensuring adequate monetary control.

Let me close with a minor disagreement with Professor McKinnon about his otherwise excellent paper: I should prefer to impose the Eurocurrency reserve requirements on M1 transaction balances on a currency-by-currency basis rather than on a bank-location basis. Impos-

[6] Kenneth C. Froewiss and John P. Judd, "Optimal Control and Money Targets: Should the Fed Look at 'Everything'?" *Federal Reserve Bank of San Francisco Economic Review*, Fall 1979; Richard G. Davis, "Broad Credit Measures as Targets for Monetary Policy," *Federal Reserve Bank of New York Quarterly Review*, vol. 4, no. 2 (Summer 1979).

ing reserve requirements according to the location of a bank would merely offer an incentive to shift the location of the bank. If, instead, all dollar M1 balances were subject to the same reserve requirements throughout the world—regardless of the location or nationality of the bank—then the control over the monetary aggregates by the Federal Reserve would certainly be enhanced. Given the desire of the Federal Reserve to reduce the inflation rate by holding down the growth of the dollar supply, such an arrangement can be only beneficial for all parties.

A. D. Crockett

John Williamson's paper is characteristically lucid, well reasoned, and thought-provoking. He argues—convincingly, in my opinion—that regulation of international reserves is an unpromising avenue by which to pursue a global counterinflationary policy. The demand for reserves is, for the reasons he gives, unlikely to be sufficiently stable to be a satisfactory fulcrum for international economic policy. Furthermore, the supply of reserves cannot become an exogenously determined policy instrument without major changes in the institutional arrangements governing international capital flows—arrangements whose very flexibility has been found to have great benefits for international trade and welfare. Thus, I conclude with Williamson that the necessary preconditions for "international reserve monetarism"—a stable demand function and exogenously determined supply—are present only in such attenuated degree that they are very weak reeds on which to lean in the attempt to restrain inflation.

If the foregoing is accepted, it follows that more direct methods are required if the growth of the world money supply is to be brought under effective control. Williamson suggests targets agreed-upon collectively for expansion of domestic credit as a means of achieving a target growth rate for the global money supply. Perhaps it is worth pausing here to consider whether controlling monetary growth is an objective that has to be pursued collectively, as Williamson asserts it is. His contention is that interdependence among economies is such that monetary targets have to be jointly set. In my opinion, this case is overstated. With floating exchange rates, individual countries can to a considerable extent achieve the degree of financial stability they desire. Although policy making is undoubtedly easier when other countries have achieved financial stability than when they are suffering from double-digit inflation, it should not be overlooked that some countries—Germany,

The views expressed in these comments do not necessarily represent those of the International Monetary Fund.

Austria, Switzerland, Japan—have achieved significant success in restraining inflation, even in the absence of effective control of the world money supply. A more modest goal than the one Williamson sets would be to devise international monetary arrangements that try to ensure that the stabilization objectives of countries are not actually impeded by the policies pursued by their trading partners. This, indeed, is the purpose of the internationally agreed guidelines for surveillance.

Even if one were to accept that collective target setting could be a useful way of adding substance to the present rather ad hoc surveillance procedures, I see a number of difficulties in Williamson's proposal. Some of these are common to all proposals that involve declaring policies in advance, according to some formula. They are well known and need not be gone into further here. I also see difficulties both of technique and of principle in the novel aspect of Williamson's proposal—namely, that the monetary objective should be expressed through expansion of domestic credit rather than the money supply. First, a technical problem: It is not true that, simply through redefinition of reserves, expansion of domestic credit summed over all countries would necessarily become equal to the increase in the world money supply. The increase in the broadly defined money supply of a country is, to simplify only slightly, equal to the banking system's acquisition of domestic assets plus its acquisition of foreign assets. It is not true, however, as Williamson seems to imply, that the net foreign assets of one banking system are the liability of another. Because both central and commercial banks can have foreign claims on nonbanks, their total assets, and hence the monetary liabilities they issue, can increase even in the absence of domestic credit expansion. In order to control the world money supply, therefore, further understandings would have to be reached governing the acquisition by banks of foreign assets.

Perhaps a more fundamental objection to Williamson's proposal is that it would require monetary authorities in individual countries to aim at a domestic credit objective, when theoretical and empirical evidence suggests that the more stable economic relation is between national income and money. Upward pressure on the exchange rate could be resisted only at the cost of more rapid domestic monetary expansion, whereas an attempt to support a weak currency would require much slower than intended monetary expansion. It may well be the case that such policy responses will often seem desirable; but it will not always be so, and the implied one-to-one association between intervention and changes in the domestic money supply is likely to be regarded as unduly constraining. It is true that in a fixed-rate world, a monetary target can hide the fact that creation of excessive credit is leaking out in a balance-of-payments deficit—but that should surely not govern the way in which targets are set under floating.

For the reasons just given, I do not believe that Williamson's proposal is likely to serve as an effective blueprint for a more managed international monetary system. Nevertheless, it contains certain ideas that could perhaps be borrowed to help improve the functioning of present arrangements. A first such aspect is the internationalization of the decision-making process. Nearly all major countries presently set targets for the growth rates of their money supplies. By and large, these monetary targets are set with the avowed intention of accommodating real growth, gradually reducing inflation, and helping the working of the international adjustment process. Enhanced international cooperation could well involve some standardization of the ways in which targets are expressed, together with mutual consultation before targets are declared. Such consultation would be a more overt signal of collaborative intent than presently exists and might even have the effect of stiffening the resolve of national authorities to adhere to targets and increasing the credibility of official policy declarations.

A second aspect of the Williamson proposal that differs from existing arrangements is its overt recognition of the balance-of-payments adjustment process, through setting targets for domestic credit expansion (DCE) rather than the money supply. It is, of course, good that policy makers should be reminded of the external dimension of monetary policy, but Williamson's proposal would do little to alleviate what is now perceived as the main problem in this area—namely, excessive exchange rate volatility. Indeed, his proposal might aggravate the problem if it made countries unwilling to engage in market intervention that could not be sterilized. Reasons of analytical tidiness aside, however, there is no reason that a *pure* monetary or a *pure* credit target has to be pursued. The authorities of a country could establish a "conditional" monetary growth target that would be predicated on a certain path for the exchange rate (or balance of payments). If the exchange rate diverged from this path, the monetary growth target could be adjusted in a manner designed to minimize the movement of the exchange rate away from the targeted path. This strategy could be publicly declared, so that market participants would know that exchange-rate weakness would normally be automatically followed by some tightening of domestic monetary policy. Thus, there could be a "graduated response" to unexpected exchange market developments that might help avoid the need for a dramatic policy package when exchange market weakness goes beyond a certain point.

Regardless of the particular way in which it is achieved, however, it would seem desirable for countries to determine in advance, and to communicate in a credible way to market participants, a monetary policy strategy that promised reasonable consistency among the policies of individual countries and, in particular, a stabilizing policy response to exogenous disturbances and other unexpected developments.

Finally, let me stress that, however scientific the empirical basis for a given monetary target, its successful employment as an instrument of policy remains an art. The purpose of targets is to provide a firmer and more consistent basis for the expectations that are now generally recognized to be the principal determinants of financial and exchange market conditions. If the targets are sensible, and are flexible enough that they can be adhered to without undue stress, they will have a valuable stabilizing influence.

John R. Karlik

As one who entered graduate school the year Robert Triffin published *Gold and the Dollar Crisis* and who grew up under the cloud of "liquidity, adjustment, and confidence," it is a bit breathtaking to contemplate, as John Williamson does in his paper, that reserves do not matter. I am not about to argue for international reserve monetarism, but Robert Heller has indicated a few respects in which reserves do seem to matter. Some developing countries that are unable to find the wherewithal to pay for oil imports during the next year will disagree with Williamson, but he would probably say that the problem in these cases is the distribution of reserves or the inability to service additional external debt.

John Williamson would have the major industrial countries, or at least those with important international financial markets, agree to and observe appropriate rates of domestic credit expansion. Williamson suggests that domestic credit-expansion targets be used as a base for the exercise of International Monetary Fund (IMF) surveillance. Perhaps I am anticipating, but I thought this objective was already being pursued by the IMF. More important, Williamson suggests four elements upon which the target rate of domestic credit expansion for each country would be based. These are (1) the nation's demand for money to finance its own real growth, (2) an allowance for decelerating inflation, (3) a contribution to anticyclical policy, and (4) a similar contribution toward promoting desired current-account adjustments.

I have the following difficulties with this proposal. First, if these limits on domestic credit expansion are to be effective, should they not also include Eurocurrency bank liabilities that are close substitutes for domestic credit? Thus, Williamson implicitly seems to advocate regulation of Eurocurrency markets. Second, the adjustments to the basic rate of credit expansion needed to finance domestic growth are unlikely to be all in the same direction. Even in theory, how are these upward and downward adjustments to be calculated? Third, in practice, the room for error in calculating these adjustments and for differences of opinion among various analysts, policy makers, and international organizations is large enough so that any sleepy bureaucrat of less than average intelligence with only one eye open could still make the target rate come out wherever his political leaders desired. Not that I am unsympathetic toward Williamson's objective—it is just that he seems to have adjusted it until it could well become unrecognizable.

Dale Henderson and Douglas Waldo have painstakingly constructed a model of the Eurocurrency market and used it to investigate the probable consequences of introducing reserve requirements in that market. Such an exercise is absolutely essential to determination of the circumstances under which Eurocurrency reserve requirements would be practicable and whether their introduction would be worth the effort. I am willing to take their technical conclusions (substantiated by their appendix B, which I have not seen) on faith.

I should like to see their exposition clarified in two respects, however. Their discussion is unclear as to whether there is only one interest rate in the model or more than one and, if the latter, as to how they move together. Initially, they assume that all interest rates in each country equal the local treasury rate and that these two treasury rates are equal. Consequently, they say that "all interest rates move together in lockstep." Further on, they say that the model really only contains one interest rate. To exercise the model, however, they imagine "a shift in U.S. nonbanks' portfolio preferences away from dollar demand deposits at U.S. banks and toward short-term Eurodollar deposits." According to my understanding, a shift in asset preferences must be motivated by some change in the risk/return trade-off. If interest rates are all equivalent, however, what would prompt such a change in asset preferences under fixed exchange rates? Even under the flexible exchange rate case, "all private agents *expect* the exchange rate to remain unchanged." I fail to see what gets the events that the model is constructed to analyze in motion. What makes this horse run? Do the assumptions rigidly predestine all the conclusions? Perhaps there is some simple explanation that could be illustrated in an example.

Ronald McKinnon has produced an instructive and original paper on offshore markets for foreign currencies and on the way these markets are related to national monetary control. The analysis regarding Singapore is new and highly relevant. His application to Britain and to the United States of the lessons derived from the Singapore example is persuasive.

Because of differences in the openness and size of the British and the U.S. economies, McKinnon's policy recommendations for the two countries run in opposite directions. British authorities must follow the Singapore example rather literally if monetary stability is to be achieved. In contrast, the United States—according to McKinnon—cannot permit the development of substantial unregulated markets for foreign currencies within its borders (1) because the U.S. current account will not adjust sufficiently rapidly to errors in demand management to avoid surges of inflation and (2) because the U.S. money supply cannot be allowed to fluctuate in response to variations in the current account and in capital flows. The same foundation underlies these two reasons: First, the domestic U.S. economy is very large relative to international goods and services transactions and relative to international capital flows involving the United States; hence, not much excess domestic purchasing power can be vented through importing. Second—continuing to adhere to McKinnon's analysis—the United States should act as the balance wheel that stabilizes the international monetary system; thus, the U.S. money supply should not respond passively to the effect of external events.

Let me present my own reactions to McKinnon's analysis. There is little with which I disagree, but in some respects I should like to see the analysis pushed farther.

In referring to the Bank of England, McKinnon suggests that " 'tight' money should be redefined in terms of the exchange rate rather than in terms of a constant rate of growth in some purely domestic monetary aggregate." I ask, To what extent is it appropriate to apply the same definition to the United States, using, say, a weighted average of other major industrial nations' currencies? Perhaps this objective is essentially the same as striving to hold the increase in a particular domestic price index below a stated maximum. I believe that identifying the relationship between these two objectives is important in the light of the desirability that the United States perform a constructive international balance-wheel function and in the light of the recent inability of U.S. authorities to achieve McKinnon's macroeconomic objectives—namely, "the balancing of aggregate demand and supply in U.S. commodity markets must be internally managed by appropriate counter-cyclical fiscal policy, on the one hand, and by careful matching of the supply of and the demand for dollars held by American residents on the other." This objective sounds like fine-tuning to me, and I

379

question the extent to which it can be achieved with the available instruments.

McKinnon recognizes that this objective will not always be met and that, in addition, changes in banking regulations, more rapid inflation in the United States, or a significant reduction in the costs of international communications could make doing business in foreign currencies or Eurodollars much more attractive to U.S. residents than has been the case in the past. If the dollar is to remain foremost among the currencies of the major industrial nations and serve as a balancing intermediary, it must win the continuing competition among currencies. Policy errors will occur again in the future. To ensure the attractiveness of the dollar to U.S. residents, McKinnon would have the Federal Reserve System pay a market rate of interest on required reserves. I wish he had gone a step or two further to specify his instrument of monetary control. Would he suggest a penalty rate of interest on borrowed reserves? Some other tool(s)? What would prevent costless switching by banks between money-market assets and borrowed reserves? What cost to banks would inhibit them, rather than the Federal Reserve, from determining the rate of monetary growth?

Rainer S. Masera

As we all know, when a commentator says he agrees with most—or indeed all—of what has been written in the papers he has been asked to comment upon and then goes on to present his own views on the subject, he has usually not read the papers. My case is the exception that confirms the rule: I do agree with most of what John Williamson, Dale Henderson and Douglas Waldo, and Ronald McKinnon wrote, *and* I have read their papers. This must be especially hard to believe because the paper by Henderson and Waldo and that by McKinnon were supposed to present conflicting views of the case for official control of private international liquidity; I shall, however, argue that they are really addressing two different questions.

Let me start with my comments on Williamson's paper. I share his views on the theoretical and empirical weaknesses of the international monetary base approach during the period of floating. Under present circumstances, no realistic mechanical aggregation can be made of the various components that add up to total official liquidity, and there is no automatic link whereby the growth of each country's money stock is broadly set by the growth in its international reserves; a fortiori, estab-

The views expressed in this comment are those of the author and should not be interpreted as reflecting the views of the Banca d'Italia.

lishing causal links between global reserves and world inflation appears very difficult.

In addition to the various arguments put forward by Williamson, I should like to stress that the link between the variation in the foreign component of the domestic monetary base and the change in external reserves is also broken by valuation adjustments: The change in the stock valued in terms of the appropriate unit of account is no longer equal to the new flow. This seemingly trivial statement does provide what I consider a useful clue to the question of gold. This is an area in which I disagree with Williamson to a certain extent: The effects of the increase in the price of gold in 1979 on world official liquidity deserve, I submit, more attention than he seems prepared to give them.

In the 1960s official reserves rose from $60 billion to $90 billion; at the end of 1979 they had climbed to some $830 billion, with gold valued at market prices ($512 an ounce). In absolute figures the approximately 1 billion ounces of gold held as reserves increased in value by more than $300 billion during the year. Gold accounted for 65 percent of total reserves in 1959, for 50 percent ten years later, and for nearly 60 percent at the end of 1979. True enough, gold is not "liquid," but I would contend that this is so mainly because central banks do not want to *sell* it—even at present prices. It must also be acknowledged that, when signs of stress develop in the solidity of the Eurocurrency system, the "outside" asset character of gold must have an obvious appeal to countries in structural surplus, especially when account is taken of their perfectly rational desire to diversify in any event their reserve holdings. In this respect, the fact that the oil price of gold is now broadly the same as thirty years ago—that is, twenty barrels an ounce—cannot be ruled out as totally insignificant.[1]

The gold reserves of the main central banks obviously no longer represent the fundamental international monetary base,[2] but it is still a fact that gold retains a role as an important component of world official reserves. Thus, even if gold will not be remonetized—and I am

[1] Note here that, with a relative price of this order, the industrial countries and the oil exporting countries (OPEC) could use gold as a partial means of settlement for oil-related payments imbalances for quite a few years. On reasonable assumptions about this complementary form of recycling, gold could be used to this purpose into the next century, by which time the problem of oil will have to be largely "solved," one way or another.

[2] As they did in the previous period of floating—during the first part of the 1930s—when the currency turmoil, set in motion by the collapse of the pound at the end of 1931, led mainly to the writing up of the international monetary base by two-thirds. In fact, the dollar price of gold was raised in 1933 from $20.67 to $35 an ounce, and by 1936—after the Tripartite Agreement—relative prices among the major currencies had settled down near to the previously existing parities.

confident it will not—and although there is no automatic link between its appreciation in relation to paper currencies and the volume of creation of domestic moneys, I would neither underestimate the possible inflationary consequences of the gold price rise, as a result of delays in the adjustment process in certain countries, nor underplay the potentially beneficial effects that gold might still have in the working of the international monetary system—witness its possible use to guarantee in some form the Substitution Account.

In more general terms, of course, one cannot but highlight the dissatisfaction with this haphazard and extremely volatile form of creation of international liquidity, with regard to both the volume and the distribution of world reserves. Concerning the latter point, I have never accepted the link argument, but, even so, one can see that developing countries will now have a new reason to complain about the inadequacy of present international monetary arrangements.

A second point I want to make concerning the severing of the automatic link between domestic monetary-base creation and growth of official reserves has to do with the practice of "liability financing" on the part of many monetary authorities after the 1973 oil price explosion. Williamson does draw attention to the importance of this question; I simply want to add that (1) in certain countries, such as Italy, no compensatory borrowing had a direct monetary base counterpart, because the proceeds were wholly sterilized and (2) in many instances, creditworthiness in international markets depends heavily on the volume of owned gross reserves. A change in gross reserves is thus very different from one in *net* reserves—which tends to be matched by a variation in the domestic monetary base.

There are further reasons that it is logically questionable to continue to apply a quantity theory framework to international liquidity creation. Under present circumstances, the quantity of foreign-exchange reserves is largely market-determined, as can be explained along the lines of a "credit model" approach.[3] In this context Williamson is right in emphasizing the importance of the fact that reserves bear a market rate of interest. In passing, let me remark that in the recent past, while most countries resorted to liability financing of their external deficits, the United States shifted to asset financing (in part) both in terms of gold and in terms of foreign currencies: With the new U.S. approach, the European Monetary System (EMS) in operation, and liability financing (now also by "strong" currency countries), the modus operandi of the

---

[3] As, for example, in the seminal work by Knut Wicksell, *Interest and Prices* (London: Macmillan, 1936) or by Ralph G. Hawtrey, *The Gold Standard in Operation* (London: Longmans, Green, 1939).

international monetary system has undergone very significant changes and a clear shift away from free floating.

Before coming to the issue of the Euromarkets, I wish to make a final point regarding Williamson's proposal for domestic credit expansion (DCE) targets. I rather share his own doubts as to the practical chances of the scheme being accepted throughout the world, even assuming recourse to a crawling peg regime—that is, allowing for different rates of inflation. Yet it would clearly be an appropriate approach in the case of countries that adhere to regional monetary arrangements: It must be slightly ironic to record that the initial operation of the EMS has been accompanied by more widespread, and stricter, adherence to money-stock targeting in member countries, which is of course theoretically consistent with freely floating exchange rates.

I turn now to McKinnon's paper. Again, I must start by saying that I am in broad agreement with both the theoretical background and the policy conclusions of the paper. I myself argued nearly ten years ago that a naive money-multiplier approach was not applicable to the workings of the Eurocurrency system, which was best understood along "credit theory" lines, even if the focus of the analysis was on the substitution character of the market. In the past few years we have seen substantial progress in both theoretical and empirical analyses of the market: the paper by McKinnon and a recent paper by Swoboda, prepared for the Group of Thirty,[4] provide what I would regard as conclusive arguments, which, though they improve the analytical apparatus, also substantially confirm the basic validity of what I might perhaps be allowed to call the BIS view of the market.

Even though there is no simplistic "magic" of multiple credit creation based upon the injection of an exogenously determined zero-yield monetary base for the system as a whole, and even though the wholesale character of Eurobanking, coupled with the freedom of each bank not to accept deposits, implies significant differences compared with all traditional domestic financial intermediaries, it is easy to see that, with the abolition of capital controls between major countries and the growing financial and real interdependence of economies, Eurobanks can increasingly provide a substitute for a class of domestic liquid financial assets. As McKinnon rightly pointed out, events in 1979—to repeat, a higher inflation tax on bank reserves, especially in the U.S. domestic market; heavy new marginal reserve requirements on the "managed liabilities" of U.S. banks; and the abolition of British

[4] Alexander K. Swoboda, *Credit Creation in the Euromarket: Alternative Theories and Implications for Control* (New York: Group of Thirty, 1979).

exchange controls—all make for a more pronounced substitution threat stemming from the Eurocurrency system.

In general terms I find it useful to approach the issue as follows. At the world level total private liquidity can be separated into two components: $L = M + QM$, where L = liquidity, M = monetary assets, and QM = all other liquid assets. These aggregates should be identified on the basis of three keys (i, j, k), where i indicates that the assets are held by residents of country i, j denotes the currency of denomination of the deposits, and k indicates that the assets in question represent liabilities of a financial intermediary domiciled in country k.[5] If the index 1 refers to the United States and to the U.S. dollar, for instance, $M_{1,1,1}$ stands for monetary assets held by U.S. residents in U.S. dollars with U.S.-domiciled financial intermediaries.

To follow this approach, if the stock of world money is regarded as an important control variable, it would make sense to impose consistent reserve requirements on both domestic deposits and Eurodeposits with monetary characteristics—that is, checkable deposits and sight and very-short-term maturity deposits, which in the Eurosector might imply deposits with less than a one-month maturity—in order to avoid easy circumvention. Two points should be stressed here: In the first place, if the objective is to eliminate or at least to reduce the competitive advantage of the Eurosystem over its domestic intermediaries, what must really be achieved is harmonization of domestic monetary control techniques between countries. The second point is that, in order to achieve consistency in the Eurosystem proper, either interest-bearing reserve requirements should be adopted or, in the case of a zero-interest-bearing requirement, the coefficient should in principle vary for each currency inversely with the market interest rates of the different currencies; it can easily be shown in fact that, considering, for instance, two currencies, the extra cost per unit of deposit that a bank must bear, because of the reserve requirement, by operating in the currency characterized by the

---

[5] Superficial observers often quote figures for the so-called gross size of the Euro-currency market, now approaching some $1,000 billion, as an aggregate that should somehow be added to total identified domestic money stocks. This only shows the basic misunderstandings that can exist about the market. McKinnon, quoting Helmut Mayer, indicates that, at the end of 1978, Eurocurrency holdings by nonbanks totaled $79 billion—that is, 2.3 percent of total world identified money, plus quasi-money. Wallich recently gave, for the same date, slightly higher estimates: According to him, "stateless money in the Eurocurrency market, that which is not counted in national monetary statistics, is of the order of $100 billion to $120 billion." (See Henry C. Wallich, "The Need for Control over the Eurocurrency Market," this volume.) Even if we take the higher figure, the order of magnitude is still such as to imply that Euroholdings are a relatively minor fraction of the sum of national monetary aggregates.

higher nominal interest rate is given by the product of the (common) reserve coefficient and the interest rate differential.

I also agree with McKinnon when he points out that there is some inconsistency in the U.S. proposal to apply a uniform (non-interest-bearing) reserve requirement on all Eurocurrency deposits when, domestically, broad money-supply aggregates are not generally controlled by means of a reserves operating target. To recall some figures recently published by the Federal Reserve, in June 1978, the proportion of the M3 aggregate in the U.S. subject to reserve requirements was 41.8 percent. In the discussions that have taken place in Basel on the question of Euromarket controls, I have often argued that it would be appropriate to rely mainly on a reserves operating target for all monetary (M1) deposits—whether in the Euromarkets or, especially, in nonmember banks domiciled in the United States. Control over broad money aggregates would depend mainly on an interest rate operating target. In a stable and logically consistent institutional setup, where the stability of the public's demand for the aggregates would make forecasts easier, the sensitivity to changes in interest rates would provide a reliable basis for controlling "liquid" assets. I cannot therefore but endorse McKinnon's analysis of this general area.

I come finally to the point of being more of a commentator by dissenting from McKinnon with regard to his apparently unqualified faith in the "adequacy" of Eurolending in the face of the new OPEC crisis. To use the word employed in the title of this volume, I would not underestimate the risk of serious stresses developing in the market from the prudential side, mainly as a consequence of country risk and of the degree of transformation that took place in 1978–1979: The very size of interbank transactions means that local stresses might easily build up into global difficulties. These dangers are heightened both by the prospect of more durable OPEC surpluses and, to some extent, by the very prospect of a stronger dollar and higher interest rates, which may increase the burdens for debtor countries. For these reasons I would advocate, first, taking some of the onus of recycling from the Eurosystem by means of direct OPEC lending and by encouraging international institutions, notably the International Monetary Fund, to be still more active, and, second, I would advocate more active concern about the macroprudential aspects of the Eurosystem on the part of the monetary authorities of the countries in the Group of Ten. This would imply a consolidated, worldwide approach to risk management and to the adequacy of capital resources in the monitoring of the international lending activity of the Eurobanks. On this prudential side, let me remark that I find it slightly odd that faith in the Eurosystem's ability to fully recycle OPEC surpluses without strain is especially strong on the U.S.

side of the Atlantic, when it is precisely the U.S. banks that are already encountering some difficulties in the process, because of capital constraints and country-risk limitations.

I conclude my comments by referring briefly to the paper by Henderson and Waldo. Time does not allow me to do full justice to what is an excellent piece of work, rich in analytical insights. I found, however, that both the financial and the real models presented in the paper are based on a set of stylized facts that are too rarefied to provide us with firm clues with regard to the practical question we are discussing. As McKinnon—rightly, I believe—pointed out, the main financial functions for which the Eurosystem provides highly beneficial services are to be found in the foreign-exchange (forward cover) aspect and in the transfer of funds from surplus areas to deficit areas. Neither of these aspects is present in Henderson and Waldo's paper. Nonetheless, I suggest that their scheme deserves careful attention in view of its implications for the crucial—and not well developed—question of monetary coordination between two major financial centers.

Summary of the Discussion

Two topics dominated the discussion from the floor: the degree of useful distinction between money and credit, and the extent of influence of changes in international reserve aggregates on world inflation.

Commenting on the first topic, Ronald McKinnon pointed out that some specific length of time to maturity of an asset, frequently used as the basis for distinction between money and credit, is hardly relevant. He suggested that a proper criterion for whether an asset should be classified as money or as credit is whether one can draw a check on it—that is, can use it directly as a means of payment. He also argued that the distinction is more important under flexible than under fixed exchange rates because under the former each country becomes more directly responsible for conducting an independent monetary policy.

Fritz Machlup suggested in this connection that, given the fuzziness of the concept of credit, some other term, such as nonliquid deposits perhaps, should be used for making the distinction to which McKinnon was alluding.

Although there was clear recognition of the difficulties of distinguishing operationally between money and credit, Karl Brunner suggested that few economists would have difficulty delineating the set of assets in which they would willingly accept repayment of previously extended loans. This set would be defined as money. The function of econometric studies in drawing the line in practice between money and credit was also emphasized. One can specify equations describing demand for various assets, for example, and see for which assets the influence of the level of transactions on their demand is significant and positive.

In regard to the effect of changes in totals of international reserves on global inflation, a wide range of opinions was voiced. Several participants expressed doubts about John Williamson's view that reserve aggregates were not of major importance in this regard. The discussion made clear the need to distinguish between two different propositions: that changes in international reserve levels have little influence on economic behavior and that totals of international reserves are important independent of the distribution of reserves.

Few would argue that the reserve positions of countries will never influence their behavior, but neither will the influence of a given change in aggregate reserves be independent of the way the change is distributed among different types of countries. John Bilson and Thomas Willett reported the results of recent econometric studies that suggest the importance of considering causality of a disaggregated level. Willett reported on disaggregate analysis, which found a much weaker relationship between reserve increases and monetary expansion in individual countries during the international liquidity explosion of the early 1970s than is suggested by aggregate relationships. Bilson reported on empirical results that confirm that countries do systematically respond to reserve changes but suggest that there are significant differences in the responses of surplus and deficit countries as well as in those of industrial and developing countries.

Subsequent discussion emphasized that not only whether reserve changes influence government behavior must be considered, but also what behavior is influenced. It makes a considerable difference, for example, whether the response to a loss of reserves is a tightening of monetary policy or the initiation of borrowing abroad. It was also emphasized that there were reasons for the creation of special drawing rights (SDR), even if aggregate global reserves are not believed to be important. Under current arrangements SDRs cannot be properly considered a mechanism for controlling aggregate international liquidity, but they can meet the demands of countries for growth in owned international reserves with the passage of time without the need for borrowing or for accumulating reserve currencies.

John Williamson's proposal for coordinating rates of national monetary expansion was also discussed. Willett argued that even under flexible exchange rates countries would have an interest in one another's rate of monetary expansion. Very high rates of monetary expansion would be likely to generate high and variable rates of inflation. The resultant variability and uncertainty would be likely to cause fluctuations in real exchange rates, which would export instability from high-inflation countries to their trading partners with lower rates of inflation. Thus, even under flexible rates countries would have an interest in attempting to limit high rates of monetary expansion in other nations.

What Can We Learn from the Past?

Luncheon Address

Introductory Remarks

Arthur F. Burns

At an occasion like this, lively conversations develop at the luncheon table, which some would like to continue. At the same time, all of us are eager to hear from our distinguished guest, Dr. Emminger. He is known to all of us; he requires no introduction. He has been a frequent visitor to this country. He knows Washington and New York City better than most Americans do. I just asked Dr. Emminger how many times he has flown across the Atlantic, and he simply responded, "More than a hundred times." Being a conservative, he gave—I think—a very conservative reply.

Dr. Emminger's active participation in international economic affairs covers the entire period since World War II. He first represented the German government in negotiations that led to the establishment of the European Payments Union. I do not think there has been an international financial meeting since then at which Dr. Emminger did not take a prominent part.

Much has happened in the thirty-five years since the end of World War II. Throughout this period Germany has been blessed with strong and extraordinarily capable economic leaders. The German economic miracle is largely attributable to this fact. And Dr. Emminger, I need hardly add, has been at the forefront of the formation of economic policies in his country in all these years.

I first had the pleasure of meeting Dr. Emminger in 1954 in Paris. I remember that meeting vividly. My knowledge of the international arena was very limited, but I already had great respect for the way in which the Germans were proceeding to rebuild their economy. During that meeting of the OEEC, a predecessor of OECD, one foreign representative after another was critical of Germany's financial policy. They kept urging Dr. Emminger to persuade his government, in the interest of the international economy, to reduce taxes, to increase government spending, to run deficits, to ease credit conditions—in short, to share in the incipient inflationary wave that was elsewhere under way. I was

391

deeply impressed by the courtesy, the patience, and particularly the firmness of character that he displayed in resisting these pressures. And the last time that I attended a formal international meeting with Dr. Emminger was in February 1978, again in Paris. Once again I listened, this time no longer astonished, to the representatives of other countries urging the Germans to expand their economy faster by practicing deficit finance on a more liberal scale and by easing up credit conditions. There was only one difference between the meeting in Paris in 1978 and the meeting in 1954. This time the Americans also urged the Germans to expand their economy faster. But Dr. Emminger did not change; he was just as patient, just as courteous, just as scholarly, just as well informed, just as firm in resisting pressure from the inflationists as he was at my very first meeting with him.

Dr. Emminger has brought sound economic thought and continuity to Germany's economic policy. He understood from the beginning that monetary order is essential to a country's economic and political strength and that an independent central bank was essential to the maintenance of monetary order.

I want to say just one thing more about Dr. Emminger. He not only knows this country, but he is a friend of the United States. He knows our literature, he knows our economic problems, he understands and at times even sympathizes with our political concerns. During the years that I served in the government, when we had a financial problem or needed to speak frankly about some international matter, we could always turn to Dr. Emminger. And when we needed assistance, which has occurred a little too often in recent times, Dr. Emminger was always a friend on whom we could count. That does not mean that he applauded America's financial policy. He was too good a friend, too understanding an economist and financier to do that; but he was always ready to render constructive assistance. I have the greatest admiration for this man, whom I consider the outstanding and most distinguished central banker of the world.

What Can We Learn from the Past?

Otmar Emminger

Preliminary Remarks

First of all I have to express my deep gratitude for having been invited to this conference. I must associate myself with what Professor Machlup said at the end of this morning's meeting, that this was one of the best discussions of the exchange rate problems and international monetary problems he has experienced. I must confess if I had heard some years ago all that I heard this morning, I might have conducted a better exchange rate policy.

I am particularly grateful to you, Arthur, for introducing me in such a nice way. You will permit me as a central banker to a central banker, or former central banker to a former central banker, to take your very flattering words with some discount, and I have to take the present high American rediscount rate for that purpose. I remember that you, Arthur, and I were once linked together about three years ago in an article or commentary by a very well known American Nobel Prize winning economist. It must have been in 1977 when he wrote in his column, probably in *Newsweek,* that Dr. Emminger was pursuing a supertight monetary policy in Germany for which Arthur Burns would have been lynched in the United States. And that was particularly funny because we were at that time really at the height of loosening up our German monetary policy and had already very low interest rates.

I consider my assignment today to talk in a general way about the international monetary system under stress because that is the title of the conference. But of course I thought I would have to say something about my personal experience with this international monetary system because I have had a very long experience in this field. I don't

Otmar Emminger is the former president of the Deutsche Bundesbank. The text of this speech is available as *The International Monetary System under Stress: What Can We Learn from the Past?* Reprint No. 112 (Washington, D.C.: American Enterprise Institute, 1980).

want to dwell at length on the historical evolution; we have had a very lucid historical introduction this morning from Professor Haberler. But I want to draw some conclusions from my experience as a practical central banker.

I

Looking back over the past ten years, one cannot but call it a turbulent decade. Apart from political turmoil—from Vietnam and Watergate to Iran and Afghanistan—it brought us the breakdown of the dollar-based system of fixed exchange rates, two oil price explosions, and the worst recession and the most stubborn inflation of the postwar period.

How has our international economic and monetary system stood up to all these disturbances and challenges? Some people would probably interject here, What system? Do we have an international monetary system at all? Isn't it all in shambles? To which I would reply, No, it isn't. And it has performed remarkably well in the face of all these turbulences. It is better than its reputation. This reminds me of what Mark Twain is reported to have said about Richard Wagner's music: "It's better than it sounds."

The reputation of the present world monetary system is not good. A few weeks ago, a leading European statesman blamed all our monetary woes on the bad international monetary system. But is it the system, or rather are bad national policies at fault? Politicians, of course, always have the tendency—and the privilege—to look for a convenient scapegoat.

II

How can we measure the performance of the system? I shall do it in a broadbrush way, by examining whether it has hampered or promoted free world trade and payments, whether it has contributed to better international equilibrium, whether it has helped stability or fostered inflation, and other issues.

Let us take a look at the facts: In the 1970s the gross national product (GNP) of the industrial countries increased in real terms at an average annual rate of a little over 3 percent, while their volume of foreign trade increased by 6 to 7 percent annually. To be sure, these average annual growth rates were lower than in the happy 1960s. This was partly due to the recession of 1974–1975, which cannot be blamed on the international monetary system; it had more to do with the oil price explosion at the end of 1973 and with bad economic management in the preceding years.

394

Under the circumstances, the average growth rate of the industrial countries at a little over 3 percent annually was not too bad. I wish we could be reasonably sure of a similar growth over the next five years—bearing in mind the worldwide slowdown in productivity growth, the likely drag on growth from scarce and expensive supplies of oil and other commodities, and the inevitable sluggishness implicit in a long-drawn-out struggle against deeply entrenched inflation.

The main point I want to make, however, is that the external trade of the industrial countries expanded nearly twice as fast as their domestic production—a creditable performance in view of all the disturbances of this period. Also it should not be forgotten that floating and the adjustment of overvalued exchange rates sometimes alleviated the fight against protectionism and enabled several major countries to eliminate capital controls—Germany in 1973–1974, the United States in 1974, and Britain last year.

On the positive side of the ledger we can also put the evolution of international capital markets. While many people had feared crippling effects from the transition to widespread floating in 1973, capital movements have risen to enormous—some may even say excessive—levels. And as concerns the recycling of the oil surpluses and the financing of payments deficits, the international financial system has performed perhaps too well, because it has engendered both excessive indebtedness and complacency in a number of countries.

Another field where the experience of recent years has refuted the critics of the present system is its effect on the adjustment of payments disequilibria. Apart from the special circumstances which produced a rapid reduction of the OPEC (Organization of Petroleum Exporting Countries) surpluses between 1974 and 1978, the large payments imbalances among the major industrial countries were reduced or reversed over the last few years. To mention a few outstanding examples:

- the improvements in the current account of the United States first in 1974–1976, then again in 1979–1980
- second, the surprising reversal of the external balances of Italy, France, and Britain from very large deficits in 1974 (with the total current account deficits of these three countries amounting to over $22 billion in 1974) to surpluses or equilibrium in 1978
- third, the almost violent swing-around of the external balances of Japan and Germany from large surpluses on current account in 1977–1978 to equally large deficits in 1979–1980

In all these cases there has been some "overshooting" in exchange rate depreciation or appreciation and an important contribution from cyclical divergences. But this just confirms that changes in exchange rates can

395

only affect trade and payments balances significantly if they lead to a "real" change in the exchange rate (that is, go beyond the mere offsetting of divergences in inflation) and if they are supported by appropriate domestic policies.

Furthermore, such adjustments usually take some time and first go through a perverse phase because of the so-called *J*-curve effect. If properly handled, however, they do not necessarily lead to a vicious circle. At any rate, a vicious circle is not an unalterable fate; a country is free to achieve a "virtuous circle" by appropriate domestic monetary policies. The examples of Britain and Italy, which experienced a considerable real appreciation of their currencies over the last twelve months, show that this alone is not sufficient to produce a virtuous circle.

As a result of the evening out of obstinate deficit positions, the present balance-of-payments pattern of the larger industrial countries appears to be better suited to withstand the payments impact of the new oil shock.

Finally, the position of the dollar as the key currency of the system: no other system but floating could have coped with the enormous short-term swings in the U.S. balance on current account—from a surplus of $18 billion in 1975 to deficits of $14 billion in each of the years 1977 and 1978 (magnified further by large net capital exports). It is true that the latent conflict between the still dominant role of the dollar and its recurrent weaknesses makes the international monetary system vulnerable and will continue to do so until the United States has regained domestic stability. But recent experience has shown that the dollar remains indispensable as the key currency and as the transactions currency for oil payments.

With the elimination of the current account deficit in 1979 and the high interest rate policy being pursued by the U.S. authorities, the dollar has recently performed remarkably well—remarkable when viewed against the worldwide discussion about "diversification" and the psychological fallout from the gold boom, from Iran, and from other difficulties. The process of dollar strengthening began in 1979. From the end of 1978 to the end of 1979 the dollar declined against the DMark by about 5 percent, less than would have been justified by the inflation differential between the two countries. Against a weighted basket of major currencies, the dollar was up by about 2 percent from end-1978 to end-1979; in view of the high inflation rate in the United States, this represented a "real" appreciation of 3 to 5 percent. Since the end of 1979 the dollar has risen further, so that now, at the end of February 1980, its "real" rate has nearly regained the level of 1973. It is also remarkable that the relative strength of the dollar has only been recognized since the turn of the year; whereas in 1979 the public image of the dollar fell victim to Gresham's law applied to the news media, that is, bad news drives out good news. But as concerns the future exchange value of the dollar, I keep my fingers crossed, in view of the present bad inflation record of the United States with its possible lagged effect on the dollar rate.

III

Where the world economy has performed badly is in the field of inflation. The average rate of inflation in the industrial countries, measured by consumer price increases, reached a peak of over 14 percent in 1974, came down to a little below 8 percent at the beginning of 1979, and has since gone up into the double-digit realm again. Of course, a large part of this latter rise has been due to vastly increased prices of oil and other commodities since the beginning of 1979. But domestically generated inflation has aggravated the situation.

Is there a connection between worldwide inflation and the present international monetary system? Some people believe that floating, or currency uncertainties, are per se contributing to inflation. I see the connection more the other way around: inflation in major countries has been one of the main causes of external currency instability. This is mainly due to the fact that high inflation is inevitably accompanied by disruptive inflation differences between major countries, as countries are very unequal in their proneness to inflation. There seems to have evolved a more or less fixed pattern of high, middle, and low inflation countries, with occasional, but rare, shifts by one country into another camp.

Apart from bad national policies, I see one particular inflationary element built into our present system, namely where attempts are made to stabilize exchange rates between countries with widely divergent inflation rates. The prime example is the European Monetary System (EMS) where, as we have seen over the last year, there is a great resistance to adjusting in time the exchange rate relations to inflation differentials. This has already led to the transmission of higher inflation to the low inflation countries. It is far easier to "harmonize" inflation rates upward than downward. This has been one of the major drawbacks of the EMS. According to its charter of December 1978, it was intended as an instrument not only for more exchange rate stability but also for more domestic stability all around. It has performed reasonably well as a zone of exchange rate stability but up to now has completely failed as an instrument for inducing all-around progress toward domestic stability. The range between the lowest and highest inflation rates among the partner countries is at present between 5½ percent (Germany) and 21 percent (Italy); while at the beginning of 1979 it was between 3 and

13 percent. In the longer run, the EMS will only succeed if these differences can be reduced in a downward direction and a real "zone of stability" can be established.

A similar transmission of inflation from high to low inflation countries takes place when floating exchange rates of high inflation countries do not respond to inflation differentials, as has recently been the case for the exchange rates of sterling and the dollar, be it because of very high interest rates or for other reasons. At any rate, Germany and other European countries have recently suffered from this import of inflation via unadjusted or sticky exchange rates (which have led to a considerable undervaluation of the DMark since the beginning of 1979).

On the other hand, our experience in Germany has clearly shown that in the past, free floating, far from having an inflationary effect, shielded us against imported inflation. Germany and Switzerland went over to floating in early 1973 not primarily with the aim of adjusting their payments balances but in order to shield their monetary systems against destabilizing inflows of foreign exchange (such as capital flight). From the middle of 1973 to the middle of 1977 we had, on balance, no net inflows from the dollar area. And up to 1978, a number of countries —among them Germany, Switzerland, Austria, the Benelux countries, and Japan—managed to reduce their inflation rates below the rates ruling before the price explosion of 1972–1973, largely thanks to their floating currencies.

Fluctuating exchange rates cannot, of course, shield a country's price level from a doubling of the oil price. Nor could a country like Germany secure full monetary autonomy when it was faced in 1977–1978 with violent swings in the external balance of the United States and extreme pressure on the exchange rate of the dollar.

A few of the low inflation countries—I mention the Netherlands, Belgium, and Austria—regained better domestic stability after the inflation explosion of 1973–1974 largely by pegging their currencies to the DMark (or the DMark and the Swiss franc), that is to say, by clinging to a system of fixed but adjustable exchange rates and adjusting their domestic policies accordingly. Thus one can regain and maintain relative stability either by using a floating rate as a shield against international inflation or by maintaining a fixed (but adjustable) rate vis-à-vis a relatively stable currency. But in both cases the prime condition has been to give domestic stability a high priority. Unfortunately, the DMark has no stable currency of reference to which it could attach itself.

IV

Another field where the international monetary system has laid itself open to criticism is the volatility of exchange rates and occasional over-

OTMAR EMMINGER

reaction of floating rates. I shall limit myself to a few general remarks on exchange rate policy.

First, we have learned that the so-called overshooting, a movement of the exchange rate going beyond the inflation differential, may be justified and even desirable in a given particular case. The German monetary authorities deliberately accepted the "real" appreciation of the DMark during the years 1977–1978 (4½ percent against a weighted basket of currencies, and 15 percent against the dollar alone, on the basis of industrial wholesale prices).[1] In accepting this "real" adjustment, we also conformed to the advice of the International Monetary Fund (IMF). Even in cases where the "overshooting" went beyond a justified change in the "real" rate, it occasionally performed a useful role by prompting a country to adopt necessary domestic adjustment measures. Well-known examples are the abrupt fall of sterling in 1976 and of the dollar in October 1978. This is what I have learned to call "the positive side of currency crises"—indeed, a crisis can be a productive event if properly used.

Second, as concerns the volatility of floating exchange rates, the critics have undoubtedly a good point. It can have served no useful purpose when, for instance, the "effective" (average) exchange rate of the Japanese yen shot up by about 26 percent between March and August 1978, only to tumble down again in the subsequent fifteen months by about 28 percent. The Swiss franc experienced a similar volatility. As compared with those currencies, the exchange rate movements of the dollar, the DMark, or the French franc in 1979 were models of relative stability, if measured in terms of the average movement against a number of other major currencies.[2]

Third, I find it remarkable how well the business community has adjusted to fluctuating exchange rates. A recent survey of market opinion (by the Group of Thirty) came to the conclusion that major corporations have accepted the floating rates regime as one that has led neither to large-scale disruption of their international activity nor to disillusionment over future investment opportunities.

Fourth, from my own very direct experience with foreign exchange markets under a regime of floating I have drawn the conclusion that for major currencies, in particular the dollar, some management of floating is appropriate, and that besides day-to-day smoothing operations there may be a case for counteracting too violent movements of the exchange

[1] These appreciations during 1977-1978 have been offset by the "real" depreciation (!) of the DMark in 1979 and in the first few months of 1980.
[2] During 1979 the dollar fluctuated within a range of 10½ percent in relation to the DMark, but within a range of only 3½ percent in relation to a weighted basket of major currencies.

rate over the medium term. I do not believe, however, that it is useful, or even practicable, to have agreed target zones for the dollar rate. Lack of time prevents me from going any further into the problems of exchange rate management and my practical experiences with it.

Fifth, competitive depreciations, which were so much feared after the first oil shock of 1973, have not materialized. On the contrary, exchange rates are being more and more used not as an instrument of payments adjustment, but as a weapon against inflation, and there is more and more resistance against a downward adjustment of the exchange rate even where it is justified. Germany has even met great resistance from other members of the European Monetary System against a well-justified appreciation of the DMark ("competive non-depreciation," or occasionally even "competitive appreciation"). I was in the middle of this battle when last September we tried to achieve an exchange rate adjustment in the EMS.

V

As the DMark has in recent years become the main counterpart currency to the dollar, in the sense of being the chief intervention currency for the dollar and the chief reserve currency of the United States, let me make a brief digression to explain our exchange rate policy in relation to the dollar.

It has sometimes been imputed to us that we had intervened massively in order to limit the appreciation of the DMark to benefit our exports. Ironically, nearly at the same time we were suspected of pursuing exactly the opposite policy, that is, letting the dollar fall in order to cheapen import prices in terms of the DMark. In reality we did neither of the two. We kept to the rule of the IMF that exchange rates should not be artificially manipulated either way, but that one should intervene if this was necessary to prevent disorderly market conditions and to counter disruptive exchange rate movements, without opposing basic trends. We are not interested in large-scale interventions; quite the contrary, because they are apt to undermine our domestic monetary policy. What has often not been fully understood is that exchange market intervention by the Federal Reserve in the New York market with DMarks obtained from the Bundesbank (or from American deposits held at the Bundesbank) has the same effect on our domestic money supply as if the Bundesbank itself had purchased dollars against newly created DMarks. There were periods, for example in the summer and autumn of 1979, when nearly all the interventions in support of the dollar were made by the Federal Reserve alone.

In the exchange rate relationship between the DMark and the dollar, the two sides have to share responsibility concerning intervention and

400

exchange rate policies in general. There is a sort of joint management. It is, therefore, important that the U.S. and German authorities see eye to eye on the main principles involved. From my personal experience I can say that this has been the case, apart from very temporary differences in nuances. In addition to close technical cooperation day by day, there has been a consensus between the two partners that mere intervention in the exchange markets cannot have a lasting effect on the exchange value of the dollar, that it all really depends on the fundamental factors. I think one could also say there is a sort of tacit understanding that in the longer run exchange rates should somehow reflect differences in inflation rates. To quote Mr. Volcker, "Stability of the exchange markets ultimately rests on U.S. ability to cope with inflation"; or Mr. A. Solomon, "Overcoming inflation is the key to maintaining the stability of the dollar."

What the Bundesbank would like to achieve over the medium term is to let the exchange rate of the DMark move by and large in line with the differences in inflation rates between West Germany and a weighted average of other major countries. This would mean that we would, in relation to our industrial partner countries, neither import nor export inflation via the exchange rate. This goal is not easy to achieve because in the short run other influences can exert a more powerful influence on exchange rates than inflation differentials. Just look at the present curious anomaly; both the United States and Britain have at present much higher rates of inflation than Germany and Switzerland. And yet the dollar and the pound sterling have been riding high on the exchange markets in relation to the DMark and the Swiss franc. Other influences—cyclical forces on the current account balances, interest rate differentials, North Sea oil, the use of the dollar for the payment of much higher oil bills—have been stronger. Which side will in the end win in this game of inflation differentials versus the rest? My guess is: relative inflation rates. But in the meantime difficult problems arise for exchange rate policy, and there may be a lot of forced "upward harmonization" of inflation rates at the expense of the present low inflation countries.

VI

Let me quickly mention in passing some other influences on the exchange rate.

Relative money supplies may in the longer run help explain the evolution of exchange rates, perhaps mainly because in the long run they influence relative inflation rates. In the short run they provide little help for explaining (or forecasting) the development of bilateral exchange rates (as I could easily demonstrate by practical examples). The EEC Commission once thought one could ensure stable exchange rate relationships among member countries by prescribing to them coordinated money supply goals; this was, however, an oversimplification, apart from the immense difficulties of achieving such goals in practice.

Another factor which has drawn particular public attention upon itself has been relative levels of interest rates. Last year some American observers held the view that an international "interest rate war" was going on with the aim of influencing the exchange rate to one's advantage. One well-known American expert even went so far last autumn as to maintain that American interest rate policy was made more in Frankfurt than in Washington. This sounds far-fetched in view of the very large differences in interest rates between the United States and Germany. It also represented a curious reversal of a view put forward ten years ago by Milton Friedman (the Nobel Prize winner) at a discussion in Frankfurt, namely that German monetary policy was in reality made in Washington. As concerns recent interest rate movements, I think it has become clear and accepted that both the Bundesbank and the Federal Reserve did nothing but respond, as best they could, to the inflationary pressures in their own domestic fields. If there has been an international escalation of interest rates, it was in response to an international escalation of inflation. At present, it is the Federal Reserve which is the leader in the international escalation of interest rates, reflecting the strength of inflationary pressures in the United States.

What happened to the diversification out of the dollar into other currencies? We have occasionally felt its disturbing effect on the exchange rate of the DMark over a few months. But over the last twelve months as a whole there has been little net movement out of the dollar or into the DMark. On the contrary, since the beginning of 1979 Germany has experienced a significant net outflow of foreign exchange, approximately in line with our current account deficit, so that the inflows and outflows of capital have more or less netted out. At present at least, I do not see any reason for getting alarmed about the "reserve role" of the DMark. Can we perhaps lay the problem of reserve diversification at rest and forget altogether about the proposed substitution account? I do not think so. Things may change if the OPEC countries accumulate such large surpluses of foreign exchange that the urge to diversify in order to spread the risk over various currencies will be a natural reaction. Therefore, it may still be useful to supplement our reserve system by a substitution account, as a safety valve for such an eventuality.

VII

Summing up my experiences: Some things have gone badly, some have gone well. But overall, the system has shown a great shock absorption capacity. Its rather pragmatic evolution and its diversity have been the natural answer to the many and very diverse external shocks and challenges to which it was exposed during the 1970s.

Should the international monetary system be reformed, or improved, and *can* it be improved?

There are two fields where improvement or reform has long been sought after—better control over international liquidity and a reform of the reserve system to get away from the one-sided dependence on the dollar. In both directions, I see little practical chance for major changes. As concerns control over international liquidity, this is particularly true after the recent gold price boom, which has inflated international liquidity in an explosive way (if and when the higher book value of national gold reserves is mobilized, that is, translated into higher collateral values for currency credits).

Perhaps the following can be achieved:

- to establish a substitution account in the IMF as a safety valve for the largely dollar-based reserve system
- to make the fund's surveillance of exchange rate policies more effective
- to ensure more transparency and possibly more prudential control over international financial markets (Euromarkets)

But these are marginal matters compared with the main problems besetting the system. The real dangers to the world monetary system are connected with:

- the oil shock
- worldwide inflation and concomitant inflation differentials
- the declining purchasing power of the world's key currency, the dollar

VIII

Let me make some brief comments on these major problems.

The first is the oil price explosion with its tremendous financial and economic impact on the balances of payments, the financing of payments deficits, inflation, and growth. There are several differences between the present and the previous oil shock. The major one may turn out to be that this time the global payments imbalance between the oil-exporting and oil-importing countries is not likely to be reduced so quickly as after 1974, as oil prices are more likely to continue rising while oil-exporting countries are unlikely to increase their imports as fast as after the first oil shock. Should this scenario turn out to be true, the financing of deficits may require some new approaches, including a greater role of the IMF and more direct lending by the OPEC countries to the deficit countries.

Perhaps we shall also at some point have to invent new kinds of assets to offer to the OPEC countries in order to guarantee them a better maintenance of their real income, so as to ensure that they will not succumb too much to the temptation to leave their oil in the ground. Note: it is not so much the insecurity of the foreign exchange value of the dollar but the "real" purchasing power of the dollar (and of other currencies) that is the decisive factor for the motivation of the OPEC countries.

Overall, despite the aggravations due to the accumulated heavy indebtedness of some countries and the likely continuation of high oil surpluses, the financing problems appear to be still manageable although probably requiring some new approaches.

What looks less manageable is the inflationary impact. The cost push from oil prices, added to the unsolved domestic inflation problem, has confronted major countries with their worst inflation headache ever. Some major countries are beyond the point where a "gradualist" approach still promises success, and a more forceful therapy may be required. Inflation, like dictatorship, has to be fought before it seizes power. Once it becomes entrenched in the system, it is terribly difficult and painful to squeeze it out. The IMF, in its latest annual report, has warned that the strategy of gradualism in the fight against inflation has failed in high inflation countries. Why? Because it is too difficult to maintain it consistently over long stretches of time, and because excessively gentle gradualism is ill suited to breaking the inflationary expectations of a public that has become cynical toward mere lip service to price stability. When I was recently asked what I would do if I had some responsibility in this country, my instinctive reaction was to quote the well-known reply of the Irishman who was asked the way toward a faraway street: "If a were you, I wouldn't start from here."

We cannot afford to let inflation at present levels drag on for very much longer. Quite apart from the domestic consequences, the United States—and the world—cannot afford it because this would lead to a continuous weakening of the dollar, and of America's position in the world; and it would exert enormous pressures on the world payments system, undermining both the oil-pricing moderation and the dollar-asset preference of OPEC countries. Europe cannot afford to continue the present inflation because this would inevitably perpetuate, perhaps even widen, the existing inflation differences among European countries, and disrupt over the longer run any attempt at monetary and exchange rate stabilization inside Europe.

IX

It is a fairly safe bet that, with the present energy and inflation problems on our hands, the shocks and challenges to our international monetary system will become not less but perhaps even greater. This leads me to the conclusion that we shall need elastic defenses. On the occasion of the first oil shock, Mr. Witteveen, then the managing director of the IMF, said in a major policy speech in January 1974: "In the present situation, a large measure of floating is inavoidable and indeed desirable." I think this is still valid today, after the second oil shock.

We have perhaps learned since 1974 how to manage the system better, both in a worldwide context and in the context of regional currency areas. One particular lesson has been that exchange rate stability cannot be based merely on intervention in the exchange markets, but only on domestic stability, and that too much intervention is apt to lead to unrealistic exchange rates and to spread inflation from one country to another. We must have the courage and the skill for judicious and elastic adaptation of exchange rates, be it in a managed floating system or in a regional currency bloc like the EMS. As I have already mentioned, I do not see a realistic prospect of establishing a target zone for the dollar.

We have also learned more about the interdependence of our economies and economic policies. Under the present more difficult circumstances we shall need even more international cooperation (with the proviso that cooperation should not consist merely of an adjustment upward to higher inflation elsewhere).

My experience of thirty years of activity in the domestic and international monetary field has made me confident that our countries have always risen to the occasion when they were severely challenged. It may well be that in a democratic system necessary but unpopular decisions can only be taken under the pressure of a crisis, in our case, a monetary crisis. But we have overcome, more or less successfully, all the many previous crises, and shall do it again.

It is on the basis of such past experiences that I have become an optimist, in a rather moderate sense, it is true. I do not believe that all goes well, but I believe that not everything will go wrong.

Part Five

The Outlook for the Dollar and Other International Assets

Introductory Remarks

Whereas part 4 was devoted to a discussion of monetary instability because of the presumed lack of control over the volume of international liquidity, part 5 is focused on monetary turbulence allegedly arising from an evolution of the monetary system and, more specifically, from a drift toward a multiple-currency reserve system.

The presumption that a monetary system based on more than one reserve asset is inherently unstable has a long history. The demise of the dollar as the only reserve asset, accompanied by the rise of a few other national currencies as components of official reserve holding, a renewed effort to promote the SDR (special drawing rights), and the emergence of the European Monetary System gave rise to increased apprehensions about the future stability of international monetary arrangements and contributed to an intensified search for alternative solutions. Papers presented in part 5 blend an evaluation of prospects for alternative future monetary arrangements and an assessment of their respective advantages and disadvantages.

Edward Bernstein focuses on the future of the dollar and other national currencies in the role of international reserve assets. He also discusses the future of the SDR, especially in the light of a proposal to establish a Substitution Account at the International Monetary Fund. Michele Fratianni concentrates on an arrangement based on regional currency blocs as exemplified by the European Monetary System.

Among the commentators, Helen Junz focuses specifically on the merits of a Substitution Account proposal, and Giovanni Magnifico addresses a number of points raised in Fratianni's paper. Ralph Bryant discusses the prospects for alternative monetary arrangements against a broader background of world economic and political evolution, and Fritz Machlup evaluates renewed suggestions to restore the monetary position of gold.

The Future of the Dollar and Other Reserve Assets

Edward M. Bernstein

Financing the U.S. Payments Deficit

The international monetary system is far different from that established at Bretton Woods. The main reason is that the United States has not performed the stabilizing role that is the function of a reserve center. The deterioration in the U.S. payments position and the inflation in the United States made it impossible to maintain a stable foreign exchange value for the dollar. The inability of the United States to adjust its balance of payments, in spite of two devaluations, compelled an abandonment of the par value system and the introduction of a regime of floating exchange rates. The recent experience with floating rates has not been satisfactory, and it would be desirable to modify the present regime in a way that would help to stabilize the dollar. That can be done only if the United States accepts greater responsibility for the foreign exchange value of the dollar, not merely through intervention but in its fiscal and monetary policies.

The decline of the dollar occurred gradually over an extended period. From 1951 to 1957, the United States had a large surplus on goods and services that was just about balanced by U.S. economic grants and government credits. Private capital outflow was small, except in 1956–1957, and foreign capital inflow was minimal. The deficit on an official reserve basis was about $4.5 billion (U.S. billion), although the concept is not meaningful during the period that the United States was giving Marshall Plan aid. The situation changed in the following twelve years. The current account was in surplus by about $33 billion, including reinvested earnings of direct investment enterprises. In the meantime, U.S. private foreign investments increased enormously in spite of restraints intended to hold down capital outflow and attempts to finance more of the investment with funds raised abroad. Foreign capital inflow,

410

excluding official funds, also increased considerably and was especially large in 1968–1969 when the tight monetary policy induced U.S. banks to draw heavily on the Eurocurrency market. The deficit on an official reserve basis was about $14.5 billion in these twelve years.

From 1970 to the first quarter of 1973, the dollar was under intermittent pressure. The current account in these thirteen quarters was in deficit by $4.8 billion, with a modest surplus in the recession of 1970. The distinctive feature of the balance of payments was not the deficit on current account but the increase in U.S. capital outflow and the return of foreign private funds, including repayment of the Eurodollar credits. In much of this period there was a flight from the dollar. As a result, the deficit on an official reserve basis was nearly $60 billion. It was especially large in 1971 ($29.7 billion) and during the first quarter of 1973 ($10 billion) when devaluations of the dollar occurred.

Since March 1973, the dollar has been a floating currency. In spite of this, there have been unusually large changes in the current and capital accounts. The current account was in surplus by $32.2 billion from the second quarter of 1973 to 1976 but in deficit by $27.9 billion in 1977–1979. The current balances include $67.6 billion of reinvested earnings of U.S. corporations and $12.3 billion of reinvested earnings of foreign corporate affiliates in the United States from the second quarter of 1973 to the fourth quarter of 1979. The U.S. capital outflow in this period, excluding official reserve assets, averaged $43.7 billion a year but exceeded $60 billion in both 1978 and 1979. Foreign capital inflow, excluding official assets, was very much less. As a result, the deficit on an official reserve basis was $85.7 billion from the second quarter of 1973 to the end of 1978, of which $66.8 billion was in 1977–1978. In 1979 the official reserve balance was in surplus by $15.6 billion, according to preliminary data.

The deterioration in the payments position was accompanied by a weakening of the dollar. Until 1969 this manifested itself in a growing preference for taking gold rather than dollars in settlement of the deficit. From 1951 to 1957 all of the deficit was financed by an increase in official holdings of dollars. U.S. gold reserves increased slightly because of the gold investment of the International Monetary Fund (IMF), and other U.S. reserve assets increased moderately. From 1957 to 1969 U.S. gold reserves decreased by $11 billion in spite of the additional gold investment by the IMF. Other U.S. reserve assets increased considerably, mainly because of drawings by other countries on their swap lines with the Federal Reserve. Foreign official assets in the United States increased by $5.9 billion. (See table 1.)

411

TABLE 1

CHANGES IN U.S. RESERVE ASSETS AND FOREIGN OFFICIAL ASSETS IN THE UNITED STATES, 1951–1979

Year or Period	U.S. Reserve Assets (increase +)					Foreign Official Assets in U.S. (increase −)
	Total	Gold[a]	Special drawing rights	Reserve position in IMF	Foreign currencies	
1951–57	0.57	0.04[b]	—	0.53	—	−4.70
1958–69	−7.88	−11.00[b]	—	0.34	2.78	−5.89
1970	−2.48	−0.79	0.85[c]	−0.39	−2.16	−7.36
1971	−2.35	−0.87[b]	0.25[c]	−1.35	−0.38	−27.39
1972	0	−0.55[b]	0.70[c]	−0.15	0	−10.29
1973I	−0.21	—	—	0.01	−0.23	−9.77
1973II–IV	0.06	—	−0.01	0.02	0.04	4.68
1974	1.47	—	0.17	1.27	0.03	−10.24
1975	0.85	—	0.07	0.47	0.32	−5.26
1976	2.56	—	0.08	2.21	0.27	−13.07
1977	0.38	0.12	0.12	0.29	−0.16	−35.42
1978	−0.73	0.07	−1.25	−4.23	4.68	−31.00
1979	1.11	0.07	1.14	0.19	−0.28	14.44

NOTE: Dash (—) indicates no changes observed.

[a] At official monetary price of $35 until 1972, $38 until February 1973, and $42.22 thereafter.

[b] Includes gold investment of the International Monetary Fund of $2.00 million at end of 1957 and $800 million at end of 1969, all repaid by 1972. Changes reflect gold restitution of IMF but not gold auctions of U.S. Treasury.

[c] Includes allocations of $2.29 billion in 1970-1972 and $1.14 billion in 1979.

SOURCE: Author. Compare *International Financial Statistics*, Yearbook 1981, pp. 438-39, which gives slightly revised figures for U.S. holdings of foreign currencies and foreign official assets in the United States.

The enormous official reserve deficit of 1970–1971 was financed almost entirely by the increase of $34.7 billion in foreign official assets. U.S. gold reserves decreased by only $1.7 billion. Very little of the deficit was settled in gold because it was understood that large-scale conversions would necessitate the termination of gold convertibility. Other reserve assets fell by $3.2 billion in spite of the creation of special drawing rights (SDR) and the substantial allocation to the United States. In 1972 and the first quarter of 1973, when there was a renewed flight from the dollar, foreign official holdings increased by $20.1 billion. U.S. gold reserves decreased by $550 million in 1972 (still valued at $35 an ounce) in repayment of the rest of the gold investment of the IMF. Other U.S. reserve assets increased somewhat in 1972 because of a new allocation of SDRs and fell slightly in the first quarter of 1973.

Floating Exchange Rates

Since the adoption of floating exchange rates in March 1973, the strength or weakness of the dollar has been reflected partly in the change of the foreign exchange value of the dollar and partly in the change of U.S. reserve assets and foreign official holdings of assets in the United States. From the end of March 1973 to the end of 1978, foreign official holdings of U.S. assets increased by $90.3 billion. About three fourths of the total ($66.4 billion) was accumulated in 1977–1978. The huge deficit was due to the sharp deterioration in the trade balance and to the flight from the dollar as it depreciated in 1977–1978. There was a small increase in U.S. gold reserves from restitution by the IMF, a large increase in foreign currency holdings because of borrowing of DMarks and Swiss francs in 1978, a moderate decrease in SDRs, and virtually no change in the reserve position in the IMF because of large drawings in 1978. In 1979, the balance on an official reserve basis was in surplus by $15.6 billion because of the return of funds to cover short positions in the dollar. Foreign official holdings of dollars fell by $14.4 billion, and U.S. reserve assets increased by $1.1 billion as a result of a new allocation of SDRs.

The purpose of floating exchange rates was to have changes in exchange rates absorb some of the pressure on the dollar rather than depend on the drawing down of U.S. reserve assets or the accumulation of foreign official assets in the United States. From March 1973 to the third quarter of 1975, the dollar rates of exchange for the currencies of the Group of Ten and Switzerland fluctuated sharply with little net change in the average over these thirty months. The dollar fell moderately against the DMark and the guilder and sharply against the Swiss franc, but this was offset by a rise against sterling, the yen, and the lira. There was relatively little accumulation of assets in this country by foreign official institutions ($8.5 billion), and nearly all of that was by the oil-exporting countries. Although the fluctuations in exchange rates were large, they did hold down the official reserve deficit.

In the following two years to September 1977, the average foreign exchange value of the dollar fell very slightly in terms of the currencies of the Group of Ten and Switzerland, weighted by their exports. The dollar was lower relative to the Swiss franc, the yen, and the currencies in the European joint float, but it was higher relative to the lira, sterling, the French franc, and the Swedish krona. Furthermore, the fluctuations in this period were relatively small. Foreign official institutions accumulated about $35 billion in assets in the United States, but nearly three fourths of that amount was accumulated by the oil-exporting countries. The Western European countries also added considerably to their dollar holdings, mainly the United Kingdom, France, and Italy, countries that had drawn down their reserves in previous years. On the whole, the regime of floating exchange rates worked very well from the third quarter of 1975 to the third quarter of 1977.

The situation changed abruptly in the following thirteen months from the end of September 1977 to the end of October 1978. In this short period, the dollar fell by an average of about 20 percent against the currencies of the Group of Ten and Switzerland. The fall was very large relative to the Swiss franc (36 percent), the yen (32.6 percent), the DMark (24.2 percent), and the other currencies in the European joint float, and almost as large against the French franc, sterling, and the Swedish krona. Such a large fall of the dollar in so short a period could not have been due to changes in underlying economic conditions. The inflation accelerated in the United States, but no more than in some other countries. The payments position did deteriorate sharply, with a large trade deficit in 1977 and 1978, and this stimulated an outflow of funds in anticipation of the depreciation of the dollar. From September 1977 to October 1978, foreign official assets in the United States increased by $36 billion, nine-tenths in holdings of Western Europe and Japan.

Until the end of October 1978, it was the policy of the United States not to intervene in the exchange market except to avoid disorderly fluctuations. On November 1, 1978, the secretary of the Treasury and the chairman of the Federal Reserve announced a new policy aimed at preventing excessive depreciation of the dollar, and for that purpose the United States mobilized large resources to be used for intervention in the exchange market if necessary. Apart from drawings on the swaps and use of resources of the IMF, the Treasury borrowed DMarks and Swiss francs in the capital markets of Germany and Switzerland and sold gold at auction. In the fourth quarter of 1978, the United States used more reserve assets than in any quarter since 1971. At the same time, the Federal Reserve raised the discount rate by one percentage point, the first time this had been done since 1933. This was an acknowledgment that the behavior of exchange rates is an integral part of monetary policy.

These measures restored confidence in the dollar and induced a large backflow of funds to cover short positions. The inflow continued until about the end of May 1979 and had a great effect on the foreign exchange markets. In these seven months, the foreign exchange value of the dollar rose by an average of about 10 percent against the currencies of the Group of Ten and Switzerland, with the increase considerably more against the yen and the Swiss franc. Foreign official assets in the United States were reduced by $21.2 billion in the first five months of 1979. As the improvement of the payments position was mainly in the form of capital flows to cover short positions, it could not last very long. In the four months to the end of September 1979, the dollar fell by an average of about 6 percent, and foreign official assets increased by $8.7 billion, nearly all in the holdings of the industrial countries. The fall of the dollar in the final weeks of this period was so rapid that it disrupted the exchange markets.

Because of the fall of the dollar, the Federal Reserve raised the discount rate in steps of half a percentage point in July, August, and September, and on October 6, 1979, the Federal Reserve raised the discount rate again by one percentage point and imposed marginal reserve requirements on the increase in certain money market liabilities of member banks. The dollar recovered in October and early November, and the industrial countries were able to reduce their holdings about as much as they had increased them from May to September. The dollar weakened again after mid-November, in large part because of adverse international developments. This was accompanied by a sharp rise in the price of gold from early November to late January 1980, not only in dollars but in all other currencies as well. Because of the accelerated inflation, the Federal Reserve raised the discount rate once more, by a full percentage point, on February 15. Thus, because the policy of more active support for the dollar was adopted on November 1, 1978, there have been three increases of the discount rate in steps of one percentage point and three in steps of one half of a percentage point that have brought the rate from 8.5 to 13 percent in sixteen months.

Federal Reserve policy in this period was directed as much or more to slowing the inflation as to supporting the dollar in the exchange market. The fact is that a monetary policy that is directed to one objective is helpful in achieving the other. Over the sixteen months since November 1978 that the policy of managed floating has been in effect, the dollar has risen and fallen within a range of about 10 percent. On February 25, 1980, the average foreign exchange value of the dollar in terms of the currencies of the Group of Ten and Switzerland, weighted by their global trade in 1978, was 6.5 percent higher than it had been on October 31, 1978. Most of this large average appreciation of the dollar was due to a rise of 38.8 percent against the yen and of 11.5 percent against the Swiss franc, only partly offset by a fall of 8.8 percent against sterling. Relative to the currencies in the European Monetary System, the dollar rose by an average of 2.2 percent in this period. (See table 2.)

U.S. Assets of Foreign Official Institutions

Because of the importance of U.S. financial markets, foreign banks and business firms and other private foreigners hold a large amount of funds in the United States. At the end of November 1979, U.S. banks reported liabilities to them of $113.1 billion. By far the larger part of these liabilities was to foreign banks ($94.9 billion), mainly the foreign offices of banks in the United States, with a considerable amount due to other private foreigners ($18.2 billion). In addition, a relatively small amount of assets was held by international institutions ($2.7 billion). Although private holdings of assets in the United States doubled in 1978–1979, they are not excessive. All of these funds are needed as working balances and as cover for liabilities and commitments in dollars.

The U.S. assets of foreign official institutions reached a peak of $157.1 billion at the end of January 1979 and then declined to $143 billion at the end of December 1979. By far the greater part of these funds is held by the central banks of Western Europe, Japan, Canada, and other developed countries. In January 1979 their holdings made up about 75 percent of total U.S. liabilities to foreign official institutions, although the proportion declined to less than 70 percent by the end of November. The members of the Organization of Petroleum Exporting Countries (OPEC) are also very large holders of official funds in the United States. Data are not available on the precise amount of their holdings, but the balance-of-payments reports on the change in their official assets in 1972–1979 would indicate that they held more than 25 percent of the total at the end of December 1979. Thus, the

TABLE 2

FOREIGN EXCHANGE VALUE OF THE DOLLAR IN TEN CURRENCIES, 1973–1980

	Foreign Units per Dollar, End of Month						Percentage Change in Dollar to[a]				
	Mar. 19, 1973	Sept. 1975	Sept. 1977	Oct. 1978	Sept. 1979	Feb. 25, 1980	Sept. 1975	Sept. 1977	Oct. 1978	Sept. 1979	Feb. 25, 1980
Belgium	39.635	39.920	35.742	27.580	28.220	28.580	0.72	−10.47	−22.84	2.32	1.28
France	4.5351	4.5126	4.9033	4.0028	4.0925	4.1320	−0.50	8.66	−18.37	2.24	0.97
Germany	2.8241	2.6466	2.3074	1.7490	1.7410	1.7615	−6.29	−12.82	−24.20	10.46	1.18
Italy	563.77	686.81	882.25	794.50	802.00	814.95	21.82	28.46	−9.95	0.94	1.61
Neth.	2.8969	2.7241	2.4565	1.8925	1.9310	1.9406	−5.90	−9.82	−22.96	2.03	0.50
Canada[b]	1.0028	0.9750	0.9316	0.8597	0.8617	0.8687	2.85	4.66	8.36	−0.23	−0.81
Japan	262.81	302.76	265.43	178.95	224.45	248.34	15.20	−12.33	−32.58	25.43	10.64
Sweden	4.2781	4.4964	4.8327	4.1800	4.1260	4.1960	5.10	7.48	−13.51	−1.29	1.70
Switz.	3.2500	2.7439	2.3385	1.4963	1.5535	1.6690	−15.57	−14.77	−36.01	3.82	7.43
U.K.[b]	2.4063	2.0433	1.7465	2.0770	2.2038	2.2765	17.77	16.99	−15.91	−5.75	3.30

[a] Rise or fall (−) of the dollar from preceding date.

[b] U.S. dollars per foreign currency unit.

SOURCE: Author.

417

amount of official funds held in the United States by the non-oil-developing countries is not very large. Of course, official agencies also hold a large amount of assets denominated in dollars outside the United States.

Nearly nine-tenths of the present holdings of foreign official assets in the United States were accumulated in the ten years to the end of 1979. Originally, all of these assets were held as monetary reserves, and even now they are a major form of reserves in many countries, particularly the non-oil-developing countries. Though some of the U.S. assets of the members of OPEC fulfill the function of reserves—that is, they are intended for use in international settlements—a large part of their holdings is of an investment character. The U.S. assets of a number of industrial countries are also more than they need for reserve purposes, but they were not acquired as investments. The large increase in Western European holdings occurred in two periods, 1971–1973, when these countries added $32.1 billion to their U.S. assets, and 1977–1978, when they added $47.1 billion to their U.S. assets. In the earlier period they accumulated U.S. assets to facilitate the establishment and maintenance of a new par value for the dollar as part of the Smithsonian Agreement. In the later period they accumulated these assets in order to avoid an excessive depreciation of the dollar in terms of their currencies. (See table 3.)

The real value of the foreign official assets in the United States has been greatly reduced by the inflation in the United States and the depreciation of the dollar. Over the ten years to 1979, the unit value of U.S. exports rose by 140 percent. Over the same period, the dollar depreciated by an average of 25 percent against the currencies of the Group of Ten and Switzerland, weighted by their exports. The depreciation has been especially large against the deutsche mark (53 percent) and the Swiss franc (63 percent). If allowance is made for the rise in prices in the other countries of the Group of Ten and Switzerland, the value of dollar reserves in paying for imports from these countries has fallen even more. These ten-year comparisons exaggerate the real loss to official holders of dollars, as much of the present holdings were acquired in the past three years.

Although the real value of their dollar reserves has fallen, many non-oil-developing countries have been beneficiaries of the U.S. inflation and the depreciation of the dollar. A very large part of their debts is denominated in dollars, and the rise in the dollar prices of their export goods has greatly reduced the real burden of their indebtedness—that is, the volume of exports needed to meet interest and amortization. Some developing countries whose currencies are linked to the dollar, however, have incurred debts in the currencies that have appreciated,

418

TABLE 3

U.S. LIABILITIES TO OFFICIAL INSTITUTIONS, 1950–1979

(billions of dollars)

End of Year	Total Foreign Countries[a]	Western Europe[b]	Can-ada	Latin America and Caribbean Republics	Asia	Africa	Other Coun-tries[c]
1950	5.40[d]	—	—	—	—	—	—
1955	8.76[d]	—	—	—	—	—	—
1960	11.09[d]	—	—	—	—	—	—
1965	15.82	8.83	1.70	1.55	3.31	0.19	0.24
1966	14.89	7.77	1.33	1.31	3.95	0.28	0.25
1967	18.19	10.32	1.31	1.58	4.43	0.25	0.30
1968	17.34	8.06	1.87	1.86	5.00	0.25	0.30
1969	16.00	7.07	1.62	1.91	4.55	0.55	0.29
1970	23.78	13.62	2.95	1.68	4.71	0.41	0.41
1971	50.65	30.13	3.98	1.43	13.82	0.42	0.87
1972	61.53	34.20	4.28	1.73	17.58	0.78	2.96
1973	66.86	45.76	3.85	2.54	10.89	0.79	3.03
1974	76.82	44.33	3.66	4.42	18.63	3.16	2.63
1975	80.71	45.70	3.13	4.45	22.55	2.98	1.90
1976	91.98	45.88	3.41	4.91	34.11	1.89	1.78
1977	126.08	70.75	2.33	4.63	45.68	1.74	0.95
1978	156.75	93.01	2.49	5.04	53.05	2.41	0.75
1979	142.98	85.50	1.90	6.36	46.31	2.41	0.50

NOTE: Dash (—) indicates that data for individual countries not available for 1950, 1955, 1960.

[a] Includes effect of valuation changes in liabilities denominated in foreign currencies.

[b] Includes Bank for International Settlements and European Fund.

[c] Includes countries in Oceania, Eastern Europe, and Western European dependencies in Latin America.

[d] Estimated.

SOURCE: Author. See *Federal Reserve Board Bulletin,* October 1981, table 3.14, p. A58, for minor revisions in these data.

and the depreciation of the dollar may have increased the real burden of such debts. In calculating the gains and losses from changes in exchange rates, moreover, the non-oil-developing countries assume that if they had shifted their reserves from dollars to other currencies they could have benefited as debtors from the depreciation of the dollar without incurring a loss as holders of dollar assets.

The oil-exporting countries are large holders of dollar assets, and although some of them have large debts denominated in dollars, others do not. The low absorbers among these countries regard their dollar assets as long-term investments. For them, the depreciation of the dollar relative to certain other currencies means that their dollar investments have been much less profitable than their investments denominated in other currencies. As a consequence, they have reduced their preference for holding dollar assets relative to other assets. This is seen in the way they invest their official reserve surplus. In 1974, the members of OPEC invested all of their U.S. surplus in this country and transferred large sums from other areas to invest here. In the first three quarters of 1979, the members of OPEC transferred all their U.S. surplus to other areas and reduced their official holdings in the United States, but in the fourth quarter they added $4.8 billion to their U.S. assets. There were, however, large unreported capital flows of the oil-exporting countries, mainly capital inflow, which have contributed to the huge statistical discrepancy since 1975.

The dollar assets of some industrial countries are far in excess of their reserve needs. They were acquired as a result of official intervention to avoid large fluctuations in the dollar exchange rates for their currencies. In theory, the policy was to buy dollars when the dollar was weak and to sell dollars when the dollar was strong. In 1973–1976, intervention was moderate and the Western European monetary authorities were successful in reversing their intervention. In 1977–1978, however, they acquired an enormous amount of dollars and were able to dispose of only a moderate part of them in 1979. For the Western European countries with strong currencies, the depreciation of the dollar in 1977–1978 involved very large losses. In its latest annual report, the Bundesbank said: "The valuation of the monetary reserves and other foreign currency positions necessitated write-downs totaling DM10,574.9 million in the 1978 annual accounts (1977: DM7,880.2 million)." In 1979, the dollar fell relatively little against European currencies other than sterling, so that their exchange loss on official holdings was very small that year.

Maintaining the Foreign Exchange Value of Dollar Reserves

A country can properly perform the function of a reserve center only if its currency is as attractive as other reserve assets. If foreign monetary authorities come to prefer other reserve assets, the country's balance of payments will be weakened and the exchange rate for its currency undermined. The shift in preference from dollars to gold in 1958–1970 contributed to the weakness of the dollar that compelled its devaluation, and the change to preference for deutsche marks and Swiss francs as reserve assets contributed to the depreciation of the dollar in 1978–1979.

The change to preference for other reserve assets did not manifest itself to a significant extent in a reduction of official holdings of dollars. Rather, it took the form of an unwillingness to add to existing holdings of dollars. This is particularly important under present conditions. In order to balance its payments, the United States must have an inflow of foreign capital sufficient to finance the balance on current account, plus U.S. foreign loans and investments. The foreign capital inflow could include official funds from the oil-exporting countries and some official funds from other countries but should consist mainly of private capital.

The weakness in the balance of payments that led to the large depreciation of the dollar in 1977–1978 originated in the current-account deficit, particularly the huge trade deficit. It was aggravated by an excessive outflow of private U.S. capital and an inadequate inflow of foreign capital, much of it in anticipation of a depreciation of the dollar. The change in official capital inflow, other than the funds of the industrial countries, also contributed to the weakness of the dollar. Members of OPEC increased their official U.S. assets by $6.4 billion in 1977, but they transferred about $11.5 billion of their U.S. receipts to other areas. In 1978 they transferred about $16.7 billion to other areas, including $725 million that they drew down from the official U.S. assets. The non-oil-developing countries added $1.5 billion to their official U.S. assets in 1977 and only $200 million in 1978. The industrial countries, in contrast, added $28.8 billion to their official assets in 1977 and $34.3 billion in 1978 in order to support the dollar.

If the foreign exchange value of the dollar were more stable, members of OPEC would be disposed to invest more of their official funds in the United States, and other developing countries would be willing to add to their dollar reserves in this country. The restoration of confidence in the dollar is a long-run process requiring greater recognition by the United States of its responsibility for the foreign exchange value of the dollar. The measures taken by the Federal Reserve and the Treasury on November 1, 1978, are indications of a major change in the U.S. attitude toward the foreign exchange value of the dollar. This was reaffirmed by the action of the Federal Reserve on October 6, 1979, and again on February 15, 1980, when the discount rate was raised by one percentage point.

The time is favorable for considering what further steps can be taken to give foreign monetary authorities greater confidence in the

421

dollar. One measure that has been frequently proposed is the establishment of a Substitution Account in the International Monetary Fund in which countries could place some or all of their dollar reserves. A number of complex legal and political problems will have to be resolved before such an account can be established, but the economic aspects are relatively clear. A participating country would transfer to the account whatever dollar assets it does not wish to retain, and it would receive in return a credit balance in the account denominated in special drawing rights. The account in turn would transfer these assets to the U.S. Treasury in exchange for a new series of interest-bearing securities whose SDR value would be guaranteed in one way or another. Thus, the value of the balances in the account in terms of the dollar would change continuously with the dollar exchange rates for the currencies in the SDR.

The present method of valuing a unit of special drawing rights as equivalent to a collection of sixteen currencies was adopted on July 1, 1974, when these currencies had a value of U.S.$1.20635 per unit of SDRs. The currency composition of the unit was changed slightly on July 1, 1978, without affecting its foreign exchange value at that time. Since this method of determining the value of a unit of SDRs was adopted, its monthly average value in U.S. dollars has ranged between a low of $1.1438 in June 1976 and a high of $1.32559 in October 1978. Thus, at its monthly average low, a unit of SDRs was 5.2 percent below its initial dollar value, and at its monthly average high it was 9.9 percent above its initial dollar value. Four-fifths of the fall of the dollar from its initial value in SDRs occurred in the four months from June to October 1978, and nearly half of the fall was in the last month before the new exchange-rate policy was adopted. (See table 4.)

The Substitution Account would provide participating members with an automatic diversification of their foreign-exchange reserves in the sixteen currencies that compose a unit of SDRs in proportion to their importance in that unit. At present exchange rates, the U.S. dollar is 30 percent of the value of a unit of SDRs, the other nine currencies of the Group of Ten are 58 percent of its value, and the remaining six currencies are 12 percent of its value. The changes in the dollar value of a unit of SDRs are almost entirely due to fluctuations in the dollar exchange rates for the other nine currencies of the Group of Ten. It is interesting to note that the value of the dollar in terms of the other fifteen currencies in a unit of SDRs has changed about as much as the Federal Reserve index of the average foreign exchange value of the dollar in terms of the other currencies in the Group of Ten and Switzerland. In general, the value of the dollar has been slightly higher relative to the other currencies in a unit of SDRs than in the Federal Reserve

TABLE 4

VALUE OF SDR AND FOREIGN EXCHANGE VALUE OF THE DOLLAR,
1974–1979

(monthly average)

Date	Dollars per Unit of SDRs	Value of Dollar in Other SDR Currencies[a]	Foreign Exchange Value of Dollar[b]
1974:			
June	1.20635	100.00	100.02
Sept.	1.18713	102.44	102.91
Dec.	1.22450	97.80	98.59
1975:			
Mar.	1.24747	95.15	93.93
June	1.24650	95.26	94.79
Sept.	1.16427	105.51	103.04
Dec.	1.17066	104.63	103.51
1976:			
Mar.	1.15767	106.42	105.12
June	1.14380	108.41	107.05
Sept.	1.15366	106.99	105.70
Dec.	1.15588	107.48	105.33
1977:			
Mar.	1.15756	106.44	105.19
June	1.16220	105.79	104.35
Sept.	1.16126	105.92	103.77
Dec.	1.20097	100.67	98.36
1978:			
Mar.	1.22979	97.17	94.80
June	1.22977	97.18	94.74
Sept.	1.27367	92.29	89.51
Dec.	1.28434	95.50	88.52
1979:			
Mar.	1.28693	90.91	88.39
June	1.27705	91.94	89.56
Sept.	1.30451	89.15	86.73
Dec.	1.31215	88.40	86.32

[a] The dollar value of the other fifteen currencies in a unit of SDRs is equal to the dollar value of the unit minus forty U.S. cents. The inverse of this value on a June 1974 base is the index of the change in the value of the dollar in the other fifteen currencies.

[b] Federal Reserve index of the foreign exchange value of the dollar in the currencies of the Group of Ten and Switzerland, weighted by their global trade in 1972-1976; March 1973 = 100.

SOURCES: *Federal Reserve Bulletin,* August 1978, p. 700, and subsequent issues. *International Financial Statistics,* February 1980. The same data are in the issue of October 1981, p. 10. The method of valuing the SDR was changed on January 1, 1981, without affecting its previous value.

index. That is mainly due to the currency composition, particularly the inclusion of the Swiss franc in the Federal Reserve index, and partly due to the weighting.

The purpose of the Substitution Account is to avoid large changes in the currency composition of reserves. Countries that participate in the account, however, must be able to use their SDR-denominated reserve assets in balance-of-payments settlements in much the same way as they now use their dollar reserves. In order to use these assets, however, the participating countries would have to convert them into a currency that is widely used in the exchange market, precisely as they now do with the SDRs in the Special Account. Although participating countries may need other currencies, they are most likely to want dollars. The United States is the one country that can undertake to convert the SDR-denominated assets into dollars. If the U.S. Treasury were to buy assets held in the Substitution Account, it could either become a holder of such assets itself or retire them in exchange for an equivalent amount of U.S. securities held by the account. Some other countries holding or acquiring dollars might also be willing to sell them for a balance in the account. Although the IMF holds the currencies that participants would need, it could not buy the SDR-denominated balances in the account under its present powers.

Countries that use their balances in the Substitution Account would have to receive the current value of the SDRs in dollars or another currency. The dollar value of the securities held by the account, however, would fluctuate with changes in the dollar value of a unit of SDRs. The unrealized changes in the dollar value of these assets would present no immediate problem, although there would be profits or losses if the account were liquidated in the future. Another country that acquired a balance in the account from a participating country, moreover, would want assurance that it would not have to bear part of the unrealized loss, if any, that had accrued previously. It has been suggested that some formula should be devised for sharing the exchange risk among the United States and the participants in the account or that the IMF accept some of the risk on behalf of all its members.

At present, a country can escape the exchange risk inherent in holding dollar assets only by selling them for other currencies and shifting the risk to others. By participating in the Substitution Account, however, it would be sharing the exchange risk with the United States. In effect, it would accept the risk that the dollar component of the SDR (30 percent of the total) may fall in value relative to the other fifteen currencies. If the United States were to guarantee the SDR value of the assets in the Substitution Account, it would be taking the risk that the value of the other fifteen currencies (70 percent of the total) may rise relative to the dollar. As a practical matter, the United States is already taking the same or a greater risk in order to support the foreign exchange value of the dollar. When the United States uses its own holdings of SDRs or draws on the IMF in order to acquire foreign currencies, it is accepting precisely the same exchange risk that it would in the Substitution Account. When the United States draws other currencies under its reciprocal currency arrangements or borrows deutsche marks and Swiss francs in the capital markets of these countries, as it has done, it is accepting a greater exchange risk than is involved in maintaining the SDR value of official dollar assets placed in the Substitution Account.

The emphasis on the exchange risk in the Substitution Account is misplaced because it neglects the general benefits that would accrue from establishing such an account. It is in the interest of the United States to avoid the disruption in the exchange market that would result from large-scale shifts of official dollar holdings to other currencies by countries that want to diversify their foreign exchange reserves. It is in the interest of the countries that want to diversify their foreign-exchange reserves to do so by placing the dollars in a Substitution Account rather than depressing the dollar by selling their holdings in the exchange market. It is no encouragement to countries that might wish to participate in a Substitution Account to make their participation dependent on their sharing the exchange risks inherent in a floating dollar. As a practical matter, the discussion of this point greatly exaggerates the exchange risks for the United States and the participating countries. From July 1974 to December 1977, the value of the dollar in SDRs rose 2 percent above its initial value. All the decline in the SDR value of the dollar occurred in the first ten months of 1978. Since November 1978 the SDR value of the dollar has fluctuated in a range of 3.3 percent.

Another question involved in the establishment of a Substitution Account is the interest rate that would be paid by the United States on the assets the account would hold. This is related to the question of exchange risk and could be linked to it. If the United States were to give the Substitution Account an SDR-denominated obligation, the interest rate on such securities should be somewhat less than the rate on dollar obligations, although not as low as the rate set by the IMF on the SDRs in the Special Account. A reasonable rate would be about 2 percent a year less than the market rate on three-month treasury bills. If the United States is troubled about the possibility of a fall in the dollar relative to the SDR, it could place the 2 percent differential in the interest rate in a reserve account that could be used to meet any supplementary payments that might be necessary if the SDR value of the dollar were to fall. That would have been enough for this purpose in 1974–1979.

It has been suggested that the establishment of a Substitution Account would be the most important step that could be taken at this time to restore a more orderly international monetary system. Those who hold this view would like to have the IMF take a very active role in the account, even becoming the guarantor of the SDR value of the assets in the account. Those who advocate such a guarantee believe that the account could be a step in the evolution of an international monetary system based on SDRs. Under its present statutes, the IMF can be no more than an administrator of the account, although it may be possible to use the profits from some of its gold holdings to meet any shortfall in the SDR value of the assets in the account. It is difficult, however, to see what justification there can be for using the resources of the IMF to underwrite the SDR value of the currency of one member, even if that currency is the U.S. dollar.

Strengthening the International Monetary System

The establishment of a Substitution Account could contribute to greater stability of the international monetary system, but only if the United States were to take responsibility for the SDR value of the assets in the account. The United States did not accept responsibility for the foreign exchange value of the dollar after it abandoned gold convertibility. In the Smithsonian Agreement the members of the Group of Ten and Switzerland undertook to support the new par value of the dollar without any obligation by the United States. This was an arrangement that could not work. The United States had no inducement to direct its monetary and fiscal policies toward maintaining the par value of the dollar. The other members of the Group of Ten and Switzerland could not be expected to continue to accumulate dollars on a large scale, and early in 1973 they abandoned this undertaking. For a time, the United States took the view that with the floating of the dollar there was no need to be concerned at all with the behavior of exchange rates.

Since November 1, 1978, the United States has committed itself to preventing excessive depreciation of the dollar. The Federal Reserve is giving greater weight to the behavior of the exchange market than at any time since 1973. This has not resulted in a very high degree of exchange rate stability—that was not its objective—but it has succeeded in preventing a sustained fall in the foreign exchange value of the dollar relative to the currencies of the other industrial countries. The Treasury and the Federal Reserve should now be willing to go one step further by setting a reasonable and attainable objective for the foreign exchange value of the dollar. The maintenance of the SDR value of the dollar is such an objective, and the establishment of a Substitution Account would underline the commitment of the United States to attaining it.

The hope that the Substitution Account can evolve into a new system of more or less fixed par values based on the SDR is illusory. A country that links its currency to the SDR would have to accept for itself the average rate of inflation of the countries whose currencies compose a unit of SDRs. Consider what this would mean for Germany and the countries in the European Monetary System. On June 30, 1974, when the present method of valuing the SDR was adopted, a unit of SDRs was equal to DM3.083. On February 25, 1980, a unit of SDRs was equal to DM2.302. Over this period, the SDR depreciated by slightly more than 25 percent against the DMark and somewhat less against most other currencies in the European Monetary System. For the dollar, which depreciated by 7.7 percent in relation to a unit of SDRs, the maintenance of the SDR value of the dollar is a reasonable initial objective.

The establishment of the Substitution Account would contribute to the importance of the SDR as a reserve asset. Although the IMF has resumed the issue of SDRs and will add SDR13 billion in 1979–1981 to the SDR 9.3 billion issued in 1969–1971, SDRs would still constitute a small part of aggregate monetary reserves, even excluding gold. The balances in the account would not be SDRs in the same sense as those issued by the IMF, but because they would have a fixed value in SDRs they would be the equivalent of SDRs. As the reserve position in the IMF is also denominated in SDRs, the aggregate of reserves linked to the SDR would be substantial. Nevertheless, they would be considerably less than the total of foreign-exchange reserves, including dollars not placed in the Substitution Account, and at the present free-market price of gold they would be far less than the gold reserves outside the Communist countries.

With the present price of gold about $650 an ounce, the value of the monetary stock of gold, including holdings of the IMF and the European Monetary Cooperation Fund, has increased to $725 billion. The U.S. gold reserves of 265 million ounces are now worth $170 billion. This has spawned some fanciful ideas about the strength of the dollar and what could be done with the international monetary system. The U.S. gold reserves, it is pointed out, are considerably more than the liabilities to foreign official institutions. Thus, the United States could repay all of these liabilities and still have larger gold reserves measured in dollars than at the peak, when they amounted to $24.8 billion at the end of August 1949. There is also a view that, because of the enormous increase in the dollar value of U.S. gold reserves, the dollar must be stronger than it seems to be on the exchange market.

427

It has been suggested that the world could quickly achieve monetary stability by restoring a gold standard. There is more to restoring the gold standard, however, than adopting gold parities and having enormous gold reserves. Any system of fixed parities requires a firm commitment to making the maintenance of the parity the primary objective of economic policy. Moreover, in order to maintain a pattern of international payments that would enable the gold standard to work, all of the large trading countries would have to follow a common monetary policy. The only monetary policy that could be generally acceptable to them would be one directed toward achieving a high degree of price stability. As the experience of the past ten years has shown, this is at present beyond the capability of most countries, including the United States. Under the circumstances, the deficits and surpluses that would emerge could be very large, much larger than at present with floating rates.

Under a gold standard, balance-of-payments settlements would have to be made in gold or in gold plus other reserve assets earmarked in a Reserve Settlement Account. The transfer of reserve assets would result in an automatic expansion of the money supply in the surplus countries and a contraction of the money supply in the deficit countries. If the surpluses and deficits were large, few countries would be willing to accept such an automatic change in their money supply. Furthermore, there is the difficult problem of private holdings of gold. Under present conditions, the volatility of private demand manifests itself in a sharp rise or fall in the price of gold. Under a gold standard, the volatility in the demand for gold could manifest itself in large purchases from or sales to the monetary authorities. Indeed, if countries were to succeed in restoring monetary stability, the huge amount of gold that speculators would then sell the monetary authorities would result in a monetary expansion that could become the basis for a renewed inflation.

There is no way in which the world can return to a system of fixed parities under present conditions. The huge current account surplus of the oil-exporting countries makes an acceptable pattern of international payments impossible. Too many countries feel impelled to compensate for their increased deficits with the oil-exporting countries by restricting their imports from other oil-importing countries or greatly expanding their exports to them. Under these conditions, the United States could become the residual absorber of that part of the aggregate deficit with the oil-exporting countries that others are unwilling or unable to bear. Even if the oil payments problem were somehow to become less disruptive, the inflation in the large trading countries would prevent them from establishing and maintaining a system of par values.

The practical objective at this time should be to improve the regime of floating exchange rates. The United States has already taken a major step in this direction by preventing excessive depreciation of the dollar. The next forward step could be to accept an objective of keeping the SDR value of the dollar reasonably stable. That would require the United States to follow monetary and fiscal policies that are no more expansive than those of the other countries whose currencies are included in the SDR. This is not too much to expect if the Treasury and the Federal Reserve mean to halt the inflation in the United States. The establishment of a Substitution Account would help to focus the attention of the U.S. government—the administration and the Congress—on the importance of such policies.

The Dollar and the ECU

Michele Fratianni

This paper deals with the decline of the dollar as the world dominant money and the prospects for the ECU, the European artificial currency, to replace this function of the dollar. For the time being, these prospects are considered dim. The European Monetary System (EMS), which elevated the ECU to official parallel currency in the European Economic Community (EEC), is not a significant innovation with respect to the objective of achieving monetary union in the Community. Without monetary union, Europe cannot seriously challenge the leading position in the world of the depreciating dollar; yet, international trade would benefit immensely from a new and stable dominant money. The public-good nature of money suggests a tendency for underprovision of the good.

The ECU as a parallel currency suffers from inherent weaknesses, and the EMS added to these weaknesses by legislating explicit restrictive provisions. Because room for improvement is ample, I conclude this paper by offering in a programmatic fashion a menu of "do's" aimed at enhancing the acceptability of the ECU in the marketplace.

Dominant Money

History records a propensity for one currency to dominate others as the international medium of exchange. Cipolla recounts that the Byzantine *nomisma* was the unchallenged coin from the fifth century to the seventh.[1] The nomisma was displaced by the Islamic *dinar* in the Low Middle Ages and by the Florentine *fiorino* and the Venetian *ducato* in the higher Middle Ages. These coins shared three attributes: large weight (high unitary value), high intrinsic (purchasing power) stability, and the feature that the coin issuer enjoyed a leading position in international trade. In more recent time, 1870–1914, the British

[1] Carlo M. Cipolla, *Money, Prices, and Civilization in the Mediterranean World* (Princeton, N.J.: Princeton University Press, 1956).

430

pound rose to the status of hegemonial currency, in part because Britain was the only country on the gold standard and in part because of British supremacy in banking and in trade, particularly merchant shipping.[2]

The vacuum left by a declining empire and pound was in time filled by the United States and the dollar. Gaps are not closed quickly; transition periods may last years, if not decades. Kindleberger laments this situation and argues that U.S. reluctance in assuming the international responsibility that had been borne by the British Empire was the principal cause of the 1929 world depression.[3] This hypothesis has implications of immediate relevance. It suggests that, with the dollar declining as the world's dominant money and with no other money emerging as a suitable replacement, the international monetary system will remain in turmoil, which will in turn hamper trade growth and possibly favor a return to bilateralism and barter.

Before we review the salient facts of the deteriorating dollar standard, it is useful to explore the theoretical case for a dominant money. For Brunner and Meltzer, money is a commodity or an asset with a comparative advantage in absorbing and disseminating information concerning the transaction domain of the consumer.[4] The degree of predictability of the exchange rate of money for commodities determines this comparative advantage. Various assets have moneylike properties. The kind and quantities of moneys held depend on their marginal productivity and marginal costs. Inflation raises the variance of the exchange ratios, thus raising the marginal productivity of moneys, but inflation also raises the marginal cost of holding (non-interest-bearing) moneys. Some of the evidence available suggests that inflation must reach high values before individuals replace high-inflating with lower-inflating mediums of exchange. Robert Barro, for example, finds that an inflation rate of 10 percent a month in the hyperinflation of the 1920s induced currency substitutions of approximately 5 percent of total transactions.[5]

---

[2] M. de Cecco, *Money and Empire* (Totowa, N.J.: Rowman and Littlefield, 1974).

[3] Charles P. Kindleberger, *The World in Depression, 1929-1939* (Berkeley and Los Angeles: University of California Press, 1973). Kindleberger's notion of responsibility goes beyond the provision of a stable international medium of exchange. The dominant-currency country must provide a market for so-called distress goods, be willing to lend in a countercyclical fashion, and perform the role of lender of last resort.

[4] Karl Brunner and Allan H. Meltzer, "The Uses of Money: Money in the Theory of an Exchange Economy," *American Economic Review,* vol. 61 (December 1971), pp. 784-805.

[5] On this point, see Benjamin Klein, "Competing Monies: A Comment," *Journal of Money, Credit and Banking,* November 1976, pp. 513-19.

This tenacity in holding onto rapidly depreciating moneys indicates that the benefits derived from the use of a dominant money are presumably high. The obvious extension is that the search for a viable alternative to the dollar is costly; and much higher rates of inflation will have to be reached before the dollar will lose its hegemonial position.

Additional insights into how moneys compete can be gained by considering Klein's model,[6] whose main virtue is the distinction between the effects of anticipated inflation from those of unanticipated inflation on money holdings. Consumers are indifferent between moneys of different anticipated inflation rates as long as the money-producing industry is competitive and the implied rental price of the monetary services of money is identical. Money holders receive an interest rate that incorporates the expected rate of inflation. Markets cannot impound unanticipated rates of inflation. Therefore, a money producer can profit by oversupplying the product. Costly information, however, does not allow the money producer to deceive without what Klein aptly calls loss of brand capital. The strategy of gaining short-run profits by overissuing runs against the constraint that losses of brand capital are capitalized and thus raise the marginal cost of producing money in the longer run.

Neither in the Brunner and Meltzer nor in the Klein model is there anything to suggest that one money will eventually prevail. Brunner and Meltzer emphasize the point that moneys possessing lower cost of information replace moneys with higher cost of information. In steady state, the distinction between money and nonmoney assets disappears. Klein stresses the loss of wealth and dominance resulting from overissuing. Given the competitive nature of Klein's model, there is no reason to expect the emergence of one money. Yet, there is agreement that a one-money world is to be preferred to a multiple-money world. Society saves the resources used to acquire information about changes in the relative prices of moneys as well as the resources devoted to money-changing activity. Speculating and hedging against unanticipated movements of exchange rates are resource-absorbing activities that could be eliminated if one money prevailed. Exchange controls that lower the marginal efficiency of resources disappear in a one-money world.[7]

[6] B. Klein, "The Competitive Supply of Money," *Journal of Money, Credit and Banking,* November 1974, pp. 423-53.

[7] Allan H. Meltzer, "The Dollar as an International Money," *Banca Nazionale del Lavoro Quarterly Review,* March 1973, pp. 21-28.

The traditional manner of arriving at a theoretical justification of a hegemonial money is to appeal to large economies of scale in the production of information about the reliability of money.[8]

Although the case for a hegemonial money is strongest for a monetary union, there are still benefits in selecting a dominant currency in a multiple-currency system. In a world of N countries there are $N(N-1)/2$ exchange rates. With one money acting as a pivot (the Nth currency), each central bank has to aim at target exchange rates defined only in terms of the Nth currency; triangular arbitrage ensures that cross rates fall into line. This is the well-known $N-1$ problem emphasized by McKinnon.[9] The world gains the organizational ease of targeting on one money as opposed to several moneys and the smaller amount of international reserves required to make the system work. In addition, the arrangement ensures that targeting will yield consistent outcomes. A corollary of this proposition is that the Nth country can pursue policies that deliberately ignore the external balance constraint. The dollar performed the role of the Nth money in the Bretton Woods system. The United States acted independently of the rest of the world, whereas the converse was not true. Pegging one's currency to the dollar meant relinquishing the independent use of monetary and fiscal instruments. To a first approximation, the United States was determining the world rate of inflation. The rest of the world had either to accept this outcome or to adjust its exchange rate vis-à-vis the dollar.

It is well understood that the benefits of such an arrangement depend on the ability of the dominant-money country to stabilize prices of tradable goods. The United States has manifestly failed in meeting this objective. In the next section I explore the reasons for this failure by making use of the theory of collective action.

The Weakening Dollar Standard

A Few Facts. There is widespread agreement among experts that the strong dollar standard of the 1950s and the 1960s has evolved into a weak dollar standard. I start the analysis by summarizing a few perti-

[8] Klein, "The Competitive Supply of Money," p. 444; Roland Vaubel, *Strategies for Currency Unification: The Economics of Currency Competition and the Case for a European Parallel Currency* (Tübingen, Germany: J. C. B. Mohr; Paul Siebeck, 1978), pp. 72-74.

[9] Ronald I. McKinnon, *Private and Official International Money: The Case for the Dollar,* Essays in International Finance, no. 74 (Princeton, N.J.: Princeton University, 1969); idem, *Money in International Exchange: The Convertible Currency System* (Oxford and New York: Oxford University Press, 1979), chap. 2.

TABLE 1
FUNCTIONS OF THE DOLLAR

Roles of the Dollar	Economic Operators	
	Private	Official
Unit of account	Invoice	Parities
Medium of exchange	Vehicle currency	Intervention currency
Store of value	Investment	Reserves

nent facts. For this purpose consider table 1, the 3 × 2 classification table (proposed by Peter Kenen and Paul Krugman) concerning the different functions performed by the dollar.

Before the 1970s the dollar fulfilled all six roles indicated in the matrix, even though the invoice function turned out, under careful empirical scrutiny, to be much less significant than originally believed.[10] In the last ten years the parity role has vanished, and the investment role has diminished appreciably. Tables 2 and 3 show data bearing on the relative importance of the dollar as an investment currency for the private sector. It is clear that the U.S. currency has steadily lost ground to the detutsche mark (DM) in the Eurocurrency market, although with a market share of 70 percent it remains by far the principal investment currency. The relative decline of the dollar is more pronounced, as one would expect, in assets with a longer-term maturity. The dollar value of DM-denominated Eurobonds in 1978, for example, was about as large as the value of Eurodollar bonds. Although it is true that currency denomination is subject to sharp short-run fluctuations, the trend is definitely in favor of Euro-DM bonds.

Table 4 considers official holdings of foreign exchange as a combined proxy of the "intervention currency" and "reserves" functions. Here the dollar is holding its own ground, in part reflecting the continuation of dollar-support programs by surplus countries. The market share of the dollar in 1978 is not different from that prevailing in 1970–1971. As is true for the private operator, central banks have

[10] In the market for primary commodities the dollar prevails as the unit of account. In the other markets invoices are denominated in the currencies of exporters and importers. Grassman found that only 10 percent of Swedish trade was invoiced in dollars; more recent research confirms this finding for major trading countries. S. Grassman, *Exchange Reserves and the Financial Structure of Foreign Trade* (Westmead, England: Saxon House, 1973); S. P. Magee and R. K. S. Rao, "Vehicle and Nonvehicle Currencies in International Trade," *American Economic Review: Papers and Proceedings,* vol. 70, no. 2 (May 1980), pp. 368-73.

TABLE 2
EXTERNAL LIABILITIES OF REPORTING EUROPEAN BANKS
IN DOLLARS AND OTHER FOREIGN CURRENCIES, 1968–1978
(billions of U.S. dollars)

Year	Total	Dollars	Ratio, Dollar/Total	DM	Ratio, DM/Total
1968	33.710	26.870	0.80	3.010	0.089
1969	56.720	46.200	0.81	4.640	0.081
1970	75.290	58.700	0.78	8.080	0.107
1971	97.720	70.750	0.72	14.630	0.15
1972	131.930	96.730	0.73	19.540	0.148
1973	192.100	131.380	0.684	32.020	0.166
1974	220.770	156.430	0.708	34.380	0.156
1975	258.670	189.470	0.732	39.940	0.154
1976	310.650	230.040	0.74	47.230	0.152
1977	396.200	278.840	0.703	68.680	0.173
1978	510.810	348.590	0.68	93.080	0.18

SOURCE: Bank for International Settlements (BIS), *Annual Reports*, 1977, 1979. The share of the DM tends to be overstated as a result of the sharp depreciation of the dollar. If one were to adjust for this depreciation, the share of the DM would be smaller; see BIS, *Annual Report*, 1979, p. 117.

shown increased interest in DM holdings. The Bundesbank calculates that the average share of deutsche marks in official exchange reserves rose from 7.6 percent in 1974 to 11.3 percent in 1978.[11]

In sum, the dollar remains the vehicle and investment currency par excellence as private and official operators increasingly diversify toward stronger currencies. The slowness of this diversification process is indicative of the high marginal productivity of the dominant money.

An Interpretation. Since the end of World War II, the United States has provided the Western world with two complementary public goods, defense and a key money.[12] The complementarity between defense and money is based on the basic proposition that "production of national defense not only yields some monetary confidence as a by-product, but production of monetary confidence also yields national defense services."[13] Historically, governments have found it more expedient to

[11] Bundesbank, "The Deutsche Mark as an International Investment Currency," *Monthly Report*, vol. 31, no. 11 (1979), pp. 26-34.
[12] This section draws on Michele Fratianni and John C. Pattison, "The Economics of International Organizations," *Kyklos*, vol. 32, fasc. no. 2 (1982).
[13] Klein, "Competitive Supply of Money," p. 449.

TABLE 3

Eurobond Issues, 1974–1978
(in the equivalent of millions of U.S. dollars)

	1974	1975	1976	1977	1978	Total	%
U.S. dollars	1,036.0	3,365.5	8,625.6	10,215.0	5,538.6	28,807.6	57.8
Deutsche marks	213.7	1,723.1	2,018.7	3,833.4	4,922.1	12,711.0	25.5
Canadian dollars	58.0	575.0	1,378.0	641.0	—	2,652.0	5.3
Dutch guilders	342.4	500.5	418.3	402.6	384.5	2,048.3	4.1
Other European currencies	13.1	305.3	38.0	216.0	421.7	1,039.1	2.1
Composite and dual currencies	222.2	585.8	102.2	33.0	198.7	1,141.9	2.3
Middle East currencies	51.3	181.4	288.5	137.0	464.3	1,122.5	2.2
Far East currencies	—	—	18.7	263.7	79.4	361.8	0.7
Total $ equivalent	1,936.7	7,281.6	12,915.0	15,741.7	12,009.2	49,884.2	
U.S. dollars as % of total	53.5	46.2	67.0	64.9	46.1		

NOTE: New issue volume for 1979 (up to October 30): U.S. dollars, 7,297.5 (U.S. dollars equivalent, millions), 60.9%; deutsche marks, 3,016.9, 25.2%; Canadian dollars, 421.5, 3.5%; others, 1,242.6, 10.4%; total, 11,978.5.

SOURCE: Wood Gundy, *Financing in the Eurobond Market,* November 1979.

436

TABLE 4
OFFICIAL HOLDINGS OF FOREIGN EXCHANGE
(billions of SDRs)

	1968	1969	1970	1971
Official claims on U.S.	17.3	16.0	23.8	46.7
Eurodollars	3.8	4.9	10.5	10.4
Total dollars	21.1	20.9	34.3	57.1
Ratio, total dollars/total official holdings	0.66	0.63	0.76	0.76
Others	10.9	12.1	11.1	17.9
Total official holdings	32.0	33.0	45.4	75.0
	1972	1973	1974	1975
Official claims on U.S.	56.7	55.4	62.7	68.9
Eurodollars	16.8	18.5	31.8	38.0
Total dollars	73.5	73.9	94.5	106.9
Ratio, total dollars/total official holdings	0.77	0.73	0.75	0.78
Others	22.4	27.9	31.8	30.0
Total official holdings	95.9	101.8	126.3	136.9
	1976	1977	1978	
Official claims on U.S.	79.2	103.8	120.2	
Eurodollars	45.6	53.6	47.7	
Total dollars	124.8	157.4	167.9	
Ratio, total dollars/total official holdings	0.78	0.79	0.76	
Others	35.0	42.7	52.9	
Total official holdings	159.8	200.1	220.8	

SOURCE: International Monetary Fund, Annual Reports, 1975, 1976, 1979.

finance wars by levying an inflation tax rather than an explicitly legislated one. The public-good nature of defense is well understood and widely accepted. The public-good nature of money can be justified in terms of the basic proposition emphasized by Brunner and Meltzer: The use of a common money lowers information and transaction costs for all economic operators, although the choice of what money to hold is a private decision.[14] In the international context, the dollar as the

[14] Brunner and Meltzer, "Uses of Money," pp. 784-805. Hamada makes extensive use of this notion in his writings. The argument is advanced that "once a monetary system is built, once an asset is chosen as its money by a society, or once a mutual confidence emerges in the use of a particular commodity or currency as the common money, then the benefit from this public (implicit) consensus becomes a public good." Koichi Hamada, "On the Political Economy of Monetary Integration: A Public Economics Approach," in Robert Z. Aliber, ed., The Political Economy of Monetary Reform (Chicago: University of Chicago Press, 1977), pp. 13-31.

TABLE 5
GROSS NATIONAL PRODUCT WEIGHTS FOR INDIVIDUAL COUNTRIES,
1955–1977
(as a percentage of OECD GNP)

Country	1955	1960	1970	1977
United States	57.8	52.5	46.7	46.9
Japan	5.6	7.9	12.6	11.3
Germany	9.9	13.2	13.9	14.0
France	6.7	7.1	7.6	8.2
United Kingdom	5.8	5.2	4.2	3.8
Italy	2.8	3.0	3.3	3.4
Canada	3.9	3.8	3.9	4.7
Netherlands	1.9	2.0	2.2	2.4
Sweden	2.0	1.8	1.8	1.7
Belgium	1.8	1.7	1.7	1.8
Switzerland	1.6	1.7	1.8	1.6

SOURCE: International Monetary Fund, *International Financial Statistics,* various issues. GNP figures were converted to constant dollar values by applying 1977 exchange rates.

undisputed intervention currency has enabled central banks to save the cost of carrying a diversified portfolio of currencies; and it has provided a solution to the redundancy or N — 1 currency problem.[15]

The theory of collective action sheds useful insights on the fundamental question of whether the dominant-currency country has an incentive in supplying the goods. This theory, when applied to the context of international monetary arrangement, generates the following implications.[16] The larger the number of countries participating in the arrangement, the larger the spread between the world and the dominant country's marginal benefit resulting from the acceptance of a dominant money, the larger the share of the cost in providing the public good borne by the dominant-currency country, the larger will be the shortfall in the provision of the public good with respect to its optimum amount. The costs to the United States of making defense and a stable

[15] The interested reader may want to consult McKinnon, *Money in International Exchange,* chap. 2, for a lucid discussion of the N — 1 currency issue.
[16] See, for example, Mancur Olson, Jr., *The Logic of Collective Action: Public Goods and the Theory of Groups* (Cambridge: Harvard University Press, 1965); Hamada, "Political Economy of Monetary Integration"; Hamada, "On the Coordination of Monetary Policies in a Monetary Union," unpublished paper; Fratianni and Pattison, "Economics of International Organizations."

TABLE 6
AREA COMPOSITION OF WORLD TRADE: EXPORTS, 1960–1977
(percent)

Country	1960	1970	1977[a]
United States	16.0	13.7	11.8
Germany	8.9	11.0	11.7
Benelux	6.1	7.5	8.0
Japan	3.2	6.2	8.0
Canada	4.3	5.4	4.1
European Community (6)	23.3	28.4	31.0
World	100.0	100.0	100.0

[a] First nine months.

SOURCES: Organization for Economic Cooperation and Development, *Policy Perspectives for International Trade and Economic Relations,* 1972; U.N. Monthly Statistics, April 1978, for 1977. Note that figures relating to the European Community include intracommunity trade, which accounted for approximately 35% of Community trade in 1960 and 51% in 1977.

dollar available to the world are the explicit expenditures of manufacturing weapons and maintaining weapons and troops around the world as well as the opportunity cost implied by a zero-inflation-rate policy. This latter cost is zero in the long run but positive over relatively brief periods of time. More importantly, it is nonzero for politicians, whose planning horizon is notoriously short. The benefits to the United States are the higher standards of living resulting from an orderly and more efficient economic system and the seigniorage that can be extracted on the stock of dollars held abroad.

The gradual weakening of the dollar, it is argued, stems from the falling net benefits accruing to the United States from supplying the two public goods. Because there is no direct way to quantify these net benefits, let me resort to some qualitative judgments. Assume that the U.S. share of gross benefits from a dollar standard *cum* defense is positively related to (1) either the U.S. share of world output or the U.S. share of world trade and (2) the ability of the United States to levy a seigniorage on foreign-held dollars. Consider assumption 1 first. Table 5 shows percentage distributions of gross national products (GNPs) of countries belonging to the Organization for Economic Cooperation and Development (OECD) over the period 1953–1977; Table 6 gives country shares in world trade. Both sets of figures indicate that the U.S. weight has been declining while the relative importance of Japan, Germany, and the European Community as a whole has been rising. The data are consistent with a diminished incentive for the United States to supply the public goods. In addition, the emergence and development of the Eurodollar market have eroded the power of the United States to levy a tax on dollar balances held abroad. Competition for funds has prompted European and non-European banks to bid away most of the monopoly profits accruing to the U.S. banking system.[17]

Unable to levy a predictable tax on money holdings, the United States has resorted to levying an unpredictable tax. Anticipated rates of inflation are embedded in competitively determined rates of interest; unanticipated rates of inflation are not.

Unanticipated rates of price-level change produce real-sector effects because they catch economic operators by surprise. In the international context, variable inflation rates alter the composition of output between a given country and the rest of the world. More specifically, an unanticipated rate of depreciation of the purchasing power of the dollar causes not only a depreciation of the dollar in terms of foreign exchange but also a depreciation of the dollar real exchange rate (that is, the nominal exchange rate adjusted for inflation differentials). Because the determinants of trade flows are, among other things, real rather than nominal rates of exchange, the United States can expand national output at the expense of rest-of-the-world output by pursuing a policy of unanticipated inflation.

Table 7 shows changes in the nominal and real effective exchange rates of the U.S. dollar for the period 1967II to 1978III. Figure 1 plots the variance of the real effective exchange rate changes and of the U.S. inflation rate calculated on an eight-quarter moving average. Although these data are informative in many respects, I shall limit myself to only two considerations. First, nominal and real effective exchange rate changes display a sharp statistical break sometime in the middle of 1971. This is the year Richard Nixon formally announced that the U.S. government was no longer committed to converting dollars into gold; this is the year wage and price controls were instituted. Second, there is a remarkable positive association between the variance of the real exchange rate change and the variance of the U.S. inflation rate, a proxy of unanticipated inflation. This evidence is consistent with the hypothesis that domestic policies were responsible (at least in part) for the increased volatility of exchange rates. The alternative hypothesis that the oil embargo of 1973 and the big price jump in crude oil in the following year are to blame for nominal and real exchange rate volatility does not square with the timing of the sharp

---

[17] Seigniorage is extracted on U.S. monetary base held abroad either in the form of coins and notes or in possible dollar reserves backing Eurodollar deposits.

TABLE 7
NOMINAL AND REAL EFFECTIVE EXCHANGE RATE CHANGES OF THE U.S. DOLLAR, 1967–1978

Date	Nominal Effective Exchange Rate Change	U.S. Inflation Rate	World Inflation Rate	Real Effective Exchange Rate Change
1967II	−0.612	2.61	3.063	−1.065
1967III	−0.627	4.53	4.020	−0.117
1967IV	8.061	3.20	4.177	7.084
1968I	0.539	5.08	4.149	1.470
1968II	−0.441	4.39	2.429	1.520
1968III	−1.055	4.34	5.089	−1.804
1968IV	−0.182	4.91	3.581	1.147
1969I	1.188	6.06	5.442	1.806
1969II	0.696	6.57	5.351	1.915
1969III	1.709	5.29	3.518	3.481
1969IV	−3.970	5.80	4.397	−2.567
1970I	−0.670	5.71	6.490	−1.450
1970II	−5.712	6.20	3.583	−3.095
1970III	3.043	4.44	3.406	−2.009
1970IV	−1.045	5.49	3.345	1.100
1971I	−1.430	2.17	5.973	−5.223
1971II	0.751	5.92	6.716	−0.045
1971III	−11.973	2.12	5.782	−15.595
1971IV	−10.599	3.17	3.824	−11.253
1972I	−7.728	2.62	5.102	−10.210
1972II	−0.999	3.12	4.900	−2.779
1972III	1.696	4.13	7.751	−1.925
1972IV	3.354	3.58	5.609	1.325
1973I	−22.797	7.59	9.509	−24.716
1973II	−15.749	7.95	11.348	−19.147
1973III	3.717	9.74	10.402	3.095
1973IV	19.023	8.56	11.556	16.027
1974I	−10.450	13.50	16.850	−13.800
1974II	2.510	10.36	14.369	−1.499
1974III	9.119	13.17	11.702	10.587
1974IV	−8.866	9.78	12.820	−11.906
1975I	−6.234	6.22	9.617	−9.631
1975II	8.150	6.95	12.503	2.597
1975III	20.187	7.63	8.887	18.930
1975IV	−2.724	6.70	7.541	−3.565

(table continues)

TABLE 7 (continued)

Date	Nominal Effective Exchange Rate Change	U.S. Inflation Rate	World Inflation Rate	Real Effective Exchange Rate Change
1976I	−0.172	2.71	8.640	−6.102
1976II	0.763	6.16	8.924	−2.001
1976III	−2.962	6.07	6.917	−3.809
1976IV	3.999	3.73	7.594	0.135
1977I	4.670	8.88	10.272	3.278
1977II	−1.805	8.33	9.220	−2.695
1977III	−0.689	4.61	6.037	−2.116
1977IV	−17.084	4.56	5.083	−17.607
1978I	−4.746	7.97	7.415	−4.191
1978II	−2.781	11.89	7.613	1.496
1978III	−6.838	7.92	5.515	−4.433

NOTE: The effective exchange rate is defined by the units of foreign exchange required to purchase one dollar. Negative signs indicate a devaluation of the U.S. dollar in terms of a weighted average of the currencies of the following countries: Germany, France, Italy, the Netherlands, Belgium-Luxembourg, the United Kingdom, Switzerland, Japan, and Canada. The weights are calculated using the U.S. export shares in this group of countries. The U.S. inflation rate is measured by the annual percentage change of the consumer price index (CPI). The world rate of inflation is the weighted average of the annual percentage change of the CPIs of the above-mentioned countries with weights based on export shares. Finally, the real effective exchange rate change is equal to the nominal effective exchange rate change, plus the U.S. rate of inflation, minus the world rate of inflation.

SOURCES: Harris Bank, "International Money Markets and Foreign Exchange Rates," *Weekly Review*, and Organization for Economic Cooperation and Development, *Main Economic Indicators*, various issues.

rise in the variances that took place in the period from 1971 to 1973 (see figure 1).

In sum, the higher deviations of exchange rate movements from their implied purchasing power parity values can in part be attributed to a less predictable rate of U.S. inflation, which in turn has produced a marginal loss of confidence in the dollar. The continuation of high and variable rates of inflation in the United States would further erode the world public's confidence in the dollar and encourage additional currency shifts in favor of more stable moneys. The return to a strong dollar standard (that is, the provision of the public good) requires that U.S. monetary policy stabilize the dollar price of traded goods, which in turn implies refraining from moving along short-run Phillips curves. A reading of current policy making does not lead us to conclude that a return to a strong dollar standard is in the making. There are two

FIGURE 1
Variance of the Real Exchange Rate Change and
U.S. Inflation Rate, 1969–1978

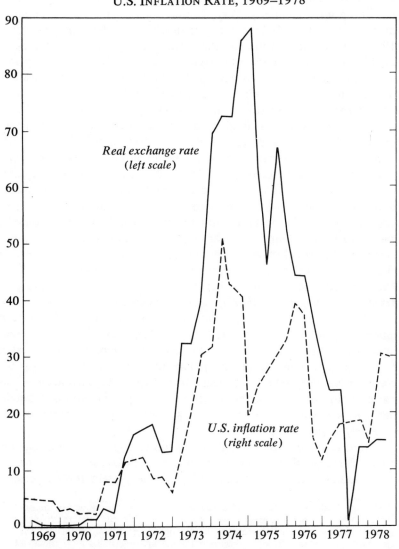

Source: Author.

reasons for this. First, Keynesian economics still constitutes the philosophical core of economic policy. Second, the United States, partly in response to military and strategic setbacks, is objecting to the large amount of free riding and the high costs of providing the two international public goods.

443

European Monetary Union and the ECU

Since 1969 monetary union has been one of the principal objectives of the European Community. Yet, despite a spate of official pronouncements, the celebrated Werner report of 1970, the Basel Agreement of 1972, which instituted the so-called snake arrangement, and the newly implemented EMS, the goal of monetary union is no closer today than it was in 1969. Why such a failure? The theory of collection action predicts that monetary union, as in the case of dominant money, would be underprovided with respect to its social optimum supply.[18] Hamada offers the following explanation for the underprovision of monetary union.[19] The benefits derived from this arrangement stem from the notion that the enlargement of the monopoly power to issue the public-good money has a positive value. The costs for a high-inflation country to join a monetary union are equivalent to the costs—measured in terms of lost output—associated with any disinflationary program. These costs are positive in the short run and zero in the long run. The politician, with a short planning horizon—that is, low discount rates for events occurring before elections, high discount rates for events after the election—attaches a higher present value to the cost of the disinflationary program than to the benefit of a common money—hence, the resistance to monetary union by member countries.

There is an alternative explanation for the failure of monetary union to gain popular acceptance: the existence of a bureaucratic interest that need not coincide with, and often opposes, the so-called public interest. Bureaucrats manipulate and feed information to politicians so as to preserve or aggrandize their number, income, and power.[20] In other words, the provision of the public good is not independent of whether the public good will affect national bureaucracies positively or negatively.

Regardless of whether one or the other hypothesis best explains reality, it is clear that monetary union is not an easy task. The question to be addressed here is whether EMS in the present form represents

[18] The shortfall of the supply is predicted to be less for monetary union than for a world dominant money. Two reasons are adduced: the relatively small number of countries participating in the European monetary union, and the fact that most of the benefits of a common money are internalized by the residents of the monetary union area. See Hamada, "Political Economy of Monetary Integration."

[19] Hamada, "Coordination of Monetary Policies."

[20] See Albert Breton, *The Economic Theory of Representative Government* (London: Macmillan & Co., 1974); Charles Kershaw Rowley and A. T. Peacock, *Welfare Economics: A Liberal Restatement* (London: Martin Robertson, Halsted Press, 1975), chap. 6.

a significant step toward European monetary union or, at least, provides an arrangement whose artificial currency may replace the dollar as the world's dominant money. The short answer to this question is no; let us see why.

EMS and the Snake. Four features distinguish EMS from the old snake arrangement: the introduction of ECU as a parallel currency, the indicator of divergence, the European Monetary Fund, and regional income distribution.[21] ECU is an artificial money defined in terms of fixed quantities of Community moneys. ECU is to function as a numéraire, as a means of settlement among central banks, and as an indicator of divergence. The reasons for choosing an artificial money are in part political and in part economic. The political reason is that no country is ready to acknowledge the superiority of one Community currency (read, monetary policy). The economic rationale is based on the notion that a parallel currency may in time replace national moneys and thus become the money of the United States of Europe. In addition, an "average" European currency such as ECU permits—so it is argued by the creators of EMS—the burden resulting from adjusting to balance-of-payments disequilibriums to be more equitably distributed among surplus and deficit countries than was the case in the snake system.

This latter feature is formally incorporated in the so-called indicator of divergence, which aims at forcing *the* "deviant" country, as opposed to two countries in the snake, to undertake corrective policies so as to bring its exchange rate back into the permissible band of fluctuation. During the negotiating phase of EMS, Italy and the United Kingdom claimed that the snake system discriminated in favor of surplus (low-inflation) countries. Deficit (high-inflation) countries had to adjust their policies to those prevailing in surplus countries and not vice versa. ECU, functioning as an indicator of divergence, aims at rectifying this alleged asymmetry.

The European Monetary Fund (EMF) is a legal entity that will replace the existing European Monetary Cooperation Fund. Two stages in the development of EMF are envisioned. In the first stage, which has already taken place, the Fund relabels 20 percent of gold and dollars owned by Community central banks in ECUs. There is no creation of international reserves.[22] In the yet to be implemented second

---

[21] For a more comprehensive treatment of this topic, consult Michele Fratianni, "The European Monetary System: A Return to an Adjustable-Peg Arrangement," *Journal of Monetary Economics,* Supplement 13 (Summer 1980), pp. 139-72.

[22] Gold is valued at lagged market values rather than at $42.50 an ounce. The revaluation of gold, it should be noted, is not a creation of reserves attributable to the Fund.

stage the Fund will create ECUs against deposits of Community currencies, thus acquiring the institutional core of a supranational European central bank.

Finally, EMS acknowledges openly the principle that progress toward monetary union requires redistribution of resources from the rich to the poor regions.

Is ECU a Viable Parallel Currency? The basic weaknesses of EMS originate from ECU in its role of parallel currency and indicator of divergence. ECU, in its present form, has a low probability of succeeding as a store of value and even less as a medium of exchange. As a store of value it is likely to fail because it excludes world currencies that can contribute significantly to risk diversification and includes several currencies that are redundant in light of their comovements with the DM. This point can be illustrated with the aid of table 8, a correlation matrix of the rates of return on various currencies, measured by their quarterly appreciation or depreciation vis-à-vis the U.S. dollar. The sample period is 1968I–1978III. It is clear that there is little to be gained in holding the Dutch guilder and the Belgian franc, once allowance is made for the DM. On the other hand, there is potential loss of risk diversification in excluding from a currency portfolio the Japanese yen and the Canadian dollar. Levy and Sarnat arrive at a similar conclusion in deriving an optimally diversified portfolio of non-interest-bearing foreign currencies for the period 1970–1973.[23] This portfolio would have included only DMs (29 percent) and Japanese yen (71 percent). Strong currencies such as the guilder and the Swiss franc did not make it in the asset mix because of their high positive covariance with the DM.

One cannot exclude a priori, however, the possibility that small savers who face relatively high unitary transaction costs in the foreign exchange market may find ECU deposits attractive assets.

The development of ECUs as a medium of exchange is hampered by (1) the self-imposed restriction of limiting this artificial currency to central bank transactions, (2) the interest rate provision, and (3) relatively high information costs in using ECUs. Concerning the first limitation, there is little to say except that this provision is contrary to the spirit of EMS and of promoting the diffusion of ECUs in the marketplace. Net holders (users) of ECUs receive (pay) an interest rate that is a weighted average of the discount rates in member countries. Be-

[23] Haim Levy and Marshall Sarnat, "Exchange Rate Risk and the Optimal Diversification of Foreign Currency Holdings," *Journal of Money, Credit and Banking*, vol. 10, no. 4 (November 1978), pp. 453-63.

cause most of these rates are administratively set below market rates, the provision tends to subsidize borrowing, consequently depressing the demand for ECUs by surplus countries. That this is the case is evidenced by the constraint that a creditor central bank may refuse to accept ECUs when these amount to 50 percent or more of the claim being settled. Finally, the artificiality of ECU generates an information cost problem. The bulk of exports is invoiced in the currency of the exporter (see note 10). The hedging exporter specializes in gathering information about one rate of exchange with the aim of converting exports proceeds into assets denominated in domestic currency. Similar considerations hold for the importer. If the introduction of ECU does not alter the preferred monetary habitat of exporters and importers, the use of ECUs as an intermediate money imposes on the trader that he be informed about seven exchange rates as opposed to one. This additional information cost will discourage the denomination of contracts in ECUs. There is, of course, the possibility that ECUs may be more stable in value than the moneys of two trading partner countries and, to the extent that the resource saving from a more stable money exceeds the additional information cost, contracts may be denominated in ECUs. The observation that special drawing rights (SDRs), an artificial currency that includes the world's representative currencies, have not made it in the marketplace does not augur well for the dissemination of ECUs.

Let us now evaluate ECU as an indicator of divergence. The claim that the snake system forced surplus and deficit countries to bear asymmetric adjustments is false. If the DM and the Italian lira were to reach the upper and lower intervention limits, respectively, either the Bundesbank or the Banca d'Italia or both would buy liras and sell DMs. The effect of these interventions in the foreign exchange markets on the national money stocks is unequivocal. In the absence of sterilization policies the German money stock would rise whereas the Italian money stock would contract. The adjustments are symmetrical.

The objection to the snake was not the lack of symmetry but the fact that the Bundesbank, unwilling to accept a higher rate of inflation, would let its currency appreciate vis-à-vis other snake currencies. The indicator of divergence aims at abolishing the pivotal role of the DM in Europe and at forcing low-inflation countries to inflate at some unspecified average European rate of inflation. An unagreed average inflation rate solution is deemed politically more European than asking high-inflation countries to lower their rate of price increases to the rate prevailing in the lowest-inflation-rate country. Besides being inferior from a welfare viewpoint, the average solution will be resisted by those

TABLE 8
INTERCOUNTRY CORRELATION MATRIX OF THE EXCHANGE RATE CHANGES, 1968–1978

	D R1	F R2	I R3	NL R4	B R5	UK R6
R1 D	1.000000	0.692354	0.284792	0.920256	0.937769	0.523764
R2 F	0.692354	1.000000	0.511040	0.681222	0.722187	0.470326
R3 I	0.284792	0.511040	1.000000	0.383681	0.333092	0.322883
R4 NL	0.920256	0.681222	0.383681	1.000000	0.958620	0.519670
R5 B	0.937769	0.722187	0.333092	0.958620	1.000000	0.571800
R6 UK	0.523764	0.470326	0.322883	0.519670	0.571800	1.000000
R7 SW	0.774808	0.617993	0.236690	0.715782	0.764623	0.453940
R8 J	0.497686	0.482208	0.242312	0.499706	0.524487	0.450638
R9 CN	−0.192912	−0.269428	−0.325109	−0.245137	−0.248834	−0.138564
	(1)	(2)	(3)	(4)	(5)	(6)

	SW R7	J R8	CN R9
R1 D	0.774808	0.497686	−0.192912
R2 F	0.617993	0.482208	−0.269428
R3 I	0.236690	0.242312	−0.325109
R4 NL	0.715782	0.499706	−0.245137
R5 B	0.764623	0.524487	−0.248834
R6 UK	0.453940	0.450638	−0.138564
R7 SW	1.000000	0.596239	−0.273638
R8 J	0.596239	1.000000	−0.239603
R9 CN	−0.273638	−0.239603	1.000000
	(7)	(8)	(9)

NOTE: Exchange rate changes were computed as $[(ex)_t - (ex)_{t-1}]/(ex)_{t-1}$, using the end-of-quarter bid spot rates reported by the Harris Bank in the *International Money Markets and Foreign Exchange Rates*. All rates are expressed in U.S. dollars per foreign currency unit. $X = $ D (Germany), F (France), I (Italy), NL (Netherlands), B (Belgium), UK (United Kingdom), SW (Switzerland), J (Japan), CN (Canada).

SOURCE: Author.

countries that are asked to inflate to a higher but unknown inflation rate. It is easy to predict that the spirit of the divergence indicator will not be adhered to and that member countries will resort often to parity changes.[24]

To sum up, EMS is not the innovation the public has been led to believe. Some of the weaknesses of the system are inherent; others have been legislated. In the next section I examine ways to improve on the prospects of ECU as a viable parallel currency and as an alternative to the dollar.

Confidence, ECU, and the European Monetary Fund

Confidence in a product's quality can be built by repeated performance. A new product must overcome the fact that there is no history of past performances. Producers often resort to money-back guarantees as a quick way to inject confidence among prospective buyers. ECU is a new product and faces similar difficulties. The All Saints' Day Manifesto and Vaubel argue that renewed interest in monetary unification in Europe offers a unique opportunity for a monetary reform (injection of confidence) that would launch an inflation-proof (money-back guarantee) ECU.[25] An indexed money eliminates the cost money holders bear in incorrectly predicting the rate of inflation. With a guarantee of a zero real rate of return, governments cannot penalize money holders and, therefore, cannot profit from generating unanticipated rates of inflation. The main advantage of the proposal is that the cost of adjusting to a common inflation rate will not be as sudden as it would be if exchange rates were to be set rigidly at a given date.

Two principal objections have been raised to the manifesto's program. First, monetary integration cannot precede political and fiscal integration.[26] Hamada notes that in Italy and Zollverein "political leadership in the sense of entrepreneurship functioned as a catalyst in realizing the public good character of money." [27] The second objection concerns the effect of a zero real rate of return on money on the demand for other assets. Balassa and Magnifico, among others, argue that the introduction of an indexed money would create an excess demand for the new money and an excess supply of other assets, including physical

---

[24] One parity realignment took place on September 24, 1979.

[25] "A Currency for Europe," *The Economist,* November 1, 1975, pp. 33-38; Vaubel, *Strategies for Currency Unification.*

[26] David Laidler, "Difficulties with European Monetary Union," in Michele Fratianni and Theo Peeters, eds., *One Money for Europe* (London: Macmillan, 1978), pp. 52-68.

[27] Hamada, "Political Economy of Monetary Integration," p. 24.

capital.[28] The outcome would be deflationary and would lead to a sudden substitution of the indexed money for national moneys. Coming to a different conclusion is Klein, who finds the inflation-proof guarantee insufficient to drive European national currencies out of circulation quickly.[29] Klein's argument is based on the empirical proposition that confidence in a new money cannot be built suddenly but evolves gradually.

This is not the place to discuss the relative merits of the manifesto's proposal, a discussion that has taken place elsewhere.[30] Suffice it to say that political union may be an important condition for monetary union in the specific sense that the instillation of confidence in Europe's new money may require the power of the state to provide the complementary public goods, defense and money, and to supply the latter in a manner consistent with a zero rate of inflation. In the absence of such an ideal state of affairs, second-best considerations suggest that the present charter of EMS be amended with the aim of enhancing the acceptability of ECU in the marketplace. The following list of suggestions, far from being exhaustive, is indicative of where improvements should be made.

First, current restrictions on the use of ECUs should be eliminated. In addition to the self-imposed limitation of using ECUs as a means of settlement among central banks, legislation or regulation in some member states still prohibits domestic contracts from being denominated in foreign currencies. Germany does not allow banks to open accounts in European units of accounts (EUAs—note that ECU is equal to EUA). Denmark, France, Ireland, and Italy do not permit their residents to maintain accounts with foreign banks. The acquisition of financial assets denominated in foreign currencies is similarly restricted.

Second, interest rates on ECUs should be market determined. To the extent that ECUs face a confidence problem and do not constitute an optimally diversified portfolio of world currencies, an interest rate subsidy may be in order to attract customers.[31]

[28] Bela Balassa, "Monetary Arrangements in the European Common Market," *Banca Nazionale del Lavoro Quarterly Review,* vol. 119 (December 1976), pp. 291-308; Giovanni Magnifico, *Una moneta per l'Europe* (Rome: Laterza, 1976).

[29] Benjamin Klein, "Competing Monies, European Monetary Union, and the Dollar," in Fratianni and Peeters, *One Money for Europe,* pp. 69-101.

[30] Fratianni and Peeters, *One Money for Europe;* Vaubel, *Strategies for Currency Unification.*

[31] The idea of making a parallel currency more attractive than a national currency is not new. See, for example, Giovanni Magnifico, *European Monetary Unification* (London: Macmillan, 1973), for specific proposals; Vaubel, *Strategies for Currency Unification,* pp. 106-8, provides a critical synthesis of the literature.

Third, national banking systems should be relied upon to issue ECU-denominated deposits. Some banks already do so, covering for their deposits by buying the underlying currencies in the foreign exchange markets. The cost of this cover could be reduced if the EMF were to issue ECU deposits to banks. The resource savings to society are the possible economies of scale—transaction costs and risk diversification—enjoyed by the Fund. In time, EMF may set reserve requirements on ECU-denominated liabilities.

Fourth, parity changes in the EMS should not be left to political discretion but ought to follow a rule known to market participants. One such rule could be the type of purchasing power parity (PPP) proposed in Optica II and further analyzed by Basevi and De Grauwe.[32] The resolution establishing EMS refers explicitly to the aim of creating a "zone of monetary stability in Europe." This is to be interpreted as price stability rather than exchange rate stability.[33] Because national economic policies are largely responsible for national rates of inflation, a PPP rule would codify the extent to which member states' policies diverge. Parity realignments would decrease in frequency and size as national economic policies converged to each other.

Fifth, the EMF could be entrusted with the function of smoothing out large deviations of exchange rate movements from their PPP values. To prevent the Fund from sustaining a fundamentally weak currency, that is, one that requires a parity adjustment, the operations of the Fund could be constrained so that the currency composition of its assets must remain approximately the same over the long run.

Sixth, the EMF could be empowered to issue ECU liabilities of different maturities. This would enable the Fund to operate in both the ECU money and the bond markets. The Fund could, for example, purchase Italian lira bonds with the proceeds of a new issue of ECU bonds of the same maturity. The transaction would not add to the European stock of base money; it would simply redistribute assets in favor of assets denominated in ECUs.

Finally, with a developed asset market in ECUs, the Fund could be entrusted with the exchange rate policy of the Community. As an example, consider an inflow of dollars into country A which, in an effort

[32] Commission of the European Communities, *Inflation and Exchange Rates: Evidence and Policy Guidelines for the European Community*, Optica II Report (Brussels, 1977); Giorgio Basevi and Paul de Grauwe, "Vicious and Virtuous Circles and the Optica Proposal," in Fratianni and Peeters, *One Money for Europe*, pp. 144-57.

[33] T. Padoa-Schioppa, "The EMF: Topics for Discussion," paper presented to the Second International Seminar on European Economic and Monetary Union (Geneva, December 7-8, 1979).

to keep a stable rate of exchange of its currency with the dollar, creates additional money. The Fund could float ECU-denominated bonds in country A and use the proceeds to buy dollars in the foreign exchange market. If this were done, the money stock in country A would be restored to the level prevailing before the inflow of dollars, and the rate of exchange between currency A and the dollar would be kept stable.[34]

Conclusions

The existence of a dominant money enhances world trade by facilitating its being monetized and multilateral. The dollar standard is weakening, and there is no indication that U.S. monetary policy will restore price stability in the near future. On the other hand, no other national money is capable of replacing the dollar as dominant money. The economies of the European Community as a group could provide such an alternative. Monetary union in Europe is a long way off; and without monetary union Europe cannot produce a money that can challenge the key position of the dollar. ECU, the parallel currency created by EMS, has weaknesses that are in part congenital and in part legislated. Even though the short-run prospects for ECU to emerge as an important store of value and medium of exchange are slim, European policy makers could do a great deal to make this artificial currency more attractive than it is at present.

[34] The example is only illustrative. A policy of this kind has little to recommend it, for it would encourage larger U.S. deficits. The Fund would bear the risk of capital losses resulting from a depreciation of the dollar.

Commentary

Ralph C. Bryant

The papers by Edward Bernstein and Michele Fratianni contain perceptive comments about the role of the dollar as an international reserve asset and, in Bernstein's case, insights about the balance of payments of the United States. Instead of focusing my discussion on points with which I disagree, I shall amplify several of the themes raised by the papers and in so doing try to extend the argument and put the issues in a broader perspective. My remarks also have a bearing on several of the topics discussed elsewhere in this volume.

Political Pluralism and Economic Interdependence. Fratianni speaks of a "weakening of the dollar standard" and the increasing failure of the dollar to play the role of a "dominant money." Bernstein, too, although in a less sweeping way and with more qualifications, sees a relative decline in the role of the dollar as an official reserve asset. I believe it is important to analyze the changes in the dollar's status against the background of a pervasive secular trend characteristic of all aspects of international relations. That trend could be described, to use the shorthand cliché, as the declining political hegemony of the United States. A more accurate characterization, however, would be "increasing political pluralism"—a situation in which one nation or a few nations no longer effectively dominate international decision making.[1]

[1] It is germane to recall that the Bretton Woods agreement establishing the International Monetary Fund and the World Bank was effectively negotiated by just two nations, Great Britain and the United States. Gardner's book on those negotiations of the 1940s starts by quoting a little rhyme he says he found on a yellow scrap of paper in the British archives: "In Washington Lord Halifax / Once whispered to Lord Keynes / It's true *they* have all the money bags / But we have all the brains." Whatever the distribution of brains and money in 1945-1946, it is abundantly clear that the situation is very different some thirty or forty years later. To appreciate the difference, one need only contrast the Committee of Twenty and the Interim Committee discussions of recent years with the tenor of the negotiations at that earlier time. See Richard N. Gardner, *Sterling-Dollar Diplomacy*, expanded ed. (New York: McGraw-Hill, 1969).

454

The fact that economic and political power is today diffused more widely among the industrialized Western nations and the Soviet Union than in the 1940s needs no elaboration. It does need to be stressed for some American readers, however, that the diffusion of wealth and power extends well beyond the Soviet Union, Europe, and Japan. That broader diffusion, moreover, is not due solely to the dramatic increase in the political and economic muscle of the oil-exporting countries. It was true in the 1970s, and could well continue to be true in the 1980s, that a number of advanced non-oil-developing countries grew more vigorously than the traditional industrial powers.

The trend toward greater political pluralism means that a significantly larger number of nations must be involved in policy decisions affecting the world polity and economy—for virtually any area of policy issues one cares to consider.

For reasons spelled out in the literature on game theory, decision making in large groups is more difficult than in smaller groups. Game-theoretic indeterminacies, moreover, are endemic to the interaction of national policies. The problems and tensions that can arise are analogous to those that occur in oligopolistic markets and industries.

The greater international diffusion of economic and political power has an important bearing on the ability of the world as a whole to reach cooperative decisions. If only a few nations needed to be involved in critical negotiations, each could easily learn about the probable behavior of the others, including the likelihood of cooperative decision making. The outcome of bargaining would be more likely to be determinate, and the potential value of cooperation could be more readily perceived. If many nations must be involved, however, with none dominant, any learning process has to be more protracted. Perceptions of the potential mutual benefits of cooperation will be less clear, and the outcomes of bargaining may not be determinate.

Is cooperation important? We know both from practical experience and from the formal analysis in game theory that it can be very important. When cooperative and noncooperative games are compared, for example, it is evident that noncooperative decisions can easily lead to outcomes that are far outside the efficient set attainable through explicit bargaining and cooperation.

The difficulties for collective decision making arising from a large rather than a small number of participating nations are exacerbated by the tendency of most nations to perceive themselves as "small" and to assume that their behavior does not significantly affect the rest of the world. From the theoretical analysis of similar situations at the microeconomic level, we know that this attitude can lead to quite undesirable outcomes for the world as a whole. Even if each individual nation behaves rationally in the light of its own objectives and even if all nations share some objectives, the tendency to ignore the consequences of one's actions for others can collectively produce a suboptimal outcome. The larger the group of nations involved, the greater the probability that some nations will act as "free riders," and hence the *less* likely it is that the group of nations will further their common interests.

Another pervasive secular trend in the world economy is related to increasing political pluralism but deserves separate billing, namely, the *increasing interdependence of national economies*. The ratio of international trade in goods and services to world output has been rising fairly steadily throughout the last four decades, and financial interdependence among nations has increased even faster than trade interdependence in the 1960s and 1970s.

The increases in economic interdependence have far-reaching consequences for national economic policies. Policy actions taken in a home nation, for example, spill over to a greater extent into the rest of the world (commonly having a smaller impact at home than when the economy was less open); this reduction in policy autonomy complicates home policy decisions. Policy actions taken abroad and nonpolicy disturbances originating abroad tend to spill over into the home economy to a greater extent than before. Macroeconomic policy for a single nation thus becomes more difficult to make and more uncertain in its consequences. Furthermore, the customary distinction between "domestic" economic policy and "international" economic policy becomes more and more elusive as the national economy becomes progressively more open.[2]

The combination of increasing political pluralism and increasing economic interdependence creates a strong prima facie case for greater efforts toward collective decision making in the global economy. The increasing openness of economies and the greater cross-national impact of policy actions increase the potential gains from coordination. The growing pluralism exacerbates the free-rider problem and raises the probability that things will fall between stools in the absence of greater efforts toward collective decision making.

Unlike Fratianni, I do not see "money" problems (more precisely, the reserve-asset characteristics of the international monetary system) as the main area in which we need to apply these insights from the theory of public goods and collective action. Indeed, I would argue

[2] These consequences of increasing interdependence are analyzed carefully in Ralph C. Bryant, *Money and Monetary Policy in Interdependent Nations* (Washington, D.C.: Brookings Institution, 1980).

that it is international cooperation itself that is the public good par excellence in the global economy. Problems requiring such cooperation are especially noteworthy in the areas of energy (for example, contingency planning for shortfalls in world oil supplies), coordination of macroeconomic policies (for example, guidelines for nations' demand-management policies following the 1980–1981 world slowdown), and regulatory policies (for example, discussion of the disparities in national antitrust policies).

Furthermore, I do not believe the United States *can* dominate international decisions and institutions as it once did. The United States would not have that capacity even if it followed superconservative monetary and fiscal policies and brought the U.S. inflation rate below that in all other countries. Trying to turn the clock back is fruitless. The sooner we stop yearning for the day when one nation or a few nations were dominant, the sooner we can make progress in improving the oligopolistic global environment that will characterize the 1980s.

Alternative Evolutions of the Dollar and the International Monetary System. Against the preceding background, I shall now comment more specifically about the dollar as a reserve asset and about Bernstein's views on the proposed Substitution Account.

Bernstein makes many sensible observations about the diversification of official reserves away from the dollar. As he points out, diversification that has occurred to date is more subtle, and somewhat less extensive, than is often claimed. The most striking trends evident in the aggregate data on official reserve holdings are the increasing importance of the deutsche mark, the Swiss franc, and the yen and the declining importance of sterling; the share of dollar-denominated assets in official reserves has not changed greatly. Nonetheless, particularly for a number of individual nations outside the Group of Ten, there are perceptible indications of the declining relative importance of the reserve-currency role of the dollar. The world seems to have embarked, albeit not yet very dramatically, on an evolutionary path leading to a multiple-currency-asset system of reserve holdings.

Can we envisage an alternative evolution of the reserve-asset characteristics of the world monetary system that involves a declining role for the dollar? If we are prepared to be visionary, we can. Instead of the multiple-currency-asset system (which is, in effect, a multiple-*inside*-reserve system), it is conceivable that the world could gradually move toward what may be called a single-*outside*-reserve system.

If that alternative evolutionary path were followed, national governments would look for and seize opportunities to increase the amount of

457

outside reserves relative to reserve currencies (inside reserves).[3] As much as possible of incremental reserve growth would take the form of special drawing rights (SDR) or some outside asset of a similar nature. In addition, opportunities would be taken to substitute outside reserves for existing amounts of inside reserves. Eventually, after a long transition, the bulk of world reserves would be held in the form of a single outside asset.

In Fratianni's discussion of the "weakening dollar standard," the only alternative considered is *replacing* the dollar with a European reserve asset, say, the European currency unit (ECU). Fratianni does not grapple with the issues raised by a multiple-inside-reserve system or alternatives to it. Nor does Bernstein explicitly discuss the broader problems of a multiple-inside-reserve system.

It is not possible here to compare carefully the alternative evolutionary paths. Let me just assert my own view that a single-outside-reserve system, if it could be implemented, would prove superior to the multiple-inside-reserve system. I hold that view even though a multiple-inside-reserve system could be made reasonably tolerable if reserve-center nations acted cooperatively to offset asset switching and even though a single-outside-reserve system would require a much higher degree of international collective action.

I prefer to think of the proposed Substitution Account as a modest step that keeps open the possibility of gradually moving toward a single-outside-reserve system. I see the Substitution Account as an innovation with potential benefits for all nations—an international public good—and therefore something that in principle should involve a collective sharing of rights and responsibilities.

Bernstein does not present the Substitution Account in this way.[4] Instead, he describes the account as a "further" step the *United States* could take "to give foreign monetary authorities greater confidence in the dollar" and as part of "taking responsibility" for the external value of the dollar. I do not want to exaggerate our differences about the Substitution Account. Bernstein has become a supporter of the account;

---

[3] The distinction between outside reserves and inside reserves is analogous to the distinction between outside money and inside money in John G. Gurley and Edward S. Shaw, *Money in a Theory of Finance* (Washington, D.C.: Brookings Institution, 1960). Outside reserves in the world monetary system are those official reserve assets that do *not* have a reserve liability of a reserve-center nation as a counterpart; the two important types of outside reserves at present are gold and special drawing rights (SDR). Inside reserve assets held by one nation *do* have a counterpart reserve liability owed by a reserve-center nation.

[4] Despite any appearances to the contrary, this is indeed the same Edward Bernstein who drafted the visionary plan in the early 1970s for a Reserve Settlement Account, which would have been de facto a single-outside-reserve system.

I certainly am; we agree on many of its features. Our different emphases, however, do generate conflicting views on at least two points.

One disagreement concerns the valuation and interest-rate features of the account. Bernstein believes that the United States must "take responsibility for the SDR value of the assets in the account"—that is, denominate the liabilities of the United States to the account in SDRs rather than the dollar and thus have the United States assume the entire burden of the "red-ink problem" (that is, the discrepancy between the value of the assets and the liabilities of the account that would exist if the assets were denominated in dollars or other national currencies, the liabilities were denominated in SDRs, and the SDR values of the national currencies changed). Because I see the account in the wider context of a modest start toward a single-outside-reserve system, and because I am anticipating how the red-ink problem will eventually have to be handled when gold and nondollar national currency assets are also consolidated in the account (or successor accounts), I believe that a different solution to the valuation and interest-rate problems is preferable. In principle, the assets of the account should be denominated in the national currency of the country whose reserve liabilities have been "substituted," and the nations participating in the account should share the valuation (and interest rate) risk in an agreed manner.

My second disagreement with Bernstein arises because he urges the Treasury and Federal Reserve to "maintain" the SDR value of the dollar and to link the Substitution Account directly to this exchange-rate commitment. In my view, stabilization of the SDR value of the dollar would be a poor general guideline for U.S. external monetary policy. To be sure, I share with Bernstein the notion that the United States should feel "responsibility" for the external value of the dollar. ("Responsibility" does not have an unambiguous meaning in this context. The external value of the dollar depends on policy actions and nonpolicy disturbances originating abroad as well as on U.S. policy actions and nonpolicy disturbances originating in the United States. Even so, like Bernstein I favor management of dollar exchange rates and oppose a policy of no exchange-market intervention. I even oppose a policy that restricts intervention solely to "disorderly market conditions.") I would not, however, carry managed floating so far as to commit the United States to a policy of pegging the value of the dollar against any single foreign currency or against an average of all major currencies (such as the SDR). Circumstances can and will arise when it is appropriate—certainly for the narrow interests of the United States, and probably also for the interests of other nations—for the average value of the dollar (and hence the SDR value) to change, either up or down.

459

As emphasized earlier, the hegemonic power of the United States has declined and may continue to decline. Because of the worldwide use of the dollar as a reserve asset, the United States cannot and should not try to achieve "symmetry" with other countries—in exchange-rate policy or in any other area. Neither should it try to behave as asymmetrically as it once could and did. It would be excessive asymmetry to saddle the United States and the rest of the world with a commitment to maintain the external value of the dollar unchanged, even against an average of major foreign currencies.

Keeping the International Monetary System in Perspective. Although I am a strong supporter of the Substitution Account, I want to conclude by voicing a worry that some of the account's proponents may be overselling it.

An unfortunate tendency exists, among both economists and policy makers, to place too much emphasis on "the international monetary system" and to analyze it in isolation, as though it were a separately definable entity with an important life of its own. One also frequently encounters the view that, if governments can devise the "right" international monetary system, that alone can play a major role in getting the world economy back on the track to prosperity and harmony.

In truth, however, the international monetary system is not so important in itself as often thought. The benefits of increasing interdependence will occur, and the constraints it imposes on national economic policies will bind strongly, *regardless of the nature of the international monetary system.* In particular, national policy makers will have increasing difficulty conducting macroeconomic policy, regardless of the degree and manner of exchange rate variability endorsed in the International Monetary Fund Articles of Agreement. All of the most difficult international economic problems we shall have to face in this decade will plague us, whether we are in the multiple-inside-reserve world or set out vigorously on an evolutionary path to a single-outside-reserve system. The fundamental issues generated by increasing interdependence and increasing political pluralism concern, for example, the interaction of the *domestic* as well as the external economic policies of nations and the discrepancies between the national regulatory environments applied to *domestic* transactions and to external transactions.

Giovanni Magnifico

In discussing Michele Fratianni's paper, "The Dollar and the ECU," I shall confine my remarks to the sections that deal with the European monetary system (EMS) and the European currency unit (ECU) in particular.

The section on the EMS is an analysis of the arrangements signed in Brussels in December 1978. It opens with such blunt statements as "the goal of monetary union is no closer today than it was in 1969"; "The short answer to this question [whether the EMS in its present form represents a significant step toward European monetary union] is no." The analysis leaves the reader with no doubt that the EMS and the ECU are not viable, both because of faulty basic conception and for the many technical flaws.

The same reader cannot help being surprised, however, when he reaches the section on confidence and the ECU, where Fratianni examines ways and means of improving the prospects of the ECU, both as a viable parallel currency and as an alternative to the dollar. There the reader discovers that the European Monetary Fund (EMF) "could be entrusted with the exchange rate policy of the Community"; that it "could float ECU-denominated bonds"—that is, that it could intervene on the exchange and capital markets of the Community; and, finally (in the concluding section), that "European policy makers could do a great deal to make this artificial currency more attractive than it is at present."

But the question is bound to be asked, How can "nonsense" be made "more attractive"? If something can be made more attractive, it must surely already have some attractive qualities.

What I have just said is certainly not meant to imply that whereas the EMS makes a lot of sense, Fratianni's paper does not. I think that the dissonance in the general tone of the section on the EMS, on the one hand, and the section on the ECU, on the other, is a consequence of Fratianni's effort to stress his main (and legitimate) point: namely, that there is still a long way to go before we can speak of European monetary union and a European currency. In order to make this point forcefully, in my view, he dramatizes in the former section the nature of the weakness in the EMS construction as it now exists. In what follows I shall attempt to demonstrate some of the flaws in that part of Fratianni's paper.

Fratianni lists four features as distinguishing the EMS from the "snake": (1) the introduction of the ECU as a parallel currency; (2) the indicator of divergence; (3) the European Monetary Fund; and (4) regional income redistribution. He fails, however, to take into consideration an important new element, the different EMS philosophy with regard to exchange rates.

The "snake" was a rigid exchange-rate arrangement that aimed at preserving on a regional basis the kind of exchange-rate system that had prevailed under the International Monetary Fund (IMF) Articles

461

of Agreement or—more precisely—under the interpretation the Articles of Agreement had been given during the first twenty or so years of their implementation. According to that interpretation, exchange-rate changes were to be made only in cases of "fundamental disequilibrium." Although there are theoretical grounds on which the notion of fundamental disequilibrium could be defined, a definition was never agreed upon, so that parity changes were de facto largely ruled out as an instrument in the adjustment process. In the mid-1960s I was a member of a study group set up by the Organization for Economic Cooperation and Development (OECD) that was supposed to produce recipes for improving the adjustment process. In the terms of reference, however, there was no mention of parity changes or changes in the gold price; in fact, the study group was told that it should not consider such instruments.

The 1972 "snake" arrangement aimed at freezing the structure of intra-European exchange rates. At that time the parity system was crumbling under the cumulative disequilibriums caused by the fact that governments, which in theory were bound by a fixed-rate system, for years had pursued policies that in fact ignored the fixed-exchange-rate constraint and thus behaved as if there were a floating-rate system.

On the other hand, the EMS, though tending to stabilize exchange rates, does not rule out exchange-rate changes as an instrument in the adjustment process. It recognizes that such changes will have to be resorted to as long as inconsistent national cost trends persist and that such trends cannot be made consistent simply by locking exchange rates.

The philosophy underlying the EMS implies that changes in central rates will be allowed by "mutual agreement" insofar as they are consistent with the differential evolution of fundamental economic variables. This, in turn, implies an undertaking by participating countries to keep the effects of accidental, seasonal, and cyclical factors on their exchange rates within the admitted margins of fluctuation around central rates. As is the case when countries announce money or credit targets, the announcement of compulsory intervention points has a stabilizing effect on expectations. Markets are told that short-term factors, such as short-term capital movements, cannot make exchange rates move beyond the margins. Consequently, when an EMS country whose currency is weak pays a higher interest rate, there can be no expectation that capital flowing in will benefit from both the interest-rate differential and a short-term appreciation of the exchange rate, which the capital inflow by itself would tend to bring about. Markets know that when an EMS country with a structurally weak balance of payments is confronted with a capital inflow it will have to intervene so as not to allow its exchange rate to appreciate beyond the restricted margins, because appreciation of the central rate would by hypothesis be inconsistent with the medium-term equilibrium rate. Rather, the EMS philosophy would suggest a downward adjustment in the medium term; because it would not be known when this might take place, the capital inflow would be dampened by the fact that the cost of forward cover would tend to offset the interest rate gain.

Countries whose currencies are not subject to a comparable exchange-rate constraint find it more difficult to avail themselves of this self-equilibrating market mechanism. Thus, speculative and, in general, short-term factors tend to have a disproportionate influence and to lead to "overshooting" of exchange rates and capital movements. In short, the EMS tends to curb the amplitude of exchange-rate changes. In my view, it tends to do this because it helps to (a) avoid "overshooting" under the pressure of speculative capital movements triggered by extrapolative and anticipatory expectations; (b) harmonize business cycle policies in the European Economic Community (to the extent that discrepancies in the business cycle require differentiated stabilization policies, these can be accommodated within the band);[1] and (c) prevent competitive devaluations and revaluations.

Far from being of little significance, the EMS marks a change in the attitudes of governments disillusioned by the experience of floating rates between 1973 and 1978 and worried about the consequences of their volatility for resource allocation and the propensity of businessmen to invest. External monetary instability implies welfare losses analogous to those caused by domestic price instability. In the light of the measures taken by the U.S. government in 1978 (and subsequently), the EMS may be regarded as part of a worldwide attempt to move away from free floating and toward more external stability—that is, a return to the notion that external and domestic stability are but two faces of the same coin.

I am speaking of a change in attitudes and of an attempt to stabilize exchange rates. As to whether this attempt will succeed, we have conflicting evidence so far.

It is fair to say that recently there has been more coherence (or less incoherence, if you prefer) in monetary policies, particularly as regards interest rates. This is an aim of EMS. I have attended meetings of the European Economic Community (EEC) Monetary Committee and of the Committee of Central Bank Governors throughout the seventies, and I think I am right in saying that, since the inception of the EMS,

---

[1] Italy requested and obtained the option of a wider band by pointing to the difficulty of integrating the four largest EEC economies compared with the difficulty involved in integrating a group of smaller economies with the Federal Republic of Germany; after the United Kingdom, Italy, and France quit the "snake," this became truly a deutsche mark (DM) area.

monetary (and other) policies pursued by member countries have been under much closer scrutiny. In some cases it has been explicitly acknowledged that the discussions in these EEC bodies and the conclusions reached were used to influence the decisions of national authorities. More coherent monetary policies and the effect on expectations of the announcement of intervention points for EMS currencies may explain why in 1979 there were no important destabilizing capital movements.

On the negative side, we find the acceleration of inflation and the accompanying increase in the dispersion of national inflation rates revealed by comparing national consumer price indexes (CPI). The picture is one of less divergence when industrial wholesale prices are compared, but measures will have to be taken in the high-inflation countries with widespread indexation mechanisms to prevent the higher speed of consumer prices from affecting producers' prices in the medium term. The effect of shifts in world demand determined by factors other than relative prices, moreover, should be taken into account. Italy's performance in 1979, with its quota of world exports increasing while its prices were rising more rapidly, cannot be completely explained without positing such a shift in world demand for Italian exports. A differential increase in world demand for a country's exports creates room for differential price increases that do not jeopardize the exchange-rate structure; it means that the rest of the world is ready to pay more for goods produced by that country. For the price increase to take place, it is not necessary to assume full employment in the exporting country; if company profits are low (under the pressure of cost push), companies can be expected to seize the occasion of brisk external demand to increase prices, and profits, before capacity is fully used.

These qualifications regarding the most widely used measure of divergence are not intended to play down the problems that shocks such as the cumulative oil price rises create for countries whose ability to adjust still differs considerably. They do point to the limited usefulness of the approach centered on purchasing power parity (PPP) in exchange-rate determination. I do not accept the proposition suggested by Fratianni that central rate changes should follow a PPP rule, partly because a domestic policy that produces a slowdown of prices can help a country to get back in line with the other industrial countries when their average rate of inflation is as high as it is now. In other words, the "ratchet effect" argument—according to which, once price levels in different countries have got out of line, it is difficult to get back to a consistent structure of exchange rates unless these are changed— loses much of its force if all a country has to do to get back in line is to engineer a slowdown of its rate of price increase and not a cut in the price level. Any automatic formula, moreover, makes it easier for speculators to bank on impending central rate changes.

Fratianni argues that there was symmetry in the adjustment process under the "snake" arrangement. I would say that it is difficult to make a prima facie case for the symmetry of a system when three of the four main participating countries left the system and all three were deficit countries. To make his point, Fratianni has to assume the absence of policies to sterilize the effects of exchange interventions on national money stocks. This is a very important proviso—but also an unrealistic one. Surplus countries have tended to sterilize the *domestic* sources of liquidity, thereby offsetting excess creation through the *external* component; we know that the Deutsche Bundesbank supplied the German banking system with the liquidity it needed by buying dollars, rather than by rediscounting domestic paper. Compensatory policies on the part of surplus countries made it necessary for deficit countries to have more restrictive policies. The system was also asymmetrical in that the cost, in reserve losses, of intervention carried out by surplus and deficit countries was in the end borne by the latter: The exhaustion of reserves and of external creditworthiness is a more stringent constraint than the subjective willingness or unwillingness to accumulate reserves. That deficit countries were obliged to adjust first tended to loosen the surplus countries' constraint. In the end, weak-currency countries had to quit, and that allowed them to continue to indulge in compensatory policies and inflation. The outcome was a widening of the gulf between the performances of strong-currency and weak-currency countries.

I do not quite follow Fratianni's argument that the ECU imposes an additional information cost on traders, who have to be informed about seven currencies (instead of one), and that this is likely to discourage its use. For one thing, he rightly points to the inclusion in the basket of currencies, such as the guilder, with a high positive covariance with the deutsche mark (DM). Thus, these currencies tend to behave as one currency, which reduces the number of currencies to "watch." Currencies with a high DM covariance raise the DM weight in the basket; they are not redundant, as Fratianni seems to argue. Because the number of units of each currency is fixed, the weights in the ECU basket change as central rate changes take place: The weight of appreciating currencies increases cumulatively, conversely for depreciating ones.

In short, an investor in ECU assets knows that because the ECU conversion rate will follow the average performance of the currencies in the basket, he will be spared the vagaries to which single currencies are liable in conditions of great instability; he also knows that because

465

the weight of strong currencies in the ECU is likely to increase, the ECU exchange rate will exhibit a growing tendency to move in line with the strong currencies in the basket. When uncertainty prevails as a result of swings such as those seen recently in the DM/dollar rate, moreover, a monetary unit based on the average performance of a number of currencies tends to become attractive, even compared with "the" strong currency in the basket.

I think that there is sufficient ex ante information here to meet the needs of operators who are not trying to make quick profits through currency speculation. In any case, I do not see how a speculator can do better than average if he confines his information to just one currency (other than his own).

Finally, may I be allowed to recall that the idea of a composite currency unit to minimize risk is a very old one? W. S. Jevons, in *Money and the Mechanism of Exchange,* asks, "Can we not conceive a multiple legal tender, which would be still less liable to variation? . . . All these commodities will, of course, fluctuate in their relative values, but if the holder of the note loses upon some, he will in all probability gain upon others, so that on the average his note will remain steady in purchasing power." [2]

Fratianni writes that the European Monetary Fund "could float ECU-denominated bonds in country *A* and use the proceeds to buy dollars in the foreign exchange market." This is very close to an idea that I developed in two articles written for the *Journal of Commerce.*[3]

I agree with Fratianni that self-imposed restrictions on the use of the ECUs should be done away with. EEC monetary authorities should make the ECU a full-fledged official currency. It should also be eligible for use outside the circle of EEC central banks and should be held by members of the Organization of Petroleum Exporting Countries, who would invest part of their oil surpluses with an important group of their trading partners. The ECU would thus produce diversification of flows and help to solve the problem of too much international debt being denominated in dollars.

[2] W. S. Jevons, *Money and the Mechanism of Exchange* (London: Kegan Paul, 1878), pp. 327-28.

[3] It was argued there that the European Monetary Fund should be given the functions of a European open market committee. It would be enabled to carry out operations aimed at mopping up excess liquidity on the market of strong-currency countries in the Community that had happened to buy dollars in order to prevent excess appreciation of their currencies and/or jeopardizing of EEC internal cohesion. The Fund would do this by selling on those markets ECU-denominated securities bearing interest that would make them competitive with national paper. The Fund would then convert its European currency proceeds into dollars at the issuing central bank. Giovanni Magnifico, "Open Market Operation for Europe?" *Journal of Commerce,* April 26, 1979.

I also agree with Fratianni that interest rates on ECUs should be market determined. There should be more than just one interest rate; indeed, there should be different rates for different risks. This is not, however, contrary to the rule to which Fratianni objects, which applies the weighted average of discount rates in member countries to central bank borrowing. These are short-term operations, and central banks are a better risk than market risks. There is, thus, no subsidization and, consequently, no depressing effect on central bank demand for ECUs. Rather, at least in the short term, official demand for ECUs is bound to be depressed because of questions concerning the convertibility of the ECU and the constraints on its use for settlements outside the EEC.

I would change the present rule, moreover, according to which interest is paid only on *net* positions by net users to net holders—an arrangement reminiscent of the special drawing right and one that detracts from the notion of the ECU as a currency in its own right. Unlike Fratianni, I should not like to see reserve requirements imposed on ECU-denominated liabilities. It seems to me that if we wish an "infant currency" to have a chance of competing on private markets with well-established currencies, such as the dollar and the DM, we should not burden it with more controls than apply to the latter.

Despite all the arguments I have attempted to present in favor of the ECU, I am under no illusion that the spontaneous evolution of international monetary relations is leading to a *dollar/DM standard;* indeed, if the United States persists in its present antiinflationary stance and finally subdues inflation, there will be a consolidation of that standard. From an economic point of view, this should not necessarily strain the EMS; if it led to a more stable dollar/DM rate, it might even help. On the other hand, it increases the risk that the "common" dollar policy, which is needed to maintain cohesion within the EEC, will actually satisfy the policy requirements of just one country—and this would create tensions.

Again, I realize that tensions are bound to develop and that they might jeopardize the very existence of the EMS. By joining a monetary union a country with a high propensity to inflation suffers costs in terms of lost output, such as are usually associated with disinflationary programs. Fratianni argues—not unexpectedly, in light of his monetarist views—that "such costs are positive in the short run and zero in the long run." I should think that in the short run not only are they positive but they can also be very high—which is one reason why governments are not inclined to enact strong disinflationary policies.

I think that for EMS to survive a dramatic change is needed in the present approach. The emphasis of EEC actions and programs has to

467

shift from exchange rate arrangements and facilities for financing balance-of-payments deficits to common policies of balanced growth, industrial investment, and labor relations, so that the adjustment posited by recent changes in relative scarcities and prices at the world level can be carried out with efficiency and in a less painful way.

Fritz Machlup

The *spiritus rector* of this conference, Gottfried Haberler, suggested to me that, instead of looking for points to criticize in the papers of Edward Bernstein and Michele Fratianni, I should deal with a question only briefly touched upon by Bernstein: the question of the high price of gold and its economic significance. Because it would be quite difficult to find any weak spots in the two papers, I am glad to accept Haberler's suggestion. As a veteran participant in discussions about gold, who has sometimes been accused of having said quite foolish things about it, I shall gladly address myself to "The High Price of Bullion," although I cannot hope to make a contribution on a level comparable to that of a famous pamphlet published, not by me, under that title in 1812.

Two years ago, on January 20, 1978, gold sold in London for $173 an ounce; on January 19, 1979, the price was $231; on January 18, 1980, it was $835. On September 21, 1979, when the price was $369, Charles Stahl, the gold expert, wrote in his *Commodity Market Comments* a piece under the title "14 Tulips for 1 Ounce of Gold." At the price reached on January 18, 1980, speculators and investors paid twenty-six tulips of 1635 vintage for one ounce of gold. The reference, of course, is to the famous tulip craze of the seventeenth century.

Bernstein mentions, near the end of his paper, some of the crazy things proposed by the chrysophiles, including the suggestion that the world reintroduce a gold standard with the price of gold fixed at the present market level. Bernstein is much too polite to say what he thinks about the proponents of such schemes, but he does state that the proposal is completely unrealistic, not just because none of the countries would be prepared to accept it but mainly because its acceptance would subject the world to an intolerable inflation of money and price levels. He refers chiefly to the sales of gold out of private hoards that would follow the restoration of monetary stability when people would no longer have to fear inflation and, therefore, their demand for holding gold as an inflation hedge or as an appreciating asset would disappear. If the monetary authorities were to purchase the gold disgorged by private holders, and if they paid for it with newly created national money, the resulting inflation would make our current inflation look pale in comparison.

I fear that, even without a return to a gold standard and without new gold acquisitions by our monetary authorities, the revaluation of the gold reserves by several central banks may have inflationary effects. One does not have to be an international-reserve monetarist to expect that some central banks will conduct more expansionary, or less restrictive, monetary policies when their books show a superabundance of reserves. This temptation may not be effective at the German Bundesbank and a few other central banks that are similarly determined to keep inflation down; for most central banks, however, we must expect that their reluctance to adopt unpopular restrictions in credit policy will be further increased when they are flush with reserve assets. Strong reserve positions favor monetary expansion: The authorities will far more easily part with special drawing rights (SDR) and U.S. dollars when their gold reserves are large. The gold stock held by monetary authorities (including international authorities) is at present 1.15 billion ounces or, at $650 an ounce, about $750 billion. A year ago, the same gold holdings amounted to only $288 billion.

There is a tendency, in many markets, for people to accept a price reached after a strong and consistent upward movement as something like an ordained value, reflecting long-run conditions of supply and demand. People assume that such a price movement cannot reverse itself. When the price of gold has been above $600 an ounce for eight or ten weeks, many "experts" cannot conceive of the possibility that it may recede to, say, $250, although it had always been below $250 until May 1979. People in this frame of mind should take note of some facts, especially in regard to the cost of production of gold by the largest producer of gold outside the Soviet Union. According to the South African Chamber of Mines, the average cost of production of South African gold mines for the year 1979 was US$125.45 an ounce, which is 50 percent of $250, 31 percent of $400, 21 percent of $600, and 16 percent of $800. The production cost in 1972 had been only $27.35 an ounce. At that time, richer ores were mined, yielding 12.69 grams of gold per ton. By 1979, with the higher selling prices of gold, the mines had turned to lower grades of ore, yielding only 8.22 grams of gold per ton.

It is important to bear in mind that the supply of gold does not conform to the textbook model of supply in a competitive market. The two largest producers of gold in the world are the Soviet Union and South Africa; together they produce almost 80 percent of the world output. The Soviet Union sells only that portion of its annual output that it needs to pay for necessary imports not financed by loans from abroad. A higher price of gold, therefore, will reduce the physical volume of their gold sales. The South Africans do not find it wise to expand their work force; instead, they switch labor from mining high-grade ores to mining low-grade ores when the price is high. Again, this lowers the physical output at higher prices. If a naive theorist thinks that this is irrational conduct, let him know that fuller information about the situation can make the observed behavior conform to the principle of long-run profit maximization.

The demand side of the market for gold has also some rather unusual and interesting features. Gold is demanded for use in jewelry and arts, in industrial products, and in dental work. These three groups are fabricators of gold. Then there are nonfabricators, who buy gold for investment, hoarding, and speculation; all three purchase gold for storage. The demand for gold for fabrication, taking up more than half but less than two-thirds of annual output, is a demand for physical gold, and the quantities demanded vary inversely with price, except for short periods when the fabricators increase or reduce their inventories. The elasticity of demand is different in different uses. The demand by nonfabricators, however, has a very unusual characteristic: It is a demand not for physical quantities but for "money's worth" of gold. This implies that an unchanged physical quantity of gold can satisfy demand even if that demand doubles, quadruples, or expands indefinitely.

Assume that all wealthy and many not so wealthy people have been advised by their bankers and financial wizards to hold 10 percent of their wealth in gold and have followed this advice. Now, the bankers and similar wizards become more gold-bullish and tell their clients to hold 20 percent of their wealth in gold. As the advisees rush to buy more gold, the price increases. Perhaps some of the fabricators will buy a little less of the more precious metal and thus give up some quantities to the gold storekeepers. This would not be necessary, however, because the increase in the price of gold will automatically increase the money value of the asset until the ounces owned reach a value equal to 20 percent of the owner's wealth. We have here the possibility of self-fulfilling aspirations, or of demand creating its own matching supply, because what is demanded is not a quantity of a physical good but an amount of money value, and this value can be boosted indefinitely by the competitive bids of the would-be buyers.

If you ask why I tell you such a bull story, I answer that it helps explain what has happened, or at least what we find recorded. Total net private purchases of gold, for fabrication and for storage, were in 1979 almost exactly the same as they were in 1978 in terms of physical weight—1,740 metric tons—but were probably as much as 100 percent higher in dollars. The fabricators did give up some gold to the non-fabricators, as their purchases declined by some 12 percent from the quantity bought in 1978, but the supply of newly mined Western gold was unchanged, sales by the Soviets declined, and the dishoarding by monetary authorities was modest. Consequently, the increase in the nonfabricators' demand had to be satisfied by sharp increases in price. Not much of the demand for gold for storage was "squeezed out" of the market by the spectacular rise in price; instead, the demand was "satisfied" in that it was not the physical metal but its money value that the nonfabricators were anxious to increase.

In saying that sales of official holdings of gold were modest, I was referring to sales to private buyers. The International Monetary Fund (IMF) did sell a part of its gold holdings, but much of it went to national monetary authorities, that is, to official hoarders and speculators, not to private ones. Gold sales by the U.S. Treasury in 1979 amounted to 13.3 million ounces, which is 4.8 percent of its gold stock at the beginning of the year. (The U.S. gold stock declined by less, because of the gold received from the IMF distributions.) Gold sales by all monetary authorities together provided the market with 17 million ounces in 1979. This is less than 1.5 percent of the gold holdings of all monetary authorities. If official gold sales go on at this rate, the authorities will still have some gold left for the next sixty-eight years.

This brings me to the question of unmined gold deposits. The South African Chamber of Mines expects the South African gold deposits to last for another fifty years at the present rate of extraction; but Stahl's estimate comes to a larger figure. The gold deposits in the Soviet Union, estimated to be 5 billion ounces, would last almost four hundred years, if the rate of extraction remained at 400 metric tons, or 12.86 million ounces, a year. What matters much more, however, is the fact that the Russian output sold to the West, at a price of $600 an ounce, would bring the Russians $7.72 billion a year. This is a very high price that our gold lobby is willing to pay to the Soviets for supplying an inflation hedge to our asset holders. Almost $8 billion of the annual savings of the free world are to be "invested" in Russian gold instead of being used for the formation of productive capital. I cannot convince myself that this is sound policy. We surely can think of less costly ways to protect our portfolios against inflation than to hand over $8 billion a year to the Russians just to fill our cellars with sterile stocks of gold. The Russians' threat that they will bury us may still come true: They may bury us in an avalanche of gold.

What is incredible is the lack of understanding on the part of elected representatives of the people. A few years ago, in 1974, there was a bill in Congress to repeal the prohibition on American residents to own gold. I testified in favor of that bill, because I believe in freedom and find it distasteful to prohibit private actions that do no harm to anybody. The right of Americans to own gold was restored on January 1, 1975. The same legislators, however, who fought for the freedom of private ownership of gold now have a bill pending in Congress to prohibit the Treasury from selling gold to private citizens. Thus, the people should be free to buy gold, but the government is to sit tight on its gold hoard and is not to sell any part of it to satisfy private demand. This shows clearly that the intent of the proposed legislation is not to give our citizens a chance to buy the gold they want but, instead, to keep the price of gold high or perhaps, if the demand increases further, to drive the price still higher.

I find it outrageous that public authorities should withhold huge stocks of a nonnoxious commodity when so many people are eager to acquire it. The gold hoards of the monetary authorities of the Western world are enormously large. Their combined stocks are twenty-five times the annual world output of gold, or thirty-six times the annual output of the noncommunist world. Can we imagine governments' holding as much as two years' output of any commodity and refusing to sell any part of it when private demand increases? We have been told that the ancient Egyptians, on Joseph's advice, accumulated large stocks of grain, not in order to sit tight on it, but to sell it off when grain became short. I can see absolutely no justification for the public authorities to withhold their gold stocks from those who want to buy them.

Lest someone accuse me of recommending government intervention in the gold market for the purpose of lowering the price of gold, I can answer only that the decision *not* to sell gold in the face of a large demand is also an intervention. The point is that the idea of government's insisting on continuing national ownership of this commodity and refusing to sell to private buyers is indefensible in a society founded on the principles of individual freedom and private property. This does not mean that all government-owned gold should be thrown on the market at once, but it ought to be sold gradually during a period of twenty-five or thirty years.

Helen B. Junz

I have been asked to concentrate on the comments made about the proposal for a Substitution Account in the International Monetary Fund (IMF). I believe that the development of such an account is a very

472

timely one, in one major respect: The fact that so much high-powered talent could have labored so long and so hard to produce this proposal fits very well with the recent development in productivity trends, especially in the United States. In other ways, unfortunately, it seems to me that the proposal is one the time for which may already have passed.

The establishment of a Substitution Account in the IMF, in which countries would deposit part of their dollar holdings in return for an internationally guaranteed asset, has been discussed since the early 1960s. At that time the question of how to achieve the orderly creation of international liquidity formed the focus of the discussion. That question clearly still is with us, but the most recent impetus for the establishment of a Substitution Account derives from the increased potential for monetary strain associated with the large investable surpluses of the Organization of Petroleum Exporting Countries (OPEC) and the desire of official holders of financial assets to diversify their portfolios.

The principal advantages cited for the Substitution Account proposal are: (1) that it would bring into being a system based on special drawing rights (SDR) rather than on a multicurrency system; (2) that it would allow diversification of reserve assets to proceed without disrupting the market; and (3) that it would move the SDR toward the center of the international financial system.

With regard to the first point, the choice really no longer is between the establishment of *either* a multicurrency reserve *or* an SDR system. A multicurrency reserve system is already evolving. The deutsche mark (DM), yen, Swiss franc, and other nontraditional currency components in the official holdings of reserves have risen appreciably over the past several years, and this process has accelerated with the recent reemergence of large OPEC surpluses. Data on the structure of official reserve portfolios are unsatisfactory, to say the least, but crude estimates suggest that by 1979 deutsche marks may have constituted about 10 percent, Swiss francs and Japanese yen perhaps 5 percent each, sterling and French francs approximately 2 percent each, and other currencies about 2 percent of official reserve holdings. Since the end of 1979 it has become quite clear that the appearance of relatively large current account deficits for Germany and Switzerland not only has made the authorities in these countries less reluctant to allow an increase in the reserve role of their currencies but has actually motivated them to seek official investment actively in their currencies.

The ability of a Substitution Account to mitigate potential destabilization of foreign exchange markets as holders of official reserve assets either diversify existing portfolios or invest their current surpluses is limited at best. A large proportion of official reserve assets apparently is invested with an eye both to obtaining the highest possible returns and to matching asset and liability structures. This is particularly true in the case of those developing and smaller industrial countries for whom borrowed reserves constitute an important part of official holdings. Accordingly, SDR-denominated securities may be attractive mainly to those monetary authorities who in any event do not constitute the volatile segment among asset holders. In addition, the Substitution Account as currently envisaged would not meet the major requirements of high liquidity and relative anonymity stressed by a significant number of holders of official reserve assets. Thus, the initial size of the proposed account—some SDR50 billion—may be realistic in terms of probable demand but is dwarfed by the projected OPEC reserve accumulation—twice that amount for 1980 alone—and even more so by the size of existing official portfolios.

Although the Substitution Account proposal seems inadequate to deal with the problem of the portfolio balancing objective of official asset holders, the negotiation process could become expensive politically as well as economically. The question of the division of costs and exchange risks, for example, is an exceedingly difficult one to solve and could absorb a fair amount of political capital. Perhaps more important, general acceptance depends upon the support of not only the reserve rich but also the reserve poor.

In this respect, the developing countries, rightly or wrongly, are likely to construe the Substitution Account proposal as a willingness of the international community to "bail out" the United States when it has been unwilling to move similarly to fund debt of developing countries. Proposals to use a portion of the Fund's gold as backing for the Substitution Account, particularly at a time when Fund auctions—the source of finance for the Trust Fund—are to end, would further add to this perception. At a minimum, the pressure to link new SDR allocations to aid or to provide other unconditional liquidity to developing countries is likely to increase. This would inhibit the proper functioning of the adjustment process—as it would tend to postpone adoption of needed adjustment measures—and it would not enhance the role of the SDR as the main reserve asset.

In fact, there is some question as to the extent to which the Substitution Account would help move the SDR toward a more central position. If I were Stanley Black's neighbor in Nashville, I would say that if God wanted us to have an SDR system she would have created one. What I will say is, if the market had wanted SDR-denominated instruments it would have generated them. Recent attempts in the private market to issue SDR-denominated assets have not met with notable success, however, indicating that present investment objectives do not favor them. The somewhat, albeit not distinctively, greater response to ECU-denominated instruments may imply that a currency-basket approach is successful only if it overlaps the liability structure of investors to a significant extent. The SDR as it is now constituted would not meet that requirement in most instances.

In these circumstances, there is some risk that promotion of the SDR as the main diversification asset through mechanisms such as the Substitution Account could actually set back rather than promote the generally accepted goal of moving the SDR toward the center of the international monetary system. All this leads one to ask whether, in the search for greater stability in the international monetary system, the Substitution Account deserves the attention and energy of high officials that it is being accorded. In a world of unlimited resources, perhaps, but in the world we live in energies should be spent on the difficulties of recycling funds from surplus to deficit countries and of ensuring smooth and adequate adjustment. The IMF has an important function to perform in this process, not least through its surveillance function. Giving greater content to that function surely should rank high among the pressing issues that face the international economic community.

William C. Hood

Edward Bernstein has offered a thoughtful, closely reasoned contribution on an important topic. I am going to confine my comment to that part of his paper concerned specifically with the Substitution Account. Let me first summarize the essence of Bernstein's argument as I understand it; then I shall comment upon this argument.[1]

Bernstein's Argument. The essence of Bernstein's argument appears to me to consist of the following propositions:

• In the face of a weak U.S. balance of payments, especially the trade deficit, monetary authorities of surplus countries have increasingly sought to invest their accretions to reserves in currencies other than the U.S. dollar, and this has contributed to disorderly exchange markets.

[1] It goes without saying that in offering these comments I speak for myself and not for the International Monetary Fund.

• To restore confidence in the U.S. dollar, the U.S. authorities must emphasize their responsibility for the exchange value of the dollar further than has been done through actions taken heretofore.

• The United States should set a reasonable and attainable objective for the exchange value of the U.S. dollar. The maintenance of the SDR (special drawing right) value of the dollar is such a target. Establishment of the Substitution Account would underline the commitment of the United States to this exchange rate objective.

Comments. I think that the establishment of a Substitution Account, and the commitment of *all* participants to it, will *help* to restore confidence in the system, confidence in the dollar in particular. I do not challenge this view of Bernstein's; indeed, I applaud it.

I think that a U.S. commitment to the Substitution Account will add a constraint on U.S. policy, which will be useful and constructive in its effect.

I do not think, however, that a commitment to a Substitution Account will, of itself, produce the basic changes in policy and attitude that will set right the fundamental factors at work in depressing the dollar's acceptability and value. These factors are the deep-running forces of inflation in the U.S. economy. The inflation almost certainly has to be addressed directly by policies that shift the attitudes of the entire nation. A commitment to a Substitution Account will be a useful spur to government to direct its policies against inflation, but I do not think that more should be expected of it in this area.

Bernstein has argued that a useful target in present circumstances would be for the United States to commit itself to maintaining the SDR value of the U.S. dollar. I have mixed feelings about this particular idea. Let me say, though, that I do not have a fixation against targets. Quite the contrary, I believe that targets are an essential aspect of policy, particularly in a period of explosive expectations. Targets can have the effect of dampening expectations and can be very useful in mustering support for specific policy measures and in providing the focus for the coordinating and monitoring of policy. Thus, I am not opposed to setting targets in certain circumstances. I wonder, though, if pegging the SDR value of the dollar is the right approach. It might be a useful intermediate target; I could concede that. It means, however, fixing the U.S. inflation rate at the average of the inflation rates of fifteen (or some other number) countries. This is, of course, a moving target, which could be hard to chase. I should think, however, that the United States would want ultimately to fix its sights higher than this target. I should hope that the United States would want to strive for an inflation rate lower than the average for other industrial countries. I should have thought the United States would especially want to do better than this average if inflation rates in the other countries are *rising* on the average.

Bernstein appears to assume that the assets of the Substitution Account that will be liabilities of the United States will be denominated in SDRs, or at least that their SDR value will be guaranteed by the United States. I think that he argues this way because he feels that the discipline which participation in the account will impose on the United States will be maximized if the United States has the entire responsibility for maintaining the SDR value of the account's assets.

It is debatable whether the discipline on the United States is significantly reduced if it shares responsibility for guaranteeing the SDR value of the account's assets. It is also debatable whether the United States should be asked by itself to guarantee the SDR value of the assets. The ultimate guarantee will be the performance of the U.S. economy, as I argued above, but there is also the question of a proximate guarantee, such as can be written into meaningful contracts. The Substitution Account is for the benefit of the world, not just the United States. It will be agreed to only if that is perceived. If it provides more stability to the world's chief reserve currency, if it moves the system toward greater acceptability and use of SDR-denominated assets, these will be benefits to all participants in the account and to others, too. There is therefore a case for sharing the obligations of ensuring the liquidity of the account and the integrity of its assets. One way of achieving this sharing is, as Bernstein has suggested, through earmarking a portion of the International Monetary Fund's gold for this purpose. Another method is by establishing a residual obligation of participants.

I am puzzled by what Bernstein says in his paragraph on the interest rate that the United States would pay on the assets held by the account. In this paragraph Bernstein explicitly assumes that the United States would give the account SDR-denominated obligations. Because of this, the United States should pay a rate substantially lower than the rate on dollar obligations—perhaps 2 percent lower.

This implies that the rate paid by the account on the SDR claims it issues to depositors should be at least 2 percent lower—and presumably a little more than 2 percent lower—than the market rate on dollar obligations. The question is, would the market judge that the diversification of exchange risks embodied in the SDR is worth two percentage points or more of interest? The fact is, there is no good market in these claims now, nor will there be immediately after the setting up of the account. If the account is to be launched successfully, it may be

477

necessary to offer a better rate to depositors than is implied by Mr. Bernstein's argument.

In any event, the question is probably academic, inasmuch as it seems unlikely that the United States will issue SDR-denominated obligations. The view that the risk of maintaining the SDR value of the assets of the account should be shared among participants appears to be widely accepted. The likelihood is therefore that the account will expect to earn on its assets a rate equal to a market rate on U.S. dollar obligations and to pay on its liabilities a rate very close to or equal to the average of the market rates in that group of countries whose currencies are part of the SDR claim. There remain, of course, complicated questions. For example, there are questions as to whether the former rate is for short-term or long-term U.S. dollar obligations and questions of protecting the capacity of the account to pay its interest obligations. I shall not pursue these matters here, however.

I conclude by repeating that I found Bernstein's paper stimulating and challenging. I am personally pleased to find him among the supporters of the Substitution Account.

Summary of the Discussion

Echoing the themes expounded in the papers and invited commentaries, the subsequent floor discussion focused upon the trend toward increased pluralism in the world economy, the resultant decline in the international importance of the dollar, and the possible alternatives to the dollar as the linchpin of the international monetary system.

The prospects for a strengthened European Monetary System (EMS) and its common currency—the European currency unit (ECU) —received a great deal of attention. Although notable differences of opinion were expressed about the significance of the latest efforts toward European monetary integration and their chances for success, the near-term and medium-term prospects for a widely used common European currency do not appear great. Several reasons were offered in support of this skeptical assessment of the future of the ECU.

One such reason is that transfer of true national sovereignty (meaning, in this context, a degree of control over monetary policy) from member governments of the European Economic Community (EEC) to a supranational body, such as the proposed European Monetary Fund, does not seem very likely in the foreseeable future. Second, even if the ECU were to coexist with national currencies, it would be unlikely to be widely used in domestic transactions. Its universal use in international transactions also seems doubtful. Even its acceptance as a generally preferred investment vehicle is far from certain. Third, short of a complete economic and political integration of EEC members, the EMS will remain essentially an adjustable peg system with all of the known difficulties and problems associated with timely adjustments of the peg. Fourth, there is no inherent reason why the ECU should be a more desirable reserve asset than the dollar. If, in the long run, the battle to subdue inflation proves to be more successful in the United States than in Western Europe, apprehensions about the exchange value of the dollar would simply disappear, and so would the urgent need perceived by a number of monetary authorities to shift some portion of their reserve holdings from dollars into ECUs. Central banks that wish to diversify out of dollars, moreover, may decide to acquire one or more national EMS currencies rather than switch to ECUs.

Many discussants were careful to point out that their doubts regarding the potential of the ECU as a reserve asset for third countries have to be distinguished from the prospects for the ECU as an intra-EEC unit of account, an intergovernmental transaction medium, or an instrument for settlement of debts among the EEC central banks.

In regard to a Substitution Account at the International Monetary Fund (or a similar arrangement aimed at consolidation of the so-called dollar overhang), the main question discussed was whether such a facility could be instrumental in allowing official reserve holders to diversify out of dollars into special drawing rights (SDR), thereby enhancing the importance of the SDR and simultaneously avoiding potentially disruptive exchange-market pressures from attempts at asset switching.

Though there was some support for the creation of such a facility, two quite different rationales for it were offered, which have quite different implications for the specific design of the facility. There was rather general agreement among discussants, moreover, that the prospective benefits from implementation would be likely to be of marginal rather than of major importance.

Some of the commentators argued for the substitution facility primarily as a further step by which the United States could take responsibility for and bolster confidence in the dollar. Others, however, questioned the extent of commitment to the external value of the dollar that the United States should make and emphasized the potential mutuality of interests of the U.S. government and foreign official dollar holders in creating a facility for allowing reserve diversification without contributing to international monetary instability. Important questions were raised about the extent to which the SDR would fit the demands of many of those seeking to diversify, and concern was expressed that many of those countries most likely to be actively engaged in asset switching on a sizable scale would be some of the least interested in substantially increasing their SDR holdings. Although there are some distinct advantages to a simple international reserve asset, prospects for such a development in the near or medium term seem rather dim.

The discussion about the future monetary role of gold turned out to be quite lively, but there was no substantial support among discussants for proposals to return to a gold standard.

In general, the papers and commentaries presented in Part 5 support the view that the basic structure of the present international monetary system is fundamentally sound. Although much more centralized systems that might score higher in economic efficiency can be imagined, our current institutional arrangements are not nearly so deficient or so fragile as has been occasionally asserted. There are proposals for marginal reforms such as the Substitution Account that should be considered seriously, and attention to more ambitious long-run reforms should certainly not be completely abandoned, but there was a rather strong degree of consensus among the conference participants—and it is certainly the view of the editors—that in the short and medium term the primary focus of policy makers should be on the creation of more stable underlying macroeconomic conditions within the framework of the present international monetary system.

Part Six

National Economic Policies in an
Interdependent World

Introductory Remarks

Throughout the conference a great many measures were suggested that were aimed at improving the operation of the international monetary system and, more specifically, at achieving greater stability of the international economy. The participants in the conference were in virtual agreement that the absolutely necessary condition for a more stable international environment is the pursuit of appropriate policies by authorities of (at least) the major industrial countries. No amount of tinkering with the international monetary system will result in its stability unless national economies themselves become much more stable.

At the same time, as it was clearly emphasized at the conference, flexible exchange rates, though providing a good deal of insulation among national economies (as compared to a fixed-rates regime), by no means eliminate completely interdependence among the policies and developments in various national economies. This interdependence gave rise in recent years to an intense controversy over the need for greater policy coordination among major countries. It has been suggested that a failure to coordinate sufficiently national macroeconomic policies contributed significantly to the stagflation and exchange-rate instability of recent years. Many specific private and official proposals for coordinated policy strategies, the locomotive and convoy strategies being most prominent among them, have been passionately promoted.

Such issues were the topic of the concluding session of the conference. This session, part 6, is organized differently from parts 1–5. Instead of invited papers and commentaries on specific subjects, a background paper in which Jacob Dreyer outlines major issues arising in discussions of the optimal scope of coordination of national economic policies is offered. These issues are then debated by a panel of experts consisting of Sven Arndt, Rudiger Dornbusch, Armin Gutowski, and Allan Meltzer. The session concludes with extensive floor discussion.

National Financial Policies in an Interdependent World: Background for Discussion

Jacob S. Dreyer

One of the frequent lines of criticism directed at the monetary arrangements that emerged in the wake of the demise of the Bretton Woods system of "stable but adjustable" exchange rates has been the absence of discernible rules of the new game. Aside from verbal and printed squabbles about whether or not the post-1973 international monetary relations are sufficiently codified to deserve being called a system, it is beyond dispute that the rules spelling out international responsibilities in the monetary sphere (not quite clear-cut even during the Golden Age of Bretton Woods) have become much looser since the inception of floating exchange rates.

One reflection of looser—that is, less clearly defined and adhered to—rules has been a diminution in the scope, frequency, and intensity of international coordination of economic policies. Two broad explanations for the loosening of the rules and the attendant curtailment of international coordination of policies have been advanced in public discussions, each coupled with a different evaluation of the need for international coordination in the new monetary environment.

In one view, the loosening of the rules is ascribed to what is perceived as aborted attempts to replace the Bretton Woods agreement with a comparably tight and comprehensive international monetary constitution suited to the new economic and financial environment. What was endorsed in Jamaica in 1976 does not, in this view, constitute an institutional framework highly enough organized for nations' rights and obligations to be realistically defined. Consequently, exponents of this view argue, it should come as no surprise that incentives for international monetary cooperation as well as penalties for noncooperation have become much diluted, resulting in less coordinated national policies and, hence, in more unstable economic and financial conditions.

The other explanation for relaxation of the rules of behavior in the international monetary sphere in general and for reduction in coordination of national economic policies in particular is economic rather than institutional. In this view, because exchange-rate flexibility, by allowing greater economic independence, is supposed to limit the scope and incidence of individual actions that may result in injury to other parties, it is only natural that the rules governing national monetary behavior be more relaxed than they were under the fixed exchange rate system.

Whichever explanation for the loosening of the rules of international behavior under flexible exchange rates is accepted, questions remain as to whether or not the currently observed degree and modes of international coordination of economic, especially financial, policies are conducive to ensuring greater economic stability in the world and, if not, which methods of international cooperation ought to be adopted and at what cost in order to attain this goal.

Clearly, one's judgment about the desirability of tighter rules and more comprehensive international cooperation would depend, among other things, on one's assessment of the performance of the present system of flexible exchange rates. Nonetheless, whatever the differences in perceptions and evaluation of the working of the present exchange rate system among its students may be, three propositions do not at present appear controversial:

• Floating exchange rates do not follow closely the differences among national rates of inflation.
• Floating exchange rates only partially insulate the domestic economy from foreign disturbances.
• Floating rates do not free monetary policy from external constraints in pursuing domestic targets even though, as compared with a pegged-rate regime, they make this pursuit easier.

For the purpose of subsequent discussion, there would be no advantage in analyzing whether flexible rates are more volatile, have stronger insulating properties, or afford a greater degree of monetary independence than was expected of them prior to 1973 and therefore whether the performance of flexible rates has vindicated the predictions of their advocates or those of their critics. The fact remains that we have witnessed in recent years substantial volatility in real exchange rates in the short and medium runs, that national economies remain highly vulnerable to both real and monetary foreign disturbances, with business cycles perhaps even more synchronized among countries than in the 1960s, and that from the point of view of national authorities longing for their monetary independence the exchange-rate constraint replaced to a large extent the balance-of-payments constraint.

Effects, and implicitly costs, of exchange-rate variability are discussed in some detail elsewhere in this volume. Opinions understandably vary as to their severity, but there is no denial that exchange-rate fluctuations have *some* negative effect on the growth of trade, investment, and, perhaps, productivity because of greater uncertainty and that they may also be responsible for unnecessary adjustment costs and reduction in allocative efficiency as a result of reversible movements in relative prices. Moreover, despite the lack of conclusive evidence, there is widespread belief that flexible rates transmit possibly asymmetrical price impulses through imports. Finally, in a different realm, when the float becomes heavily managed, inconsistencies in national exchange rate policies are likely to arise with all their consequences for economic conflict and political friction.

Given this assessment of reality, various proposals have been advanced with the broad aim of retaining the benefits of flexible exchange rates while eliminating their drawbacks or, at least, alleviating some harmful consequences thereof. Because the problems caused by (undesirable) exchange-rate movements are inherently multilateral, these proposals imply various degrees of international cooperation, especially (but not exclusively) in the domain of financial policies.

The purpose of our discussion is to review the validity, as well as the desirability and implementability, of arguments for various modes of international coordination, especially of financial policies, in light of the nature of international interdependence that has emerged under the currently existing exchange rate arrangements. In order to facilitate the subsequent discussion, the topics to be discussed are grouped in six categories: (1) the nature of international interdependence under flexible rates; (2) the commonly advanced arguments for international coordination of policies; (3) coordination strategies; (4) consistency of coordination policies; (5) special problems for the United States; and (6) cost and implementability of coordinated policies.

Because the principal purpose of this paper is to stimulate an exchange of views rather than to provide definitive answers, in many instances, instead of advancing my own conclusions, I have deliberately limited myself to asking what I consider to be relevant questions.

The Nature of Interdependence

The Long Run. A widely accepted proposition is that in the long run market forces have to be right—that is, they are bound to force exchange rates toward their (constantly changing, of course) equilibrium values. It is true, however, that (be it through their effects on expectations or directly on the level and composition of output) monetary and—even more so—fiscal policies would affect a country's future productivity and hence the terms of trade. Is there a real sense, therefore, in which separately pursued national policies affect in the long run other countries' welfare? If the answer is in the affirmative, is there any conceivable scheme of international coordination of policies that would take into account long-term market interdependence of this sort? Is there any rationale for such coordination?

The Medium-Long Run. Medium-term departures of exchange rates from their equilibrium values are the result of both government policies and the behavior of private parties, as well as of the structure of markets. Some government policies that cause such departures are fairly obvious: capital controls and import deposit schemes, official or quasi-official borrowing in offshore markets, persistent intervention on the same side in the foreign-exchange market. In principle, at least, these policies can be incorporated into an international code of good conduct, even though, probably, unenforced. There are, however, other policies, with much more emphasis on domestic objectives, that are likely to produce medium-term divergences of exchange rates from their equilibrium levels, such as, for instance, aggressive income policies or changes in the tax structure. The question arises whether or not policies aimed at purely domestic targets can be realistically expected to be codified in a world of sovereign states. If the answer is negative and if, indeed, such nonfinancial policies have a strong influence on medium-term exchange-rate variability, does this not imply that coordination of financial policies alone (even if deemed desirable) may exacerbate rather than alleviate medium-term disequilibriums?

As for divergences of exchange rates from their equilibrium levels that originate in the private sector (such as the length of foreign trade contracts and duration of labor contracts, the degree of competitiveness of markets for goods, and the inelasticity of supply of speculative funds in foreign exchange markets), is there room for coordinated financial policies designed to shorten and smooth the path of adjustment of exchange rates to their equilibrium levels? Is it at all clear that rapid movement of exchange rates toward these levels is preferable to a slower, more gradual approach to equilibrium? Is it established, in other words, that benefits derived from an early elimination of inefficiencies imputable to a disequilibrium exchange rate outweigh the costs of disruptions stemming from a fast adjustment?

The Short Run. Variability of exchange rates in the short run has been attributed to a variety of factors resulting in so-called overshooting or to the occurrence of inefficiencies in the foreign-exchange market. The latter cause, to the extent that it can be identified, is thought to justify official intervention. There is less agreement on whether or not monetary authorities ought to step in and smooth the transition of the exchange rate from the old equilibrium level to a new one, that is, to prevent the variability associated with the overshooting phenomenon. One basic question to be addressed is the direct effect of very short-run fluctuations in exchange rates on real variables (that is, over and above their possible psychological damage or, in general, their contribution to a more uncertain economic environment). Assuming that short-term variability of real rates is costly in current or future losses in output, frictional unemployment, and the like, are all causes of such variability to be dealt with by means of coordinated policies, or only some of them? In particular, do disturbances originating in the private sector deserve the same concern on the part of monetary authorities as those caused by government actions? Should a similar distinction be made with respect to monetary versus transitory real disturbances, or with respect to those originating within versus those originating outside the area over which coordination of policies is envisaged? More fundamentally, will coordinated policies aimed at reducing exchange rate fluctuations in the short run truly reduce vulnerability of a closely integrated open economy against shocks from abroad, or will they just lead to other channels of transmission being opened?

Arguments for Coordination

Editorial writers, especially when turmoil engulfs foreign exchange markets, tend to equate the need for coordination of financial policies with the need to undertake joint action aimed at stabilizing nominal exchange rates. Arguments for international coordination of policies advanced in analytical literature and even in some official documents are, however, more numerous and subtle. These arguments, although intertwined, fall into the following five classes.

1. The externality argument (popularized by Assar Lindbeck) treats foreign spillovers of domestic policies as externalities to the community. A low German rate of inflation, for example, is a free public good to the community of nations, but low German growth would be an imposed public "bad," over and above the advantages and disadvantages, respectively, for Germany itself. These externalities are said to be nonappropriable; that is, there is no mechanism by which

Germany would be able to extract from the international community remuneration for providing it with cheaper imports, nor is there one by which its trading partners could impose a penalty on Germany for not absorbing enough of their exports. It follows then that keeping the rate of inflation in Germany low while accelerating its rate of real growth becomes a common economic objective of the whole community to be achieved by means of a coordinated effort.

One question that requires a good answer in connection with this argument is why, if higher rates of growth would certainly benefit Germany more than its neighbors, German authorities would not want to undertake the necessary actions on their own. Another question is why coordination of monetary policies and, consequently, more limited variations in the German mark bilateral exchange rates should result in higher real growth at an *unchanged* inflation rate in Germany.

A related argument (advanced in various guises in a number of documents of the Organization for Economic Cooperation and Development, or OECD) refers to "free riders." The opportunity for free riders arises when one group of countries undertakes, for instance, policies aimed at domestic expansion even at the risk of exacerbating domestic inflationary pressures, whereas another group of countries benefits from export-led growth without having to stimulate domestic demand and thus, purportedly, to endure additional inflation as a by-product.

Sure enough, faster growth of world income is a common good, and it makes eminent sense to call upon all members of the community to join in efforts to achieve it. Should a group of countries refuse to join in the common effort, however, their opportunity to take a free ride would not in the long run be a great one. All depends on the methods employed to achieve faster growth in the cooperating countries. If fiscal stimulus is used as the main tool of expansion (and the debt increment is not fully monetized), potential free riders would enjoy both income and a price-induced export boom. At the same time, however, depreciation of their currencies would subject them to greater inflationary pressure, avoidance of which was the reason for their non-cooperation in the first place. If monetary policy is the main tool used to stimulate output by a group of expanding countries, effects of real appreciation of free riders' currencies may in time more than offset the initial positive effect of higher foreign income growth on their exports.

2. The good-behavior or good-neighbor argument for coordination of financial policies (of major concern to the International Monetary Fund) invokes a particular country's possible desire to affect the

pattern of exchange rates temporarily and thereby extract a transitional gain to itself at the expense of others. A temporary abrupt increase in the rate of monetary expansion, leading to a short-term increase in income, is one example of internationally disruptive behavior of the kind discussed. Another example is intervention in the foreign-exchange market designed to achieve a temporary depreciation of one's own currency. Because the gains obtained through such destabilizing policies must ultimately be surrendered when the policies are reversed, it is difficult to see why any country would want to engage in such seemingly irrational behavior. Be it for the reasons emphasized by political-cycle theorists or for any other motives, occurrences of unstable floating and active exchange-rate manipulation by governments have been too frequent to be dismissed as aberrations. Note that the injury inflicted on others by unstable floaters or exchange rate manipulators may be magnified by the very nature of the dynamic exchange rate adjustment process—that is, the injury may be reinforced and prolonged by possible oscillations in real exchange rates. In any event, the potential harm of these beggar-thy-neighbor policies has been recognized as sufficiently serious to make safeguards against such behavior (at least on paper) the substance of the International Monetary Fund (IMF) "Principles for the Guidance of Members' Exchange Rate Policies."

3. The strategic interdependence argument (of which Koichi Hamada is the most explicit proponent) relies on the proposition that the number of countries whose policies affect the community in a major way is so small that they must behave like oligopolists; that is, they must take into account each others' policies when formulating their own. Drawing on the results of the standard theory of oligopoly, this argument comes down to the conclusion that noncoordinated policies will result in suboptimal (Cournot or Stackelberg) solutions as compared with a solution arrived at by means of joint maximization. The textbook exposition of the oligopoly problem teaches us that the Cournot solution will be reached if each duopolist (all participants) desires to act as a follower, knowing that the other will also act as a follower. If one of them desires to be the leader and the other the follower, a Stackelberg equilibrium will be reached that (relative to the Cournot solution) is advantageous to the leader and disadvantageous to the follower.

Perhaps even more important, it is likely that attainment of noncoordinated solutions will be preceded by oligopolistic warfare, stemming from incompatibility of policies (Stackelberg disequilibrium). A Stackelberg disequilibrium will occur if both duopolists desire to be leaders and each assumes that the other's responses are governed by his reaction function. In fact, however, neither of the reaction functions is observed, and the distribution of welfare gains among duopolists constantly changes. The real-world reflection of a Stackelberg disequilibrium is an economic conflict, for example, competitive depreciations or the recently advertised international interest rate war. Equilibrium is achieved when one party loses—that is, succumbs to the leadership of the other—or when a collusive agreement that maximizes joint welfare (a point lying on the contract curve) is reached. Whether the former or the latter equilibrium solution would be easier to reach would depend on the relative strength of the participants and the circumstances at hand. Insofar as Stackelberg disequilibrium represents the worst of all possible outcomes and the danger of its occurrence is real, *some* remedial collective action is clearly called for.

Although dismissed by many as irrelevant, or even pernicious, in my judgment this is an argument deserving more than a casual dismissal.

4. Efficiency arguments (expounded years ago by Richard Cooper) invoke the possibility of a more efficient pairing of policy instruments and targets in an international context and the probability of a faster and smoother approach to the desired targets. The first of these arguments raises the possibility of a more efficient international matching of instruments and policies; the second, of a higher speed of convergence toward desired targets.

Crudely put, the first argument refers to a possibility that, say, the monetary policy of country A would be more efficient in influencing the external position of country B than any other instrument in either A's arsenal or B's. According to this argument all national targets and all instruments could be arrayed in a "cosmopolitan" matrix, and (provided that the overall number of targets does not exceed the number of instruments) targets and instruments could be paired according to the principles of effective market classification, irrespective of their "nationality." The Bretton Woods arrangement under which U.S. monetary policy was sometimes said to be directed toward controlling the world rate of real growth is cited as an example of such an assignment.

Although "cosmopolitan" assignment sounds attractive, I personally doubt its relevance. First, common sense and all empirical evidence confirm the fact of the comparative—let alone the absolute—advantage of domestic instruments over foreign instruments in their effects on domestic macroeconomic variables. Second, even if it were true, for example, that German monetary policy is more efficient (at the margin) in restoring balance on the French current account, the resulting assignment would certainly encounter a very unkind reception among German voters. Given that domestic authorities are likely to be more responsive to their own constituents than to foreign governments (and international organizations), it is rather doubtful that "cosmopolitan" assignment schemes have much of a future.

The second argument for international coordination of policies in this category is based on a proposition that the speed with which desired targets are reached may be greater when policies are coordinated than otherwise. This argument is theoretically sound, and (leaving the problem of implementation aside) any set of policies that would reduce the oscillations typical for the exchange rate adjustment process must be welcome.

Still, too many questions arise. One question is whether or not active coordination—that is, a negotiated set of policies, is indeed indispensable in order to achieve common targets. Would a simple exchange of information regarding unilaterally planned policies be sufficient for the purpose? Second, if active coordination is needed, would not a multilateral commitment to a set of policies be too unwieldly for making the necessary adjustments when the circumstances change, mistakes are discovered, or targets are revised?

5. The equity argument, discernible in the European Economic Community (EEC) Commission pronouncements, goes one step beyond economists' traditional preoccupation with efficiency and optimality. Proponents of this argument observe that countries with lesser economic and political clout would be more likely to obtain their "fair share" of benefits accruing to the community if the distribution of these benefits were negotiated, then implemented by means of a set of coordinated policies.

This argument starts with the obvious fact that economic power of nations is very uneven. Therefore, because Denmark has no choice but to accept Germany's leadership, it is condemned to make do with Stackelberg equilibrium solutions, which from the followers' standpoint are, as was indicated earlier, inferior to Cournot solutions (more likely to emerge under less unequal distribution of power), to say nothing of Pareto solutions. In terms of policy decisions, it means that if Denmark finds fluctuations in its terms of trade with Germany too disruptive to its economy, it is compelled to align its rate of excess credit creation with that of Germany, irrespective of whether this rate is perceived to be appropriate for the Danish economy. According to the equity argument, negotiations between Germany and Denmark not only may lead to the agreed upon rate of credit expansion that would be best for the two countries jointly but would also give special consideration to Denmark's needs. In other words, instead of a Stackelberg equilibrium solution determined by the relative power of the bargaining parties,

494

both countries would move to the contract curve along the highest attainable Danish indifference curve so that, in fact, collective increase in welfare would accrue to Denmark alone.

Acceptance of this argument hinges primarily on one's concept of fairness. Viewed in isolation and provided that some elements of Rawlsian concepts of fairness postulating interdependent utility functions (increase in A's welfare positively affecting B's welfare) are taken axiomatically, this argument would have some merit. Yet, apart from philosophical considerations, it is not clear that smaller countries are necessarily worse off overall. Most likely they derive gains disproportionate to their size from close integration with larger economies; often play the role of swing members in coalitions, which allows them to have greater voice in collective decisions than their relative size would justify otherwise; and obtain noneconomic benefits from their association with larger neighbors. Once all dimensions of a relationship between big and small partners are examined, the case for international coordination of policies on equity grounds becomes much more debatable.

These brief summaries do not exhaust the long list of questions that can be raised about the arguments for coordination enumerated above. First, some of the arguments (for example, those invoking externalities) encountered theoretical objections (by Roland Vaubel, for example). Second, what is the real-world relevance of most of these arguments? Is it clear, for instance, that negotiated coordination of policies would lead to internalization of externalities rather than just their redistribution? If international equity (in some definable sense) is deemed to be desirable from the community's point of view, is not coordination for this purpose just one method (probably a relatively inefficient one) of concealing the underlying income transfer from national electorates? In regard to the efficiency argument, there can be little doubt that domestic instruments are better suited—that is, they have a comparative advantage over foreign instruments—to tackle domestic problems. If this is so, what would be the benefit of having a greater number of *potentially* available instruments if the *actual* assignment is not affected?

Finally, even if some or all of the arguments for coordination were defensible, selection of appropriate and implementable coordination strategies to achieve the postulated goals would remain a major problem.

Coordination Strategies

Coordination strategies analyzed in academic literature and proposed in official pronouncements are geared, of course, toward the attainment of one or more goals implied by various arguments discussed in the preceding section. Although the distinctions are frequently blurred, coordination strategies can be divided into active strategies and passive strategies. Basically, active coordination strategies require prior agreement on objectives to be achieved and a set of policies, negotiated in advance, presumed to facilitate the achievement of these objectives. Success of an active strategy presupposes the willingness and ability of each party to fulfill its obligations. Passive strategies, on the other hand, require only that each party have knowledge of everybody else's current and intended policies. With information of this kind available to everybody, each government can adjust its own policies in the light of those pursued or to be pursued by the others.

In descending order of "activism," various coordination strategies can be classified as follows:

1. binding agreements on exchange rate targets (coupled if necessary with restrictions on capital flows), with monetary and exchange-rate policies used in support of this agreement (the Bretton Woods arrangement, for example)

2. agreements on adjustable exchange rate targets, accompanied by understandings regarding official borrowing, short- and medium-term financing, payment imbalances, and provisions regarding multilateral consultations on various policy issues (the European Monetary System [EMS] arrangement, for example)

3. agreements on *negotiated* steady rates of monetary expansion, implying predictable long-run evolution of nominal exchange rates and long-run relative stability of real exchange rates (the Ronald McKinnon "tripartite" proposal)

4. agreements on medium-term expenditure policies either coupled with preannounced monetary targets (the OECD approach, for example) or not (the "locomotive" proposal, for example)

5. agreements on short-term exchange rate management policies —that is, joint intervention either mandated by a formula or the width of the band (the old "snake" arrangement, for example) or discretionary (intermittent joint countering of "disorderly market conditions," for example)

6. occasional common actions, such as public pronouncements of mutual assistance, supported by provision or augmentation of bilateral facilities, such as swap lines, loans, and so on (the dollar support package of November 1, 1978, for example)

7. unilaterally chosen but preannounced and informally binding targets for the rates of growth of monetary aggregates, with neither interest nor exchange rate targets (passive coordination)

8. exchange of economic information, including forecasts and policy intentions (institutionalized to some extent by some international organizations, mainly the OECD)

This list of coordination strategies, although far from exhaustive, provides sufficient evidence that coordination means to different people different actions to be undertaken in order to attain different objectives. I shall omit discussion of the various objectives postulated in various quarters. Suffice it to say that they range from "equitable" sharing of balance-of-payments deficits caused by high petroleum prices to "equitable" distributions of the burden of balance-of-payments adjustment among surplus and deficit countries, with the adjective "equitable" being used much more frequently than the adjective "efficient."

As to the coordination strategies themselves, I cannot resist the urge to point out that just in the course of this conference a number of participants (all of them seemingly in favor of coordination) produced dramatically different implicit definitions of what international coordination of national policies would entail. It is important, therefore, when favoring or opposing international coordination, to specify meticulously and precisely the concrete actions to be jointly undertaken and the goals they are supposed to help achieve.

Consistency of Coordination Strategies

Among advocates of international cooperation, the questions of mutual consistency of various policies to be coordinated are frequently brushed aside. These questions are, however, of truly primary importance, especially when international coordination of *financial* policies is advocated. Once it is recognized, for instance, that monetary targets and exchange-rate targets cannot be set independently, a number of troubling questions arise regarding mutual consistency among various coordination strategies (as well as among the various objectives they are supposed to attain). If, for instance, the primary objective of coordination is to reduce uncertainty about future monetary policies, then strategy 8—negotiated steady rates of monetary expansion (provided that they can be negotiated and enforced)—or strategy 7—unilaterally preannounced targets for monetary growth—could be employed. Neither strategy will, however, eliminate short-term fluctuations in real exchange rates, even though these strategies, if credible, are likely to reduce the amplitude of these fluctuations. Similarly, strategy 4—agreements on medium-term fiscal policies, especially in the "locomotive" version—even though it may prevent free rides, will do nothing to ensure greater stability of exchange rates in the medium run and may actually amplify their fluctuations in the short run.

497

Given that "pure" strategies generally cannot assure attainment of all desired objectives simultaneously, a more general question is: Does it make sense to employ "mixed" strategies? Would it be advisable, for instance, to set targets for steady monetary expansion but to fiddle on the side with short-term movements in exchange rates so as to smooth their fluctuations? Would not such a pair of coordination strategies, even though perhaps technically implementable, soon lose their credibility and result in even greater uncertainty than existed before their inception? More generally, can one rely on less than perfect equivalence between the impacts of open-market operations and foreign-exchange-market operations to pursue a long-term or medium-term monetary policy and a short-term exchange-rate policy?

Another question deserving attention is whether, with predictable monetary policy, exchange-rate management (for the purpose of smoothing short-term fluctuations) is necessary at all. Would not such a predictable policy encourage enough stabilizing speculation to eliminate most oscillations in exchange rates commonly associated with overshooting phenomena?

Finally, if a principal cause of exchange-rate fluctuations is unstable expectations and if, therefore, a major purpose of policy coordination is to reduce uncertainty, are coordinated actions demonstrably superior in this respect to unilateral policies? True, coordinated policies may be (or may just appear to be) more focused and forceful. On the other hand, they are probably perceived as intrinsically less enduring than policies undertaken by a single government. To this author it is by no means self-evident which one of these perceptions prevails in affecting people's expectations.

Problems Specific to the U.S. Situation

A number of questions related to the problem of international coordination acquire additional dimension when allowance is made for the special place of the United States in the world economy. Though every government doubtless bases its decision to enter into cooperative arrangements with other countries on some sort of a cost/benefit calculus, the United States has to contemplate a number of additional factors on both the cost and the benefit sides. I submit that the following factors are, or ought to be, considered in deciding the degree, intensity, and modalities of coordination of policies between the United States and other countries.

• Because of its *size*, the U.S. economy is more able to absorb the effects of external disturbances than any other industrial country, and, conversely, the U.S. economy is relatively less able to soften the effects of domestic disturbances by "exporting" these effects. Therefore, a smaller country would derive a relatively greater benefit than the United States would from, say, a bilateral effort to stabilize the real dollar exchange rate of its currency.

• Because of its small *share of foreign trade* in gross national product and its relative self-sufficiency (as compared with other industrial countries) in basic raw material inputs, the United States is exposed to foreign disturbances less frequently and with less intensity than its industrial partners. With disruptions caused by foreign disturbances likely to be less severe, the incentives for the United States to coordinate its policies with its industrial partners are accordingly weaker.

• On the other side of the coin, the United States, as the issuer of the principal *intervention currency,* has often to endure the consequences of unexpected dollar exchange-rate fluctuations due to foreign-exchange-market intervention undertaken by foreign entitites—that is, to actions beyond the control of the U.S. monetary authorities. As a consequence, other things being equal, the United States may be more interested in, say, an international code governing intervention practices.

• In the same vein, the *openness* and international character of the American money and capital markets render the United States more vulnerable to uncertainty-generated short-term capital flows in comparison with those countries whose money and capital markets are tightly regulated by the authorities.

• In a different dimension (examined in greater detail in Michele Fratianni's paper in this volume), *American leadership* of the free world gives the United States disproportionately high stakes in maintaining monetary stability and in averting political discord.

Needless to say, the significance of these factors cannot be quantified easily. Nonetheless, it may be worth pondering whether or not any one of them taken separately or all of them taken jointly provide sufficient additional incentives to the United States to be more eager or more reluctant than other countries to subject its own policies to the unavoidable restrictions entailed by international coordination.

Cost and Implementability
of Various Coordination Strategies

The questions raised thus far referred to the reasons for and the desirability of various coordination policies without regard to their cost or the likelihood of their implementation. These may in fact turn out to be crucial factors in any decision to embark upon a course of international coordination of policies. I find it useful, for the purpose of discussion, to group various objections to international policy coordination in four categories.

1. As a general proposition, each active coordination strategy entails greater informational requirements than a passive strategy. A relevant question, for instance, is whether it is at all possible to collect information necessary to make a judgment about, say, the sustainability of a set of internationally negotiated rates of money growth in different countries. How much more do we have to know about international transmission processes to keep future "locomotives" from derailment?

With very few exceptions, questions of informational requirements for particular coordination strategies have been largely ignored by both opponents and, especially, proponents of closer international coordination of economic policies. This omission is regrettable because it seems obvious that different coordination schemes presuppose the availability of information that is different in kind, reliability, and degree of detail.

2. Although passive-coordination policies (essentially consultations and exchange of information among governments) can be accommodated within the framework of existing institutions, it is likely that a substantial increase in the scope and intensity of international coordination will necessitate creation of new or expansion of existing institutions. Executive time and resources would have to be diverted to studying the merits of coordinated actions and negotiating their implementation. Scores of economists would have to be engaged in preparatory staff work and many more in monitoring the compliance or, more probably, the reasons for noncompliance of national governments with the agreed upon policies. It is by no means self-evident that this arrangement, apart from being costly, would not lead to petty squabbling among involved governments which would heighten rather than abate tensions among them.

No less important, the evolution toward closer and more comprehensive international coordination is bound, for better or worse, to be accompanied by a gradual shift of power from national to supranational decision-making bodies. Even though an analysis of the (possibly far-reaching) consequences of a world economy managed by supranational technocracies is clearly beyond the scope of this conference, they should be kept in mind when the pros and cons of various coordination strategies are discussed.

3. Even with the best information available, policy mistakes are bound to be made and unpredictable events to occur. Should this happen, instead of a rapid approach to the right targets, the outcome of coordinated policies may be a rapid approach to wrong or obsolete targets. Instead of leading the international community out of an expected recession, for instance, multilateral expansion may find countries

reciprocally committed to priming the pump in spite of rising inflationary pressures. Unless the supranational coordinating body is given the power—awesome, in my judgment—to delay, adjust, reverse, or otherwise amend the previously negotiated deal, can it be hoped that the negotiated arrangement would be flexible enough to induce the governments involved to make, individually or collectively, timely corrections? Is there not danger that a policy arrived at through complex negotiations involving several power centers is inherently too rigid to be responsive to rapid changes in circumstances? What kind of machinery would be needed to rid internationally coordinated policies of such a rigidity?

4. The most serious obstacle to successful implementation of actively coordinated policies is, in my opinion, a conspicuous lack of a commonly accepted economic philosophy. As John Williamson has pointed out elsewhere, old differences in relative priorities attached to conflicting economic objectives have become reinforced in recent years by a breakdown of Keynesian orthodoxy, with no new universally accepted doctrine emerging in its place. As a result, economic establishments in different countries tend to give widely differing advice to their respective governments, thus making an international consensus on specific objectives to be attained through international coordination of policies all the more difficult to achieve. Agreements on exchange-rate targets, for instance, are clearly dependent on individual countries' evaluation of costs of medium-term exchange-rate variability; agreements on common short-term exchange-rate support are predicated upon countries' endorsement of the idea of aggressive exchange-rate management; steady money-growth targets, multilaterally negotiated or otherwise, presuppose abandonment of monetary policy tools for the purpose of short-term demand management, not to mention that defining monetary policy in terms of money-supply targets rather than interest-rate targets is not yet universally accepted. Moreover, various countries' trade-offs among different objectives—inflation, unemployment, external balance, exchange rate stability, high growth rate, and so on—remain as disparate as ever, with no sign of meaningful and permanent rapprochement in sight.

One may wonder if it is rational to search for "best" international policy coordination strategies before agreeing upon what these strategies are supposed to achieve.

Commentary

Sven W. Arndt

Jacob Dreyer's paper begins with a discussion of international economic interdependence and proceeds from there to macroeconomic policy coordination. This is an appropriate sequence insofar as the call for coordination is typically based on the fact of interdependence and occasionally on its purported increase.

That countries are economically interdependent none will deny; that they have become increasingly interdependent in recent years, as Ralph Bryant has suggested in these pages, may be true but is far from evident; but that interdependence—its level or rate of increase—creates a presumption in favor of *greater* coordination does not follow at all. It does not follow for several reasons, including the possibility that coordination may be the cause of global economic instabilities.

It is therefore not clear that interdependence requires more coordination and surveillance than we already have. Instead of letting interdependence dictate the degree of coordination, a country may wish to let the available *quality* of coordination determine how much of it it wants, then choose the degree of interdependence that goes with it. When countries concluded that coordination under Bretton Woods had become too costly and burdensome, they opted for floating rates. It is, of course, widely agreed that until countries can coordinate their inflation preferences exchange rates will have to remain flexible, but flexibility is also required in order to accommodate divergent growth and productivity trends and to manage the various shocks that are visited upon the system from time to time.

In addition to the question of whether interdependence or coordination came first, more careful attention needs to be given to the precise form coordination is to take and the purposes for which it is to be undertaken. Those who have criticized existing international monetary arrangements as a "nonsystem" often appear to be concerned mainly with the absence of rules and with international civil servants; whereas those who have thought about the object of coordination have sometimes been too preoccupied with the volatility and reversibility of exchange rates. Not enough attention has been paid in this context to the causes of exchange-rate variability and to the economic and political structures within which it occurs. There is often an implicit assumption that governments with dismal records in stabilizing their own economies are now ready to take on the greater task of stabilizing the world economy. To accept this proposition, one has to believe (1) that inadequate coordination has been the principal—or at least a major—cause of global instability or (2) that concerted action at the international level can induce governments to follow the paths they have always known to be righteous but were too weak and timid to adopt on their own.

There is no strong, systematic evidence to support the former argument, but the latter offers some tantalizing possibilities. The promised fruits of coordination—stable prices and exchange rates, reduced cyclical volatility, and steady rates of growth—are surely worthy of pursuit, but they are that in their own right, and they are attainable—as some countries have shown—even in the absence of concerted global action. Still, nations everywhere have displayed in their actual behavior and in the conduct of their official policies a curious preference for high rates of inflation, volatile exchange rates, slow growth, and cyclical instability. What is it that prevents the United States or Italy or the United Kingdom from supping at the tree of plenty? Surely not the absence of international coordination. The problem is one of national consensus and political will. One is led to hope that coordination and pressure from the "international community" will give divided and weak governments the strength to impose discipline on their fractious citizens. One must hope that coordination at the intergovernmental level will work in a world in which citizens find it difficult to cooperate with one another.

That argument is not to be dismissed altogether. Groups do from time to time achieve what individuals may not. Pressure from the community may indeed be the sole means of returning order and stability to the affairs of some countries. That would be an easier task, however, if the dominant member of the community—the United States—were itself a model of stability and good behavior. The United States has been a major destabilizing influence in recent years; it has also shown itself to be particularly insensitive to the approbation of the community. It is vain to hope that the disruptions brought on by the loss of national consensus and by attitudinal, structural, and institutional changes may be excised by concerted international action at the macroeconomic level.

On a more technical, less political issue, it is important to keep in mind that flexibility of exchange rates is essential and their volatility not inappropriate in a world in which adjustment processes are slow. We know from recent work in disequilibrium economics that price movements in auction markets are influenced by rigidities in contract markets. The exchange rate is an auction price whose movements in the short run are governed by, among other things, rigidities in labor and commodity markets. Far from representing economic inefficiency, such movements serve as early shock absorbers and thereby give the rest of the economy the additional time needed to adjust to disturbances.

An exchange-rate movement that occurs in part because adjustment elsewhere in the economy is temporarily retarded is not without economic value. Indeed, in this respect the conventional rule of thumb that exchange rate fluctuations should not exceed in degree the variations in the fundamentals misses the point when applied to the short run. The ability of many advanced economies to adjust in the short run has been reduced in a variety of ways, often by the purposeful intervention of the state.

These considerations are relevant to the widely held concern with the allocative effects of reversible exchange rate movements. To the extent that an exchange rate displays greater variability *because* other parts of the system cannot adjust immediately, the fear that other markets will be forced to engage in a series of unnecessary resource reallocations is unwarranted. In such cases it would be inappropriate to view the exchange rate as an independent source of instability or to see its variability as anything other than a symptom.

It is thus crucial to distinguish between exchange rate changes that represent the system's response to exogenous disturbances and the exchange rate as an independent source of change. This distinction requires information, including information about the lasting and transient components of a disturbance. Inasmuch as governments are the principal purveyors of information as well as important sources of economic change, a first step in the search for economic stability might usefully be to improve the conduct of public policy. In too many countries, public policy has been inconstant, its signals erratic and unreliable, and its intentions confused and unpredictable. There are, of course, powerful and deep-seated reasons for this state of affairs, but the volatility of exchange rates is surely more the result than the cause.

The difficulty, therefore, with the various rationales in Dreyer's comprehensive survey is that they constitute more a hope that further coordination will somehow solve all our nasty little problems than a demonstration that they will. We appear to have learned little from recent experience. Failure of governments to achieve eminently worthy goals at the national level in no way diminishes enthusiasm and support for global intervention.

504

Rudiger Dornbusch

Jacob Dreyer's paper provides a thoughtful account of the merits and demerits of international macroeconomic coordination. He leaves little doubt that he is skeptical about an effective coordination policy and comes out in favor of noncoordination, whatever that may mean in practical terms. Though I share broadly that conclusion, I find myself in substantial disagreement with his assessment of the costs of pursuing coordination policies, and I shall comment briefly on my differences with his views.

Does coordination have greater information requirements than a passive strategy, as we are told by Dreyer? I would certainly believe that one of the substantial merits of coordination is not only to know what other countries plan to do but actually to achieve agreements that these plans will be carried out.

I will pass over Dreyer's concern for executive time and resources by paraphrasing James Tobin to ask how many Treasury deputies fit in an Okun gap. The more serious argument of an overburdening of the decision-making process strikes me also as exaggerated because macroeconomic decisions have to be made one way or the other.

The argument that coordinated decision making on the international scene might lead to dramatic overshooting, such as in 1973, has received wide support. There is little doubt that coordination is in no way an assurance against errors, even sizable ones, but one would expect the risks to be reduced in comparison with a situation where less information is being used. The 1930s serve as a reminder of the transmission of disturbances and beggar-thy-neighbor policies in an uncoordinated environment where countries independently, but altogether, erred on the down side.

Finally, as I shall detail below, I do not believe that there remain important differences in economic philosophy. On the contrary, the United States has joined Europe in the belief that persistently accommodating policies are inconsistent with price stability or even stability of inflation.

Even though I disagree with some of Dreyer's reasons for rejecting coordination, I do join him in seeing active coordination as an undesirable direction for policy. The process is so political that active coordination might well increase uncertainty about policies that will actually be agreed upon, and increased uncertainty, I believe, is to be avoided. The accompanying chart (figure 1) is perhaps the best evidence for the highly undesirable results of "coordination policies." Here we show for Japan the actual current account, six-month-ahead forecasts of the current account by the Organization for Economic Cooperation

FIGURE 1

JAPAN: CURRENT ACCOUNT AND THE YEN EXCHANGE RATE

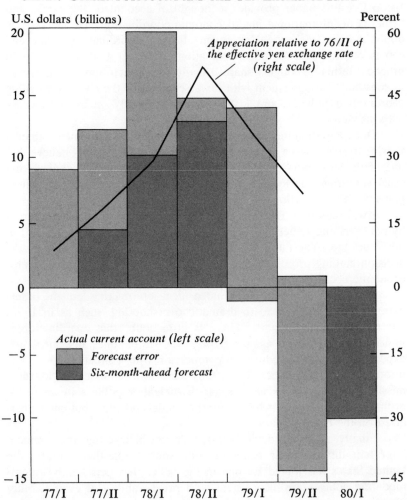

SOURCE: Organization for Economic Cooperation and Development, *Economic Outlook*, various issues.

and Development (OECD), and changes in the effective yen rate. Figure 1 reveals massive swings in the actual current account, vast forecast errors, and substantial exchange rate overshooting.

The origin of these facts is, of course, international macroeconomic diplomacy that, faced with a large Japanese surplus, felt that Japan should have a massive fiscal expansion together with a substantial real appreciation of the yen. Against the threat of increasing trade controls, Japan did pursue these policies on a scale larger than anticipated. The real appreciation, moreover, worked much better and faster than had been anticipated. As a consequence, a substantial deficit and depreciation of the yen soon developed. There is little doubt that the instability introduced by these policies both in Japan and abroad served very little purpose and would have been less without shotgun coordination.

A framework that yields greater stability is one that emphasizes built-in stabilizers and leaves less room for large, active, and unanticipated policy moves. What are the essential ingredents of a framework that places substantial emphasis on built-in stabilizers? I would distinguish here the medium-term and cyclical perspectives. In the medium term there is relatively little need for coordination except in three respects, the first of which is to maintain and increase the openness of the world trade system. I should think that this is most particularly a challenge to continental Europe. Increased manufacturers' exports from developing countries have found their way increasingly into the United States, Japan, and the United Kingdom. They have had little success in Europe, thus pointing to a grievous protectionism in place.[1]

The second medium-term requirement is to achieve an increasing openness of capital markets, not only across national boundaries but, more particularly, on the national scene. It remains true that most countries in continental Europe as well as Japan maintain highly regulated and repressed financial markets that are the vehicles of administrative protectionism but are also an obstacle to cyclical policies.

The third requirement is that of maintaining flexibility of *real* exchange rates. The substantial overvaluation of the dollar that occurred in the 1960s and the subsequent real depreciation remind us that shifting comparative advantage requires relative price adjustments. Flexible rates are an important vehicle in achieving these adjustments.[2]

Coordination is mainly seen as an international extension of activist domestic macroeconomic policies. An alternative approach, of course, is to achieve a framework for economic stability that substantially dispenses with the need for policy activism.[3] Monetary and fiscal rules replace fine tuning and, though they do not guarantee full stability, they

---

[1] See *Cambridge Economic Review*, no. 5 (April 1979), and Organization for Economic Cooperation and Development, *The Impact of the Newly Industrializing Countries* (Paris, 1979).

[2] H. S. Houthakker, "The Breakdown of Bretton Woods," in Werner Sichel, ed., *Economic Advice and Executive Policy: Recommendations from Past Members of the Council of Economic Advisors* (New York: Praeger Publishers, 1978), pp. 45-64.

[3] Milton Friedman, *A Program for Economic Stability* (New York: Fordham University Press, 1956).

507

at least reduce uncertainties about the stance of policies. Furthermore, because these rules can be given either an activist or a cyclical stance, they can make a contribution toward reducing the variability of output, demand, current accounts, and exchange rates.

It is my impression that a substantial part of the current-account instability and the accompanying instability arises from a lack of sufficient built-in stabilizers in countries such as Japan. The most critical question, in the context of built-in stabilizers, is whether the real exchange rate should be one of them. There are two arguments, the first being that lags in response to real exchange rate changes are both long and variable. This is the traditional argument against the activist use of an instrument and would lead us to maintain rates constant over the business cycle. The argument is certainly reinforced when we recognize that real exchange rate variability may interfere with trend growth in world trade and that adjustment costs in marginal industries are high.

The above represents a strong argument against the use of exchange rates as built-in stabilizers. Does it present enough of a case to make us turn toward active intervention policy so as to maintain cyclically stable exchange rates? I do not take that view. The requirements for maintaining medium-term flexibility in real exchange rates imply that any kind of fixing arrangements will interfere with the efficient adjustments process to shifting comparative advantage. Moreover, with built-in fiscal stabilizers and less monetary and fiscal activism, we should expect speculation (capital flaws) to provide a substantial stabilizing function. This view is all the stronger if indeed the uncertainties associated with policy activism are the cause for the large exchange-rate volatility that has been observed.

Otmar Emminger in his remarks has rightly emphasized that as long as the U.S. inflation has not been brought under control the world at large cannot regain economic stability. I share that view and shall briefly consider the possibilities for stabilizing inflation in America. The proper framework of analysis is that set out by Fellner and since formalized in macroeconomic models such as that of Taylor.[4] The Fellner–Taylor analysis draws out the fact that sticky wage behavior is the consequence of the expectation of *accommodating* macroeconomic policies. A government that pursues a full-employment policy forsakes all price discipline, and indeed the price level becomes a random walk.

The United States has experienced accommodating macroeconomic

[4] William Fellner, *Towards a Reconstruction of Macroeconomics* (Washington, D.C.: American Enterprise Institute, 1976); John Taylor, "Staggered Wage Setting in a Macro Model," *American Economic Review*, vol. 69, no. 2 (May 1979), pp. 108-13; and Rudiger Dornbusch and Stanley Fischer, *Macroeconomics*, 2d ed. (New York: McGraw-Hill Book Co., 1980).

TABLE 1
U.S. INFLATION, 1974–1979
(percent)

	1974	1975	1976	1977	1978	1979
Hourly compensation	9.1	10.0	8.7	8.1	9.3	8.5
Intermediate materials	23.8	10.5	5.2	6.6	6.8	12.6
Crude materials	28.6	0.0	12.9	10.6	11.0	21.5
Producer prices	18.9	9.2	4.6	6.1	7.8	12.5

policies for more than thirty years, and it comes as no surprise that under these conditions restrictive policies are viewed as "cyclical and short-lived" rather than as determined efforts to cope with inflation. Because they are viewed in this way, they have little effect on wage settlements, they create unemployment, and they therefore lead rapidly to a collapse of policy determination. The U.S. inflation process is brought out by table 1, which shows wage inflation, materials costs, and the rate of increase of the producer price index.

Table 1 shows that the rate of wage inflation moves very little either over the business cycle or in response to accelerations or decelerations in inflation. Wage *inertia,* which Fellner has emphasized, makes inflation unresponsive to short-lived macroeconomic restraint such as is compatible with a progressive democratic society. What then is the solution to the U.S. inflation problem?

I would favor a four-point program. The first point is to forgo, henceforth, monetary policy. The Federal Reserve should commit itself—or be committed—to a monetary aggregates policy that removes all temptation to use monetary policy for cyclical purposes. The second point is to move toward substantial net fiscal restraint through increased personal taxes, combined with some tax reductions that favor capital formation, skill building, and research and development. The fiscal restraint will slow down real growth to between zero and 1 percent and will be maintained until the rate of unit-labor-cost inflation has reached zero. The third point, given the first two, is to implement comprehensive, temporary wage-price controls. Only through direct controls of wage and price setting can the inflationary process shown in table 1 be stopped without a massive, long recession. The costs of wage-price controls are small in comparison with, for example, the costs of the 1974–1975 recession or of a policy to reduce inflation without controls. Indeed, the more credible the policy commitment to end inflation, the less inhibiting the controls will prove to be. Short of such a determination, it is useless to create a short recession without ultimate success in inflation control.

U.S. inflation is a world problem, and stabilization of the U.S. economy is well recognized to be not only in the interest of the United States but also in that of its partners abroad. They should accordingly take a share in the substantial costs of eliminating inflation. One way to assess their share is to seek their agreement to forgo a year's interest on foreign official holdings of U.S. government liabilities. Foreign sharing of the costs of stabilization is important not only as a point of principle but also to reinforce the domestic commitment to achieve stabilization. The more visibly and forcefully the administration is *seen* to be committed to stabilization, the less costly and more rapid it will be. It is for this reason that stabilization should be attempted only if there is indeed a major policy commitment actually to end inflation. It should serve as a warning that in the United States inflation has risen over every business cycle (measured peak to peak). Every time inflation is fought, and after the courage collapses, we have had higher, not lower, rates of inflation. Against that pattern of policies an alternative of restraint with controls is well worth trying. Unlike Fellner, I believe that this is indeed the time to go ahead.

Armin Gutowski

In this volume national financial policies in an interdependent world are considered. It is not self-evident that this implies coordination of national policies if the world economy is to function. Under a fixed exchange rate system policy coordination is no doubt necessary in the sense that in the medium and long runs all countries accept a common rate of inflation (with the qualification that the price levels of nontradable goods might develop differently because of different rates of increase in productivity between countries and between sectors within individual countries). One should, perhaps, not call this policy coordination but call it rather an agreement on a set of rules that necessitate certain policy actions without consultations.

The Bretton Woods system broke down because countries were not willing or able to stick to the rules. They felt that some policy objectives such as full employment or growth could be reached only if they sacrificed the rules. They considered short-run trade-offs more important than the long-run advantages of abiding by the rules of the system.

Certainly it was an illusion to believe that with the introduction of floating exchange rates each country would be in a position to pursue its own policies without affecting the economies of other countries.

Again, policy coordination in a strict sense is not necessary to prevent adverse effects on the world economy from policy actions of individual countries. All that is necessary for a floating exchange rate system to work smoothly and efficiently—that is, without overshooting and undershooting of exchange rates and without triggering vicious and virtuous circles (which we have discussed at length), is that economic policies of all major countries be fairly predictable—in other words, that these countries succeed in stabilizing medium-term expectations. It is quite possible then that individual countries pursue policies that lead to different rates of inflation, but there should be no uncertainty as to which policy actions in an individual country have to be expected under given circumstances.

This condition is presently not fulfilled in our real world under the regime of floating exchange rates. Therefore, the question arises whether—and, if at all, to what extent—a single country can isolate its domestic economy from disturbances caused by other countries whose actions are not fairly predictable and, if not, whether policy coordination could prevent the detrimental effects from arising. I am convinced that perfect isolation from such influences in a world with free trade and free capital movements is impossible. Uncertainty as to whether a country will sustain an announced monetary policy to bring down the rate of inflation or will change this policy as soon as the rate of unemployment goes up, combined with confidence that other countries will stick to their stabilization policies, would give rise to international capital movements into the currencies that are expected to be more stable. This would cause an appreciation of these currencies in real terms. If the confidence differential persists for a while, the higher real value of these currencies will lower the competitiveness of the tradable goods in these countries with the consequence that structural adjustments would have to be made.

The problems arising from an appreciation in real terms caused by such an inflow of funds from abroad are not easily solved. Let us suppose that there is a confidence differential between the dollar and the deutsche mark. Dollar holders wish to switch into deutsche marks, which they consider a bettter store of value in the long run. (To the extent that the inflowing capital consists of cash balances held by multinational corporations or of official foreign exchange reserves of other countries, this has to be dealt with differently; but time does not permit me to go into this here.) The real value of the deutsche mark goes up. This causes competitive pressure on tradable goods industries and consequently dampens the rate of increase of the price level. The rate of inflation will be lower than previously expected. This, again, means that the level of real wages will be higher than expected when the wages were negotiated, resulting in unemployment and slower growth. Unemployment will persist until the rate of interest is low enough to stimulate investment. Because capital in Germany will be cheaper in real terms than in the United States, the structure of the economy will become more capital intensive. Full employment can be reached again.

The whole process of adjustment, including a period of possibly severe unemployment, would have been caused solely by the confidence differential that emerged from uncertainty as to the course of monetary policy in the United States. If this differential persists, the process of structural adjustment is unavoidable, insofar as it is impossible for a single country to isolate itself against influences from abroad under a flexible exhange rate regime. Whether unemployment can be avoided during the process of structural adjustment is a different matter. I believe this to be possible if the monetary authority acts in a different way. Suppose, again, that dollar holders want to switch into Dmarks. The Bundesbank could then expand its money supply beyond its target rate in order to offset the deflationary pressure from inflowing capital. Real wages would then not rise unexpectedly, interest rates would fall, and investment into more capital-intensive production would be stimulated. The structural change would be brought about without the economy's having to pass through a period of unemployment. The structure of production, however, has to adjust to the change in relative factor prices caused by capital movements into the currency of higher confidence. Of course, if the confidence in the dollar strengthens again, the adjustment process would have to be reversed (and the Bundesbank would have to restrict money supply quickly in order to offset the inflationary pressure).

It is obvious that, although an individual country can find strategies to offset detrimental effects from the outside on its price level and employment, the world would incur losses from the misallocation of resources because of the failure of some countries to pursue a policy of stabilizing medium-term expectations. This shows that there are real costs to the system, but there is no less costly alternative. Going back to a system of fixed exchange rates is certainly no way out. I doubt, for example, that the European Monetary System will be able to prevent distortions within the European Community. It has too much in common with the Bretton Woods system. The member countries failed to produce a set of rules that would harmonize domestic policies, particularly monetary policies.

Because we live in an interdependent world and no country can isolate itself fully from the effects of other countries' policies, even under a regime of flexible exchange rates, there is a case for policy coordination. Having said this, however, I hasten to add that there is no substitute for sound domestic economic policies in each and every country. Experience has shown that this cannot be brought about by simply establishing one or the other exchange rate regime. Policy coordination would have to go to the roots of the problem, that is, medium- and long-term monetary and possibly fiscal policies.

Allan H. Meltzer

Economists and policy makers usually complain that prices and particularly wages do not respond quickly enough or do not change enough to clear markets. When the discussion turns to exchange rates, this complaint is reversed. Policy makers, and some economists, complain that exchange rates are "too volatile"—change too much, too often, and too quickly. Of course, inflexible wages and highly flexible exchange rates are not unrelated in a general equilibrium model. If wages are more flexible, exchange rates are less volatile. Relatively constant policies that require fewer adjustments of beliefs also require fewer adjustments of prices and, therefore, reduce the volatility of exchange rates.

Several years have passed since major countries permitted exchange rates to float. Public and academic discussion does not reveal great depth of understanding about the operation of the current system, and we are far from a consensus about the net benefits of the system. On one side are those who write, or talk, as if the criterion for success of a system of floating exchange rates is the stability of exchange parities between freely floating currencies or between currencies subject to episodic official intervention. On the other side is the claim that exchange rate fluctuations are dominated by actual or anticipated monetary policies. The claim is, at times, accompanied by a prediction that exchange rate stability would be achieved if central banks and governments would renounce exchange rate intervention.

The benefits of stable exchange rates are not in dispute. I believe there is general agreement that variability is costly, even if the cost is not easily documented. Generally, low variability of exchange rates cannot be achieved by monetary policy if there are unanticipated real shocks to spending or to production. It is an open question whether intervention increases or reduces the variability of exchange rates. There are no doubt instances in which central bank intervention stabilizes exchange rates, just as there are cases in which intervention delays adjustments that eventually occur. The average or expected value of intervention will not be positive unless the central bank is able to identify the type of shock that occurs and its duration with a high degree of reliability. I do not believe this can be done, in general, and I am certain that there is no useful evidence that it has been done. I shall develop the argument in the next section of my comments.

If the world or groups of countries want stable exchange rates, they can peg exchange rates and adopt a commodity standard. The advocates of a return to the gold standard press their case regularly, many would say zealously, so repetition is not required. If the main aim of policy is to stabilize exchange rates, I believe a commodity standard like the gold standard is a more reliable means of achieving that aim than central bank intervention or harmonization or coordination of policies.

Recent experience seems to show that one common argument against the gold standard is not correct. We did not avoid the social costs of mining and storing gold by abandoning the gold standard. Countries can avoid these costs, but few choose to do so. The gold price did not fall after 1968, as some expected; desired gold holding has not declined; and gold mining has not ceased.

The case against fixed exchange rates reflects a preference for price stability over exchange rate stability, as Friedman pointed out years ago.[1] Because neither prices nor exchange rates are stable in an absolute sense, I believe it is more useful to express the choice as a preference for achieving as much exchange rate stability as is consistent with price stability rather than achieving as much price stability as is consistent with exchange rate stability. That, however, is a quibble with Friedman. The more basic problem is that neither price nor exchange rate stability can be achieved fully because there are unforeseen real shocks, and the shocks are uncertain in their timing and have uncertain duration.

To show the problems that arise in a system of fluctuating exchange rates, I adapt the model developed by Brunner, Cukierman, and Meltzer to a world with floating exchange rates.[2] The distinctive feature of the model is that there are permanent and transitory shocks to productivity, to aggregate demand, and to money. Expectations are rational in the sense of Muth. The model suggests why efforts to reduce the variability of freely floating exchange rates by coordinating economic policies are not likely to be successful.

A more useful approach is to adopt stabilizing policies. Two main steps are required. First, governments should rely on preannounced monetary policies, perhaps supplemented by preannounced fiscal policies. The former fix the average or maintained rate of inflation, and the latter fix the relative size of government and thus reduce this source of uncertainty about after-tax real rates of return to capital and labor.

---

[1] Milton Friedman, *Capitalism and Freedom* (Chicago: University of Chicago Press, 1962), p. 53.

[2] Karl Brunner, Alex Cukierman, and Allan Meltzer, "Stagflation, Persistent Unemployment, and the Permanence of Economic Shocks," *Journal of Monetary Economics,* vol. 6 (October 1980), pp. 467-92.

Second, governments should remove the remaining controls on capital, prohibition of interest payments on deposits, and other restrictions that induce relatively large capital movements to avoid actual or anticipated restrictions.[3]

Real Effects on Exchange Rates. To analyze exchange rates, I use a simplified equilibrium model. Two economies can be described, using the model in Brunner, Cukierman, and Meltzer.[4] Each has different structural parameters, and both economies are small, open economies subject to three types of shocks—to money, productivity, and aggregate demand. All markets clear. All expectations are rational, and everyone knows the deterministic and stochastic structure.

Money is neutral. In fact, the systems are dichotomized, so everyone knows that monetary shocks cannot change real variables. This assumption implies that there is never any confusion between observed exchange rates and underlying real exchange rates.

There is, however, confusion between the permanent and transitory values of each of the shocks. When a shock occurs, generally, no one knows whether it will persist or vanish next period. The duration of the shock becomes more apparent as time passes, so information about all past observations is useful when forming anticipations about current values. Actual permanent values are, of course, never observed.

The perceived permanent value of the exchange rate is the value that incorporates all information about the deterministic and stochastic structure of the economy and past shocks. Let s_t^p be the perceived permanent value of the exchange rate measured in units of home currency per unit of foreign currency. In the appendix to this paper, I show that s_t^p is determined by

$$s_t^p = K_s^p + A_1 E \Psi_t^p + A_2 (l_t^p + E u_t^p) + A_3 E \varepsilon_t^p$$
$$+ A_4 r_t^{*p} - A_1 p_t^{*p} \tag{1}$$

with $A_1, A_3, A_4 > 0; A_2 < 0$. Because real shocks, u_t and ε_t, affect the domestic price level, the perceived permanent values of real shocks $E u_t^p$ and $E \varepsilon_t^p$, affect the perceived permanent value s_t^p. Other variables are defined in the appendix.

[3] A more detailed analysis of preannounced monetary growth with floating can be found in Allan Meltzer, "The Conduct of Monetary Policy under Current Monetary Arrangements," *Journal of Monetary Economics,* vol. 4, no. 2 (April 1978), pp. 371-88.

[4] Brunner, Cukierman, and Meltzer, "Stagflation, Persistent Unemployment, and the Permanence of Economic Shocks." The equations for permanent values of the open economy, discussed here, are stated explicitly in the appendix to this comment.

Equation 1 shows that in this simplified model, with purchasing power parity expected to hold, we obtain Dreyer's second proposition: Floating rates only partially insulate economies from foreign disturbances.

On examination of equation 1, Dreyer's proposition turns out to be a restatement of the familiar proposition that real exchange rates change whenever there are changes in tastes, productivity, population, and other determinants of real interest rates and relative prices at home and abroad. An increase in foreign interest rates, r^{*p}_t, raises s^p_t and depreciates home currency. Increases in permanent, home or foreign, productivity or in perceived aggregate demand also change the exchange rate and the perceived permanent price levels at home and abroad. If the shocks occur in foreign countries, real interest rates and price levels transmit part of the real shock to the home country by changing s^p_t.

Gottfried Haberler and others have made this point on many occasions, and it is restated in Haberler's paper in this volume. Once again, real exchange rates are stable exchange rates only if there are no real shocks. The problem, then, is to replace shock-amplifying with shock-absorbing institutions if we are to reduce the effects of shocks on exchange rates and countries' economies.

I am not sure how to interpret Jacob Dreyer's third proposition. Monetary policy can keep the price level stable in any model in which money is neutral. Inflation permanently changes real variables but only as a result of the inflation tax, or other nonindexed taxes, and not as a result of floating. Using equation 1, we see that the variance of the log of the perceived *permanent* value of the exchange rate depends on the variances of $E\varepsilon^p$, Eu^p and $E\Psi^p$ and similar terms for the rest of the world.[5] The variances of nominal and real shocks in the rest of the world affect the (log of the) rest of the world's perceived permanent price level, p^{*p}, and s^p.

Within each country shocks to aggregate demand and productivity are independent, provided governments do not try to use fiscal policy (for example, ε^p) to change aggregate demand when productivity shocks (u) change output.[6] Efforts to use fiscal policy to offset real shocks introduce covariance between the shocks and open the problem Friedman raised years ago.[7] To stabilize the exchange rate, the policy maker

[5] Foreign variables p^{*p} and r^{*p} depend on productivity and aggregate demand in the rest of the world and therefore depend on E^{*p} and Eu^{*p}.

[6] Because the model is dichotomized and everyone knows the structure, monetary policy cannot offset real shocks.

[7] Milton Friedman, "The Effects of Full-Employment Policy on Economic Stability: A Formal Analysis," in *Essays in Positive Economics* (Chicago: University of Chicago Press, 1953), pp. 117-32.

must know both the magnitude of the effect and the timing of the response to fiscal policy and to the productivity shock. If his information is incomplete, policy may increase the variance of exchange rates.

The oil shock was not unique to the United States, so there are additional effects to consider. Eu^* is a determinant of r^{*p} and p^{*p}. The variance of s^p depends on the relative variances of u^p and u^{*p}, on the relative variances of fiscal and monetary policies, and on the covariances between these terms. The variance of the trade-weighted exchange rate was almost certainly increased by the oil shock and subsequent policies. The data on trade-weighted exchange rates show substantial variability. The trade-weighted dollar fell sharply both before and after adjustment for changes in relative price indexes. Later, in 1975, the dollar recovered much of its fall.

The data are also consistent with the view that fiscal and monetary policies altered the effects of the worldwide productivity shock after 1974. The Ford administration policy of vetoing spending bills and the reduction in the growth rate of money in the United States during 1975 and 1976 appear to have lowered s^p. The fiscal and monetary expansion of 1977 and the misguided locomotive policy of 1977 and 1978 contributed to the later fall in the exchange value of the dollar (increase in s^p). These policies also contributed to the variance of s^p over time.

An Alternative to Coordination. I have considered only permanent effects. In practice, activist policy makers must separate permanent and transitory effects of home-country and rest-of-the-world policies.

If we invoke rational expectations and ignore differences in information, s^p_t is the value at which everyone expects the exchange rate to settle on the basis of information available today. This rate cannot be known with certainty because we observe actual, not permanent, values. In a world of rational expectations, policy makers can intervene to stabilize exchange rates only if they possess superior information about permanent values. This is, of course, a standard problem and is not unique to exchange rates, whether freely floating or managed.

I do not dissent from Dreyer's "universally accepted proposition" that in the long run market forces produce an equilibrium value of the exchange rate. I go farther. The market produces an equilibrium exchange rate every day, but the equilibrium rate is subject to change whenever the market receives new information. Equilibrium rates are not constant rates.

What can central banks do? We are now twenty years into the era of rational expectations, so we should begin to absorb the main lessons. There are, I believe, four main lessons: (1) Because there are risks inherent in nature, trade, and social arrangements, prices and quantities fluctuate; large shocks can have large effects on prices, employment, and exchange rates. (2) The best we can do currently is design institutions or arrangements that minimize the cost of adjusting to shocks. (3) Generally, central banks do not have superior information about real and nominal, permanent and transitory effects. Unless they have superior information about shocks and their effects through time, they cannot expect to stabilize exchange rates. (4) Agents of the central bank often mistake the temporary effect of central bank intervention, arising from the reluctance of speculators to bet against the momentary effects of intervention, for longer-term effects on the value of a currency.

Central bankers and governments have contributed to, and even created, high and variable inflation, low growth, and high unemployment by inappropriate policies during the past two decades. Their past mistakes do not give us reason to believe that they have information about prices, economic activity, interest rates, and other variables that permits them to stabilize exchange rates by means of coordinated efforts in the exchange market.

The time passed long ago when we should have shifted our focus from attempts to fine-tune prices, output, interest rates, and exchange rates to the more important problem of finding arrangements that reduce risks arising from shocks inherent in nature and resulting from social arrangements. The list of such arrangements begins with a monetary rule, adds a fiscal rule setting the maximum ratio of government spending to output or setting the anticipated growth of taxes and spending, and includes removal of remaining impediments to capital and to trade.

Policies of this kind establish procedures to which markets adapt. They eliminate the risks arising from destabilizing shifts in policy. Known procedures and credible preannounced policies permit the type of coordination, through the action of informed traders and speculators, that reduces variability in markets. Variability of exchange rates will be "low," however, under constant policies only if real shocks are small.

Appendix

The perceived permanent values of the variables are obtained from the equations for the output market (A.1), the money market (A.2), the production function (A.3), and the belief that purchasing power parity holds for permanent values (A.4). The fact that the model is dichotomized removes permanent effects of unanticipated inflation on real variables.

$$y_t^p = k + \alpha y_t^p + \beta_1 r_t^p + \beta_2 s_t^p + E\varepsilon_t^p \qquad \text{(A.1)}$$

$$m + E\Psi_t^p = B + p_t^p + y_t^p + b_1 r_t^p + b_2 r_t^{*p} - \theta_1 E\varepsilon_t^p \qquad \text{(A.2)}$$

$$y^p_t = \delta l^p_t + Eu^p_t \tag{A.3}$$

$$s^p_t = p^p_t - p^{*p}_t \tag{A.4}$$

The symbols are perceived permanent values of: y^p_t = output; r^p_t = market rate of interest; s^p_t = spot exchange rate; l^p_t = labor force (a given). The expected values of perceived permanent shocks to productivity, aggregate demand, and money stock are Eu^p_t, $E\varepsilon^p_t$ and $E\Psi^p_t$ respectively. The actual values of the shocks, u, ε, and Ψ, include permanent and transitory components. Parameters α, θ_1, and δ are positive; b_1, b_2, β_1, and β_2 are negative. Asterisks indicate foreign or rest-of-the-world variables; for example, p^{*p}_t is the permanent price level in the rest of the world.

The solution for s^p_t is equation 1 of the text:

$$s^p_t = K^p_s + A_1 E\Psi^p_t + A_2(\delta l^p_t + Eu^p_t) + A_3 E\varepsilon^p_t$$
$$+ A_4 r^{*p}_t - A_1 P^{*p}_t$$

where K^p_s is a constant and $A_1 = (-\beta_1)/D > 0$; $A_2 = [b_1(1 - \alpha) + \beta_1]/D < 0$; $A_3 = -(b_1 + \beta_1 \theta_1)/D > 0$; $A_4 = (\beta_1 b_2)/D > 0$; $D = \beta_2 b_1 - \beta_1 > 0$.

Summary of the Discussion

Given a history of controversy over the "locomotive" and "convoy" proposals for coordinated economic expansion and, in general, over advantages and disadvantages of establishing a permanent institutional framework for coordination of national economic policies, the extent of general agreement among the participants of the conference on a number of major issues was somewhat surprising. Still, some participants, most notably Robert Solomon, maintained that closer coordination of economic policies in 1972–1973 could have prevented the worldwide boom that then developed and that led to an explosion in commodity prices, contributed to the oil price boosts of 1973–1974, and ultimately resulted in a painful global slump. Even this premise was challenged, however. Helen Junz held that the explosive economic growth of 1972–1973 was, at least partially, due to excessive consultations and implicit coordination of policies among nations. Every government underestimated at that time the strength of its own economy and, consequently, unintentionally misinformed its partners about the true conditions. Thus, errors of judgment became compounded, and every government continued to pursue highly expansionary policies on the assumption that increments to the global growth of demand for resources due to such policies would not be excessive. Thomas Willett pointed out in this connection that international coordination of macroeconomic policies would be more defensible if, indeed, governments had a superior forecasting ability. He claimed, however, that this ability is, if anything, rather inferior because of the inherent bias of politicians toward overoptimism. Moreover, Willett contended that because coordination is likely to be based on governments' discretion, as distinct from predetermined rules, political considerations are certain to influence the outcome, not necessarily in a desirable manner.

Rainer Masera addressed the issue of structural differences among countries and of how they impinge on a coordination process. He pointed out that not only are certain prices sticky and others flexible but that the degree of their stickiness is very different among countries. After all, institutional settings for determination of wages are different

520

among countries, methods of monetary control are different, and, most of all, functions of the public sector are very different, not to mention the differences in the tax structures across countries. Masera remarked that in the absence of a longer-term effort to coordinate structural evolution of the cooperating countries the scope for macroeconomic coordination among countries would remain very limited.

On the whole, however, issues of international coordination of policies per se were deemphasized relative to the problems of reestablishing greater stability in national macroeconomic policies. There was little opposition to the view that there is an ideal case for international policy coordination in the face of particular types of shocks, but at the same time skepticism was frequently expressed regarding the extent to which macroeconomic policy making should focus on such discretionary fine-tuning. The past history of macroeconomic policy mistakes and the general trend toward ever more accommodative policies that has led to the common occurrences of double-digit inflation appeared to be the major concern of a majority of participants.

As a consequence, there was a remarkably high degree of support for views that our major priorities should be to adopt rules that would discipline macroeconomic behavior and to rely on automatic stabilizers rather than discretionary policy strategies aimed at attempting to limit the severity of effects of economic disturbances. Though of course such views were not fully shared by everyone, the proportion of speakers putting primary emphasis on the need for more steadiness in policies was extremely high. Indeed, the most hotly debated topic did not even involve issues of exchange rate and macropolicy coordination but centered on whether attempts to reduce the current high rate of inflation should be gradual or abrupt.

The debate on this topic was triggered by the proposal contained in Rudiger Dornbusch's comment. Though a number of speakers recognized the merits of an antiinflationary jolt to the U.S. economy as a means of making the government's policy credible from the outset, many commentators, notably Jacob Dreyer and Armin Gutowski, felt that the present situation does not justify—at least not yet—the necessity of incurring the enormous cost inevitably involved with dislocations associated with any attempt to end inflation abruptly. William Fellner noticed, in particular, that, because most contracts were entered into under expectations of continuing high inflation, a policy of ending inflation abruptly, say, within one year, would have to be accompanied by legislative action that would allow renegotiation of all existing contracts. Nonetheless, Dornbusch's suggestion to suspend for one year all interest payments on foreign-held claims on the U.S. government encountered strong opposition. John Bilson argued against it on legal

521

and ethical grounds, and other participants pointed out that such a suspension of its obligations by the U.S. government, whether decreed unilaterally or forced diplomatically upon its foreign creditors, would destroy its creditworthiness for a very long time.

Dornbusch's proposal to impose a wage and price freeze proved to be even more controversial. Steven Kohlhagen wondered how Dornbusch's advocacy of wage and price controls can be reconciled with his advocacy of free trade and capital flows. Kohlhagen remarked that a wage and price freeze would shift more of the equilibrating burden from goods and labor markets to capital and foreign exchange markets, resulting in even greater volatility of interest and exchange rates. Apart from inefficiency arguments levied against a wage and price freeze, however, a number of participants questioned even their value as a signal of the authorities' seriousness and determination to bring the rate of inflation down. Roland Vaubel argued that a wage and price freeze, far from imparting credibility to an antiinflation program, may have the perverse effect of being interpreted as a sign of the authorities' reluctance to pursue a monetary policy of necessary restraint. Edward Bernstein expanded on this theme by invoking the historical record of inflation usually accelerating once the freeze is lifted. If rational expectations are prevalent, a wage and price freeze would make people believe that the future rate of inflation will be higher, not lower. Dornbusch replied to this criticism that the wage and price freeze he proposes is to be applied in conjunction with drastic monetary restraint and fiscal restraint pursued sufficiently long to produce stable unit labor costs. Such a combination of policies would no doubt throw the United States into a deep recession, which would be the price the United States would have to pay for restoring price stability. Because price stability in the United States is clearly beneficial to the rest of the world, however, other countries could be expected to shoulder part of the burden by forgoing one year's worth of interest receipts on their claims on the U.S. government.

This discussion should be interpreted not as saying that issues of macro and exchange rate policy coordination are of no consequence but rather as saying that, given the current danger of high and escalating inflation, the major focus of attention needs to be on the reestablishment of stability in the national financial policies of the major industrial countries. If and when that objective is accomplished, one can turn more safely to focusing on possible residual improvements in economic performance through discretionary policy coordination.

As a number of participants pointed out, this suggests that for the near term the focus of international coordination should be on maintaining an open trading system and mutual reinforcement of the need to restore economic stability in each of the major countries. Although pegged exchange rates may be a rational component of such a strategy among particular countries or groups of countries along optimum-currency-area arguments, attempts to restore a general system of pegged rates are neither a necessary nor a sufficient part of such a strategy. As success is achieved in restoring national economic stability, flexible exchange rates will themeslves become less volatile, and the current stresses on the international monetary system will abate. If efforts to restore stability were to fail in some countries, then flexible rates would become all the more essential for insulation of those countries in which progress is being made.

The proceedings of this conference have reinforced our view that the current stresses on the international monetary system are primarily (although, of course, not exclusively) the results of the failures of national economic policies rather than deficiencies in present international monetary arrangements and that it is to the improvement of national economic policies that we must give our greatest attention in order to restore international monetary stability.

A Note on the Book

*This book was edited by the
Publications Staff of the American Enterprise Institute.
The staff also designed the cover and format, with Pat Taylor.
The figures were drawn by Hördur Karlsson.
The text was set in Times Roman, a typeface designed by Stanley Morison.
Hendricks-Miller Typographic Company, of Washington, D.C.,
set the type, and R. R. Donnelley & Sons Company,
of Harrisonburg, Virginia, printed and bound the book,
using paper made by the S. D. Warren Company.*

Selected AEI Publications

The AEI Economist, Herbert Stein, ed., published monthly (one year, $18; single copy, $1.50)

Meeting Human Needs: Toward a New Public Philosophy, Jack A. Meyer, ed. (469 pp., paper $13.95, cloth $34.95)

The Gateway: U.S. Immigration Issues and Policies, Barry R. Chiswick, ed. (476 pp., paper $12.95, cloth $22.95)

Wage-Price Standards and Economic Policy, Jack A. Meyer (80 pp., $4.95)

Mergers in Perspective, Yale Brozen (88 pp., paper $6.95, cloth $14.95)

Low Pay, Occupational Mobility, and Minimum-Wage Policy in Britain, David Metcalf (83 pp., $4.25)

Unemployment Insurance Financing: An Evaluation, Joseph M. Becker (169 pp., paper $6.25, cloth $14.25)

Rethinking Federalism: Block Grants and Federal, State, and Local Responsibilities, Claude E. Barfield (99 pp., $4.25)

Money and Housing, John Charles Daly, mod. (31 pp., $3.75)

A Conversation with Dr. Ezra Sadan: Combating Inflation in Israel (18 pp., $2.25)

Prices subject to change without notice.

AEI Associates Program

The American Enterprise Institute invites your participation in the competition of ideas through its AEI Associates Program. This program has two objectives:

The first is to broaden the distribution of AEI studies, conferences, forums, and reviews, and thereby to extend public familiarity with the issues. AEI Associates receive regular information on AEI research and programs, and they can order publications and cassettes at a savings.

The second objective is to increase the research activity of the American Enterprise Institute and the dissemination of its published materials to policy makers, the academic community, journalists, and others who help shape public attitudes. Your contribution, which in most cases is partly tax deductible, will help ensure that decision makers have the benefit of scholarly research on the practical options to be considered before programs are formulated. The issues studied by AEI include:

- Defense Policy
- Economic Policy
- Energy Policy
- Foreign Policy
- Government Regulation
- Health Policy
- Legal Policy
- Political and Social Processes
- Social Security and Retirement Policy
- Tax Policy

For more information, write to:

AMERICAN ENTERPRISE INSTITUTE
1150 Seventeenth Street, N.W.
Washington, D.C. 20036

Date Due